Autism Spectrum Disorders: Characteristics and Effective Strategies

Autism Spectrum Disorders: Characteristics and Effective Strategies

Edited by Annabell Gibson

STATES
ACADEMIC PRESS
www.statesacademicpress.com

States Academic Press,
109 South 5th Street,
Brooklyn, NY 11249, USA

Visit us on the World Wide Web at:
www.statesacademicpress.com

ISBN: 978-1-63989-064-4

Cataloging-in-Publication Data

Autism spectrum disorders : characteristics and effective strategies / edited by Annabell Gibson.
p. cm.
Includes bibliographical references and index.
ISBN 978-1-63989-064-4
1. Autism spectrum disorders. 2. Autism spectrum disorders--Treatment. 3. Autism.
4. Developmental disabilities. I. Gibson, Annabell.
RC553.A88 A88 2022
616.858 82--dc23

Table of Contents

Preface

This book aims to highlight the current researches and provides a platform to further the scope of innovations in this area. This book is a product of the combined efforts of many researchers and scientists, after going through thorough studies and analysis from different parts of the world. The objective of this book is to provide the readers with the latest information of the field.

Autism spectrum disorders cover a collection of conditions which fall under the umbrella of neurodevelopmental disorders. People who suffer from these disorders exhibit difficulty in communicating socially. Other symptoms are unusual reactions to external stimuli and difficulty in moving from one task to another. There are other disorders which can exist along with autism such as epilepsy, intellectual disabilities and learning disabilities. The strategies for the management of autism spectrum disorders focus on reducing the connected deficits and family distress. Major goals of these strategies are to increase the quality of life as well as the functional independence. This book unravels the recent studies in the field of autism spectrum disorders. It outlines the characteristics and effective strategies for the management of these disorders in detail. The book is appropriate for students seeking detailed information in this area as well as for experts.

I would like to express my sincere thanks to the authors for their dedicated efforts in the completion of this book. I acknowledge the efforts of the publisher for providing constant support. Lastly, I would like to thank my family for their support in all academic endeavors.

Editor

1

Impact of Sensory Sensitivity on Physiological Stress Response and Novel Peer Interaction in Children with and without Autism Spectrum Disorder

Blythe A. Corbett[1,2], Rachael A. Muscatello[2] and Scott D. Blain[3]*

[1] Department of Psychiatry and Behavioral Sciences, Vanderbilt University, Nashville, TN, USA, [2] Vanderbilt Brain Institute, Neuroscience Graduate Program, Vanderbilt University, Nashville, TN, USA, [3] Department of Psychology and Human Development, Vanderbilt University, Nashville, TN, USA

Edited by:
Benjamin Gesundheit, Cell El Ltd., Israel

Reviewed by:
Alka Anand Subramanyam, Topiwala National Medical College & BYL Nair Charitable Hospital, India
Om Sai Ramesh Vallamkonda, Lady Hardinge Medical College, India

****Correspondence:***
Blythe A. Corbett
blythe.corbett@vanderbilt.edu

Background: For many children with Autism Spectrum Disorder (ASD), social interactions can be stressful. Previous research shows that youth with ASD exhibit greater physiological stress response during peer interaction, compared to typically developing (TD) peers. Heightened sensory sensitivity may contribute to maladaptive patterns of stress and anxiety. The current study investigated between-group differences in stress response to peer interaction, as well as the role of sensory sensitivity.

Methods: Participants included 80 children (40 ASD) between 8 and 12 years. Children participated in the peer interaction paradigm (PIP), an ecologically valid protocol that simulates real-world social interaction. Salivary cortisol was collected before and after the 20 min PIP. Parents completed questionnaires pertaining to child stress (*Stress Survey Schedule*) and sensory sensitivity (*Short Sensory Profile*). Statistical analyses included *t*-tests and ANCOVA models to examine between-group differences in cortisol and play; Pearson correlations to determine relations between cortisol, play, and questionnaire scores; and moderation analyses to investigate interactions among variables.

Results: Controlling for baseline cortisol values, children with ASD showed significantly higher cortisol levels than TD peers, in response to the PIP [$F_{(1, 77)} = 5.77$, $p = 0.02$]. Cortisol during play was negatively correlated with scores on the SSP ($r = -0.242$, $p = 0.03$), and positively correlated with SSS ($r = 0.273$, $p = 0.02$) indicating that higher cortisol was associated with greater sensory sensitivity (lower SSP reflects more impairment) and enhanced stress in various contexts (higher SSS reflects more stress). Furthermore, diagnosis was a significant moderator of the relation between cortisol and SSP, at multiple time points during the PIP ($p < 0.05$).

Conclusions: The current study extends previous findings by showing that higher physiological arousal during play is associated with heightened sensory sensitivity and a pattern of increased stress in various contexts. Results are discussed in a broader context, emphasizing the need to examine relationships between social, behavioral, and physiological profiles in ASD to enhance understanding and improve treatments aimed at ameliorating stress and sensory dysfunction, while enhancing social skills.

Keywords: autism, stress, cortisol, sensory, peer interaction, social, auditory

INTRODUCTION

Impaired social communication is a primary characteristic of Autism Spectrum Disorder (ASD) (American Psychiatric Association, 2013) and may be the result of limitations in social cognition (e.g., Baron-Cohen, 1995) or social motivation (Chevallier et al., 2012). Underlying physiological factors may also impact the extent to which individuals with ASD engage with others in social situations. For example, there is considerable evidence that social interactions are highly stressful for children with ASD (Lopata et al., 2008; Corbett et al., 2010). It may be this exaggerated stress response that drives, in part, reductions in social engagement. There is also significant prevalence of sensory dysfunction in ASD (Rogers et al., 2003; Kern et al., 2006; Tomchek and Dunn, 2007; Ben-Sasson et al., 2009), and these hyper- and/or hypo- sensory sensitivities may further contribute to atypical patterns of social interaction.

Compared to typically developing (TD) peers, children with ASD tend to interact less with other children (Corbett et al., 2010, 2012) and engage in less cooperative play (Corbett et al., 2014b), instead showing a preference to engage in self-play (Humphrey and Symes, 2011). There is also evidence that individuals with ASD have abnormal preferences for interpersonal distance (IPD), including both standing too close or preferring more distance relative to TD peers (Kennedy and Adolphs, 2014; Lough et al., 2015; Perry et al., 2015). As children with ASD become more aware of their limitations in social skills with age (Knott et al., 2006), later peer interactions may be characterized by exacerbated social stress (Schupp et al., 2013). As a result of this stress, these children may display increased avoidance behaviors characterized by decreased social motivation to interact with peers. This notion is supported by research showing that higher cortisol response to a novel social interaction was associated with reduced social communication among children with ASD (Corbett et al., 2014b).

The hypothalamic-pituitary-adrenal (HPA) axis is a highly regulated system that is responsible for maintaining homeostasis via maintenance of a diurnal rhythm, activation in response to stress or threat, and restoration of basal activity via negative feedback mechanisms. Cortisol, an important stress hormone, serves as a measurable indicator of HPA regulation, increasing in concentration after exposure to stressors (Herman and Cullinan, 1997). Cortisol also shows a diurnal rhythm of fluctuating concentration, throughout the day. Typically, diurnal cortisol values are at peak levels in the morning and slowly decline to lowest levels in the evening. In ASD, the diurnal rhythm appears to be altered, such that children with ASD have lower morning cortisol and higher evening cortisol values relative to TD children (Corbett et al., 2008, 2009). Further, many children with ASD show an increased response to stress, as indicated by higher cortisol levels, when interacting with unfamiliar peers (Lopata et al., 2008; Corbett et al., 2010). This stress response appears to be tied to level of social cognition, as those with highest cortisol values tend to show less social motivation (Corbett et al., 2014b). It is important to note, however, that this response is considerably variable within the ASD population (Lopata et al., 2008; Schupp et al., 2013). This suggests the possibility of interactions with other characteristics, which may explain part of the high variability in psychosocial stress response as seen in ASD.

Sensory processing abnormalities are now considered a core symptom of ASD under the Restrictive and Stereotypic Behaviors criteria of the DSM-5 (American Psychiatric Association, 2013). Sensory behaviors have historically been divided into four patterns, including sensory hypo-reactivity, hyper-reactivity, sensory seeking, and sensory avoidance (Dunn, 2001; Ben-Sasson et al., 2009). Complexity arises from the fact that many individuals with ASD will show several of these patterns at one time, with mixed patterns being displayed across sensory domains (Baranek et al., 2006; Tomchek and Dunn, 2007; Lidstone et al., 2014). Recent conceptualizations, therefore, have attempted to classify sensory processing abnormalities in ASD into specific subtypes (Lane et al., 2011, 2014; Uljarević et al., 2016), such as sensory adaptive, sensory moderate, and sensory severe (Uljarević et al., 2016).

Emerging research demonstrates a relationship between sensory sensitivities and arousal/anxiety in ASD. In one study, children with ASD showed lower morning cortisol relative to TD peers, which was associated with higher parent-reported stress as measured by the Stress Survey Schedule (SSS) (Corbett et al., 2009). Similarly, morning cortisol was associated with various domains of sensory functioning derived from the Short Sensory Profile—a parent-reported indicator of sensory sensitivities—(SSP; Dunn, 1999) painting a complex picture based on individual profiles (Corbett et al., 2009). Other studies investigating sensory profiles in ASD have also found relationships between sensory responsivity and anxiety (Green et al., 2012; Lidstone et al., 2014; Wigham et al., 2015; Uljarević et al., 2016), repetitive behaviors and stereotyped movements (Gabriels et al., 2008; Gal et al., 2010; Lidstone et al., 2014), and intolerance of uncertainty (Chamberlain et al., 2013; Wigham et al., 2015). Furthermore, a sample of TD young adults showed a correlation between sensory sensitivity and increased interpersonal distance (Perry et al., 2016), suggesting some role of sensory processing in social behavior. Currently, however, there is limited research that attempts to elucidate the impact of sensory dysfunction on social motivation and communication, especially in a naturalistic play setting.

The current study sought to investigate between-group differences in biobehavioral profiles of psychosocial stress following play with unfamiliar peers, in conjunction with sensory profiles. In order to elucidate the impact of sensory dysfunction on stress and social interaction, the current study sought to measure social engagement during a Peer Interaction Paradigm (PIP) (Corbett et al., 2010) and then to compare social behavior to stress and sensory profiles, as indicated by measures of cortisol and parent reports of stress and sensory sensitivity. It was hypothesized that children with ASD would have greater cortisol in response to play, relative to TD peers. Furthermore, it was hypothesized that cortisol response would be positively correlated with both increased parent-reported stress and sensory sensitivity.

MATERIALS AND METHODS

Participants

The sample included 80 un-medicated, pre-pubertal, children between the ages of 8-to 12 years, including 40 with ASD (mean = 9.65 years) and 40 TD (mean = 9.79 years). The gender composition included 14 females (6 = ASD, 8 = TD) and 66 males (34 = ASD, 32 = TD). ASD diagnosis was based on the Diagnostic and Statistical Manual (DSM-5) criteria (American Psychiatric Association, 2013) and established by all of the following: (1) a previous diagnosis by a psychologist, psychiatrist, or behavioral pediatrician with ASD expertise; (2) current clinical judgment; and (3) corroborated by the ADOS (Lord et al., 2000), administered by research-reliable personnel. For inclusion in the study all participants were required to have an estimated IQ of 80 or above, as measured by the Wechsler Abbreviated Scale of Intelligence (Wechsler, 1999). In addition, pubertal status was determined by the Pubertal Development Scale (Petersen et al., 1988) to confirm that the child had not yet entered puberty.

The Vanderbilt University Institutional Review Board approved the study. The investigation was performed in accordance with the Helsinki Declaration for research involving human subjects. Prior to inclusion in the study, informed written consent from parents and verbal assent from research participants were obtained. Participants were recruited by IRB approved flyers and several recruitment systems via clinics, subject tracking systems, resource centers, support groups, schools, and recreational facilities.

As described below, the study also included children who served as confederates (actor that participates in the study), who were of the same age and gender as the ASD and TD children. Parents of the confederates provided informed consent for them to train for and participate in the study. Confederates were selected based on demonstrated strong social skills, genuine desire to play and interact with children with and without disabilities, and an ability to follow research personnel instructions and translate them into age appropriate play behaviors. All confederates underwent several training procedures, including reading an instruction manual, direct skills modeling, and playground practice. The majority of the confederates had previously participated in research or served as a peer helper for children with disabilities.

Peer Interaction Playground Paradigm

The Peer Interaction Paradigm examines social exchanges between children with and without ASD within a naturalistic playground environment (Corbett et al., 2010). The playground is a 130 by 120 ft. fenced in play area that is part of the Susan Gray Preschool. The 20-min paradigm consisted of periods of free play and opportunities for cooperative play, which was facilitated by an age- and gender-match TD confederate. The trained confederate followed cues provided by research personnel through an earpiece with a remote transmitter, in order to provide structure to play by simultaneously soliciting play with both research participants. Use of a confederate permitted each interactive sequence of free or solicited play to occur within an otherwise natural setting, while also maintaining an even level of play to prevent increased aerobic activity, which could affect cortisol levels. In addition to the confederate, the paradigm involved one child with ASD and one TD child, all three of whom were unfamiliar with each other prior to the interaction. Each participant only took part in one 20-min session, such that the exposure represented a novel social experience. During the protocol, research personnel remained in the building in order to facilitate more natural play behavior.

The paradigm was divided into four 5-min time (T) periods of intermittent free play and solicited play (see **Figure 1**). The first period (T1) consisted of unsolicited free play. During the second period (T2), the confederate was instructed to solicit interaction for cooperative play on the playground equipment. During the third period (T3), the confederate returned to unsolicited free play. During the fourth period (T4), the confederate was instructed to once again solicit the two participants to engage in a cooperative game involving toys.

Interactions were recorded using state-of-the-art video equipment, including four professional Sony EVI D70 (Sony, New York, NY, USA) remotely operated cameras housed in glass cases, which were affixed to the four corners of the playground's fence. The cameras contain pan, tilt, and zoom features allowing full capture of the playground. To record remote audio communication, Motorola MC22OR GMRS-FRS (Motorola, Libertyville, IL, USA) and Audio-Technica (Audio-Technica, Stow, Ohio, USA) transmitters and receivers functioning as battery-operated microphones were clipped to each child's shirt. Audio was recorded using an eight-channel mixing board.

Behavior Coding

The Observer XT Version 8.0 software was used for the collection and analysis of the observational social interaction data (Noldus, 2008). Data were analyzed based on a predefined list of operationalized behaviors (Corbett et al., 2010; Schupp et al., 2013) by research-reliable raters who were unaware of the current study aims. Behaviors were analyzed using a transactional approach (i.e., *who does what to whom*) based on predefined operationalized behaviors (Mendoza and Mason, 1989; Lyons et al., 1990, 1992; Mason et al., 1993). Inter-rater reliability was calculated using Cohen's Kappa at $K = 0.80$, while test-retest reliability was $K = 0.89$. Cooperative play interactions were calculated as percentage of time engaged (verbal 90% and $K = 0.85$; group play 91% and $K = 0.89$). Variables such as cooperative play and verbal interaction were operationalized based upon previously described definitions and as part of a larger study (Corbett et al., 2014b). For the purpose of this study, cooperative play was defined as the percentage of time engaged in a reciprocal activity for enjoyment that involved and relied on the participation of two or more

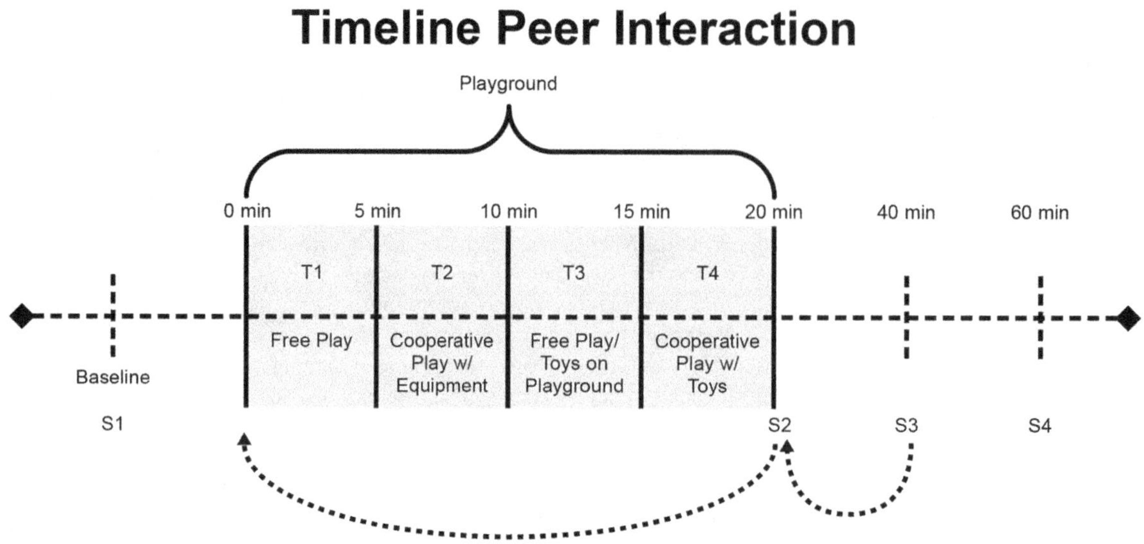

FIGURE 1 | Peer interaction paradigm timeline of events. The 20-min paradigm consists of four 5-min periods of free play (T1), solicited play with equipment (T2), free, unsolicited play (T3), and solicited cooperative play with toys (T4). Salivary cortisol measures were taken at baseline (S1), immediately after the paradigm (S2), 20-min after the paradigm (S3), and 40-min after (S4).

children (e.g., hide and seek). For an expanded description of the behavior coding protocol and operationalized variables, see previous studies (Corbett et al., 2010, 2014b; Schupp et al., 2013).

Salivary Cortisol Sampling

Basal levels of salivary cortisol were collected from home to ascertain the child's afternoon baseline over 3 days, using established methods, as part of a larger study (Corbett et al., 2008). For the purpose of this study, only playground cortisol levels were analyzed.

It is important to note that there is an approximate 20-min time lag between when an event occurs and when a related change in cortisol can be detected in saliva (Kirschbaum and Hellhammer, 1989). The peer interaction included four salivary cortisol samples taken 20 min apart for each subject: S1–(baseline), S2–(immediately post-play), S3–(20 min post-play), and S4–(40 min post play). The S2 measurement taken immediately after the peer interaction represents circulating cortisol levels at the start of the paradigm, while the S3 measurement is representative of levels at the end of the peer interaction (see **Figure 1**). All peer interactions were held in the afternoon between 13:00 and 16:00, for comparison to afternoon baseline values.

Immediately before and following the playground paradigm, the ASD and TD participants were each assigned to an individual room and sat with a research assistant for cortisol sampling. A similar bag of toys and activities was provided to each child in order to maintain consistency in experience across all participants. Samples were collected following the standardized drool procedures outlined in previous studies (Corbett et al., 2008, 2010).

Cortisol Assay

The salivary cortisol assay was performed using a Coat-A-Count® radioimmunoassay kit (Siemens Medical Solutions Diagnostics, Los Angeles, CA) modified to accommodate lower levels of cortisol in human saliva relative to plasma. Saliva samples, which had been stored at −20°C, were thawed and centrifuged at 3460 rpm for 15 min to separate the aqueous component from mucins and other suspended particles. The coated tube from the kit was substituted with a glass tube into which 100 μl of saliva, 100 μl of cortisol antibody (courtesy of Wendell Nicholson, Vanderbilt University, Nashville, TN), and 100 μl of ^{125}I-cortisol were mixed. After incubation at 4°C for 24 h 100 μl of normal rat serum in 0.1% PO4/EDTA buffer (1:50) and precipitating reagent (PR81) were added. The mixture was centrifuged at 3460 rpm for 30 min, decanted, and counted. Serial dilution of samples indicated a linearity of 0.99. Interassay coefficient of variation was 10.4%.

Dependent Measures

Short Sensory Profile (SSP; Dunn, 1999)

The SSP is a parent-report questionnaire designed to assess sensory sensitivity across seven sensory domains, such as auditory sensitivity, tactile sensitivity, and underresponsive/seeks sensation. Parents are asked to rate the frequency with which their child engages in behaviors related to sensory sensitivity in each domain. Possible scores range from 5 points to 1 point, ranging from "never responds in this manner" (5 points) to "always responds in this manner" (1 points). High raw scores indicate typical performance, while lower scores on the SSP are indicative of greater sensory dysfunction. The primary variable of interest for analysis was total raw score.

Stress Survey Schedule (SSS; Groden et al., 2001)

The SSS is a 60-item, parent-report survey designed to measure the daily stress of individuals with ASD and other developmental disabilities. The survey addresses eight domains of stress: Anticipation/Uncertainty, Changes and Threats, Unpleasant Events, Pleasant Events, Sensory/Personal Contact, Food Related Activity, Social/Environmental Interactions, and Ritual Related Stress. Parents are asked to rate intensity of stress for each item on a five-point Likert scale, ranging from none to mild stress (1) to severe stress (5). Internal consistency correlations range from 0.70 to 0.87. Higher total scores are indicative of enhanced stress, and total raw score was used for analysis.

Salivary Cortisol

The primary outcome variable of interest for characterizing the stress response was salivary cortisol. Samples were analyzed for S1–S4, as described above. Because salivary cortisol measurements are positive and skewed toward large values, a log transformation was performed to achieve approximate normality. Log-transformed values were used in all analyses.

Social Behavior

The primary outcome variable for social behavior was percent time spent in cooperative play during solicited play at T4 of the PIP.

Statistical Analysis

Descriptive statistics were calculated for demographic information, as well as parent-report measures of sensory functioning (SSP) and child stress (SSS); possible group differences in these variables were examined using independent samples t-tests. Analysis of covariance (ANCOVA) models were utilized to examine group differences in salivary cortisol response, controlling for baseline cortisol values. Pearson product moment correlations were conducted to examine associations between the sensory and stress measures. Moderation analyses were conducted to determine whether diagnosis was a moderator of the relation between SSP and cortisol response.

All statistical analyses were conducted using SPSS Version 22.0 (IBM Corp, 2013). The PROCESS application for SPSS was used to conduct moderation analyses (Hayes, 2013).

RESULTS

Demographic information for each group is presented in **Table 1**, including age, cognitive, and diagnostic information. Descriptive statistics for SSP, SSS, and cooperative play (separated by group) are listed in **Table 2**. Using independent samples t-tests, there were significant between-group differences on the SSP [$t_{(78)} = 140.44$, $p < 0.0001$] and the SSS [$t_{(77)} = 109.32$, $p < 0.0001$], showing greater parent-reported stress and sensory sensitivity in the ASD group, compared to the TD group.

In order to assess group differences in social behavior, the percent duration of cooperative play during the solicited play period T4 of the PIP was compared between groups, using independent samples t-tests. Results revealed a significant difference between groups in percent duration of cooperative play [$t_{(83)} = 8.349, p = 0.005$], showing that children with ASD engage in significantly less cooperative play than TD peers.

TABLE 1 | Demographics.

Variable	ASD mean (SD)	TD mean (SD)	*P*-value
Age	9.65 (1.485)	9.79 (1.631)	0.699
SCQ total	20.72 (7.229)	2.37 (2.123)	<0.0001
Performance IQ	111.03 (53.394)	112.45 (12.831)	0.973
Verbal IQ	108.72 (62.858)	112.16 (13.997)	0.240
WASI estimated IQ	101.22 (22.505)	119.47 (13.123)	<0.001

ASD, Autism spectrum disorder; IQ, intelligence quotient; TD, typical development; SCQ, social communication questionnaire; WASI, Weschler abbreviated scale of intelligence.

TABLE 2 | Descriptive statistics for parent-report measures and play.

Variable	ASD mean (SD)	TD mean (SD)	*P*-value
TOTAL SCORES			
Short sensory profile	122.28 (21.393)	172.82 (16.629)	<0.0001
Stress survey schedule	122.02 (30.243)	62.59 (18.823)	<0.0001
PERCENT TIME INTERACTING			
Cooperative play	55.15 (36.08)	74.54 (24.13)	0.005

TABLE 3 | Descriptive statistics for log cortisol at baseline, in response to the PIP, and after the PIP.

Cortisol value	ASD mean (SD)	TD mean (SD)
Baseline cortisol (S1)	−0.1515 (0.333)	−0.1034 (0.267)
Cortisol during play (S3)	−0.1284 (0.303)	−0.2730 (0.373)
Cortisol after play (S4)	−0.2190 (0.293)	−0.3148 (0.266)

Descriptive statistics for cortisol at baseline, during play, and after play are shown in **Table 3**. Analysis of covariance (ANCOVA) was conducted to examine the effect of group on stress (cortisol levels during cooperative play with peers), while controlling for baseline values. Results indicate a significant group difference in cortisol during play (S3) with peers [$F_{(1,\ 77)} = 5.77$, $p = 0.02$]. There was also a significant group difference in cortisol after play (S4) [$F_{(1,\ 77)} = 4.78, p = 0.03$].

In consideration of these group differences, Pearson product correlations were calculated to assess the relations between physiological stress (cortisol), sensory functioning (SSP), and parent-report stress (SSS). Cortisol during play was negatively correlated with scores on the SSP ($r = -0.24$, $p = 0.03$) and positively correlated with scores on the SSS ($r = 0.27, p = 0.02$). Therefore, as cortisol levels increased during the PIP, SSP scores decreased (indicating greater sensory dysfunction) and global stress as measured by the SSS increased.

Moderation analysis was conducted to examine the impact of diagnosis on the relation between stress (cortisol) and sensory (SSP) functioning. Results show that diagnosis was a significant moderator of the association between SSP and cortisol at baseline (S1) [$\Delta R^2 = 0.01$, $F_{(1,\ 76)} = 8.46$, $p = 0.0047$], the beginning

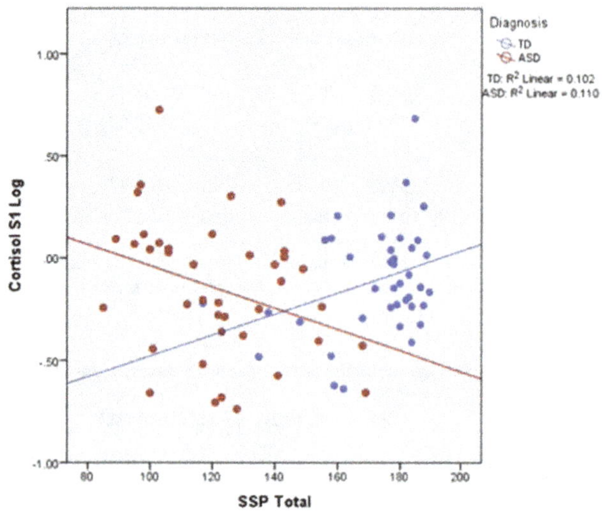

FIGURE 2 | Relationship between cortisol and sensory profile in children with ASD and TD peers.

of play (S2) [$\Delta R^2 = 0.06$, $F_{(1, 76)} = 4.85$, $p = 0.03$], during play (S3) [$\Delta R^2 = 0.02$, $F_{(1, 76)} = 3.94$, $p = 0.05$], and after play (S4) [$\Delta R^2 = 0.05$, $F_{(1, 76)} = 3.95$, $p = 0.05$]. **Figure 2** shows the moderating effect of diagnosis on the relation between SSP and cortisol, indicating that the negative correlation observed between cortisol and sensory functioning in the total sample is driven by the ASD group, whereas the opposite trend appears to hold true for the TD group.

In order to examine the impact of sensory sensitivity on play, we examined the association between SSP score and percent duration spent in cooperative play during the solicited play period, T4. There was a trend level positive association between cooperative play and total SSP ($r = 0.197$, $p = 0.07$). This association suggests that more sensory impairment was associated with less time spent in cooperative play (lower scores on the SSP are indicative of greater sensory dysfunction).

In an effort to further assess the impact of sensory sensitivity on play, *post-hoc* correlational analyses were conducted for individual domains of the SSP along with time spent in cooperative play. Scores on the Auditory domain were significantly positively correlated with cooperative play ($r = 0.218$, $p = 0.04$), while Underresponsive/Seeks Sensation correlated with play at a trend level ($r = 0.196$, $p = 0.07$).

DISCUSSION

While challenges in reciprocal social interaction are synonymous with ASD, sensory dysfunction and heightened stress are often found as well. Thus, the current study sought to examine the impact of sensory dysfunction on stress and social engagement with unfamiliar peers in children with and without ASD. The study utilized measures of social interaction (cooperative play) and physiological arousal (cortisol) during peer play using the PIP (Corbett et al., 2010) to assess the associations of social behavior and physiological stress with parent reports of stress and sensory sensitivity. It was hypothesized that children with ASD would show greater levels of salivary cortisol in response to play, relative to TD peers. Furthermore, it was hypothesized that cortisol response would be positively correlated with both increased parent-reported stress and sensory sensitivity. Therefore, the current study sought to further investigate biobehavioral profiles following play with unfamiliar peers with an emphasis on the impact of sensory sensitivity.

Autism is characterized by prevalence of sensory dysfunction (Rogers et al., 2003; Kern et al., 2006; Tomchek and Dunn, 2007; Ben-Sasson et al., 2009) and increased stress, especially during social interactions (Lopata et al., 2008; Corbett et al., 2010). In the current study, children with ASD showed both increased sensory dysfunction and parent-reported stress, relative to their TD peers. Research has shown that both altered sensory sensitivity and stress have deleterious effects on the overall functioning of children with ASD, especially given their potential associations with a variety of challenges, such as poor response to change (e.g., Chamberlain et al., 2013; Wigham et al., 2015) and anxiety (Green et al., 2012; Lidstone et al., 2014; Wigham et al., 2015; Uljarević et al., 2016).

In addition to group differences in sensory sensitivity and parent-reported stress, differences in salivary cortisol response were observed. Consistent with previous reports (Corbett et al., 2010, 2012, 2014b; Schupp et al., 2013), the ASD group had significantly greater physiological arousal in response to social interaction relative to the TD group, as indicated by higher cortisol levels both during and after the PIP. The increased arousal suggests that children with ASD may perceive social interaction with peers to be more stressful, compared to TD peers. Moreover, cortisol response was significantly correlated with parent-reported stress suggesting that heightened physiological reactions to peer interaction are also associated with a global pattern of elevated stress. Findings add to a growing body of work showing dysregulated patterns of stress in youth with ASD, both in terms of global and diurnal stress (Corbett et al., 2008, 2009), as well as stress in response to social interaction (e.g., Corbett et al., 2014b).

In light of observing group differences for both physiological stress and sensory sensitivity, we explored correlations between these variables. Significant associations were found between cortisol and SSP, such that higher cortisol in response to play was associated with greater sensory impairment. Moderation analyses were conducted to determine whether the correlation was driven by group status. Results showed that ASD diagnosis was a significant moderator of this relation, such that sensory dysfunction was associated with increased salivary cortisol response to peer interaction in the ASD group only. Moreover, this relationship held for cortisol levels at each time point of collection, including baseline cortisol as well as before, during, and after play. Interestingly, the TD group appeared to have the opposite relationship between cortisol and sensory functioning (**Figure 2**), implying that the negative impact of sensory sensitivity on stress reactivity during play is unique to ASD. In other words, greater levels of sensory dysfunction in ASD may lead to increased physiological stress. Thus, it appears that the symptom profile of ASD ostensibly contributes to enhanced reactivity to the environment, which can be manifested in both sensory and physiological functioning. The question still remains whether or not these relationships between stress and sensory sensitivity are bi-directional or whether a uni-directional model exists, such that one symptom precedes and drives the other.

When assessing group differences in cooperative play, the ASD group engaged in significantly less cooperative play, relative to the TD group. This is in line with previous findings that children with ASD tend to engage less than their TD peers during the PIP (e.g., Corbett et al., 2014b). While factors such as social cognition (Baron-Cohen, 1995; Corbett et al., 2014a) and social motivation (Chevallier et al., 2012; Corbett et al., 2014b) appear to play a significant role in explaining group differences in social engagement, sensory dysfunction may also have an impact on social behavior. For example, sensory sensitivity was recently shown to associate with interpersonal distance in TD individuals (Perry et al., 2016). In order to better understand the potential impact of sensory sensitivity on play behavior in ASD, duration spent in cooperative play was analyzed along with sensory processing scores. While overall sensory dysfunction was not associated with play behavior, auditory sensitivity was significantly correlated with play.

Adults with ASD have shown impairments in auditory localization through an inability to use prior perceptual experience to locate sounds (Skewes and Gebauer, 2016). Difficulties in auditory processing and orienting to a stimulus may be linked to emergence of impairments in social and communication behaviors early in development (Osterling et al., 2002). As such, children with ASD fail to orient to stimuli, especially critical social stimuli such as response to their own name (Dawson et al., 1998). It is possible that the inability to attend to stimuli is due, in part, to altered auditory processing, resulting in reduced early social interactions through a lack of joint attention with the caregiver. According to the Enactive Mind hypothesis (Klin et al., 2003), limited early social experiences may contribute to the social communication deficits that characterize ASD. Therefore, if sensory sensitivity alters one's experience in the physical world, interactions in the social world may be absent, incomplete, or unpredictable among children with ASD, thus leading to difficulties in social communication and cognition. While this is an intriguing theory for connecting the sensory and social symptoms of ASD, a great deal of empirical evidence is needed to test for direct links between sensory and social functioning in ASD.

Limitations and Future Directions

The study had several strengths, including a relatively large sample size and use of a validated protocol for observing play behavior in a naturalistic playground setting. Some limitations do exist. Although parent-reports are the most commonly used measure of sensory profile in ASD and provide a useful representation of sensory dysfunction, future studies would benefit from more objective tests of sensory sensitivity such as assessment of various sensory domains (e.g., auditory, tactile) or through clinician-based observations. Furthermore, this study assessed only one novel exposure, representing everyday experiences of interacting with new people. A limitation of the current study is the lack of repeated exposure, which would allow for assessing stress response across several repeat social encounters. The study was also limited to one measure of physiological arousal (i.e., cortisol). Use of other measures such as respiratory sinus arrhythmia (e.g., Benevides and Lane, 2013) could provide a more detailed, continuous assessment of regulation and arousal throughout the protocol.

Novel social experiences are only one aspect of daily social interactions. The current study focused on these novel experiences. Results were consistent with previous reports (Corbett et al., 2010, 2012, 2014b; Schupp et al., 2013) suggesting that when exposed to new peers for the first time, children with ASD experience greater physiological stress and tend to engage in less cooperative play with those new people, relative to their TD peers. However, social interactions are not solely reliant on single interactions with new people. Children interact with the same peers on a daily basis at school, and physiological stress or sensory sensitivity could have significant effects on how children with ASD interact with familiar peers in a setting such as the classroom. Therefore, future studies should investigate the role of sensory sensitivity and physiological stress during repeat exposure.

The findings that sensory dysfunction may negatively impact social behavior is notable and warrants further investigation. It would be helpful to discern whether targeting sensory symptoms via treatment could indirectly improve social motivation in individuals with ASD. While results show several interactions are present between physiological stress, sensory sensitivity, and parent-report stress, the directionality among these variables remains unclear. Future studies are needed to determine the extent to which change in one variable leads to change in another. The findings that the association between cortisol and sensory sensitivity was driven by the ASD group requires further investigation to enhance understanding of the mechanisms behind the purported link, which appears specific to ASD. Finally, while auditory sensitivity and cooperative play were correlated, further research is needed to determine any possible causal impact of sensory sensitivity on social motivation.

Summary

The primary objective of the current study was to examine the impact of sensory sensitivity on stress response and peer interaction in children with and without ASD. Results show that cortisol response to play is elevated in children with ASD and that higher physiological arousal during play is associated with greater sensory sensitivity and parent-reported stress. Additionally, ASD diagnosis confers risk for atypical sensory and stress reactivity, which may further contribute to the core social deficits. Taken together, results provide evidence for important interactions among social, sensory, and physiological profiles in ASD. Characterizing and assessing such profiles may better predict global outcomes, while also serving to inform more effective methods for intervention.

AUTHOR CONTRIBUTIONS

The named authors made significant contributions to the investigation and manuscript. Specifically, BC conceptualized the study design, outlined the organization of the manuscript, guided the literature search, ran data analysis, provided interpretation to the findings, and made significant contributions to the final manuscript. RM read the extant literature, synthesized the results, contributed to interpretation of the findings, and co-wrote the initial draft of the manuscript. SB participated in the acquisition, analysis, and interpretation of the physiological and behavioral data, and contributed to the writing of the manuscript. All authors read and approved the content of the work.

FUNDING

This work was supported by National Institute of Mental Health R01 MH085717 awarded to BC.

REFERENCES

American Psychiatric Association (2013). *Diagnostic and Statistical Manual of Mental Disorders, 5th Edn (DSM-5).* Washington, DC: American Psychiatric Association. doi: 10.1176/appi.books.9780890425596

Baranek, G. T., David, F. J., Poe, M. D., Stone, W. L., and Watson, L. R. (2006). Sensory Experiences Questionnaire: discriminating sensory features in young children with autism, developmental delays, and typical development. *J. Child Psychol. Psychiatry* 47, 591–601. doi: 10.1111/j.1469-7610.2005.01546.x

Baron-Cohen, S. (1995). *Mindblindness: An Essay on Autism and Theory of Mind.* Cambridge, MA: MIT Press.

Benevides, T. W., and Lane, S. J. (2013). A review of cardiac autonomic measures: considerations for examination of physiological response in children with autism spectrum disorder. *J. Autism Dev. Disord.* 45, 560–575. doi: 10.1007/s10803-013-1971-z

Ben-Sasson, A., Hen, L., Fluss, R., Cermak, S. A., Engel-Yeger, B., and Gal, E. (2009). A meta-analysis of sensory modulation symptoms in individuals with autism spectrum disorders. *J. Autism Dev. Disord.* 39, 1–11. doi: 10.1007/s10803-008-0593-3

Chamberlain, P. D., Rodgers, J., Crowley, M. J., White, S. E., Freeston, M. H., and South, M. (2013). A potentiated startle study of uncertainty and contextual anxiety in adolescents diagnosed with autism spectrum disorder. *Mol. Autism* 4, 31. doi: 10.1186/2040-2392-4-31

Chevallier, C., Kohls, G., Troiani, V., Brodkin, E. S., and Schultz, R. T. (2012). The social motivation theory of autism. *Trends Cogn. Sci.* 16, 231–239. doi: 10.1016/j.tics.2012.02.007

Corbett, B. A., Mendoza, S., Wegelin, J. A., Carmean, V., and Levine, S. (2008). Variable cortisol circadian rhythms in children with autism and anticipatory stress. *J. Psychiatry Neurosci.* 33, 227–234.

Corbett, B. A., Newsom, C., Key, A. P., Qualls, L. R., and Edmiston, E. K. (2014a). Examining the relationship between face processing and social interaction behavior in children with and without autism spectrum disorder. *J. Neurodev. Disord.* 6, 1. doi: 10.1186/1866-1955-6-35

Corbett, B. A., Schupp, C. W., and Lanni, K. E. (2012). Comparing biobehavioral profiles across two social stress paradigms in children with and without autism spectrum disorders. *Mol. Autism* 3, 13. doi: 10.1186/2040-2392-3-13

Corbett, B. A., Schupp, C. W., Levine, S., and Mendoza, S. (2009). Comparing cortisol, stress, and sensory sensitivity in children with autism. *Autism Res.* 2, 39–49. doi: 10.1002/aur.64

Corbett, B. A., Schupp, C. W., Simon, D., Ryan, N., and Mendoza, S. (2010). Elevated cortisol during play is associated with age and social engagement in children with autism. *Mol. Autism* 1, 13. doi: 10.1186/2040-2392-1-13

Corbett, B. A., Swain, D. M., Newsom, C., Wang, L., Song, Y., and Edgerton, D. (2014b). Biobehavioral profiles of arousal and social motivation in autism spectrum disorders. *J. Child Psychol. Psychiatry* 55, 924–934. doi: 10.1111/jcpp.12184

Dawson, G., Meltzoff, A. N., Osterling, J., Rinaldi, J., and Brown, E. (1998). Children with autism fail to orient to naturally occurring social stimuli. *J. Autism Dev. Disord.* 28, 479–485. doi: 10.1023/A:1026043926488

Dunn, W. (1999). *Short Sensory Profile.* San Antonio, TX: Psychological Corporation.

Dunn, W. (2001). The sensations of everyday life: empirical, theoretical, and pragmatic considerations. *Am. J. Occup. Ther.* 55, 608–620. doi: 10.5014/ajot.55.6.608

Gabriels, R. L., Agnew, J. A., Miller, L. J., Gralla, J., Pan, Z., Goldson, E., et al. (2008). Is there a relationship between restricted, repetitive, stereotyped behaviors and interests and abnormal sensory response in children with autism spectrum disorders? *Res. Autism Spectr. Disord.* 2, 660–670. doi: 10.1016/j.rasd.2008.02.002

Gal, E., Dyck, M. J., and Passmore, A. (2010). Relationships between stereotyped movements and sensory processing disorders in children with and without developmental or sensory disorders. *Am. J. Occup. Ther.* 64, 453–461. doi: 10.5014/ajot.2010.09075

Green, S. A., Ben-Sasson, A., Soto, T. W., and Carter, A. S. (2012). Anxiety and sensory over-responsivity in toddlers with autism spectrum disorders: bidirectional effects across time. *J. Autism Dev. Disord.* 42, 1112–1119. doi: 10.1007/s10803-011-1361-3

Groden, J., Diller, A., Bausman, M., Velicer, W., Norman, G., and Cautela, J. (2001). The development of a stress survey schedule for persons with autism and other developmental disabilities. *J. Autism Dev. Disord.* 31, 207–217. doi: 10.1023/A:1010755300436

Hayes, A. F. (2013). *Introduction to Mediation, Moderation, and Conditional Process Analysis.* New York, NY: Guilford Press.

Herman, J. P., and Cullinan, W. E. (1997). Neurocircuitry of stress: central control of the hypothalamo-pituitary-adrenocortical axis. *Trends Neurosci.* 20, 78–84. doi: 10.1016/S0166-2236(96)10069-2

Humphrey, N., and Symes, W. (2011). Peer interaction patterns among adolescents with autistic spectrum disorders (ASDs) in mainstream school settings. *Autism* 15, 397–419. doi: 10.1177/1362361310387804

IBM Corp. (2013). *IBM SPSS Statistics for Windows, Version 22.0.* Armonk, NY: IBM Corp.

Kennedy, D. P., and Adolphs, R. (2014). Violations of personal space by individuals with autism spectrum disorder. *PLoS ONE* 9:e103369. doi: 10.1371/journal.pone.0103369

Kern, J. K., Trivedi, M. H., Garver, C. R., Grannemann, B. D., Andrews, A. A., Savla, J. S., et al. (2006). The pattern of sensory processing abnormalities in autism. *Autism* 10, 480–494. doi: 10.1177/1362361306066564

Kirschbaum, C., and Hellhammer, D. H. (1989). Salivary cortisol in psychobiological research: an overview. *Neuropsychobiology* 22, 150–169. doi: 10.1159/000118611

Klin, A., Jones, W., Schultz, R., and Volkmar, F. (2003). The enactive mind, or from actions to cognition: lessons from autism. *Philos. Trans. R. Soc. Lond. B Biol. Sci.* 358, 345–360. doi: 10.1098/rstb.2002.1202

Knott, F., Dunlop, A.-W., and Mackay, T. (2006). Living with ASD: how do children and their parents assess their difficulties with social interaction and understanding? *Autism* 10, 609–617. doi: 10.1177/1362361306068510

Lane, A. E., Dennis, S. J., and Geraghty, M. E. (2011). Brief report: further evidence of sensory subtypes in autism. *J. Autism Dev. Disord.* 41, 826–831. doi: 10.1007/s10803-010-1103-y

Lane, A. E., Molloy, C. A., and Bishop, S. L. (2014). Classification of children with autism spectrum disorder by sensory subtype: a case for sensory-based phenotypes. *Autism Res.* 7, 322–333. doi: 10.1002/aur.1368

Lidstone, J., Uljarević, M., Sullivan, J., Rodgers, J., McConachie, H., Freeston, M., et al. (2014). Relations among restricted and repetitive behaviors, anxiety and sensory features in children with autism spectrum disorders. *Res. Autism Spectr. Disord.* 8, 82–92. doi: 10.1016/j.rasd.2013.10.001

Lopata, C., Volker, M. A., Putnam, S. K., Thomeer, M. L., and Nida, R. E. (2008). Effect of social familiarity on salivary cortisol and self-reports of social anxiety and stress in children with high functioning autism spectrum disorders. *J. Autism Dev. Disord.* 38, 1866–1877. doi: 10.1007/s10803-008-0575-5

Lord, C., Risi, S., Lambrecht, L., Cook, E. H. Jr., Leventhal, B. L., DiLavore, P. C., et al. (2000). The Autism diagnostic observation schedule—generic: a standard measure of social and communication deficits associated with the spectrum of autism. *J. Autism Dev. Disord.* 30, 205–223. doi: 10.1023/A:1005592401947

Lough, E., Hanley, M., Rodgers, J., South, M., Kirk, H., Kennedy, D. P., et al. (2015). Violations of personal space in young people with autism spectrum disorders and williams syndrome: insights from the social responsiveness scale. *J. Autism Dev. Disord.* 45, 4101–4108. doi: 10.1007/s10803-015-2536-0

Lyons, D., Mason, W. A., and Mendoza, S. P. (1990). Beyond the ethogram: transactional analysis of behavior in primate social interchanges. *Am. J. Primatol.* 20, 209.

Lyons, D. M., Mendoza, S. P., and Mason, W. A. (1992). Sexual segregation in squirrel monkeys (*Saimiri sciureus*): a transactional analysis of adult social dynamics. *J. Comp. Psychol.* 106, 323–330. doi: 10.1037/0735-7036.106.4.323

Mason, W. A., Long, D. D., and Mendoza, S. P. (1993). "Temperament and mother–infant conflict in macaques: a transactional analysis," in *Primate Social Conflict*, ed W. M. S. Mendoza (Albany, NY: State University of New York Press), 205–227.

Mendoza, S. P., and Mason, W. A. (1989). Behavioral and endocrine consequences of heterosexual pair formation in squirrel monkeys. *Physiol. Behav.* 46, 597–603. doi: 10.1016/0031-9384(89)90338-7

Noldus (2008). *The Observer XT.* Vol. 10.5. Wageningen: Noldus Information Technology.

Osterling, J. A., Dawson, G., and Munson, J. A. (2002). Early recognition of 1-year-old infants with autism spectrum disorder versus mental retardation. *Dev. Psychopathol.* 14, 239–251. doi: 10.1017/S0954579402002031

Perry, A., Levy-Gigi, E., Richter-Levin, G., and Shamay-Tsoory, S. G. (2015). Interpersonal distance and social anxiety in autistic spectrum disorders: a behavioral and ERP study. *Soc. Neurosci.* 10, 354–365. doi: 10.1080/17470919.2015.1010740

Perry, A., Nichiporuk, N., and Knight, R. T. (2016). Where does one stand: a biological account of preferred interpersonal distance. *Soc. Cogn. Affect. Neurosci.* 11, 317–326. doi: 10.1093/scan/nsv115

Petersen, A. C., Crockett, L., Richards, M., and Boxer, A. (1988). A self-report measure of pubertal status: reliability, validity, and initial norms. *J. Youth Adolescence* 17, 117–133. doi: 10.1007/BF01537962

Rogers, S. J., Hepburn, S., and Wehner, E. (2003). Parent reports of sensory symptoms in toddlers with autism and those with other developmental disorders. *J. Autism Dev. Disord.* 33, 631–642. doi: 10.1023/B:JADD.0000006000.38991.a7

Schupp, C. W., Simon, D., and Corbett, B. A. (2013). Cortisol responsivity differences in children with autism spectrum disorders during free and cooperative play. *J. Autism Dev. Disord.* 43, 2405–2417. doi: 10.1007/s10803-013-1790-2

Skewes, J. C., and Gebauer, L. (2016). Brief report: suboptimal auditory localization in autism spectrum disorder: support for the bayesian account of sensory symptoms. *J. Autism Dev. Disord.* 46, 2539–2547. doi: 10.1007/s10803-016-2774-9

Tomchek, S. D., and Dunn, W. (2007). Sensory processing in children with and without autism: a comparative study using the short sensory profile. *Am. J. Occup. Ther.* 61, 190–200. doi: 10.5014/ajot.61.2.190

Uljarević, M., Lane, A., Kelly, A., and Leekam, S. (2016). Sensory subtypes and anxiety in older children and adolescents with autism spectrum disorder. *Autism Res.* doi: 10.1002/aur.1602. [Epub ahead of print].

Wechsler, D. (1999). *Wechsler Abbreviated Scale of Intelligence.* San Antonio, TX: Psychological Corporation.

Wigham, S., Rodgers, J., South, M., McConachie, H., and Freeston, M. (2015). The interplay between sensory processing abnormalities, intolerance of uncertainty, anxiety and restricted and repetitive behaviours in autism spectrum disorder. *J. Autism Dev. Disord.* 45, 943–952. doi: 10.1007/s10803-014-2248-x

2

A Preference for Biological Motion Predicts a Reduction in Symptom Severity 1 Year Later in Preschoolers with Autism Spectrum Disorders

Martina Franchini[1,2], Hilary Wood de Wilde[1], Bronwyn Glaser[1], Edouard Gentaz[2], Stephan Eliez[1,3] and Marie Schaer[1,4]*

[1] Office Médico-Pédagogique, University of Geneva, Geneva, Switzerland, [2] Psychology and Educational Sciences, University of Geneva, Geneva, Switzerland, [3] Department of Medical Genetics, Geneva University Medical School, Geneva, Switzerland, [4] Stanford Cognitive & Systems Neuroscience Laboratory, Stanford University, Palo Alto, CA, USA

Edited by:
Roberto Canitano, University Hospital of Siena, Italy

Reviewed by:
David Cochran, University of Massachusetts Medical Center, USA
Yang Xu, Washington University in St. Louis, USA

***Correspondence:**
Martina Franchini
martina.franchini@unige.ch

Recent research has consistently demonstrated reduced orienting to social stimuli in samples of young children with autism spectrum disorders (ASD). However, social orienting greatly varies between individual children on the spectrum. Better understanding this heterogeneity in social orienting may contribute to our comprehension of the mechanisms underlying autistic symptoms thereby improving our ability to intervene. Indeed, children on the autism spectrum who show higher levels of interest in social stimuli demonstrate reduced clinical symptoms and increased adaptive functioning. However, longitudinal studies examining the influence of social orienting on subsequent outcome are critically lacking. Here, we aim to explore the relationship between social interest at the age of 3 and changes in severity of autistic symptoms over the subsequent year, in 20 children with ASD and 20 age-matched typically developing (TD) children. A visual preference for social stimuli was measured using an eye-tracking task at baseline, consisting of a previously studied visual preference paradigm presenting biological and geometric motion side-by-side. The task was altered for the current study by alternating presentation side for each type of stimuli to keep visual perseveration from influencing participants' first fixation location. Clinical data were collected both at baseline and 1 year later at follow-up. As a group, we observed reduced interest for biological motion (BIO-M) in children with ASD compared to TD children, corroborating previous findings. We also confirmed that a preference for BIO-M is associated with better adaptive functioning in preschoolers with ASD. Most importantly, our longitudinal results showed that a preference for BIO-M strongly predicted decreased severity of diagnostic symptoms. Participants who preferred social stimuli at the age of 3 showed drastic reductions in their severity level of autistic symptoms 1 year later, whereas participants who preferred geometric stimuli showed autistic symptoms that were unchanged

Abbreviations: ASD, autism spectrum disorders; BIO-M, biological motion; BVMP, biological motion visual preference task; GEO-M, geometric motion; GR, geometric responders; SR, social responders; TD, typically developing.

or more severe after 1 year. As a whole, our results suggest that a preference for BIO-M may be key to understanding the behavioral phenotype of young children with ASD, and may represent a promising candidate behavior for predicting early developmental trajectories and outcome.

Keywords: autism spectrum disorders, early development, social orienting, eye-tracking, symptom severity, adaptive functioning

INTRODUCTION

Autism spectrum disorders (ASD) comprise behavioral symptomatology with significant heterogeneity (1–3). This heterogeneity is evident from the first year of life, when behavioral signs of autism are first detectable (4). Also, developmental trajectories of young individuals with ASD have been shown to be varied and related on the behavioral features noted when the diagnosis of autism was established (5–7). For example, the rare, but consistent, longitudinal studies of outcome predictors, which are based on symptoms in children with ASD during early development, suggest that higher levels of early adaptive, cognitive and socio-communicative functioning predict better clinical outcomes [e.g., Ref. (5, 7)].

Several studies aimed at disentangling the heterogeneity of ASD symptoms have searched for biomarkers for autism with inconsistent results [for a review, see Ref. (8)]. Eye-tracking represents a promising way to measure early and specific visual exploration patterns in ASD that are different from those of children with typical development or developmental delay [for a review, see Ref. (9)]. Most eye-tracking studies on young children with autism have used stimuli with a high social content, such as faces or biological motion (BIO-M) (human movement) [e.g., Ref. (10–12)]. These investigations using social stimuli have consistently reported reduced attention to social stimuli in individuals with ASD [for a meta-analysis see Ref. (13)], though this reduction is inconsistent in preschoolers with ASD and appears to be related to adaptive or cognitive functioning [e.g., Ref. (14–17)]. These initial findings provide evidence for a relationship between reduced social interest in young children on the spectrum and their development. However, it is important to keep in mind that paradigm design also can greatly influence attention to social stimuli. An elegant meta-analysis by Chita-Tegmark (13) recently described different eye-tracking paradigms used to assess visual attention to social stimuli in ASD. This implies, for instance, social scenes used to measure preference for socially salient stimuli (e.g., faces) or on non-socially salient stimuli (e.g., objects). Also, existing research used visual preference paradigms opposing social stimuli to non-social stimuli (e.g., BIO-M vs. non-BIO-M). Measures of preference are both considered as visual exploration (e.g., time spent on stimuli) or latency to fixate social stimuli (e.g., reaction time). The authors point out that non-central aspects of these paradigms, including motion (e.g., static vs. dynamic stimuli), social content and communicative intention (e.g., number of people in a social scene and their social engagement), ecological validity, and multimodal presentation (e.g., conjunction with audio inputs) can significantly affect the allocation of social attention.

The *social motivation hypothesis of autism* [for a review, see Ref. (18)] considers a lack of social interest as the trigger for a behavioral cascade leading to the emergence of ASD symptomatology (19, 20). Accordingly, studies that further explore the relationship between reduced social interest and autistic symptoms deepen our understanding of early development of ASD in individuals. However, to the best of our knowledge, researchers have yet to explore the relationship between social interest and the development of severity of diagnostic symptoms in preschoolers with ASD over time.

Here, we explore how reduced social interest impacts ASD symptomatology in a group of 20 preschoolers with ASD and in 20 typically developing (TD) children of the same age. Pierce and colleagues (10, 16) previously demonstrated the validity of using visual preference patterns for BIO-M to assess social interest in preschoolers with ASD. Their task inspired our eye-tracking paradigm of visual preference for BIO-M (Franchini et al., submitted)[1], redesigned for the current study. In addition to the eye-tracking paradigm, we also evaluated participants on severity of diagnostic symptoms during a diagnostic assessment and adaptive functioning using parent reports to investigate whether visual preference, clinical, and/or adaptive features predict severity of diagnostic symptoms 1 year later.

First, we would expect that preschoolers with ASD would spend a lower percentage of their time looking at BIO-M than TD preschoolers; second, that the time ASD and TD participants spend on the BIO-M would correlate with their clinical and adaptive functioning. Third, we hypothesize that a preference for BIO-M will be positively related to a reduction in severity of diagnostic symptoms after 1 year.

MATERIALS AND METHODS

A total of 20 participants with ASD (all boys) were included in the study. A first visit (Time 1) was planned as soon as possible after a clinical diagnosis was made and a follow-up visit (Time 2) was organized 12 months later. An age-matched group (all boys) of TD children was compared to our group of children with ASD at Time 1 only. Participants with ASD were recruited through French-speaking parent associations and specialized clinical centers. TD participants were recruited through announcements in the Geneva community. At Time 1, the children's ages ranged between 22 and 51 months. The groups did not differ by age ($t = 0.38, p = 0.71$, see **Table 1**). At Time 2, ASD participants

[1]Franchini M, Wood de Wilde H, Glaser B, Gentaz E, Eliez S, Schaer M. Social orienting and joint attention in preschoolers with Autism Spectrum Disorders. Submitted.

TABLE 1 | Comparison between ASD and TD children on their clinical, adaptive, and social orienting features at Time 1.

	ASD – mean (SD) $n = 20$, males	TD – mean (SD) $n = 20$, males	*t*-Value	*p*-Value
Age (in months)	35.00 (9.47)	33.84 (9.52)	0.38	0.71
Severity Score	6.80 (0.39)	1.05 (0.05)	14.31	<0.0001***
Adaptive Behavior Composite	73.15 (1.87)	102.6 (2.78)	8.87	<0.0001***
Communication	73.00 (2.08)	104.8 (2.28)	9.86	<0.0001***
Daily Living Skills	75.90 (2.45)	102.4 (2.43)	7.68	<0.0001***
Socialization	74.45 (1.59)	99.84 (3.16)	7.58	<0.0001***
Motor Skills	83.37 (2.64)	98.95 (2.57)	4.23	0.0002***
Preference for BIO-M (%)	44.83 (4.98)	68.30 (2.29)	4.21	0.0002***

***$p < 0.001$.

were between 33 and 63 months of age (mean age = 47.13, SD = 9.54). As expected, the children in the ASD group and the TD groups differed on measures of severity of symptoms and adaptive behavior (further details in **Table 1**). The Institutional Review Board of the University of Geneva approved the study protocol for all participants, and participants' parents gave their informed consent prior to inclusion in the study.

Measures

To measure adaptive behavior, we used the Vineland Adaptive Behavior Scales, 2nd edition (21). The VABS-II is a standardized parent report interview that provides a standardized Adaptive Behavior Composite and four domain scores: Communication, Daily Living Skills, Socialization, and Motor Skills.

To assess the severity of autistic symptoms, we used the Autism Diagnostic Observation Schedule – Generic (ADOS-G) (22), which gives a diagnostic score that is derived from the sum of each symptom score according to diagnosis of ASD in the DSM-5 (23). The ADOS-G diagnostic score was then transformed according to Gotham et al.'s algorithm (24) to obtain a Severity Score ranging from 1 to 10. Severity Scores allow further comparison of the severity of autism spectrum symptoms between the ADOS-G evaluations of each participant. All participants performed the Module 1 of the ADOS-G (module adapted to children with "Few to No Words" or "Some Words") or Module 2 (adapted to children with "Phrase Speech").

Finally, to quantify participants' preference for BIO-M, we designed a Biological Motion Visual Preference eye-tracking task (BVMP, see text footnote 1), inspired from the paradigm proposed by Pierce et al. (10). This passive 1-min task consists of the simultaneous presentation of dynamic geometric motion (GEO-M) on one side of the eye-tracking screen, and dynamic BIO-M on the other side. For the GEO-M, we used moving geometric shapes, similar to the classic abstract screen savers taken from MacOS screensavers or available under General Public License.[2] For the BIO-M, we recorded standardized sequences of one child moving and dancing in front of a white wall (to minimize opportunities for distraction). In contrast to the stationary sequence of 60 s used by Pierce et al. (10), the stimuli in our study alternated between the left and right sides. Between each segment, a turning wheel brought the child's gaze to the middle of the screen. Of the six segments of children moving and dancing, three sequences were of a boy and three were of a girl.

The task was administered using Tobii Studio software[3] with the TX300 Tobii eye-tracker. The sampling rate of the machine was 300 Hz and the video resolution was 1920 × 1080 pixels. As recommended by Tobii, participants sat on a parent's lap or alone on a chair at approximately 60 cm from the screen to minimize the impact of head movement on the gaze data. Before administering the task, all participants completed a five-point calibration procedure adapted to toddlers to detect eye motion and eye gaze.

Data analysis was done with Tobii Studio, version 3.1.6. The software automatically counts a fixation point every time a participant spends at least 100 ms within a 30-pixel circle. Areas of interests (AOIs) were drawn on the paradigm videos to delineate BIO-M and GEO-M. For each kind of stimuli (BIO-M and GEO-M), we calculated the total sum of fixation duration (the total looking time). The percentage of time spent on each stimulus type (BIO-M and GEO-M) was calculated by dividing the total fixations on in each AOI (or per stimulus type) by the total fixations on the entire screen. Visual preference for BIO-M was defined by whether a child looked at least 50% of the time at the video of a child moving and dancing.

Analysis Strategy

We first performed descriptive analyses of the groups' behavior and scores at Time 1. Children with ASD and TD children were compared on time spent on BIO-M at Time 1 by means of a *t*-test. To explore the relationship between variables in the ASD and the TD groups at Time 1, we correlated preference for BIO-M with standard VABS-II domain scores. In the ASD group, we additionally correlated Severity Score from the ADOS-G with VABS-II domain scores and with a preference for BIO-M (this was not performed in the TD group because all but one TD participant received the lowest possible Severity Score of 1). Subsequently, according to previous work [Pierce and colleagues (10, 16) and see text footnote 1], we split our group of children with ASD into two sub-groups: Social Responders (SR-ASD, who spent more than 50% of their total time on BIO-M) and Geometric Responders (GR-ASD, who spent more than 50% of their total time on GEO-M). Using *t*-tests, we compared GR-ASD and SR-ASD groups on

[2]http://www.reallyslick.com/screensavers

[3]www.tobii.com

the VABS-II domain scores and on the Severity Score from the ADOS-G.

Second, in the ASD group only, we correlated VABS-II scores and percent time spent on BIO-M at Time 1 with percent of change in Severity Score between Time 1 and Time 2. Correlation analyses were performed using Pearson correlation coefficients. Using a *t*-test, we then compared GR-ASD and SR-ASD children on their percent of change in Severity Score between Time 1 and Time 2. We then observed GR-ASD and SR-ASD improvements on each ADOS-G item contributing to the Severity Score. We, therefore, separated GR-ASD and SR-ASD into three groups for chi-square analysis of each item in the Severity Score: participants who showed a reduction on the item, participants who demonstrated no change on the item and participants with increased severity on the item. Three items were not included in our analyses because they contributed to the Severity Score in either Module 1-Few to No Words or Module 1-Some Words and, thus, did not allow for sufficient data. The specific items were "Pointing" ($n = 7$), "Responding to Joint Attention" ($n = 4$), and "Intonation of Vocalizations or Verbalizations" ($n = 4$). Results were considered significant at a *p*-value of 0.05. For the correlations between the VABS-II domains and related variables (preference for BIO-M, Severity Score, and percent change in Severity Score), we applied a Benjamini–Hochberg correction for multiple comparisons.

RESULTS

Cross-Sectional Observations: A Reduced Preference for Biological Motion in ASD Preschoolers Compared to TD Preschoolers

The ASD and TD groups differed on time spent on BIO-M ($t = 4.21$, $p < 0.001$) during the BVMP task (see **Table 1**). All TD children showed a preference for BIO-M (they spent more than 50% of the total time on BIO-M). By contrast, in the group of children with ASD, 12 preferred GEO-M (thus comprising the GR-ASD sub-group) and 8 preferred BIO-M (comprising the SR-ASD sub-group).

Time spent on BIO-M correlated with the VABS-II Adaptive Behavior Composite scores in the group of children with ASD ($r = 0.75$, $p < 0.001$, $df = 18$) but not in the TD group ($r = 0.45$, 0.05, $df = 18$) in which we observed a trend toward significance. We then examined the relationship between a preference for BIO-M and VABS-II domain scores in both groups.

After applying a Benjamini–Hochberg correction ($p < 0.0125$), we observed a positive relationship in the ASD group between time spent on BIO-M and scores on the Daily Living Skills ($r = 0.55$, $p = 0.0117$, $df = 18$) and the Socialization ($r = 0.84$, $p < 0.001$, $df = 18$) domains. We observed a non-significant trend between time spent on BIO-M and scores on the Motor Skills ($r = 0.51$, $p = 0.02$, $df = 18$) and Communication ($r = 0.68$, $p = 0.047$, $df = 18$) domains. In the TD group, we did not observe any significant relationship between preference for BIO-M and scores on the Communication ($r = 0.29$, $p = 0.22$, $df = 18$), Daily Living Skills ($r = 0.03$, $p = 0.89$, $df = 18$), Socialization ($r = 0.16$, $p = 0.51$, $df = 18$) or Motor Skills ($r = 0.51$, $p = 0.03$, $df = 18$) domains, though we observed a trend toward significance in the latter.

When we correlated severity of symptoms and VABS-II scores in the ASD group, we observed a trend toward a negative correlation between Severity Score and the Adaptive Behavior Composite ($r = -0.40$, $p = 0.08$, $df = 18$). Correcting the *p*-values for multiple comparisons at the threshold of $p < 0.0125$, the correlation between the Severity Score and the VABS-II socialization score did not survive ($r = -0.44$; $p = 0.05$, $df = 18$); none of the other correlations survived either between the Severity Score and the VABS-II Communication ($r = -0.29$, $p = 0.22$, $df = 18$), Motor Skills ($r = -0.38$, $p = 0.11$, $df = 18$) or Daily Living Skills ($r = -0.41$, $p = 0.07$, $df = 18$) scores. Time spent on BIO-M in the ASD group was not correlated with Symptom Severity ($r = -0.22$, $p = 0.36$, $df = 18$).

We subsequently compared SR-ASD and GR-ASD children. Despite the small sample sizes, we observed a significant difference between the groups. The SR-ASD children showed higher adaptive functioning compared to GR-ASD for the Adaptive Behavior Composite, Communication, and Socialization domains ($t = 2.13$, $p = 0.047$; $t = 2.14$, $p = 0.047$; $t = 3.39$, $p < 0.01$), but not for the Daily Living Skills and Motor Skills domains ($t = 1.17$, $p = 0.26$; $t = 1.01$, $p = 0.33$). We did not, however, observe a significant difference between SR-ASD and GR-ASD children ($t = 0.67$, $p = 0.51$) on Severity Score.

Longitudinal Analyses: A Preference for Biological Motion Predicts Reduced Symptom Severity 1 Year Later

We first correlated time spent on BIO-M at T1 and VABS-II adaptive behavior scores at T1 with percent change (between T1 and T2) in Severity Score on the ADOS-G (results are shown in **Table 2**). The results suggest that time spent on BIO-M at T1 predicts reduction in Severity Score 1 year later in the ASD group ($r = -0.67$, $p = 0.001$, $df = 18$, see **Figure 1**). In other words, children who spent the majority of their time on BIO-M during the eye-tracking BMVP task at baseline were the individuals who showed the most clinical improvement, as measured by the Symptom Severity score 1 year later.

A correlation between VABS-II Communication score and percent change in Severity Score survived the uncorrected

TABLE 2 | Predictors of changes in symptom severity 1 year later.

Adaptive behavior or preference for BIO-M at Time 1	Reduction in Severity Score from Time 1 to Time 2	
	r	*p*-value
Adaptive Behavior Composite	−0.31	0.18
Communication	−0.47	0.037
Daily Living Skills	−0.07	0.78
Socialization	−0.31	0.19
Motor Skills	−0.10	0.66
Preference for BIO-M (%)	−0.67	0.001**

**$p < 0.01$.

FIGURE 1 | Screenshots representing examples from the BMVP task.

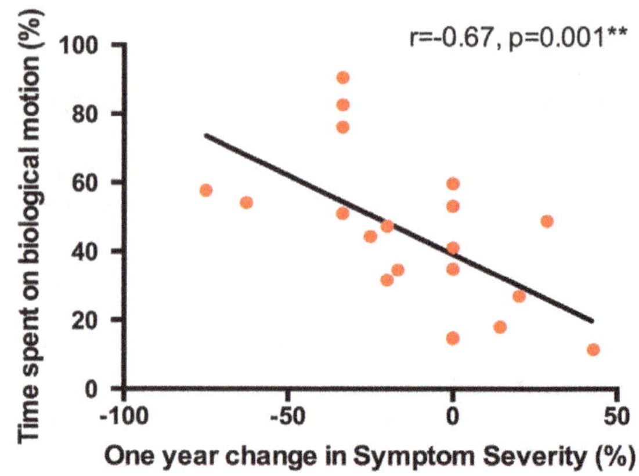

FIGURE 2 | Time spent on biological motion strongly predicts 1-year reduction of Symptom Severity in the group of preschoolers with ASD.

significance threshold, but did not survive our correction for multiple comparisons ($r = -0.47$, $p = 0.037$, $df = 18$).

We then looked at differences between the SR-ASD and GR-ASD sub-groups on the change in Symptom Severity between Time 1 and Time 2, and found a group difference. SR-ASD children showed greater improvement in Symptom Severity than GR-ASD children ($t = 3.38$, $p = 0.003$). After that, we looked at inter-group differences between GR-ASD and SR-ASD children for each item that contributed to the Symptom Severity score. Two participants were administered a Module 2 ADOS-G at one or both of the two visits and were, thus, excluded from analysis of items "Frequency of Spontaneous Vocalization Directed to Others" and "Integration of Gaze and Other Behaviors during Social Overtures," items that count toward the Severity Score in Module 1 only. A significant difference, with SR-ASD children showing more improvement than GR-ASD children, was detected on the following items: "Shared Enjoyment in Interaction" ($X^2 = 7.78$, $p = 0.02$), "Showing" ($X^2 = 13.13$, $p = 0.001$), and "Spontaneous Initiation of Joint Attention" ($X^2 = 7.82$, $p = 0.02$). For details, see **Table 3**.

DISCUSSION

Our results showing reduced interest in BIO-M in preschoolers with ASD compared to TD children, corroborate previous results by Pierce and colleagues (10, 16) and by our research group (see text footnote 1). Our ASD group also demonstrated a wide variance in their preferences for BIO-M, with percentage of visual preference for BIO-M ranging from 11.6 to 90.17% between participants. As previously observed in children with autism [(10, 16), see text footnote 1], this heterogeneity was related to their adaptive functioning. Based on these cross-sectional observations, we subsequently explored whether measures of adaptive functioning and social interest could predict symptom development in preschoolers on the spectrum. Longitudinal analyses revealed that a child's preference for BIO-M predicted a reduction in the severity of symptomatology after 1 year. Moreover, children with ASD with a stronger preference for BIO-M (SR-ASD) showed improvement on "Shared Enjoyment in Interaction," "Showing," and "Spontaneous Initiation of Joint Attention."

The implications of reduced social interest overall during the early development of children with ASD and the relationship between social interest (a preference for BIO-M) and reductions in certain ASD symptoms will be discussed in the following sections.

Reduced Preference for Biological Motion in ASD Children Compared to Their TD Children

In the present study, we confirmed previous findings (10, 16) that preschoolers with ASD orient less often toward BIO-M than TD children. As discussed in Franchini et al. (see text footnote 1),

TABLE 3 | Change in ASD Symptom Severity after 1 year according to preference for BIO-M at Time 1.

ADOS-G Symptoms	Preference for BIO-M	Change in Symptom Severity			X^2	*p*-Value
		Reduction (*n*)	No change (*n*)	Increasing (*n*)		
SOCIAL AFFECT						
Communication						
Frequency of Spontaneous Vocalization Directed to Others	SR-ASD (*n* = 6)	5	1	0	4.06	0.13
	GR-ASD (*n* = 12)	4	7	1		
Gestures	SR-ASD (*n* = 8)	5	2	1	1.25	0.54
	GR-ASD (*n* = 12)	5	6	1		
Reciprocal social interaction						
Unusual Eye Contact	SR-ASD (*n* = 8)	1	7	0	0.06	0.79
	GR-ASD (*n* = 12)	2	10	0		
Facial Expression Directed to Others	SR-ASD (*n* = 8)	2	6	0	0.06	0.79
	GR-ASD (*n* = 12)	3	6	3		
Integration of Gaze and Other Behaviors during Social Overtures	SR-ASD (*n* = 6)	4	2	0	2.00	0.38
	GR-ASD (*n* = 12)	5	4	3		
Shared Enjoyment in Interaction	SR-ASD (*n* = 8)	5	3	0	7.78	0.02*
	GR-ASD (*n* = 12)	1	7	4		
Showing	SR-ASD (*n* = 8)	6	1	1	13.13	0.001**
	GR-ASD (*n* = 12)	0	9	3		
Spontaneous Initiation of Joint Attention	SR-ASD (*n* = 8)	5	1	2	7.82	0.02*
	GR-ASD (*n* = 12)	1	8	3		
Quality of Social Overtures	SR-ASD (*n* = 8)	3	5	0	2.55	0.28
	GR-ASD (*n* = 12)	1	11	0		
RESTRICTED AND REPETITIVE BEHAVIOR						
Unusual Sensory Interest in Play Material/Person	SR-ASD (*n* = 8)	2	6	0	3.34	0.16
	GR-ASD (*n* = 12)	3	5	4		
Hand and Fingers and Other Complex Mannerisms	SR-ASD (*n* = 8)	2	6	0	4.47	0.11
	GR-ASD (*n* = 12)	2	5	5		
Unusually Repetitive Interests or Stereotyped Behavior	SR-ASD (*n* = 8)	4	2	2	3.61	0.16
	GR-ASD (*n* = 12)	2	8	2		

*$p < 0.05$, **$p < 0.01$.

these results demonstrate that visual preference paradigms for BIO-M can serve as consistent and valid biomarkers for visual exploration patterns in young children with ASD. Moreover, presentation side of BIO-M and GEO-M stimuli changed often during the BMVP task to avoid visual exploration patterns associated with "sticky attention," which are characterized by a difficulty disengaging from GEO-M, a behavior that may be characteristic of individuals on the autism spectrum (25). Pierce and collaborators (10, 16) did not alternate the stimuli presentation during their task, which could potentially result in the young participants' attention to get "stuck." Accordingly, social orienting may, thus, be a better indicator of an initial preference for social or geometric stimuli, rather than a participant's main interest during the task. As we hypothesized, a preference for BIO-M was related to adaptive functioning in participants on the autism spectrum, lending support to the idea that interest in social stimuli is related to the behavioral phenotype of young children with ASD.

It is important to note that there are studies on social attention in ASD that did not report a difference between the visual preferences of ASD and TD children for social stimuli [for reviews, see Ref. (13, 26)]. Specific social content of stimuli used in tasks, as well as the salience of non-social stimuli can influence visual attention patterns in individuals with ASD [for a review, see Ref. (26)] and contribute to differences between studies. However, as Chita-Tegmark suggested in a review (13), tasks that display moving biological and geometric stimuli on opposite sides of the display, such as the task used in the current study and the one used by Pierce et al. (10, 16), have the advantage of clearly demarcating a visual preference for BIO-M or GEO-M in children with ASD.

A Preference for Biological Motion Predicts a Reduction in Symptom Severity 1 Year Later

To date, only a few research studies using limited samples have explored the evolution of Symptom Severity in young children with ASD. One such study demonstrated the idea that superior adaptive behavior is associated with better outcome in preschoolers with ASD (5). Also, better adaptive functioning has indeed been shown to be predictive of a small subset of young children who show "optimal progress" between ages 2 and 4, including those who no longer meet criteria for diagnosis at age 4 (7). In our study, we found that the best predictor of clinical improvement in Symptom Severity was a preference for BIO-M. Despite our small sample size, our results suggest that a preference for BIO-M may be a key to predicting early developmental trajectories and outcome.

Finally, our results point to specific criteria within the diagnostic assessment (ADOS-G) that were most improved in children with a preference for BIO-M. These items are "Shared Enjoyment in Interaction," "Showing," and "Spontaneous Initiation of Joint Attention," Interestingly, these three items account for the "Social Affect" domain of the ADOS-G. According to a recent publication by Mundy et al. (27), these three criteria measure the initiation of joint attention behaviors, which also are described as "*infants' use of gestures and eye contact to direct others' attention to objects, to events, and to themselves*" [(28), p. 269]. The initiation of joint attention in early development of children with ASD is an example of a spontaneous and natural attention-sharing behavior that is intrinsically related to both social attention and social learning [for a review, see Ref. (28)]. Accordingly, increased social interest, as measured by a preference for BIO-M in the current study, may be related to early improvements in joint attention behaviors, thus resulting in improved early socio-communicative development (19, 20). These results corroborate the *social motivation hypothesis of autism* [for a review, see Ref. (18)], in that a preference for early social interest appears to support ensuing socio-communicative learning in young children with autism.

Limitations and Perspectives

The present study has several limitations. First, our sample size was relatively small. However, despite our small sample size, our results demonstrate that clinical differences can be detected during a 60-s standardized video, a quick and easy screening idea that warrants replication and further exploration. Second, this study explores clinical outcome of children with ASD during a 1-year period only. While future investigations should try to explore the influence of early social interest over a longer developmental period and with more participants, we are convinced that the strength of our statistical results reflects the importance of social orienting in ASD during preschool, a period that appears to be particularly ripe for developmental changes. Finally, subsequent studies may wish to explore the relationship between social interest and Symptom Severity taking into account baseline behavioral features of children with ASD, as well as specific therapeutic interventions, to better understand the factors moderating the longitudinal change.

CONCLUSION

Social attention plays an important role in early life, and may be a pivotal factor for individuals on the autism spectrum. Measures of social interest, as the one described in this study, offer the potential to better understand clinical features and outcome during early development in children with ASD. Our results provide support for this idea, by demonstrating a way of operationalizing social interest in young children to better understand and follow the heterogeneous phenotype between individuals on the spectrum. The resulting data are especially useful for the conceptualization of individualized early intervention in ASD and the assessment of progress during intervention.

AUTHOR CONTRIBUTIONS

MF, HW, BG, SE, and MS designed the study; MF, HW, and MS acquired the data; MF and MS analyzed the data and wrote the first draft of the article; MF, HW, BG, EG, SE, and MS contributed to the interpretation of the results and the writing of the manuscript. All authors have approved the final manuscript.

ACKNOWLEDGMENTS

The authors would like to thank all the families who kindly participated in the study, as well as Stéphanie Baudoux, Léa Chambaz, Sophie Diakonoff, Nada Kojovic, Matthieu Mansion, and Isaline Mottet for their help with data collection. This study was supported by the National Center of Competence in Research "Synapsy," financed by the Swiss National Science Foundation (SNF, Grant number: 51AU40_125759) and by the "Fondation Pôle Autisme" (http://www.pole-autisme.ch). Marie Schaer is further supported by an individual fellowship from the SNF (#145760 & #158831).

REFERENCES

1. Kim SH, Macari S, Koller J, Chawarska K. Examining the phenotypic heterogeneity of early Autism spectrum disorder: subtypes and short-term outcomes. *J Child Psychol Psychiatry* (2015) 57:93–102. doi:10.1111/jcpp.12448
2. Georgiades S, Szatmari P, Boyle M, Hanna S, Duku E, Zwaigenbaum L, et al. Investigating phenotypic heterogeneity in children with autism spectrum disorder: a factor mixture modeling approach. *J Child Psychol Psychiatry* (2013) 54:206–15. doi:10.1111/j.1469-7610.2012.02588.x
3. Lenroot RK, Yeung PK. Heterogeneity within Autism spectrum disorders: what have we learned from neuroimaging studies? *Front Hum Neurosci* (2013) 7:733. doi:10.3389/fnhum.2013.00733
4. Ozonoff S, Iosif A-M, Baguio F, Cook IC, Hill MM, Hutman T, et al. A prospective study of the emergence of early behavioral signs of autism. *J Am Acad Child Adolesc Psychiatry* (2010) 49:.e1–2. doi:10.1097/00004583-201003000-00009
5. Peter Szatmari MD, Katarzyna Chawarska P, Geraldine Dawson P, Stelios Georgiades P, Rebecca Landa PC-S, Catherine Lord P, et al. Prospective longitudinal studies of infant siblings of children with autism: lessons learned and future directions. *J Am Acad Child Adolesc Psychiatry* (2016) 55(3):179–87. doi:10.1016/j.jaac.2015.12.014
6. Fountain C, Winter AS, Bearman PS. Six developmental trajectories characterize children with autism. *Pediatrics* (2012) 129(5):e1112–20. doi:10.1542/peds.2011-1601
7. Moulton E, Barton M, Robins DL, Abrams DN, Fein D. Early characteristics of children with ASD who demonstrate optimal progress between age two and four. *J Autism Dev Disord* (2016) 46(6):2160–73. doi:10.1007/s10803-016-2745-1
8. Walsh P, Elsabbagh M, Bolton P, Singh I. In search of biomarkers for autism: scientific, social and ethical challenges. *Nat Rev Neurosci* (2011) 12:603–12. doi:10.1038/nrn3113
9. Falck-Ytter T, Bölte S, Gredebäck G. Eye tracking in early autism research. *J Neurodev Disord* (2008) 5:693–716. doi:10.1146/annurev.psych.60.110707.163514
10. Pierce K, Conant D, Hazin R, Stoner R, Desmond J. Preference for geometric patterns early in life as a risk factor for autism. *Arch Gen Psychiatry* (2011) 68:101–9. doi:10.1001/archgenpsychiatry.2010.113
11. Chawarska K, Klin A, Volkmar F. Automatic attention cueing through eye movement in 2-year-old children with autism. *Child Dev* (2003) 74:1108–22. doi:10.1111/1467-8624.00595
12. Jones W, Klin A. Attention to eyes is present but in decline in 2-6-month-old infants later diagnosed with autism. *Nature* (2013) 504(7480):427–31. doi:10.1038/nature12715

13. Chita-Tegmark M. Social attention in ASD: a review and meta-analysis of eye-tracking studies. *Res Dev Disabil* (2016) 48:79–93. doi:10.1016/j.ridd.2015.10.011
14. Klin A, Jones W, Schultz R, Volkmar F, Cohen D. Visual fixation patterns during viewing of naturalistic social situations as predictors of social competence in individuals with autism. *Arch Gen Psychiatry* (2002) 59:809–16. doi:10.1001/archpsyc.59.9.809
15. Chawarska K, Macari S, Shic F. Context modulates attention to social scenes in toddlers with autism. *J Child Psychol Psychiatry* (2012) 53:903–13. doi:10.1111/j.1469-7610.2012.02538.x
16. Pierce K, Marinero S, Hazin R, McKenna B, Barnes CC, Malige A. Eye tracking reveals abnormal visual preference for geometric images as an early biomarker of an Autism spectrum disorder subtype associated with increased symptom severity. *Biol Psychiatry* (2016) 79(8):657–66. doi:10.1016/j.biopsych.2015.03.032
17. Gliga T, Jones EJH, Bedford R, Charman T, Johnson MH. From early markers to neuro-developmental mechanisms of autism. *Dev Rev* (2014) 34:189–207. doi:10.1016/j.dr.2014.05.003
18. Chevallier C, Kohls G, Troiani V, Brodkin ES, Schultz RT. The social motivation theory of autism. *Trends Cogn Sci* (2012) 16:231–9. doi:10.1016/j.tics.2012.02.007
19. Dawson G, Toth K, Abbott R, Osterling J, Munson J, Estes A, et al. Early social attention impairments in autism: social orienting, joint attention, and attention to distress. *Dev Psychol* (2004) 40:271–83. doi:10.1037/0012-1649.40.2.271
20. Dawson G, Bernier R, Ring RH. Social attention: a possible early indicator of efficacy in autism clinical trials. *J Neurodev Disord* (2012) 4(1):11. doi:10.1186/1866-1955-4-11
21. Sparrow SS, Cicchetti VD, Balla AD. *Vineland Adaptive Behavior Scales*. 2nd ed. Minnesota: American Guidance Service (2005).
22. Lord C, Risi S, Lambrecht L, Cook EH, Leventhal BL, DiLavore PC, et al. The autism diagnostic observation schedule-generic: a standard measure of social and communication deficits associated with the spectrum of autism. *J Autism Dev Disord* (2000) 30:205–23. doi:10.1023/A:1005591205002
23. American Psychiatric Association. Neurodevelopmental disorders. In: *Diagnostic and Statistical Manual of Mental Disorders*. 5th ed. (2013). doi:10.1176/appi.books.9780890425596.dsm01
24. Gotham K, Pickles A, Lord C. Standardizing ADOS scores for a measure of in Autism spectrum disorders. *J Autism Dev Disord* (2008) 39:693–705. doi:10.1007/s10803-008-0674-3
25. Elsabbagh M, Fernandes J, Jane Webb S, Dawson G, Charman T, Johnson MH, et al. Disengagement of visual attention in infancy is associated with emerging autism in toddlerhood. *Biol Psychiatry* (2013) 74:189–94. doi:10.1016/j.biopsych.2012.11.030
26. Guillon Q, Hadjikhani N, Baduel S, Rogé B. Visual social attention in autism spectrum disorders: insights from eye tracking studies. *Neurosci Biobehav Rev* (2014) 42:279–97. doi:10.1016/j.neubiorev.2014.03.013
27. Mundy PC. *Autism and Joint Attention*. New York: Guilford Publications (2016).
28. Mundy P, Newell L. Attention, joint attention, and social cognition. *Curr Dir Psychol Sci* (2007) 16:269–74. doi:10.1111/j.1467-8721.2007.00518.x

3

Premutation in the Fragile X Mental Retardation 1 (*FMR1*) Gene Affects Maternal Zn-milk and Perinatal Brain Bioenergetics and Scaffolding

Eleonora Napoli*[1]*, Catherine Ross-Inta*[1]*, Gyu Song*[1]*, Sarah Wong*[1]*, Randi Hagerman*[2,3]*, Louise W. Gane*[2]*, Jennifer T. Smilowitz*[4]*, Flora Tassone*[2,5] *and Cecilia Giulivi*[1,2]*

[1] Department of Molecular Biosciences, School of Veterinary Medicine, Davis, CA, USA, [2] Medical Investigations of Neurodevelopmental Disorders Institute, University of California, Davis, Davis, CA, USA, [3] Department of Pediatrics, University of California Davis Medical Center, Sacramento, CA, USA, [4] Department of Food Science and Technology and Foods for Health Institute, University of California, Davis, Davis, CA, USA, [5] Department of Biochemistry and Molecular Medicine, School of Medicine, University of California, Davis, Davis, CA, USA

Edited by:
Yuri Bozzi,
University of Trento, Italy

Reviewed by:
Andreas Martin Grabrucker,
Ulm University, Germany
Barbara Bardoni,
Centre National de la Recherche Scientifique UMR7275 Institut de Pharmacologie Moléculaire et Cellulaire, France

***Correspondence:**
Cecilia Giulivi
cgiulivi@ucdavis.edu

Fragile X premutation alleles have 55–200 CGG repeats in the 5′ UTR of the *FMR1* gene. Altered zinc (Zn) homeostasis has been reported in fibroblasts from >60 years old premutation carriers, in which Zn supplementation significantly restored Zn-dependent mitochondrial protein import/processing and function. Given that mitochondria play a critical role in synaptic transmission, brain function, and cognition, we tested FMRP protein expression, brain bioenergetics, and expression of the Zn-dependent synaptic scaffolding protein SH3 and multiple ankyrin repeat domains 3 (Shank3) in a knock-in (KI) premutation mouse model with 180 CGG repeats. Mitochondrial outcomes correlated with FMRP protein expression (but not *FMR1* gene expression) in KI mice and human fibroblasts from carriers of the pre- and full-mutation. Significant deficits in brain bioenergetics, Zn levels, and Shank3 protein expression were observed in the Zn-rich regions KI hippocampus and cerebellum at PND21, with some of these effects lasting into adulthood (PND210). A strong genotype × age interaction was observed for most of the outcomes tested in hippocampus and cerebellum, whereas in cortex, age played a major role. Given that the most significant effects were observed at the end of the lactation period, we hypothesized that KI milk might have a role at compounding the deleterious effects on the *FMR1* genetic background. A higher gene expression of *ZnT4* and *ZnT6,* Zn transporters abundant in brain and lactating mammary glands, was observed in the latter tissue of KI dams. A cross-fostering experiment allowed improving cortex bioenergetics in KI pups nursing on WT milk. Conversely, WT pups nursing on KI milk showed deficits in hippocampus and cerebellum bioenergetics. A highly significant milk type × genotype interaction was observed for all three-brain regions, being cortex the most influenced. Finally, lower milk-Zn levels were recorded in milk from lactating women carrying the premutation as well as other Zn-related outcomes (Zn-dependent alkaline phosphatase activity and lactose biosynthesis—whose limiting step is the Zn-dependent β-1,4-galactosyltransferase). In premutation carriers, altered

Zn homeostasis, brain bioenergetics and Shank3 levels could be compounded by Zn-deficient milk, increasing the risk of developing emotional and neurological/cognitive problems and/or FXTAS later in life.

Keywords: bioenergetics, brain, *FMR1*, milk, mitochondria, premutation, Shank3, zinc

INTRODUCTION

A 55–200 expanded CGG nucleotide repeats in the 5′-UTR of the fragile X mental retardation one gene (*FMR1*) constitutes the genetic hallmark of premutation carriers (OMIM#300623), whereas >200 repeats give rise to Fragile X syndrome (FXS; OMIM#300624), the leading inherited form of cognitive impairment (Kogan et al., 2008; Tassone et al., 2012; Battistella et al., 2013). Later in life, premutation carriers may have an increased risk of developing a neurodegenerative disorder known as Fragile X-associated tremor/ataxia syndrome [FXTAS (Kogan et al., 2008; Hagerman and Hagerman, 2013)]. Initially, this prevalent allelic variant was thought to be free of phenotypic traits; however, neurodevelopmental problems like autism spectrum disorder (ASD), attention deficit hyperactivity disorder (ADHD), anxiety, and other types of psychopathologies (Farzin et al., 2006; Tassone et al., 2012; Winarni et al., 2012; Wong et al., 2012; Battistella et al., 2013; Chonchaiya et al., 2013) have been reported in some young carriers, but not as often as in Fragile X syndrome [i.e., incidence of ASD in FXS is ~4-fold of that in premutation carriers (Farzin et al., 2006; Garcia-Nonell et al., 2008; Harris et al., 2008; D'Hulst et al., 2009; Zingerevich et al., 2009; Hagerman et al., 2010; Chonchaiya et al., 2013)].

Unlike the full mutation alleles, which undergo repeat-mediated gene silencing (Pieretti et al., 1991; Sutcliffe et al., 1992), premutation alleles are active and actually show normal or elevated *FMR1* mRNA levels (Tassone et al., 2000a,b, 2007). It is still not clearly understood how the premutation pathology arises and research to date has focused on how premutation alleles might trigger neurodegeneration through a gain-of-function (toxicity) RNA mechanism (Tassone et al., 2004; Hagerman and Hagerman, 2013). It has been suggested that the "excess" of premutation transcript may bind and sequester factors important for cell function (Sellier et al., 2010, 2013). Previous work from our laboratory conducted on fibroblasts from premutation individuals has shown that zinc (Zn) might also be included among these factors (Napoli et al., 2011). It has been shown that while *FMR1* gene expression could be high in some carriers, its product FMRP can be low (Tassone et al., 2000c; Tassone and Hagerman, 2003) which has been attributed to a reduced translation efficiency (Tassone and Hagerman, 2003). However, critical aspects of the pathology cannot be explained purely by an RNA-mediated process but rather to a protein-mediated neurodegeneration (Todd et al., 2013). Recently, the paradox of the RNA- mediated vs. protein-mediated toxicity in FXTAS, although still controversial (Banez-Coronel et al., 2012), has been partly explained by demonstrating that CGG repeats trigger repeat-associated non-AUG-initiated (RAN) translation (Todd et al., 2013) of a cryptic polyG-containing protein, FMRPolyG. Accumulation of FMRPolyG has been seen in ubiquitin-positive inclusions in *Drosophila*, mammalian cell cultures carrying the expansion, and brains of patients that died of FXTAS (Todd et al., 2013) and this lengthy polyglycine tract seems to be toxic to a number of cell types (Todd et al., 2013; Oh et al., 2015). So far, the relative contribution of RNA sequestration (of essential factors), low FMRP expression or RAN translation (of the toxic FMRPolyG) to the premutation pathology is unknown.

Adding to these mechanisms, bioenergetic deficits with increased oxidative stress biomarkers have been observed in post-mortem brain samples (Ross-Inta et al., 2010) and fibroblasts from premutation carriers (Ross-Inta et al., 2010; Napoli et al., 2011) and altered mitochondrial dynamics have been noted in neurons from a knock-in (KI) mouse model of *FMR1* premutation (Kaplan et al., 2012). These deficits seem to precede the occurrence of ubiquitin-positive intranuclear inclusions [considered a hallmark of FXTAS; (Greco et al., 2006)], and correlate with both CGG repeat expansion and severity of the phenotype (Ross-Inta et al., 2010; Napoli et al., 2011). Fibroblasts from >60 years old asymptomatic premutation carriers presented altered protein expression of the Zn transporters ZnT6/ZnT4 (Napoli et al., 2011) accompanied by mitochondrial dysfunction (MD; Ross-Inta et al., 2010; Napoli et al., 2011). This MD was mainly evidenced by an accumulation of precursor over mature mitochondrial proteins encoded by the nuclear DNA. This scenario was significantly reversed upon Zn supplementation, which allowed Zn-dependent import/processing pathways of nuclearly-encoded mitochondrial proteins to occur (Napoli et al., 2011).

Abnormal behavior (i.e., over-responsivity and hyperactivity-like behavior with acute Zn deficiency; ASD-like behavior secondary to prenatal Zn deficiency) was reported in young Zn-deficient mice with altered scaffolding elements within the postsynaptic density of excitatory synapses (Grabrucker et al., 2014). Indeed, it has been proposed that the ~50% incidence of Zn deficiency in children with ASD (Yasuda et al., 2011) has the potential to contribute to the etiology and/or morbidity of ASD via dysregulation of the synaptic Shank scaffolding (Grabrucker et al., 2014). Furthermore, some symptoms of ASD seem to lessen with Zn supplementation (Russo and Devito, 2011).

Collectively these studies suggest that the *FMR1* premutation affects Zn homeostasis, and that Zn deficits have a detrimental effect on behavior, opening the door for evaluating the effect of environmental stressors (such as Zn deficits) at compounding or initiating MD early in life and, possibly, predisposing young carriers to develop ASD, ADHD, and/or FXTAS at older age (Tassone et al., 2012; Winarni et al., 2012; Wong et al., 2012; Battistella et al., 2013).

Thus, we hypothesized that *FMR1* premutation would alter brain Zn homeostasis, bioenergetics, and protein expression of Zn-dependent scaffolding protein SH3 and multiple ankyrin repeat domains 3 (Shank3), outcomes which could be further affected by nursing on milk from premutation carriers. To test our hypothesis, *FMR1* gene expression, Fragile X mental retardation protein 1 (FMRP) protein expression, bioenergetics, Zn levels, and Shank3 protein expression were evaluated at post-natal days (PND) 0, 9 (or 7), 21, and 210 in cerebellum, hippocampus (both areas rich in Zn-containing neurons) as well as in cortex from a KI premutation mouse model. This murine model recapitulates some of the molecular, histological, and neurobehavioral deficits observed in premutation carriers (i.e., elevated *FMR1* mRNA, FMRP protein levels reduced or normal), and with age they develop intranuclear inclusions in neurons and astrocytes, ataxia-like mild motor dysfunctions, anxiety, and cognitive impairments (Hunsaker et al., 2009, 2011, 2012; Wenzel et al., 2010). To evaluate the effect of carriers' milk on the offspring's brain bioenergetics, a cross-fostering experiment was designed in which brain mitochondrial function was tested in suckling WT and KI pups at PND21. To complement the mouse model studies, Zn and Zn-associated outcomes were evaluated in breast milk from control and premutation nursing mothers.

Given the key role of Shank3 in post-synaptic neuron scaffolding and the contribution of mitochondria to the regulation of synaptic transmission, brain function, and cognition, we propose that early nutritional Zn interventions may represent a new preventive strategy in newborns of premutation mothers with the potential of lowering the risk of developing emotional or neurological symptoms later in life, emphasizing the interdependence between genetics and nutrition.

MATERIALS AND METHODS

Animals

This study was approved by the IACUC Committee at the University of California Davis, which is accredited by the American Association for the Accreditation of Laboratory Animal Care (IACUC-approved protocol number 17896). All animals were treated accordingly to the guidelines established by the NIH and the UCD animal welfare committee. Mice were monitored daily during the length of the experiments. Mice with signs of stress, weight loss >20%, paralysis, or any other serious disease, would have been euthanized immediately to avoid unnecessary pain or discomfort. However, none of the animals showed these signs of distress or were euthanized. No animal procedure was attempted without prior approval from the NIH and the UCD animal welfare committee, as well as all personnel was trained to handle animals under the current regulations. Wild-type female C57BL/6J mice were obtained commercially (Charles River, Wilmington, MA) and the knock-in (KI) mouse model of the premutation in the same genetic background (Wenzel et al., 2010) was from Dr. Robert Berman (University of California, Davis). The mice were housed in polycarbonate cages and fed *ad libitum*. Zn content of the diet used (Purina Pico chow 5058) was 1200 ppm, which with an average adult body weight of 30 g/mouse and a food intake of 2–5 g/mouse equals to 10–20 mg Zn/kg body weight *per diem*. Female mice during pregnancy increase their food intake by about two-fold and during lactation by about four-fold resulting in 20–40 mg Zn/kg body weight *per diem* during pregnancy and 40–60 mg Zn/kg body weight per day during lactation [reference values = 10 mg/kg and 30 mg/kg for adult and pregnant/lactating mice, respectively (Knapka et al., 1974; Luecke and Fraker, 1979; Beach et al., 1982)]. Mice were maintained on a 12 h light/dark cycle under controlled temperature and humidity. Mice were bred and allowed to deliver naturally. At PND0, 9 (or 7), 21, and 210, mitochondria were isolated from hippocampus, cerebellum and cortex from WT and KI male mice ($n = 9$–13 at each time point for a total of 54 WT and 55 KI). For the cross-fostering experiments (performed twice), at birth KI pups (males; $n = 12$; CGG repeats = 196 ± 6) and WT pups (males; $n = 12$; CGG repeats = 9.3 ± 0.2) were randomly foster-nursed either on KI dams (173 ± 4 CGG repeats) or on WT dams, with six pups on each dam. The KI pups were fed with the same frequency as WT animals. At PND21, WT, and KI dams were removed from pups for 2 h to control for effects of suckling on Zn transporter expression and localization, and subsequently were euthanized by CO_2 asphyxiation. Mammary glands from lactating dams were removed and either snap-frozen in liquid nitrogen or stored in RNA later. At PND21 pups were also euthanized by CO_2 asphyxiation. Euthanasia was performed by an experienced technician by way of inhalation of 30% CO_2 (compressed gas cylinder). This method is considered acceptable by the 2000 Report of American Veterinary Medical Association (AVMA) Panel on Euthanasia and it has been approved by IACUC. The cortex, cerebellum, and hippocampus were removed post-mortem and processed immediately to isolate mitochondria.

Isolation and Purification of Mitochondria from Brain Regions

Enriched mitochondrial fractions were obtained from cortex, cerebellum and hippocampus at PND0 ($n = 13$ WT and 13 KI), PND7 ($n = 9$ WT and 9 KI), PND21 ($n = 12$ WT and 12 KI), and PND210 ($n = 11$ WT and 12 KI). Intact, highly purified, non-synaptosomal mitochondria from the same brain tissues were isolated through a Percoll gradient as previously described in detail (Napoli et al., 2012, 2013), resuspended in iso-osmotic 150 mM KCl and immediately used for oxygen consumption measurements. Western blots to actin (cytosolic protein) and beta-ATPase (mitochondrial protein) showed a cytosolic contamination of the mitochondrial fraction of less than 2% [see (Napoli et al., 2013)].

Primary Neuronal Cultures

To assess the contribution of glia to brain mitochondrial outcomes [as previously shown in Napoli et al. (2012)], isolated, intact primary neurons were obtained from WT and KI pups at PND0, using an established methodology (Brand, 1990; Jekabsons and Nicholls, 2004). Cultures of dissociated neurons were prepared as described in Kaplan et al. (2012) and kindly provided by Dr. Eitan Kaplan. Intact (non-permeabilized) neurons suspended in PBS supplemented with 10 mM glucose were used for evaluation of oxygen consumption followed by sequential additions of 5 μg/ml oligomycin and 20 μM FCCP

(Napoli et al., 2011). The RCR under uncoupling conditions or RCRu in intact cells was calculated as the oxygen uptake ratio of State 3u (with FCCP) over that of oligomycin-induced State 4.

Mitochondrial Outcomes

Enriched mitochondrial fractions or in intact, purified mitochondria were used for evaluation of oxygen consumption using a Clark-type oxygen electrode (Hansatech, King's Lynn, UK) as described (Napoli et al., 2013). An aliquot (0.1–0.3 mg protein/ml) of mitochondria was added to the oxygen chamber in a buffer containing 0.22 M sucrose, 50 mM KCl, 1 mM EDTA, 10 mM KH_2PO_4, and 10 mM HEPES, pH 7.4. Oxygen consumption rates were evaluated in the presence of (i) 1 mM ADP plus 1 mM malate–10 mM glutamate followed by the addition of 5 μM rotenone; (ii) 10 mM succinate followed by the addition of 10 mM malonate; (iii) 10 mM α-glycerophosphate followed by addition of 3.6 μM antimycin A; and (iv) 10 mM ascorbate and 0.2 mM *N,N,N′,N′*-tetramethyl-*p*-phenylenediamine followed by the addition of 1 mM KCN. The activities of mitochondrial NADH oxidase, succinate oxidase, and cytochrome *c* oxidase were evaluated as the difference of oxygen uptake recorded before and after the addition of rotenone, malonate, antimycin A, and KCN respectively, and normalized by the activity of citrate synthase (a marker of mitochondrial mass). Citrate synthase activity was evaluated spectrophotometrically as described elsewhere (Napoli et al., 2013) using 1–2 μg of mitochondrial protein. The respiratory control ratio (RCR) with malate/glutamate as a substrate was calculated as the ratio between oxygen uptake rates in State 3 (with ADP or under phosphorylating conditions) and State 4 [rotenone-resistant oxygen uptake or non-phosphorylating conditions; (Napoli et al., 2013)].

Western Blots

For quantification of FMRP, Shank3, cytochrome *c* oxidase subunit IV (CCOIV), ATPase *β*-subunit (ATPB), *β*-actin, GAPDH, and tubulin expression levels, brain regions (hippocampus, cerebellum, and cortex) at PND9, 21, and 210 from WT and KI mice were homogenized in cold 20 mM HEPES, pH 7.4, added with protease and phosphatase inhibitor cocktails (Sigma, St. Louis, MO), and centrifuged at 13,000 × *g* for 10 min to eliminate particulate matter. A second set of Shank3 immunoblots (shown in Supplementary Figure 1) was carried out by using acetone precipitation to concentrate and partly delipidate the samples as previously described (Fujisawa et al., 2015). Thirty to fifty microgram of proteins were solubilized in SDS sample buffer (Life Technologies, Grand Island, NY) and loaded onto a 4–12% bis-tris gel (Life Technologies) as previously described (Napoli et al., 2013). After transferring proteins with an iBlot apparatus (Life Technologies), membranes were blocked with LI-COR blocking buffer (LI-COR Biosciences, Lincoln, NE) for 1 h at room temperature and subsequently probed with anti-FMRP antibody (Sigma, St. Louis, MO; 1:700 dilution), anti-Shank3 antibody (Santa Cruz Biotechnologies, Dallas, TX; 1:500 dilution), anti-CCOIV antibody (Cell Signaling, Danvers, MA, 1:1000 dilution), anti ATPB (BD Biosciences, San Jose, CA, 1:3000 dilution) overnight at 4°C, and with anti-*β*-actin (Sigma, St. Louis, MO; 1:20,000 dilution) for 1 hour at room temperature. Tubulin (Proteintech, Chicago, IL; 1:1,000 dilution) and GAPDH (Santa Cruz Biotechnology, Dallas, TX, 1:300 dilution) were used as loading controls. Secondary antibodies were from LI-COR (Lincoln, NE; 1:10,000 dilution). Membranes were visualized with the use of the Odyssey Infrared Imaging System (LI-COR) and densitometry analysis carried out with the Carestream software (Napoli et al., 2013).

Gene Expression of *ZnT4/T6* In Mammary Glands from Lactating WT and KI Dams

RT-qPCR performed with three different sets of commercially available primers from Life Technologies showed low specificity and efficiency. Thus, the gene expression of *ZnT4* and *ZnT6* was assessed by PCR. Total RNA was isolated from homogenized mammary gland following the manufacturer's instructions (Qiagen). Concentration and purity of RNA was measured at an absorbance of 260 nm and 280 nm using the Tecan i-control 1.6 software (v.1.6.19.2) on Tecan infinite M200 Nanoquant (Tecan, Austria). Following RNA isolation, 2 μg of the RNA was used to make cDNA with the Qiagen Quantitech RT Kit following the manufacturer's instructions. Following cDNA synthesis, *ZnT4*, and *ZnT6* gene expression was performed by Touchdown PCR in a 96-well plate in a 25 μl reaction volume containing: 100 ng of cDNA, 2.5 μl of 10x Advantage 2 PCR buffer (Clontech, Mountain View, CA), 0.5 μl of 50X Advantage 2 Polymerase Mix (Clontech), 1 μl of 10 mM dNTPs (Life Technologies, Grand Island, NY), and 0.5 μl of each 10 mM forward and reverse primer. Mouse primers for *ZnT4* were: forward 5′-CTCCAGGCCGACGATGACT-3′; reverse 5′-GTGTCCACTAGATACCATGCTTGG-3′. Primers for *ZnT6* were: forward 5′-CAGACCTTAGCCGCAGCTTG-3′; reverse 5′-GGTCTGAGAAGTTTAGGACGTTGG-3′. PCR cycling parameters were: 95°C for 3 min; 10 cycles of: 94°C for 15 s, 65°C for 30 s (with 1°C decrease at each cycle), and 72°C for 40 s; 30 cycles of: 95°C for 15 s, 55°C for 30 s, and 72°C for 40 s; 5 min at 72°C, 15°C hold step. PCR was performed on a Mastercycler EP Realplex thermocycler (Eppendorf, Westbury, NY). PCR products were separated in a 1.3% agarose gel in the presence of ethidium bromide, and the fragments had the expected sizes of 585 bp (*ZnT4*) and 537 bp (*ZnT6*). Gene expression of *ZnT4* and *ZnT6* was normalized by that of *GAPDH*. Expression of *GAPDH* was performed in a 96-well PCR plate by Real Time RT PCR with 100 ng of cDNA, TaqMan Universal PCR Mastermix (Life Technologies, Grand Island, NY), and 0.5x *GAPDH* primer-probe mix (Life Technologies, Grand Island, NY). Amplification was performed using the default cycling parameters of 2 min at 50°C, 10 min at 95°C, and 40 cycles of 15 s at 95°C, and 60 s at 60°C. PCR product was separated in a 3% agarose gel electrophoresis in the presence of ethidium bromide with an expected fragment size of 107 bp.

Human Subjects and Breast Milk Samples

Control breast milk samples were obtained from 25 healthy women who gave birth to healthy term infants enrolled in the UC Davis Foods for Health Institute Lactation Study (ClinicalTrials.gov Identifier: NCT01817127). Donors filled out detailed health history questionnaires regarding demographics, anthropometrics, pregnancy history, current, and prior health history, current dietary intake habits and restrictions, physical activity level, as well as medication and supplementation intake history during the third trimester of pregnancy and 1 year postpartum. Half of the control donors reported intake of prenatal vitamins and minerals during the post-partum period. Breast milk was also obtained from one control and five premutation lactating mothers seen through the Fragile X Treatment and Research Center at the M.I.N.D. Institute at the University of California Davis Medical Center. All milk samples (5–30 ml) were obtained between 8 and 20 lactation weeks. These women delivered their infants between 38 and 41 weeks of gestation. Fresh milk samples were collected using hand expression at the conclusion of a morning breastfeed (between 09.00 and 12.00 h). All milk samples were frozen within 1 h of expression at –20°C, and transferred to –80°C until analyzed. Genotyping for these individuals was performed by extracting gDNA from milk samples and following the procedure described before (Tassone et al., 2012). The UC Davis Institutional Review Board approved all aspects of the study (IRB # 200917212-1) and informed consent was obtained from all donors.

Activity of Milk Alkaline Phosphatase

ALP activity was measured in breast milk and the method optimized using unpasteurized cow's milk (from Trader Joe's, Davis, CA). ALP activity was evaluated in 6 μl (correspondent to ~12–13 μg of protein) of breast milk samples using the QuantiChrom™ Alkaline Phosphatase Assay Kit (BioAssay Systems, Hayward, CA). The assay utilizes *p*-nitrophenyl phosphate that is hydrolyzed by ALP into a color product, which is measured at $\lambda = 405$ nm for 5 min at 37°C. Total protein concentration of breast milk was measured with the Pierce BCA Protein Assay kit (Thermo Scientific, Waltham, MA). ALP activity was expressed either as μmol $\times$ (min $\times$ l milk)$^{-1}$ or nmol $\times$ (min $\times$ mg protein)$^{-1}$. The detection limit of this assay was (mean $\pm$ SEM) 0.050 $\pm$ 0.001μmol $\times$ (min $\times$ l)$^{-1}$ ($n = 16$) and the inter-assay CV was 8.1% ($n = 32$).

Milk Lactose Determination

Lactose was determined by an enzymatic spectroscopic method according to the manufacturer's instructions (Biovision, Milpitas, CA). The recovery of a known amount of lactose added to the milk samples was (mean $\pm$ SEM) 101 $\pm$ 0.9 % ($n = 12$). The detection limit of this assay was 0.025 $\pm$ 0.002 nmol galactose ($n = 12$) and the inter-assay CV was 10.2% ($n = 42$).

Determination of Zn Levels in Murine Brain and Human Milk

Measurements of Zn in murine brain regions and human milk were carried out with the Zn fluorophore zinquin (Sigma-Aldrich, St. Louis, MO) essentially as previously described (Zalewski et al., 2006) with some modifications. To evaluate total Zn levels in mouse brain regions, homogenized samples for Western blot analysis were used. One-hundred microgram of brain protein was added to each well of a 96-well-microplate to a final volume of 100 μl in the presence of 10 μM zinquin dissolved in Zn-free Hank's balanced salt solution (HBSS, in mM: 0.03 Na_2HPO_4, 0.4 KH_2PO_4, 4.2 $NaHCO_3$, 5.4 KCl, 5.6 D-glucose, 137 NaCl; pH 7.4) following the addition of Zn-free ovalbumin to a final concentration of 0.3 mg/ml (to prevent precipitation of the lipophilic zinquin from aqueous solutions). Samples were incubated in the dark for 40 min at 22°C, and fluorescence was evaluated at excitation and emission wavelengths of 365 and 510 nm, respectively.

For the determination of Zn in milk, 5 μl of milk were used and the assay carried out essentially as described for brain samples, but with and without 10 mM EGTA. EGTA-containing samples were used to obtain the non-labile Zn fluorescence, as EGTA removes any free Zn-related fluorescence. Free Zn concentrations were evaluated by subtracting the fluorescence in the presence of EGTA by the total fluorescence without EGTA, and converting fluorescence values into Zn concentrations using the linear part of a calibration curve performed with 1 to 25 μM $ZnSO_4$. To confirm that milk or brain samples did not display any intrinsic fluorescence at the excitation and emission wavelengths used, blanks without zinquin were prepared. No unspecific fluorescence was recorded in any of the samples in the absence of zinquin.

Human Fibroblasts Collection and Outcomes

Skin biopsies from controls, premutation and full mutation carriers were obtained from subjects recruited through the Fragile X Treatment and Research Center at the M.I.N.D. at the University of California Davis Medical Center. The UC Davis Institutional Review Board approved all aspects of the study and informed consent was obtained from the parents of the children. All fibroblasts were grown in Minimum Essential Medium (MEM) supplemented with 15% FBS, 2 mM glutamine and 1 mM sodium pyruvate. FMRP levels were evaluated by Western blots upon lysis of whole cells in RIPA (25 mM MOPS, 150 mM NaCl, 1 mM EDTA, 1% Triton, 0.1% SDS, and 1% DOC, pH 7.5), and centrifugation at 12,000 $\times$ *g* for 10 min. For *FMR1* gene expression, RNA was isolated from 10^6 fibroblasts using the RNeasy Plus Mini Kit from Qiagen (cat. no. 74134) following the manufacturer's protocol. cDNA was synthesized from the RNA using Qiagen's Quantitect RT kit following manufacturers recommendations. RNA and cDNA concentrations were determined using the Tecan Infinite M200 Nanoquant plate reader (Tecan, Austria). Primer/probe mix was purchased from Life Technologies (Grand Island, NY, USA) for *FMR1* and *XRCC5* (housekeeping gene) were also obtained by Life Technologies. Sequences of commercial primers and probes are proprietary. cDNA was diluted to 5 ng/μl and served as stock template for QRTPCR. QRTPCR was performed in a Mastercycler EP Realplex thermocycler (Eppendorf, Westbury, NY). Amplification was performed using the following cycling parameters: 2 min at 50°C, 95°C for 10 min, followed by 40 cycles of 15 s at 95°C and 1 min of at 60°C. The mean cycle time was obtained by double derivatives (CalqPlex algorithm; Eppendorf, Westbury, NY) and designated as Ct. Each sample was analyzed in triplicates, and positive and negative controls were run on each plate. Coefficient of variation (CV) was 0.3% or less on average. The gene expression of *FMR1* was determined by the comparative Ct method using the following equation: 2ΔCt, where $\Delta Ct = Ct_{Target} - Ct_{Housekeeper}$. The gene expression fold change (premutation or full muation/Control) was determined using the ΔΔCt method using the following equation: $2^{(\Delta CtFXTAS - \Delta CtControl)}$. Fold changes were calculated based on their age matched controls. Values were converted to positive or negative values to indicate up or down gene regulation. Coupling between electron transport and ATP production were tested in whole, intact cells as previously described (Napoli et al., 2011).

Statistical Analysis

Data are expressed as mean ± SEM. Statistical analysis was performed either by Student's *t*-test (for comparisons between WT and KI), or by Two-way ANOVA, followed by the Tukey's HSD *post-hoc* test for multiple comparisons with the GraphPad Prism 6.0 software (San Diego, CA). Significance was set at $p \leq 0.05$. Unless otherwise noted, experiments were run in triplicates (technical replicates) and performed at least in 2–3 separate occasions (biological replicates). To determine the minimum number of mice/group, we used an a priori G test (software STATsimple; v. 2.0.5) with selected mitochondrial outcomes that indicated 4 mice as optimal given an alpha of 0.05 with an actual power of 0.993. Considering the yield of mitochondria from mouse brain (a limiting step), sample needed for assay in triplicates, and the assay parameter (polarography) that requires the largest amount of sample, 5 mice/group were used at a minimum for each time point, unless otherwise stated.

RESULTS

Decreased FMRP Protein Levels in Brain from Young KI Mice

Male, hemizygous KI mice were used as a murine model of the *FMR1* premutation [CGG repeat expansion = 196 ± 6; (Wenzel et al., 2010)]. This model recapitulates most deficits observed in premutation carriers (Hunsaker et al., 2009, 2011, 2012; Wenzel et al., 2010). Despite the relatively high CGG expansions, the expression of the *FMR1* gene product FMRP, was still detectable at PND9, PND21, and PND210 in hippocampus, cerebellum, and cortex and not absent as observed in models of Fragile X syndrome [(Zalfa et al., 2003); **Figures 1A,B**]. Consistent with other reports (Ludwig et al., 2014), FMRP protein expression decreased with age in all brain areas in WT (**Figure 1B**); conversely, no age-dependent effect was observed on FMRP expression of KI mice in any of the brain regions tested. At PND9, 40-50% of FMRP control values were observed in hippocampus, cerebellum, and cortex of KI mice, effect that lasted into PND21 for the first two tissues (**Figure 1B**).

Interestingly, in all three-brain regions the expression levels of FMRP were followed by those of β-actin (**Figure 1C**). The correlation between actin and FMRP protein levels is consistent with the role of FMRP as regulator of actin filaments organization and dynamics (Castets et al., 2005; Nolze et al., 2013), a key process in the morphogenesis of dendritic spines (Castets et al., 2005), influencing the effect of actin on mitochondria distribution and function (Kusano et al., 2000; Xu et al., 2001; Dugina et al., 2009), mitochondrial fission (Korobova et al., 2013; Hatch et al., 2014; Li et al., 2015), short-distance mitochondrial movements (Boldogh and Pon, 2006), mitochondria quality control (Higuchi et al., 2013), mitochondria clustering and reactive oxygen species (ROS) generation (Li et al., 2004).

Deficits in Bioenergetics in Brain Regions from Young KI Mice

Different segments of the electron transport chain from brain mitochondria (hippocampus, cerebellum, and cortex) were tested for their capacity to generate ATP in WT and KI mice: NADH oxidase (using NAD-linked substrates such as glucose and comprising Complex I, III, IV, and V), succinate oxidase (using FAD-linked substrates such as fatty acids and comprising Complex II, III, IV, and V), as well as citrate synthase activity as a normalizing marker of mitochondrial mass. Complex IV, or cytochrome *c* oxidase (CCO), activity, and coupling between ATP synthesis and electron transfer (as judged by the RCR) were also tested.

At PND0-7, no statistically significant differences were observed in mitochondrial outcomes between WT and KI pups in any of the brain regions tested (**Figure 2**). At PND21, hippocampus was the most affected brain area in KI pups, with significant decreases in NADH oxidase, succinate oxidase, and CCO activities, as well as increased uncoupling between ATP production and electron transfer, relative to WT (**Figure 2**). At PND21, uncoupling was also evident in cerebellum of KI pups, but to a lesser extent than hippocampus (**Figure 2**), whereas in adult age (PND210) succinate oxidase, and coupling (hippocampus) were still significantly lower in KI hippocampus than age-matched WT mice. No difference was observed in any of the outcomes in cortex at any of the time points (**Figure 2**).

Mitochondrial protein levels (relative to total protein) were evaluated by measuring the expression of the abundant protein ATPase β-subunit of Complex V [ATPB; (Elfering et al., 2004; Haynes et al., 2010), **Figure 3**]. Lower levels of ATPB were noted at PND21 and lasting into adulthood (PND210) in hippocampus of KI mice, while in cerebellum significant ATPB deficits were observed only at PND21 (**Figure 3**). No statistically significant differences were observed in cortex at any time point (**Figure 3**).

Taken together, these results point toward a generalized OXPHOS deficit in premutation pups' hippocampus, characterized by lower ATP production with both NAD- and FAD-linked substrates, accompanied by lower expression of ATPB. These deficits were less evident in cerebellum (uncoupling and lower ATPB expression were evident at PND21 only), with no apparent involvement of cortex.

The OXPHOS changes observed in brain mitochondria could not be ascribed to a specific subcellular localization (e.g., synaptosomal mitochondria derived only from the termini of neurons vs. free, non-synaptosomal mitochondria) because the majority of brain mitochondria [88% of all mitochondria

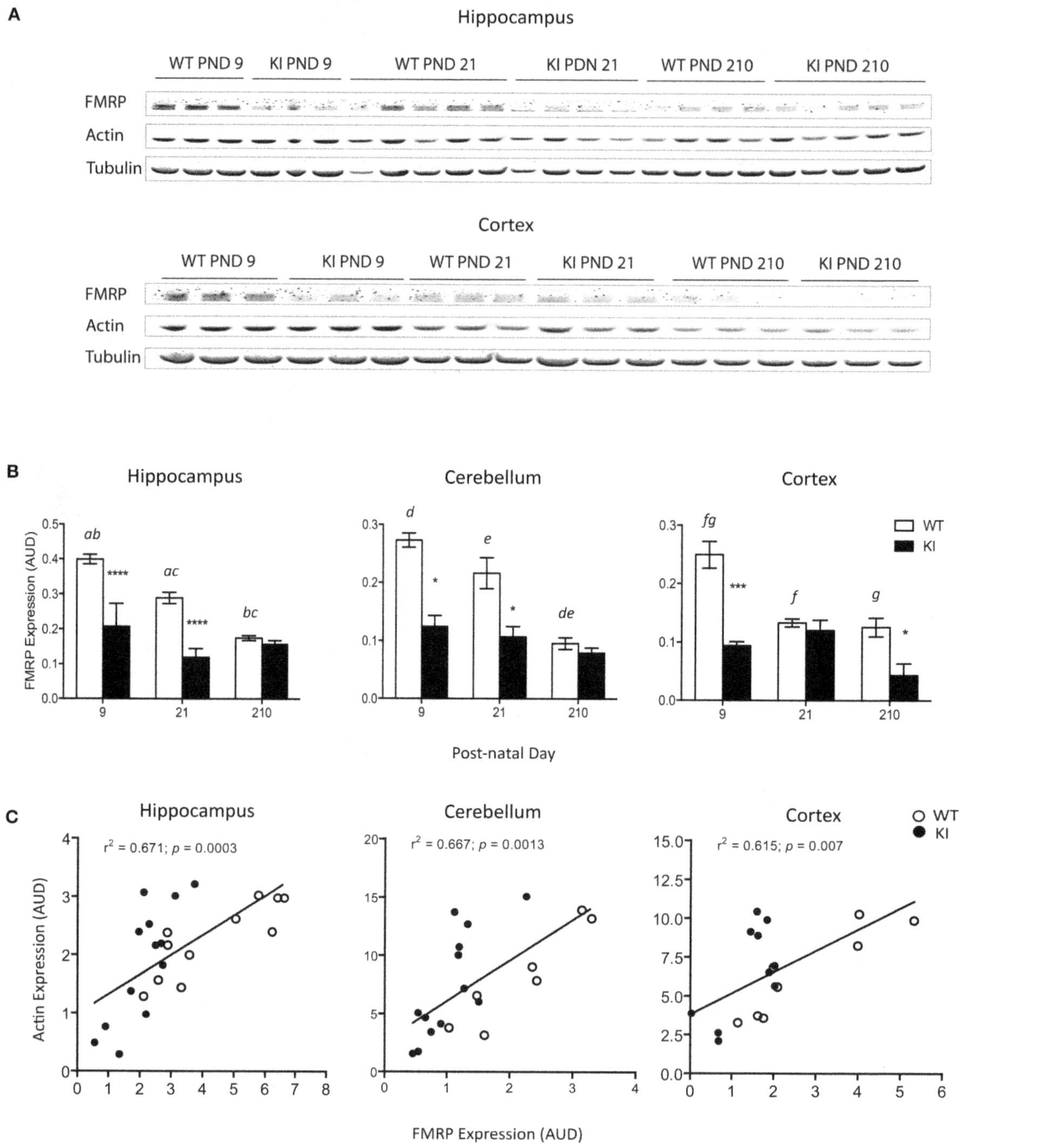

FIGURE 1 | Changes in FMRP protein expression in brain from WT and KI mice. (A) Representative Western blots of FMRP and actin protein expression levels in hippocampus and cortex of WT and KI mice. Tubulin was used as loading control. FMRP protein levels of KI mice hippocampus and cerebellum were 37 and 45% of WT at post-natal day (PND) 9, and 41 and 50% of WT at post-natal day 21. In cortex, FMRP protein levels in KI mice were 38% of WT at post-natal day 9. **(B)** Time-dependent changes in FMRP protein levels in hippocampus, cerebellum, and cortex respectively. Data are reported as mean ± SEM, $n = 3$–5 per genotype per time point. Statistical analysis was performed by Two-way ANOVA. *Post-hoc* analysis performed by Tukey's HSD test revealed significant differences between WT and KI, indicated in the figure by asterisk as follows. Hippocampus: $^{****}p < 0.0001$; Cerebellum: $^{*}p = 0.0110$; Cortex: $^{**}p = 0.0003$, $^{*}p = 0.0363$, $^{***}p = 0.0001$. Statistically significant differences among time points are indicated by letters with the following p values. $p = 0.0029$ (*a*), $p < 0.0001$ (*b*), $p = 0.0009$ (*c*), $p = 0.0260$ (*d*), $p = 0.0101$ (*e*), $p = 0.0033$ (*f*), $p = 0.0020$ (*g*). For more statistical details on the genotype, age, and genotype × age effect see **Table 3**. **(C)** Correlation between FMRP and actin in the same brain areas. AUD, Arbitrary Units of Densitometry.

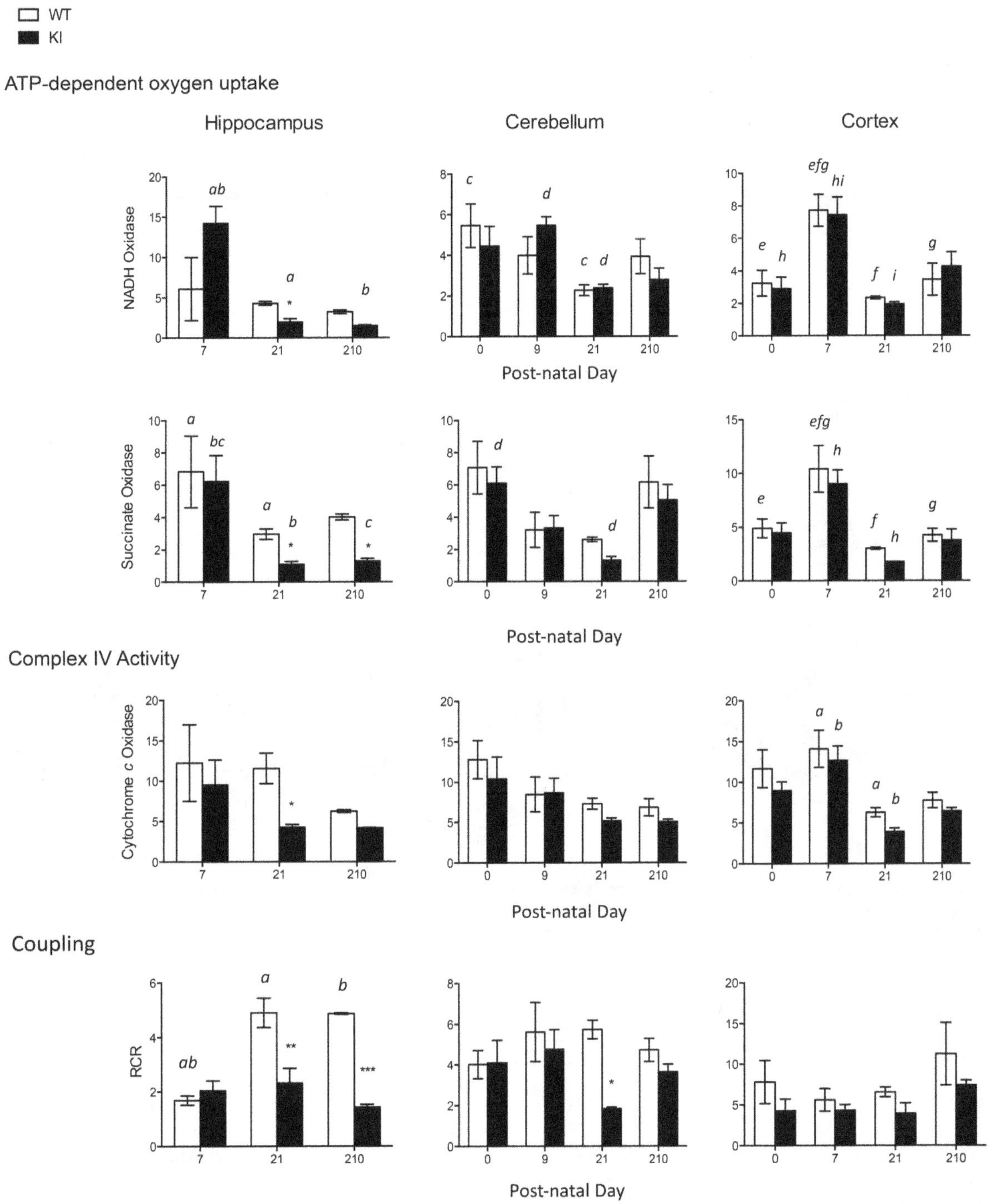

FIGURE 2 | Brain bioenergetics of KI mice during neurodevelopment and adulthood. Mitochondria were isolated from cortex, cerebellum, and hippocampus of WT and KI pups as described in the Methods section. Activities of NADH oxidase, succinate oxidase, and cytochrome *c* oxidase (CCO), and respiratory control ratio (RCR) were evaluated at PND0 (cerebellum and cortex only, due to the scarcity of hippocampal tissue), PND7, PND21, and PND210. Data are reported as mean ± SEM, $n = 3$–7 per genotype per time point. Statistical analysis was performed by Two-way ANOVA. *Post-hoc* analysis performed by Tukey's HSD test revealed significant differences between WT and KI indicated by asterisks as follows NADH oxidase: $^{*}p = 0.0468$; Succinate oxidase: $^{*}p = 0.0466$ at PND21, $^{*}p = 0.0423$ at PND210; Cytochrome *c* oxidase: $^{*}p = 0.0484$; Coupling: $^{**}p = 0.001$, $^{***}p = 0.0004$, $^{*}p = 0.0496$. Letters indicate statistically significant differences amongst time points as follows. NADH oxidase: $p = 0.0291$ (*a*), $p = 0.0033$ (*b*), $p = 0.0166$ (*c*), $p = 0.0320$ (*d*), $p = 0.0036$ (*e*), $p = 0.0001$ (*f*), $p = 0.0113$ (*g*), $p = 0.0032$ (*h*), $p = 0.0004$ (*i*); Succinate oxidase: $p < 0.0001$ (*a*), $p = 0.0002$ (*b*), $p = 0.0240$ (*c*), $p = 0.0434$ (*d*), $p = 0.0283$ (*e*), $p = 0.0009$ (*f*), $p = 0.0250$ (*g*), $p = 0.0013$ (*h*); Cytochrome *c* oxidase: $p = 0.0053$ (*a*), $p = 0.0035$ (*b*). Coupling: $p = 0.0003$ (*a*), $p = 0.0010$ (*b*). Further statistical details on the genotype, age, and genotype × age effect can be found in the legend of **Table 3**.

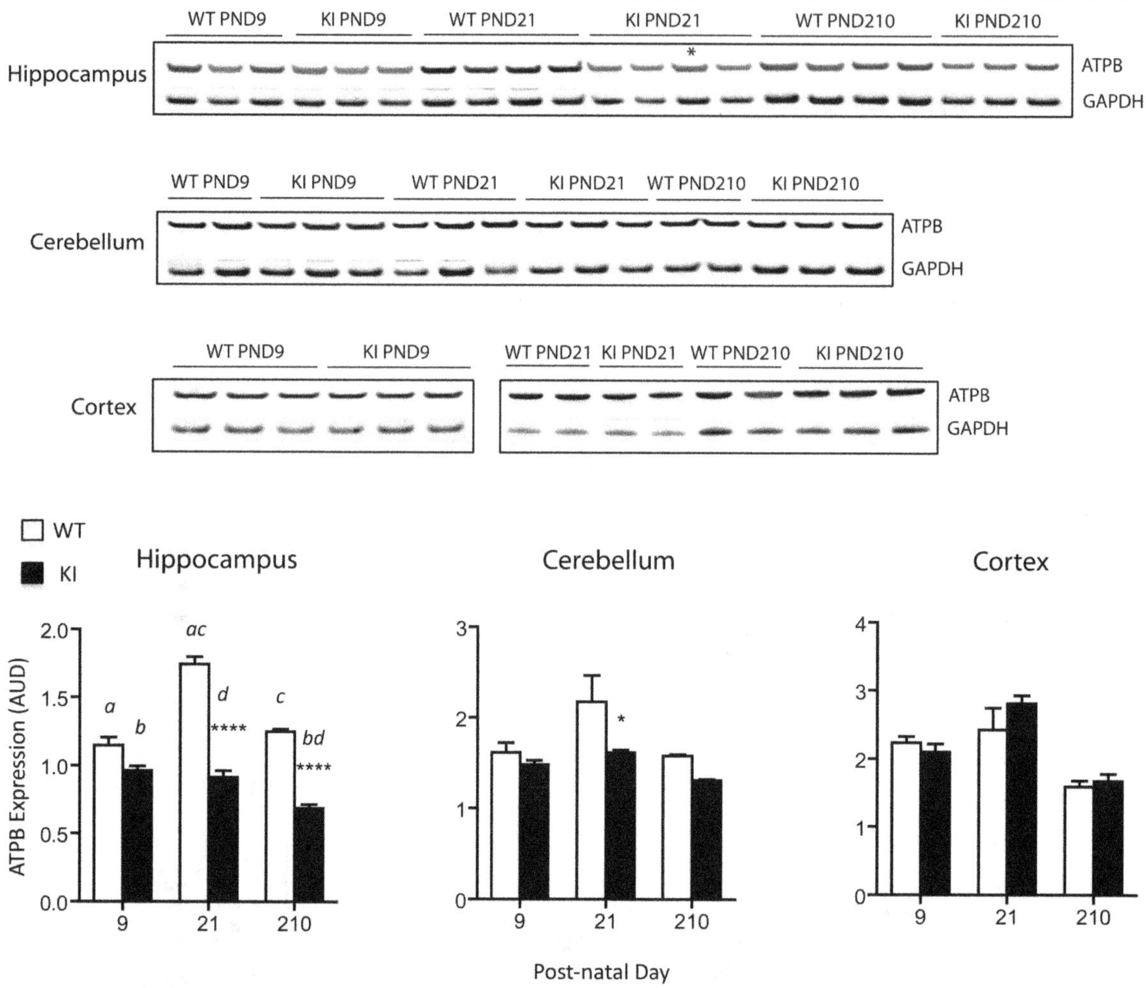

FIGURE 3 | Protein expression levels of mitochondrial ATPase β-subunit in brain from KI mice. ATPase β-subunit protein expression (normalized to GAPDH) was evaluated at PND9, 21 and 210 in hippocampus, cerebellum, and cortex lysates. Asterisk in the immunoblot image of hippocampus denotes a 90 CGG KI sample. Densitometry data for this sample have not been taken into account for averages calculation of KI. Cortex samples were ran in two different gels (PND9 and PND21-210) and are shown separately. Data are reported as mean ± SEM, $n = 3–5$ per genotype per time point, ran in triplicates. Statistical analysis was performed by Two-way ANOVA. *Post-hoc* analysis was performed by Tukey's HSD test for multiple comparisons. Significant difference between WT and KI are indicated by asterisks as follows. $^{****}p < 0.0001$; $^{*}p < 0.0492$. Statistically significant differences among time points are indicated by letters as follows: $p < 0.0001$ (*a, c*), $p = 0.0087$ (*b*), $p = 0.0222$ (*d*). Further, statistical details on the genotype, age, and genotype × age effect can be found in **Table 3**. AUD, Arbitrary Units of Densitometry.

(Rendon and Masmoudi, 1985)] are non-synaptosomal (Napoli et al., 2012). As such, no OXPHOS differences were observed between mitochondria-enriched fractions and highly purified, non-synaptosomal mitochondria at PND21 in any brain region from WT and KI (**Table 1**).

Isolated Neurons Recapitulate the Mitochondrial Deficits Observed in KI Brain Regions

Non-synaptosomal mitochondria as well as mitochondria-enriched fractions are, by necessity, removed from their cytoplasmic environment with the potential of altering their function through the purification process. To address this issue, in parallel we tested mitochondrial function in a system retaining cellular specificity and with an intact intracellular milieu. OXPHOS was directly evaluated in isolated, intact hippocampal, cerebellar, and cortical neurons obtained from 4–6 pooled WT and KI mice at PND0 (**Table 2**). Glucose-sustained basal respiration of intact neurons, followed by the addition of the ATPase inhibitor oligomycin, was recorded to establish the ATP production linked to oxygen uptake. Subsequent addition of FCCP, an uncoupler of ATP production and electron transfer, allowed evaluating the maximum mitochondrial oxygen uptake capacity. ROS-mediated oxygen uptake and membrane proton leak (oligomycin-resistant oxygen uptake rates), oxygen uptake linked to ATP production (oligomycin-sensitive), and spare respiratory capacity (FCCP-mediated maximal respiration rate) were expressed as a fraction of the basal oxygen consumption rate for both WT and KI neurons (**Table 2**). At PND0, a deficiency in the ATP-driven oxygen uptake was already evident in isolated KI

TABLE 1 | Comparison of outcomes in mitochondria-enriched fractions vs. purified, non-synaptosomal mitochondria from cerebellum and cortex at PND21 in WT and KI mice.

Outcomes	Cerebellum				Cortex			
	Total mitochondria		Non-synaptosomal mitochondria		Total mitochondria		Non-synaptosomal mitochondria	
	WT	KI	WT	KI	WT	KI	WT	KI
OXYGEN UPTAKE RATES								
NADH oxidase	5.38 ± 0.01	4.5 ± 0.3	52.4 ± 1.3	58.3 ± 5.6	8.8 ± 3.3	8.4 ± 1.0	50 ± 11	45 ± 6
Succinate oxidase	6.31 ± 0.02	2.33 ± 0.01**	47.1 ± 1.0	26 ± 2**	8.1 ± 0.8	6.5 ± 1.0*	74 ± 15	45 ± 2*
ACTIVITIES								
Cytochrome *c* oxidase	14.3 ± 0.1	10 ± 1**	168 ± 28	116 ± 19**	27 ± 1	16 ± 1**	149 ± 17	64 ± 4**
Citrate synthase	274 ± 52	293 ± 31	2314 ± 305	2400 ± 320	263 ± 27	282 ± 39	2258 ± 360	2324 ± 199

*All activities were expressed as nmol oxygen consumed × (min × mg protein)$^{-1}$. Citrate synthase was expressed as nmol × (min × mg protein)$^{-1}$. Statistical analysis was carried out with the Student's t-test. The p-values are as follows: *< 0.05, **< 0.01.*

TABLE 2 | Mitochondrial coupling and respiratory capacity in intact, isolated neurons from WT and KI mice at PND0.

Outcomes	Hippocampus		Cerebellum		Cortex	
	(% Basal rate)					
Oxygen consumption rates	**WT**	**KI**	**WT**	**KI**	**WT**	**KI**
Oligomycin-sensitive	90 ± 1	85 ± 1**	89 ± 3	80 ± 6	84 ± 2	77 ± 3
Oligomycin-resistant	0.33 ± 0.33	6.9 ± 0.5***	-0.22 ± 0.22	0.9 ± 0.2*	3 ± 5	19 ± 3*
Spare respiratory capacity	128 ± 12	62 ± 2**	102 ± 30	74 ± 42	110 ± 17	67 ± 12
Coupling	**Hippocampus**		**Cerebellum**		**Cortex**	
RCRu	11 ± 2	3.4 ± 0.8*	9 ± 1	1.7 ± 0.4**	7 ± 1	0.9 ± 0.3***

*Oxygen consumption rates under basal conditions (in the presence of glucose only) were not statistically significant different between WT and KI in any of the brain regions [average of WT and KI = 6.5 ± 0.7; 3.4 ± 0.9; and 3.1 ± 0.5 nmol oxygen consumed × (min × 10^{6} cells)$^{-1}$ for cortex, cerebellum and hippocampus, respectively]. Oxygen uptake linked to ATP production (oligomycin-sensitive mitochondrial oxygen uptake), ROS-mediated oxygen uptake and membrane proton leak (oligomycin-resistant mitochondrial oxygen uptake), and spare respiratory capacity (FCCP-mediated maximal respiration rate) were expressed as a fraction of the basal oxygen consumption rate. The RCRu represents the ratio between FCCP and oligomycin-resistant oxygen uptake rates. Data (from three separate preparations run in duplicates) are shown as mean ± SEM. Statistical comparison between WT and KI was performed with the Student's t-test. The p-values are as follows: *< 0.05; **< 0.005; ***< 0.0005.*

hippocampal neurons, consistent with this area being the most affected.

Interestingly, KI neurons show a dramatically lower spare respiratory capacity than WT, capacity defined as the mitochondrial ability to meet increased energy demand with increased respiration (**Table 2**). This may indicate a lower capacity to adapt to stressful situations with increased ATP need. The coupling (as judged by the RCRu) and the oligomycin-resistant oxygen uptake were significantly different (3–5-fold lower and 4–20-fold higher, respectively, than controls) in KI compared to WT in all brain areas (**Table 2**). The lower RCRu and spare respiratory capacity of hippocampal KI cells are of significant biological relevance because energy deficits generated by an imbalance between bioenergetic reserve and demand, play a critical role in the survival of neurons under stress conditions (Nicholls, 2008) and can lead to disrupted synaptic network (Selkoe, 2002; Yadava and Nicholls, 2007).

The apparent discrepancy between the marked deficits observed at PND0 in KI isolated neurons (**Table 2**) relative to the ones at PND7 in KI non-synaptosomal mitochondria (**Table 1**) or total mitochondrial fractions (**Figure 2**) can be bridged taking into account the absence of supporting cells (glia) in a neuron-only culture system (Iwata-Ichikawa et al., 1999; Bélanger and Magistretti, 2009), which could be even more critical for neurons with an already compromised genetic background. Alternatively, neuronal mitochondria might be more affected than those of glia, masking the effect when both are tested in mitochondria-rich fractions from brain.

Coupling Between Electron Transport and ATP Synthesis Correlates with FMRP But Not *FMR1* Expression Levels In Human Fibroblasts

As a proof of concept, to test whether *FMR1* gene or FMRP protein expression influence mitochondrial outcomes, we turned to human primary skin fibroblasts from premutation and full mutation carriers, as commercially available *FMR1* KO mice are

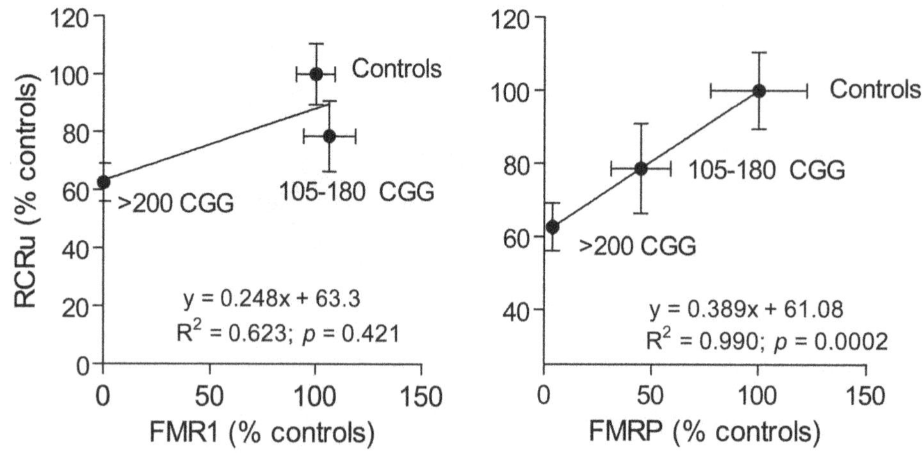

FIGURE 4 | Correlation between mitochondrial outcomes and FMRP or *FMR1* expression levels. The correlation between FMRP and *FMR1* expression with a mitochondrial outcome (i.e., coupling between ATP synthesis and electron transfer or RCRu) was carried out using human primary dermal from controls, premutation carriers (105–180 CGG), and full mutation carriers (>200 CGG repeats). RCRu, *FMR1*, and FMRP levels were expressed as percentage of control values. Data are shown as mean ± SEM for controls, permutation, and full mutation carriers.

on a different genetic background (FVB129 or FVB129/NJ) than the ones used in this study (C57BL/6J) making the comparison invalid [see as an example for Huntington's disease, another triplet-nucleotide repeat disease (Menalled et al., 2009)]. In addition, KO mice may not recapitulate the full mutation seen in humans, since humans show no expression of FMRP over time as a result of a repeat-mediated gene silencing sometime during early development (Pieretti et al., 1991; Sutcliffe et al., 1992). To this end, *FMR1* and FMRP expression were assessed in fibroblasts from controls, premutation (105–180 CGG matching the range of CGG in KI mice), and full mutation (>200 CGG repeats) carriers (**Figure 4**). Fibroblasts from premutation carriers showed normal or marginally elevated *FMR1* transcript levels with ~50% FMRP levels of controls; in contrast, fibroblasts from full mutation carriers showed no gene or protein expression. When the link between *FMR1* and FMRP expression and bioenergetics (as judged by coupling between ATP synthesis and electron transfer, RCRu) was investigated in these samples, a strong direct correlation was observed between RCRu and FMRP levels but not *FMR1* mRNA levels (**Figure 4**).

Further studies are warranted by including either a wider array of outcomes or more subjects, however, these results are consistent with the association between bioenergetics and FMRP protein expression rather than to *FMR1* transcript levels.

Zn Concentrations, Bioenergetics, and Shank3 Deficiencies in KI Brain

The bioenergetic deficits observed in brains from KI mice were similar to those reported in previous studies performed on primary dermal fibroblasts from older premutation carriers (Napoli et al., 2011). That study ascribed the bioenergetic deficits to altered ZnT6 protein level and lower transport of cytoplasmic Zn (Napoli et al., 2011), which resulted in deficient Zn-mediated import/processing of nuclearly-encoded mitochondrial subunits (Napoli et al., 2011). As a result of the defective Zn-dependent processing/import of nuclear DNA (nDNA)-encoded mitochondrial proteins, higher ratios of precursor-to-mature mitochondrial proteins were observed in fibroblasts and brain samples of premutation carriers.

To test whether the import/processing of nDNA-encoded mitochondrial proteins was also affected in the KI mouse model, providing an explanation for the observed defects in OXPHOS, we evaluated the protein expression levels of mature and precursor cytochrome *c* oxidase subunit IV (CCOIV, **Figure 5**) in brains from WT and KI mice. The CCOIV Precursor-to-Mature ratios (P:M) were significantly increased in hippocampus (PND21 and PND210) and cerebellum (PND21) of KI mice (**Figure 5**), consistent with our previous reports.

To test for Zn homeostasis, Zn levels in brain were evaluated in parallel. Lower Zn concentrations were observed in hippocampus and cerebellum of KI mice at PND21 and lasting into PND210 for both brain regions (**Figure 6**). Interestingly, these regions are the ones with the highest Zn concentrations (average two-fold of cortex; **Figure 6**), consistent with their higher fraction of Zn-containing neurons (Sawashita et al., 1997) and neuron-to-glia ratios (Napoli et al., 2012). In agreement with the findings previously obtained with fibroblasts from older premutation carriers (Napoli et al., 2011), a positive correlation was also observed between Zn levels and mitochondrial outcomes (namely, activities of Complex IV and citrate synthase and coupling; **Figure 7**). Taken together, these results confirmed the lower import/processing capacity of nDNA-encoded proteins to mitochondria in premutation and the occurrence of altered Zn bioavailability.

Zn deficits are linked not only to altered mitochondrial protein import (Tokatlidis et al., 2000; Napoli et al., 2011) but also to dysregulation of Shank2/3 scaffolding (Grabrucker

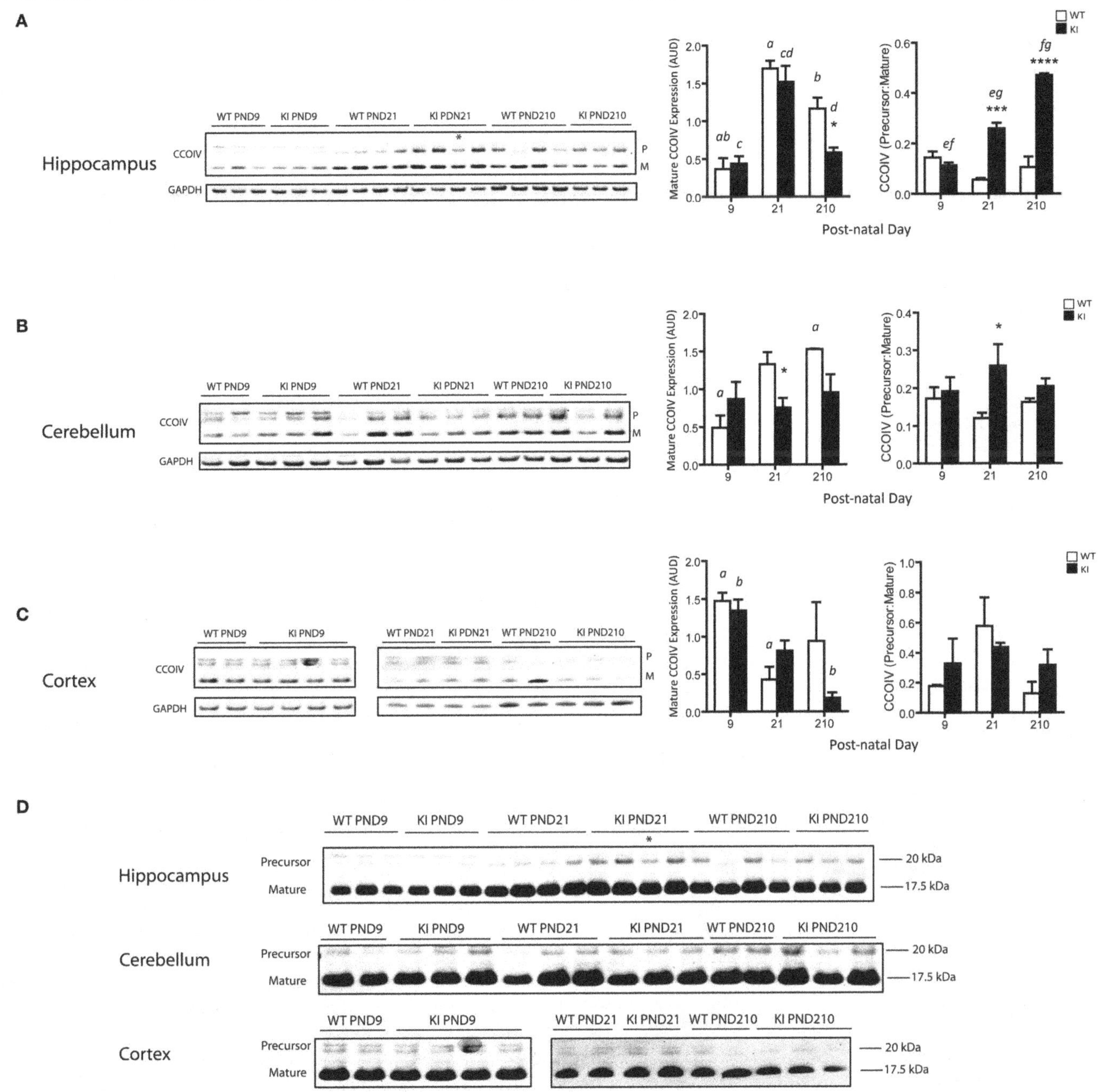

FIGURE 5 | Protein expression of precursor and mature CCOIV in brains from KI mice. Representative Western blots of CCOIV (precursor and mature proteins) in hippocampus **(A)**, cerebellum **(B)** and cortex **(C)** of WT and KI mice. The densitometry for all the samples is also shown. Data were expressed as Arbitrary Densitometry Units and reported as mean ± SEM. Mature form of CCO4 was normalized by GAPDH. Data are reported as mean ± SEM, $n = 3$–5 per genotype per time point, ran in triplicates. Statistical analysis was performed by Two-way ANOVA, followed by Tukey *post-hoc* test for multiple comparisons. Statistically significant differences between WT and KI are indicated by asterisks as follows. Hippocampus: *$p = 0.0416$; ***$p = 0.0002$; ****$p < 0.0001$. Cerebellum: *$p = 0.0212$ for mature CCO at PND21; *$p = 0.0197$ for P:M at PND21. Statistically significant differences among time points are indicated by letters as follows. Hippocampus: $p = 0.0002$ (*a*), $p = 0.0172$ (*b*), $p = 0.0013$ (*c*), $p = 0.0047$ (*d*), $p = 0.0086$ (*e*), $p < 0.0001$ (*f*), $p = 0.0003$ (*g*). Cerebellum: $p = 0.0459$ (*a*). Cortex: $p = 0.0391$ (*a*), $p = 0.0113$ (*b*). Further statistical details on the genotype, age, and genotype × age effect can be found in **Table 3**. **(D)** Uncropped version of the Western blot image showing the intensity and mobility of the precursor band relative to the mature protein. The observed molecular weights for the CCOIV precursor and mature forms were, respectively, 20.0 and 17.5 kDa, as extrapolated by the Molecular Weight markers with the use of the Carestream software. This 2.5 kDa difference was close to the theoretical calculated molecular weight (2.4 kDa) of the 22 residues of amino acids (MLATRVFSLVGKRAISTSVCVR) present in the precursor form, which is cleaved by mitochondrial matrix peptidases (Isaya et al., 1991) to produce the mature mitochondrial form of the protein (UniProtKB P13073). Asterisk in the immunoblot image of hippocampus (panels A and D) denotes a 90 CGG KI sample. Densitometry data for this sample have not been included in the averages for KI. For cortex, samples were run in two separate gels (PND9 and PND21-210). AUD, Arbitrary Units of Densitometry.

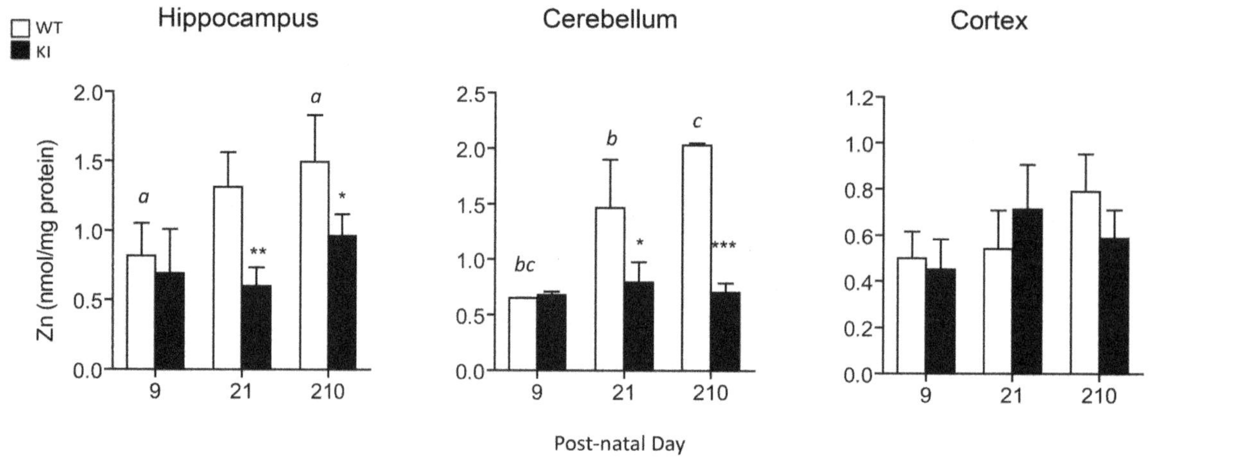

FIGURE 6 | Brain Zn concentrations in WT and KI mice. Total Zn levels were measured in whole hippocampus, cerebellum and cortex homogenates from WT and KI mice. Data are shown as mean ± SEM, $n = 3$–6 individuals *per* genotype, *per* time point, ran individually. Statistical analysis was performed by Two-way ANOVA, followed by Tukey's HSD post-hoc test for multiple comparisons. Statistically significant differences between WT and KI at individual time-points are indicated by asterisks as follows: Hippocampus: $^{*}p = 0.0425$; $^{**}p = 0.0070$; Cerebellum: $^{*}p = 0.0158$; $^{***}p = 0.0003$. Statistically significant differences among time points are indicated by letters as follows: $p = 0.0190$ (*a*), $p = 0.0144$ (*b*), $p = 0.0003$ (*c*). Further statistical details on the genotype, age, and genotype × age effect can be found in **Table 3**.

et al., 2014). Indeed, Shank3 transcript—as actin transcript—has been identified as one of the main mRNAs interacting with FMRP (Darnell et al., 2011) and both FMRP and *FMR1* mRNA are normally present in ribosomes associated to postsynaptic dendritic sites, location shared by Shank3 (Weiler et al., 1997).

Deficits in Shank3 protein expression—evaluated by Western blots—were noticeable at PND9, PND21, and PND210 in hippocampus and cerebellum from KI mice (**Figure 8** and Supplementary Figure 1). These results are consistent with other studies reporting Shank3 protein expression being brain-region/cell-type specific and developmentally regulated (Wang et al., 2014). Of note, although Shank3 is a postsynaptic density protein, several studies have shown that Shank3 expression pattern in whole brain areas mirrors that observed at the synaptic regions (Han et al., 2013; Kouser et al., 2013) providing support for the Shank3 expression in total homogenates from brain regions. Furthermore, the amount of tissue collected from each pup, especially at early time points—i.e., PND9 and PND21—would not have been sufficient as starting material for postsynaptic density preparations.

Given that Zn deficits were observed after those in Shank3, it could be inferred that the reduced levels of FMRP at early time points affects mainly Shank3 translation whereas later, both Shank3 protein expression and Zn-dependent scaffolding seem affected. In brains of WT and KI mice, statistically significant positive correlations were noted between FMRP and Shank3 (**Figure 8C**), FMRP and Zn levels (**Figure 7B**) and between Shank3 and Zn levels (**Figure 7C**), reinforcing the concept of the crosstalk between FMRP, Shank3, and Zn homeostasis.

Interaction between Genotype and Age on FMRP Levels, Bioenergetics, Zn, and Shank3 in Brains of WT and KI Mice

To test the putative interaction between genotype and age, a Two-way ANOVA analysis was performed for each of the outcomes tested at different time-points (**Table 3**). A statistically significant genotype × age interaction was observed in hippocampus for FMRP, most of the mitochondrial outcomes tested (five of eight; NADH oxidase activity, uncoupling, citrate synthase activity, and ATPB and COXIV expression), and Shank3, whereas in cerebellum the interaction was statistically significant for FMRP, only one mitochondrial outcome (COXIV), Zn levels and Shank3 (**Table 3**). In cortex, the interaction of age and genotype was statistically significant only for FMRP levels (**Table 3**). Thus, the tissue that showed the most evident gene × age interaction was hippocampus, followed by cerebellum and then cortex (**Table 3**). Simple main effect analysis showed that the overall changes observed in hippocampus and cerebellum could be equally attributed to genotype and age, whereas in cortex age had a more prominent effect (**Table 3**).

In terms of outcomes, FMRP expression was the only parameter that showed a strong interaction between genotype and age in all three-brain regions, with a bigger contribution of genotype than age (**Figure 1** and **Table 3**). Differences recorded in mitochondrial outcomes appeared to be determined by both genotype and age in hippocampus, while age played a bigger role in cerebellum and cortex (**Figure 2** and **Table 3**). Differences observed in Zn levels in hippocampus and cerebellum seemed mainly due to genotype more than age (**Figure 6** and **Table 3**). Finally, Shank3 expression seemed to be influenced by genotype and age in hippocampus and cerebellum (**Figure 8** and **Table 3**), and mainly by age in cortex. Taken together, this analysis

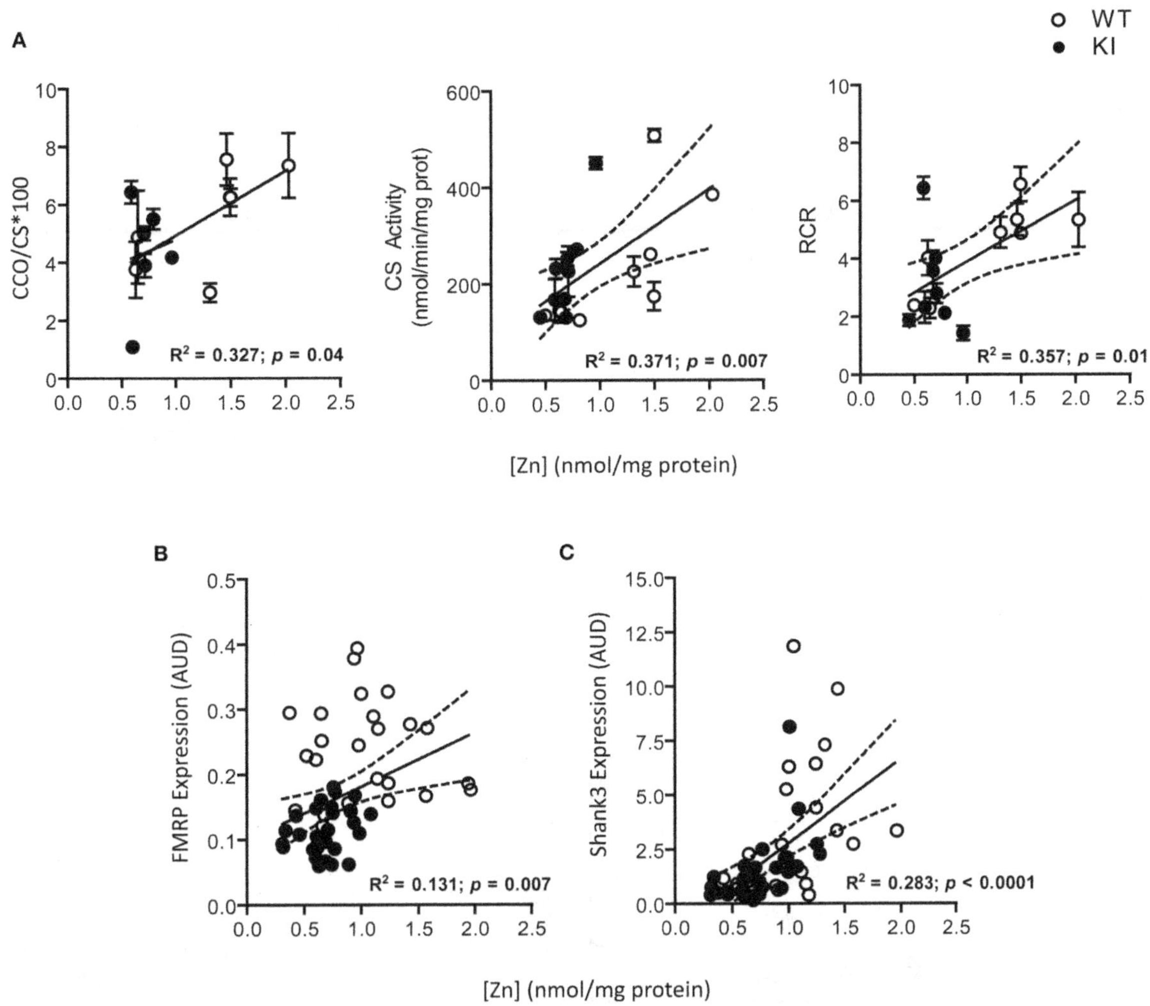

FIGURE 7 | Correlations among Zn levels, selected mitochondrial outcomes, and protein expression of FMRP and Shank3, in brain of WT and KI mice. A significant direct correlation was noted between average Zn levels and activities of CCO and CS and RCR for all the time points analyzed **(A)**. CCO and CS activities were expressed as nmol × (min × mg protein)$^{-1}$. CCO activity has been normalized to citrate synthase and multiplied by 100. All the other mitochondrial outcomes did not show a correlation with Zn. A direct correlation was also observed between Zn levels and both FMRP and Shank3 protein expression (individual values) in brains of WT and KI when all time points were combined **(B,C)**. Dotted lines illustrate the 95% CI obtained with WT and KI values.

indicates a stronger effect of the KI genotype than age on the outcomes evaluated in hippocampus, about equal for cerebellum and mostly age-dependent effects in cortex.

Altered ZnT Gene Expression in Lactating Mammary Glands from KI Dams

While some of the Zn, Shank3, and mitochondrial deficits lasted into PND210 in hippocampus and cerebellum (**Figures 2–8**), the finding that most of the mitochondrial outcomes were significantly different at PND21 (at the end of the nursing period) and that some amelioration was observed between PND21 and PND210 in cortex and cerebellum, suggested that lactation (nursing from KI dams vs. post-weaning diet constituted by vitamin- and mineral-balanced murine chow) might have compounded the early deficits. Due to the unsuccessful attempts to collect sufficient murine milk to evaluate Zn levels or any other biochemical analyses, as a surrogate for Zn homeostasis we tested the gene expression of *ZnT4* and *ZnT6* in lactating mammary glands from control and KI dams. *ZnT4* and *ZnT6* gene expression was evaluated by PCR, followed by separation of the products in a 1.3% agarose gel, visualized by using ethidium bromide. (Commercially available dual-labeled probes for these transporters resulted unspecific).

In lactating mammary glands from WT dams, both *ZnT4* and *ZnT6* (normalized to *GAPDH*) were expressed with a ratio of *ZnT6/ZnT4* equal to 15 (**Figure 9A**). The gene expression of both ZnTs was significantly higher (two-fold) in KI than WT, with no significant changes in the *ZnT6/ZnT4* expression ratio compared to WT (**Figure 9B**). These results suggested a disrupted ZnT expression, which may affect Zn efflux in milk, and as a consequence, the Zn status of the suckling pups.

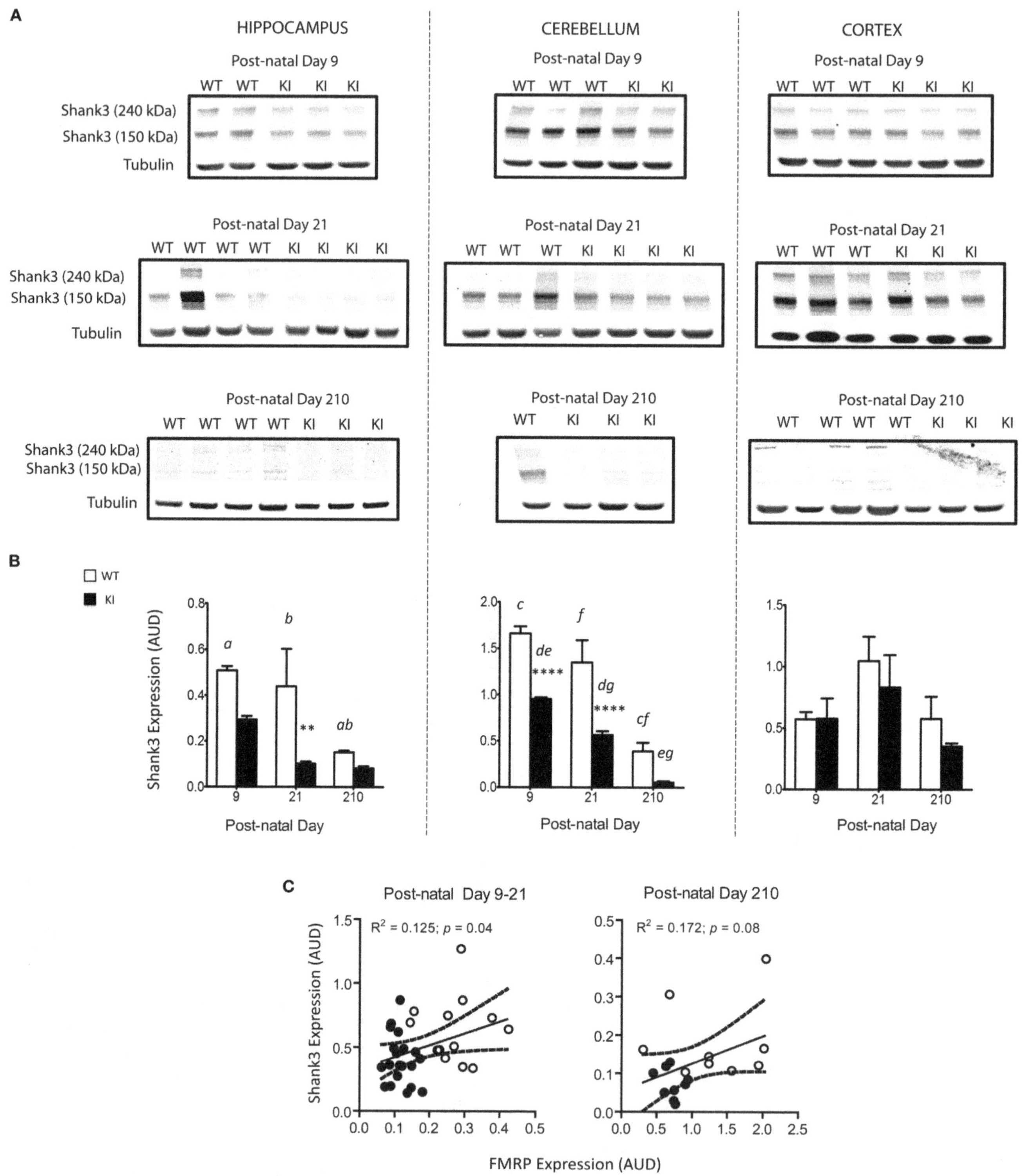

FIGURE 8 | Brain Shank3 protein levels in WT and KI mice. (A) Western blots for Shank3 protein expression levels in hippocampus, cerebellum, and cortex were performed at PND 9, 21, and 210 from WT (white) and KI (black) mice as described in details in the Materials and Methods Section. Further, images taken with acetone-precipitated samples and normalized by either tubulin or GADPH are found under Supplementary Figure 1. **(B)** Densitometry data is shown as mean ± SEM, $n = 4$–5 individuals *per* genotype, *per* time point, ran individually. Statistical analysis was performed by two-way ANOVA, followed by Tukey's HSD *post-hoc* test for multiple comparisons. Statistically significant differences between WT and KI are indicated by asterisks as follows: Hippocampus: $^{**}p = 0.0054$; Cerebellum: $^{****}p < 0.0001$. Statistically significant differences among time points are indicated by letters as follows: $p = 0.0074$ (*a*), $p = 0.0267$ (*b*), $p < 0.0001$ (*c, e, f*), $p = 0.0217$(*d*),

(Continued)

FIGURE 8 | Continued
$p = 0.0041$ (*g*). Further, statistical details on the genotype, age, and genotype × age effect can be found in **Table 3**. **(C)** Correlation between FMRP levels and Shank3 protein expression in brain of WT and KI mice. Both proteins have been normalized by tubulin, used as loading control. Shown are individual data points collected in cerebellum, hippocampus, and cortex of WT and KI mice at PND9, PND21, and PND210. PND210 is shown in a separate plot due to the difference in protein expression of both FMRP and Shank3 at this time point, relative to the previous ones. Dotted lines are 95% CI constructed with WT and KI values. AUD, Arbitrary Units of Densitometry.

TABLE 3 | Effect of genotype, age, and genotype × age interaction on outcomes evaluated in hippocampus, cerebellum, and cortex of WT and KI mice.

	Genotype × age interaction	Genotype effect	Age effect
HIPPOCAMPUS			
FMRP	$F_{(2, 17)} = 23.42$ **$p < 0.0001$**	$F_{(1, 17)} = 105.3$ **$p < 0.0001$**	$F_{(2, 17)} = 16.24$ **$p = 0.0001$**
NADH oxidase	$F_{(2, 18)} = 8.466$ **$p = 0.0026$**	$F_{(1, 18)} = 2.435$ **$p = 0.0464$**	$F_{(2, 18)} = 17.12$ **$p < 0.0001$**
Succinate oxidase	$F_{(2, 19)} = 0.6392$ $p = 0.5387$	$F_{(1, 19)} = 6.180$ **$p = 0.0224$**	$F_{(2, 19)} = 16.02$ **$p < 0.0001$**
Cytochrome *c* oxidase	$F_{(2, 18)} = 1.099$ $p = 0.3545$	$F_{(1, 18)} = 5.245$ **$p = 0.0343$**	$F_{(2, 18)} = 2.915$ $p = 0.0801$
RCR	$F_{(2, 22)} = 9.284$ **$p = 0.0012$**	$F_{(1, 22)} = 27.45$ **$p < 0.0001$**	$F_{(2, 22)} = 8.578$ **$p = 0.0018$**
Citrate synthase	$F_{(3, 47)} = 1.307$ $p = 0.283$	$F_{(1, 47)} = 2.162$ $p = 0.1481$	$F_{(3, 47)} = 8.239$ **$p = 0.0002$**
ATPB	$F_{(2, 15)} = 26.74$ **$p < 0.0001$**	$F_{(1, 15)} = 214.1$ **$p < 0.0001$**	$F_{(2, 15)} = 39.95$ **$p < 0.0001$**
COXIV	$F_{(2, 15)} = 2.362$ $p = 0.1283$	$F_{(1, 15)} = 3.582$ $p = 0.0779$	$F_{(2, 15)} = 34.88$ **$p < 0.0001$**
COXIV (P:M)	$F_{(2, 15)} = 30.14$ **$p < 0.0001$**	$F_{(1, 15)} = 78.45$ **$p < 0.0001$**	$F_{(2, 15)} = 23.12$ **$p < 0.0001$**
[Zn]	$F_{(2, 17)} = 2.588$ $p = 0.1045$	$F_{(1, 17)} = 19.94$ **$p = 0.0003$**	$F_{(2, 17)} = 7.303$ **$p = 0.0051$**
Shank3	$F_{(2, 20)} = 2.559$ **$p = 0.1024$**	$F_{(1, 20)} = 16.50$ **$p = 0.0006$**	$F_{(2, 20)} = 10.23$ **$p = 0.0009$**
CEREBELLUM			
FMRP	$F_{(2, 15)} = 4.768$ **$p = 0.0250$**	$F_{(1, 15)} = 28.64$ **$p < 0.0001$**	$F_{(2, 15)} = 13.16$ **$p = 0.0005$**
NADH oxidase	$F_{(3, 48)} = 1.471$ $p = 0.2341$	$F_{(1, 48)} = 0.08211$ $p = 0.7757$	$F_{(3, 48)} = 6.907$ **$p = 0.0006$**
Succinate oxidase	$F_{(3, 44)} = 0.2040$ $p = 0.893$	$F_{(1, 44)} = 1.196$ $p = 0.2802$	$F_{(3, 44)} = 8.347$ **$p = 0.002$**
Cytochrome *c* oxidase	$F_{(3, 42)} = 1.198$ $p = 0.3221$	$F_{(1, 42)} = 0.1964$ $p = 0.6559$	$F_{(3, 42)} = 2.490$ $p = 0.0733$
RCR	$F_{(3, 40)} = 1.493$ $p = 0.2312$	$F_{(1, 40)} = 4.457$ **$p = 0.0411$**	$F_{(3, 40)} = 1.044$ $p = 0.3835$
Citrate synthase	$F_{(3, 57)} = 7.890$ $p = 0002$	$F_{(1, 57)} = 0.9931$ $p = 0.2323$	$F_{(3, 57)} = 43.11$ **$p < 0.0001$**
ATPB	$F_{(2, 12)} = 1.194$ $p = 0.3427$	$F_{(1, 12)} = 7.348$ **$p = 0.0219$**	$F_{(2, 12)} = 5.603$ **$p = 0.0233$**
COXIV	$F_{(2, 12)} = 5.355$ **$p = 0.0262$**	$F_{(1, 12)} = 4.313$ $p = 0.0645$	$F_{(2, 12)} = 4.394$ **$p = 0.0427$**
COXIV (P:M)	$F_{(2, 12)} = 3.523$ $p = 0.0695$	$F_{(1, 12)} = 8.816$ **$p = 0.0141$**	$F_{(2, 12)} = 0.3843$ $p = 0.6906$

(Continued)

TABLE 3 | Continued

	Genotype × age interaction	Genotype effect	Age effect
[Zn]	$F_{(2, 11)} = 12.09$ **$p = 0.0017$**	$F_{(1, 11)} = 37.88$ **$p < 0.0001$**	$F_{(2, 11)} = 13.61$ **$p = 0.0011$**
Shank3	$F_{(2, 18)} = 4.293$ **$p = 0.0299$**	$F_{(1, 18)} = 85.27$ **$p < 0.0001$**	$F_{(2, 18)} = 95.15$ **$p < 0.0001$**
Cortex			
FMRP	$F_{(2, 12)} = 9.336$ **$p = 0.0036$**	$F_{(1, 12)} = 38.50$ **$p < 0.0001$**	$F_{(2, 12)} = 14.01$ **$p = 0.0007$**
NADH oxidase	$F_{(3, 41)} = 0.2289$ $p = 0.8757$	$F_{(1, 41)} = 0.0008$ $P = 0.9286$	$F_{(3, 41)} = 19.52$ **$p < 0.0001$**
Succinate oxidase	$F_{(3, 46)} = 0.09088$ $p = 0.9647$	$F_{(1, 46)} = 1.045$ $P = 0.3120$	$F_{(3, 46)} = 15.24$ **$p < 0.0001$**
Cytochrome *c* oxidase	$F_{(3, 46)} = 0.09514$ $p = 0.9623$	$F_{(1, 46)} = 3.203$ $p = 0.0801$	$F_{(2, 46)} = 12.30$ **$p < 0.0001$**
RCR	$F_{(3, 45)} = 0.2112$ $p = 0.8881$	$F_{(1, 45)} = 4.890$ **$p = 0.0321$**	$F_{(3, 45)} = 2.388$ $p = 0.0813$
Citrate synthase	$F_{(3, 55)} = 1.983$ $p = 0.1272$	$F_{(1, 55)} = 1.983$ $p = 0.3405$	$F_{(3, 55)} = 213.7$ **$p < 0.0001$**
ATPB	$F_{(2, 11)} = 1.249$ $p = 0.3246$	$F_{(1, 11)} = 0.6066$ $p = 0.4525$	$F_{(2, 11)} = 15.49$ **$p = 0.0006$**
COXIV	$F_{(2, 12)} = 3.819$ $p = 0.0630$	$F_{(1, 12)} = 1.054$ $p = 0.3313$	$F_{(2, 12)} = 12.72$ **$p = 0.0024$**
COXIV (P:M)	$F_{(2, 12)} = 1.018$ $p = 0.3993$	$F_{(1, 12)} = 0.4778$ $p = 0.5069$	$F_{(2, 12)} = 3.047$ $p = 0.0976$
[Zn]	$F_{(2, 12)} = 1.913$ $p = 0.1979$	$F_{(1, 12)} = 0.1174$ $p = 0.7389$	$F_{(2, 12)} = 3.011$ $p = 0.0947$
Shank3	$F_{(2, 12)} = 0.4705$ $p = 0.6322$	$F_{(1, 12)} = 1.679$ $p = 0.2114$	$F_{(2, 12)} = 9.085$ **$p = 0.0019$**

Statistical parameters reported in the table were calculated by Two-way ANOVA. In bold are statistically significant effects. Between parentheses are values of F(DFn, DFd). Further, statistical details are reported in the figure legend of each outcome tested.

Studies have shown that Zn deficiency in rodents results in anorexia (with about 50% of the body weight gained under physiological conditions), poor hair coat, scaly paws, and reproductive defects (Brody, 1999), none of which have been observed in either KI dams or pups, supporting the idea of a localized Zn homeostasis deficit related to the premutation (probably linked to the tissue expression of FMRP), rather than a generalized one.

Detrimental Effect of KI Milk on Brain Bioenergetics

On the basis of the findings shown thus far we hypothesize that Zn-deficient milk of KI dams would be detrimental on the suckling pups' bioenergetics requirements, whereas milk from WT dams might rescue some of the deficits observed in the premutation mice. To test this hypothesis we designed a cross-fostering experiment in which KI pups nursed on WT dams (WT milk) and WT pups nursed on KI dams (KI milk; **Figure 10**). We tested mitochondrial outcomes at PND21 from WT and KI in the pups (male hemizygous) nursing on KI milk to elucidate the effect of KI milk on the brain bioenergetics of WT pups, or nursing on WT milk to elucidate the effect of WT milk on the brain bioenergetics of KI pups (**Figure 10**).

A detrimental effect on brain bioenergetics was observed in WT pups nursing on KI milk, characterized by significantly lower mitochondrial outcomes relative to WT pups nursing on WT milk in all three brain areas, with the highest effect observed in hippocampus showing, deficits in four of the five measured outcomes. On average, the most affected outcome was ATP-dependent oxygen uptake sustained by NAD-linked substrate (NADH oxidase activity), followed by ATP-dependent oxygen uptake sustained by an FAD-linked substrate (succinate oxidase activity), CCO activity, and coupling (**Figure 10**). Furthermore, the hippocampus of WT pups nursing on KI milk showed a significant decrease in mitochondrial mass. Of note, although the detrimental effects of the KI milk on the mitochondrial outcomes in WT pups were significant (–29 ± 8% average of all outcomes), they were not severe enough to match the deficits observed in KI pups nursed on KI milk (–46 ± 11%, mean ± SEM). KI pups nursing on WT milk compared to KI pups nursed on KI milk exhibited some mitochondrial improvement, as judged by a partial recovery of succinate oxidase activity in cerebellum (from 60 to 82% of WT) and complete recovery of succinate oxidase and

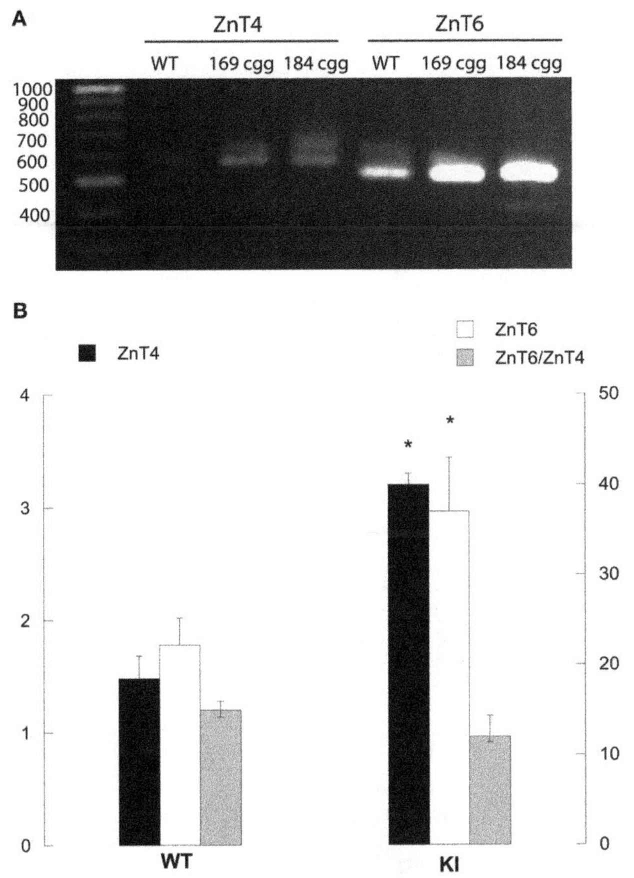

FIGURE 9 | *ZnT4* and *ZnT6* gene expression in mammary glands from lactating WT and KI dams. Representative image of the PCR products (obtained by RT-qPCR as described under Methods) that were separated in a 1.3% agarose gel and visualized with ethidium bromide **(A)**. The fragments exhibited the expected sizes of 585 bp (*ZnT4*) and 537 bp (*ZnT6*). *GAPDH* PCR product was separated in a 3% agarose gel electrophoresis with ethidium bromide resulting in a product of the expected of 107 bp (not shown). Intensities of *ZnT4* and *ZnT6* bands were obtained in a Kodak Imager were normalized by that of *GAPDH* **(B)**. Bars represent averages ± SEM of 4 individuals/genotype. Statistical analysis was carried out with the Student's *t*-test between WT and KI. $^*p < 0.05$.

coupling in cortex (**Figure 10**). None of the measured outcomes showed a significant recovery in hippocampus (**Figure 10**).

The effect of the diet (KI vs. WT milk) and genotype on mitochondrial outcomes was evaluated by Two-way ANOVA (**Table 4**). A significant milk type × genotype interaction on bioenergetics was observed in all brain regions, with the main effects being attributed to genotype in hippocampus and cerebellum, and to both genotype and milk type in cortex (**Table 4**).

Taken together these results suggest that, despite the presence of a susceptible genetic background conferred by the *FMR1* premutation, brain mitochondrial outcomes were modulated by a nutritional intervention (KI milk) mainly in cortex, the least Zn-enriched brain region. While the impact of cross-fostering on offspring's brain bioenergetics could not be explained by differences in caloric intake because there were no statistical differences in body weight gain or brain weight gain between the two groups (not shown), the changes in mitochondrial brain OXPHOS in both WT and KI mice were consistent with a compounding effect of an altered Zn homeostasis in milk from premutation carriers (**Table 4**). While WT pups nursing on KI milk resulted in MD (hippocampus and cerebellum), KI pups nursing on WT milk improved some of the mitochondrial outcomes (cortex). The lack of a significant improvement in all of the brain regions tested could be explained by their different brain Zn requirements (Sawashita et al., 1997), limitations of a non-optimized intervention on a specific genetic background, or inability of achieving a complete recovery of some of the components involved in post-synaptic scaffolding and bioenergetics beyond PND21.

Zn Deficits in Breast Milk from Premutation Carriers

To complement and further confirm the experiments performed with the premutation mouse model, experiments were extended to test the quality of milk from lactating women carrying the premutation. Zn concentrations were determined in mature human milk [i.e., 8–20 weeks of lactation (Worth et al., 1981)] from asymptomatic premutation women (milk CGG repeats = 63–119) and age-matched controls (**Table 5**). Furthermore, we tested selected Zn-associated outcomes, namely activity of milk alkaline phosphatase (ALP), a Zn-requiring enzyme that contributes with 20% of total milk Zn (Fransson and Lonnerdal, 1984), and concentrations of lactose, whose biosynthesis is dependent on the Zn-requiring enzyme β-1,4-galactosyltransferase (McCormick and Kelleher, 2012), the rate limiting enzyme in the lactose biosynthetic pathway (Jagoda and Rillema, 1991).

Milk from healthy donors had an average Zn concentration of 26 ± 2 μM (1.7 ± 0.1 mg/l), within the normal range reported before [1.0–1.7 mg/l at 3–5 months of lactation evaluated by atomic absorption spectrometry (Krebs et al., 1995)], with 86% of the Zn being in the labile form. In agreement with data previously reported (Nagra, 1989; Krebs et al., 1995), milk Zn concentrations from control and premutation women were reciprocally correlated with the postpartum period (**Figure 11A**), following a pseudo-first order kinetics with a biological half-life of 8 weeks (**Figure 11**). Although 10 of the 25 control donors were taking vitamins and mineral supplements (including Zn) during lactation, no significant differences in Zn concentrations were observed between these two groups, in agreement with the observed lack of correlation between milk or plasma Zn concentrations and maternal Zn intake (Krebs et al., 1995). In samples from premutation carriers, the average milk Zn concentration at 3–5 months of lactation was 56% of control values (14 ± 3 μM; $p = 0.020$). Specifically, milk Zn concentrations from two carriers at 8–9 lactation weeks and from one carrier at 19–20 weeks were significantly lower than the 95% CI (**Figure 11A**, **Table 6**). Zn levels in the remaining premutation milk samples, obtained after week 15, followed the decrease observed in control milk (**Figure 11A**, **Table 6**).

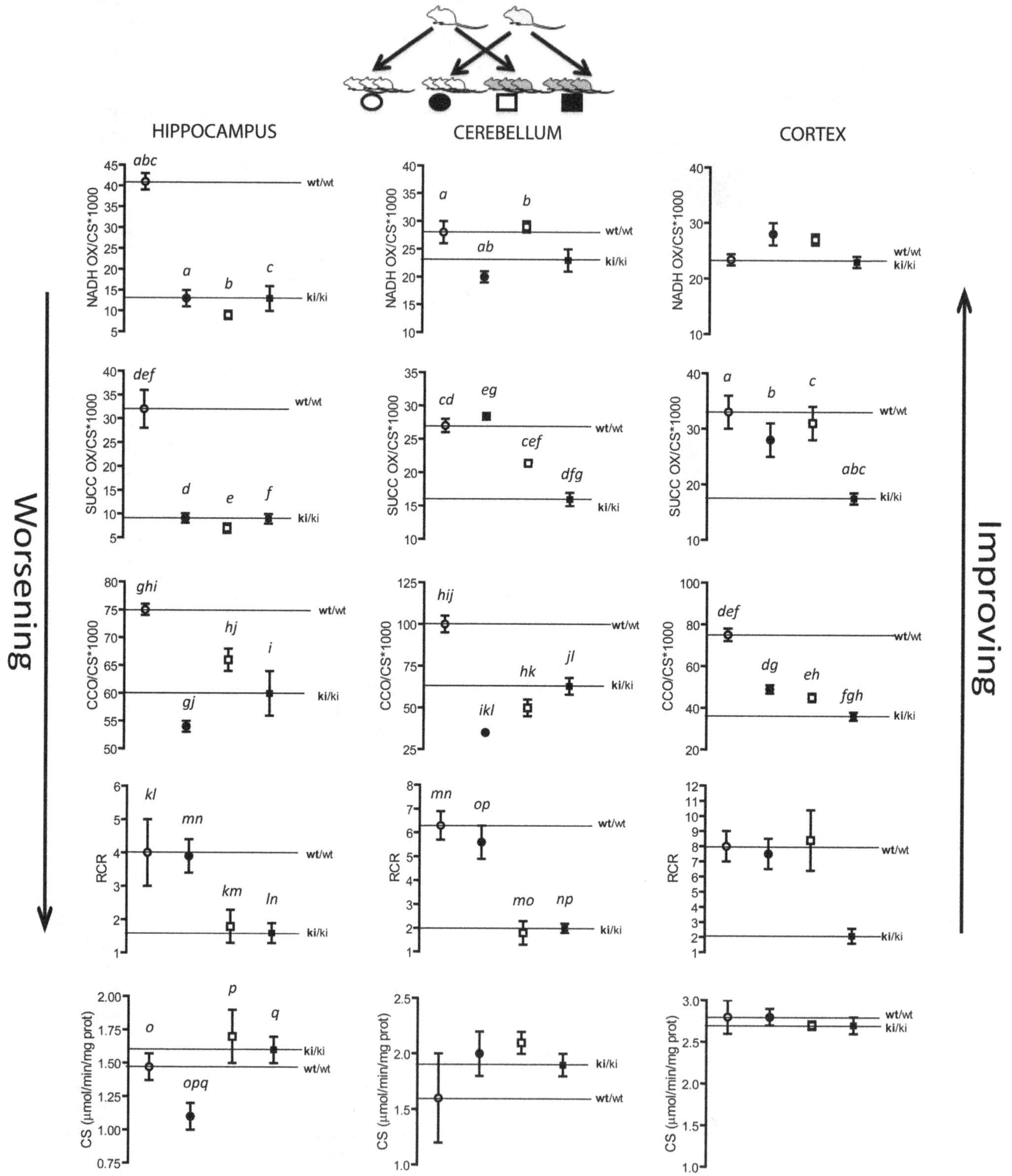

FIGURE 10 | Changes in mitochondrial outcomes in hippocampus, cerebellum and cortex of suckling WT and KI pups nursed on WT or KI dams. At birth, KI pups ($n = 24$) and WT pups ($n = 24$) were foster-nursed either on KI dams or WT dams, six pups on each dam. After 21 days, mitochondria were isolated from cortex, cerebellum, and hippocampus and activities of NADH oxidase, succinate oxidase, cytochrome *c* oxidase, and citrate synthase and RCR were evaluated as described in the Methods section. wt/wt = WT pups nursing on WT milk; ki/ki = KI pups nursing on KI milk. Circles represent WT pups, squares represent KI pups. White symbols represent WT milk and black symbols represent KI milk. Upward or downward arrows represent improvement or worsening, respectively, upon nursing on WT milk or KI milk. Activities (NADH oxidase, succinate oxidase, cytochrome *c* oxidase) were expressed as nmol × (min × mg protein)$^{-1}$, normalized by citrate

(Continued)

FIGURE 10 | Continued
synthase activity and multiplied by 1000. Data are shown as mean ± SEM (from technical replicates of pooled samples). Statistical analysis was performed by Two-way ANOVA, followed by Tukey's *post-hoc* test for multiple comparisons. The p values are as follows. Hippocampus: $p < 0.0001$ (*a, b, c, g, i, p, q*), $p = 0.0004$ (*d, o*), $p = 0.0002$ (*e, f*), $p = 0.0025$ (*h*), $p = 0.0008$ (*j*), $p = 0.0027$ (*k*), $p = 0.0006$ (*l*), $p = 0.0262$ (*m*), $p = 0.0082$ (*n*); Cerebellum: $p = 0.0296$ (*a*), $p = 0.0301$ (*b*), $p = 0.0039$ (*c*), $p < 0.0001$ (*d, g, h, i, j, k, l, m, n, o, p*), $p = 0.0023$ (*e*); $p = 0.0086$ (*f*); Cortex: $p < 0.0001$ (*a, b, c, d, e, f*), $p = 0.0047$ (*g*), $p = 0.0468$ (*h*). Further statistical details on the genotype, age, and genotype × age effect can be found in **Table 4**.

TABLE 4 | Effect of genotype, diet, and genotype × diet interaction on outcomes evaluated in hippocampus, cerebellum, and cortex of cross-fostered WT and KI pups.

	Genotype × diet interaction	Genotype effect	Diet effect
HIPPOCAMPUS			
NADH oxidase	$F_{(1, 11)} = 58.03$ **$p < 0.0001$**	$F_{(1, 11)} = 57.52$ **$p < 0.0001$**	$F_{(1, 11)} = 32.05$ **$p = 0.0001$**
Succinate oxidase	$F_{(1, 11)} = 20.96$ **$p = 0.0008$**	$F_{(1, 11)} = 20.49$ **$p = 0.0009$**	$F_{(1, 11)} = 14.15$ **$p = 0.0031$**
Cytochrome *c* oxidase	$F_{(1, 11)} = 29.96$ **$p = 0.0002$**	$F_{(1, 11)} = 1.501$ $p = 0.2462$	$F_{(1, 11)} = 97.53$ **$p < 0.0001$**
RCR	$F_{(1, 11)} = 0.1242$ $p = 0.7312$	$F_{(1, 11)} = 39.29$ **$p < 0.0001$**	$F_{(1, 11)} = 1.039$ $p = 0.3298$
Citrate synthase	$F_{(1, 11)} = 10.35$ **$p = 0.0082$**	$F_{(1, 11)} = 26.72$ **$p = 0.0003$**	$F_{(1, 11)} = 67.89$ **$p < 0.0001$**
CEREBELLUM			
NADH oxidase	$F_{(1, 11)} = 0.6863$ $p = 0.4250$	$F_{(1, 11)} = 15.68$ **$p = 0.0022$**	$F_{(1, 11)} = 1.384$ $p = 0.2642$
Succinate oxidase	$F_{(1, 11)} = 12.75$ **$p = 0.0044$**	$F_{(1, 11)} = 97.54$ **$p < 0.0001$**	$F_{(1, 11)} = 5.300$ **$p = 0.0419$**
Cytochrome *c* oxidase	$F_{(1, 11)} = 905.1$ **$p < 0.0001$**	$F_{(1, 11)} = 69.16$ **$p < 0.0001$**	$F_{(1, 11)} = 403.2$ **$p < 0.0001$**
RCR	$F_{(1, 11)} = 14.28$ **$p = 0.0031$**	$F_{(1, 11)} = 1146$ **$p < 0.0001$**	$F_{(1, 11)} = 4.768$ $p = 0.0515$
Citrate synthase	$F_{(1, 11)} = 1.582$ $p = 0.2290$	$F_{(1, 11)} = 0.8701$ $p = 0.3667$	$F_{(1, 11)} = 0.3943$ $p = 0.5401$
CORTEX			
NADH oxidase	$F_{(1, 11)} = 98.63$ **$p < 0.0001$**	$F_{(1, 11)} = 4.235$ $P = 0.0641$	$F_{(1, 11)} = 0.5049$ $p = 0.4921$
Succinate oxidase	$F_{(1, 11)} = 34.47$ **$p = 0.0001$**	$F_{(1, 11)} = 61.96$ **$P < 0.0001$**	$F_{(1, 11)} = 149.0$ **$p < 0.0001$**
Cytochrome *c* oxidase	$F_{(1, 11)} = 16.45$ **$p = 0.0019$**	$F_{(1, 11)} = 109.7$ **$p < 0.0001$**	$F_{(1, 11)} = 71.65$ **$p < 0.0001$**
RCR	$F_{(1, 11)} = 60.13$ **$p < 0.0001$**	$F_{(1, 11)} = 44.72$ **$p < 0.0001$**	$F_{(1, 11)} = 84.89$ **$p < 0.0001$**
Citrate synthase	$F_{(1, 11)} = 2.068$ $p = 0.1724$	$F_{(1, 11)} = 0.1195$ $p = 0.7347$	$F_{(1, 11)} = 0.0441$ $p = 0.8367$

Statistical parameters reported in the table were calculated by Two-way ANOVA. Outcomes were measured in 24 mice (12 WT and 12 KI). Due to the scarce amount of tissue collected from hippocampus and cerebellum, material from four animals belonging to the same genotype and nursed from the same dam were pooled. The cross-fostering experiment was repeated twice, for a total of 48 mice used. In bold are statistically significant effects. Between parentheses are values of F(DFn, DFd). Further, statistical details are reported in the figure legend of each outcome tested.

Although the sample size is small, the incidence of low Zn concentration was higher in carriers compared to controls (60% vs. 24%; test for one proportion $p = 0.0595$; 95% CI = 0.2307–0. 8824).

The ALP activity in human breast milk from control donors increased almost linearly from eight to 18–20 weeks, in agreement with other reports (Chanda et al., 1951; Stewart et al., 1958; Worth et al., 1981) and with published values (Worth et al., 1981; Coburn et al., 1992; **Figure 11B**, **Table 6**). As observed with milk Zn concentrations, ALP activities in controls were not affected by vitamin supplementation. Changes in milk ALP activity with lactation week from premutation donors paralleled those of controls, with only one carrier showing a 51% ALP activity of control values at 19 weeks (**Figure 11B**, **Table 6**).

TABLE 5 | Details of the study population.

Premutation carrier	Milk CGG repeats	Maternal age at sample collection (y)	Lactation week at sample collection
1	29, 63	38	20
2	20, 80	34	9
3	29, 91	34	16
4	30, 93	23	19
5	29, 119	34	8
		MEAN ± SEM	
Premutation women ($n = 5$)	89 ± 9	33 ± 2	14 ± 2
Control women ($n = 25$)	27 ± 2 ($p = 0.002$)	31 ± 1	13.1 ± 0.5

CGG repeats were evaluated by extracting total genomic DNA from milk samples and following the procedure described before (Tassone et al., 2012). The mean CGG for premutation patients represent that of the longer allele only.

In terms of protein and lactose concentrations, the mean nutrient composition of milk samples was not different between controls and premutation individuals and remained fairly constant throughout the evaluated period, consistent with published concentrations for controls [[protein] in g/l: this study = 12.8 ± 0.5, 95%CI 12-13, literature = 12 ± 1.5 (Tudehope, 2013); [lactose] in mM: this study = 205 ± 3 95%CI 199-210, literature = 196 ± 15 (Nagra, 1989; Mohammad et al., 2012; Tudehope, 2013)]. However, the incidence of either low protein or low lactose concentrations was higher in premutation carriers than controls (**Table 6**). Interestingly, these observations are consistent with the findings obtained in HC11 cells in which overexpression of ZnT4 lowers both β-1,4-galactosyltransferase activity (McCormick and Kelleher, 2012) and lactose concentration by compromising the incorporation of Zn into Zn-requiring proteins.

Taken together, these results show lower milk Zn concentrations in premutation women, consistent with an altered Zn homeostasis as observed in mammary glands from KI dams, supporting the idea that adequate gene expression of *ZnT4* and *ZnT6* may be required during the switch from the non-lactating to the lactating condition to support normal Zn efflux into milk.

DISCUSSION

Our study reports the contribution of FMRP protein expression to the development of brain bioenergetics, cytoskeleton structure, and post-synaptic scaffolding protein Shank3 in *FMR1* premutation carriers at early stages of life. In support of this concept, we found (i) mitochondrial deficits at PND0 in isolated neurons from hippocampus, cerebellum and cortex of KI pups likely reflecting an embryonic (pre-natal) FMRP-dependent dysfunction; (ii) deficits in bioenergetics, Zn concentrations and Shank3 protein, mainly in hippocampus and cerebellum (Zn-rich brain areas) of KI pups at PND21, with some of these deficits lasting into adulthood; and (iii) defective import/processing of nDNA-encoded mitochondrial subunits secondary to impaired Zn homeostasis. A strong genotype × age interaction was observed for most of the outcomes tested in hippocampus and cerebellum, whereas in cortex, age played a major factor.

The effect of maternal milk Zn on offspring bioenergetics highlights the influence of genetics × nutrition on the premutation supported by the altered gene expression of *ZnT6/T4* in lactating KI mammary glands, the KI milk-dependent detrimental effect on KI and WT brain bioenergetics, and the lower milk Zn content in breast milk from lactating premutation women. A highly significant milk type × genotype interaction was observed for all three-brain regions being cortex the most influenced.

Brain Zn concentrations change with age, reflecting its function as a neuromodulator and as a required element for brain development (Sawashita et al., 1997), especially in regards to synaptic transmission and bioenergetics (Ho et al., 2003; Kogan et al., 2008; Grabrucker et al., 2014; Hara et al., 2014; Picard and McEwen, 2014). Our study is consistent with the reported detrimental effect of milk Zn deficiency on perinatal outcomes in the lethal milk (*lm*) mice (Huang and Gitschier, 1997), and in agreement with the proposed role of FMRP as modulator of synaptogenesis through actions on cytoskeletal proteins, by interacting with specific mRNAs [such as Shank3 or actin (Brown et al., 2001; Darnell and Richter, 2012; Han et al., 2013)] or via the Rac1 pathway (Bardoni and Mandel, 2002). The lower milk Zn concentration found in premutation women and the altered *ZnT4/ZnT6* gene expression in lactating KI murine mammary gland may account for the effect of KI milk on the brain bioenergetics of both WT and KI offspring, but more evident in KI pups. Given the heavy reliance of brain on mitochondrial ATP as well as on *de novo* synthesis of Krebs cycle-associated neurotransmitter amino acids [i.e., Glu, Asp, and GABA (Butterworth and Heroux, 1989; Navarro et al., 2008)], mitochondrial and synaptic scaffolding deficits are likely to increase the risk for some of the neurological symptoms observed in pediatric carriers. Indeed, altered brain bioenergetics and those of the post-synaptic scaffolding protein Shank3 during perinatal periods may explain the abnormal behavior observed

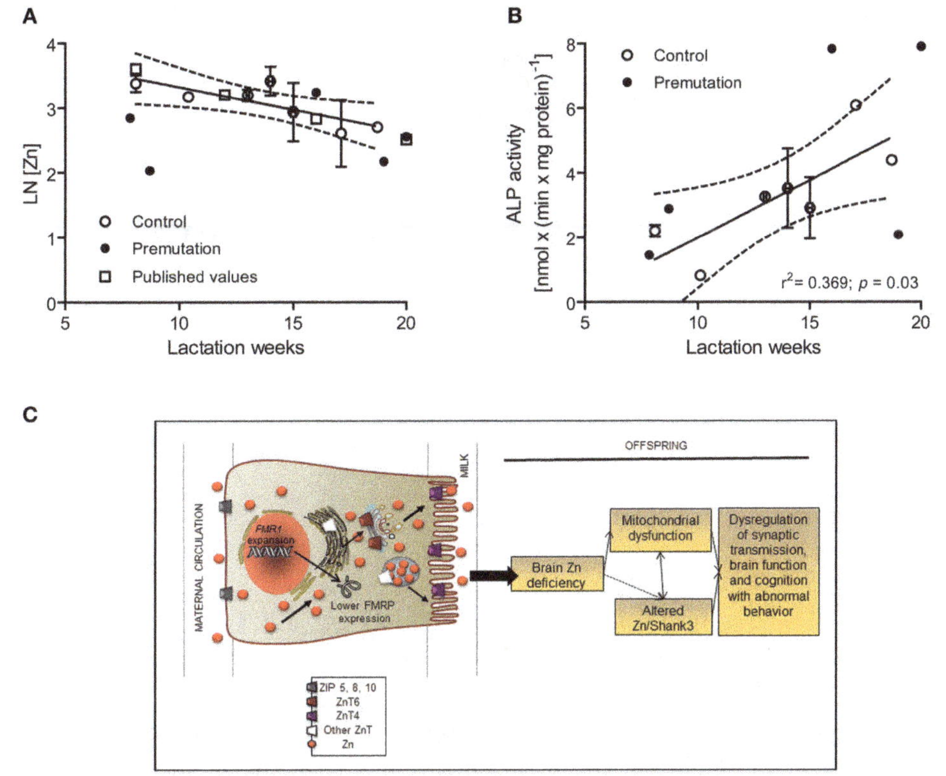

FIGURE 11 | Role of milk Zn in brain bioenergetics and synapse scaffolding in premutation carriers. Milk-Zn concentrations followed a pseudo-first order kinetics over the lactation period **(A)**. Milk Zn concentrations from control and premutation donors decreased with the post-partum period, ranging from 30 ± 3 μM at 6–8 weeks to 15 ± 2 μM at 18–20 weeks. The LN values of the Zn concentrations (in μM) were plotted against lactation week. The published values were obtained from Nagra et al. (Nagra, 1989) and shown as white squares. Regression parameters are as follows: for published [Zn], $r^2 = 0.997$, $y = -0.09x + 4.3$; for this study, $r^2 = 0.647$, $y = -0.07x + 4.0$. P value for slopes = 0.458; P value for intercepts = 0.986. ALP activity [expressed as nmol × (min × mg protein)$^{-1}$] in human breast milk from control donors increased linearly from 8 to 18–20 weeks **(B)**. The average ALP activity of controls was 3.3 ± 0.3 nmol × (min × mg protein)$^{-1}$ or 46 ± 1 μmol × (min × l)$^{-1}$ and within reported values [40 to 60 μmol × (min × l)$^{-1}$; (Worth et al., 1981; Coburn et al., 1992)]. Linear regression analyses were performed with control values (reported as mean ± SEM) for both outcomes ($r^2 = 0.638$ and 0.639 for Zn concentration and ALP activity, respectively). The 95% CIs performed with control values are shown with dotted lines. Individual premutation carriers' values for Zn concentrations and ALP activities are shown in **Table 5**. ALP activities in controls were not affected by vitamin and mineral supplementation [supplemented: 3.7 ± 0.4 vs. not supplemented: 3.2 ± 0.4 nmol × (min × mg protein)$^{-1}$; $p = 0.624$]. A model integrating experimental data based on altered Zn homeostasis, mitochondrial dysfunction [current study and (Ross-Inta et al., 2010; Napoli et al., 2011)], and the putative effect of defective synaptic scaffolding in premutation individuals is shown in **(C)**. During lactation, Zn uptake is exerted by ZIP5, 8 and 10, then excreted to milk via ZnT4/ZnT2 with a lower flux through ZnT6 (ZnT10) in the Golgi [Adapted from (Kelleher et al., 2012)]. The presence of the CGG expansion in *FMR1*, as it is the case with premutation carriers, may ensue in a lower expression of FMRP, which may affect the cytoskeleton (e.g., actin, Shank3), and the expression or function of membrane transporter such as ZnT4/T6. This situation would ensue in the suboptimal delivery of Zn into milk, mitochondrial dysfunction, and synaptic dysregulation. The arrows indicate the direction of Zn transport from maternal blood to milk.

in KI mice later in life [12 and 24 weeks; (Van Dam et al., 2005; Hunsaker et al., 2009, 2012)], similar to the spatial processing defects observed in humans with FXTAS (Hunsaker et al., 2012).

While the relative contribution of RNA sequestration of essential factors, low FMRP expression and RAN translation (of the toxic FMRPolyG) to the premutation pathology is still unknown, this study supports the notion that that lower levels of wild-type FMRP [as observed in this study and most premutation carriers (Kenneson et al., 2001), with or without the generation of aberrant FMRP isoforms (Todd et al., 2013)] may provide a disrupted cellular background that affects cytoskeleton/scaffolding (actin, Shank3) and Zn homeostasis allowing environmental factors (e.g., quality of the breast milk) to further affect synaptogenesis and mitochondrial function early in life (**Figure 11C**).

In support of this concept, FMRP protein expression—and not *FMR1* mRNA levels—correlates positively with mitochondrial outcomes (ATP-driven oxygen uptake and coupling) in both the KI mouse model and primary dermal fibroblasts from premutation and full mutation carriers. Furthermore, the incidence of neurodevelopmental disorders like ASD, ADHD, anxiety, and other types of psychopathologies (Farzin et al., 2006; Tassone et al., 2012; Winarni et al., 2012; Wong et al., 2012; Battistella et al., 2013; Chonchaiya et al., 2013) observed in young carriers seem to follow the FMRP protein expression [e.g., incidence of ASD in FXS is 60% (Garcia-Nonell et al., 2008; Harris et al., 2008; D'Hulst et al., 2009; Zingerevich et al., 2009; Hagerman et al., 2010) and in premutation carriers is ~15% (Farzin et al., 2006; Chonchaiya et al., 2013)]. In this regard, and consistent with our findings, the expression levels of a subset of

TABLE 6 | Characteristics of mature breast milk from premutation individuals.

Premutation carrier	[Zn] (μM) [mg/l]	ALP activity [nmol × (min × mg)$^{-1}$]	[Protein] (mg/ml)	[Lactose] (mM)
1	13 ± 1 [0.84 ± 0.08]	7.9 ± 0.6	12.2 ± 0.4	213 ± 3
2	**8 ± 2 [0.50 ± 0.05]**	2.9 ± 0.3	**6.0 ± 0.1**	**160 ± 4**
3	25 ± 2 [1.67 ± 0.13]	7.3 ± 1.0	**11.4 ± 0.4**	231 ± 1
4	**9 ± 1 [0.57 ± 0.09]**	**2.1 ± 0.3**	17.7 ± 0.7	**196 ± 2**
5	**17.2 ± 4 [1.13 ± 0.91]**	**1.5 ± 0.1**	19.9 ± 2.0	208 ± 1
(Mean ± SEM)	14 ± 3 [0.94 ± 0.21]	4 ± 2	13 ± 3	202 ± 13
<95% CI	3 of 5	1 of 5	2 of 5	2 of 5
p-value	0.001	n.s.	0.054	0.054
Controls (mean ± SEM)	26 ± 2 [1.68 ± 0.12]	4 ± 1	12.8 ± 0.5	205 ± 3
95% CI			12–13	199–210

For samples from premutation carriers, each outcome was expressed as mean ± SD, reflecting technical variability of triplicates. In bold, values below the 95% CI calculated with control values. For Zn concentrations and ALP activities, outcomes that change with the lactation week, the 95% CIs are shown in ***Figures 9A,B****. No significant correlation was obtained between lactation week and lactose or protein concentrations, thus the 95%CIs were calculated using all control data regardless of lactation week. The p-values correspond to the test for one proportion. n.s., not significant. A post-hoc analysis to calculate the power of the analysis for the means of milk-Zn concentration from each group was 1.00, whereas for all others was 0.504 or lower (G*power software; v. 3.0.10).*

miRNAs involved in learning, memory and autistic behavior have been shown to be deregulated in FXTAS (Zongaro et al., 2013; Nguyen et al., 2016).

While additional studies will be necessary to estimate Zn requirements for breast-fed only premutation carriers' babies and assess potential benefits of Zn-fortified milk (while controlling for confounding factors and monitoring for potential adverse effects), our findings emphasize that early nutritional interventions to prevent MD seem critical for the management of premutation carriers at high risk of developing emotional and neurological/cognitive problems (including autism) and/or FXTAS later in life (Tassone et al., 2012; Winarni et al., 2012; Wong et al., 2012; Battistella et al., 2013; Kim et al., 2013). This is largely relevant considering the independence of milk-Zn concentrations on maternal diet (Moore et al., 1984; Krebs et al., 1995), and consistent with the fact that infants born to the lowest milk Zn-producing mothers (among other feeding factors) are more stunted than infants of women with higher milk Zn concentrations (Krebs et al., 1995; Umeta et al., 2000; Krebs and Hambidge, 2007).

AUTHOR CONTRIBUTIONS

EN measured mitochondrial outcomes in mice at PND21 and 210, Zn, FMRP, and Shank3 levels, Zn in milk, run all western blots from rodents and human cells, analyzed the data, helped drafting, and reviewed the manuscript; CI measured mitochondrial outcomes isolated neurons and in mice at PND0-9 and PND21; GS measured ALP activity, proteins, and lactose levels in human milk and reviewed the manuscript; SW evaluated the *FMR1* expression in fibroblasts and *ZnTs* gene expression, and reviewed the manuscript; LG recruited the patients, collected the medical history, and the premutation milk samples; JS provided all milk samples from controls; FT determined the CGG repeats in fibroblasts and milk samples from gDNA extracted by Wong; CG conceptualized the work, wrote, and reviewed the manuscript.

FUNDING

Support for this study was provided by the National Institutes of Health (ES020392, HD040661, and HD036071) and Simons Foundation (#271406). The funders had no role in study design, data collection and analysis, decision to publish, or preparation of the manuscript. The authors of this publication declare that they have no financial relationships relevant to this article to disclose.

ACKNOWLEDGMENTS

We wish to thank all milk donors that made this study possible and Ms. Lucia Goin for editing the manuscript.

REFERENCES

Bañez-Coronel, M., Porta, S., Kagerbauer, B., Mateu-Huertas, E., Pantano, L., Ferrer, I., et al. (2012). A pathogenic mechanism in Huntington's disease involves small CAG-repeated RNAs with neurotoxic activity. *PLoS Genet.* 8:e1002481. doi: 10.1371/journal.pgen.1002481

Bardoni, B., and Mandel, J. L. (2002). Advances in understanding of fragile X pathogenesis and FMRP function, and in identification of X linked mental retardation genes. *Curr. Opin. Genet. Dev.* 12, 284–293. doi: 10.1016/S0959-437X(02)00300-3

Battistella, G., Niederhauser, J., Fornari, E., Hippolyte, L., Gronchi Perrin, A., Lesca, G., et al. (2013). Brain structure in asymptomatic FMR1 premutation carriers at risk for fragile X-associated tremor/ataxia syndrome. *Neurobiol. Aging* 34, 1700–1707. doi: 10.1016/j.neurobiolaging.2012.12.001

Beach, R. S., Gershwin, M. E., and Hurley, L. S. (1982). Gestational zinc deprivation in mice: persistence of immunodeficiency for three generations. *Science* 218, 469–471. doi: 10.1126/science.7123244

Belanger, M., and Magistretti, P. J. (2009). The role of astroglia in neuroprotection. *Dialogues Clin. Neurosci.* 11, 281–295.

Boldogh, I. R., and Pon, L. A. (2006). Interactions of mitochondria with the actin cytoskeleton. *Biochim. Biophys. Acta* 1763, 450–462. doi: 10.1016/j.bbamcr.2006.02.014

Brand, M. D. (1990). The contribution of the leak of protons across the mitochondrial inner membrane to standard metabolic rate. *J. Theor. Biol.* 145, 267–286. doi: 10.1016/S0022-5193(05)80131-6

Brody, T. (1999). *Nutritional Biochemistry*. San Diego, CA: Academic Press.

Brown, V., Jin, P., Ceman, S., Darnell, J. C., O'Donnell, W. T., Tenenbaum, S. A., et al. (2001). Microarray identification of FMRP-associated brain mRNAs and altered mRNA translational profiles in fragile X syndrome. *Cell* 107, 477–487. doi: 10.1016/S0092-8674(01)00568-2

Butterworth, R. F., and Heroux, M. (1989). Effect of pyrithiamine treatment and subsequent thiamine rehabilitation on regional cerebral amino acids and thiamine-dependent enzymes. *J. Neurochem.* 52, 1079–1084. doi: 10.1111/j.1471-4159.1989.tb01850.x

Castets, M., Schaeffer, C., Bechara, E., Schenck, A., Khandjian, E. W., Luche, S., et al. (2005). FMRP interferes with the Rac1 pathway and controls actin cytoskeleton dynamics in murine fibroblasts. *Hum. Mol. Genet.* 14, 835–844. doi: 10.1093/hmg/ddi077

Chanda, R., Owen, E. C., and Cramond, B. (1951). The composition of human milk with special reference to the relation between phosphorus partition and phosphatase and to the partition of certain vitamins. *Br. J. Nutr.* 5, 228–242. doi: 10.1079/BJN19510029

Chonchaiya, W., Tardif, T., Mai, X., Xu, L., Li, M., Kaciroti, N., et al. (2013). Developmental trends in auditory processing can provide early predictions of language acquisition in young infants. *Dev. Sci.* 16, 159–172. doi: 10.1111/desc.12012

Coburn, S. P., Mahuren, J. D., Pauly, T. A., Ericson, K. L., and Townsend, D. W. (1992). Alkaline phosphatase activity and pyridoxal phosphate concentrations in the milk of various species. *J. Nutr.* 122, 2348–2353.

Darnell, J. C., and Richter, J. D. (2012). Cytoplasmic RNA-binding proteins and the control of complex brain function. *Cold Spring Harb. Perspect. Biol.* 4:a012344. doi: 10.1101/cshperspect.a012344

Darnell, J. C., Van Driesche, S. J., Zhang, C., Hung, K. Y., Mele, A., Fraser, C. E., et al. (2011). FMRP stalls ribosomal translocation on mRNAs linked to synaptic function and autism. *Cell* 146, 247–261. doi: 10.1016/j.cell.2011.06.013

D'Hulst, C., Heulens, I., Brouwer, J. R., Willemsen, R., De Geest, N., Reeve, S. P., et al. (2009). Expression of the GABAergic system in animal models for fragile X syndrome and fragile X associated tremor/ataxia syndrome (FXTAS). *Brain Res.* 1253, 176–183. doi: 10.1016/j.brainres.2008.11.075

Dugina, V., Zwaenepoel, I., Gabbiani, G., Clement, S., and Chaponnier, C. (2009). Beta and gamma-cytoplasmic actins display distinct distribution and functional diversity. *J. Cell Sci.* 122, 2980–2988. doi: 10.1242/jcs.041970

Elfering, S. L., Haynes, V. L., Traaseth, N. J., Ettl, A., and Giulivi, C. (2004). Aspects, mechanism, and biological relevance of mitochondrial protein nitration sustained by mitochondrial nitric oxide synthase. *Am. J. Physiol. Heart Circ. Physiol.* 286, H22–H29. doi: 10.1152/ajpheart.00766.2003

Farzin, F., Perry, H., Hessl, D., Loesch, D., Cohen, J., Bacalman, S., et al. (2006). Autism spectrum disorders and attention-deficit/hyperactivity disorder in boys with the fragile X premutation. *J. Dev. Behav. Pediatr.* 27, S137–S144. doi: 10.1097/00004703-200604002-00012

Fransson, G. B., and Lonnerdal, B. (1984). Iron, copper, zinc, calcium, and magnesium in human milk fat. *Am. J. Clin. Nutr.* 39, 185–189.

Fujisawa, Y., Napoli, E., Wong, S., Song, G., Yamaguchi, R., Matsui, T., et al. (2015). Impact of a novel homozygous mutation in nicotinamide nucleotide transhydrogenase on mitochondrial DNA integrity in a case of familial glucocorticoid deficiency. *Proc. Natl. Acad. Sci. U.S.A.* 3, 70–78. doi: 10.1016/j.bbacli.2014.12.003

Garcia-Nonell, C., Ratera, E. R., Harris, S., Hessl, D., Ono, M. Y., Tartaglia, N., et al. (2008). Secondary medical diagnosis in fragile X syndrome with and without autism spectrum disorder. *Am. J. Med. Genet. A* 146A, 1911–1916. doi: 10.1002/ajmg.a.32290

Grabrucker, S., Jannetti, L., Eckert, M., Gaub, S., Chhabra, R., Pfaender, S., et al. (2014). Zinc deficiency dysregulates the synaptic ProSAP/Shank scaffold and might contribute to autism spectrum disorders. *Brain* 137, 137–152. doi: 10.1093/brain/awt303

Greco, C. M., Berman, R. F., Martin, R. M., Tassone, F., Schwartz, P. H., Chang, A., et al. (2006). Neuropathology of fragile X-associated tremor/ataxia syndrome (FXTAS). *Brain* 129, 243–255. doi: 10.1093/brain/awh683

Hagerman, R., and Hagerman, P. (2013). Advances in clinical and molecular understanding of the FMR1 premutation and fragile X-associated tremor/ataxia syndrome. *Lancet Neurol.* 12, 786–798. doi: 10.1016/S1474-4422(13)70125-X

Hagerman, R., Hoem, G., and Hagerman, P. (2010). Fragile X and autism: intertwined at the molecular level leading to targeted treatments. *Mol. Autism* 1:12. doi: 10.1186/2040-2392-1-12

Han, K., Holder, J. L. Jr., Schaaf, C. P., Lu, H., Chen, H., Kang, H., et al. (2013). SHANK3 overexpression causes manic-like behaviour with unique pharmacogenetic properties. *Nature* 503, 72–77. doi: 10.1038/nature12630

Hara, Y., Yuk, F., Puri, R., Janssen, W. G., Rapp, P. R., and Morrison, J. H. (2014). Presynaptic mitochondrial morphology in monkey prefrontal cortex correlates with working memory and is improved with estrogen treatment. *Proc. Natl. Acad. Sci. U.S.A.* 111, 486–491. doi: 10.1073/pnas.1311310110

Harris, S. W., Hessl, D., Goodlin-Jones, B., Ferranti, J., Bacalman, S., Barbato, I., et al. (2008). Autism profiles of males with fragile X syndrome. *Am. J. Ment. Retard.* 113, 427–438. doi: 10.1352/2008.113:427-438

Hatch, A. L., Gurel, P. S., and Higgs, H. N. (2014). Novel roles for actin in mitochondrial fission. *J. Cell Sci.* 127, 4549–4560. doi: 10.1242/jcs.153791

Haynes, V., Traaseth, N. J., Elfering, S., Fujisawa, Y., and Giulivi, C. (2010). Nitration of specific tyrosines in FoF1 ATP synthase and activity loss in aging. *Am. J. Physiol. Endocrinol. Metab.* 298, E978–E987. doi: 10.1152/ajpendo.00739.2009

Higuchi, R., Vevea, J. D., Swayne, T. C., Chojnowski, R., Hill, V., Boldogh, I. R., et al. (2013). Actin dynamics affect mitochondrial quality control and aging in budding yeast. *Curr. Biol.* 23, 2417–2422. doi: 10.1016/j.cub.2013.10.022

Ho, E., Courtemanche, C., and Ames, B. N. (2003). Zinc deficiency induces oxidative DNA damage and increases p53 expression in human lung fibroblasts. *J. Nutr.* 133, 2543–2548.

Huang, L., and Gitschier, J. (1997). A novel gene involved in zinc transport is deficient in the lethal milk mouse. *Nat. Genet.* 17, 292–297. doi: 10.1038/ng1197-292

Hunsaker, M. R., Arque, G., Berman, R. F., Willemsen, R., and Hukema, R. K. (2012). Mouse models of the fragile x premutation and the fragile X associated tremor/ataxia syndrome. *Results Probl. Cell Differ.* 54, 255–269. doi: 10.1007/978-3-642-21649-7_14

Hunsaker, M. R., von Leden, R. E., Ta, B. T., Goodrich-Hunsaker, N. J., Arque, G., Kim, K., et al. (2011). Motor deficits on a ladder rung task in male and female adolescent and adult CGG knock-in mice. *Behav. Brain Res.* 222, 117–121. doi: 10.1016/j.bbr.2011.03.039

Hunsaker, M. R., Wenzel, H. J., Willemsen, R., and Berman, R. F. (2009). Progressive spatial processing deficits in a mouse model of the fragile X premutation. *Behav. Neurosci.* 123, 1315–1324. doi: 10.1037/a0017616

Isaya, G., Kalousek, F., Fenton, W. A., and Rosenberg, L. E. (1991). Cleavage of precursors by the mitochondrial processing peptidase requires a compatible mature protein or an intermediate octapeptide. *J. Cell Biol.* 113, 65–76. doi: 10.1083/jcb.113.1.65

Iwata-Ichikawa, E., Kondo, Y., Miyazaki, I., Asanuma, M., and Ogawa, N. (1999). Glial cells protect neurons against oxidative stress via transcriptional up-regulation of the glutathione synthesis. *J. Neurochem.* 72, 2334–2344. doi: 10.1046/j.1471-4159.1999.0722334.x

Jagoda, C. A., and Rillema, J. A. (1991). Temporal effect of prolactin on the activities of lactose synthetase, alpha-lactalbumin, and galactosyl transferase in mouse mammary gland explants. *Proc. Soc. Exp. Biol. Med.* 197, 431–434. doi: 10.3181/00379727-197-43278

Jekabsons, M. B., and Nicholls, D. G. (2004). *In situ* respiration and bioenergetic status of mitochondria in primary cerebellar granule neuronal cultures exposed continuously to glutamate. *J. Biol. Chem.* 279, 32989–33000. doi: 10.1074/jbc.M401540200

Kaplan, E. S., Cao, Z., Hulsizer, S., Tassone, F., Berman, R. F., Hagerman, P. J., et al. (2012). Early mitochondrial abnormalities in hippocampal neurons cultured from Fmr1 pre-mutation mouse model. *J. Neurochem.* 123, 613–621. doi: 10.1111/j.1471-4159.2012.07936.x

Kelleher, S. L., Velasquez, V., Croxford, T. P., McCormick, N. H., Lopez, V., and MacDavid, J. (2012). Mapping the zinc-transporting system in mammary cells: molecular analysis reveals a phenotype-dependent zinc-transporting network during lactation. *J. Cell. Physiol.* 227, 1761–1770. doi: 10.1002/jcp.22900

Kenneson, A., Zhang, F., Hagedorn, C. H., and Warren, S. T. (2001). Reduced FMRP and increased FMR1 transcription is proportionally associated with CGG repeat number in intermediate-length and premutation carriers. *Hum. Mol. Genet.* 10, 1449–1454. doi: 10.1093/hmg/10.14.1449

Kim, S. Y., Hashimoto, R., Tassone, F., Simon, T. J., and Rivera, S. M. (2013). Altered neural activity of magnitude estimation processing in adults with the fragile X premutation. *J. Psychiatr. Res.* 47, 1909–1916. doi: 10.1016/j.jpsychires.2013.08.014

Knapka, J. J., Smith, K. P., and Judge, F. J. (1974). Effect of open and closed formula rations on the performance of three strains of laboratory mice. *Lab. Anim. Sci.* 24, 480–487.

Kogan, C. S., Turk, J., Hagerman, R. J., and Cornish, K. M. (2008). Impact of the Fragile X mental retardation 1 (FMR1) gene premutation on neuropsychiatric functioning in adult males without fragile X-associated Tremor/Ataxia syndrome: a controlled study. *Am. J. Med. Genet. B Neuropsychiatr. Genet.* 147B, 859–872. doi: 10.1002/ajmg.b.30685

Korobova, F., Ramabhadran, V., and Higgs, H. N. (2013). An actin-dependent step in mitochondrial fission mediated by the ER-associated formin INF2. *Science* 339, 464–467. doi: 10.1126/science.1228360

Kouser, M., Speed, H. E., Dewey, C. M., Reimers, J. M., Widman, A. J., Gupta, N., et al. (2013). Loss of predominant Shank3 isoforms results in hippocampus-dependent impairments in behavior and synaptic transmission. *J. Neurosci.* 33, 18448–18468. doi: 10.1523/JNEUROSCI.3017-13.2013

Krebs, N. F., and Hambidge, K. M. (2007). Complementary feeding: clinically relevant factors affecting timing and composition. *Am. J. Clin. Nutr.* 85, 639S–645S.

Krebs, N. F., Reidinger, C. J., Hartley, S., Robertson, A. D., and Hambidge, K. M. (1995). Zinc supplementation during lactation: effects on maternal status and milk zinc concentrations. *Am. J. Clin. Nutr.* 61, 1030–1036.

Kusano, H., Shimizu, S., Koya, R. C., Fujita, H., Kamada, S., Kuzumaki, N., et al. (2000). Human gelsolin prevents apoptosis by inhibiting apoptotic mitochondrial changes via closing VDAC. *Oncogene* 19, 4807–4814. doi: 10.1038/sj.onc.1203868

Li, J., Li, Q., Xie, C., Zhou, H., Wang, Y., Zhang, N., et al. (2004). Beta-actin is required for mitochondria clustering and ROS generation in TNF-induced, caspase-independent cell death. *J. Cell Sci.* 117, 4673–4680. doi: 10.1242/jcs.01339

Li, S., Xu, S., Roelofs, B. A., Boyman, L., Lederer, W. J., Sesaki, H., et al. (2015). Transient assembly of F-actin on the outer mitochondrial membrane contributes to mitochondrial fission. *J. Cell Biol.* 208, 109–123. doi: 10.1083/jcb.201404050

Ludwig, A. L., Espinal, G. M., Pretto, D. I., Jamal, A. L., Arque, G., Tassone, F., et al. (2014). CNS expression of murine fragile X protein (FMRP) as a function of CGG-repeat size. *Hum. Mol. Genet.* 23, 3228–3238. doi: 10.1093/hmg/ddu032

Luecke, R. W., and Fraker, P. J. (1979). The effect of varying dietary zinc levels on growth and antibody-mediated response in two strains of mice. *J. Nutr.* 109, 1373–1376.

McCormick, N. H., and Kelleher, S. L. (2012). ZnT4 provides zinc to zinc-dependent proteins in the trans-Golgi network critical for cell function and Zn export in mammary epithelial cells. *Am. J. Physiol. Cell Physiol.* 303, C291–C297. doi: 10.1152/ajpcell.00443.2011

Menalled, L., El-Khodor, B. F., Patry, M., Suarez-Farinas, M., Orenstein, S. J., Zahasky, B., et al. (2009). Systematic behavioral evaluation of Huntington's disease transgenic and knock-in mouse models. *Neurobiol. Dis.* 35, 319–336. doi: 10.1016/j.nbd.2009.05.007

Mohammad, M. A., Hadsell, D. L., and Haymond, M. W. (2012). Gene regulation of UDP-galactose synthesis and transport: potential rate-limiting processes in initiation of milk production in humans. *Am. J. Physiol. Endocrinol. Metab.* 303, E365–E376. doi: 10.1152/ajpendo.00175.2012

Moore, M. E., Moran, J. R., and Greene, H. L. (1984). Zinc supplementation in lactating women: evidence for mammary control of zinc secretion. *J. Pediatr.* 105, 600–602. doi: 10.1016/S0022-3476(84)80430-8

Nagra, S. A. (1989). Longitudinal study in biochemical composition of human milk during first year of lactation. *J. Trop. Pediatr.* 35, 126–128. doi: 10.1093/tropej/35.3.126

Napoli, E., Hung, C., Wong, S., and Giulivi, C. (2013). Toxicity of the flame-retardant BDE-49 on brain mitochondria and neuronal progenitor striatal cells enhanced by a PTEN-deficient background. *Toxicol. Sci.* 132, 196–210. doi: 10.1093/toxsci/kfs339

Napoli, E., Ross-Inta, C., Wong, S., Hung, C., Fujisawa, Y., Sakaguchi, D., et al. (2012). Mitochondrial dysfunction in Pten haplo-insufficient mice with social deficits and repetitive behavior: interplay between Pten and p53. *PLoS ONE* 7:e42504. doi: 10.1371/journal.pone.0042504

Napoli, E., Ross-Inta, C., Wong, S., Omanska-Klusek, A., Barrow, C., Iwahashi, C., et al. (2011). Altered zinc transport disrupts mitochondrial protein processing/import in fragile X-associated tremor/ataxia syndrome. *Hum. Mol. Genet.* 20, 3079–3092. doi: 10.1093/hmg/ddr211

Navarro, D., Zwingmann, C., and Butterworth, R. F. (2008). Region-selective alterations of glucose oxidation and amino acid synthesis in the thiamine-deficient rat brain: a re-evaluation using 1H/13C nuclear magnetic resonance spectroscopy. *J. Neurochem.* 106, 603–612. doi: 10.1111/j.1471-4159.2008.05410.x

Nguyen, L. S., Lepleux, M., Makhlouf, M., Martin, C., Fregeac, J., Siquier-Pernet, K., et al. (2016). Profiling olfactory stem cells from living patients identifies miRNAs relevant for autism pathophysiology. *Mol. Autism* 7, 1. doi: 10.1186/s13229-015-0064-6

Nicholls, D. G. (2008). Oxidative stress and energy crises in neuronal dysfunction. *Ann. N.Y. Acad. Sci.* 1147, 53–60. doi: 10.1196/annals.1427.002

Nolze, A., Schneider, J., Keil, R., Lederer, M., Huttelmaier, S., Kessels, M. M., et al. (2013). FMRP regulates actin filament organization via the armadillo protein p0071. *RNA* 19, 1483–1496. doi: 10.1261/rna.037945.112

Oh, S. Y., He, F., Krans, A., Frazer, M., Taylor, J. P., Paulson, H. L., et al. (2015). RAN translation at CGG repeats induces ubiquitin proteasome system impairment in models of fragile X-associated tremor ataxia syndrome. *Hum. Mol. Genet.* 24, 4317–4326. doi: 10.1093/hmg/ddv165

Picard, M., and McEwen, B. S. (2014). Mitochondria impact brain function and cognition. *Proc. Natl. Acad. Sci. U.S.A.* 111, 7–8. doi: 10.1073/pnas.1321881111

Pieretti, M., Zhang, F. P., Fu, Y. H., Warren, S. T., Oostra, B. A., Caskey, C. T., et al. (1991). Absence of expression of the FMR-1 gene in fragile X syndrome. *Cell* 66, 817–822. doi: 10.1016/0092-8674(91)90125-I

Rendon, A., and Masmoudi, A. (1985). Purification of non-synaptic and synaptic mitochondria and plasma membranes from rat brain by a rapid Percoll gradient procedure. *J. Neurosci. Methods* 14, 41–51. doi: 10.1016/0165-0270(85)90113-X

Ross-Inta, C., Omanska-Klusek, A., Wong, S., Barrow, C., Garcia-Arocena, D., Iwahashi, C., et al. (2010). Evidence of mitochondrial dysfunction in fragile X-associated tremor/ataxia syndrome. *Biochem. J.* 429, 545–552. doi: 10.1042/BJ20091960

Russo, A. J., and Devito, R. (2011). Analysis of copper and zinc plasma concentration and the efficacy of zinc therapy in individuals with asperger's syndrome, pervasive developmental disorder not otherwise specified (PDD-NOS) and autism. *Biomark. Insights* 6, 127–133. doi: 10.4137/BMI.S7286

Sawashita, J., Takeda, A., and Okada, S. (1997). Change of zinc distribution in rat brain with increasing age. *Brain Res. Dev. Brain Res.* 102, 295–298. doi: 10.1016/S0165-3806(97)00107-7

Selkoe, D. J. (2002). Alzheimer's disease is a synaptic failure. *Science* 298, 789–791. doi: 10.1126/science.1074069

Sellier, C., Freyermuth, F., Tabet, R., Tran, T., He, F., Ruffenach, F., et al. (2013). Sequestration of DROSHA and DGCR8 by expanded CGG RNA repeats alters microRNA processing in fragile X-associated tremor/ataxia syndrome. *Cell Rep.* 3, 869–880. doi: 10.1016/j.celrep.2013.02.004

Sellier, C., Rau, F., Liu, Y., Tassone, F., Hukema, R. K., Gattoni, R., et al. (2010). Sam68 sequestration and partial loss of function are associated with splicing alterations in FXTAS patients. *EMBO J.* 29, 1248–1261. doi: 10.1038/emboj.2010.21

Stewart, R. A., Platou, E., and Kelly, V. J. (1958). The alkaline phosphatase content of human milk. *J. Biol. Chem.* 232, 777–784.

Sutcliffe, J. S., Nelson, D. L., Zhang, F., Pieretti, M., Caskey, C. T., Saxe, D., et al. (1992). DNA methylation represses FMR-1 transcription in fragile X syndrome. *Hum. Mol. Genet.* 1, 397–400. doi: 10.1093/hmg/1.6.397

Tassone, F., Beilina, A., Carosi, C., Albertosi, S., Bagni, C., Li, L., et al. (2007). Elevated FMR1 mRNA in premutation carriers is due to increased transcription. *RNA* 13, 555–562. doi: 10.1261/rna.280807

Tassone, F., Greco, C. M., Hunsaker, M. R., Seritan, A. L., Berman, R. F., Gane, L. W., et al. (2012). Neuropathological, clinical and molecular pathology in female fragile X premutation carriers with and without FXTAS. *Genes Brain Behav.* 11, 577–585. doi: 10.1111/j.1601-183X.2012.00779.x

Tassone, F., and Hagerman, P. J. (2003). Expression of the FMR1 gene. *Cytogenet. Genome Res.* 100, 124–128. doi: 10.1159/000072846

Tassone, F., Hagerman, R. J., Loesch, D. Z., Lachiewicz, A., Taylor, A. K., and Hagerman, P. J. (2000a). Fragile X males with unmethylated, full mutation trinucleotide repeat expansions have elevated levels of *FMR1* messenger RNA. *Am. J. Med. Genet.* 94, 232–236. doi: 10.1002/1096-8628(20000918)94:3<232::AID-AJMG9>3.0.CO;2-H

Tassone, F., Hagerman, R. J., Taylor, A. K., Gane, L. W., Godfrey, T. E., and Hagerman, P. J. (2000b). Elevated levels of *FMR1* mRNA in carrier males: a new mechanism of involvement in the fragile-X syndrome. *Am. J. Hum. Genet.* 66, 6–15. doi: 10.1086/302720

Tassone, F., Hagerman, R. J., Taylor, A. K., Mills, J. B., Harris, S. W., Gane, L. W., et al. (2000c). Clinical involvement and protein expression in individuals with the *FMR1* premutation. *Am. J. Med. Genet.* 91, 144–152. doi: 10.1002/(SICI)1096-8628(20000313)91:2<144::AID-AJMG14>3.0.CO;2-V

Tassone, F., Iwahashi, C., and Hagerman, P. J. (2004). FMR1 RNA within the intranuclear inclusions of fragile X-associated tremor/ataxia syndrome (FXTAS). *RNA Biol.* 1, 103–105. doi: 10.4161/rna.1.2.1035

Todd, P. K., Oh, S. Y., Krans, A., He, F., Sellier, C., Frazer, M., et al. (2013). CGG repeat-associated translation mediates neurodegeneration in fragile X tremor ataxia syndrome. *Neuron* 78, 440–455. doi: 10.1016/j.neuron.2013.03.026

Tokatlidis, K., Vial, S., Luciano, P., Vergnolle, M., and Clémence, S. (2000). Membrane protein import in yeast mitochondria. *Biochem. Soc. Trans.* 28, 495–499. doi: 10.1042/bst0280495

Tudehope, D. I. (2013). Human milk and the nutritional needs of preterm infants. *J. Pediatr.* 162, S17–S25. doi: 10.1016/j.jpeds.2012.11.049

Umeta, M., West, C. E., Haidar, J., Deurenberg, P., and Hautvast, J. G. (2000). Zinc supplementation and stunted infants in Ethiopia: a randomised controlled trial. *Lancet* 355, 2021–2026. doi: 10.1016/S0140-6736(00)02348-5

Van Dam, D., Errijgers, V., Kooy, R. F., Willemsen, R., Mientjes, E., Oostra, B. A., et al. (2005). Cognitive decline, neuromotor and behavioural disturbances in a mouse model for fragile-X-associated tremor/ataxia syndrome (FXTAS). *Behav. Brain Res.* 162, 233–239. doi: 10.1016/j.bbr.2005.03.007

Wang, X., Xu, Q., Bey, A. L., Lee, Y., and Jiang, Y. H. (2014). Transcriptional and functional complexity of Shank3 provides a molecular framework to understand the phenotypic heterogeneity of SHANK3 causing autism and Shank3 mutant mice. *Mol. Autism* 5, 30. doi: 10.1186/2040-2392-5-30

Weiler, I. J., Irwin, S. A., Klintsova, A. Y., Spencer, C. M., Brazelton, A. D., Miyashiro, K., et al. (1997). Fragile X mental retardation protein is translated near synapses in response to neurotransmitter activation. *Proc. Natl. Acad. Sci. U.S.A.* 94, 5395–5400. doi: 10.1073/pnas.94.10.5395

Wenzel, H. J., Hunsaker, M. R., Greco, C. M., Willemsen, R., and Berman, R. F. (2010). Ubiquitin-positive intranuclear inclusions in neuronal and glial cells in a mouse model of the fragile X premutation. *Brain Res.* 1318, 155–166. doi: 10.1016/j.brainres.2009.12.077

Winarni, T. I., Chonchaiya, W., Sumekar, T. A., Ashwood, P., Morales, G. M., Tassone, F., et al. (2012). Immune-mediated disorders among women carriers of fragile X premutation alleles. *Am. J. Med. Genet. A* 158A, 2473–2481. doi: 10.1002/ajmg.a.35569

Wong, L. M., Goodrich-Hunsaker, N. J., McLennan, Y., Tassone, F., Harvey, D., Rivera, S. M., et al. (2012). Young adult male carriers of the fragile X premutation exhibit genetically modulated impairments in visuospatial tasks controlled for psychomotor speed. *J. Neurodev. Disord.* 4:26. doi: 10.1186/1866-1955-4-26

Worth, G. K., Retallack, R. W., Gutteridge, D. H., Jefferies, M., Kent, J., and Smith, M. (1981). Serum and milk alkaline phosphatase in human lactation. *Clin. Chim. Acta* 115, 171–177. doi: 10.1016/0009-8981(81)90073-5

Xu, X., Forbes, J. G., and Colombini, M. (2001). Actin modulates the gating of Neurospora crassa VDAC. *J. Membr. Biol.* 180, 73–81. doi: 10.1007/s002320010060

Yadava, N., and Nicholls, D. G. (2007). Spare respiratory capacity rather than oxidative stress regulates glutamate excitotoxicity after partial respiratory inhibition of mitochondrial complex I with rotenone. *J. Neurosci.* 27, 7310–7317. doi: 10.1523/JNEUROSCI.0212-07.2007

Yasuda, H., Yoshida, K., Yasuda, Y., and Tsutsui, T. (2011). Infantile zinc deficiency: association with autism spectrum disorders. *Sci. Rep.* 1:129. doi: 10.1038/srep00129

Zalewski, P., Truong-Tran, A., Lincoln, S., Ward, D., Shankar, A., Coyle, P., et al. (2006). Use of a zinc fluorophore to measure labile pools of zinc in body fluids and cell-conditioned media. *BioTechniques* 40, 509–520. doi: 10.2144/06404RR02

Zalfa, F., Giorgi, M., Primerano, B., Moro, A., Di Penta, A., Reis, S., et al. (2003). The fragile X syndrome protein FMRP associates with BC1 RNA and regulates the translation of specific mRNAs at synapses. *Cell* 112, 317–327. doi: 10.1016/S0092-8674(03)00079-5

Zingerevich, C., Greiss-Hess, L., Lemons-Chitwood, K., Harris, S. W., Hessl, D., Cook, K., et al. (2009). Motor abilities of children diagnosed with fragile X syndrome with and without autism. *J. Intellect. Disabil. Res.* 53, 11–18. doi: 10.1111/j.1365-2788.2008.01107.x

Zongaro, S., Hukema, R., D'Antoni, S., Davidovic, L., Barbry, P., Catania, M. V., et al. (2013). The 3′ UTR of FMR1 mRNA is a target of miR-101, miR-129-5p and miR-221: implications for the molecular pathology of FXTAS at the synapse. *Hum. Mol. Genet.* 22, 1971–1982. doi: 10.1093/hmg/ddt044

4

Neuropathological Mechanisms of Seizures in Autism Spectrum Disorder

Richard E. Frye[1,2], Manuel F. Casanova[3], S. Hossein Fatemi[4], Timothy D. Folsom[4], Teri J. Reutiman[4], Gregory L. Brown[5], Stephen M. Edelson[6], John C. Slattery[1,2] and James B. Adams[7]*

[1] Autism Research Program, Arkansas Children's Research Institute, Little Rock, AR, USA, [2] Department of Pediatrics, University of Arkansas for Medical Sciences, Little Rock, AR, USA, [3] Department of Biomedical Sciences, University of South Carolina School of Medicine Greenville, Greenville, SC, USA, [4] Department of Psychiatry, University of Minnesota Medical School, Minneapolis, MN, USA, [5] Serenity Health Care Center, Waukesha, WI, USA, [6] Autism Research Institute, San Diego, CA, USA, [7] School for Engineering of Matter, Transport, and Energy, Arizona State University, Tempe, AZ, USA

Edited by:
Joshua Pesach Rosenzweig, Cell-El, Israel

Reviewed by:
Bashkim Kadriu, Albert Einstein College of Medicine at Bronx-Lebanon Hospital Center, USA
Andrew Walter Zimmerman, UMass Medical School, USA

****Correspondence:***
Richard E. Frye
refrye@uams.edu

This manuscript reviews biological abnormalities shared by autism spectrum disorder (ASD) and epilepsy. Two neuropathological findings are shared by ASD and epilepsy: abnormalities in minicolumn architecture and γ-aminobutyric acid (GABA) neurotransmission. The peripheral neuropil, which is the region that contains the inhibition circuits of the minicolumns, has been found to be decreased in the post-mortem ASD brain. ASD and epilepsy are associated with inhibitory GABA neurotransmission abnormalities including reduced $GABA_A$ and $GABA_B$ subunit expression. These abnormalities can elevate the excitation-to-inhibition balance, resulting in hyperexcitablity of the cortex and, in turn, increase the risk of seizures. Medical abnormalities associated with both epilepsy and ASD are discussed. These include specific genetic syndromes, specific metabolic disorders including disorders of energy metabolism and GABA and glutamate neurotransmission, mineral and vitamin deficiencies, heavy metal exposures and immune dysfunction. Many of these medical abnormalities can result in an elevation of the excitatory-to-inhibitory balance. Fragile X is linked to dysfunction of the mGluR5 receptor and Fragile X, Angelman and Rett syndromes are linked to a reduction in $GABA_A$ receptor expression. Defects in energy metabolism can reduce GABA interneuron function. Both pyridoxine dependent seizures and succinic semialdehyde dehydrogenase deficiency cause GABA deficiencies while urea cycle defects and phenylketonuria cause abnormalities in glutamate neurotransmission. Mineral deficiencies can cause glutamate and GABA neurotransmission abnormalities and heavy metals can cause mitochondrial dysfunction which disrupts GABA metabolism. Thus, both ASD and epilepsy are associated with similar abnormalities that may alter the excitatory-to-inhibitory balance of the cortex. These parallels may explain the high prevalence of epilepsy in ASD and the elevated prevalence of ASD features in individuals with epilepsy.

Keywords: autism spectrum disorder, seizures, epilepsy, genetic syndrome, metabolic disorders, excitatory-to-inhibitory cortical balance, gamma-aminobutyric acid

INTRODUCTION

Autism spectrum disorders (ASD) is a behaviorally defined disorder that has recently been estimated to affect as many as 1 out of 45 individuals (Zablotsky et al., 2015). Although, ASD is defined by behavioral features, it is associated with co-occurring medical conditions. For example, epilepsy is more prevalent in ASD than in the typically developing children with a prevalence ranging from 5 to 38% (Deykin and Macmahon, 1979; Volkmar and Nelson, 1990; Tuchman and Rapin, 2002; Danielsson et al., 2005; Hara, 2007). Data from surveys performed by the Autism Research Institute on over 1200 participants suggests that the prevalence is between 15 and 19%. Epilepsy is one of the most disabling ASD co-morbidities as children with ASD and epilepsy are more likely to have intellectual disability (Tuchman, 2013) and increased mortality (Shavelle et al., 2001; Pickett et al., 2011) as compared to children with ASD without epilepsy. In addition, epilepsy in ASD tends to be more treatment-resistant as compared to epilepsy in typically developing children (Sansa et al., 2011).

One of the major questions in ASD research is its etiology. Much ASD research concentrates on genetic causes (Rossignol and Frye, 2012b) even though inherited single gene and chromosomal defects only account for a minority of ASD cases (Schaefer et al., 2013). However, genetic etiologies may be overrepresented in children with ASD and epilepsy as many genetic syndromes and gene mutations associated with ASD include epilepsy as a common feature (Murdoch and State, 2013; Tuchman et al., 2013).

Although some have suggested that clinical seizures do not have any special causative significance in ASD (Tuchman and Rapin, 1997), ASD coexists with epilepsy in several disorders (see Section Specific Medical Disorders Associated with Both ASD and Epilepsy) suggesting that the same neuropathology may result in both ASD and epilepsy. Thus, this manuscript reviews the shared biological abnormalities in ASD and epilepsy in two sections. The section called Basic Neuropathological Mechanisms of Seizures in ASD discusses two neuropathological mechanisms that have been described in ASD that can also cause epilepsy. Both mechanisms involve an abnormal reduction in inhibitory mechanisms of the brain, thereby resulting in an increase in the excitatory-to-inhibitory balance. The section called Specific Medical Disorders Associated with Both ASD and Epilepsy will review specific clinical disorders that have been described in both ASD and epilepsy with special reference to underlying neuropathological mechanisms that can cause seizures.

Overall, our review finds that many disorders associated with ASD increase the excitatory-to-inhibitory balance by either (1) reducing inhibitory circuits in the brain through a decrease in the inhibitory neurotransmitter γ-aminobutyric acid (GABA), or (2) increasing excitatory circuits in the brain through an increase in glutamate neurotransmission. Elevation in the excitatory-to-inhibitory balance in the brain can lead to seizures. By carefully outlining these disorders, insight into the etiologies that underlie ASD may be better understood.

Abbreviations: AMPA, α-amino-3-hydroxy-5-methyl-4-isoxazolepropionic acid; NMDA, N-methyl-D-aspartate; ASD, autism spectrum disorder; ATP, adenosine-5′-triphosphate; CNS, central nervous system; GABA, γ-aminobutyric acid.

BASIC NEUROPATHOLOGICAL MECHANISMS OF SEIZURES IN ASD

Several neuropathological processes associated with ASD are also associated with epilepsy. Here we review two such neuropathological processes: (1) minicolumn architecture and (2) GABA neurotransmission.

Minicolumn Architecture

The minicolumn is a radially-oriented assembly of neurons and cellular elements considered to be an elemental modular microcircuit of the neocortex (Buxhoeveden and Casanova, 2002; Casanova et al., 2006). The minicolumn core contains pyramidal cell arrays surrounded by a peripheral neuropil space that contains GABAergic inhibitory interneurons and other cells such as the double-bouquet cell (Mountcastle, 1997; Buxhoeveden and Casanova, 2002; Defelipe, 2005). Double-bouquet cells feature axonal bundles which provide a vertical stream of inhibition (Mountcastle, 1997). This inhibitory stream insulates the minicolumn core from the excitation from other surrounding minicolumns (Defelipe et al., 1990; Favorov and Kelly, 1994; Defelipe, 1999).

The peripheral neuropil space has been shown to be reduced in post-mortem brain tissue from ASD individuals (Buxhoeveden and Casanova, 2002), with this reduction most prominent over the prefrontal cortex (Casanova et al., 2006). The neuropil space is reduced within the region that contains the inhibition circuits of minicolumns (Defelipe et al., 1990; Favorov and Kelly, 1994; Defelipe, 1999). These architectural changes should, theoretically, disrupt the normal balance between excitation and inhibition influences within the columnar organization of the cortex (Casanova et al., 2003). A reduction of GABAergic inhibitory activity has been proposed to result in hyperexcitability of minicolumn circuits and can explain some of the symptomatology observed in ASD, including the high incidence of seizures and auditory-tactile hypersensitivity (Rubenstein and Merzenich, 2003). Networks of inhibitory interneurons acting as GABA gated pacemakers are also critically involved in gamma oscillations (Grothe and Klump, 2000). Abnormalities in gamma oscillations are associated with problems with binding and the coactivation of neural assemblies. A deficit in binding and gamma oscillations has been proposed to explain many of the symptoms related to ASD (e.g., visuoperceptual defects, understanding and using context; Grice et al., 2001; Brock et al., 2002; Brown et al., 2005; Rippon et al., 2007; Tommerdahl et al., 2007).

GABA Transmission

GABA is the major inhibitory neurotransmitter of the central nervous system (CNS). Abnormalities in GABA neurotransmission have been associated with epilepsy. GABBR1A, GABBR1B, and GABBR2 receptor subunits are reduced in the hippocampi of patients with temporal lobe epilepsy (Princivalle et al., 2003), and animal models have also shown a link between GABA receptor expression and epilepsy (Schuler et al., 2001; Han et al., 2006). Individuals with ASD have been shown to have abnormalities in GABAergic brain systems (Blatt et al., 2001; Dhossche et al., 2002; Fatemi, 2008), as well as a reduction in $GABA_A$(Fatemi et al., 2009) and $GABA_B$ (Fatemi et al., 2009) receptor subunits in both the frontal and parietal cortices, as compared to controls, with the ASD group also demonstrating a markedly higher rate of epilepsy than the controls. In addition, the GABA subunits found to be reduced in individuals with ASD (i.e., GABRα1 and GABBR1) have been associated with childhood absence epilepsy, juvenile myoclonic epilepsy, and atypical absence seizures (Delgado-Escueta, 2007; Kang et al., 2009).

SPECIFIC MEDICAL DISORDERS ASSOCIATED WITH BOTH ASD AND EPILEPSY

Genetic Disorders

The neurobiological mechanisms leading to seizures in genetic syndromes that are associated with ASD are diverse and complex. Imbalances in GABA and glutamate have been suggested to underlie CNS dysfunction in several of these genetic syndromes. Defects in $GABA_A$ function has been implicated in Fragile X (D'hulst and Kooy, 2007) and recent studies on Fragile X suggest that mGluR5 dysfunction results in heightened excitability and secondary alterations in GABA function (Frye, 2014). Dysfunction in $GABA_A$ receptor function has also been implicated in Angelman syndrome (Pelc et al., 2008). Indeed, a cluster of genes coding for three $GABA_A$ receptor subunits lie adjacent to the critical Angelman region (i.e., UBE3A). Mutations within the Rett syndrome gene (i.e., MECP2) decreases expression of GABRB3, a gene responsible for encoding the $beta_3$ subunit of the $GABA_A$ receptor, and DLX5, a gene which regulates the production of enzymes responsible for GABA production.

Some genetic syndromes associated with epilepsy and ASD are associated with metabolic abnormalities. For example, mouse models of both Angelman and Rett syndromes demonstrate mitochondrial dysfunction (Kriaucionis et al., 2006; Su et al., 2011) and mitochondrial dysfunction is reported in a Rett syndrome case (Condie et al., 2010). Phelan-McDermid Syndrome (PMS) and duplication of the 22q13 region are both associated with ASD and mitochondrial dysfunction (Frye, 2012b; Frye et al., 2016a). As mentioned below, disruption of mitochondrial metabolism can result in changes to the excitatory-to-inhibitory balance.

Single gene disorders associated with both ASD and epilepsy have been associated with abnormalities in the excitatory- to-inhibitory balance (Srivastava and Schwartz, 2014). Mutations in CNTNAP2 (Peñagarikano et al., 2011) or CNTNAP4 (Karayannis et al., 2014) result in reduced GABAergic neurotransmission. The SYNGAP1 haploinsufficiency animal model shows an increase in neuronal excitability and an increase in seizure susceptibility (Clement et al., 2012). Other genes are associated with a relative decrease in the excitatory-to-inhibitory balance. Animal model with NLGN3 mutations demonstrates increased inhibitory neurotransmission (Tabuchi et al., 2007). Cellular (Shcheglovitov et al., 2013) and animal models (Bangash et al., 2011; Wang et al., 2011b) demonstrate a reduction in excitatory neurotransmission when SHANK3 is disrupted. Animal models with decreased synapsin I (SYN1) demonstrate reduced glutamate release (Li et al., 1995).

Metabolic Disorders

Disorders of Energy Metabolism

Disorders of energy metabolism have been associated with ASD (Giulivi et al., 2010; Frye and Naviaux, 2011; Frye, 2012c; Rose et al., 2014a,b) and epilepsy (Frye, 2015). Some children with ASD have mitochondrial dysfunction that is different than classic mitochondrial disease (Frye and Rossignol, 2011; Rossignol and Frye, 2012a; Frye, 2012a). Of children with mitochondrial disease and ASD, 41% have seizures (Rossignol and Frye, 2012a).

Other disorders of energy metabolism are associated with ASD and epilepsy, including disorders of creatine metabolism (Póo-Argüelles et al., 2006; Longo et al., 2011) and adenylosuccinate lyase deficiency (Spiegel et al., 2006; Jurecka et al., 2008). Creatine and phosphocreatine play important roles in energy storage and transmission of high-energy phosphates. Adenylosuccinate lyase deficiency is a rare autosomal disorder of *de novo* purine synthesis (Spiegel et al., 2006; Jurecka et al., 2008). The purine nucleotide cycle regulates cellular metabolism by controlling levels of fumarate, a citric acid cycle intermediate, and adenosine, the precursor to adenosine-5′-triphosphate (ATP) (Spiegel et al., 2006).

An energy deficiency can result in seizures. Neurons with high firing rates, such as inhibitory GABA interneurons (Anderson et al., 2008), are disproportionally affected by an energy deficit. In addition, processes critically involved in the release and reuptake of neurotransmitters and maintenance of the neuronal resting potential, such as calcium homeostasis, are critically dependent on mitochondrial function (Li et al., 2004; Quiroz et al., 2008; Chen and Chan, 2009).

Disorders of GABA Neurotransmission

Several metabolic disorders directly lead to GABA metabolism abnormalities. Pyridoxine and its primary biologically active form, pyridoxal-5-phosphate, are essential cofactors for over 110 enzymes, including glutamic acid decarboxylase (GAD), the enzyme that produces GABA from glutamate. Pyridoxal-5-phosphate depletion reduces GAD activity which, in turn, increases glutamate, decreases GABA synthesis and decreases cortical inhibition (Gospe et al., 1994; Gospe, 2002; Mills et al., 2006). This occurs in pyridoxine dependent seizures.

Succinic semialdehyde dehydrogenase deficiency is an autosomal recessive disorder of GABA metabolism. It results from a defect in the aldehyde dehydrogenase gene (ALDH5A1; Jakobs et al., 1981). Aldehyde dehydrogenase is partially responsible for the degradation of GABA and when this enzyme is deficient GABA is degraded through an alternative pathway, resulting in the formation of gamma-hydroxybutyric acid and GABA elevations in the brain. Positron emission tomography studies suggest that chronic elevation in GABA down-regulates

$GABA_A$ receptors, leading to a deficit in cortical inhibition and an elevation in the excitatory-to-inhibitory balance (Pearl et al., 2009a,b).

Disorders of Glutamate Neurotransmission

Two types of metabolic disorders (urea cycle defects and phenylketonuria) may result in dysfunction of glutamate neurotransmission. Glutamate is the major excitatory cortical neurotransmitter and excess glutamate results in an elevation in the excitatory-to-inhibitory balance, leading to seizures.

Urea cycle defects result in ammonia elevations. Astrocytes exposed to ammonia do not express glutamate reuptake transporters that normally reduce extracellular glutamate (Rose, 2006). Thus, increased ammonia levels in the brain can result in elevated extracellular glutamate.

Neurological consequences of phenylketonuria are usually avoided by dietary treatment starting at birth (Williams et al., 2008). However, epilepsy and ASD may develop in untreated children and in those noncompliant to the prescribed diet (Baieli et al., 2003). Such children demonstrate high levels of phenylalanine in the brain. Phenylalanine antagonizes both N-methyl-D-aspartate (NMDA) and non-NMDA glutamate receptors (i.e., α-amino-3-hydroxy-5-methyl-4-isoxazolepropionic acid (AMPA) receptors; Glushakov et al., 2003). Chronic elevation in phenylalanine leads to an upregulation of several NMDA and AMPA receptor subunits (Glushakov et al., 2005), increased glutamate receptor density and increased glutamate release (Martynyuk et al., 2005). Such changes in glutamate neurotransmission predispose the brain to heightened excitability and seizures, especially if the phenylalanine level is transiently lowered (Martynyuk et al., 2005).

Mineral Deficiencies

Magnesium is essential in neurotransmitter metabolism and in modulating neurotransmitter receptor function. Ionized magnesium is important in seizure control. Ionized magnesium is a NMDA antagonist (Ault et al., 1980; Hallak, 1998) and may be a factor in some epilepsies (Hallak et al., 1992; Mathern et al., 1998; Mikuni et al., 1999). NMDA receptor activation by glutamate results in calcium influx (Macdermott et al., 1986; Delorenzo and Limbrick, 1996), which is pro-epileptogenic (Delorenzo, 1986; Heinemann and Hamon, 1986). Low ionized magnesium or altered balance between ionized magnesium and ionized calcium may precipitate seizures (Chaistitwanich et al., 1987). Patients with epilepsy have been shown to have significantly lower mean ionized magnesium levels and an increase in the ionized calcium to ionized magnesium ratio in spite of normal total serum magnesium levels (Sinert et al., 2007).

The role of zinc in epilepsy is not clear. Low zinc levels has been associated with seizures in children (Ganesh and Janakiraman, 2008; Mollah et al., 2008) and in the EL epileptic mouse (Fukahori and Itoh, 1990). Zinc acts as an anticonvulsant (Williamson and Spencer, 1995; Cole et al., 2000) and decreases seizure susceptibility (Fukahori and Itoh, 1990). However, zinc has been shown to be proconvulsant in a mouse model (Pei et al., 1983). Zinc co-localizes with glutamate where it inhibits the reuptake of synaptic GABA, thereby increasing the cortical inhibitory tone (Cohen-Kfir et al., 2005). Thus, a zinc deficiency could increase the relative excitatory-to-inhibitory balance.

Vitamin Deficiencies

Children with ASD have been shown to have abnormalities in cobalamin dependent pathways (Frye and James, 2014), and cobalamin supplementation improves metabolites in these pathways (James et al., 2009a; Adams et al., 2011; Frye et al., 2013a; Hendren et al., 2016) and behavior (Adams et al., 2011; Frye et al., 2013a,b; Hendren et al., 2016). The exact mechanism in which cobalamin deficiency causes seizures is unclear but infants with cobalamin deficiency manifest seizures (Benbir et al., 2007; Erol et al., 2007). Cobalamin is essential for myelin synthesis and methylation (Kumar, 2004). Neurons with damaged myelin sheaths are more susceptible to the excitatory effects of glutamate (Akaike et al., 1993).

Cerebral folate deficiency (CFD) is characterized by low 5-methyltetrahydrofolate in the CNS and is associated with ASD and seizures (Ramaekers et al., 2002; Ramaekers and Blau, 2004). Children with idiopathic ASD have a high prevalence of folate receptor alpha autoantibodies that causes CFD (Frye et al., 2013c, 2016b). Folate is essential in a wide range of metabolic processes, including redox and homocysteine metabolism and gene methylation (Obeid et al., 2007). Disruption in these processes could disrupted redox metabolism, thereby depleting glutathione which, in turn, can decreased glutamate degradation, leading to increased cortical excitability (Deepmala et al., 2015).

Heavy Metals

Several epidemiologic studies support a relationship between ASD and exposure to mercury or other heavy metals (Rossignol et al., 2014). Epilepsy has been associated with exposure to toxic levels of heavy metals including lead (Silbergeld et al., 1979; Swartzwelder, 1985; Lockitch et al., 1991; Arrieta et al., 2005) and mercury (Torres et al., 2000). Heavy metals may have toxic effects on the brain by reducing mitochondrial function (James et al., 2009b; Belyaeva et al., 2011; Wang et al., 2011a; Rose et al., 2015), causing apoptosis (Wang et al., 2011a; Pal et al., 2012), and increasing levels of reactive oxygen species (James et al., 2009b; Furieri et al., 2011; Wang et al., 2011a). Although the mechanism(s) by which heavy metals cause epilepsy are not clear, both mitochondrial dysfunction (Rossignol and Frye, 2012a) and high levels of reactive oxygen species (Riazi et al., 2010; Specchio et al., 2010; Waldbaum and Patel, 2010), have been linked to epilepsy.

Immune Dysregulation

Multiple studies have demonstrated evidence of abnormal immune system activation in individuals with ASD. Unusually high levels of proinflammatory cytokines have been found in the cerebrospinal fluid of individuals with ASD (Vargas et al., 2005). Abnormal activation of the intrinsic immune system in the cerebral cortex, white matter, and cerebellum has been demonstrated in individuals with ASD at autopsy (Vargas et al., 2005).

Children with ASD manifest autoantibodies implicated in childhood epilepsy syndromes associated with language regression (Connolly et al., 2006) and cognitive and behavioral changes (Ganor et al., 2004; Vincent et al., 2004) and drug-resistant epilepsy (Majoie et al., 2006) as well as autoantibodies to critical brain elements, such as myelin basic protein, brain derived neurotrophic factor and endothelial cells (Connolly et al., 1999). GAD65 autoantibodies are associated with several neurological disorders including drug-resistant epilepsy (Blanc et al., 2009). One study found GAD65 autoantibodies in 15% of children with ASD (Rout et al., 2012) but other studies have failed to find these autoantibodies in ASD children (Kalra et al., 2015).

Certain autoantibodies, such as the folate receptor alpha autoantibody, could result in specific syndromes like CFD and a recent study suggests that the folate receptor alpha autoantibody may also interfere with cobalamin metabolism (Frye et al., 2016b). Autoantibodies associated with specific seizure syndromes could also result in the dysfunction of specific neural elements. Autoantibodies can also be an epiphenomenon of underlying immune dysregulation.

SUMMARY

Many of these disorders associated with both seizures and ASD increase the excitatory-to-inhibitory balance. Some disorders reduce brain inhibition by reducing the inhibitory neurotransmitter GABA by a reduction in GABA production, metabolic failure of inhibitory GABA neurons or dysfunction of GABA receptors. Other disorders increase brain excitation by increasing the excitatory neurotransmitter glutamate through increased production, alterations in degradation, or altering glutamate receptors. Independent of these disorders, neuropathological research on ASD points to abnormalities in inhibitory GABA pathways.

A few studies suggest that some gene mutations are associated with a reduction in the excitatory-to-inhibitory balance. This appears to contradict the classic association of seizures with cortical excitability. It may be that these changes cause instability in neuronal networks or compensatory changes at the neuronal level that may create abnormalities in neural excitability. For example, although brain GABA is increased in patients with succinic semialdehyde dehydrogenase deficiency, GABA receptors are down regulated, leading to an elevation in the excitatory-to-inhibitory balance (Pearl et al., 2009a,b).

Clearly further research examining these pathways in more detail could help guide the development of targeted treatments and improve our understanding of the clinical implication of these changes. This review suggests that neurological dysfunction in at least a subset of children with ASD is based on alterations in the excitatory-to inhibitory balance in the brain.

AUTHOR CONTRIBUTIONS

This manuscript was developed as part of the Elias Tembenis Seizure Think Tanks at the Autism One Meeting in Chicago in May of 2009 and 2010 and at the Autism Canada Meeting in Toronto, Canada in October of 2009. These Think Tanks included scientists and clinicians with expertise in seizures related to ASD. The participants represented a wide variety of researchers and practitioners who treat ASD. Individual participants who provided written text for the supplement or contributed in the editing of the document are recognized as authors. Dr. Fatemi's research fellows assisted with the writing despite not attending the Think Tank so they are recognized as authors.

ACKNOWLEDGMENTS

This research has been supported by a National Institute of Child Health and Development grant to SF. This manuscript was supported by the Elias Tembenis Seizure Think Tanks conducted at the Autism One Meetings, the Autism International Association and the Autism Research Foundation.

REFERENCES

Adams, J. B., Audhya, T., McDonough-Means, S., Rubin, R. A., Quig, D., Geis, E., et al. (2011). Effect of a vitamin/mineral supplement on children and adults with autism. *BMC Pediatr.* 11:111. doi: 10.1186/1471-2431-11-111

Akaike, A., Tamura, Y., Sato, Y., and Yokota, T. (1993). Protective effects of a vitamin B12 analog, methylcobalamin, against glutamate cytotoxicity in cultured cortical neurons. *Eur. J. Pharmacol.* 241, 1–6. doi: 10.1016/0014-2999(93)90925-8

Anderson, M. P., Hooker, B. S., and Herbert, M. R. (2008). Bridging from cells to cognition in autism pathophysiology: biological pathways to defective brain function and plasticity *Am. J. Biochem. Biotechnol.* 4, 167–176. doi: 10.3844/ajbbsp.2008.167.176

Arrieta, O., Palencia, G., García-Arenas, G., Morales-Espinosa, D., Hernández-Pedro, N., and Sotelo, J. (2005). Prolonged exposure to lead lowers the threshold of pentylenetetrazole-induced seizures in rats. *Epilepsia* 46, 1599–1602. doi: 10.1111/j.1528-1167.2005.00267.x

Ault, B., Evans, R. H., Francis, A. A., Oakes, D. J., and Watkins, J. C. (1980). Selective depression of excitatory amino acid induced depolarizations by magnesium ions in isolated spinal cord preparations. *J. Physiol.* 307, 413–428. doi: 10.1113/jphysiol.1980.sp013443

Baieli, S., Pavone, L., Meli, C., Fiumara, A., and Coleman, M. (2003). Autism and phenylketonuria. *J. Autism Dev. Disord.* 33, 201–204. doi: 10.1023/A:1022999712639

Bangash, M. A., Park, J. M., Melnikova, T., Wang, D., Jeon, S. K., Lee, D., et al. (2011). Enhanced polyubiquitination of Shank3 and NMDA receptor in a mouse model of autism. *Cell* 145, 758–772. doi: 10.1016/j.cell.2011.03.052

Belyaeva, E. A., Korotkov, S. M., and Saris, N. E. (2011). In vitro modulation of heavy metal-induced rat liver mitochondria dysfunction: a comparison of copper and mercury with cadmium. *J. Trace Elem. Med. Biol.* 25(Suppl. 1), S63–S73. doi: 10.1016/j.jtemb.2010.10.007

Benbir, G., Uysal, S., Saltik, S., Zeybek, C. A., Aydin, A., Dervent, A., et al. (2007). Seizures during treatment of Vitamin B12 deficiency. *Seizure* 16, 69–73. doi: 10.1016/j.seizure.2006.10.016

Blanc, F., Ruppert, E., Kleitz, C., Valenti, M. P., Cretin, B., Humbel, R. L., et al. (2009). Acute limbic encephalitis and glutamic acid decarboxylase antibodies: a reality? *J. Neurol. Sci.* 287, 69–71. doi: 10.1016/j.jns.2009.09.004

Blatt, G. J., Fitzgerald, C. M., Guptill, J. T., Booker, A. B., Kemper, T. L., and Bauman, M. L. (2001). Density and distribution of hippocampal neurotransmitter receptors in autism: an autoradiographic study. *J. Autism Dev. Disord.* 31, 537–543. doi: 10.1023/A:1013238809666

Brock, J., Brown, C. C., Boucher, J., and Rippon, G. (2002). The temporal binding deficit hypothesis of autism. *Dev. Psychopathol.* 14, 209–224. doi: 10.1017/S0954579402002018

Brown, C., Gruber, T., Boucher, J., Rippon, G., and Brock, J. (2005). Gamma abnormalities during perception of illusory figures in autism. *Cortex* 41, 364–376. doi: 10.1016/S0010-9452(08)70273-9

Buxhoeveden, D. P., and Casanova, M. F. (2002). The minicolumn hypothesis in neuroscience. *Brain* 125, 935–951. doi: 10.1093/brain/awf110

Casanova, M. F., Buxhoeveden, D., and Gomez, J. (2003). Disruption in the inhibitory architecture of the cell minicolumn: implications for autism. *Neuroscientist* 9, 496–507. doi: 10.1177/1073858403253552

Casanova, M., Van Kooten, I., Switala, A., Van Engeland, H., Heinsen, H., Steinbusch, H., et al. (2006). Abnormalities of cortical minicolumnar organization in the prefrontal lobes of autistic patients. *Clin. Neurosci. Res.* 6, 127–133. doi: 10.1016/j.cnr.2006.06.003

Chaistitwanich, R., Mahoney, A. W., Hendricks, D. G., and Sisson, D. V. (1987). Dietary calcium and phosphorus and seizure susceptibility of magnesium deficient rats. *Pharmacol. Biochem. Behav.* 27, 443–449. doi: 10.1016/0091-3057(87)90347-9

Chen, H., and Chan, D. C. (2009). Mitochondrial dynamics–fusion, fission, movement, and mitophagy–in neurodegenerative diseases. *Hum. Mol. Genet.* 18, R169–R176. doi: 10.1093/hmg/ddp326

Clement, J. P., Aceti, M., Creson, T. K., Ozkan, E. D., Shi, Y., Reish, N. J., et al. (2012). Pathogenic SYNGAP1 mutations impair cognitive development by disrupting maturation of dendritic spine synapses. *Cell* 151, 709–723. doi: 10.1016/j.cell.2012.08.045

Cohen-Kfir, E., Lee, W., Eskandari, S., and Nelson, N. (2005). Zinc inhibition of gamma-aminobutyric acid transporter 4 (GAT4) reveals a link between excitatory and inhibitory neurotransmission. *Proc. Natl. Acad. Sci. U.S.A.* 102, 6154–6159. doi: 10.1073/pnas.0501431102

Cole, T. B., Robbins, C. A., Wenzel, H. J., Schwartzkroin, P. A., and Palmiter, R. D. (2000). Seizures and neuronal damage in mice lacking vesicular zinc. *Epilepsy Res.* 39, 153–169. doi: 10.1016/S0920-1211(99)00121-7

Condie, J., Goldstein, J., and Wainwright, M. S. (2010). Acquired microcephaly, regression of milestones, mitochondrial dysfunction, and episodic rigidity in a 46,XY male with a de novo MECP2 gene mutation. *J. Child Neurol.* 25, 633–636. doi: 10.1177/0883073809342004

Connolly, A. M., Chez, M. G., Pestronk, A., Arnold, S. T., Mehta, S., and Deuel, R. K. (1999). Serum autoantibodies to brain in Landau-Kleffner variant, autism, and other neurologic disorders. *J. Pediatr.* 134, 607–613. doi: 10.1016/S0022-3476(99)70248-9

Connolly, A. M., Chez, M., Streif, E. M., Keeling, R. M., Golumbek, P. T., Kwon, J. M., et al. (2006). Brain-derived neurotrophic factor and autoantibodies to neural antigens in sera of children with autistic spectrum disorders, Landau-Kleffner syndrome, and epilepsy. *Biol. Psychiatry* 59, 354–363. doi: 10.1016/j.biopsych.2005.07.004

Danielsson, S., Gillberg, I. C., Billstedt, E., Gillberg, C., and Olsson, I. (2005). Epilepsy in young adults with autism: a prospective population-based follow-up study of 120 individuals diagnosed in childhood. *Epilepsia* 46, 918–923. doi: 10.1111/j.1528-1167.2005.57504.x

Deepmala, Slattery, J., Kumar, N., Delhey, L., Berk, M., Dean, O., et al. (2015). Clinical trials of N-acetylcysteine in psychiatry and neurology: a systematic review. *Neurosci. Biobehav. Rev.* 55, 294–321. doi: 10.1016/j.neubiorev.2015.04.015

Defelipe, J. (1999). Chandelier cells and epilepsy. *Brain* 122(Pt 10), 1807–1822. doi: 10.1093/brain/122.10.1807

Defelipe, J. (2005). "Reflections on the structure of the cortical minicolumn," in *Neocortical Modularity and the Cell Minicolumn*, ed M. F. Casanova (New York, NY: Nova Biomedical), 57–92.

Defelipe, J., Hendry, S. H., Hashikawa, T., Molinari, M., and Jones, E. G. (1990). A microcolumnar structure of monkey cerebral cortex revealed by immunocytochemical studies of double bouquet cell axons. *Neuroscience* 37, 655–673. doi: 10.1016/0306-4522(90)90097-N

Delgado-Escueta, A. V. (2007). Advances in genetics of juvenile myoclonic epilepsies. *Epilepsy Curr.* 7, 61–67. doi: 10.1111/j.1535-7511.2007.00171.x

Delorenzo, R. J. (1986). A molecular approach to the calcium signal in brain: relationship to synaptic modulation and seizure discharge. *Adv. Neurol.* 44, 435–464.

Delorenzo, R. J., and Limbrick, D. D. Jr. (1996). Effects of glutamate on calcium influx and sequestration/extrusion mechanisms in hippocampal neurons. *Adv. Neurol.* 71, 37–46.

Deykin, E. Y., and Macmahon, B. (1979). The incidence of seizures among children with autistic symptoms. *Am. J. Psychiatry* 136, 1310–1312. doi: 10.1176/ajp.136.10.1310

Dhossche, D., Applegate, H., Abraham, A., Maertens, P., Bland, L., Bencsath, A., et al. (2002). Elevated plasma gamma-aminobutyric acid (GABA) levels in autistic youngsters: stimulus for a GABA hypothesis of autism. *Med. Sci. Monit.* 8, PR1–PR6.

D'hulst, C., and Kooy, R. F. (2007). The GABAA receptor: a novel target for treatment of fragile X? *Trends Neurosci.* 30, 425–431. doi: 10.1016/j.tins.2007.06.003

Erol, I., Alehan, F., and Gümüs, A. (2007). West syndrome in an infant with vitamin B12 deficiency in the absence of macrocytic anaemia. *Dev. Med. Child Neurol.* 49, 774–776. doi: 10.1111/j.1469-8749.2007.00774.x

Fatemi, S. H. (2008). The hyperglutamatergic hypothesis of autism. *Prog. Neuropsychopharmacol. Biol. Psychiatry.* 32, 911. author reply: 912–913.

Fatemi, S. H., Reutiman, T. J., Folsom, T. D., and Thuras, P. D. (2009). GABA(A) receptor downregulation in brains of subjects with autism. *J. Autism Dev. Disord.* 39, 223–230. doi: 10.1007/s10803-008-0646-7

Favorov, O. V., and Kelly, D. G. (1994). Minicolumnar organization within somatosensory cortical segregates: II. Emergent functional properties. *Cereb. Cortex* 4, 428–442. doi: 10.1093/cercor/4.4.428

Frye, R. E. (2012a). Biomarker of abnormal energy metabolism in children with autism spectrum disorder. *North Am. J. Med. Sci.* 5, 141–147. doi: 10.7156/v5i3p141

Frye, R. E. (2012b). Mitochondrial disease in 22q13 duplication syndrome. *J. Child Neurol.* 27, 942–949. doi: 10.1177/0883073811429858

Frye, R. E. (2012c). Novel mitochondrial Cytochrome B gene polymorphisms associated with autism. *J. Pediatr. Neurol.* 10, 35–40. doi: 10.3233/JPN-2012-0530

Frye, R. E. (2014). Clinical potential, safety, and tolerability of arbaclofen in the treatment of autism spectrum disorder. *Drug Healthc. Patient Saf.* 6, 69–76. doi: 10.2147/DHPS.S39595

Frye, R. E. (2015). Metabolic and mitochondrial disorders associated with epilepsy in children with autism spectrum disorder. *Epilepsy Behav.* 47, 147–157. doi: 10.1016/j.yebeh.2014.08.134

Frye, R. E., Cox, D., Slattery, J., Tippett, M., Kahler, S., Granpeesheh, D., et al. (2016a). Mitochondrial Dysfunction may explain symptom variation in Phelan-McDermid Syndrome. *Sci. Rep.* 6, 19544. doi: 10.1038/srep19544

Frye, R. E., Delatorre, R., Taylor, H. B., Slattery, J., Melnyk, S., Chowdhury, N., et al. (2013a). Metabolic effects of sapropterin treatment in autism spectrum disorder: a preliminary study. *Transl. Psychiatry* 3:e237. doi: 10.1038/tp.2013.14

Frye, R. E., Delhey, L., Slattery, J., Tippett, M., Wynne, R., Rose, S., et al. (2016b). Blocking and binding folate receptor alpha autoantibodies identify novel autism spectrum disorder subgroups. *Front. Neurosci.* 10:80. doi: 10.3389/fnins.2016.00080

Frye, R. E., and James, S. J. (2014). Metabolic pathology of autism in relation to redox metabolism. *Biomark. Med.* 8, 321–330. doi: 10.2217/bmm.13.158

Frye, R. E., Melnyk, S., Fuchs, G., Reid, T., Jernigan, S., Pavliv, O., et al. (2013b). Effectiveness of methylcobalamin and folinic Acid treatment on adaptive behavior in children with autistic disorder is related to glutathione redox status. *Autism Res. Treat.* 2013, 609705. doi: 10.1155/2013/609705

Frye, R. E., and Naviaux, R. K. (2011). Autistic disorder with complex IV overactivity: a new mitochondrial syndrome. *J. Pediatr. Neurol.* 9, 427–434. doi: 10.3233/JPN-2011-0507

Frye, R. E., and Rossignol, D. A. (2011). Mitochondrial dysfunction can connect the diverse medical symptoms associated with autism spectrum disorders. *Pediatr. Res.* 69, 41R–47R. doi: 10.1203/pdr.0b013e318212f16b

Frye, R. E., Sequeira, J. M., Quadros, E. V., James, S. J., and Rossignol, D. A. (2013c). Cerebral folate receptor autoantibodies in autism spectrum disorder. *Mol. Psychiatry* 18, 369–381. doi: 10.1038/mp.2011.175

Fukahori, M., and Itoh, M. (1990). Effects of dietary zinc status on seizure susceptibility and hippocampal zinc content in the El (epilepsy) mouse. *Brain Res.* 529, 16–22. doi: 10.1016/0006-8993(90)90806-M

Furieri, L. B., Galán, M., Avendaño, M. S., García-Redondo, A. B., Aguado, A., Martínez, S., et al. (2011). Endothelial dysfunction of rat coronary arteries after exposure to low concentrations of mercury is dependent on reactive oxygen species. *Br. J. Pharmacol.* 162, 1819–1831. doi: 10.1111/j.1476-5381.2011.01203.x

Ganesh, R., and Janakiraman, L. (2008). Serum zinc levels in children with simple febrile seizure. *Clin. Pediatr.* 47, 164–166. doi: 10.1177/0009922807306165

Ganor, Y., Goldberg-Stern, H., Amrom, D., Lerman-Sagie, T., Teichberg, V. I., Pelled, D., et al. (2004). Autoimmune epilepsy: some epilepsy patients harbor autoantibodies to glutamate receptors and dsDNA on both sides of the blood-brain barrier, which may kill neurons and decrease in brain fluids after hemispherotomy. *Clin. Dev. Immunol.* 11, 241–252. doi: 10.1080/17402520400001736

Giulivi, C., Zhang, Y. F., Omanska-Klusek, A., Ross-Inta, C., Wong, S., Hertz-Picciotto, I., et al. (2010). Mitochondrial dysfunction in autism. *JAMA* 304, 2389–2396. doi: 10.1001/jama.2010.1706

Glushakov, A. V., Dennis, D. M., Sumners, C., Seubert, C. N., and Martynyuk, A. E. (2003). L-phenylalanine selectively depresses currents at glutamatergic excitatory synapses. *J. Neurosci. Res.* 72, 116–124. doi: 10.1002/jnr.10569

Glushakov, A. V., Glushakova, O., Varshney, M., Bajpai, L. K., Sumners, C., Laipis, P. J., et al. (2005). Long-term changes in glutamatergic synaptic transmission in phenylketonuria. *Brain* 128, 300–307. doi: 10.1093/brain/awh354

Gospe, S. M. (2002). Pyridoxine-dependent seizures: findings from recent studies pose new questions. *Pediatr. Neurol.* 26, 181–185. doi: 10.1016/S0887-8994(01)00407-6

Gospe, S. M. Jr., Olin, K. L., and Keen, C. L. (1994). Reduced GABA synthesis in pyridoxine-dependent seizures. *Lancet* 343, 1133–1134. doi: 10.1016/S0140-6736(94)90236-4

Grice, S. J., Spratling, M. W., Karmiloff-Smith, A., Halit, H., Csibra, G., De Haan, M., et al. (2001). Disordered visual processing and oscillatory brain activity in autism and Williams syndrome. *Neuroreport* 12, 2697–2700. doi: 10.1097/00001756-200108280-00021

Grothe, B., and Klump, G. M. (2000). Temporal processing in sensory systems. *Curr. Opin. Neurobiol.* 10, 467–473. doi: 10.1016/S0959-4388(00)00115-X

Hallak, M. (1998). Effect of parenteral magnesium sulfate administration on excitatory amino acid receptors in the rat brain. *Magnes. Res.* 11, 117–131.

Hallak, M., Berman, R. F., Irtenkauf, S. M., Evans, M. I., and Cotton, D. B. (1992). Peripheral magnesium sulfate enters the brain and increases the threshold for hippocampal seizures in rats. *Am. J. Obstet. Gynecol.* 167, 1605–1610. doi: 10.1016/0002-9378(92)91749-Z

Han, Y., Qin, J., Bu, D. F., Chang, X. Z., and Yang, Z. X. (2006). Successive alterations of hippocampal gamma-aminobutyric acid B receptor subunits in a rat model of febrile seizure. *Life Sci.* 78, 2944–2952. doi: 10.1016/j.lfs.2005.11.023

Hara, H. (2007). Autism and epilepsy: a retrospective follow-up study. *Brain Dev.* 29, 486–490. doi: 10.1016/j.braindev.2006.12.012

Heinemann, U., and Hamon, B. (1986). Calcium and epileptogenesis. *Exp. Brain Res.* 65, 1–10. doi: 10.1007/BF00243826

Hendren, R. L., James, S. J., Widjaja, F., Lawton, B., Rosenblatt, A., and Bent, S. (2016). Randomized, placebo-controlled trial of Methyl B12 for children with autism. *J. Child Adolesc. Psychopharmacol.* doi: 10.1089/cap.2015.0159. [Epub ahead of print].

Jakobs, C., Bojasch, M., Mönch, E., Rating, D., Siemes, H., and Hanefeld, F. (1981). Urinary excretion of gamma-hydroxybutyric acid in a patient with neurological abnormalities. The probability of a new inborn error of metabolism. *Clin. Chim. Acta* 111, 169–178. doi: 10.1016/0009-8981(81)90184-4

James, S. J., Melnyk, S., Fuchs, G., Reid, T., Jernigan, S., Pavliv, O., et al. (2009a). Efficacy of methylcobalamin and folinic acid treatment on glutathione redox status in children with autism. *Am. J. Clin. Nutr.* 89, 425–430. doi: 10.3945/ajcn.2008.26615

James, S. J., Rose, S., Melnyk, S., Jernigan, S., Blossom, S., Pavliv, O., et al. (2009b). Cellular and mitochondrial glutathione redox imbalance in lymphoblastoid cells derived from children with autism. *FASEB J.* 23, 2374–2383. doi: 10.1096/fj.08-128926

Jurecka, A., Zikanova, M., Tylki-Szymanska, A., Krijt, J., Bogdanska, A., Gradowska, W., et al. (2008). Clinical, biochemical and molecular findings in seven Polish patients with adenylosuccinate lyase deficiency. *Mol. Genet. Metab.* 94, 435–442. doi: 10.1016/j.ymgme.2008.04.013

Kalra, S., Burbelo, P. D., Bayat, A., Ching, K. H., Thurm, A., Iadarola, M. J., et al. (2015). No evidence of antibodies against GAD65 and other specific antigens in children with autism. *BBA Clin.* 4, 81–84. doi: 10.1016/j.bbacli.2015.08.001

Kang, J. Q., Shen, W., and Macdonald, R. L. (2009). Two molecular pathways (NMD and ERAD) contribute to a genetic epilepsy associated with the GABA(A) receptor GABRA1 PTC mutation, 975delC, S326fs328X. *J. Neurosci.* 29, 2833–2844. doi: 10.1523/JNEUROSCI.4512-08.2009

Karayannis, T., Au, E., Patel, J. C., Kruglikov, I., Markx, S., Delorme, R., et al. (2014). Cntnap4 differentially contributes to GABAergic and dopaminergic synaptic transmission. *Nature* 511, 236–240. doi: 10.1038/nature13248

Kriaucionis, S., Paterson, A., Curtis, J., Guy, J., Macleod, N., and Bird, A. (2006). Gene expression analysis exposes mitochondrial abnormalities in a mouse model of Rett syndrome. *Mol. Cell. Biol.* 26, 5033–5042. doi: 10.1128/MCB.01665-05

Kumar, S. (2004). Recurrent seizures: an unusual manifestation of vitamin B12 deficiency. *Neurol. India* 52, 122–123.

Li, L., Chin, L. S., Shupliakov, O., Brodin, L., Sihra, T. S., Hvalby, O., et al. (1995). Impairment of synaptic vesicle clustering and of synaptic transmission, and increased seizure propensity, in synapsin I-deficient mice. *Proc. Natl. Acad. Sci. U.S.A.* 92, 9235–9239. doi: 10.1073/pnas.92.20.9235

Li, Z., Okamoto, K., Hayashi, Y., and Sheng, M. (2004). The importance of dendritic mitochondria in the morphogenesis and plasticity of spines and synapses. *Cell* 119, 873–887. doi: 10.1016/j.cell.2004.11.003

Lockitch, G., Berry, B., Roland, E., Wadsworth, L., Kaikov, Y., and Mirhady, F. (1991). Seizures in a 10-week-old infant: lead poisoning from an unexpected source. *CMAJ* 145, 1465–1468.

Longo, N., Ardon, O., Vanzo, R., Schwartz, E., and Pasquali, M. (2011). Disorders of creatine transport and metabolism. *Am. J. Med. Genet. C Semin. Med. Genet.* 157C, 72–78. doi: 10.1002/ajmg.c.30292

Macdermott, A. B., Mayer, M. L., Westbrook, G. L., Smith, S. J., and Barker, J. L. (1986). NMDA-receptor activation increases cytoplasmic calcium concentration in cultured spinal cord neurones. *Nature* 321, 519–522. doi: 10.1038/321519a0

Majoie, H. J., De Baets, M., Renier, W., Lang, B., and Vincent, A. (2006). Antibodies to voltage-gated potassium and calcium channels in epilepsy. *Epilepsy Res.* 71, 135–141. doi: 10.1016/j.eplepsyres.2006.06.003

Martynyuk, A. E., Glushakov, A. V., Sumners, C., Laipis, P. J., Dennis, D. M., and Seubert, C. N. (2005). Impaired glutamatergic synaptic transmission in the PKU brain. *Mol. Genet. Metab.* 86(Suppl. 1), S34–S42. doi: 10.1016/j.ymgme.2005.06.014

Mathern, G. W., Pretorius, J. K., Mendoza, D., Lozada, A., Leite, J. P., Chimelli, L., et al. (1998). Increased hippocampal AMPA and NMDA receptor subunit immunoreactivity in temporal lobe epilepsy patients. *J. Neuropathol. Exp. Neurol.* 57, 615–634. doi: 10.1097/00005072-199806000-00008

Mikuni, N., Babb, T. L., Ying, Z., Najm, I., Nishiyama, K., Wylie, C., et al. (1999). NMDA-receptors 1 and 2A/B coassembly increased in human epileptic focal cortical dysplasia. *Epilepsia* 40, 1683–1687. doi: 10.1111/j.1528-1157.1999.tb01584.x

Mills, P. B., Struys, E., Jakobs, C., Plecko, B., Baxter, P., Baumgartner, M., et al. (2006). Mutations in antiquitin in individuals with pyridoxine-dependent seizures. *Nat. Med.* 12, 307–309. doi: 10.1038/nm1366

Mollah, M. A., Rakshit, S. C., Anwar, K. S., Arslan, M. I., Saha, N., Ahmed, S., et al. (2008). Zinc concentration in serum and cerebrospinal fluid simultaneously decrease in children with febrile seizure: findings from a prospective study in Bangladesh. *Acta Paediatr.* 97, 1707–1711. doi: 10.1111/j.1651-2227.2008.01001.x

Mountcastle, V. B. (1997). The columnar organization of the neocortex. *Brain* 120(Pt 4), 701–722. doi: 10.1093/brain/120.4.701

Murdoch, J. D., and State, M. W. (2013). Recent developments in the genetics of autism spectrum disorders. *Curr. Opin. Genet. Dev.* 23, 310–315. doi: 10.1016/j.gde.2013.02.003

Obeid, R., Mccaddon, A., and Herrmann, W. (2007). The role of hyperhomocysteinemia and B-vitamin deficiency in neurological and psychiatric diseases. *Clin. Chem. Lab. Med.* 45, 1590–1606. doi: 10.1515/CCLM.2007.356

Pal, P. B., Pal, S., Das, J., and Sil, P. C. (2012). Modulation of mercury-induced mitochondria-dependent apoptosis by glycine in hepatocytes. *Amino Acids* 42, 1669–1683. doi: 10.1007/s00726-011-0869-3

Pearl, P. L., Gibson, K. M., Cortez, M. A., Wu, Y., Carter Snead, O. 3rd., Knerr, I., et al. (2009a). Succinic semialdehyde dehydrogenase deficiency: lessons from mice and men. *J. Inherit. Metab. Dis.* 32, 343–352. doi: 10.1007/s10545-009-1034-y

Pearl, P. L., Gibson, K. M., Quezado, Z., Dustin, I., Taylor, J., Trzcinski, S., et al. (2009b). Decreased GABA-A binding on FMZ-PET in succinic semialdehyde dehydrogenase deficiency. *Neurology* 73, 423–429. doi: 10.1212/WNL.0b013e3181b163a5

Pei, Y., Zhao, D., Huang, J., and Cao, L. (1983). Zinc-induced seizures: a new experimental model of epilepsy. *Epilepsia* 24, 169–176. doi: 10.1111/j.1528-1157.1983.tb04876.x

Pelc, K., Boyd, S. G., Cheron, G., and Dan, B. (2008). Epilepsy in Angelman syndrome. *Seizure* 17, 211–217. doi: 10.1016/j.seizure.2007.08.004

Peñagarikano, O., Abrahams, B. S., Herman, E. I., Winden, K. D., Gdalyahu, A., Dong, H., et al. (2011). Absence of CNTNAP2 leads to epilepsy, neuronal migration abnormalities, and core autism-related deficits. *Cell* 147, 235–246. doi: 10.1016/j.cell.2011.08.040

Pickett, J., Xiu, E., Tuchman, R., Dawson, G., and Lajonchere, C. (2011). Mortality in individuals with autism, with and without epilepsy. *J. Child Neurol.* 26, 932–939. doi: 10.1177/0883073811402203

Póo-Argüelles, P., Arias, A., Vilaŝeca, M. A., Ribes, A., Artuch, R., Sans-Fito, A., et al. (2006). X-Linked creatine transporter deficiency in two patients with severe mental retardation and autism. *J. Inherit. Metab. Dis.* 29, 220–223. doi: 10.1007/s10545-006-0212-4

Princivalle, A. P., Richards, D. A., Duncan, J. S., Spreafico, R., and Bowery, N. G. (2003). Modification of GABA(B1) and GABA(B2) receptor subunits in the somatosensory cerebral cortex and thalamus of rats with absence seizures (GAERS). *Epilepsy Res.* 55, 39–51. doi: 10.1016/S0920-1211(03)00090-1

Quiroz, J. A., Gray, N. A., Kato, T., and Manji, H. K. (2008). Mitochondrially mediated plasticity in the pathophysiology and treatment of bipolar disorder. *Neuropsychopharmacology* 33, 2551–2565. doi: 10.1038/sj.npp.1301671

Ramaekers, V. T., and Blau, N. (2004). Cerebral folate deficiency. *Dev. Med. Child Neurol.* 46, 843–851. doi: 10.1111/j.1469-8749.2004.tb00451.x

Ramaekers, V. T., Häusler, M., Opladen, T., Heimann, G., and Blau, N. (2002). Psychomotor retardation, spastic paraplegia, cerebellar ataxia and dyskinesia associated with low 5-methyltetrahydrofolate in cerebrospinal fluid: a novel neurometabolic condition responding to folinic acid substitution. *Neuropediatrics* 33, 301–308. doi: 10.1055/s-2002-37082

Riazi, K., Galic, M. A., and Pittman, Q. J. (2010). Contributions of peripheral inflammation to seizure susceptibility: cytokines and brain excitability. *Epilepsy Res.* 89, 34–42. doi: 10.1016/j.eplepsyres.2009.09.004

Rippon, G., Brock, J., Brown, C., and Boucher, J. (2007). Disordered connectivity in the autistic brain: challenges for the 'new psychophysiology'. *Int. J. Psychophysiol.* 63, 164–172. doi: 10.1016/j.ijpsycho.2006.03.012

Rose, C. (2006). Effect of ammonia on astrocytic glutamate uptake/release mechanisms. *J. Neurochem.* 97(Suppl. 1), 11–15. doi: 10.1111/j.1471-4159.2006.03796.x

Rose, S., Frye, R. E., Slattery, J., Wynne, R., Tippett, M., Melnyk, S., et al. (2014a). Oxidative stress induces mitochondrial dysfunction in a subset of autistic lymphoblastoid cell lines. *Transl. Psychiatry* 4:e377. doi: 10.1038/tp.2014.15

Rose, S., Frye, R. E., Slattery, J., Wynne, R., Tippett, M., Pavliv, O., et al. (2014b). Oxidative stress induces mitochondrial dysfunction in a subset of autism lymphoblastoid cell lines in a well-matched case control cohort. *PLoS ONE* 9:e85436. doi: 10.1371/journal.pone.0085436

Rose, S., Wynne, R., Frye, R. E., Melnyk, S., and James, S. J. (2015). Increased susceptibility to ethylmercury-induced mitochondrial dysfunction in a subset of autism lymphoblastoid cell lines. *J. Toxicol.* 2015, 573701. doi: 10.1155/2015/573701

Rossignol, D. A., and Frye, R. E. (2012a). Mitochondrial dysfunction in autism spectrum disorders: a systematic review and meta-analysis. *Mol. Psychiatry* 17, 290–314. doi: 10.1038/mp.2010.136

Rossignol, D. A., and Frye, R. E. (2012b). A review of research trends in physiological abnormalities in autism spectrum disorders: immune dysregulation, inflammation, oxidative stress, mitochondrial dysfunction and environmental toxicant exposures. *Mol. Psychiatry* 17, 389–401. doi: 10.1038/mp.2011.165

Rossignol, D. A., Genuis, S. J., and Frye, R. E. (2014). Environmental toxicants and autism spectrum disorders: a systematic review. *Transl. Psychiatry* 4:e360. doi: 10.1038/tp.2014.4

Rout, U. K., Mungan, N. K., and Dhossche, D. M. (2012). Presence of GAD65 autoantibodies in the serum of children with autism or ADHD. *Eur. Child Adolesc. Psychiatry* 21, 141–147. doi: 10.1007/s00787-012-0245-1

Rubenstein, J. L., and Merzenich, M. M. (2003). Model of autism: increased ratio of excitation/inhibition in key neural systems. *Genes Brain Behav.* 2, 255–267. doi: 10.1034/j.1601-183X.2003.00037.x

Sansa, G., Carlson, C., Doyle, W., Weiner, H. L., Bluvstein, J., Barr, W., et al. (2011). Medically refractory epilepsy in autism. *Epilepsia* 52, 1071–1075. doi: 10.1111/j.1528-1167.2011.03069.x

Schaefer, G. B., Mendelsohn, N. J., Professional, P., and Guidelines, C. (2013). Clinical genetics evaluation in identifying the etiology of autism spectrum disorders: 2013 guideline revisions. *Genet. Med.* 15, 399–407. doi: 10.1038/gim.2013.32

Schuler, V., Lüscher, C., Blanchet, C., Klíx, N., Sansig, G., Klebs, K., et al. (2001). Epilepsy, hyperalgesia, impaired memory, and loss of pre- and postsynaptic GABA(B) responses in mice lacking GABA(B(1)). *Neuron* 31, 47–58. doi: 10.1016/S0896-6273(01)00345-2

Shavelle, R. M., Strauss, D. J., and Pickett, J. (2001). Causes of death in autism. *J. Autism Dev. Disord.* 31, 569–576. doi: 10.1023/A:1013247011483

Shcheglovitov, A., Shcheglovitova, O., Yazawa, M., Portmann, T., Shu, R., Sebastiano, V., et al. (2013). SHANK3 and IGF1 restore synaptic deficits in neurons from 22q13 deletion syndrome patients. *Nature* 503, 267–271. doi: 10.1038/nature12618

Silbergeld, E. K., Miller, L. P., Kennedy, S., and Eng, N. (1979). Lead, GABA, and seizures: effects of subencephalopathic lead exposure on seizure sensitivity and GABAergic function. *Environ. Res.* 19, 371–382. doi: 10.1016/0013-9351(79)90062-8

Sinert, R., Zehtabchi, S., Desai, S., Peacock, P., Altura, B. T., and Altura, B. M. (2007). Serum ionized magnesium and calcium levels in adult patients with seizures. *Scand. J. Clin. Lab. Invest.* 67, 317–326. doi: 10.1080/00365510601051441

Specchio, N., Fusco, L., Claps, D., and Vigevano, F. (2010). Epileptic encephalopathy in children possibly related to immune-mediated pathogenesis. *Brain Dev.* 32, 51–56. doi: 10.1016/j.braindev.2009.09.017

Spiegel, E. K., Colman, R. F., and Patterson, D. (2006). Adenylosuccinate lyase deficiency. *Mol. Genet. Metab.* 89, 19–31. doi: 10.1016/j.ymgme.2006.04.018

Srivastava, A. K., and Schwartz, C. E. (2014). Intellectual disability and autism spectrum disorders: causal genes and molecular mechanisms. *Neurosci. Biobehav. Rev.* 46(Pt 2), 161–174. doi: 10.1016/j.neubiorev.2014.02.015

Su, H., Fan, W., Coskun, P. E., Vesa, J., Gold, J. A., Jiang, Y. H., et al. (2011). Mitochondrial dysfunction in CA1 hippocampal neurons of the UBE3A deficient mouse model for Angelman syndrome. *Neurosci. Lett.* 487, 129–133. doi: 10.1016/j.neulet.2009.06.079

Swartzwelder, H. S. (1985). Central neurotoxicity after exposure to organic lead: susceptibility to seizures. *Neurosci. Lett.* 58, 225–228. doi: 10.1016/0304-3940(85)90168-5

Tabuchi, K., Blundell, J., Etherton, M. R., Hammer, R. E., Liu, X., Powell, C. M., et al. (2007). A neuroligin-3 mutation implicated in autism increases inhibitory synaptic transmission in mice. *Science* 318, 71–76. doi: 10.1126/science.1146221

Tommerdahl, M., Tannan, V., Cascio, C. J., Baranek, G. T., and Whitsel, B. L. (2007). Vibrotactile adaptation fails to enhance spatial localization in adults with autism. *Brain Res.* 1154, 116–123. doi: 10.1016/j.brainres.2007.04.032

Torres, A. D., Rai, A. N., and Hardiek, M. L. (2000). Mercury intoxication and arterial hypertension: report of two patients and review of the literature. *Pediatrics* 105:E34. doi: 10.1542/peds.105.3.e34

Tuchman, R. (2013). Autism and social cognition in epilepsy: implications for comprehensive epilepsy care. *Curr. Opin. Neurol.* 26, 214–218. doi: 10.1097/WCO.0b013e32835ee64f

Tuchman, R. F., and Rapin, I. (1997). Regression in pervasive developmental disorders: seizures and epileptiform electroencephalogram correlates. *Pediatrics* 99, 560–566. doi: 10.1542/peds.99.4.560

Tuchman, R., Hirtz, D., and Mamounas, L. A. (2013). NINDS epilepsy and autism spectrum disorders workshop report. *Neurology* 81, 1630–1636. doi: 10.1212/WNL.0b013e3182a9f482

Tuchman, R., and Rapin, I. (2002). Epilepsy in autism. *Lancet Neurol.* 1, 352–358. doi: 10.1016/S1474-4422(02)00160-6

Vargas, D. L., Nascimbene, C., Krishnan, C., Zimmerman, A. W., and Pardo, C. A. (2005). Neuroglial activation and neuroinflammation in the brain of patients with autism. *Ann. Neurol.* 57, 67–81. doi: 10.1002/ana.20315

Vincent, A., Buckley, C., Schott, J. M., Baker, I., Dewar, B. K., Detert, N., et al. (2004). Potassium channel antibody-associated encephalopathy: a potentially immunotherapy-responsive form of limbic encephalitis. *Brain* 127, 701–712. doi: 10.1093/brain/awh077

Volkmar, F. R., and Nelson, D. S. (1990). Seizure disorders in autism. *J. Am. Acad. Child Adolesc. Psychiatry* 29, 127–129. doi: 10.1097/00004583-199001000-00020

Waldbaum, S., and Patel, M. (2010). Mitochondria, oxidative stress, and temporal lobe epilepsy. *Epilepsy Res.* 88, 23–45. doi: 10.1016/j.eplepsyres.2009.09.020

Wang, L., Wang, H., Li, J., Chen, D., and Liu, Z. (2011a). Simultaneous effects of lead and cadmium on primary cultures of rat proximal tubular cells: interaction of apoptosis and oxidative stress. *Arch. Environ. Contam. Toxicol.* 61, 500–511. doi: 10.1007/s00244-011-9644-4

Wang, X., Mccoy, P. A., Rodriguiz, R. M., Pan, Y., Je, H. S., Roberts, A. C., et al. (2011b). Synaptic dysfunction and abnormal behaviors in mice lacking major isoforms of Shank3. *Hum. Mol. Genet.* 20, 3093–3108. doi: 10.1093/hmg/ddr212

Williams, R. A., Mamotte, C. D., and Burnett, J. R. (2008). Phenylketonuria: an inborn error of phenylalanine metabolism. *Clin. Biochem. Rev.* 29, 31–41.

Williamson, A., and Spencer, D. (1995). Zinc reduces dentate granule cell hyperexcitability in epileptic humans. *Neuroreport* 6, 1562–1564. doi: 10.1097/00001756-199507310-00024

Zablotsky, B., Black, L. I., Maenner, M. J., Schieve, L. A., and Blumberg, S. J. (2015). *Estimated Prevalence of Autism and Other Developmental Disabilities Following Questionnaire Changes in the 2014 National Health Interview Survey.* Hyattsville, MD: National Center for Health Statistics. National Health Statistics Reports No. 87.

5

The Broad Autism (Endo)Phenotype: Neurostructural and Neurofunctional Correlates in Parents of Individuals with Autism Spectrum Disorders

Lucia Billeci[1], *Sara Calderoni*[2*], *Eugenia Conti*[1,3], *Camilla Gesi*[1], *Claudia Carmassi*[1], *Liliana Dell'Osso*[1], *Giovanni Cioni*[1,2], *Filippo Muratori*[1,2] *and Andrea Guzzetta*[1,2]

[1] Department of Clinical and Experimental Medicine, University of Pisa, Pisa, Italy, [2] IRCCS Stella Maris Foundation, Pisa, Italy, [3] Department of Sciences for Health Promotion and Mother and Child Care G. D'Alessandro, University of Palermo, Palermo, Italy

Edited by:
Yuri Bozzi,
University of Trento, Italy

Reviewed by:
José A. Alda,
Hospital Sant Joan de Deu Barcelona, Spain
Deepak Kumar,
Institute of Human Behavior and Allied Sciences, India

***Correspondence:**
Sara Calderoni
sara.calderoni@inpe.unipi.it

Autism Spectrum Disorders (ASD) are a set of neurodevelopmental disorders with an early-onset and a strong genetic component in their pathogenesis. According to genetic and epidemiological data, ASD relatives present personality traits similar to, but not as severe as the defining features of ASD, which have been indicated as the "Broader Autism Phenotype" (BAP). BAP features seem to be more prevalent in first-degree relatives of individuals with ASD than in the general population. Characterizing brain profiles of relatives of autistic probands may help to understand ASD endophenotype. The aim of this review was to provide an up-to-date overview of research findings on the neurostructural and neurofunctional substrates in parents of individuals with ASD (pASD). The primary hypothesis was that, like for the behavioral profile, the pASD express an intermediate neurobiological pattern between ASD individuals and healthy controls. The 13 reviewed studies evaluated structural magnetic resonance imaging (MRI) brain volumes, chemical signals using magnetic resonance spectroscopy (MRS), task-related functional activation by functional magnetic resonance imaging (fMRI), electroencephalography (EEG), or magnetoencephalography (MEG) in pASD.The studies showed that pASD are generally different from healthy controls at a structural and functional level despite often not behaviorally impaired. More atypicalities in neural patterns of pASD seem to be associated with higher scores at BAP assessment. Some of the observed atypicalities are the same of the ASD probands. In addition, the pattern of neural correlates in pASD resembles that of adult individuals with ASD, or it is specific, possibly due to a compensatory mechanism. Future studies should ideally include a group of pASD and HC with their ASD and non-ASD probands respectively. They should subgrouping the pASD according to the BAP scores, considering gender as a possible confounding factor, and correlating these scores to underlying brain structure and function. These types of studies may help to understand the genetic mechanisms involved in the various clinical dimension of ASD.

Keywords: Autism Spectrum Disorders, parents, Broader Autism Phenotype, magnetic resonance imaging, magnetic resonance spectroscopy, electroencephalography, magnetoenchephalography

INTRODUCTION

Autism Spectrum Disorders (ASD) are a set of early-onset neurodevelopmental disorders that are characterized by a disrupted development of brain connectivity with several cascading effects on neuropsychological functions (Narzisi et al., 2013; Kana et al., 2014). A clinical dyad, comprising social communication difficulties and repetitive, stereotyped behavior must be present for a diagnosis of ASD (American Psychiatric Association, 2013). The exact cause of ASD is still unknown (Levy et al., 2009). Although, only 20% of ASD cases can be explained by a specific genetic cause, such as identifiable genetic syndromes, genetic mutations or de novo copy number variants (Jeste and Geschwind, 2014), recent twin studies estimate an heritability between 64 and 91% (Tick et al., 2016), suggesting an interaction between genetic vulnerability and environmental factors (Rossignol et al., 2014).

Genetic epidemiological data suggest that personality traits similar to, but not as severe as those of ASD, are also heritable (Freitag, 2007). This group of "sub-threshold" features, which are believed to be milder manifestations of ASD (Dell'Osso et al., 2016), have been indicated as the broader autism phenotype (BAP) (Piven et al., 1997). BAP includes peculiar social, communication, and cognitive processes, strong persistent interests, and rigid and aloof personality traits (Gerdts and Bernier, 2011; Sucksmith et al., 2011). Interestingly, it was shown that BAP traits are more prevalent in first-degree relatives of individuals with ASD than in other groups, supporting the hypothesis that ASD have a significant genetic component (Bailey et al., 1998; Losh et al., 2008).

Kanner and Asperger were the first to report behavioral features in parents that were similar in kind to those of their autistic offspring. In particular, Kanner (1943) observed that both first and second degree relatives of children with "early infantile autism" had common characteristics of late speech, mild obsessiveness and uninterest in people. Similarly, Asperger (1944) described a group of parents of children with autism as withdrawn, pedantic, eccentric, and loners, who had problems relating to the outside world. Later studies have shown that the expression of ASD traits in relatives concerns not only behavioral traits, but also social cognition abilities (e.g., Baron-Cohen and Hammer, 1997), neurocognitive functioning (e.g., Koczat et al., 2002) or biological dimensions (e.g., Lainhart et al., 2006) and that these aspects could relate to or explain the clinical presentation of the BAP.

The biological dimension of ASD has been largely investigated in the last decades, thanks to the growing availability of brain imaging techniques and analysis methods for *in vivo* examination of brain structure and function. All in all, these studies reported abnormal neuroanatomical and neurofunctional profiles in individuals with ASD, suggesting a dysfunction of key brain areas underlying the core impairments of ASD (Amaral et al., 2008; Bellani et al., 2013a,b; Billeci et al., 2013; Calderoni et al., 2014). As such, there has been great interest in evaluating whether these neurological profiles also characterize the relatives of autistic probands. Indeed, should the same brain abnormalities of ASD patients be present in their direct relatives, their heritable origin would be strongly supported together with their role as endophenotypes of the disorder (Sullivan et al., 2003; Palmen et al., 2005a). This is particularly true for studies exploring correlations in parents. In fact, while sibling and twin studies are suitable for detecting brain abnormalities under genetic control, studies on parents allow mitigating the role of the shared (pre- and perinatal) environment (Sullivan et al., 2003; Palmen et al., 2005a). Thus, if brain abnormalities are observed in parents, they are more likely to be of heritable origin and consequently reflect endophenotypes of the disorder. To assess the strength of this hypothesis, we provide here a critical revision of all studies exploring the neuroanatomical and neurofunctional profile of parents of individuals with ASD.

METHODS

To find papers concerning neuroimaging studies in parents of individuals with ASD, a sensitive search strategy was conducted in two relevant article databases: PubMed and ScienceDirect. Search terms included database subject headings for the concepts of pervasive developmental disorders (e.g. "autism," "autism spectrum disorder," "pervasive developmental disorders"), neuroimaging (e.g., "MRI," "MRS," "EEG," "MEG") and parents ("parents," "relatives," "fathers," "mothers," "broader phenotype"). The reference lists of the retrieved papers were searched to identify additional articles.

Studies adhering to the following criteria were incorporated in this review: (1) parents of individuals with ASD were the population under study; (2) Magnetic Resonance Imaging (MRI), Magnetic Resonance Spectroscopy (MRS), Electroencephalography (EEG) and Magnetoencephalography (MEG) were used to investigate neurostructural and neurofunctional correlates in parents of individuals with ASD; (3) empirical findings about neural substrates were reported by the authors; (4) studies were published before March 30, 2016; (5) studies were published in an English peer-reviewed journal.

RESULTS

Thirteen published studies meeting the inclusion criteria were identified. **Table 1** summarizes the studies included in this review.

Structural MRI

Only three studies used sMRI to assess brain structure in parents of autistic probands.

Rojas et al. (2004) assessed total brain, hippocampus, and amygdala volumes in adults with ASD, parents of children with ASD (pASD) and healthy controls (HC), defined as adults with no personal or familial history of ASD. The left hyppocampus was found significantly larger in the ASD group in comparison to both the pASD and the HC group, and in the pASD group in comparison to the HC group. In the three groups, hyppocampus enlargement was more pronounced in males than in females. The right amygdala was smaller in the ASD group in comparison

TABLE 1 | Neuroanatomical and neurofunctional characteristics associated to the BAP in the parents of individuals with ASD.

Study (year)	Participants (nr, M/F, mean age ± SD in years)	BAP Questionnaires	Method	Results	Correlations with BAP scores and behavior
STRUCTURAL STUDIES					
Rojas et al., 2004	15 ASD (6/9) 30.3 ± 9.1	None	ROI manual tracing (HYP, AMY total brain)	ASD>pASD>HC left HYP	–
	17 pASD (15/2) 44.75 ± 4.4				
	17 HC (8/9) 43.6 ± 4.3			ASD<pASD, HC right AMY	
Palmen et al., 2005a	38 pASD (19/19) 50.3 ± 3.4	AQ	ROI semi-automatic tracing	No significant differences in volume	Positive correlations between AQ scores and intracranial and ventricular volume in pASD
	40 HC (20/20) 52.0 ± 4.1				
Peterson et al., 2006	23 pASD (8/15) 39.6 ± 6.0	None	VBM	pASD>HC in several GM regions (i.e. right precentral gyrus, right superior parietal lobule, and superior temporal gyri)	–
	23 HC (8/15) 38.3 ± 6.4			pASC<HC anterior portion of the left cerebellar hemisphere	
fMRI STUDIES					
Baron-Cohen et al., 2006	12 pASD (6/6) M: 39.1 ± 6.0	None	Visual Search Task (EFT) and Emotion Recognition Task (ET)	Females>Males>Fathers = Mothers in BA 19 in EFT task Females>Males>Fathers=Mothers in BA 21 e BA 44 in ET task	–
	F: 37.3 ± 5.9				
	12 HC (6/6) M: 23.1 ± 0.6				
	F: 21.6 ± 0.8				
Greimel et al., 2010	15 ASD (15/0) 14.9 ± 1.6	AQ	Empathy: other-task and self-task	pASD<pHC AMY other-task	No significant correlations between brain activity and AQ scores
				pASD<pHC FG other-task	
				ASD<HC FG other-task and self-task	
					Positive correlation between FG activation and GEM score in ASD
	15 HC (15/0) 15.0 ± 1.4			ASD<HC IFG self-task	
	11 pASD (11/0) 43.9 ± 5.1				
					Positive correlation between insula activation and BEES score in pASD and pHC
	9 pHC (9/0) 47.7 ± 5.3				
Wilson et al., 2013	16 pASD (6/10) 43.7 ± 8.1	AQ	Phonological processing: homophones vs pseudohomophone	pASD>HC pseudohomophone several regions (i.e. IC, STG, SMG, SMA, cerebellum)	Positive correlations between IFG activation and CTOPP scores in pASD and HC
	18 HC (6/12) 41.0 ± 8.1			pASD<HC left STG and left SMG phonological priming	
					Positive correlations between IC activation and CTOPP scores in pASD

(Continued)

TABLE 1 | Continued

Study (year)	Participants (nr, M/F, mean age ± SD in years)	BAP Questionnaires	Method	Results	Correlations with BAP scores and behavior
Yucel et al., 2014	40 pASD (20/20) 40.6 ± 0.7	BAPQ MPAS-R	Face processing	pASD>HC AMY	BAP+ >BAP−,HC LOC
				pASD>HC FG	
	15 BAP+ 40.9 ± 1.4			pASD<HC INS	
	25 BAP− 42.1 ± 1.28				
	20 HC (6/12) 39.8 ± 1.6				
MRS STUDIES					
Brown et al., 2013	13 ASD (9/4) 41.2 ± 6.9	AQ	Level of Glu, NAA, Cr in auditory cortex	ASD>HC Glu, NAA, Cr	Positive correlation, uncorrected for multiple comparisons, between left NAA and the SRS and left Glu and the AQ
		SRS		No differences between pASD and ASD or HC	
	15 pASD (11/4) 41.0 ± 8.1				
	15 HC (6/9) 41.1 ± 6.8				
EEG AND MEG STUDIES					
Dawson et al., 2005	21 pASD (10/11) 38.5 ± n.d.	None	Face processing ERPs	pASD<HC N170 right amplitude to faces	Positive correlation between N170 amplitude to faces and WMS Immediate and Delay task in HC
				pASD<HC N170 latency difference chairs-faces	
	21 HC (8/13) 38.9 ± n.d.				
Rojas et al., 2008	11 ASD (9/2) 42.6 ± 5.1	None	Auditory stimulation	pASD,ASD>HC induced tGBR	–
			Evoked, induced and total power tGBR	pASD,ASD<HC evoked tGBR, PLF, anterior-posterior asymmetry	
	16 pASD (9/7) 31.5 ± 9.3				
			PLF tGBR	No differences between pASD and ASD	
			Source Localization		
	16 HC (7/9) 43.1 ± 6.7				
Rojas et al., 2011	21 pASD (7/13) 43.7 ± 7.3	AQ	Auditory stimulation	pASD<HC total and evoked power, PLF ASSR	Negative correlation between ASSR PLF and AQ communication subscale
	20 HC (6/15) 43.8 ± 6.9	SRS	Evoked, induced and total power tGBR	No differences in tGBR	
			PLF tGBR		Negative correlation between tGBR and ASSR evoked power and SRS scores
			Evoked, induced and total power ASSR		
			PLF ASSR		
McFadden et al., 2012	23 pASD (8/15) 35.8 ± 10.0	None	Language auditory stimulation	pASD>HC evoked and total gamma SMG, LOC	Significant but different correlations between gamma or beta activity and language measures (expressive, receptive, figurative language and phonological processing) in pASD and HC

(Continued)

TABLE 1 | Continued

Study (year)	Participants (nr, M/F, mean age ± SD in years)	BAP Questionnaires	Method	Results	Correlations with BAP scores and behavior
			Evoked, induced and total power gamma and beta	pASD>HC evoked and total gamma SMG, LOC	
	28 HC (12/16) 38.7 ± 6.3				
			PLF gamma and beta	pASD>HC left lateralization	
Buard et al., 2013	12 ASD (?/?) 28.3 ± 13.3	None	Picture-naming task	ASD<HC high-gamma in right STG, evoked high-beta/low-gamma in left IFG and PLF beta in OCC	No significant correlation between MEG measures and language scores
	14 pASD (?/?) 37.9 ± 5.9				
			Evoked, induced and total power gamma and beta	pASD>HC high-gamma in left STG and evoked high-beta/low-gamma in left FG	
	35 HC (?/?) 34.2 ± 11.9				
			PLF gamma and beta	ASD>HC connectivity between IFG and FG and between STG and OCC in both gamma and beta band	
			Granger Causality		

BAP, Broader Autism Phenotype; ASD, Autism Spectrum Disorders; HC, healthy controls; pASD, parents of individuals with ASD; SD, standard deviation.

AQ, Autism Quotient; BEES, Balanced Emotional Empathy Scale; BAPQ, Broad Autism Phenotype Questionnaire; MPAS-R, Modified Personality Assessment Schedule —Revised; SRS, Social Responsiveness Scale.

ROI, region of interest; VBM, voxel-based morphometry; EFT, "Adult Embedded Figures" test; ET, "Reading the Mind in the Eyes" (or Eyes) test; Glu, glutamate; NAA, n-acetyl aspartate + n-acetyl aspartyl; Cr, phosphocreatine and creatine; ERPs, evoked response potentials; tGBR, transient gamma-band response; ASSR, auditory steady-state response; PLF, phase locking factor; CTOOP, Comprehensive Test of Phonological Processing; WMS, Wechsler Memory Scale.

HYP, hippocampus; AMY, amygdala; GM, gray matter; BA, Broadmann area; FG, fusiform gyrus; IFG, inferior frontal gyrus; IC, insular cortex, STG, superior temporal gyrus, SMG, supramarginal gyrus; SMA, supplementary motor area; INS, insula; LOC, lateral occipital cortex; OCC, occipital lobe.

to both the pASD and the HC group, while no significant differences were found between pASD and HC. No differences were detected in the total brain volume among the three groups.

Palmen et al. (2005a) compared couples of pASD with known increased brain volumes with HC couples for volume differences in total brain, cortical lobes, cerebral and cortical gray matter (GM) and white matter (WM), cerebellum, and ventricles. The overt aim of the study was to investigate whether the cerebral enlargement observed in ASD probands (Palmen et al., 2005b) extended also to parents, and in this case whether fathers and mothers were equally affected and if the same regions, as those of the autistic probands, were interested in the enlargement. The authors found no group or gender differences in any of the brain volumes, including the volume of intracranium, total brain, GM and WM of the cerebrum, frontal, temporal, parietal, and occipital GM and WM, cerebellum, third and lateral ventricle. Nevertheless, within the pASD group significant positive correlations were found between the Autism Quotient (AQ) (Baron-Cohen et al., 2001a) scores and intracranial and ventricular volumes, suggesting that autistic traits might be associated to an enlargement in these structures.

In the third study, Peterson et al. (2006) compared regional GM volume in pASD and in HC, reporting an increase in several GM regions in pASD (e.g., superior temporal gyri, inferior and middle frontal gyri, superior parietal lobule, anterior cingulate). A single large relative decrease was observed in the anterior portion of the left cerebellar hemisphere in pASD compared with HC. Males showed increased GM compared with females in both groups, while no between-group differences respect to gender emerged.

It is worth noting that in the three above mentioned studies three different procedures were applied for data analysis. Specifically, Rojas et al. (2004) used manual tracing for selecting hippocampus and amygdala, Palmen et al. (2005a) applied a semi-automatic procedure to obtain a segmentation of the brain in the structure of interest and Peterson et al. (2006) applied an approach based on voxel-based morphometry (VBM).

Magnetic Resonance Spectroscopy

Only one study used Magnetic Resonance Spectroscopy (MRS) to assess brain chemistry in parents of individuals with ASD (Brown et al., 2013). The aim of the study was therefore to determine whether the parents of ASD patients show higher levels of Glutamate (Hyperglutamate Theory) as compared to controls (Fatemi, 2008). The level of Glutamate (Glu), together with other potentially interesting molecules, including n-acetyl-aspartate (NAA), choline (Cho), myoinositol (mI) and creatine (Cr), was measured in the auditory cortex of subjects with ASD, pASD and HC. BAP traits in pASD were assessed by AQ and by Social Responsiveness Scale (SRS) (Constantino, 2002). While ASD subjects had increased levels of Glu compared with both pASD and HC, no differences were found between pASD and HC. Although not significantly different, the mean levels of the explored molecules in the pASD group were found to be intermediate between the HC and the ASD group. A significant positive correlation between left NAA and the SRS as well as between left Glu and the AQ was observed, but these correlations did not remain significant after multiple comparison correction. Both ASD and pASD did not exhibit sex differences in any of the MRS measures.

Functional MRI (fMRI)

The first study that evaluated the BAP in pASD through fMRI technique was performed by Baron-Cohen et al. (2006). In this investigation, the authors used the visual search task "Adult Embedded Figures Test" (EFT) (Witkin et al., 1962), and the advanced emotion recognition task test "Reading the Mind in the Eyes" (or Eyes) (ET) (Baron-Cohen et al., 2001b) in order to see if the parents showed the same atypical brain function observed in the autistic children (Baron-Cohen et al., 1999; Ring et al., 1999). They also preliminarily explored the influence of sex on brain functioning during these two tasks in a small sample of six males and six females. Results indicated that pASD showed atypical brain activity compared with HC; moreover sex differences in neural underpinnings of both tests were found. As far as the EFT task is concerned, pASD showed less activity in the visual cortex while a reduced activity in the mid-temporal gyrus, and the inferior frontal gyrus was observed using the ET task.

As regards sex differences in the EFT, female controls displayed increased activity in middle occipital gyrus than male controls while both mothers and fathers showed even less activity in this area than sex-matched controls. In the ET, female controls exhibited more activity in the left medial temporal gyrus and left dorsolateral prefrontal cortex than male controls, while both mothers and fathers of children with ASD showed a brain activity similar to that of male controls. Mothers and fathers had comparable brain activation. One of the region identified as atypically activated in the ET task (B44) overlaps with a region previously identified as involved in "theory of mind" (Frith and Frith, 1999).

Greimel et al. (2010) explored in ASD boys and in their fathers (pASD) aspects related to the social domain of ASD, and in particular to the mechanism of empathy. Two aspects of empathy were evaluated related to (1) inferring how another person feels (other-task), and (2) responding appropriately to emotions of others (self-task). Comparison groups consist of age-matched typically developing boys (HC) and their fathers (pHC). Brain activation was analyzed in three predefined ROIs, the fusiform gyrus (FG), the inferior frontal gyrus (IFG) and the AMY and correlations with behavioral traits were evaluated. Empathic abilities were assessed by the Griffith Empathy Measure (GEM) in ASD and by the Balanced Emotional Empathy Scale (BEES) in pASD.

Despite a normal performance in reference to the number of correct/incorrect responses and even a faster response than pHC, pASD showed an abnormal brain activation. Specifically, both boys with ASD and their fathers obtained reduced anterior FG activation during the other-task, and boys with ASD additionally exhibited reduced FG activation during the self-task compared to HC. Interestingly, the activation within the FG occurred outside the well-known fusiform face area leading to exclude that differences of activation detected in this area were ascribable to a deficit in face processing. This hypothesis was corroborated also by the recording of the gaze during the fMRI task that showed an intact gaze pattern in scanning faces both in the adolescents with ASD and in their fathers. A diminished activation was also found in AMY in fathers of boys with ASD compared to control fathers when inferring others' emotions from weak cues, while in the ASD group this result was only obtained at an uncorrected threshold. The author hypothesized that fathers activated strategies to compensate for FG and AMY dysfunction. An involvement of the mirror neuron system (MNS) was also observed mainly in the ASD adolescents who showed a reduced activation of the IFG during the self-task. In both pASD and ASD groups a significant correlation between behavioral measures of empathy and brain activation was detected: specifically, in the ASD group the correlation was significant with activation of FG while in the pASD group with activation of the insula. However, no significant correlation was found between brain activity and AQ scores in pASD.

Together with social impairments, language dysfunction is another well-known hallmark of ASD. Extending the boundaries, language ability, specifically phonological processing ability, has been proposed to be one of six candidate BAP traits (Dawson et al., 2002).

Wilson et al. (2013) explored the neural correlates of phonological processing ability in a group of parents of children with ASD and in a group of age-matched controls. The task proposed consisted of prime-target word pairs differing in terms of their phonological relatedness including both word-word homophone and pseudoword-word pseudohomophone. Brain activation was also correlated with a behavioral measure of phonological processing ability obtained by the non-word repetition subtest of the Comprehensive Test of Phonological Processing (CTOPP) (Wagner et al., 1999).

Despite non-significant differences in terms of task performances and CTOPP scores and low AQ scores, pASD showed significantly higher hemodynamic responses than controls for pseudohomophone compared with homophone priming. Several cortical regions were involved in this abnormal activation, including the left anterior insular cortex (IC), the bilateral cerebellum and thalamus, left postcentral gyrus, precentral gyrus, and supplementary motor area (SMA), right superior temporal gyrus (STG) and supramarginal gyrus (SMG): interestingly, most of these regions had been previously implicated in language processing (Baddeley, 1992; Ackermann and Riecker, 2004; Hickok and Poeppel, 2007; Ghosh et al.,

2008). Significant positive correlations were also observed between greater hemodynamic response and CTOPP in right STG, left IFG and IC in pASD and in several regions in controls (i.e. bilateral occipital gyrus, parietal lobule, postcentral gyrus, lingual gyrus, and IFG).

Moreover, parents of boys with ASD exhibited increased hemodynamic suppression in response to phonological priming compared with controls in several cortical regions including both the left lateralized STG and SMG. Both groups expressed a significant left lateralization in the ROI selected for the analysis.

The more recent fMRI study conducted in parents of individuals with ASD investigated neural substrates of face processing (Yucel et al., 2014). This is the only study which subset the parents on BAP traits. Specifically, in order to investigate the characteristics of a specific endophenotype linked to social behavior, the parents were classified in a group having "aloof personality" (BAP+) and a group having "non-aloof personality" (BAP−). The classification was based on the Broad Autism Phenotype Questionnaire (BAPQ) and the Modified Personality Assessment Schedule—Revised (MPAS-R) specifically designed to determine the presence or absence of "aloof personality." Using two face activation paradigms, one based on face memory and the other based on emotional matching, the authors found that pASD had a higher activation of AMY and FG and a lower activation of right insula compared with HC, while no significant difference in activation was observed between BAP+ and BAP− in these regions. Conversely, BAP+ and BAP− parents significantly differ in terms of activation of the lateral occipital cortex (LOC). Indeed, BAP+ parents showed a bilateral hyper-activation in the LOC compared with both BAP− and HC.

Neurophysiology (Electroencephalography and Magnetoencephalography)

The first electrophysiological study in pASD was performed by Dawson et al. (2005) who evaluated event-related brain potentials to face and non-face stimuli. Specifically, upright and inverted faces or chairs were presented to a group of pASD and HC and N170 amplitude and latency was measured at the inferior right and left posterior temporal regions. While HC showed the typical pattern of higher right than left N170 amplitude in response to faces (Bentin et al., 1996), pASD exhibited reduced right N170 amplitude resulting in bilaterally distributed brain activity to faces. In addition, HC had the expected faster N170 response to upright faces compared to upright chairs (Itier et al., 2006), while pASD showed no differences in latency in response to the two types of stimuli. Abnormalities in brain activity in pASD compared to controls were also associated to lower performances in behavioral tests (face recognition and object memory).

Subsequent studies explored brain activity in pASD in response to different stimuli using magnetoencephalography (MEG), focusing on high-frequency bands.

First, Rojas et al. (2008) investigated both evoked and induced components of the *transient gamma-band response (tGBR)*, elicited by auditory stimulation in subjects with ASD, in pASD and in a comparison group of healthy subjects. Source localization of the data was performed on MRI data acquired on the subjects enrolled in the study (Peterson et al., 2006). In addition to evoked and induced power, the authors also computed the *phase locking factor (PLF)* as a measure of phase consistency across trials.

Both pASD and the ASD groups showed bilaterally higher induced tGBR response compared with controls, while evoked tGBR was found bilaterally reduced in the same comparison. The PLF was also bilaterally reduced in both the pASD and the ASD group compared with HC. Moreover, both the pASD and the ASD group had a reduced anterior-posterior asymmetry of the magnetic sources compared with controls. In this study, no differences between pASD and ASD were found: such findings could be attributable to the low statistical power, but could also suggest that parents had the familial liability relevant to gamma-band disturbances.

Later, Rojas et al. (2011) extended the results of their previous work analyzing not only the tGBR component of gamma-band power, but also the *auditory steady-state response (ASSR)*, in response to auditory stimulation. A group of pASD was compared with a control group of HC. In this study, authors also correlated MEG results with scores indicative of BAP−traits (AQ and SRS). The group of pASD exhibited reduced evoked power, total power (left hemisphere) and PLF (left hemisphere) of the ASSR component relative to the HC group. However, the authors were not able to replicate their previous findings relative to tGBR (Rojas et al., 2008), as they did not found any significant differences between pASD and HC.

Interestingly, an inverse correlation between ASSR PLF and the AQ communication subscale was found in pASD, confirming an association of gamma-band activity to perception of speech sounds and lexicality (Kaiser, 2004; Basirat et al., 2008). An inverse correlation was also observed in pASD between SRS scores and tGBR and ASSR gamma-band evoked power suggesting an indirect relationship between auditory gamma-band dysfunction and social traits of ASD.

In another investigation (McFadden et al., 2012), gamma-band response was analyzed in pASD and in HC in response to auditory language stimuli, rather than to simple auditory stimuli. In this contest, beta band activity was also examined since it has been suggested to be involved in language processing (Shahin et al., 2009). While in the previous two investigations (Rojas et al., 2008, 2011) pASD showed decreased evoked gamma-band response compared with HC, in this study pASD exhibited increased evoked power. In addition, there was an increase in pASD of total gamma power compared with controls. Source localization analysis showed that this increase was mainly localized in the SMG, in the lateral occipital cortex (LOC), and in the FG.

Beta evoked activity was also found increased in pASD compared with controls mainly in SMG, but also in LOC and FFG possibly reflecting differences in cognitive function during language processing. While in both groups the task generally elicited left lateralized responses, pASD showed greater left lateralization than controls, confirming also in this case an atypical lateralization of the brain in pASD. Significant but different correlations were found between gamma or beta band activity and language measures.

Gamma and beta band responses were also assessed in pASD compared with HC during a picture-naming task (Buard et al., 2013). Subjects were instructed to sub-vocalize (to reduce motion artifacts) the name of the object depicted in the image they were shown. Due to their involvement in language function and in visual processing, FG, STG, IFG and occipital lobe (OCC) were considered as the regions of interest. As in the three previous studies (Rojas et al., 2008, 2011; McFadden et al., 2012), evoked and induced power together with PLF were computed. In addition, Granger causality function, as a measure of effective connectivity among the activated regions, was measured.

Interestingly, the ASD group and the pASD showed different patterns of activation both in gamma and beta bands. While the ASD group exhibited reduced evoked high-gamma activity in the right STG, increased evoked high-beta/low-gamma in the left IFG and reduced PLF beta in the OCC, the pASD group showed increased evoked high-gamma in the left STG and evoked high-beta/low-gamma in the left FG.

Functional connectivity abnormalities were only observed in the ASD group compared with the control group: specifically, over-connectivity was found in the left hemisphere between IFG and FG and between STG and OCC in both gamma and beta band. This altered functional connectivity from anterior to posterior language and visual areas may partially explain the impaired activation of these regions in the ASD group, ascribable to alterations in long-range neural synchronization.

DISCUSSION

The main leading hypothesis tested in this review is that pASD present with a number of neuroanatomical and neurofunctional characteristics observed in individuals with ASD, but to a lesser extent. This hypothesis is supported by previous studies demonstrating intermediate levels of biochemical, immunological, morphological and neuropsychological endophenotypes/biomarkers in pASD (Ruggeri et al., 2014).

In some cases, the results of the studies, using different methodological approaches, have supported the primary hypothesis, while in other cases different results have emerged.

Are pASD Different from HC?

All of the 13 reviewed studies compared the pASD with a sample of HC.

(a) No differences in total brain volumes between pASD and controls were found in any of the three sMRI studies (Rojas et al., 2004; Palmen et al., 2005a; Peterson et al., 2006). This finding is not surprising when considering that even within the ASD population many/most adults, unlike children, do not differ from controls in overall brain volume. Indeed, there is increasing evidence that brain growth trajectory is abnormal in subjects with ASD and that they have differences in the timing of both initiation and cessation of overall brain growth, resulting in larger brain volumes during childhood followed by later normalization (Courchesne et al., 2001, 2003; Dawson et al., 2007).

(b) More inconsistent findings were reported for the single brain structures. While Palmen et al. (2005a) found no differences between pASD and HC groups in any of the volumes considered, including cortical lobes, cerebral GM and WM, cerebellum, and ventricles, increased volumes were found in the left hippocampus (Rojas et al., 2004) or in a number of GM regions (Peterson et al., 2006). The different approach in analyzing brain regions (global brain structures—Palmen et al., 2005a—vs. focal structures—Rojas et al., 2004—vs. whole brain approach—Peterson et al., 2006) prevents a comparison among studies. Overall, the inconsistency of these results reflects that of the studies on subjects with ASD (Ameis and Catani, 2015). Methodological differences between investigations and the potential for heterogeneity of underlying brain alterations in ASD likely contribute to the inconsistency of these results.

(c) Functional studies showed some atypicalities in face processing, empathy and language/auditory processing in pASD compared with HC.

Face

The study by Dawson et al. (2005) support the social motivation impairment showing an abnormal N170 response to faces both in its latency and amplitude with a pattern resembling that observed for subject with ASD (Apicella et al., 2013). Yucel et al. (2014) observed an increased activation in pASD compared with controls during an emotion recognition task in regions that are specialized for face processing, i.e., the fusiform gyrus and the amygdala.

Empathy

An opposite pattern was found by Greimel et al. (2010) who explored empathy during the presentation of emotional stimuli in pASD and found a decreased activation in the same regions. It is possible that the two different types of task lead to different brain activations. Moreover, the different results could be explained by the fact that the sample of Greimel study is composed of males only who are generally less empathic than females (Klein and Hodges, 2001), and therefore process emotion to a lesser extent than females. In addition it is worth noting that Yucel et al. (2014) found a decreased activation of the insula, which is known to be linked to empathic abilities (Carr et al., 2003) as also suggested by the positive correlation found in Greimel et al. (2010) between insula activation and the BEES. Emotion recognition impairments in pASD also emerged from the study of Baron-Cohen et al. (2006) who observed a decreased activation in the left IFG of pASD compared with controls during an emotion recognition test.

Language

Wilson et al. (2013) showed that pASD compared with HC exhibit a greater hemodynamic response to pseudohomophones respect to homophones and an enhanced hemodynamic suppression in response to phonological priming. Interestingly, Peterson et al. (2006) observed both cerebellar enhancements and reductions, although in different cerebellar regions than those differently activated in the phonological task, and larger left STG and SMG GM volumes in pASD relative to HC. These regions are known to be involved in language and phonological processing (Turkeltaub and Coslett, 2010) and to be functionally impaired in ASD (Mostofsky et al., 2009).

Abnormalities associated to language processing have been shown also by MEG studies, mainly associated to gamma-band response. In particular, gamma-band deficit, which has been suggested as a biomarker of ASD (Jamal et al., 2013; Rojas and Wilson, 2014), exists also in pASD, and abnormalities seem to extend also to the beta band. In ASD individuals, dysfunctional gamma-band response has been associated with GABAergic inhibitory deficits (Hussman, 2001; Fatemi et al., 2009). Conversely, multiple evidences suggest an increased neuronal excitability in ASD, involving a higher than normal serum glutamate (Shinohe et al., 2006), and increased metabotropic glutamate receptor expression (Fatemi et al., 2011). Overall, these evidences have been summarized in the excitation/inhibition imbalance (EI) theory of ASD (Rubenstein and Merzenich, 2003).

Rojas et al. (2008, 2011) explored gamma band response to auditory stimulation in pASD. Induced response has been found increased in pASD (Rojas et al., 2008), while evoked response and PLF were decreased (Rojas et al., 2011) compared with HC in response to simple auditory stimulus. However, more complex stimuli activate a different pattern as observed in subsequent investigations (McFadden et al., 2012; Buard et al., 2013). In both these studies, pASD showed an increased evoked gamma band response compared with HC, which extended also to beta band in Buard et al. (2013). The different findings among these studies might be explained by the different level of complexity of the tasks: specifically, subjects were requested to be engaged in higher order cognitive processes including language and sustained attention (McFadden et al., 2012; Buard et al., 2013), or only passive listening to a simple auditory stimulus was required (Rojas et al., 2008, 2011).

The studies exploring auditory/language processing suggest that when pASD are involved in higher cognitive function they activate a higher brain response compared to that of controls, possibly as a compensatory mechanism in absence of behavioral impairment. In the study by Wilson et al. (2013) the greater hemodynamic responses in the parent group might reflect the heavier demands requested by the pseudohomophone primes on phonological recoding and working memory skills compared with homophone primes, and it can be interpreted as an index of more effortful processing during this task. Analogously, in the studies by McFadden et al. (2012) and Buard et al. (2013) the increase in gamma and/or beta could reflect a greater cognitive effort in phonology and receptive language tasks, which determine an abnormal synchronous activation of language networks (Jerbi et al., 2009).

It is worth noting that functional abnormalities at a neural level in pASD are not always associated to behavioral impairments. For example Greimel et al. (2010) found a non-compromised empathic ability in an emotion recognition task while Wilson et al. (2013) found no difference in terms of phonological processing (CTOPP scores) between pASD and HC. Conversely in the study by Dawson et al. (2005) the authors found that neurofunctional abnormalities and neuropsychological performances in pASD were associated, suggesting that pASD are more compromised at a neural level than at a behavioral level.

How Are Parents of Individuals with ASD Compared to Other Individuals with ASD?

Only five of the 13 studies addressed the question of the overlap between pASD and other individuals with ASD (Rojas et al., 2004, 2008; Greimel et al., 2010; Brown et al., 2013; Buard et al., 2013). All reported similarities in some aspects of brain structure and function consistent with the hypothesis of a continuum of some ASD features expressed in pASD, with milder but qualitatively similar brain alterations to those detected in ASD.

In particular, structural (Rojas et al., 2004) and spectroscopy (Brown et al., 2013) studies revealed a brain endophenotype in pASD intermediate between ASD patients and HC. Specifically, Rojas et al. (2004) found that hippocampus enlargement interested also pASD, but to a lesser extent than ASD individuals. Vice-versa, the amygdala was smaller in ASD patients compared to pASD. Brown et al. (2013) showed that the mean levels of the explored molecules in the parent group were intermediate between ASD individuals and HC. However, these findings were not statistically significant possibly due to the small sample size and/or to the low scores at the AQ and the SRS of the pASD subjects.

The fMRI study exploring the neural correlates of empathy (Greimel et al., 2010) reported a reduced activation in the right anterior fusiform gyrus in both adolescents with ASD and pASD compared to age and IQ matched controls. Finally, using EEG a reduced early auditory gamma-band response shared by both adults with ASD and pASD in comparison to HC was detected (Rojas et al., 2008).

Several other patterns of brain activity were not shared by pASD and ASD patients, potentially suggesting a lesser role of these aspects as endophenotypes of the disorder. For example, in the same fMRI study exploring empathy (Greimel et al., 2010), reduced amygdala activity was found in pASD but not in ASD. Also, using MEG during a picture naming task, Buard et al. (2013) found that gamma-band activity showed opposite profiles in pASD and in ASD subjects relative to controls, being increased in the former and reduced in the latter.

All in all, the limited number of studies addressing this question does not allow for definitive conclusions although it seems to be conceivable that some aspects of brain structure and function are shared by pASD and ASD patients, supporting their possible role as endophenotype of the disorder.

How Are Parents of Individuals with ASD Compared to Their Probands?

The study by Greimel et al. (2010) was the only one that enrolled both the probands and their fathers to explore the transmission of neural substrates. The results confirmed the primary hypothesis of a neurofunctional pattern in pASD intermediate between HC and ASD. In particular, pASD showed an abnormal neural activation during the other-task similar to their probands, expressed by a reduced hemodynamic response in FG – a tempo-occipital brain region primarily involved in face processing-. Conversely, unlike their probands, pASD showed a normal response during the self-task. It is of interest that a reduced activation of regions previously associated to the MNS, namely IFG, was found in ASD probands but not in their fathers. These results support the hypothesis that FG dysfunction in ASD is genetically influenced (Polk et al., 2007).

Are the Neurostructural and Neurofunctional Alterations Reported in Parents of Individuals with ASD Specifically Related to BAP Features?

Six of the reviewed studies (Palmen et al., 2005a; Greimel et al., 2010; Rojas et al., 2011; Brown et al., 2013; Wilson et al., 2013; Yucel et al., 2014) assessed the BAP characteristics of the pASD applying instruments such as the AQ, the BAPQ or the SRS. Significant correlations between scores at the questionnaires and the brain structural and functional indexes were found in almost all these studies. In particular, Palmen et al. (2005a) found a significant positive correlation between AQ scores and intracranial and ventricular volume in pASD, while Brown et al. (2013) found a significant, uncorrected, positive correlation between left NAA and the SRS and left Glu and the AQ. Both studies did not report significant differences in pASD compared to HC (Palmen et al., 2005a; Brown et al., 2013); however, the fact that pASD scored very low at questionnaires assessing BAP could represent a possible bias leading to negative findings. Interestingly, in both studies a positive correlation between neurostructural results and BAP features was found, suggesting that enlarged brain volume or increased Glu level respectively could still be associated to the autistic phenotype.

Notably, Wilson et al. (2013) found significant differences in brain activation during a language task in the pASD sample, despite low scores at the AQ. This result could suggest that deficits in neural substrates of language processing could be associated with autistic traits, confirming it as one of the core impairment of ASD.

This is confirmed by the investigation of Rojas et al. (2011) in which a negative correlation between ASSR PLF and AQ communication subscale as well as between SRS scores and tGBR/ASSR evoked power was observed. ASSR PLF and evoked power were found decreased in pASD compared to HC: therefore, it can be argued that deficits in auditory gamma band are correlated to problems in communications (AQ) and socials skills (SRS). Despite the authors did not find significant differences regarding tGBR, a significant correlation between SRS scores and this feature was observed in pASD suggesting a possible association with the autistic phenotype, as proposed in their previous study (Rojas et al., 2008).

Greimel et al. (2010) did not find any significant correlation between brain activation and AQ in pASD, while a brain-behavior relationship was detected with empathic scores (BEES).

The paper by Yucel et al. (2014) was the only one subgrouping the parent sample according to BAP traits. Interestingly, the authors observed that while an atypical activation of face processing regions was common to both groups of parents, BAP+, but not BAP− parents showed an hyper-activation of lateral occipital cortex. The hyper-activation of LOC in BAP+ could reflect an aberrant "compensatory" activation of these regions in BAP+ parents. These data suggest that while neural circuitry abnormalities in the regions specific for face processing are necessary for the occurrence of the BAP, they are not sufficient to result in autism-related social behavior.

Overall, these findings suggest a possible link between the subclinical dimension of BAP and neurobiological expression of brain function and structure.

Does Gender Influence Neurostructural and Neurofunctional Results in Parents of Individuals with ASD?

Previous studies have reported sex differences in brain in healthy populations and these processes have shown to differ in people with ASD. In particular, sexual dimorphism in brain regions that are crucial to language and social abilities has been proposed (Lai et al., 2013; Retico et al., 2016).

Understanding cerebral gender differences is important, among other reasons, to explain the increased vulnerability of males to ASD. Few studies have explored gender differences in pASD in order to investigate the heritability of sex differences in brain structures and function.

From a structural point of view, it was observed that males, both pASD and HC had increased total, hippocampal and amygdala volumes (Rojas et al., 2004), as well as GM (Peterson et al., 2006) compared to pASD and HC females, but this difference did not contribute to between-groups differences. Brown et al. (2013) investigated gender differences in MRS measures both in ASD and pASD and did not find any differences as well. Conversely, Baron-Cohen et al. (2006) found significant differences in brain function related to gender. In particular, their results support the hypothesis of the "Extreme Male Brain Theory" of ASD, according to which "the male brain is programmed to systemize and the female brain to empathize" (Benenson, 2003). Indeed, both mothers and fathers showed an activation even lower than that of male controls in regions were female controls had a higher activity. The results of this study may suggest a genetic component of the hyper-masculinization of the brain.

Do Parents of Individuals with ASD Express an Atypical Lateralization of the Brain?

In typical development, lateralization of brain function underlies specialized cognitive and behavioral processes (Mesulam, 1990). In particular, several pieces of evidence exist about a left lateralization in language regions (Knecht et al., 2000), and right lateralization in attentional regions (Corbetta and Shulman, 2011) in the majority of individuals with typical development. Atypical lateralization in brain structure and function has been associated with ASD (Conti et al., 2016); more specifically, reduced left lateralization or reversed lateralization of brain structure and function in core language regions and in the WM tracts that connect them has been shown in ASD using different techniques (Kleinhans et al., 2008; Lange et al., 2010; Seery et al., 2013).

Whether the pattern of lateralization related to language processing observed in subjects with ASD is the same in their parents is not clear from the reviewed studies.

In Wilson et al. (2013), hemispheric lateralization analysis did not indicate greater right hemispheric language dominance in the pASD: in fact, both pASD and HC showed left lateralization across the selected ROIs. McFadden et al. (2012) found that pASD showed even an increased left lateralization than controls. Rojas et al. (2011) showed that differences in ASSR response in pASD was restricted to the left hemisphere, however across groups the tGBR and ASSR evoked power was increased in the right hemisphere. Rojas et al. (2008) highlighted a peculiar pattern of asymmetric activation in control subjects in which the activation of the right hemisphere was anterior to that of the left hemisphere. This pattern was not observed in ASD and was mild in pASD.

Yucel et al. (2014), observed in the face processing task a significant effect of hemisphere. Specifically, FG showed greater activation in right than left hemisphere in BAP+ compared with BAP− and HC, and right amygdala was more active than left in BAP+ compared with BAP−. Since right lateralization was observed specifically in BAP+ pASD, a compensatory mechanism of activation in these regions could be hypothesized for this subgroup of parents. Additional support for this interpretation can be found in the investigation of Rojas et al. (2004) on the basis of which pASD has reduced right amygdala volume compared with HC: it may be possible that to compensate the reduction of volume an abnormal high activation is required.

CONCLUSIONS AND FUTURE DIRECTIONS

Although, results are often unclear and contradictory, some general considerations can be done:

(i) pASD differ from HC both at a structural and functional level and these neural abnormalities are not always associated with behavioral impairments;
(ii) The neural pattern in pASD seems to be intermediate between HC and ASD probands;
(iii) More atypicalities in neural patterns of pASD seem to be associated with higher autistic traits;
(iv) The pattern of neural correlates in pASD resembles that of adult individuals with ASD or it is specific to pASD, possibly due to a compensatory mechanism;
(v) The gender might influence the results.

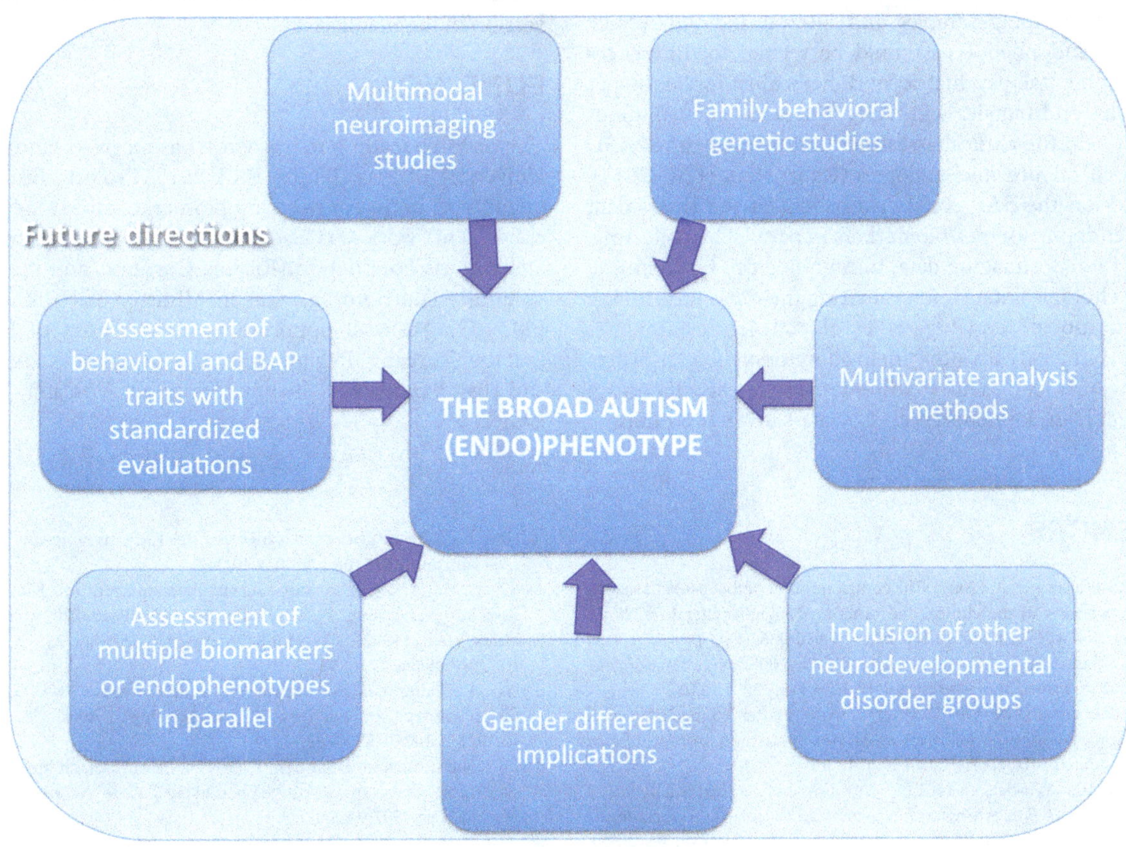

FIGURE 1 | Recommendations for future studies assessing the broader autism (endo)phenotype.

In conclusion, our review reports findings that are often non-replicated, preventing a univocal interpretation of the results.

In order to elucidate the brain structural and functional underpinnings in pASD and their potential role as endophenotype, several aspects should be considered when planning future studies (**Figure 1**).

First, neuroimaging studies should be ideally include a group of pASD and HC with their ASD and non-ASD probands, respectively. Second, a family-behavioral genetic design should be adopted in order to analyze the behavioral features as well as the genetics not only of the probands, but also of the parents and the siblings, and to link these data to underlying brain structure and function. Third, behavioral assessment as well as BAP traits evaluation should be performed using standardized questionnaires and tests in order to subgroups the probands and their relatives according to the obtained scores and to investigate a possible correlation between brain abnormalities and BAP traits and/or behavioral impairments. Fourth, multimodal imaging techniques could also be adopted to better elucidate brain correlates of BAP. For example, the integration of neuroimaging data with neurophysiological signals (EEG and MEG) offers advantages of both high spatial and temporal resolution (Ingalhalikar et al., 2012; Berman et al., 2016). The application of these methods also in pASD probands could provide new insights into the endophenotype of ASD. Fifth, since gender can influence neural substrates, this factor needs to be carefully taken into account when grouping samples and interpreting the results. Indeed, brain endophenotypes could be related to differences in the developmental, psychiatric, and medical endophenotypes between males and females with ASD. These research findings may in turn help the clinical assessment and treatment of ASD and the search for possible etiologies (Rubenstein et al., 2015). Sixth, studies on the BAP could also benefit of the assessment of multiple endophenotypes/biomarkers in parallel by collecting, in addition to neuroimaging data, immunological, biochemical, or neuropsychological data and evaluating the cross talk among the different modalities (Ruggeri et al., 2014). Seventh, the inclusion of samples with other neurodevelopmental disorders rather than ASD can help to disentangle the specific from the non-specific endophenotypes associated to each condition. Indeed brain alterations have been found in relatives of probands with Attention Deficit/Hyperactivity Disorder—ADHD—(Casey et al., 2007; Hale et al., 2010; Poissant et al., 2014; Rapin et al., 2014), language impairments (Plante, 1991; Ors et al., 2002) and learning or intellectual disabilities (Mannerkoski et al., 2009). In particular, previous literature suggests that there are cognitive and brain endophenotypes common to ASD and ADHD and that studying the similarities and differences between these two disorders might be a powerful research approach to increase our understanding of their pathophysiology (Rommelse et al., 2011). Finally the use of multivariate approaches, based for example on machine learning (Retico et al., 2014; Segovia et al., 2014), can provide more insightful results than the traditional statistical analysis methods.

In conclusion, these types of implementations may help to better elucidate the hereditary mechanisms involved in the various clinical dimension of ASD.

AUTHOR CONTRIBUTIONS

LB performed the literature-search, analyzed the data and drafted the paper, SC, EC made substantial contribution in the literature analysis and in writing the paper, CG, CC collaborated during the literature analysis, LD, GC participated in the design of the paper and supervised the wiring, FM, AG made substantial contributions to the conception of the review, and revisited the manuscript critically. All the authors read and approved the final version of the manuscript.

FUNDING

The research leading to this work has received funding from the University of Pisa, Bando PRA 2015, Project "Broader autism phenotype: brain connectivity biomarkers from the adult to the child." This work was also supported by grant from the IRCCS Stella Maris Foundation (Ricerca Corrente, and the "5 × 1000" voluntary contributions, Italian Ministry of Health to SC, GC, FM, AG). SC was supported by the Ministry of Health, Italy and by Tuscany Region with the grant "GR-2010-2317873," and by Bando FAS Salute Sviluppo Toscana -ARIANNA Project.

REFERENCES

Ackermann, H., and Riecker, A. (2004). The contribution(s) of the insula to speech production: a review of the clinical and functional imaging literature. *Brain Struct. Funct.* 214, 419–433. doi: 10.1007/s00429-010-0257-x

Amaral, D. G., Schumann, C. M., and Nordahl, C. W. (2008). Neuroanatomy of autism. *Trends Neurosci.* 31, 137–145. doi: 10.1016/j.tins.2007.12.005

Ameis, S. H., and Catani, M. (2015). Altered white matter connectivity as a neural substrate for social impairment in Autism Spectrum Disorder. *Cortex* 62, 158–181. doi: 10.1016/j.cortex.2014.10.014

American Psychiatric Association, (2013). *Diagnostic and Statistical Manual of Mental Disorders, 5th Edn.* Arlington, TX: American Psychiatric Association.

Apicella, F., Sicca, F., Federico, R. R., Campatelli, G., and Muratori, F. (2013). Fusiform gyrus responses to neutral and emotional faces in children with autism spectrum disorders: a high density ERP study. *Behav. Brain Res.* 251, 155–162. doi: 10.1016/j.bbr.2012.10.040

Asperger, H. (1944). Die autistischen Psychopathen im Kindersalter. *Arch. Psychiatr. Nervenkr.* 117, 76–136. doi: 10.1007/BF01837709

Baddeley, A. (1992). Working memory. *Science* 255, 556–559. doi: 10.1126/science.1736359

Bailey, A., Palferman, S., Heavey, L., and Couteur, A. L. (1998). Autism: the phenotype in relatives. *J. Autism Dev. Disord.* 28, 369–392. doi: 10.1023/A:1026048320785

Baron-Cohen, S., and Hammer, J. (1997). Parents of children with asperger syndrome: what is the cognitive phenotype? *J. Cogn. Neurosci.* 9, 548–554. doi: 10.1162/jocn.1997.9.4.548

Baron-Cohen, S., Ring, H., Wheelwright, S., Bullmore, E. T., Brammer, M. J., Simmons, A. C., et al. (1999). Social intelligence in the normal and autistic brain: an fMRI study. *Eur. J. Neurosci.* 11, 1891–1898. doi: 10.1046/j.1460-9568.1999.00621.x

Baron-Cohen, S., Ring, H., Wheelwright, S., Williams, S., Brammer, M., and Bullmore, E. (2006). fMRI of parents of children with Asperger Syndrome: a pilot study. *Brain Cogn.* 61, 122–130. doi: 10.1016/j.bandc.2005.12.011

Baron-Cohen, S., Wheelwright, S., Hill, J., Raste, Y., and Plumb, I. (2001b). The "Reading the Mind in the eyes" test revised version: a study with normal adults, and adults with Asperger Syndrome or High-Functioning autism. *J. Child Psychol. Psychiatry* 42, 241–252. doi: 10.1111/1469-7610.00715

Baron-Cohen, S., Wheelwright, S., Skinner, R., Martin, J., and Clubley, E. (2001a). The Autism-Spectrum Quotient (AQ): evidence from Asperger Syndrome/high-functioning autism, males and females, scientists and mathematicians. *J. Autism Dev. Disord.* 31, 5–17. doi: 10.1023/A:1005653411471

Basirat, A., Sato, M., Schwartz, J., Kahane, P., and Lachaux, J. (2008). Parieto-frontal gamma band activity during the perceptual emergence of speech forms. *Neuroimage* 42, 404–413. doi: 10.1016/j.neuroimage.2008.03.063

Bellani, M., Calderoni, S., Muratori, F., and Brambilla, P. (2013a). Brain anatomy of autism spectrum disorders I. Focus on corpus callosum. *Epidemiol. Psychiatr. Sci.* 22, 217–221. doi: 10.1017/S2045796013000139

Bellani, M., Calderoni, S., Muratori, F., and Brambilla, P. (2013b). Brain anatomy of autism spectrum disorders II. Focus on amygdala. *Epidemiol. Psychiatr. Sci.* 22, 309–312. doi: 10.1017/S2045796013000346

Benenson, J. F. (2003). Sex on the brain. *Nature* 424, 132–133. doi: 10.1038/424132b

Bentin, S., Allison, T., Puce, A., Perez, E., and McCarthy, G. (1996). Electrophysiological studies of face perception in humans. *J. Cogn. Neurosci.* 8, 551–565. doi: 10.1162/jocn.1996.8.6.551

Berman, J. I., Edgar, J. C., Blaskey, L., Kuschner, E. S., Levy, S. E., Ku, M., et al. (2016). Multimodal diffusion-MRI and MEG assessment of auditory and language system development in autism spectrum disorder. *Front. Neuroanat.* 10:30. doi: 10.3389/fnana.2016.00030

Billeci, L., Sicca, F., Maharatna, K., Apicella, F., Narzisi, A., Campatelli, G., et al. (2013). On the application of quantitative EEG for characterizing autistic brain: a systematic review. *Front. Hum. Neurosci.* 7:442. doi: 10.3389/fnhum.2013.00442

Brown, M. S., Singel, D., Hepburn, S., and Rojas, D. C. (2013). Increased glutamate concentration in the auditory cortex of persons with autism and first-degree relatives: a 1H-MRS study. *Autism Res.* 6, 1–10. doi: 10.1002/aur.1260

Buard, I., Rogers, S. J., Hepburn, S., Kronberg, E., and Rojas, D. C. (2013). Altered oscillation patterns and connectivity during picture naming in autism. *Front. Hum. Neurosci.* 7:742. doi: 10.3389/fnhum.2013.00742

Calderoni, S., Bellani, M., Hardan, A. Y., Muratori, F., and Brambilla, P. (2014). Basal ganglia and restricted and repetitive behaviours in Autism Spectrum Disorders: current status and future perspectives. *Epidemiol. Psychiatr. Sci.* 23, 235–238. doi: 10.1017/S2045796014000171

Carr, L., Iacoboni, M., Dubeau, M. C., Mazziotta, J. C., and Lenzi, G. L. (2003). Neural mechanisms of empathy in humans: a relay from neural systems for imitation to limbic areas. *Proc. Natl. Acad. Sci. U.S.A.* 100, 5497–5502. doi: 10.1073/pnas.0935845100

Casey, B. J., Epstein, J. N., Buhle, J., Liston, C., Davidson, M. C., Tonev, S. T., et al. (2007). Frontostriatal connectivity and its role in cognitive control in parent-child dyads with ADHD. *Am. J. Psychiatry* 164, 1729–1736. doi: 10.1176/appi.ajp.2007.06101754

Constantino, J. N. (2002). *The Social Responsiveness Scale.* Los Angeles, CA: Western Psychological Services.

Conti, E., Calderoni, S., Gaglianese, A., Pannek, K., Mazzotti, S., Rose, S., et al. (2016). Lateralization of Brain Networks and Clinical Severity in Toddlers with Autism Spectrum Disorder: a HARDI Diffusion MRI Study. *Autism Res.* 9, 382–392. doi: 10.1002/aur.1533

Corbetta, M., and Shulman, G. L. (2011). Spatial neglect and attention networks. *Annu. Rev. Neurosci.* 34, 569–599. doi: 10.1146/annurev-neuro-061010-113731

Courchesne, E., Carper, R., and Akshoomoff, N. (2003). Evidence of brain overgrowth in the first year of life in autism. *JAMA* 290, 337–344. doi: 10.1001/jama.290.3.337

Courchesne, E., Karns, C. M., Davis, H. R., Ziccardi, R., Carper, R. A., Tigue, Z. D., et al. (2001). Unusual growth patterns in early life in patients with autistic disorder. An MRI study. *Neurology* 57, 245–254. doi: 10.1212/WNL.57.2.245

Dawson, G., Munson, J., Webb, S. J., Nalty, T., Abbott, R., and Toth, K. (2007). Rate of head growth decelerates and symptoms worsen in the second year of life in autism. *Biol. Psychiatry* 61, 458–464. doi: 10.1016/j.biopsych.2006.07.016

Dawson, G., Webb, S. J., Wijsman, E., Schellenberg, G., Estes, A., Munson, J., et al. (2005). Neurocognitive and electrophysiological evidence of altered face processing in parents of children with autism: implications for a model of abnormal development of social brain circuitry in autism. *Dev. Psychopathol.* (Summer) 17, 679–697. doi: 10.1017/s0954579405050327

Dawson, G., Webb, S., Schellenberg, G. D., Dager, S., Friedman, S., Aylward, E., et al. (2002). Defining the broader phenotype of autism: genetic, brain, and behavioral perspectives. *Dev. Psychopathol.* (Summer) 14, 581–611. doi: 10.1017/s0954579402003103

Dell'Osso, L., Dalle Luche, R., and Maj, M. (2016). Adult autism spectrum as a transnosographic dimension. *CNS Spectr.* 21, 131–133. doi: 10.1017/S1092852915000450

Fatemi, S. H. (2008). The hyperglutamatergic hypothesis of autism. *Prog. Neuropsychopharmacol. Biol. Psychiatry* 32, 911, author reply 912–913. doi: 10.1016/j.pnpbp.2007.11.004

Fatemi, S. H., Folsom, T. D., Kneeland, R. E., and Liesch, S. B. (2011). Metabotropic glutamate receptor 5 upregulation in children with autism is associated with underexpression of both Fragile X mental retardation protein and GABAA receptor beta 3 in adults with autism. *Anat. Rec. (Hoboken).* 294, 1635–1645. doi: 10.1002/ar.21299

Fatemi, S. H., Reutiman, T. J., Folsom, T. D., and Thuras, P. D. (2009). GABA(A) receptor downregulation in brains of subjects with autism. *J. Autism Dev. Disord.* 39, 223–230. doi: 10.1007/s10803-008-0646-7

Freitag, C. M. (2007). The genetics of autistic disorders and its clinical relevance: a review of the literature. *Mol. Psychiatry* 12, 2–22. doi: 10.1038/sj.mp.4001896

Frith, C. D., and Frith, U. (1999). Interacting minds-a biological basis. *Science* 286, 1692–1695. doi: 10.1126/science.286.5445.1692

Gerdts, J., and Bernier, R. (2011). The broader autism phenotype and its implications on the etiology and treatment of autism spectrum disorders. *Autism Res. Treat.* 2011:545901. doi: 10.1155/2011/545901

Ghosh, S. S., Tourville, J. A., and Guenther, F. H. (2008). A neuroimaging study of premotor lateralization and cerebellar involvement in the production of phonemes and syllables. *J. Speech Lang. Hear. Res.* 51, 1183–1202. doi: 10.1044/1092-4388(2008/07-0119)

Greimel, E., Schulte-Rüther, M., Kircher, T., Kamp-Becker, I., Remschmidt, H., Fink, G. R., et al. (2010). Neural mechanisms of empathy in adolescents with autism spectrum disorder and their fathers. *Neuroimage* 49, 1055–1065. doi: 10.1016/j.neuroimage.2009.07.057

Hale, T. S., Smalley, S. L., Dang, J., Hanada, G., Macion, J., McCracken, J. T., et al. (2010). ADHD familial loading and abnormal EEG alpha asymmetry in children with ADHD. *J. Psychiatr. Res.* 44, 605–615. doi: 10.1016/j.jpsychires.2009.11.012

Hickok, G., and Poeppel, D. (2007). The cortical organization of speech processing. *Nat. Rev. Neurosci.* 8, 393–402. doi: 10.1038/nrn2113

Hussman, J. P. (2001). Suppressed GABAergic inhibition as a common factor in suspected etiologies of autism. *J. Autism Dev. Disord.* 31, 247–248. doi: 10.1023/A:1010715619091

Ingalhalikar, M., Parker, W. A., Bloy, L., Roberts, T. P., and Verma, R. (2012). Using multiparametric data with missing features for learning patterns of pathology. *Med. Image Comput. Comput. Assist. Interv.* 15, 468–475. doi: 10.1007/978-3-642-33454-2_58

Itier, R. J., Latinus, M., and Taylor, M. J. (2006). Face, eye and object early processing: what is the face specificity? *Neuroimage* 29, 667–676. doi: 10.1016/j.neuroimage.2005.07.041

Jamal, W., Das, S., Maharatna, K., Kuyucu, D., Sicca, F., Billeci, L., et al. (2013). "Using brain connectivity measure of EEG synchrostates for discriminating typical and Autism Spectrum Disorder," in *Neural Engineering (NER), 2013 6th International IEEE/EMBS Conference on, 6–8 Nov* (San Diego, CA), 1402–1405.

Jerbi, K., Ossandon, T., Hamame, C. M., Senova, S., Dalal, S. S., Jung, J., et al. (2009). Task-related gamma-band dynamics from an intracerebral perspective: review and implications for surface EEG and MEG. *Hum. Brain Mapp.* 30, 1758–1771. doi: 10.1002/hbm.20750

Jeste, S. S., and Geschwind, D. H. (2014). Disentangling the heterogeneity of autism spectrum disorder through genetic findings. *Nat. Rev. Neurol.* 10, 74–81. doi: 10.1038/nrneurol.2013.278

Kaiser, J. (2004). Hearing lips: gamma-band activity during audiovisual speech perception. *Cereb. Cortex* 15, 646–653. doi: 10.1093/cercor/bhh166

Kana, R. K., Uddin, L. Q., Kenet, T., Chugani, D., and Müller, R. A. (2014). Brain connectivity in autism. *Front. Hum. Neurosci.* 8:349. doi: 10.3389/fnhum.2014.00349

Kanner, L. (1943). Autistic disturbances of affective contact. *Nervous Child* 2, 217–250.

Klein, K. J. K., and Hodges, S. D. (2001). Gender differences, motivation, and empathic accuracy: when it pays to understand. *Pers. Soc. Psychol. Bull.* 27, 720–730. doi: 10.1177/0146167201276007

Kleinhans, N. M., Muller, R. A., Cohen, D. N., and Courchesne, E. (2008). Atypical functional lateralization of language in autism spectrum disorders. *Brain Res.* 1221, 115–125. doi: 10.1016/j.brainres.2008.04.080

Knecht, S., Drager, B., Deppe, M., Bobe, L., Lohmann, H., Floel, A., et al. (2000). Handedness and hemispheric language dominance in healthy humans. *Brain* 123(Pt 12), 2512–2518. doi: 10.1093/brain/123.12.2512

Koczat, D. L., Rogers, S. J., Pennington, B. F., and Ross, R. G. (2002). Eye movement abnormality suggestive of a spatial working memory deficit is present in parents of autistic probands. *J. Autism Dev. Disord.* 32, 513–518. doi: 10.1023/A:1021246712459

Lai, M.-C., Lombardo, M., Suckling, J., Ruigrok, A., Chakrabarti, B., Ecker, C., et al. (2013). Biological sex affects the neurobiology of autism. *Brain* 136, 2799–2815. doi: 10.1093/brain/awt216

Lainhart, J. E., Bigler, E. D., Bocian, M., Coon, H., Dinh, E., Dawson, G., et al. (2006). Head circumference and height in autism: a study by the collaborative program of excellence in autism. *Am. J. Med. Genet. A.* 140, 2257–2274. doi: 10.1002/ajmg.a.31465

Lange, N., Dubray, M. B., Lee, J. E., Froimowitz, M. P., Froehlich, A., Adluru, N., et al. (2010). Atypical diffusion tensor hemispheric asymmetry in autism. *Autism Res.* 3, 350–358. doi: 10.1002/aur.162

Levy, S. E., Mandell, D. S., and Schultz, R. T. (2009). Autism. *Lancet* 374, 1627–1638. doi: 10.1016/S0140-6736(09)61376-3

Losh, M., Childress, D., Lam, K., and Piven, J. (2008). Defining key features of the broad autism phenotype. *Am. J. Med. Genet. Part B.* 147B, 424–433. doi: 10.1002/ajmg.b.30612

Mannerkoski, M., Heiskala, H., Raininko, R., Aberg, L., Sarna, S., Wirtavuori, K., et al. (2009). Brain magnetic resonance imaging of siblings from families with two or more children with learning or intellectual disabilities and need for full-time special education. *Acta Radiol.* 50, 437–445. doi: 10.1080/02841850902756524

McFadden, K. L., Hepburn, S., Winterrowd, E., Schmidt, G. L., and Rojas, D. C. (2012). Abnormalities in gamma-band responses to language stimuli in first-degree relatives of children with autism spectrum disorder: an MEG study. *BMC Psychiatry* 12:213. doi: 10.1186/1471-244X-12-213

Mesulam, M. M. (1990). Large-scale neurocognitive networks and distributed processing for attention, language, and memory. *Ann. Neurol.* 28, 597–613. doi: 10.1002/ana.410280502

Mostofsky, S. H., Powell, S. K., Simmonds, D. J., Goldberg, M. C., Caffo, B., and Pekar, J. J. (2009). Decreased connectivity and cerebellar activity in autism during motor task performance. *Brain* 132, 2413–2425. doi: 10.1093/brain/awp088

Narzisi, A., Muratori, F., Calderoni, S., Fabbro, F., and Urgesi, C. (2013). Neuropsychological profile in high functioning autism spectrum disorders. *J. Autism Dev. Disord.* 43, 1895–1909. doi: 10.1007/s10803-012-1736-0

Ors, M., Lindgren, M., Blennow, G., and Rosén, I. (2002). Auditory event-related brain potentials in parents of children with specific language impairment. *Eur. J. Paediatr. Neurol.* 6, 249–260. doi: 10.1053/ejpn.2002.0607

Palmen, S. J. M. C., Hulshoff Pol, H. E., Kemner, C., Schnack, H. G., Durston, S., Lahuis, B. E., et al. (2005b). Increased gray matter volume in medication naive high-functioning children with autism spectrum disorder. *Psychol. Med.* 35, 561–570. doi: 10.1017/S0033291704003496

Palmen, S. J. M. C., Pol, H. E. H., Kemner, C., Schnack, H. G., Sitskoorn, M. M., Appels, M. C. M., et al. (2005a). Brain anatomy in non-affected parents of autistic probands: a MRI study. *Psychol. Med.* 35, 1411–1420. doi: 10.1017/S0033291705005015

Peterson, E., Schmidt, G. L., Tregellas, J. R., Winterrowd, E., Kopelioff, L., Hepburn, S., et al. (2006). A voxel-based morphometry study of gray matter in parents of children with autism. *Neuroreport* 17, 1289–1292. doi: 10.1097/01.wnr.0000233087.15710.87

Piven, J., Palmer, P., Jacobi, D., Childress, D., and Arndt, S. (1997). Broader autism phenotype: evidence from a family history study of multiple-incidence autism families. *Am. J. Psychiatry* 154, 185–190. doi: 10.1176/ajp.15 4.2.185

Plante, E. (1991). MRI findings in the parents and siblings of specifically language-impaired boys. *Brain Lang.* 41, 67–80. doi: 10.1016/0093-934X(91)90111-D

Poissant, H., Rapin, L., and Mendrek, A. (2014). Intergenerational transmission offronto-parietal dysfunction during forethought in attention deficit/hyperactivity disorder: a pilot study. *Psychiatry Res.* 224, 242–245. doi: 10.1016/j.pscychresns.2014.08.011

Polk, T. A., Park, J., Smith, M. R., and Park, D. C. (2007). Nature versus nurture in ventral visual cortex: a functional magnetic resonance imaging study of twins. *J. Neurosci.* 27, 13921–13925. doi: 10.1523/JNEUROSCI.4001-07.2007

Rapin, L., Poissant, H., and Mendrek, A. (2014). Atypical activations of fronto-cerebellar regions during forethought in parents of children with ADHD. *J. Atten. Disord.* 18, 242–251. doi: 10.1177/1087054714524983

Retico, A., Giuliano, A., Tancredi, R., Cosenza, A., Apicella, F., Narzisi, A., et al. (2016). The effect of gender on the neuroanatomy of children with autism spectrum disorders: a support vector machine case-control study. *Mol. Autism* 7, 5. doi: 10.1186/s13229-015-0067-3

Retico, A., Tosetti, M., Muratori, F., and Calderoni, S. (2014). Neuroimaging-based methods for autism identification: a possible translational application? *Funct. Neurol.* 29, 231–239. doi: 10.11138/fneur/2014.29.4.231

Ring, H., Baron-Cohen, S., Williams, S., Wheelwright, S., Bullmore, E., Brammer, M., et al. (1999). Cerebral correlates of preserved cognitive skills in autism. A functional MRI study of Embedded Figures task performance. *Brain* 122, 1305–1315. doi: 10.1093/brain/122.7.1305

Rojas, D. C., Maharajh, K., Teale, P., and Rogers, S. J. (2008). Reduced neural synchronization of gamma-band MEG oscillations in first-degree relatives of children with autism. *BMC Psychiatry* 8:66. doi: 10.1186/1471-244X-8-66

Rojas, D. C., Smith, J. A., Benkers, T. L., Camou, S. L., Reite, M. L., and Rogers, S. J. (2004). Hippocampus and amygdala volumes in parents of children with autistic disorder. *Am. J. Psychiatry* 161, 2038–2044. doi: 10.1176/appi.ajp.161.11.2038

Rojas, D. C., Teale, P. D., Maharajh, K., Kronberg, E., Youngpeter, K., Wilson, L. B., et al. (2011). Transient and steady-state auditory gamma-band responses in first-degree relatives of people with autism spectrum disorder. *Mol. Autism* 2:11. doi: 10.1186/2040-2392-2-11

Rojas, D. C., and Wilson, L. B. (2014). γ-band abnormalities as markers of autism spectrum disorders. *Biomark. Med.* 8, 353–368. doi: 10.2217/bmm.14.15

Rommelse, N. N., Geurts, H. M., Franke, B., Buitelaar, J. K., and Hartman, C. A. (2011). A review on cognitive and brain endophenotypes that may be common in autism spectrum disorder and attention-deficit/hyperactivity disorder and facilitate the search for pleiotropic genes. *Neurosci. Biobehav. Rev.* 35, 1363–1396. doi: 10.1016/j.neubiorev.2011.02.015

Rossignol, D. A., Genuis, S. J., and Frye, R. E. (2014). Environmental toxicants and autism spectrum disorders: a systematic review. *Transl. Psychiatry* 4, e360. doi: 10.1038/tp.2014.4

Rubenstein, E., Wiggins, L. D., and Lee, L. C. (2015). A review of the differences in developmental, psychiatric, and medical endophenotypes between males and females with autism spectrum disorder. *J. Dev. Phys. Disabil.* 27, 119–139. doi: 10.1007/s10882-014-9397-x

Rubenstein, J. L., and Merzenich, M. M. (2003). Model of autism: increased ratio of excitation/inhibition in key neural systems. *Genes Brain Behav.* 2, 255–267. doi: 10.1034/j.1601-183X.2003.00037.x

Ruggeri, B., Sarkans, U., Schumann, G., and Persico, A. M. (2014). Biomarkers in autism spectrum disorder: the old and the new. *Psychopharmacology (Berl).* 231, 1201–1216. doi: 10.1007/s00213-013-3290-7

Seery, A. M., Vogel-Farley, V., Tager-Flusberg, H., and Nelson, C. A. (2013). Atypical lateralization of ERP response to native and non-native speech in infants at risk for autism spectrum disorder. *Dev. Cogn. Neurosci.* 5, 10–24. doi: 10.1016/j.dcn.2012.11.007

Segovia, F., Holt, R., Spencer, M., Górriz, J. M., Ramírez, J., Puntonet, C. G., et al. (2014). Identifying endophenotypes of autism: a multivariate approach. *Front. Comput. Neurosci.* 8:60. doi: 10.3389/fncom.2014.00060

Shahin, A. J., Picton, T. W., and Miller, L. M. (2009). Brain oscillations during semantic evaluation of speech. *Brain Cogn.* 70, 259–266. doi: 10.1016/j.bandc.2009.02.008

Shinohe, A., Hashimoto, K., Nakamura, K., Tsujii, M., Iwata, Y., Tsuchiya, K. J., et al. (2006). Increased serum levels of glutamate in adult patients with autism. *Prog. Neuropsychopharmacol. Biol. Psychiatry* 30, 1472–1477. doi: 10.1016/j.pnpbp.2006.06.013

Sucksmith, E., Roth, I., and Hoekstra, R. A. (2011). Autistic traits below the clinical threshold: re-examining the broader autism phenotype in the 21st century. *Neuropsychol. Rev.* 21, 360–389. doi: 10.1007/s11065-011-9183-9

Sullivan, P. F., Kendler, K. S., and Neale, M. C. (2003). Schizophrenia as a complex trait: evidence from a meta-analysis of twin studies. *Arch. Gen. Psychiatry* 60, 1187–1192. doi: 10.1001/archpsyc.60.12.1187

Tick, B., Bolton, P., Happé, F., Rutter, M., and Rijsdijk, F. (2016). Heritability of autism spectrum disorders: a meta-analysis of twin studies. *J. Child Psychol. Psychiatry* 57, 585–595. doi: 10.1111/jcpp.12499

Turkeltaub, P. E., and Coslett, H. B. (2010). Localization of sublexical speech perception components. *Brain Lang.* 114, 1–15. doi: 10.1016/j.bandl.2010.03.008

Wagner, R. K., Togesen, J. K., and Rashotte, C. A. (1999). *Comprehensive Test of Phonological Processing.* Austin, TX: PRO-ED.

Wilson, L. B., Jason, R., Tregellas, J. R., Slason, E., Pasko, B. E., Hepburn, S., et al. (2013). Phonological processing in first-degree relatives of individuals with autism: an fMRI study. *Hum. Brain Mapp.* 34, 1447–1463. doi: 10.1002/hbm.22001

Witkin, H. A., Dyk, R. B., Faterson, H. F., Goodenough, D. G., and Karp, S. A. (1962). *Personality Through Perception.* New York, NY: Harper & Row.

Yucel, G. H., Belger, A., Bizzell, J., Parlier, M., Adolphs, R., and Piven, J. (2014). Abnormal neural activation to faces in the parents of children with autism. *Cereb. Cortex* 25, 4653–4666. doi: 10.1093/cercor/bhu147

6

Autism as a Disorder of High Intelligence

Bernard J. Crespi *

Department of Biological Sciences and Human Evolutionary Studies Program, Simon Fraser University, Burnaby, BC, Canada

A suite of recent studies has reported positive genetic correlations between autism risk and measures of mental ability. These findings indicate that alleles for autism overlap broadly with alleles for high intelligence, which appears paradoxical given that autism is characterized, overall, by below-average IQ. This paradox can be resolved under the hypothesis that autism etiology commonly involves enhanced, but imbalanced, components of intelligence. This hypothesis is supported by convergent evidence showing that autism and high IQ share a diverse set of convergent correlates, including large brain size, fast brain growth, increased sensory and visual-spatial abilities, enhanced synaptic functions, increased attentional focus, high socioeconomic status, more deliberative decision-making, profession and occupational interests in engineering and physical sciences, and high levels of positive assortative mating. These findings help to provide an evolutionary basis to understanding autism risk as underlain in part by dysregulation of intelligence, a core human-specific adaptation. In turn, integration of studies on intelligence with studies of autism should provide novel insights into the neurological and genetic causes of high mental abilities, with important implications for cognitive enhancement, artificial intelligence, the relationship of autism with schizophrenia, and the treatment of both autism and intellectual disability.

Keywords: intelligence, autism, schizophrenia, genetic correlation, pleiotropy, evolution

Edited by:
Joshua Pesach Rosenzweig, Cell-El Therapeutics Ltd., Israel

Reviewed by:
Kerstin Jessica Plessen, University of Copenhagen, Denmark
Rex Eugene Jung, University of New Mexico, USA

Correspondence:
Bernard J. Crespi
crespi@sfu.ca

INTRODUCTION

'How wonderful that we have met with a paradox. Now we have some hope of making progress.'
Niels Bohr

Autism is conventionally regarded as a neurodevelopmental disorder that involves deficits in social interaction and social communication, combined with restricted or repetitive patterns of behavior and interests. However useful this definition may be for practical purposes, it also represents a reified, more or less arbitrary, historical and societal construction that fits neither with Kanner's (1943) original description (Evans, 2013) nor with the standard medical model of disease whereby maladaptive phenotypes must be understood in terms of alteration to specific adaptive systems (Nesse and Stein, 2012; Crespi, 2016).

Autism may, alternatively, be regarded as a syndrome, a constellation of phenotypes, sets of which tend to be found together relatively often, or sets of which when found together cause particular problems for children, families, and communities (Happé et al., 2006). Any given individual "with" autism will exhibit some more or less unique collection of such phenotypes (e.g., van Os, 2009), which is due to their more or less unique genomic makeup and early developmental environment. By this simple logic, any diagnoses of autism should be regarded not as any sort of endpoint, but as a rough, initial signpost toward eventual determination of the genetic, developmental, hormonal, neurological, psychological, and/or environmental causes of each individual's altered autism-related cognition, affect and behavior.

The finding that autism has many causes (Happé and Ronald, 2008) should direct attention to improved means of differentially diagnosing its personalized bases. This process, in turn, centers on determining what adaptive neural and psychological systems has been altered, and how, to result in some set of autistic traits in some individual. Autistic phenotypes have been linked, for example, to increased protein synthesis at synapses (Bourgeron, 2009), higher excitatory to inhibitory neurotransmission (Rubenstein and Merzenich, 2003), enhanced local compared to global processing and connectivity (Happé and Frith, 2006), a bias toward systemizing over empathizing (Baron-Cohen, 2009), and enhanced perceptual functioning (Mottron et al., 2006). These patterns and theories are not mutually exclusive, but none of them includes an explicit evolutionary dimension, such that their proximate causes remain ungrounded in the one discipline that unites across all biological-psychological levels in the context of ultimate, long-term determinants of psychological adaptation and maladaptation (Crespi, 2016).

Risks for autism, like risks of cancer, diabetes, or arthritis, have evolved along the human lineage (Crespi and Leach, 2016). As such, evolutionary biology becomes a valuable conceptual and analytic tool for connecting adaptive brain systems with the ways in which they can become altered and maladaptive in psychiatric disorders (Fjell et al., 2015). So what adaptive, evolved human brain systems are changed, in what different ways, to produce the phenotypes characteristic of autism? The most prominent neurological change along the human lineage is, of course, the tripling of brain size and associated changes in brain organization and functions, and our concomitant tremendous increase in intelligence compared to other great apes (Roth and Dicke, 2005). A notable set of "brain size genes" has been demonstrated to have been subject to natural selection in humans and other mammals (Montgomery and Mundy, 2014), and variation among extant humans in intelligence is now known to be highly polygenic, underlain by hundreds to thousands of alleles each of small effect (e. g., Davies et al., 2011; Benyamin et al., 2014; Plomin and Deary, 2015).

The genetical evolution of high intelligence in humans has increased scope for two main forms of dysregulation. First, the developmental and neural systems that connect genetic variation and environments with intelligence may be subject to maladaptive alterations by purely deleterious mutations, maladapted genotypes, or harmful environments, that degrade the "intelligence development" system. This route generally leads to what we call intellectual disability (Vissers et al., 2016), with overall reductions in intelligence and the functioning of its physiological and neural subsystems. Second, the development of intelligence can be affected, by genes or environments, in the opposite direction, toward higher levels of functioning. If this change results in balanced enhancements in all of the components of high intellect, general intelligence will be increased. However, if some, or most, but not all inter-dependent general cognitive-intellectual functions are enhanced, what would we observe?

Autism has long been characterized by relatively low intelligence as measured by most standard tests (e. g., Hoekstra et al., 2009). However, a suite of recent studies, described in more detail below, has demonstrated that alleles "for" autism, that is, common alleles that each contributes slightly to its risk, overlap substantially and significantly with alleles "for" high intelligence (Bulik-Sullivan et al., 2015; Clarke et al., 2015; Hill et al., 2015; Hagenaars et al., 2016). To a notable, and well-replicated, degree, then, many "autism" alleles are "high intelligence" alleles. How can these paradoxical observations be reconciled?

In this article I describe and evaluate the hypothesis that a substantial proportion of "autism risk" is underlain by high, but more or less imbalanced, components of intelligence. First, I provide a brief overview of the genetic, developmental and neurological bases and correlates of human intelligence, from research within this particular domain, and relate the structure of intelligence in neurotypical individuals to the differences between autistic individuals and neurotypical individuals. Second, I compare the best-validated correlates of variation among humans in intelligence with established characteristics of autistic individuals, compared to controls. These two areas of study, intelligence and autism, have thus far developed virtually independently from one another; I thus integrate and synthesize them in the context of testing the hypothesis addressed here. In doing so, I also compare results for autism with those for schizophrenia, the other primary human neurodevelopmental disorder, in light of theories for how these two conditions are related to one another (Crespi and Badcock, 2008; Crespi, 2016). Finally, I develop a framework for consilience of these findings with previous theory on autism, and describe the implications of the results, with regard to the causes, treatments, and understanding of autism, and the structure and study of human intelligence. The primary novelty and usefulness of this synthesis is that it provides the first comprehensive connections of the causes and symptoms of autism with alterations to a specific human-elaborated adaptive system, intelligence, and thereby generates new insights and research questions into the natures and inter-relationships of intelligence, autism, and schizophrenia.

THE ARCHITECTURE AND CORRELATES OF HUMAN INTELLIGENCE

Human intelligence has been studied predominantly from psychometric, genetic, neurological, and psychological perspectives. Psychometric studies tracing back to Spearman (1904) have demonstrated that virtually all measures of human mental abilities are moderately to highly positively correlated with one another, such that a common factor, typically called "*g*," underlies their joint co-variation. Between the general, primary *g* factor, and the diverse, specific measures of mental abilities, is a small set of secondary factors that each statistically accounts for covariation among a larger set of functionally-similar abilities. The Verbal-Perceptual-Rotational (VPR) model of Johnson and Bouchard (2005a,b, 2007; **Figure 1**), with three such secondary factors, represents the currently best-supported psychometric description of human intelligence structure. Under this model, "Verbal" refers to verbal fluency and knowledge, "Perceptual" refers to perceptual speed and mechanical and spatial abilities other than mental rotation, and "Rotational" refers to mental rotation, which involves mental movements of imagined objects or persons, as in the classic Mental Rotation test from Vandenberg and Kruse (1978; Johnson and Bouchard, 2005b; Major et al., 2012). The components of the VPR model correspond on a broad scale with brain structural organization in that verbal skills are relatively left-hemispheric, spatial and non-verbal abilities are relatively right-hemispheric, and mental rotation depends, in part, on strongly bihemispheric functions associated with corpus callosum size (Johnson and Bouchard, 2005b; Karadi et al., 2006; Schoenemann, 2006).

In addition to its success in describing patterns of co-variation among aspects of human intelligence, the VPR model also demonstrates evidence of tradeoffs between sets of cognitive abilities: when controlling for variation in *g*, image rotation ability is inversely associated with verbal ability, and scores on tests indicative of a strong focus of attention are inversely associated with scores indicating diffuse focus (Johnson and Bouchard, 2007; **Figure 2**). These two tradeoffs also exhibit sex differences, with males over-represented at the high rotational-strong focus pole, and more females at the pole with higher verbal abilities and more-diffuse focus (Johnson and Bouchard, 2007). Such sex differences and negative correlations are important given the strong male biases found in autism (Fombonne, 2009; Baron-Cohen et al., 2011), the extensive data showing that autism involves reductions in verbal skills but (1) increases in focus of attention (e. g., Ploog, 2010; Sabatos-DeVito et al., 2016), (2) enhanced perceptual and spatial abilities [as reflected in prowess, for example, in Block Design and the Embedded Figures test (EFT); Mottron et al., 2006; Muth et al., 2014], and (3) superior ability in non-rotational (though not rotational) aspects of the mental rotation task (Zapf et al., 2015). Considered together, these findings provide evidence that the cognitive structure of autism dovetails with the structure of the independently derived best-supported model for the psychometric architecture of human intelligence, but that it is characterized by increases in some, specific, components of intelligence and decreases in others, leading to a profile that is imbalanced and reflects extremes of typical variation. As such, autism-related differences in VPR-model structured intelligence appear to reflect its evolutionary bases in altered expression of adaptive cognitive variation (Crespi, 2016), with autistic cognition mediated by

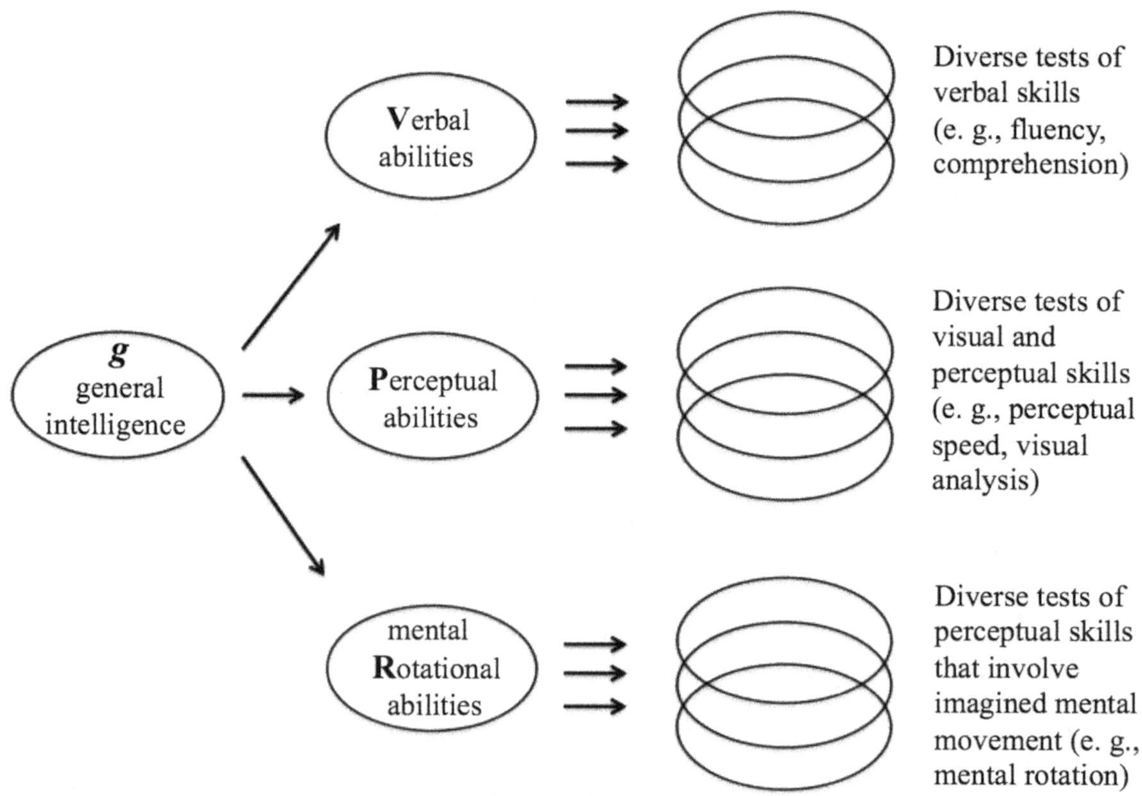

FIGURE 1 | The VPR model of intelligence. Under this model, the higher-level architecture of human intelligence, as indicated by diverse mental-ability tasks, involves one general factor, *g*, and three mid-level factors, Verbal, Perceptual, and image Rotation, that reflect variation among individuals in large-scale neural structure and processing. Adapted from Johnson et al. (2007).

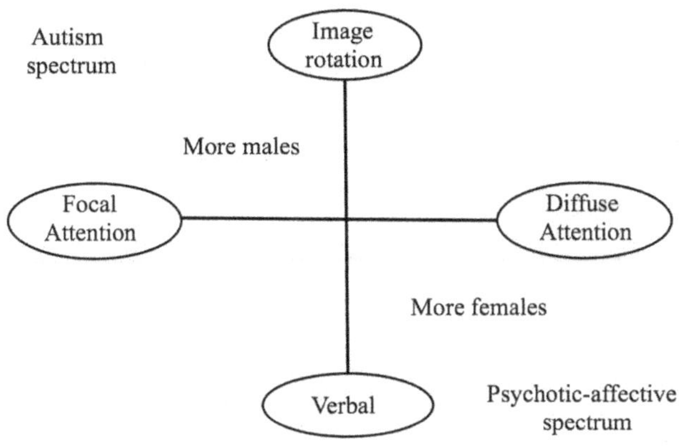

FIGURE 2 | Two orthogonal dimensions of intelligence, which emerge after the general factor *g* is statistically removed. Poles of each of the two dimensions demonstrate inverse associations with one another, indicative of neurally-based cognitive trade-offs. The psychotic-affective spectrum includes mainly schizophrenia, bipolar disorder, depression, and borderline personality disorder. Adapted from Johnson et al. (2007).

relative extremes of tradeoffs (Johnson and Bouchard, 2007, 2008). In contrast to autism, schizophrenia is characterized by a focus of attention decreased relative to controls (e.g., Morris et al., 2013), notably-poor visual-spatial relative to verbal abilities (Kravariti et al., 2006), and reduced ability in non-rotational (though not in rotational) aspects of mental rotation tasks (Thakkar and Park, 2010; Benson and Park, 2013). These patterns of findings derive directly from the VPR model, and indicate that its further application and extension will help to clarify the psychometric structure of autistic, neurotypical, and schizophrenia-associated cognition.

A second model for the higher-level psychometric structure of intelligence is its division into a "fluid" component, reflecting ability to solve novel problems, use logic, and identify patterns, in ways that are independent of acquired and cultural knowledge, and a "crystallized" component, indicative of ability to utilize acquired and learned knowledge and experience (e. g., Nisbett et al., 2012). This subdivision of intelligence fits less well than the VPR model to patterns of covariation across mental ability tests (Johnson and Bouchard, 2005a,b), but its validity and usefulness are supported by the underpinning of fluid vs. crystallized intelligence by distinct sets of genes (Christoforou et al., 2014), their different patterns of change with age (with fluid changing like physical traits, but crystallized showing little age-related decline; Deary et al., 2010), and the primacy of social learning in human cultural adaptation (Henrich, 2015). As for the VPR model, the structure of intelligence in autism reflects the fluid-crystallized dichotomy, in that fluid intelligence is relatively or absolutely enhanced in autism, but crystallized intelligence is reduced, compared to controls (Dawson et al., 2007; Hayashi et al., 2008; see also Nader et al., 2016). This pattern again indicates imbalance, and elevation, in components of intelligence in autism that correspond to its evolved and psychometrically characterized structure.

Intelligence, usually measured by strong correlates of *g*, has a clear polygenic basis, as well as established connections with neurological variation. Recent GWA studies have provided evidence that many hundreds or thousands of alleles, each of very small effect, underlie variation among individuals in *g*, although only a fraction of its high heritability can be accounted for at this point (Plomin and Deary, 2015). By contrast, data from studies of the genetic basis of intellectual disability show that it is due mainly to moderate or large effect *de novo* deleterious alleles, rather than a concentration of weakly-deleterious, small-effect, segregating alleles; these findings indicate that "high intelligence requires that everything work right, including most of the positive alleles and few of the negative alleles associated with intelligence" (Plomin and Deary, 2015, p. 103; Franić et al., 2015; Hill et al., 2015). Plomin and Deary (2015, p. 103) also point out an important question regarding such "positive genetics" of intelligence, for psychiatric disorders: if individuals at the positive end of the polygenic distribution of "risk" simply have low risk, or if they "have special powers." In this article, I am evaluating the hypothesis that such "special powers" indeed exist, in the contexts of autism and intelligence, and in comparison to schizophrenia. Finally, Plomin and Deary (2015) point out that assortative mating is notably stronger (~0.40) for intelligence than for most other human traits, which maintains additive genetic variation for this trait as well as generating more "extreme" intelligence phenotypes than otherwise expected. Increased autism risk has been attributed by Baron-Cohen et al. (2006) to assortative mating between two individuals high in "systemizing," and assortative mating is much high among individuals diagnosed with ASD than other disorders (Nordsletten et al., 2016); how might intelligence variation play a role in this process and its sequelae?

As described in detail below, the neurological basis of intelligence has been well established for a suite of phenotypes, including large brain size and high numbers of neurons, large hippocampus size, high efficacy of working memory, fast neuronal processing speed, neural efficiency, fast rates of brain growth and pruning, and specific patterns of gray matter and white matter distributions. Most broadly, high intelligence appears to reflect high functionality, speed, and integration of a fronto-parietal brain network that subserves the sensory acquisition, abstraction, alternative model-testing, and deployment of information (the Parieto-Frontal Integration Theory; Jung and Haier, 2007; Colom et al., 2010; **Figure 3**). This "intelligence network" overlaps substantially with the "task-positive network," whose activation is inversely associated with that of the "default mode" or "task-negative" network (e.g., Uddin et al., 2009), as might be expected given that mental abilities and intelligence are measured in the context of particular tasks. The general and specific functioning of this distributed, fronto-parietal network are highly compatible with the VPR psychometric model described above (Deary et al., 2010), with genetic bases to VPR abilities and fronto-parietal structure and function (Johnson et al., 2007).

In addition to its substantial psychometric and genetic basis, and neurological underpinnings, intelligence is also notably associated with two additional factors that are relevant to the autism spectrum: sensory abilities and socioeconomic status. Positive correlations of *g* with sensory abilities in the auditory,

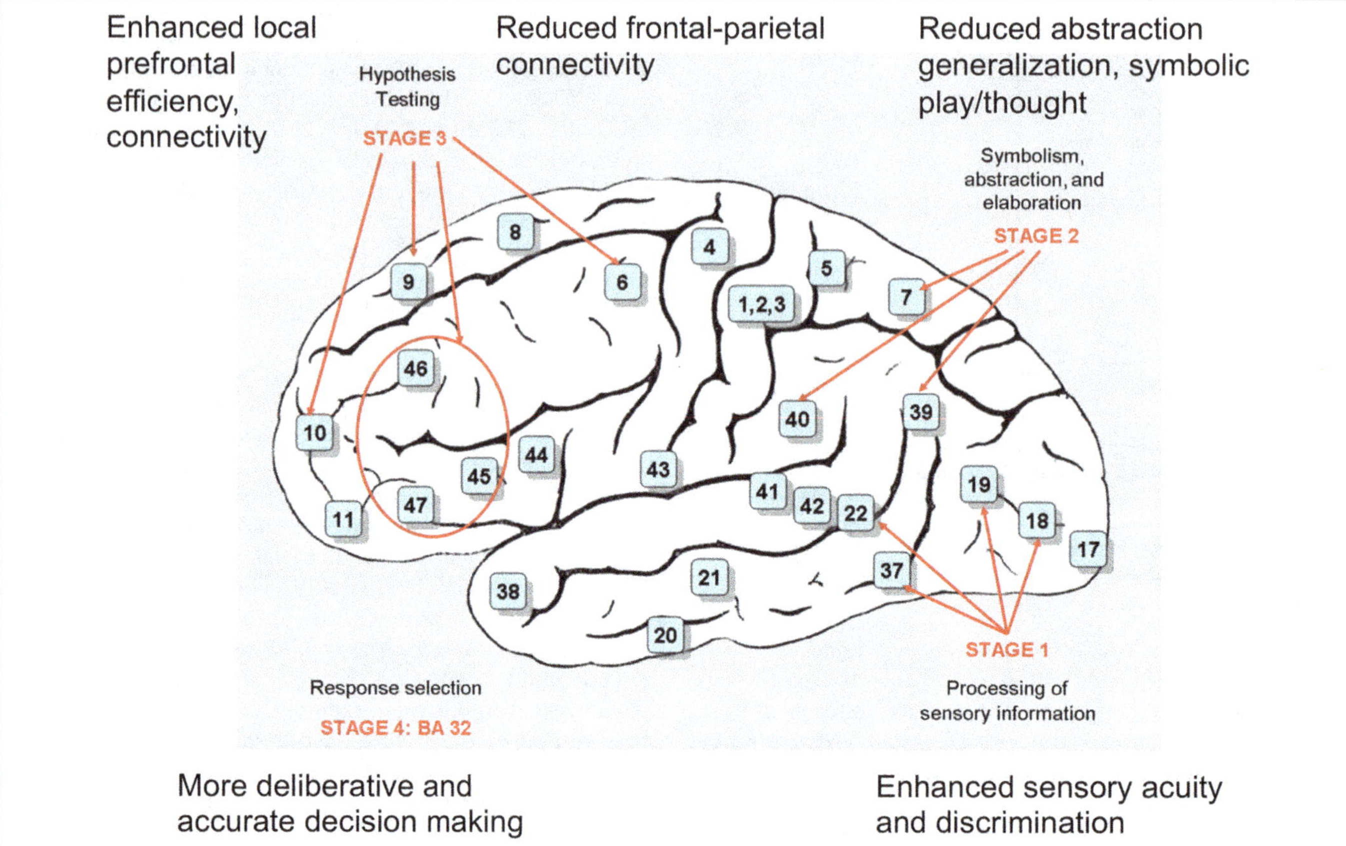

FIGURE 3 | Brain regions, and temporal stages, representing the P-FIT (Parietal Frontal Integration Theory) model of intelligence. Postulated alterations in autism, compared to control individuals, are shown along the periphery, and described in the text. Adapted from Colom et al. (2010).

visual, and tactile domains have been well documented and replicated, across over a century of testing (Deary et al., 2004). Such sensory tests include, for example, ability to discriminate closely-similar stimuli, temporal information processing skill, or sensitivity in stimulus detection, that apparently reflect aspects of processing speed, focal-attentional abilities, and ability to suppress irrelevant stimuli. As described further below, Galton (1883) and Spearman (1904, pp. 268–272) indeed virtually equated higher cognitive abilities with more-accurate sensory discrimination, and postulated "general discrimination" skills that underpinned sensory abilities across different modalities and correlated near unity with general intelligence. Genetically-based positive associations of intelligence with socioeconomic status, as well as with education levels and occupational status, have also been well documented (Marioni et al., 2014; Trzaskowski et al., 2014; Krapohl and Plomin, 2016; review in Plomin and Deary, 2015). These findings indicate that the same alleles pleiotropically mediate high intelligence and high socioeconomic status (vs. low levels of both), again through many alleles of small effect that account for a small, though statistically significant, proportion of the variance in both traits.

The upshot of these considerations from psychometrics, genetics, neuroscience, psychology, and sociology is that high intelligence involves many beneficial alleles of small effect, an absence of *de novo* deleterious mutations, high performance with balanced integration of neural subsystems (as well as large brain size and more neurons), enhanced sensory abilities, high socioeconomic status, and a notable degree of assortative mating. How, then, do these genetic and phenotypic correlates of intelligence, and associated ones, relate to the genetic basis and phenotypic correlates of autism?

GENETIC OVERLAP OF AUTISM WITH INTELLIGENCE

Recent increases in sample sizes, extensions of target phenotypes analyzed, and developments in analytic methods for genome-wide association studies, have allowed the first robust tests of the sign and magnitude of genetic correlations, due to pleiotropy and linkage disequilibrium, between intelligence and other traits including risk of psychiatric conditions. Four studies have used data from the Psychiatric Genetics Consortium (PGC) on polygenic risk for autism (Cross-Disorder Group of the Psychiatric Genomics Consortium, 2013) to assess overlap of autism risk alleles (identified from over 5000 cases) with alleles for aspects of cognitive ability and intelligence. All four of these studies, which used diverse, independent populations and tests (or correlates) of cognitive abilities, have reported significant, substantial genetically-based positive associations of autism risk with intelligence, notably including full-scale IQ and a PCA-based measure of *g* (Clarke et al., 2015), childhood IQ, college attendance, and years of education (Bulik-Sullivan et al., 2015), cognitive function in childhood and educational attainment (Hill et al., 2015), and verbal-numerical reasoning and educational level reached (Hagenaars et al., 2016). These studies indicate that polygenic, small-effect size alleles that increased risk of autism are also associated with increased intelligence (and strong correlates of intelligence, such as education level; Davies et al., 2016) among neurotypical individuals.

In direct contrast to these findings for autism, genetic risk for schizophrenia has been demonstrated to be negatively associated with measures of cognitive ability and intelligence, across a broad suite of studies (McIntosh et al., 2013; Lencz et al., 2014; Bulik-Sullivan et al., 2015; Hill et al., 2015; Hagenaars et al., 2016; Hubbard et al., 2016). These results indicate that a substantial proportion of schizophrenia risk alleles also represent alleles "for" lower intelligence. Such findings for schizophrenia accord well with large bodies of research on cognitive deficits in first-degree relatives of individuals with schizophrenia (Snitz et al., 2006), and among children who are premorbid for schizophrenia (and thus will develop it at or after adolescence; Woodberry et al., 2008).

The question of whether intelligence, or any of its components, are elevated, compared to controls, among parents, siblings, or higher-order relatives of individuals with autism has yet to be investigated systematically, although this pattern is predicted by the positive genetic correlations of autism risk with measures of IQ. Tests conducted thus far have yielded diverse results, but individuals with autism clearly exhibit a similar cognitive profile to their sibs across WAIS subtests, with high scores on Block Design and Object Assembly, and low scores on Comprehension and Coding, relative to controls (Gizzonio et al., 2014). Similarly, siblings of individuals with autism have shown better working memory (for non-social targets) than control individuals (Noland et al., 2010) and higher visual-motion sensitivity (McCleery et al., 2007), and parents of individuals with autism are faster than controls at the EFT (Baron-Cohen and Hammer, 1997). Kanner (1943) and Rimland (1964, pp. 29–30) believed that parents of individuals with autism were of higher intelligence than control parents (see Levine and Olson, 1968), but their hypotheses have apparently not been subject to robust empirical testing, with most such studies of parents focusing on social deficits and alterations. By contrast, as described above, there is clear evidence for relatively low IQ, on average, among individuals with autism, at least as measured by most standardized tests.

How can this paradox of low IQ, but positive genetic correlations of autism risk with intelligence, be resolved? None of the papers on genetic correlations of autism with intelligence discuss possible explanations, or ways to investigate the conundrum further. I have proposed here the hypothesis that autism involves high but imbalanced intelligence, such that some or many genetically-based components of intelligence are enhanced, but imbalance across components increases risk and patterns of expression for autistic phenotypes, and for diagnoses. By this hypothesis, higher intelligence may co-occur with higher risk for imbalance and cognitive and affective consequences from it, given that the components of cognitive ability are expected to interact strongly and may do so to a greater degree at the higher end of ability. The "high intelligence imbalance" hypothesis is useful because it makes clear predictions, and thus directs attention toward specific forms of existing data and new, informative future data to collect.

AUTISM AND THE CORRELATES OF INTELLIGENCE

The "high intelligence imbalance" hypothesis predicts that autism should be associated, at a phenotypic level, with substantiated correlates of intelligence. I elaborate here on the most-notable joint correlates of intelligence and autism, focusing on phenotypes that are associated with intelligence and that are over-developed or over-expressed in autism.

Brain Size and Growth

Large brain size and head circumference, especially in childhood but also adulthood, represent some of the best-substantiated phenotypic correlates of autism (e.g., Fukumoto et al., 2011; Foster et al., 2015; meta-analysis in Sacco et al., 2015). Autism-linked increases in brain size have been shown to involve higher numbers of neurons (Courchesne et al., 2013), a thicker cortex (Hardan et al., 2006; Karama et al., 2011; Ecker et al., 2013; Smith et al., 2016), increased hippocampus volume (Barnea-Goraly et al., 2014; Maier et al., 2015), increased brain growth rates in early childhood (Campbell et al., 2014), increased rate of cortical thinning in adolescence (Hardan et al., 2009; Mak-Fan et al., 2012), a combination of "accelerated expansion in early childhood" with "accelerated thinning in in later childhood and adolescence" (Zielinski et al., 2014), and increased processing of more-local, detailed information (White et al., 2009).

Faster increase in cortical thickness between ages 6 and 12, followed by faster cortical thickness deceleration between ages 12 and 18 (indicative of neuronal and synaptic pruning), has been linked with higher intelligence in typically-developing children (Shaw et al., 2006). These findings provide evidence that trajectories of brain growth rate during middle childhood to adolescence are notably associated with IQ, with an overall pattern of accelerated growth and accelerated pruning that matches trajectories reported in autism, though with different timings of growth in early childhood. Within humans (e.g., Ivanovic et al., 2004; Witelson et al., 2006; Menary et al., 2013), and among non-human primates (Deaner et al., 2007) species, brain size (and cortical thickness, for humans) are also positively correlated with measures of intelligence, an effect that appears to be mediated predominantly by numbers of neurons (Roth and Dicke, 2005; Dicke and Roth, 2016).

In contrast to these patterns in autism, brain size, hippocampus size, and cortical thickness are reduced among individuals with schizophrenia, including at first episode (e.g., Steen et al., 2006; Rais et al., 2012; Rimol et al., 2012;

Oertel-Knöchel et al., 2013). These reductions appear to be associated with reduced brain growth rates in late childhood and early adolescence (Gogtay et al., 2008), followed by increased gray matter loss in adolescence and early adulthood (e.g., Pantelis et al., 2005; Rapoport and Gogtay, 2011).

The genetic bases of brain size and growth, and intelligence, in relation to autism and schizophrenia, remain largely unknown. However, as one example of such inter-relations, numbers of repeat units of a protein domain referred to as *DUF1220* have been positively associated with a suite of characters including: (1) brain size (within humans, and across species of anthropoid primates; Dumas et al., 2012; Keeney et al., 2014), (2) IQ and mathematical aptitude (Davis et al., 2015), and (3) the severity of autism (Davis et al., 2014); by contrast, *DUF1220* repeat numbers are inversely associated with positive-symptom (though not negative-symptom) severity in schizophrenia (Quick et al., 2015). These findings indicate strongly pleiotropic effects of this molecular domain on brain size, intelligence, autism, and schizophrenia, whereby autism is linked with large brain size and high IQ, but positive symptom schizophrenia shows a diametric result.

Brain Connectivity

Low global, relative to local, structural and functional connectivity of the brain has been demonstrated in autism by a large suite of studies (reviews in Courchesne and Pierce, 2005; Maximo et al., 2014), and it follows in part, presumably, from increased brain size itself. Under the P-FIT model of intelligence (**Figure 3**), effective long-range connectivity is required for the integration of parietal and frontal brain regions that underlies IQ (Jung and Haier, 2007); "efficient" patterns of brain connectivity involving small-world network-level organization (with an optimal mix of short and long-rage connections) have thus, for example, been positively associated with measures of intelligence (van den Heuvel et al., 2009; Koenis et al., 2015; Kim et al., 2016). These findings suggest that relative reductions in long-range connectivity may represent an important constraint on general intelligence among individuals with autism, contributing to imbalances between its constituent parts. Testing of this hypothesis will, however, require analyses of local and global brain connectivity patterns in relation to both autism (compared to controls) and variation in intelligence (in each group) using the same methodology, to determine the degree to which the long-range connectivity pathways central to the P-FIT model (e.g., the arcuate fasciculus, and connections to the lateral prefrontal cortex; Jung and Haier, 2007; Cole et al., 2012) are differentially reduced in efficiency among individuals with autism.

In contrast to reduced long-range brain connectivity, increased local connectivity has been linked with enhanced ability in some domains, such as auditory pitch perception (Loui et al., 2011), which shows a notable association with the autism spectrum (Stanutz et al., 2014). Increased local connectivity, especially of the prefrontal cortex, also characterizes the valproic acid animal model of autism (Rinaldi et al., 2008) and the "intense world" theory of autism etiology (Markram and Markram, 2010), which involves perception, attention, and memory that are enhanced to levels that interfere with social functioning.

Higher local connectivity in sensory regions of the brain has been suggested as the basis for sensory hyper-sensitivities in autism (Belmonte et al., 2004) as well as hyper-developed attention to detail and systemizing (Baron-Cohen et al., 2009). Considered together, these findings suggest that increased local brain connectivity in autism is linked with specific enhanced abilities or interests, such that components or facets of general intelligence are increased whereas *g* itself is reduced. These brain network alterations in autism can be described most simply as involving increased brain modularity and parallel processing, which may enhance region-specific functions (such as sensory abilities and visual-spatial skills) but also lead to reduced general intelligence due to under-developed long-range connectivities.

Decreased local and increased long-range connectivity have been described in childhood-onset schizophrenia (Baribeau and Anagnostou, 2013), and increased connectivity has also been found within the default mode in schizophrenia across multiple studies (Whitfield-Gabrieli et al., 2009; Tang et al., 2013), with several reviews pointing out the opposite nature of this pattern compared to that found in autism (Broyd et al., 2009; Karbasforoushan and Woodward, 2012). However, robust tests of this hypothesis require joint connectivity analysis of individuals with autism and schizophrenia using the same protocols.

Neuronal Function

Synaptic plasticity represents a core component of brain function, and, in principle, it underlies on a neuronal scale the long-term macroscopic changes in cortical thickness across childhood and adolescence that have been linked with intelligence (e.g., Shaw et al., 2006). Protein synthesis in dendritic spines mediates synaptic plasticity, and has been associated with diverse aspects of cognition, learning and memory (Sutton and Schuman, 2006; Kasai et al., 2010). Evidence of exaggerated protein synthesis at dendrites has been reported in human syndromic autism and in multiple animal models of autism (Kelleher and Bear, 2008; Bourgeron, 2009; Gkogkas et al., 2013; Santini et al., 2013; Santini and Klann, 2014; review in Mottron et al., 2014), indicating that gains of function or expression in key molecular mediators of cognition may characterize the autism spectrum (e.g., Figure 1 in Kulkarni and Firestein, 2012). Increased levels of neuronal plasticity and synaptic remodeling likewise characterize some theory for autism and animal models (Markram and Markram, 2010; Isshiki et al., 2014; Oberman and Pascual-Leone, 2014).

The degree to which neuronal functions such as synaptic plasticity, dendritic spine protein synthesis levels, and dendrite dynamics including flexibility and stability influence variation in general intelligence remains unclear. However, a recent GWA study found that the strongest functional enrichment for genes linked with fluid intelligence was synaptic "efficiency," whereas for crystallized intelligence it was synaptic depression and LTD (long-term depression; Christoforou et al., 2014). These findings suggest strong associations of neuronal and synaptic function with intelligence, such that autism may commonly involve dysregulation of intelligence-associated neuronal processes toward hyper-functional dynamics. The gene *CYFIP1* represents an apparent example of a locus that mediates such effects: high expression of this gene, which coordinates mRNA translation at dendrites, has been associated with autism (Oguro-Ando et al., 2015; Wang et al., 2015); by contrast, deletions that reduce its expression have been strongly linked with risk of schizophrenia, as well as with aspects of impaired cognition (especially dyslexia and dyscalculia) among otherwise-neurotypical individuals (Stefansson et al., 2008, 2014; Tam et al., 2010).

Sensory Functions, Attention, and Special Abilities

As noted above, Galton (1883) and Spearman (1904) first described hypotheses and psychometric evidence that sensory abilities and sensory discrimination skills were strongly positively associated with high intelligence. A resurgence of interest in this phenomenon has led to consistent and diverse evidence for small to moderate links of specific sensory discrimination abilities with intelligence, but strong correlations (e.g., 0.68 and 0.92 in Deary et al., 2004) of intelligence with latent factors that integrate sensory ability variation across domains (Meyer et al., 2010). The causes of correlations between general intelligence and sensory discrimination abilities remain largely unknown, but they appear to be related to: (a) ability to focus intensely while ignoring irrelevant stimuli (Melnick et al., 2013); (b) a strong positive genetic correlation between intelligence and sensory-neural processing speed (Lee et al., 2012); (c) speed of neural oscillations, which may underlie both sensory discrimination skills and intelligence (Troche and Rammsayer, 2009a,b; Troche et al., 2009); (d) white matter structure and integrity, which are positively associated with neural processing speed (e.g., Turken et al., 2008; Kerchner et al., 2012); (e) regional or global increases in gray matter (e.g., Deary et al., 2010; Hyde et al., 2010), and (f) the role of sensory input as a limiting step in general cognitive ability, upon which all further neurological components of intelligence depend. Further evaluation of these hypotheses, through GWAS-based tests for genetic correlation and neurological studies that jointly address sensory discrimination and intelligence, are required to evaluate their robustness and generality.

A large body of evidence has shown that sensory discrimination and sensory acuity abilities are commonly enhanced in autism compared to controls, across auditory (O'Riordan and Passetti, 2006; Heaton et al., 2008; Eigsti and Fein, 2013; Stanutz et al., 2014), visual (Ashwin et al., 2009; Brosnan et al., 2012; Falter et al., 2012), and tactile (Blakemore et al., 2006; Cascio et al., 2008; Nakano et al., 2012) domains. As for the links with IQ, causation remains largely obscure. However, Blaser et al. (2014) demonstrate that the autism-associated advantage in visual search is associated with stronger phasic pupillary response, which is indicative of stronger attentional focus and implicates the locus coeruleus-norepinephrine system in (at least) visual discrimination proficiency. This finding is of especially notable interest given that autism is characterized, on a general diagnostic basis, by increased attention to detail, difficulties in switching of attention, and attentional stimulus "overselectivity" on specific aspects of the physical environment (Murray et al., 2005; Ploog, 2010). High attention to detail on the Autism Quotient test, high intelligence, and high rates of autism in family members have also been reported among child prodigies (children who display highly-advanced abilities in fields such as music, mathematics, chess, or art; Ruthsatz and Urbach, 2012). Baron-Cohen et al. (2009) describe evidence that such high attention to detail in autism is a consequence of enhanced sensory abilities, and also leads to high levels of an analytical, "systemizing" cognition. Finally, Sabatos-DeVito et al. (2016) describe experiments that link atypical sensory processing in autism to attentional engagement, suggesting that these two facets of autism share neurological and psychological links.

One visual-spatial test, the embedded-figures test (EFT), represents a paradigmatic task showing superiority in autism for speed, accuracy, or both (Happé and Frith, 2006; Muth et al., 2014; Horlin et al., 2016). This test has traditionally been considered as indicative of a local cognitive "style," but three sets of findings: (a) high positive correlations of EFT performance with measures of fluid intelligence (e, g., McKenna et al., 1986; McKenna, 1990), (b) demonstration by Khodadady and Tafaghodi (2013) that EFT performance is strongly, positively linked with intelligence, and (c) the visual-spatial search and discrimination nature of the task, suggest that it can also be interpreted as a metric of visual sensory ability and discrimination that is, like other such metrics, highly associated with intelligence, especially fluid intelligence that is often not matched in autism-control comparison studies. In contrast to the patterns of EFT enhancement found for autism, meta-analysis indicates that EFT performance is significantly and substantially reduced in schizophrenia (Panton et al., 2016). Indeed, more generally, sensory discrimination and abilities are consistently reduced in schizophrenia (Bates, 2005; Force et al., 2008; Javitt, 2009a,b), as expected under the hypothesis that they represent psychologically-diametric conditions (Crespi and Badcock, 2008; Crespi, 2016).

Considered together, these findings suggest that increased sensory discrimination ability in autism represents a component or strong correlate of intelligence that is frequently enhanced to the point of imbalance with other aspects of IQ. Indeed, under the P-FIT model (**Figure 3**), sensory abilities are represented by the first, sensory processing stage of intelligence circuitry: data acquisition and coding mainly via occipital and parietal regions of the brain. Hyper-functioning of these regions may thus result in imbalanced intelligence, whereby efficient integration with downstream regions, especially parietal regions that subserve symbolism, abstraction and categorization of sensory information, becomes dysregulated (e.g., Froehlich et al., 2012; Church et al., 2015; Eduardo Mercado et al., 2015; **Figure 3**). The gene *GABRB3*, which codes for a GABA receptor, represents a possible example of a locus that is pleiotropically linked to sensory sensitivity, autism risk, and components of intelligence, given that SNPs in this gene have been linked with tactile sensitivity, risk of Asperger syndrome, and scores on the embedded figures and mental rotation tests (Tavassoli et al., 2012; Warrier et al., 2013).

Finally, autism is the only psychiatric condition characterized by notable rates of savant skills, which in this context represent highly-structured, rule-based abilities largely restricted to a few spheres of mental ability: calendar calculating, rote memory, mathematical computation, musical memory, and realistic drawing (Howlin et al., 2009; Snyder, 2009; Treffert, 2014; Meilleur et al., 2015). Savantism appears to represent an extreme of imbalanced components of mental ability in autism, given its highly limited range of enhancements and apparent negative associations of special skills with verbal and social abilities (Crespi and Leach, 2016).

Decision-Making

Decision making, or "response selection," mediated by the anterior cingulate cortex, represents the fourth stage in the P-FIT model of intelligence (Jung and Haier, 2007; **Figure 3**). Autism has been characterized, in a recent suite of studies, by more "deliberative" decision making (compared to controls), that tends to reduce biases and errors associated with fast and intuitive, but often "irrational," decision-making (De Martino et al., 2008; Brosnan et al., 2014, 2016; South et al., 2014). Given that susceptibilities to cognitive biases are negatively associated with measures of intelligence, weakly though significantly (e.g., Teovanović et al., 2015), these findings suggest that this component of intelligence is enhanced in autism, at least in some contexts. More-deliberative decision making in autism may be associated, and underpinned, by enhanced explanatory drive to seek information in ambiguous circumstances, with regard to physical (rather than social) problems (Rutherford and Subiaul, 2015).

In contrast to these results for autism, some cognitive biases, such as "jumping to conclusions," and "bias against disconfirmatory evidence" are increased in schizophrenia compared to controls (Woodward et al., 2006; Dudley et al., 2016). Similarly, performance on the Iowa Gambling task of decision-making ability is reduced in schizophrenia (Sevy et al., 2007; Adida et al., 2011) but increased in autism (South et al., 2014), in each case compared to controls. Despite such findings, the degree to which more-deliberative or enhanced decision-making is more intelligent *per se*, and does not itself entail costs, remains unclear; for example, faster, more-intuitive decision-making may be favored in many social situations (South et al., 2014), and rationality appears to be at least partially dissociable from intelligence (Stanovich and West, 2014).

Socioeconomic Status

Socioeconomic status, intelligence, and education level achieved have been demonstrated to exhibit strong positive correlations amongst themselves, although the reasons for these associations have remained unspecified (Deary and Johnson, 2010). A recent suite of studies has shown that such links are substantially genetically based, indicating that a large number of alleles pleiotropically affect socioeconomic status, intelligence, and educational achievement (Marioni et al., 2014; Trzaskowski et al., 2014; Krapohl and Plomin, 2016). These findings are of interest in the context of autism because autism also shows significant, positive genetic correlations with educational attainment, which is strongly positively associated with socioeconomic status as well (Bulik-Sullivan et al., 2015; Hill et al., 2015; Hagenaars et al., 2016).

The hypothesis that autism risk in offspring is positively associated with high parental intelligence, and high socioeconomic status, traces to Kanner (1943, p. 248), who stated, referring to autistic children, that "they all come of highly intelligent families," at high levels of educational, socioeconomic and occupational achievement (Kanner and Lesser, 1958; Rimland, 1964). King (1975) reviewed a set of demographic studies motivated by these findings, and reported strong support for the pattern of high socioeconomic status linked with autism, including support from studies (e.g., Lotter, 1966, 1967) that checked all young children (of 8–10 years) in a given geographic area for infantile autism, and thus should be largely independent of confounding ascertainment or help-seeking biases, variation in access to relevant health care, or variation in parental awareness.

Recent studies of socioeconomic correlates of autism have generated variable results, most of which, however, find that autism is positively related to indicators or strong correlates of high socioeconomic status (Durkin et al., 2010; Van Meter et al., 2010; King and Bearman, 2011; Leonard et al., 2011; Thomas et al., 2012; Bakian et al., 2015); other studies report links with low socioeconomic conditions, or no associations (Rai et al., 2012; Sun et al., 2014). The degree to which biases and confounding factors mediate the positive associations remains largely unknown, although it is noteworthy that both mild to moderate intellectual disability, and schizophrenia, show notable patterns of association with measures of low socioeconomic status (Werner et al., 2007; Leonard et al., 2011; Emerson, 2012; Zheng et al., 2012).

Given that autism risk shows strong genetic correlations with intelligence and years of education, and that these two variables are strongly linked with higher socioeconomic status in a demographic context, the findings described above suggest that autism risk and high socioeconomic status are also expected to show a basis in pleiotropy as demonstrated by positive genetic correlation. However, this hypothesis requires direct genetic tests that take account of known confounding factors and inter-correlated traits (King and Bearman, 2011), as well as analyzing hypotheses for the causal underpinnings of the genetic and phenotypic associations.

Profession

Profession, occupation, and vocational interests have been associated with autism in the context of Baron-Cohen's theory that the autism spectrum is mediated by high "systemizing" (drive to understand non-social, mechanistic and rule-based systems) combined with low "empathizing" (drive to understand and connect with people, socially and emotionally; Baron-Cohen, 2009). Under this systemizing-empathizing theory, persons expressing high levels of autism spectrum psychological traits are predicted to engage in, or plan to enter, professions that involve systemizing, especially engineering and the physical, mathematical and technical sciences. This prediction of the theory has received considerable, though not fully unequivocal, support (Baron-Cohen et al., 1997, 1998, 2007; Windham et al., 2009; Campbell and Wang, 2012; Roelfsema et al., 2012; Spek and Velderman, 2013; Wei et al., 2013). In contrast to these results, schizophrenia and mood disorders are associated with professions in the arts and humanities, across a diverse array of studies (Nettle, 2006; Kyaga et al., 2011; Campbell and Wang, 2012; Crespi et al., 2016).

Associations of autism with technical professions, in the context of autism's links with intelligence, raise the issue of whether intelligence, as measured by tests of IQ, varies in relation to profession. This controversial topic has been addressed in a suite of studies, all of which report that more-technical professions or occupational plans, especially in engineering, the physical sciences, and mathematics, are associated with relatively high IQs or strong correlates of IQ (Wolfle and Oxtoby, 1952; Hauser, 2002; Wai et al., 2009; Eysenck, 2012 p. xi). The psychological, sociological, and economic causes of these findings are ambiguous, but the results, taken at face value and in conjunction with the vocational correlates of autism, support the hypothesis that the autism spectrum is associated in some manner with relatively high intelligence.

In the context of Baron-Cohen's systemizing-empathizing hypothesis, these findings appear somewhat problematic, because systemizing, as measured by the Systemizing Quotient questionnaire, appears to be uncorrelated with IQ (Ling et al., 2009). Given the diversity of causes of autism, this condition may, however, certainly be associated with both systemizing and high, imbalanced intelligence, even if the two are not connected in simple or direct and causal ways.

Assortative Mating

Positive assortative mating, the mating between individuals who are relatively-similar for a given phenotype or genotype, results in a disproportionate concentration of the relevant alleles among offspring, an increase in additive genetic variance for the trait, and a concomitant rise in heritability (Plomin and Deary, 2015). Humans mate positively assortatively for a wide variety of phenotypes, with intelligence as one of the traits exhibiting the highest correlation between mates, on the order of 0.40–0.60 (Escorial and Martín-Buro, 2012; Plomin and Deary, 2015). To the extent that high intelligence potentiates imbalance in the components of intelligence due to either increases or reductions in its parts, strong assortative mating for intelligence is expected to intensify its effects.

Is there also assortative mating for autism or autism spectrum traits? Baron-Cohen et al. (2006) describe evidence of assortative mating between couples who are both high in the autism-associated psychological trait of systemizing. This hypothesis is supported, for example, by findings that both fathers and mothers of children with ASD exhibit elevated rates of systemizing-related occupations in their fathers (Baron-Cohen et al., 1997), as well as both showing high performance on the EFT (Baron-Cohen and Hammer, 1997). The most direct evidence for assortative mating for autistic phenotypes comes from Nordsletten et al. (2016), who reported much higher rates of assortative mating by psychiatric diagnosis for adults with ASDs (0.45–0.48), than for any other of a large set of disorders. To the extent that autism is genetically correlated with metrics of high intelligence (as described above), these findings indicate that humans mate positively assortatively not just for intelligence, but also for the autism-associated genetic underpinnings of intelligence. Genetic consequences for offspring would thus include both high intelligence and elevated risk of autism, provided that, under the intelligence-imbalance hypothesis addressed here, this process also involved dysregulation of one or more of its components. Further evaluation of this hypothesis would benefit from determining the degree to which positive assortative mating also occurs for autism-related cognitive phenotypes in non-clinical populations, data which would indicate the generality and strength of any such effects.

DISCUSSION

Risk and expression of autism is mediated by alterations to adaptive, evolved cognitive systems, and human intelligence represents one of the most important and pervasive changes along the human lineage and a principal source of cognitive variation among individuals. In this article, I have described the novel paradox that autism is positively genetically correlated with high intelligence, even though individuals with autism tend to have substantially lower IQs than controls. I then evaluated the idea that the paradox can be resolved under the hypothesis that autism involves high yet imbalanced intelligence, such that some or most components of intelligence are increased, but in such a way that overall performance is often reduced. This hypothesis extends previous studies of intelligence in relation to autism (e.g., Dawson et al., 2007; Hayashi et al., 2008; Nader et al., 2016) by providing the first comprehensive integration of the study of intelligence with the study of this condition, in the context of a novel "high and imbalanced intelligence" model that provides specific predictions and guidance for future work. The primary conclusions and implications from testing the hypothesis are four-fold.

First, the psychometric structure of human intelligence, as encompassed by the VPR model and the fluid/crystallized dichotomy, corresponds well with the differences in cognitive profiles between individual with autism and controls. Autism thus involves absolutely or relatively enhanced abilities in the Perceptual domain, but reduced or preserved Verbal and Rotation skills, and absolutely or relatively enhanced fluid intelligence, but reduced or preserved crystallized intelligence. Given that Perceptual domain tasks and tests quantify visual-spatial, sensory discrimination, mechanistic, scientific, and attentional abilities and motivations (Johnson and Deary, 2011), such enhancements are consistent with a large body of previous work on autism but can serve to unify and connect such skills with their neurological and genetic bases. The VPR model can also help to explain the male bias in autism as related to increased focus of attention, reduced verbal skills, and enhanced image rotation ability (or components thereof), given that these patterns emerge from the VPR model once the effects of g are controlled. Considered together, these results imply that although major aspects of intelligence differ between individuals with autism and controls, the differences align with the evolved, neurologically-based axes of cognitive architecture that underlie human mental abilities. Finally, this model may help to frame hypotheses for the autism-related co-variation in perceptual abilities described by Meilleur et al. (2014), perhaps as a manifestation of the increased importance of this facet of intelligence in autistic cognition.

The main implications of these results are that they provide a non-arbitrary, well-validated context (the theory of intelligence) for the interpretation of differences between individuals with and without autism, and they should motivate novel and comprehensive integration of the study of intelligence with the study of autism. With regard to treatments for autism, such integration is useful because it indicates that imbalances in components of intelligence, and their neural underpinnings, may represent novel and malleable targets for individualized therapies that seek to increase the degree of balance, thereby reducing autism symptoms and enhancing everyday social and non-social functioning and well-being. In both phenotypic and genetic contexts, future studies of intelligence in autism might usefully focus on individuals with autism that is apparently mediated by polygenic (rather than monogenic, oligogenic, or syndromic) effects, given that only such causes of autism are expected to be directly relevant to its positive genetic correlation with intelligence. Do such individuals have "too many," or a biased neurological-associated set, of alleles for high intelligence? What developmental and molecular pathways are affected by such sets of genes, and can they also serve as foci for therapies?

Second, a broad swath of correlates of autism, including large brain size, fast brain growth, increased sensory and visual-spatial abilities, enhanced synaptic functions, increased attentional focus, high socioeconomic status, more deliberative decision-making, profession and occupational interests in engineering and physical sciences, and high levels of positive assortative mating, also represent strong correlates of intelligence (**Figure 4**). These findings broadly support the high, imbalanced intelligence hypothesis, although targeted tests are required for more-robust evaluation. Future studies can usefully focus on how these joint correlates of autism and intelligence are related to one another, especially across levels from genes to neurobiology and psychological traits.

Third, the theory and results described here are largely consilient with three of the major psychological theories of autism, systemizing-empathizing bias (Baron-Cohen, 2009), enhanced perceptual function (Mottron et al., 2006), and the intense world (Markram and Markram, 2010), although they ground the patterns supporting each theory in a specific domain of human adaptation, intelligence. This compatibility of theories need not imply that autism has one or few specific causes at the genetic, neurological, and psychological levels—it has many—but it focuses attention on what information will be most useful to collect, to differentially diagnose the causes of autism for each specific individual. What alleles are related to what components of intelligence under the VPR model, and what is their overlap with alleles underlying different phenotypes

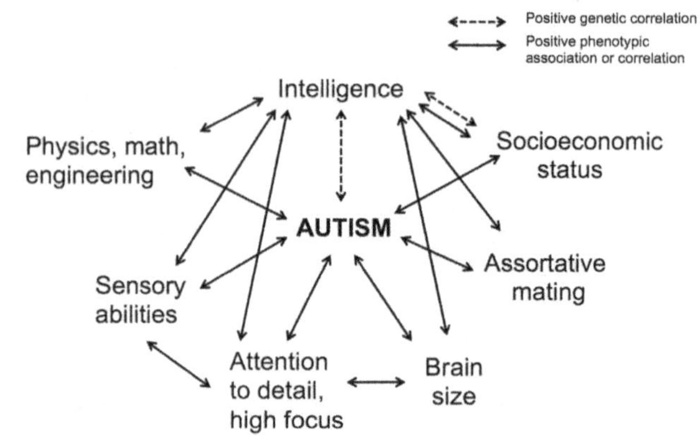

FIGURE 4 | Autism and intelligence are genetically correlated with one another, indicative of a shared genetic basis, and they share phenotypic correlations or associations with a broad suite of traits. These patterns suggest that autism risk is mediated in part by high, but imbalanced, components of intelligence.

found in autism? What neurological processes underlie negative associations between focal and diffuse attention, and verbal vs. rotational abilities (Johnson et al., 2008), and how do they relate to neurological differences among individuals with autism? More generally, what developmental and neurological components of intelligence are altered in autism, and how? And how can the genes, neurodevelopment, and psychology of each individual with autism, or subsets of individuals, be fit within these frameworks?

Fourth, comparisons of autism with schizophrenia for the genetic and phenotypic correlates of intelligence described here support the hypothesis that these two sets of conditions can be regarded as psychiatric, psychological, neurological and genetic "opposites," especially as evidenced by consistent negative genetic correlations of schizophrenia risk with measures of intelligence. Jung (2014) indeed contrasts intelligence and the autism spectrum as diametric to creativity and the schizophrenia spectrum (see also Figure 1 in Crespi et al., 2016; Krapohl and Plomin, 2016), as two major, inversely-associated domains of human cognition. Inverse associations of intelligence with personality correlates of imagination (Openness and apophenia, defined as seeing pattern where none exists) are also supported by factor-analytic studies of personality structure, and by studies that relate working memory, white matter tract integrity, and dopaminergic neurotransmission to both intelligence and imagination (DeYoung et al., 2012). To the extent that autism represents most broadly a disorder of high intelligence (and low imagination), and schizophrenia a disorder of high imagination (and low intelligence), studying these psychiatric conditions will also provide novel insights into variation among neurotypical individuals, and human cognitive architecture, at their largest and smallest scales, with important implications for such fields as artificial intelligence and cognitive enhancement (e.g., Minzenberg et al., 2008; Blaser et al., 2014).

The primary limitations of the hypotheses and predictions evaluated here are that intelligence, as measured in most standardized tests, does not quantify aspects of social and emotional phenotypes that are also highly relevant to disorders such as autism and schizophrenia. Moreover, some key questions remain unresolved, such as how and why especially-high intelligence in one domain would tend to reduce intelligence test scores overall, how and why systemizing and empathizing are related to intelligence and its components (as well as genetic underpinnings), and how autism risk is mediated by polygenic effects, many of which apparently involve alleles for high intelligence, as well as by monogenic or oligogenic effects, which are expected to be deleterious and cause dysfunctions. Addressing these and other questions will require integration of data from evolutionary biology, genetics, the study of intelligence, and autism, and testing of hypotheses that involves spanning across these levels of analysis and theory.

AUTHOR CONTRIBUTIONS

BC conceived and wrote the paper.

ACKNOWLEDGMENTS

I thank Drs Benjamin Gesundheit, Joshua Pesach Rosenzweig, and Yehuda Julyus Shoenfeld for inviting me to prepare this article, the Human Evolutionary Studies Group at Simon Fraser University for helpful discussions, and S. Read for expert technical assistance.

REFERENCES

Adida, M., Maurel, M., Kaladjian, A., Fakra, E., Lazerges, P., Da Fonseca, D., et al. (2011). Decision-making and schizophrenia. *Encephale* 37(Suppl. 2), S110–S116. doi: 10.1016/S0013-7006(11)70036-7

Ashwin, E., Ashwin, C., Rhydderch, D., Howells, J., and Baron-Cohen, S. (2009). Eagle-eyed visual acuity: an experimental investigation of enhanced perception in autism. *Biol. Psychiatry* 65, 17–21. doi: 10.1016/j.biopsych.2008.06.012

Bakian, A. V., Bilder, D. A., Carbone, P. S., Hunt, T. D., Petersen, B., and Rice, C. E. (2015). Brief report: independent validation of Autism Spectrum Disorder case status in the Utah Autism and Developmental Disabilities Monitoring (ADDM) network site. *J. Autism Dev. Disord.* 45, 873–880. doi: 10.1007/s10803-014-2187-6

Baribeau, D. A., and Anagnostou, E. (2013). A comparison of neuroimaging findings in childhood onset schizophrenia and autism spectrum disorder: a review of the literature. *Front. Psychiatry* 4:175. doi: 10.3389/fpsyt.2013.00175

Barnea-Goraly, N., Frazier, T. W., Piacenza, L., Minshew, N. J., Keshavan, M. S., Reiss, A. L., et al. (2014). A preliminary longitudinal volumetric MRI study of amygdala and hippocampal volumes in autism. *Prog. Neuropsychopharmacol. Biol. Psychiatry* 48, 124–128. doi: 10.1016/j.pnpbp.2013.09.010

Baron-Cohen, S. (2006). The hyper-systemizing, assortative mating theory of autism. *Prog. Neuropsychopharmacol. Biol. Psychiatry* 30, 865–872. doi: 10.1016/j.pnpbp.2006.01.010

Baron-Cohen, S. (2009). Autism: the Empathizing–Systemizing (E-S) theory. *Ann. N.Y. Acad. Sci.* 1156, 68–80. doi: 10.1111/j.1749-6632.2009.04467.x

Baron-Cohen, S., Ashwin, E., Ashwin, C., Tavassoli, T., and Chakrabarti, B. (2009). Talent in autism: hyper-systemizing, hyper-attention to detail and sensory hypersensitivity. *Philos. Trans. R. Soc. Lond. B Biol. Sci.* 364, 1377–1383. doi: 10.1098/rstb.2008.0337

Baron-Cohen, S., Bolton, P., Wheelwright, S., Scahill, V., Short, L., Mead, G., et al. (1998). Autism occurs more often in families of physicists, engineers, and mathematicians. *Autism* 2, 296–301. doi: 10.1177/1362361398023008

Baron-Cohen, S., and Hammer, J. (1997). Parents of children with Asperger syndrome: what is the cognitive phenotype? *J. Cogn. Neurosci.* 9, 548–554. doi: 10.1162/jocn.1997.9.4.548

Baron-Cohen, S., Lombardo, M. V., Auyeung, B., Ashwin, E., Chakrabarti, B., and Knickmeyer, R. (2011). Why are autism spectrum conditions more prevalent in males? *PLoS Biol.* 9:e1001081. doi: 10.1371/journal.pbio.1001081

Baron-Cohen, S., Wheelwright, S., Burtenshaw, A., and Hobson, E. (2007). Mathematical talent is linked to autism. *Hum. Nat.* 18, 125–131. doi: 10.1007/s12110-007-9014-0

Baron-Cohen, S., Wheelwright, S., Stott, C., Bolton, P., and Goodyer, I. (1997). Is there a link between engineering and autism? *Autism* 1, 101–109. doi: 10.1177/1362361397011010

Bates, T. C. (2005). The panmodal sensory imprecision hypothesis of schizophrenia: reduced auditory precision in schizotypy. *Pers. Indiv. Diff.* 38, 437–449. doi: 10.1016/j.paid.2004.04.021

Belmonte, M. K., Allen, G., Beckel-Mitchener, A., Boulanger, L. M., Carper, R. A., and Webb, S. J. (2004). Autism and abnormal development of brain connectivity. *J. Neurosci.* 24, 9228–9231. doi: 10.1523/JNEUROSCI.3340-04.2004

Benson, T. L., and Park, S. (2013). Exceptional visuospatial imagery in schizophrenia; implications for madness and creativity. *Front. Hum. Neurosci.* 7:756. doi: 10.3389/fnhum.2013.00756

Benyamin, B., Pourcain, B., Davis, O. S., Davies, G., Hansell, N. K., Brion, M. J., et al. (2014). Childhood intelligence is heritable, highly polygenic and associated with FNBP1L. *Mol. Psychiatry* 19, 253–258. doi: 10.1038/mp.2012.184

Blakemore, S. J., Tavassoli, T., Calò, S., Thomas, R. M., Catmur, C., Frith, U., et al. (2006). Tactile sensitivity in Asperger syndrome. *Brain Cogn.* 61, 5–13. doi: 10.1016/j.bandc.2005.12.013

Blaser, E., Eglington, L., Carter, A. S., and Kaldy, Z. (2014). Pupillometry reveals a mechanism for the Autism Spectrum Disorder (ASD) advantage in visual tasks. *Sci. Rep.* 4:4301. doi: 10.1038/srep04301

Bourgeron, T. (2009). A synaptic trek to autism. *Curr. Opin. Neurobiol.* 19, 231–234. doi: 10.1016/j.conb.2009.06.003

Brosnan, M., Chapman, E., and Ashwin, C. (2014). Adolescents with autism spectrum disorder show a circumspect reasoning bias rather than 'jumping-to-conclusions.' *J. Autism Dev. Disord.* 44, 513–520. doi: 10.1007/s10803-013-1897-5

Brosnan, M. J., Gwilliam, L. R., and Walker, I. (2012). Brief report: the relationship between visual acuity, the embedded figures test and systemizing in autism spectrum disorders. *J. Autism Dev. Disord.* 42, 2491–2497. doi: 10.1007/s10803-012-1505-0

Brosnan, M., Lewton, M., and Ashwin, C. (2016). Reasoning on the Autism Spectrum: a dual process theory account. *J. Autism Dev. Disord.* 46, 2115–2125. doi: 10.1007/s10803-016-2742-4

Broyd, S. J., Demanuele, C., Debener, S., Helps, S. K., James, C. J., and Sonuga-Barke, E. J. (2009). Default-mode brain dysfunction in mental disorders: a systematic review. *Neurosci. Biobehav. Rev.* 33, 279–296. doi: 10.1016/j.neubiorev.2008.09.002

Bulik-Sullivan, B., Finucane, H. K., Anttila, V., Gusev, A., Day, F. R., Loh, P. R., et al. (2015). An atlas of genetic correlations across human diseases and traits. *Nat. Genet.* 47, 1236–1241. doi: 10.1038/ng.3406

Campbell, B. C., and Wang, S. S. H. (2012). Familial linkage between neuropsychiatric disorders and intellectual interests. *PLoS ONE* 7:e30405. doi: 10.1371/journal.pone.0030405

Campbell, D. J., Chang, J., and Chawarska, K. (2014). Early generalized overgrowth in autism spectrum disorder: prevalence rates, gender effects, and clinical outcomes. *J. Am. Acad. Child Adolesc. Psychiatry* 53, 1063–1073. doi: 10.1016/j.jaac.2014.07.008

Cascio, C., McGlone, F., Folger, S., Tannan, V., Baranek, G., Pelphrey, K. A., et al. (2008). Tactile perception in adults with autism: a multidimensional psychophysical study. *J. Autism Dev. Disord.* 38, 127–137. doi: 10.1007/s10803-007-0370-8

Christoforou, A., Espeseth, T., Davies, G., Fernandes, C. P., Giddaluru, S., Mattheisen, M., et al. (2014). GWAS-based pathway analysis differentiates between fluid and crystallized intelligence. *Genes Brain Behav.* 13, 663–674. doi: 10.1111/gbb.12152

Church, B. A., Rice, C. L., Dovgopoly, A., Lopata, C. J., Thomeer, M. L., Nelson, A., et al. (2015). Learning, plasticity, and atypical generalization in children with autism. *Psychon. Bull. Rev.* 22, 1342–1348. doi: 10.3758/s13423-014-0797-9

Clarke, T. K., Lupton, M. K., Fernandez-Pujals, A. M., Starr, J., Davies, G., Cox, S., et al. (2015). Common polygenic risk for autism spectrum disorder (ASD) is associated with cognitive ability in the general population. *Mol. Psychiatry* 21, 419–425. doi: 10.1038/mp.2015.12

Cole, M. W., Yarkoni, T., Repovš, G., Anticevic, A., and Braver, T. S. (2012). Global connectivity of prefrontal cortex predicts cognitive control and intelligence. *J. Neurosci.* 32, 8988–8999. doi: 10.1523/JNEUROSCI.0536-12.2012

Colom, R., Karama, S., Jung, R. E., and Haier, R. J. (2010). Human intelligence and brain networks. *Dialogues Clin. Neurosci.* 12, 489–501.

Courchesne, E., Mouton, P. R., Calhoun, M. E., Ahrens-Barbeau, C., Hallet, M. J., Carter Barnes, C., et al. (2013). "An overabundance of prefrontal cortex neurons underlies early brain overgrowth in autism," in *Neurostereology: Unbiased Stereology of Neural Systems*, ed P. R. Mouton (Hoboken, NJ: Wiley-Blackwell), 73–83.

Courchesne, E., and Pierce, K. (2005). Why the frontal cortex in autism might be talking only to itself: local over-connectivity but long-distance disconnection. *Curr. Opin. Neurobiol.* 15, 225–230. doi: 10.1016/j.conb.2005.03.001

Crespi, B., and Badcock, C. (2008). Psychosis and autism as diametrical disorders of the social brain. *Behav. Brain Sci.* 31, 241–261; discussion 261–320. doi: 10.1017/s0140525x08004214

Crespi, B. J. (2016). "The evolutionary etiologies of autism spectrum and psychotic-affective spectrum disorders," in *Evolutionary Thinking in Medicine: From Research to Policy and Practice*, eds A. Alvergne, C. Jenkinson, and C. Faurie (New York, NY: Oxford University Press), 299–327.

Crespi, B., and Leach, E. (2016). "The evolutionary biology of human neurodevelopment: evo-neuro-devo comes of age," in *Evolutionary Developmental Anthropology*, eds J. Boughner and C. Rolian (Hoboken, NJ: Wiley), 205–229.

Crespi, B., Leach, E., Dinsdale, N., Mokkonen, M., and Hurd, P. (2016). Imagination in human social cognition, autism, and psychotic-affective conditions. *Cognition* 150, 181–199. doi: 10.1016/j.cognition.2016.02.001

Davies, G., Marioni, R. E., Liewald, D. C., Hill, W. D., Hagenaars, S. P., Harris, S. E., et al. (2016). Genome-wide association study of cognitive functions and educational attainment in UK Biobank ($N = 112$ 151). *Mol. Psychiatry* 21, 758–767. doi: 10.1038/mp.2016.45

Davies, G., Tenesa, A., Payton, A., Yang, J., Harris, S. E., Liewald, D., et al. (2011). Genome-wide association studies establish that human intelligence is highly heritable and polygenic. *Mol. Psychiatry* 16, 996–1005. doi: 10.1038/mp.2011.85

Davis, J. M., Searles, V. B., Anderson, N., Keeney, J., Dumas, L., and Sikela, J. M. (2014). DUF1220 dosage is linearly associated with increasing severity of the three primary symptoms of autism. *PLoS Genet.* 10:e1004241. doi: 10.1371/journal.pgen.1004241

Davis, J. M., Searles, V. B., Anderson, N., Keeney, J., Raznahan, A., Horwood, L. J., et al. (2015). DUF1220 copy number is linearly associated with increased cognitive function as measured by total IQ and mathematical aptitude scores. *Hum. Genet.* 134, 67–75. doi: 10.1007/s00439-014-1489-2

Dawson, M., Soulières, I., Gernsbacher, M. A., and Mottron, L. (2007). The level and nature of autistic intelligence. *Psychol. Sci.* 18, 657–662. doi: 10.1111/j.1467-9280.2007.01954.x

Deaner, R. O., Isler, K., Burkart, J., and Van Schaik, C. (2007). Overall brain size, and not encephalization quotient, best predicts cognitive ability across non-human primates. *Brain Behav. Evol.* 70, 115–124. doi: 10.1159/000102973

Deary, I. J., Bell, P. J., Bell, A. J., Campbell, M. L., and Fazal, N. D. (2004). Sensory discrimination and intelligence: testing Spearman's other hypothesis. *Am. J. Psychol.* 117, 1–18. doi: 10.2307/1423593

Deary, I. J., and Johnson, W. (2010). Intelligence and education: causal perceptions drive analytic processes and therefore conclusions. *Int. J. Epidemiol.* 39, 1362–1369. doi: 10.1093/ije/dyq072

Deary, I. J., Penke, L., and Johnson, W. (2010). The neuroscience of human intelligence differences. *Nat. Rev. Neurosci.* 11, 201–211. doi: 10.1038/nrn2793

De Martino, B., Harrison, N. A., Knafo, S., Bird, G., and Dolan, R. J. (2008). Explaining enhanced logical consistency during decision making in autism. *J. Neurosci.* 28, 10746–10750. doi: 10.1523/JNEUROSCI.2895-08.2008

DeYoung, C. G., Grazioplene, R. G., and Peterson, J. B. (2012). From madness to genius: the Openness/Intellect trait domain as a paradoxical simplex. *J. Res. Pers.* 46, 63–78. doi: 10.1016/j.jrp.2011.12.003

Dicke, U., and Roth, G. (2016). Neuronal factors determining high intelligence. *Phil. Trans. R. Soc. B Biol. Sci.* 371:20150180. doi: 10.1098/rstb.2015.0180

Dudley, R., Taylor, P., Wickham, S., and Hutton, P. (2016). Psychosis, delusions and the "jumping to conclusions" reasoning bias: a systematic review and meta-analysis. *Schizophr. Bull.* 42, 652–665. doi: 10.1093/schbul/sbv150

Dumas, L. J., O'Bleness, M. S., Davis, J. M., Dickens, C. M., Anderson, N., Keeney, J. G., et al. (2012). DUF1220-domain copy number implicated in human brain-size pathology and evolution. *Am. J. Hum. Genet.* 91, 444–454. doi: 10.1016/j.ajhg.2012.07.016

Durkin, M. S., Maenner, M. J., Meaney, F. J., Levy, S. E., DiGuiseppi, C., Nicholas, J. S., et al. (2010). Socioeconomic inequality in the prevalence of autism spectrum disorder: evidence from a US cross-sectional study. *PLoS ONE* 5:e11551. doi: 10.1371/journal.pone.0011551

Ecker, C., Ginestet, C., Feng, Y., Johnston, P., Lombardo, M. V., Lai, M. C., et al. (2013). Brain surface anatomy in adults with autism: the relationship between surface area, cortical thickness, and autistic symptoms. *JAMA Psychiatry* 70, 59–70. doi: 10.1001/jamapsychiatry.2013.265

Eduardo Mercado, B. A. C. III, Coutinho, M. V., Dovgopoly, A., Lopata, C. J., Toomey, J. A., and Thomeer, M. L. (2015). Heterogeneity in perceptual category learning by high functioning children with autism spectrum disorder. *Front. Integrative Neurosci.* 9:42. doi: 10.3389/fnint.2015.00042

Eigsti, I. M., and Fein, D. A. (2013). More is less: pitch discrimination and language delays in children with optimal outcomes from autism. *Autism Res.* 6, 605–613. doi: 10.1002/aur.1324

Emerson, E. (2012). Deprivation, ethnicity and the prevalence of intellectual and developmental disabilities. *J. Epidemiol. Commun. Health.* 66, 218–224. doi: 10.1136/jech.2010.111773

Escorial, S., and Martín-Buro, C. (2012). The role of personality and intelligence in assortative mating. *Spanish J. Psychol.* 15, 680–687. doi: 10.5209/rev_SJOP.2012.v15.n2.38879

Evans, B. (2013). How autism became autism: the radical transformation of a central concept of child development in Britain. *Hist. Human Sci.* 26, 3–31. doi: 10.1177/0952695113484320

Eysenck (2012). *The Measurement of Intelligence.* Berlin: Springer Science and Business Media.

Falter, C. M., Elliott, M. A., and Bailey, A. J. (2012). Enhanced visual temporal resolution in autism spectrum disorders. *PLoS ONE* 7:e32774. doi: 10.1371/journal.pone.0032774

Fjell, A. M., Westlye, L. T., Amlien, I., Tamnes, C. K., Grydeland, H., Engvig, A., et al. (2015). High-expanding cortical regions in human development and evolution are related to higher intellectual abilities. *Cereb. Cortex* 25, 26–34. doi: 10.1093/cercor/bht201

Fombonne, E. (2009). Epidemiology of pervasive developmental disorders. *Pediatr. Res.* 65, 591–598. doi: 10.1203/PDR.0b013e31819e7203

Force, R. B., Venables, N. C., and Sponheim, S. R. (2008). An auditory processing abnormality specific to liability for schizophrenia. *Schizophr. Res.* 103, 298–310. doi: 10.1016/j.schres.2008.04.038

Foster, N. E., Doyle-Thomas, K. A., Tryfon, A., Ouimet, T., Anagnostou, E., Evans, A. C., et al. (2015). Structural gray matter differences during childhood development in autism spectrum disorder: a multimetric approach. *Pediatr. Neurol.* 53, 350–359. doi: 10.1016/j.pediatrneurol.2015.06.013

Franić, S., Dolan, C. V., Broxholme, J., Hu, H., Zemojtel, T., Davies, G. E., et al. (2015). Mendelian and polygenic inheritance of intelligence: a common set of causal genes? Using next-generation sequencing to examine the effects of 168 intellectual disability genes on normal-range intelligence. *Intelligence* 49, 10–22. doi: 10.1016/j.intell.2014.12.001

Froehlich, A. L., Anderson, J. S., Bigler, E. D., Miller, J. S., Lange, N. T., DuBray, M. B., et al. (2012). Intact prototype formation but impaired generalization in autism. *Res. Autism Spectr. Disord.* 6, 921–930. doi: 10.1016/j.rasd.2011.12.006

Fukumoto, A., Hashimoto, T., Mori, K., Tsuda, Y., Arisawa, K., and Kagami, S. (2011). Head circumference and body growth in autism spectrum disorders. *Brain Dev.* 33, 569–575. doi: 10.1016/j.braindev.2010.09.004

Galton, F. (1883). *Inquiries into the Human Faculty & Its Development.* London: JM Dent and Company.

Cross-Disorder Group of the Psychiatric Genomics Consortium (2013). Genetic relationship between five psychiatric disorders estimated from genome-wide SNPs. *Nat. Genet.* 45, 984–994. doi: 10.1038/ng.2711

Gizzonio, V., Avanzini, P., Fabbri-Destro, M., Campi, C., and Rizzolatti, G. (2014). Cognitive abilities in siblings of children with autism spectrum disorders. *Exp. Brain Res.* 232, 2381–2390. doi: 10.1007/s00221-014-3935-8

Gkogkas, C. G., Khoutorsky, A., Ran, I., Rampakakis, E., Nevarko, T., Weatherill, D. B., et al. (2013). Autism-related deficits via dysregulated eIF4E-dependent translational control. *Nature* 493, 371–377. doi: 10.1038/nature11628

Gogtay, N., Lu, A., Leow, A. D., Klunder, A. D., Lee, A. D., Chavez, A., et al. (2008). Three-dimensional brain growth abnormalities in childhood-onset schizophrenia visualized by using tensor-based morphometry. *Proc. Natl. Acad. Sci. U.S.A.* 105, 15979–15984. doi: 10.1073/pnas.0806485105

Hagenaars, S. P., Harris, S. E., Davies, G., Hill, W. D., Liewald, D. C., Ritchie, S. J., et al. (2016). Shared genetic aetiology between cognitive functions and physical and mental health in UK Biobank ($N = 112\,151$) and 24 GWAS consortia. *Mol. Psychiatry.* doi: 10.1038/mp.2015.225. [Epub ahead of print].

Happé, F., and Frith, U. (2006). The weak coherence account: detail-focused cognitive style in autism spectrum disorders. *J. Autism Dev. Disord.* 36, 5–25. doi: 10.1007/s10803-005-0039-0

Happé, F., and Ronald, A. (2008). The 'fractionable autism triad': a review of evidence from behavioural, genetic, cognitive and neural research. *Neuropsychol. Rev.* 18, 287–304. doi: 10.1007/s11065-008-9076-8

Happé, F., Ronald, A., and Plomin, R. (2006). Time to give up on a single explanation for autism. *Nat. Neurosci.* 9, 1218–1220. doi: 10.1038/nn1770

Hardan, A. Y., Libove, R. A., Keshavan, M. S., Melhem, N. M., and Minshew, N. J. (2009). A preliminary longitudinal magnetic resonance imaging study of brain volume and cortical thickness in autism. *Biol. Psychiatry* 66, 320–326. doi: 10.1016/j.biopsych.2009.04.024

Hardan, A. Y., Muddasani, S., Vemulapalli, M., Keshavan, M. S., and Minshew, N. J. (2006). An MRI study of increased cortical thickness in autism. *Am. J. Psychiatry* 163, 1290–1292. doi: 10.1176/ajp.2006.163.7.1290

Hauser, R. M. (2002). *Meritocracy, Cognitive Ability, and the Sources of Occupational Success.* Madison, WI: Center for Demography and Ecology, University of Wisconsin.

Hayashi, M., Kato, M., Igarashi, K., and Kashima, H. (2008). Superior fluid intelligence in children with Asperger's disorder. *Brain Cogn.* 66, 306–310. doi: 10.1016/j.bandc.2007.09.008

Heaton, P., Hudry, K., Ludlow, A., and Hill, E. (2008). Superior discrimination of speech pitch and its relationship to verbal ability in autism spectrum disorders. *Cogn. Neuropsychol.* 25, 771–782. doi: 10.1080/02643290802336277

Henrich, J. (2015). *The Secret of Our Success: How Culture Is Driving Human Evolution, Domesticating Our Species, and Making Us Smarter.* Princeton, NJ: Princeton University Press.

Hill, W. D., Davies, G., CHARGE Cognitive Working Group, Liewald, D. C., McIntosh, A. M., and Deary, I. J. (2015). Age-dependent pleiotropy between general cognitive function and major psychiatric disorders. *Biol. Psychiatry.* doi: 10.1016/j.biopsych.2015.08.033. [Epub ahead of print].

Hoekstra, R. A., Happé, F., Baron-Cohen, S., and Ronald, A. (2009). Association between extreme autistic traits and intellectual disability: insights from a general population twin study. *Br. J. Psychiatry* 195, 531–536. doi: 10.1192/bjp.bp.108.060889

Horlin, C., Black, M., Falkmer, M., and Falkmer, T. (2016). Proficiency of individuals with autism spectrum disorder at disembedding figures: a systematic review. *Dev. Neurorehabil.* 19, 54–63. doi: 10.3109/17518423.2014.888102

Howlin, P., Goode, S., Hutton, J., and Rutter, M. (2009). Savant skills in autism: psychometric approaches and parental reports. *Philos. Trans. R. Soc. Lond. B Biol. Sci.* 364, 1359–1367. doi: 10.1098/rstb.2008.0328

Hubbard, L., Tansey, K. E., Rai, D., Jones, P., Ripke, S., Chambert, K. D., et al. (2016). Evidence of common genetic overlap between schizophrenia and cognition. *Schizophr. Bull.* 42, 832–842. doi: 10.1093/schbul/sbv168

Hyde, K. L., Samson, F., Evans, A. C., and Mottron, L. (2010). Neuroanatomical differences in brain areas implicated in perceptual and other core features of autism revealed by cortical thickness analysis and voxel-based morphometry. *Hum. Brain Mapp.* 31, 556–566. doi: 10.1002/hbm.20887

Isshiki, M., Tanaka, S., Kuriu, T., Tabuchi, K., Takumi, T., and Okabe, S. (2014). Enhanced synapse remodelling as a common phenotype in mouse models of autism. *Nat. Commun.* 5. doi: 10.1038/ncomms5742

Ivanovic, D. M., Leiva, B. P., Castro, C. G., Olivares, M. G., Jansana, J. M. M., Castro, V. G., et al. (2004). Brain development parameters and intelligence in Chilean high school graduates. *Intelligence* 32, 461–479. doi: 10.1016/j.intell.2004.07.001

Javitt, D. C. (2009a). Sensory processing in schizophrenia: neither simple nor intact. *Schizophr. Bull.* 35, 1059–1064. doi: 10.1093/schbul/sbp110

Javitt, D. C. (2009b). When doors of perception close: bottom-up models of disrupted cognition in schizophrenia. *Annu. Rev. Clin. Psychol.* 5, 249–275. doi: 10.1146/annurev.clinpsy.032408.153502

Johnson, W., and Bouchard, T. J. (2005a). Constructive replication of the visual–perceptual-image rotation model in Thurstone's (1941) battery of 60 tests of mental ability. *Intelligence* 33, 417–430. doi: 10.1016/j.intell.2004.12.001

Johnson, W., and Bouchard, T. J. (2005b). The structure of human intelligence: it is verbal, perceptual, and image rotation (VPR), not fluid and crystallized. *Intelligence* 33, 393–416. doi: 10.1016/j.intell.2004.12.002

Johnson, W., and Bouchard, T. J. (2007). Sex differences in mental abilities: g masks the dimensions on which they lie. *Intelligence* 35, 23–39. doi: 10.1016/j.intell.2006.03.012

Johnson, W., and Bouchard, T. J. (2008). Linking abilities, interests, and sex via latent class analysis. *J. Career Assess.* 17, 3–38. doi: 10.1177/1069072708325738

Johnson, W., Bouchard, T. J., McGue, M., Segal, N. L., Tellegen, A., Keyes, M., et al. (2007). Genetic and environmental influences on the Verbal-Perceptual-Image Rotation (VPR) model of the structure of mental abilities in the Minnesota study of twins reared apart. *Intelligence* 35, 542–562. doi: 10.1016/j.intell.2006.10.003

Johnson, W., and Deary, I. J. (2011). Placing inspection time, reaction time, and perceptual speed in the broader context of cognitive ability: the VPR model in the Lothian Birth Cohort 1936. *Intelligence* 39, 405–417. doi: 10.1016/j.intell.2011.07.003

Johnson, W., Jung, R. E., Colom, R., and Haier, R. J. (2008). Cognitive abilities independent of IQ correlate with regional brain structure. *Intelligence* 36, 18–28. doi: 10.1016/j.intell.2007.01.005

Jung, R. E. (2014). Evolution, creativity, intelligence, and madness: "Here Be Dragons". *Front. Psychol.* 5:784. doi: 10.3389/fpsyg.2014.00784

Jung, R. E., and Haier, R. J. (2007). The Parieto-Frontal Integration Theory (P-FIT) of intelligence: converging neuroimaging evidence. *Behav. Brain Sci.* 30, 135–154. doi: 10.1017/S0140525X07001185

Kanner, L. (1943). Autistic disturbances of affective contact. *Nervous Child. Acta Paedopsychiatr.* 35, 100–136.

Kanner, L., and Lesser, L. I. (1958). Early infantile autism. *Pediatr. Clin. North Am.* 5, 711.

Karadi, K., Kallai, J., Kover, F., Nemes, J., Makany, T., and Nagy, F. (2006). Endogenous testosterone concentration, mental rotation, and size of the corpus callosum in a sample of young Hungarian women. *Percept. Mot. Skills* 102, 445–453. doi: 10.2466/pms.102.2.445-453

Karama, S., Colom, R., Johnson, W., Deary, I. J., Haier, R., Waber, D. P., et al. (2011). Cortical thickness correlates of specific cognitive performance accounted for by the general factor of intelligence in healthy children aged 6 to 18. *Neuroimage* 55, 1443–1453. doi: 10.1016/j.neuroimage.2011.01.016

Karbasforoushan, H., and Woodward, N. D. (2012). Resting-state networks in schizophrenia. *Curr. Top. Med. Chem.* 12, 2404–2414. doi: 10.2174/156802612805289863

Kasai, H., Fukuda, M., Watanabe, S., Hayashi-Takagi, A., and Noguchi, J. (2010). Structural dynamics of dendritic spines in memory and cognition. *Trends Neurosci.* 33, 121–129. doi: 10.1016/j.tins.2010.01.001

Keeney, J. G., Dumas, L., and Sikela, J. M. (2014). The case for DUF1220 domain dosage as a primary contributor to anthropoid brain expansion. *Front. Hum. Neurosci.* 8:427. doi: 10.3389/fnhum.2014.00427

Kelleher, R. J., and Bear, M. F. (2008). The autistic neuron: troubled translation? *Cell* 135, 401–406. doi: 10.1016/j.cell.2008.10.017

Kerchner, G. A., Racine, C. A., Hale, S., Wilheim, R., Laluz, V., Miller, B. L., et al. (2012). Cognitive processing speed in older adults: relationship with white matter integrity. *PLoS ONE* 7:e50425. doi: 10.1371/journal.pone.0050425

Khodadady, E., and Tafaghodi, A. (2013). Cognitive styles and fluid intelligence: are they related? *J. Stud. Soc. Sci.* 3, 138–150.

Kim, D. J., Davis, E. P., Sandman, C. A., Sporns, O., O'Donnell, B. F., Buss, C., et al. (2016). Children's intellectual ability is associated with structural network integrity. *Neuroimage* 124, 550–556. doi: 10.1016/j.neuroimage.2015.09.012

King, M. D., and Bearman, P. S. (2011). Socioeconomic status and the increased prevalence of autism in California. *Am. Sociol. Rev.* 76, 320–346. doi: 10.1177/0003122411399389

King, P. D. (1975). Early infantile autism: relation to schizophrenia. *J. Am. Acad. Child Psychiatry* 14, 666–682. doi: 10.1016/S0002-7138(09)61465-5

Koenis, M. M., Brouwer, R. M., van den Heuvel, M. P., Mandl, R. C., van Soelen, I. L., Kahn, R. S., et al. (2015). Development of the brain's structural network efficiency in early adolescence: a longitudinal DTI twin study. *Hum. Brain Mapp.* 36, 4938–4953. doi: 10.1002/hbm.22988

Krapohl, E., and Plomin, R. (2016). Genetic link between family socioeconomic status and children's educational achievement estimated from genome-wide SNPs. *Mol. Psychiatry* 21, 437–443. doi: 10.1038/mp.2015.2

Kravariti, E., Toulopoulou, T., Mapua-Filbey, F., Schulze, K., Walshe, M., Sham, P., et al. (2006). Intellectual asymmetry and genetic liability in first-degree relatives of probands with schizophrenia. *Br. J. Psychiatry* 188, 186–187. doi: 10.1192/bjp.bp.104.008177

Kulkarni, V. A., and Firestein, B. L. (2012). The dendritic tree and brain disorders. *Mol. Cell. Neurosci.* 50, 10–20. doi: 10.1016/j.mcn.2012.03.005

Kyaga, S., Lichtenstein, P., Boman, M., Hultman, C., Långström, N., and Landén, M. (2011). Creativity and mental disorder: family study of 300 000 people with severe mental disorder. *Br. J. Psychiatry* 199, 373–379. doi: 10.1192/bjp.bp.110.085316

Lee, T., Mosing, M. A., Henry, J. D., Trollor, J. N., Lammel, A., Ames, D., et al. (2012). Genetic influences on five measures of processing speed and their covariation with general cognitive ability in the elderly: the older Australian twins study. *Behav. Genet.* 42, 96–106. doi: 10.1007/s10519-011-9474-1

Lencz, T., Knowles, E., Davies, G., Guha, S., Liewald, D. C., Starr, J. M., et al. (2014). Molecular genetic evidence for overlap between general cognitive ability and risk for schizophrenia: a report from the Cognitive Genomics consorTium (COGENT). *Mol. Psychiatry* 19, 168–174. doi: 10.1038/mp.2013.166

Leonard, H., Glasson, E., Nassar, N., Whitehouse, A., Bebbington, A., Bourke, J., et al. (2011). Autism and intellectual disability are differentially related to sociodemographic background at birth. *PLoS ONE* 6:e17875. doi: 10.1371/journal.pone.0017875

Levine, M., and Olson, R. P. (1968). Intelligence of parents of autistic children. *J. Abnorm. Psychol.* 73, 215. doi: 10.1037/h0020120

Ling, J., Burton, T. C., Salt, J. L., and Muncer, S. J. (2009). Psychometric analysis of the systemizing quotient (SQ) scale. *Br. J. Psychol.* 100, 539–552. doi: 10.1348/000712608X368261

Lotter, V. (1966). Epidemiology of autistic conditions in young children. Part I: prevalence. *Soc. Psychiatry* 1, 124–135. doi: 10.1007/bf00584048

Lotter, V. (1967). Epidemiology of autistic conditions in young children. Part II: some characteristics of the parents and children. *Soc. Psychiatry* 1, 163–173. doi: 10.1007/BF00578950

Loui, P., Li, H. C., Hohmann, A., and Schlaug, G. (2011). Enhanced cortical connectivity in absolute pitch musicians: a model for local hyperconnectivity. *J. Cogn. Neurosci.* 23, 1015–1026. doi: 10.1162/jocn.2010.21500

Maier, S., van Elst, L. T., Beier, D., Ebert, D., Fangmeier, T., Radtke, M., et al. (2015). Increased hippocampal volumes in adults with high functioning autism spectrum disorder and an IQ> 100: a manual morphometric study. *Psychiatry Res. Neuroimaging* 234, 152–155. doi: 10.1016/j.pscychresns.2015.08.002

Major, J. T., Johnson, W., and Deary, I. J. (2012). Comparing models of intelligence in Project TALENT: the VPR model fits better than the CHC and extended Gf-Gc models. *Intellig* 40, 543–559. doi: 10.1016/j.intell.2012.07.006

Mak-Fan, K. M., Taylor, M. J., Roberts, W., and Lerch, J. P. (2012). Measures of cortical grey matter structure and development in children with autism spectrum disorder. *J. Autism Dev. Disord.* 42, 419–427. doi: 10.1007/s10803-011-1261-6

Marioni, R. E., Davies, G., Hayward, C., Liewald, D., Kerr, S. M., Campbell, A., et al. (2014). Molecular genetic contributions to socioeconomic status and intelligence. *Intelligence* 44, 26–32. doi: 10.1016/j.intell.2014.02.006

Markram, K., and Markram, H. (2010). The intense world theory–a unifying theory of the neurobiology of autism. *Front. Hum. Neurosci.* 4:224. doi: 10.3389/fnhum.2010.00224

Maximo, J. O., Cadena, E. J., and Kana, R. K. (2014). The implications of brain connectivity in the neuropsychology of autism. *Neuropsychol. Rev.* 24, 16–31. doi: 10.1007/s11065-014-9250-0

McCleery, J. P., Allman, E., Carver, L. J., and Dobkins, K. R. (2007). Abnormal magnocellular pathway visual processing in infants at risk for autism. *Biol. Psychiatry* 62, 1007–1014. doi: 10.1016/j.biopsych.2007.02.009

McIntosh, A. M., Gow, A., Luciano, M., Davies, G., Liewald, D. C., Harris, S. E., et al. (2013). Polygenic risk for schizophrenia is associated with cognitive change between childhood and old age. *Biol. Psychiatry* 73, 938–943. doi: 10.1016/j.biopsych.2013.01.011

McKenna, F. P. (1990). Learning implications of field dependence-independence: cognitive style versus cognitive ability. *Appl. Cogn. Psychol.* 4, 425–437. doi: 10.1002/acp.2350040602

McKenna, F. P., Duncan, J., and Brown, I. D. (1986). Cognitive abilities and safety on the road: a re-examination of individual differences in dichotic listening and search for embedded figures. *Ergonomics* 29, 649–663. doi: 10.1080/00140138608968300

Meilleur, A. A. S., Berthiaume, C., Bertone, A., and Mottron, L. (2014). Autism-specific covariation in perceptual performances: "g" or "p" factor? *PLoS ONE* 9:e103781. doi: 10.1371/journal.pone.0103781

Meilleur, A. A. S., Jelenic, P., and Mottron, L. (2015). Prevalence of clinically and empirically defined talents and strengths in autism. *J. Autism Dev. Disord.* 45, 1354–1367. doi: 10.1007/s10803-014-2296-2

Melnick, M. D., Harrison, B. R., Park, S., Bennetto, L., and Tadin, D. (2013). A strong interactive link between sensory discriminations and intelligence. *Curr. Biol.* 23, 1013–1017. doi: 10.1016/j.cub.2013.04.053

Menary, K., Collins, P. F., Porter, J. N., Muetzel, R., Olson, E. A., Kumar, V., et al. (2013). Associations between cortical thickness and general intelligence in children, adolescents and young adults. *Intelligence* 41, 597–606. doi: 10.1016/j.intell.2013.07.010

Meyer, C. S., Hagmann-von Arx, P., Lemola, S., and Grob, A. (2010). Correspondence between the general ability to discriminate sensory stimuli and general intelligence. *J. Indiv. Diff.* 31, 46–56. doi: 10.1027/1614-0001/a0 00006

Minzenberg, M. J., Watrous, A. J., Yoon, J. H., Ursu, S., and Carter, C. S. (2008). Modafinil shifts human locus coeruleus to low-tonic, high-phasic activity during functional MRI. *Science* 322, 1700–1702. doi: 10.1126/science.1164908

Montgomery, S. H., and Mundy, N. I. (2014). Microcephaly genes evolved adaptively throughout the evolution of eutherian mammals. *BMC Evol. Biol.* 14:120. doi: 10.1186/1471-2148-14-120

Morris, R., Griffiths, O., Le Pelley, M. E., and Weickert, T. W. (2013). Attention to irrelevant cues is related to positive symptoms in schizophrenia. *Schiz. Bull.* 39, 575–582. doi: 10.1093/schbul/sbr192

Mottron, L., Belleville, S., Rouleau, G. A., and Collignon, O. (2014). Linking neocortical, cognitive, and genetic variability in autism with alterations of brain plasticity: the Trigger-Threshold-Target model. *Neurosci. Biobehav. Rev.* 47, 735–752. doi: 10.1016/j.neubiorev.2014.07.012

Mottron, L., Dawson, M., Soulieres, I., Hubert, B., and Burack, J. (2006). Enhanced perceptual functioning in autism: an update, and eight principles of autistic perception. *J. Autism Dev. Disord.* 36, 27–43. doi: 10.1007/s10803-005-0040-7

Murray, D., Lesser, M., and Lawson, W. (2005). Attention, monotropism and the diagnostic criteria for autism. *Autism* 9, 139–156. doi: 10.1177/1362361305051398

Muth, A., Hönekopp, J., and Falter, C. M. (2014). Visuo-spatial performance in autism: a meta-analysis. *J. Autism Dev. Disord.* 44, 3245–3263. doi: 10.1007/s10803-014-2188-5

Nader, A. M., Courchesne, V., Dawson, M., and Soulières, I. (2016). Does WISC-IV underestimate the intelligence of autistic children? *J. Autism Dev. Disord.* 46, 1582–1589. doi: 10.1007/s10803-014-2270-z

Nakano, T., Kato, N., and Kitazawa, S. (2012). Superior haptic-to-visual shape matching in autism spectrum disorders. *Neuropsychologia* 50, 696–703. doi: 10.1016/j.neuropsychologia.2011.12.024

Nesse, R. M., and Stein, D. J. (2012). Towards a genuinely medical model for psychiatric nosology. *BMC Med.* 10:5. doi: 10.1186/1741-7015-10-5

Nettle, D. (2006). Schizotypy and mental health amongst poets, visual artists, and mathematicians. *J. Res. Pers.* 40, 876–890. doi: 10.1016/j.jrp.2005.09.004

Nisbett, R. E., Aronson, J., Blair, C., Dickens, W., Flynn, J., Halpern, D. F., et al. (2012). Intelligence: new findings and theoretical developments. *Am. Psychol.* 67, 130. doi: 10.1037/a0026699

Noland, J. S., Reznick, J. S., Stone, W. L., Walden, T., and Sheridan, E. H. (2010). Better working memory for non-social targets in infant siblings of children with Autism Spectrum Disorder. *Dev. Sci.* 13, 244–251. doi: 10.1111/j.1467-7687.2009.00882.x

Nordsletten, A. E., Larsson, H., Crowley, J. J., Almqvist, C., Lichtenstein, P., and Mataix-Cols, D. (2016). Patterns of nonrandom mating within and across 11 major psychiatric disorders. *JAMA Psychiatry* 73, 354–361. doi: 10.1001/jamapsychiatry.2015.3192

O'Riordan, M., and Passetti, F. (2006). Discrimination in autism within different sensory modalities. *J. Autism Dev. Disord.* 36, 665–675. doi: 10.1007/s10803-006-0106-1

Oberman, L. M., and Pascual-Leone, A. (2014). Hyperplasticity in Autism Spectrum Disorder confers protection from Alzheimer's disease. *Med. Hypotheses* 83, 337–342. doi: 10.1016/j.mehy.2014.06.008

Oertel-Knöchel, V., Knöchel, C., Rotarska-Jagiela, A., Reinke, B., Prvulovic, D., Haenschel, C., et al. (2013). Association between psychotic symptoms and cortical thickness reduction across the schizophrenia spectrum. *Cereb. Cortex* 23, 61–70. doi: 10.1093/cercor/bhr380

Oguro-Ando, A., Rosensweig, C., Herman, E., Nishimura, Y., Werling, D., Bill, B. R., et al. (2015). Increased CYFIP1 dosage alters cellular and dendritic morphology and dysregulates mTOR. *Mol. Psychiatry* 20, 1069–1078. doi: 10.1038/mp.2014.124

Pantelis, C., Yücel, M., Wood, S. J., Velakoulis, D., Sun, D., Berger, G., et al. (2005). Structural brain imaging evidence for multiple pathological processes at different stages of brain development in schizophrenia. *Schizophr. Bull.* 31, 672–696. doi: 10.1093/schbul/sbi034

Panton, K. R., Badcock, D. R., and Badcock, J. C. (2016). A metaanalysis of perceptual organization in schizophrenia, schizotypy, and other high-risk groups based on variants of the embedded figures task. *Front. Psychol.* 7:237. doi: 10.3389/fpsyg.2016.00237

Plomin, R., and Deary, I. J. (2015). Genetics and intelligence differences: five special findings. *Mol. Psychiatry* 20, 98–108. doi: 10.1038/mp.2014.105

Ploog, B. O. (2010). Stimulus overselectivity four decades later: a review of the literature and its implications for current research in autism spectrum disorder. *J. Autism Dev. Disord.* 40, 1332–1349. doi: 10.1007/s10803-010-0990-2

Quick, V. S., Davis, J. M., Olincy, A., and Sikela, J. M. (2015). DUF1220 copy number is associated with schizophrenia risk and severity: implications for understanding autism and schizophrenia as related diseases. *Transl. Psychiatry* 5, e697. doi: 10.1038/tp.2015.192

Rai, D., Lewis, G., Lundberg, M., Araya, R., Svensson, A., Dalman, C., et al. (2012). Parental socioeconomic status and risk of offspring autism spectrum disorders in a Swedish population-based study. *J. Am. Acad. Child Adolesc. Psychiatry* 51, 467–476. doi: 10.1016/j.jaac.2012.02.012

Rais, M., Cahn, W., Schnack, H. G., Pol, H. H., Kahn, R. S., and van Haren, N. E. M. (2012). Brain volume reductions in medication-naive patients with schizophrenia in relation to intelligence quotient. *Psychol. Med.* 42, 1847–1856. doi: 10.1017/S0033291712000098

Rapoport, J. L., and Gogtay, N. (2011). Childhood onset schizophrenia: support for a progressive neurodevelopmental disorder. *Int. J. Dev. Neurosci.* 29, 251–258. doi: 10.1016/j.ijdevneu.2010.10.003

Rimland, B. (1964). *Infantile Autism: The Syndrome and Its Implications for a Neural Theory of Behavior.* New York, NY: Appleton-Century-Crofts.

Rimol, L. M., Nesvåg, R., Hagler, D. J., Bergmann, Ø., Fennema-Notestine, C., Hartberg, C. B., et al. (2012). Cortical volume, surface area, and thickness in schizophrenia and bipolar disorder. *Biol. Psychiatry* 71, 552–560. doi: 10.1016/j.biopsych.2011.11.026

Rinaldi, T., Perrodin, C., and Markram, H. (2008). Hyper-connectivity and hyper-plasticity in the medial prefrontal cortex in the valproic acid animal model of autism. *Front. Neural Circuits* 2:4. doi: 10.3389/neuro.04.004.2008

Roelfsema, M. T., Hoekstra, R. A., Allison, C., Wheelwright, S., Brayne, C., Matthews, F. E., et al. (2012). Are autism spectrum conditions more prevalent in an information-technology region? A school-based study of three regions in the Netherlands. *J. Autism Dev. Disord.* 42, 734–739. doi: 10.1007/s10803-011-1302-1

Roth, G., and Dicke, U. (2005). Evolution of the brain and intelligence. *Trends Cogn. Sci.* 9, 250–257. doi: 10.1016/j.tics.2005.03.005

Rubenstein, J. L. R., and Merzenich, M. M. (2003). Model of autism: increased ratio of excitation/inhibition in key neural systems. *Genes Brain Behav.* 2, 255–267. doi: 10.1034/j.1601-183X.2003.00037.x

Rutherford, M. D., and Subiaul, F. (2015). Children with autism spectrum disorder have an exceptional explanatory drive. *Autism.* doi: 10.1177/13623613156 05973. [Epub ahead of print].

Ruthsatz, J., and Urbach, J. B. (2012). Child prodigy: a novel cognitive profile places elevated general intelligence, exceptional working memory and attention to detail at the root of prodigiousness. *Intelligence* 40, 419–426. doi: 10.1016/j.intell.2012.06.002

Sabatos-DeVito, M., Schipul, S. E., Bulluck, J. C., Belger, A., and Baranek, G. T. (2016). Eye tracking reveals impaired attentional disengagement associated with sensory response patterns in children with autism. *J. Autism Dev. Disord.* 46, 1319–1333. doi: 10.1007/s10803-015-2681-5

Sacco, R., Gabriele, S., and Persico, A. M. (2015). Head circumference and brain size in autism spectrum disorder: a systematic review and meta-analysis. *Psychiatry Res.* 234, 239–251. doi: 10.1016/j.pscychresns.2015.08.016

Santini, E., Huynh, T. N., MacAskill, A. F., Carter, A. G., Pierre, P., et al. (2013). Exaggerated translation causes synaptic and behavioural aberrations associated with autism. *Nature* 493, 411–415. doi: 10.1038/nature11782

Santini, E., and Klann, E. (2014). Reciprocal signaling between translational control pathways and synaptic proteins in autism spectrum disorders. *Sci. Signal.* 7, re10. doi: 10.1126/scisignal.2005832

Schoenemann, P. T. (2006). Evolution of the size and functional areas of the human brain. *Annu. Rev. Anthropol.* 35, 379–406. doi: 10.1146/annurev.anthro.35.081 705.123210

Sevy, S., Burdick, K. E., Visweswaraiah, H., Abdelmessih, S., Lukin, M., et al. (2007). Iowa gambling task in schizophrenia: a review and new data in patients with schizophrenia and co-occurring cannabis use disorders. *Schizophr. Res.* 92, 74–84. doi: 10.1016/j.schres.2007.01.005

Shaw, P., Greenstein, D., Lerch, J., Clasen, L., Lenroot, R., Gogtay, N. E. E. A., et al. (2006). Intellectual ability and cortical development in children and adolescents. *Nature* 440, 676–679. doi: 10.1038/nature04513

Smith, E., Thurm, A., Greenstein, D., Farmer, C., Swedo, S., Giedd, J., et al. (2016). Cortical thickness change in autism during early childhood. *Hum. Brain Mapp.* 37, 2616–2629. doi: 10.1002/hbm.23195

Snitz, B. E., MacDonald, A. W., and Carter, C. S. (2006). Cognitive deficits in unaffected first-degree relatives of schizophrenia patients: a meta-analytic review of putative endophenotypes. *Schizophr. Bull.* 32, 179–194. doi: 10.1093/schbul/sbi048

Snyder, A. (2009). Explaining and inducing savant skills: privileged access to lower level, less-processed information. *Philos. Trans. R. Soc. Lond. B Biol. Sci.* 364, 1399–1405. doi: 10.1098/rstb.2008.0290

South, M., Chamberlain, P. D., Wigham, S., Newton, T., Le Couteur, A., McConachie, H., et al. (2014). Enhanced decision making and risk avoidance in high-functioning autism spectrum disorder. *Neuropsychol.* 28, 222. doi: 10.1037/neu0000016

Spearman, C. (1904). "General Intelligence," objectively determined and measured. *Am. J. Psychol.* 15, 201–292. doi: 10.2307/1412107

Spek, A. A., and Velderman, E. (2013). Examining the relationship between autism spectrum disorders and technical professions in high functioning adults. *Res. Autism Spectr. Disord.* 7, 606–612. doi: 10.1016/j.rasd.2013.02.002

Stanovich, K. E., and West, R. F. (2014). What intelligence tests miss. *Psychologist* 27, 80–83.

Stanutz, S., Wapnick, J., and Burack, J. A. (2014). Pitch discrimination and melodic memory in children with autism spectrum disorders. *Autism* 18, 137–147. doi: 10.1177/1362361312462905

Steen, R. G., Mull, C., McClure, R., Hamer, R. M., and Lieberman, J. A. (2006). Brain volume in first-episode schizophrenia. *Br. J. Psychiatry* 188, 510–518. doi: 10.1192/bjp.188.6.510

Stefansson, H., Meyer-Lindenberg, A., Steinberg, S., Magnusdottir, B., Morgen, K., Arnarsdottir, S., et al. (2014). CNVs conferring risk of autism or schizophrenia affect cognition in controls. *Nature* 505, 361–366. doi: 10.1038/nature12818

Stefansson, H., Rujescu, D., Cichon, S., Pietiläinen, O. P., Ingason, A., Steinberg, S., et al. (2008). Large recurrent microdeletions associated with schizophrenia. *Nature* 455, 232–236. doi: 10.1038/nature07229

Sun, X., Allison, C., Auyeung, B., Matthews, F. E., Zhang, Z., Baron-Cohen, S., et al. (2014). Comparison between a mandarin Chinese version of the childhood autism spectrum test and the Clancy autism behaviour scale in mainland China. *Res. Dev. Disabil.* 35, 1599–1608. doi: 10.1016/j.ridd.2014.02.005

Sutton, M. A., and Schuman, E. M. (2006). Dendritic protein synthesis, synaptic plasticity, and memory. *Cell* 127, 49–58. doi: 10.1016/j.cell.2006.09.014

Tam, G. W., van de Lagemaat, L. N., Redon, R., Strathdee, K. E., Croning, M. D., Malloy, M. P., et al. (2010). Confirmed rare copy number variants implicate novel genes in schizophrenia. *Biochem. Soc. Trans.* 38, 445–451. doi: 10.1042/BST0380445

Tang, J., Liao, Y., Song, M., Gao, J. H., Zhou, B., Tan, C., et al. (2013). Aberrant default mode functional connectivity in early onset schizophrenia. *PLoS ONE* 8:e71061. doi: 10.1371/journal.pone.0071061

Tavassoli, T., Auyeung, B., Murphy, L. C., Baron-Cohen, S., and Chakrabarti, B. (2012). Variation in the autism candidate gene GABRB3 modulates tactile sensitivity in typically developing children. *Mol. Autism* 3, 1. doi: 10.1186/2040-2392-3-6

Teovanović, P., Knežević, G., and Stankov, L. (2015). Individual differences in cognitive biases: evidence against one-factor theory of rationality. *Intelligence* 50, 75–86. doi: 10.1016/j.intell.2015.02.008

Thakkar, K. N., and Park, S. (2010). Empathy, schizotypy, and visuospatial transformations. *Cog. Neuropsych.* 15, 477–500. doi: 10.1080/13546801003711350

Thomas, P., Zahorodny, W., Peng, B., Kim, S., Jani, N., Halperin, W., et al. (2012). The association of autism diagnosis with socioeconomic status. *Autism* 16, 201–213. doi: 10.1177/1362361311413397

Treffert, D. A. (2014). Savant syndrome: realities, myths and misconceptions. *J. Autism Dev. Disord.* 44, 564–571. doi: 10.1007/s10803-013-1906-8

Troche, S. J., Houlihan, M. E., Stelmack, R. M., and Rammsayer, T. H. (2009). Mental ability, P300, and mismatch negativity: analysis of frequency and duration discrimination. *Intelligence* 37, 365–373. doi: 10.1016/j.intell.2009.03.002

Troche, S. J., and Rammsayer, T. H. (2009a). "Neural oscillations and intelligence: the temporal resolution power hypothesis," in *Chronobiology and Chronopsychology*, eds T. G. Baudson, A. Seemüller, and M. Dresler (Lengerich: Pabst Press), 62–76.

Troche, S. J., and Rammsayer, T. H. (2009b). The influence of temporal resolution power and working memory capacity on psychometric intelligence. *Intelligence* 37, 479–486. doi: 10.1016/j.intell.2009.06.001

Trzaskowski, M., Harlaar, N., Arden, R., Krapohl, E., Rimfeld, K., McMillan, A., et al. (2014). Genetic influence on family socioeconomic status and children's intelligence. *Intelligence* 42, 83–88. doi: 10.1016/j.intell.2013.11.002

Turken, U., Whitfield-Gabrieli, S., Bammer, R., Baldo, J. V., Dronkers, N. F., and Gabrieli, J. D. (2008). Cognitive processing speed and the structure of white matter pathways: convergent evidence from normal variation and lesion studies. *Neuroimage* 42, 1032–1044. doi: 10.1016/j.neuroimage.2008.03.057

Uddin, L. Q., Clare Kelly, A. M., Biswal, B. B., Xavier Castellanos, F., and Milham, M. P. (2009). Functional connectivity of default mode network components: correlation, anticorrelation, and causality. *Hum. Brain Mapp.* 30, 625–637. doi: 10.1002/hbm.20531

Vandenberg, S. G., and Kruse, A. R. (1978). Mental rotations, a group test of three-dimensional spatial visualization. *Percept. Mot. Skills* 47, 599–604. doi: 10.2466/pms.1978.47.2.599

van den Heuvel, M. P., Stam, C. J., Kahn, R. S., and Pol, H. E. H. (2009). Efficiency of functional brain networks and intellectual performance. *J. Neurosci.* 29, 7619–7624. doi: 10.1523/JNEUROSCI.1443-09.2009

Van Meter, K. C., Christiansen, L. E., Delwiche, L. D., Azari, R., Carpenter, T. E., and Hertz-Picciotto, I. (2010). Geographic distribution of autism in California: a retrospective birth cohort analysis. *Autism Res.* 3, 19–29. doi: 10.1002/aur.110

van Os, J. (2009). 'Salience syndrome' replaces 'schizophrenia' in DSM-V and ICD-11: psychiatry's evidence-based entry into the 21st century? *Acta Psychiatr. Scand.* 120, 363–372. doi: 10.1111/j.1600-0447.2009.01456.x

Vissers, L. E., Gilissen, C., and Veltman, J. A. (2016). Genetic studies in intellectual disability and related disorders. *Nat. Rev. Genet.* 17, 9–18. doi: 10.1038/nrg3999

Wai, J., Lubinski, D., and Benbow, C. P. (2009). Spatial ability for STEM domains: aligning over 50 years of cumulative psychological knowledge solidifies its importance. *J. Edu. Psychol.* 101, 817. doi: 10.1037/a0016127

Wang, J., Tao, Y., Song, F., Sun, Y., Ott, J., and Saffen, D. (2015). Common regulatory variants of CYFIP1 contribute to susceptibility for Autism Spectrum Disorder (ASD) and classical autism. *Annals Hum. Genet.* 79, 329–340. doi: 10.1111/ahg.12121

Warrier, V., Baron-Cohen, S., and Chakrabarti, B. (2013). Genetic variation in GABRB3 is associated with Asperger syndrome and multiple endophenotypes relevant to autism. *Mol. Autism* 4, 1. doi: 10.1186/2040-2392-4-48

Wei, X., Jennifer, W. Y., Shattuck, P., McCracken, M., and Blackorby, J. (2013). Science, technology, engineering, and mathematics (STEM) participation among college students with an autism spectrum disorder. *J. Autism Dev. Disord.* 43, 1539–1546. doi: 10.1007/s10803-012-1700-z

Werner, S., Malaspina, D., and Rabinowitz, J. (2007). Socioeconomic status at birth is associated with risk of schizophrenia: population-based multilevel study. *Schizophr. Bull.* 33, 1373–1378. doi: 10.1093/schbul/sbm032

White, S., O'Reilly, H., and Frith, U. (2009). Big heads, small details and autism. *Neuropsychologia* 47, 1274–1281. doi: 10.1016/j.neuropsychologia.2009.01.012

Whitfield-Gabrieli, S., Thermenos, H. W., Milanovic, S., Tsuang, M. T., Faraone, S. V., McCarley, R. W., et al. (2009). Hyperactivity and hyperconnectivity of the default network in schizophrenia and in first-degree relatives of persons with schizophrenia. *Proc. Natl. Acad. Sci. U.S.A.* 106, 1279–1284. doi: 10.1073/pnas.0809141106

Windham, G. C., Fessel, K., and Grether, J. K. (2009). Autism spectrum disorders in relation to parental occupation in technical fields. *Autism Res.* 2, 183–191. doi: 10.1002/aur.84

Witelson, S. F., Beresh, H., and Kigar, D. L. (2006). Intelligence and brain size in 100 postmortem brains: sex, lateralization and age factors. *Brain* 129, 386–398. doi: 10.1093/brain/awh696

Wolfle, D., and Oxtoby, T. (1952). Distributions of ability of students specializing in different fields. *Science* 116, 311.

Woodberry, K. A., Giuliano, A. J., and Seidman, L. J. (2008). Premorbid IQ in schizophrenia: a meta-analytic review. *Am. J. Psychiatry* 165, 579–587. doi: 10.1176/appi.ajp.2008.07081242

Woodward, T. S., Moritz, S., Cuttler, C., and Whitman, J. C. (2006). The contribution of a cognitive bias against disconfirmatory evidence (BADE) to delusions in schizophrenia. *J. Clin. Exp. Neuropsychol.* 28, 605–617. doi: 10.1080/13803390590949511

Zapf, A. C., Glindemann, L. A., Vogeley, K., and Falter, C. M. (2015). Sex differences in mental rotation and how they add to the understanding of autism. *PLoS ONE* 10:e0124628. doi: 10.1371/journal.pone.0124628

Zheng, X., Chen, R., Li, N., Du, W., Pei, L., Zhang, J., et al. (2012). Socioeconomic status and children with intellectual disability in China. *J. Intellect. Disabil. Res.* 56, 212–220. doi: 10.1111/j.1365-2788.2011.01470.x

Zielinski, B. A., Prigge, M. B., Nielsen, J. A., Froehlich, A. L., Abildskov, T. J., Anderson, J. S., et al. (2014). Longitudinal changes in cortical thickness in autism and typical development. *Brain* 137, 1799–1812. doi: 10.1093/brain/awu083

7

Comparative Gene Expression Analysis of Two Mouse Models of Autism: Transcriptome Profiling of the BTBR and En2$^{-/-}$ Hippocampus

Giovanni Provenzano[1], Zelia Corradi[1], Katia Monsorno[1], Tarcisio Fedrizzi[2], Laura Ricceri[3], Maria L. Scattoni[3] and Yuri Bozzi[1,4]*

[1] Laboratory of Molecular Neuropathology, Centre for Integrative Biology, University of Trento, Trento, Italy, [2] Bioinformatics Core Facility, Centre for Integrative Biology, University of Trento, Trento, Italy, [3] Neurotoxicology and Neuroendocrinology Section, Department of Cell Biology and Neuroscience, Istituto Superiore di Sanità, Rome, Italy, [4] National Research Council Neuroscience Institute, Pisa, Italy

Edited by:
John Vijay Sagar Kommu, National Institute of Mental Health and Neurosciences, India

Reviewed by:
Suhash Chakraborty, Hindustan Aeronautics Limited Hospital, India
Mu Yang, University of California, Davis, USA

****Correspondence:***
Giovanni Provenzano
giovanni.provenzano@unitn.it

Autism spectrum disorders (ASD) are characterized by a high degree of genetic heterogeneity. Genomic studies identified common pathological processes underlying the heterogeneous clinical manifestations of ASD, and transcriptome analyses revealed that gene networks involved in synapse development, neuronal activity, and immune function are deregulated in ASD. Mouse models provide unique tools to investigate the neurobiological basis of ASD; however, a comprehensive approach to identify transcriptional abnormalities in different ASD models has never been performed. Here we used two well-recognized ASD mouse models, BTBR T^{+} *Itpr3*^{tf}/J (BTBR) and Engrailed-2 knockout (*En2*$^{-/-}$), to identify conserved ASD-related molecular signatures. *En2*$^{-/-}$ mice bear a mutation within the EN2 transcription factor homeobox, while BTBR is an inbred strain with unknown genetic defects. Hippocampal RNA samples from BTBR, *En2*$^{-/-}$ and respective control (C57Bl/6J and *En2*$^{+/+}$) adult mice were assessed for differential gene expression using microarrays. A total of 153 genes were similarly deregulated in the BTBR and *En2*$^{-/-}$ hippocampus. Mouse phenotype and gene ontology enrichment analyses were performed on BTBR and *En2*$^{-/-}$ hippocampal differentially expressed genes (DEGs). Pathways represented in both BTBR and *En2*$^{-/-}$ hippocampal DEGs included abnormal behavioral response and chemokine/MAP kinase signaling. Genes involved in abnormal function of the immune system and abnormal synaptic transmission/seizures were significantly represented among BTBR and *En2*$^{-/-}$ DEGs, respectively. Interestingly, both BTBR and *En2*$^{-/-}$ hippocampal DEGs showed a significant enrichment of ASD and schizophrenia (SCZ)-associated genes. Specific gene sets were enriched in the two models: microglial genes were significantly enriched among BTBR DEGs, whereas GABAergic/glutamatergic postsynaptic genes, FMRP-interacting genes and epilepsy-related genes were significantly enriched among *En2*$^{-/-}$ DEGs. Weighted correlation network analysis (WGCNA) performed on BTBR and *En2*$^{-/-}$ hippocampal transcriptomes together identified six modules significantly enriched in ASD-related genes. Each of these modules showed a specific enrichment profile in neuronal and glial genes, as well as in genes associated to ASD comorbidities such as epilepsy and SCZ. Our data reveal significant transcriptional similarities and differences between the BTBR and *En2*$^{-/-}$ hippocampus, indicating that transcriptome analysis of ASD mouse models may contribute to identify novel molecular targets for pharmacological studies.

Keywords: autism, hippocampus, gene expression, microarray, WGCNA, BTBR, Engrailed, mouse

INTRODUCTION

Autism spectrum disorders (ASD) are a family of neurodevelopmental disorders characterized by a high degree of genetic heterogeneity. Recent advances in genetics and genomics allowed to attribute the heterogeneous clinical manifestations of ASD to shared pathophysiological processes (de la Torre-Ubieta et al., 2016). Integrative analysis of large-scale genetic data revealed distinct gene networks affected in ASD, mainly related to the formation and function of brain synapses. Network-based analysis of large-scale transcriptome data also highlighted that co-expression modules related to synapse development, neuronal activity and immune function are deregulated in ASD (Voineagu et al., 2011; Gupta et al., 2014; de la Torre-Ubieta et al., 2016). Thus, pathophysiological processes in ASD seem to converge on specific molecular pathways and networks, with a clear interplay between immune and synaptic functions (Estes and McAllister, 2015).

Gene transcriptional profiling in ASD is mainly performed on post-mortem brain samples, but the restricted availability of human ASD brain tissues represents a significant challenge. For this reason, ASD mouse models provide a unique tool to identify conserved pathological mechanisms at the gene expression level. BTBR T^{+} *Itpr3*^{tf}/J (BTBR) is an inbred strain of mice that incorporates behavioral phenotypes relevant to all diagnostic symptoms of ASD, including reduced social interactions in juveniles and adults, repetitive self-grooming and an unusual pattern of ultrasonic vocalizations resembling the atypical vocalizations seen in some autistic children (Scattoni et al., 2008, 2013). Moreover, BTBR mice show a severely reduced hippocampal commissure and absent corpus callosum (Wahlsten et al., 2003). Noteworthy, corpus callosum abnormalities have been reported in autistic individuals (Egaas et al., 1995; Alexander et al., 2007). However, it is important to emphasize that genetic abnormalities causing behavioral deficits in BTBR mice are still under investigation (Jones-Davis et al., 2013).

Engrailed-2 (EN2) is a homeodomain transcription factor involved in regionalization and patterning of the midbrain and hindbrain regions (Joyner et al., 1991). Genome-wide association studies revealed that EN2 is a candidate gene for ASD (Benayed et al., 2009), and an abnormal expression and methylation profile of the EN2 gene has been reported in the cerebellum of ASD patients (James et al., 2013, 2014; Choi et al., 2014). Mice lacking the homeobox domain of *En2* (*En2*$^{hd/hd}$ mice; Joyner et al., 1991; here referred to as *En2*$^{-/-}$) display neuropathological changes related to ASD. These defects include cerebellar hypoplasia and reduced number of Purkinje neurons (Joyner et al., 1991; Kuemerle et al., 1997), defective GABAergic innervation in the forebrain (Sgadò et al., 2013a; Allegra et al., 2014; Provenzano et al., 2014), reduced monoaminergic innervation to the forebrain (Brielmaier et al., 2014; Genestine et al., 2015; Viaggi et al., 2015) and ASD-like behavioral traits such as decreased sociability, spatial learning deficits, and increased seizure susceptibility (Cheh et al., 2006; Tripathi et al., 2009; Brielmaier et al., 2012; Provenzano et al., 2014).

So far, a comprehensive approach to identify common and distinct abnormalities in ASD models has been conducted by brain imaging-based neuroanatomical phenotyping (Ellegood et al., 2015; Ellegood and Crawley, 2015). However, few efforts have been made to identify conserved genes signatures at the transcriptome level in brain tissues from ASD mice. The hippocampal and cortical transcriptome has been examined in BTBR mice (Daimon et al., 2015; Kratsman et al., 2016), while we evaluated the gene expression signature of the *En2*$^{-/-}$ hippocampus and cerebellum (Sgadò et al., 2013b). Similar studies have been performed on brains from *Fmr1* (Prilutsky et al., 2015) and *Pten* (Tilot et al., 2016) mutant mice. However, a comprehensive approach to identify transcriptional abnormalities in ASD mouse models has never been performed so far. Here we compared the transcriptome profile of the BTBR and *En2*$^{-/-}$ hippocampus, and describe common and distinct transcriptional signatures for these two ASD mouse models.

MATERIALS AND METHODS

Animals

Experiments were conducted in conformity with the European Community Directive 2010/63/EU and were approved by the Animal Welfare Committee of University of Trento, Istituto Superiore di Sanità and Italian Ministry of Health. Animals were housed in a 12 h light/dark cycle with food and water available *ad libitum*, and all efforts were made to minimize animal suffering during the experiments. *En2* mutants were originally generated on a mixed 129Sv x C57BL/6 genetic background (Joyner et al., 1991) and then backcrossed at least five times into a C57BL/6 background. *En2*$^{+/+}$ and *En2*$^{-/-}$ mice used in this study were obtained by heterozygous mating (*En2*$^{+/-}$ x *En2*$^{+/-}$) and genotyped by PCR as previously described (Sgadò et al., 2013a). BTBR T^{+} *Itpr3*^{tf}/J (BTBR) and C57Bl/6J (B6) inbred mice were purchased from the Jackson Laboratory (Bar Harbour, ME, USA) and bred in the mouse vivarium of the Istituto Superiore di Sanità (Rome, Italy). A total of 32 adult (3–5 months old) mice were used: 4 BTBR and 4 B6 mice for microarray experiments, and 6 mice per strain/genotype (BTBR, B6, *En2*$^{+/+}$ and *En2*$^{-/-}$) for quantitative RT-PCR.

Microarrays and Single-Gene Differential Expression Analysis

In this study, we aimed to identify common and distinct molecular signatures across the hippocampi of BTBR and *En2*$^{-/-}$ mice. To obtain a comparable and reliable hippocampal transcriptomic profile of BTBR mice and reduce any source of variability during microarray analysis, which might arise from pre-scanning and/or post-scanning steps (Kadanga et al., 2008), we applied the same experimental procedures previously described for the transcriptome analysis of *En2*$^{-/-}$ hippocampus (Sgadò et al., 2013b). Briefly, hippocampal RNAs from BTBR and B6 mice ($n = 4$ per experimental group) were purified using standard column purification according to the manufacturer's protocol (RNAeasy Mini Kit, QIAGEN). RNA quality was analyzed by microfluidic gel electrophoresis on RNA 6000 NanoChips using the Agilent 2100 Bioanalyzer. Only RNA with a high (>9) RNA integrity number was selected and used for subsequent retrotranscription, labeling, and array hybridization according to Agilent protocols. Mouse gene expression arrays (Agilent 4X44K slides) were hybridized and scanned with the Agilent microarray station. The images obtained from the microarray scanner were analyzed with Agilent Feature Extraction version 10.7.3.1. Hippocampal gene expression dataset of BTBR and B6 mice have been deposited in the NCBI's Gene Expression Omnibus (GEO) database (accession number GSE81501). Intensity values were processed with Agi4x44PreProcess using default parameters to remove low-quality probes. Signals were then normalized by means of the quantile normalization method. Multiple replicas of the same probes were summarized using the median. To evaluate differential expression, the Rank Product (RP) non-parametric method was used (Sgadò et al., 2013b). The RP is equivalent to calculating the geometric mean rank with a statistical method (average rank) that is slightly more sensitive to outlier data and puts a higher premium on consistency between the ranks in various lists.

Quantitative RT-PCR (qRT-PCR)

Total RNAs were extracted by Trizol reagent (Invitrogen) from explanted hippocampi. DNase-treated RNAs were purified by RNA extraction RNAeasy Kit (QIAGEN). cDNA was synthesized from pooled RNAs by SuperScript VILO cDNA Synthesis Kit (Invitrogen) according to the manufacturer' instructions. qRT-PCR was performed in a C1000 Thermal Cycler (Bio-Rad) with real-time detection of fluorescence, using the KAPA SYBR FAST Master Mix reagent (KAPA Biosystems). Mouse mitochondrial ribosomal protein L41 (mRPL41) was used as a standard for quantification. Primer sequences (Eurofins Genomics) are reported in **Supplementary Table 1**. Ratios of comparative concentrations of each mRNA with respect to L41 mRNA were then calculated and plotted as the average of three independent reactions (technical replicates) obtained from each RNA. Expression analyses were performed using the CFX3 Manager (Bio-Rad) software (Sgadò et al., 2013b). Statistical analysis of qRT-PCR was performed with Prism 6 (GraphPad) software. Values were expressed as mean ± s.e.m and quantitative gene expression differences between each autistic mouse (BTBR and *En2*$^{-/-}$) strain and their respective controls (B6 and *En2*$^{+/+}$) were assessed by Student's t-test, with the level of statistical significance set at $p < 0.05$.

Phenotype/Pathway Ontology and Enrichment Analysis on DEGs

DEGs in BTBR and *En2*$^{-/-}$ hippocampi were analyzed for "phenotype ontology" using Enrichr (http://amp.pharm.mssm.edu/Enrichr/). Enrichr is an enrichment analysis web-based tool providing various types of gene-set libraries, including the knockout mouse phenotypes ontology developed by the Jackson Lab from their Mouse Genome Informatics-Mammalian Phenotype (MGI-MP) browser (Blake et al., 2009). Mammalian phenotypes predefined by MGI are sorted by z-score considering only terms with an adjusted p-value less than 0.05. Phenotype/pathway ontology of *En2*$^{-/-}$ hippocampal DEGs was performed on our previous dataset from *En2*$^{+/+}$ and *En2*$^{-/-}$ adult mice, already deposited in NCBI's GEO database (accession number GSE51612; Sgadò et al., 2013b). In order to visualize enriched Kyoto Encyclopedia of Genes and Genomes (KEGG) pathways, we used DAVID v6.7 (http://david.abcc.ncifcrf.gov/). To focus the functional analysis on hippocampal expressed genes we used as background a list of tissue-specific expressed genes for both autistic (BTBR and *En2*$^{-/-}$) strains. These background lists were obtained by filtering the genes by the normalized expression values and excluding the ones with the lowest expression levels (<10th percentile).

We also performed the direct enrichment analysis of different gene set categories present in the DEGs from BTBR and *En2*$^{-/-}$ mice, using the hypergeometric test present in R (P-value cut-off 0.05). The background used to compute the enrichments was the same used for KEGG pathway analysis (see below for the gene lists used for enrichment analyses).

Weighted Correlation Network Analysis (WGCNA) and Enrichment on Co-expression Modules

Microarray data from the BTBR and *En2*$^{-/-}$ hippocampi were analyzed with the WGCNA R package in order to find highly correlated modules of co-expressed genes (Langfelder and Horvath, 2008). Two different batches of samples, autistic (BTBR and *En2*$^{-/-}$) vs. control (B6 and *En2*$^{+/+}$), were used to obtain an appropriate number for the WGCNA analysis. All samples were normalized and filtered using the same method described above. The R program ComBat (Johnson et al., 2007) included in the SVA package (Leek et al., 2012) was used to remove the batch effect present on different chips, in which samples were run. In order to keep the most informative probes, only the top 20% (in terms of per-probe variance) were used as input for the WGCNA analysis. The WGCNA method is based on soft threshold approach in order to obtain an adjacency matrix that describes the relations among the genes (Zhang and Horvath, 2005). The scale-free criterion is used to select the power to apply to the correlations in order to obtain the adjacency matrix, a power of 11 was chosen in this study. The Topological Overlap

Measure (TOM) is then calculated starting from the previously obtained adjacency matrix. TOM is a highly robust measure of network interconnectedness (proximity) and expresses the strength characterizing the connection between each pair of genes. Genes with high TOM are clustered into co-expression modules. kME (representing the connection strength of each gene in each module) is then calculated as the correlation of each gene to the module eigengene (ME, defined as the first principal component of the expressions of the genes within the module). The ME defines measures of module membership (MM), which quantify how close a gene is to a given module eigengene. For each expression profile, Gene Significance (GS) was calculated as the absolute value of the correlation between expression profile and trait (autistic phenotype). The statistical significance of MM and GS (denoted as p.MM and p.GS) is carried out from the correlation test p-value of the WGCNA package. All values are tabulated in **Supplementary Table 3**. Given autism is a complex and very heterogeneous group of disorders, simple correlation of the modules with the trait produced meaningless results. A different approach was hence used: the modules were ranked based on their enrichment in term of genes present in the SFARI list. Then, modules significantly enriched in ASD-associated genes were functionally characterized for enrichment in markers of specific synapse, cell and disease types, using the same method described above. Moreover, to evaluate the biological and functional relevance of ASD-associated modules we used the Enrichr web tool. We analyzed the overrepresentation of the biological processes GO category for each gene list of modules.

Gene Lists Used for Enrichment Analyses

SFARI database (https://gene.sfari.org/autdb/Welcome.do) was used to calculate enrichment with ASD-associated genes on BTBR and *En2*$^{-/-}$ hippocampal DEGs. For disease annotations, we used the following gene sets from Autworks database (http://autworks.hms.harvard.edu): epilepsy, parkinsonian disorders and schizophrenia. For searching the recurrence and overlaps with FMRP-associated genes, we used a set of 842 genes (herein termed "FMRP Interacting Genes"), from a crosslinking and immunoprecipitation (CLIP) experiment (Darnell et al., 2011). Other gene lists used in this study (neuronal markers, astrocyte markers, type 1 microglial markers, type 2 microglial markers, oligodendrocyte markers, postsynaptic density, asdM12, asdM16) are available at http://www.arkinglab.org/resources. GABAergic synapse, glutamatergic synapse, dopaminergic synapse lists were taken from http://www.genome.jp/kegg/. In addition, the following gene lists were compiled from MsigDB (http://www.broadinstitute.org/gsea/msigdb/collections.jsp#C1): GABAergic presynaptic markers (GABA synthesis, release, reuptake and degradation); GABAergic postsynaptic markers (GABA A receptor activation, GABA B receptor activation, GABA receptor activation); glutamaergic presynaptic markers (glutamate neurotransmitter release cycle); glutamaergic postsynaptic markers (glutamate receptor activity; glutamate signaling pathway); dopaminergic markers (dopamine neurotransmitter release cycle).

RESULTS

Recently, we showed by transcriptome analysis that several genes related to ASD, abnormal synaptic transmission and GABA signaling are markedly deregulated in the hippocampus of *En2*$^{-/-}$ mice (Sgadò et al., 2013b). Here we extended this analysis to the hippocampus of BTBR mice, to test the hypothesis that common and distinct downstream mechanisms may be altered in these two ASD mouse models. Hippocampi from BTBR and B6 control adult mice were assessed for differential gene expression by microarray and bioinformatic analysis, as previously reported for *En2*$^{-/-}$ mice (Sgadò et al., 2013b). We found 1016 differentially expressed genes in the hippocampus of BTBR mice compared to their B6 controls (**Figure 1A**). Among these, 436 and 580 were up- and down-regulated, respectively. **Supplementary Table 2** shows the entire list of genes differentially expressed in the BTBR hippocampus, with fold change, percentage of false prediction (pfp) and P-values calculated by RankProd. We next validated microarray findings by qRT-PCR analysis, selecting seven representative genes from the DEGs list. Except for Gabra5, for which decreased protein and mRNA levels were found in the brains of ASD patients (Fatemi et al., 2010), many of the selected genes belong to immune/inflammatory categories. All genes showed statistically significant differential expression in the BTBR hippocampus, as compared to B6 controls [chemokine (C-C motif) ligand 21A (Ccl21a) $p = 0.0424$; gamma-aminobutyric acid (GABA) A receptor, subunit alpha 5 (Gabra5) $p = 0.0069$; glial fibrillary acidic protein (Gfap) $p = 0.009$; polymerase (RNA) E (DNA directed) polypeptide E (Polr3e) $p = 0.025$; cyclin-dependent kinase inhibitor 1A (P21) (Cdkn1a) $p = 0.0052$; protein kinase C, delta polypeptide E (Polr3e) $p = 0.0029$; SLIT and NTRK-like family, member 6 (Slitrk6) $p = 0.0018$] (**Figure 1B**). In all tested genes the expression difference reported by qRT-PCR significantly correlated with microarray data (Pearson $r = 0.97$, $p < 0.0003$).

We next compared the BTBR hippocampal transcriptional profile to that of *En2*$^{-/-}$ mice. We first identified a total number of 153 commonly expressed genes between BTBR and *En2*$^{-/-}$ mice Interestingly, some of the common DEGs are related to inflammatory pathways (Aldh1a2, C2, Ccnd1, Cox7b2, Eif2ak2, Gsk3a, H2-Aa, H2-A1, H2-Bl, Map3k6, Pglyrp1, Slpi, Tia1; **Figure 2A**). qRT-PCR confirmed the differential expression of two of these genes [cyclin D1 (Ccdn1), $p = 0.0018$ and $p = 0.0051$ for BTBR and *En2*$^{-/-}$ mice, respectively; peptidoglycan recognition protein 1 (Pglyrp1), $p = 0.0052$ and $p = 0.0284$ for BTBR and *En2*$^{-/-}$ mice, respectively] (**Figure 2B**).

We next explored whether shared functional categories or common pathways were perturbed in both ASD mouse models. To increase accuracy of the functional analysis, we decided to compare the two lists of DEGs using updated databases and different bioinformatic tools, respect to those previously employed for the analysis of the hippocampal trascriptome of *En2*$^{-/-}$ mice (Sgadò et al., 2013b). We tested BTBR and *En2*$^{-/-}$ hippocampal DEGs for enrichment of mouse phenotype terms (Mouse Genome Informatics Mammalian Phenotype Level 4) using Enrichr (**Figure 3**). Two significantly

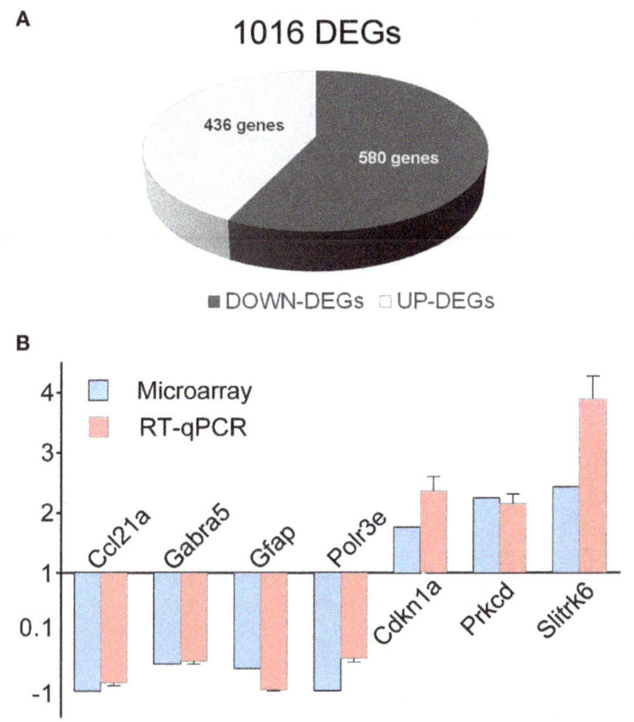

FIGURE 1 | Differentially expressed genes in the BTBR hippocampus. (A) Schematic representation of BTBR hippocampal DEGs, as compared to control B6 mice. A total of 1016 DEGs were identified, (580 down-regulated, 436 up-regulated). **(B)** qRT-PCR validation of differentially expressed genes. qRT-PCR results for all the evaluated genes were in agreement with microarray results. Values are expressed as each gene/L41 comparative quantitation ratios normalized on the expression of WT (mean ± s.e.m of three replicates from pools of six animals per genotype; $p < 0.05$, Student's *t*-test, BTBR vs. B6).

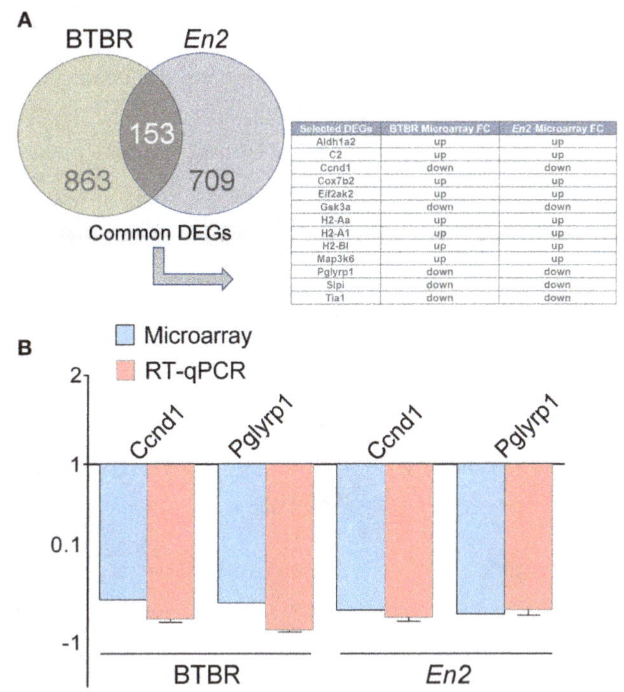

Selected DEGs	BTBR Microarray FC	*En2* Microarray FC
Aldh1a2	up	up
C2	up	up
Ccnd1	down	down
Cox7b2	up	up
Eif2ak2	up	up
Gsk3a	down	down
H2-Aa	up	up
H2-A1	up	up
H2-Bl	up	up
Map3k6	up	up
Pglyrp1	down	down
Slpi	down	down
Tia1	down	down

FIGURE 2 | DEGs commonly expressed in the BTBR and *En2*$^{-/-}$ hippocampus. (A) Venn diagram of differentially expressed genes in the BTBR and *En2*$^{-/-}$ adult hippocampus. A total of 1016 and 862 differentially expressed genes were identified in BTBR (brown) and *En2*$^{-/-}$ (gray) mice, respectively. Among these, 153 show differential expression in both strains. The table shows a subset of these common DEGs, all belonging to inflammatory pathways. **(B)** qRT-PCR validation of Ccnd1 and Pglyrp1, two genes differentially expressed in both BTBR and *En2*$^{-/-}$ hippocampi. qRT-PCR results for both genes were in agreement with microarray results. Values are expressed as each gene/L41 comparative quantitation ratios normalized on the expression of respective control (mean ± s.e.m of three replicates from pools of six animals per genotype; $p < 0.05$, Student's *t*-test, BTBR vs. B6 and *En2*$^{-/-}$ vs. *En2*$^{+/+}$).

enriched phenotypes were common to both mouse strains: abnormal behavioral responses and abnormal eating/drinking behavior. Conversely, specific phenotype ontologies enriched in BTBR were abnormal sensory capabilities, neurodegeneration, abnormal innate immunity and abnormal antigen presenting (**Figure 3A**). For *En2*$^{-/-}$ mice, we confirmed a significant enrichment for terms related to seizure and altered synaptic transmission (**Figure 3B**), as previously reported (Sgadò et al., 2013b). KEGG pathways analysis for BTBR and *En2*$^{-/-}$ hippocampal DEGs was performed with DAVID, using tissue-specific lists of expressed genes as background for each ASD mouse model (see Materials and Methods). The common pathways that were most significantly enriched across the differentially expressed genes of both ASD mouse models were related to chemokine signaling, MAPK signaling, systemic lupus erythematosus, Fc gamma receptor mediated phagocytosis and pathways in cancer (**Figure 4**).

To further reveal similarities and differences between the BTBR and *En2*$^{-/-}$ hippocampal transcriptome, we tested whether the two lists of DEGs were specifically enriched for cell-type specific markers and genes implicated in neurodevelopmental and neurodegenerative diseases (ASD, SCZ, epilepsy, Parkinson's). Remarkably, when compared to these repositories, BTBR and *En2*$^{-/-}$ hippocampal DEGs were enriched in SCZ- and ASD-related genes according to SFARI 2014 dataset (**Figure 5A**), consistent with reports showing overlap in candidate genes between ASD and SCZ (Crespi et al., 2010). Furthermore, when we separately analyzed up- and down-regulated genes, we found a significant over-representation of neuronal markers for both BTBR and *En2*$^{-/-}$ down-regulated DEGs; conversely, a significant over-representation of astrocyte markers was found in BTBR and *En2*$^{-/-}$ up-regulated DEGs (**Figure 5A**). Significant differences were also detected between the two strains. Among the genes down-regulated in the *En2*$^{-/-}$ hippocampus the following terms were significantly enriched: epilepsy, asdM12 (a neuronal module enriched for ASD-associated genes; Voineagu et al., 2011), FMR1 interacting genes, dopaminergic markers, GABAergic postsynaptic markers and glutamatergic presynaptic markers; conversely, type I microglia markers were significantly enriched among BTBR down-regulated genes (**Figures 5A,B**).

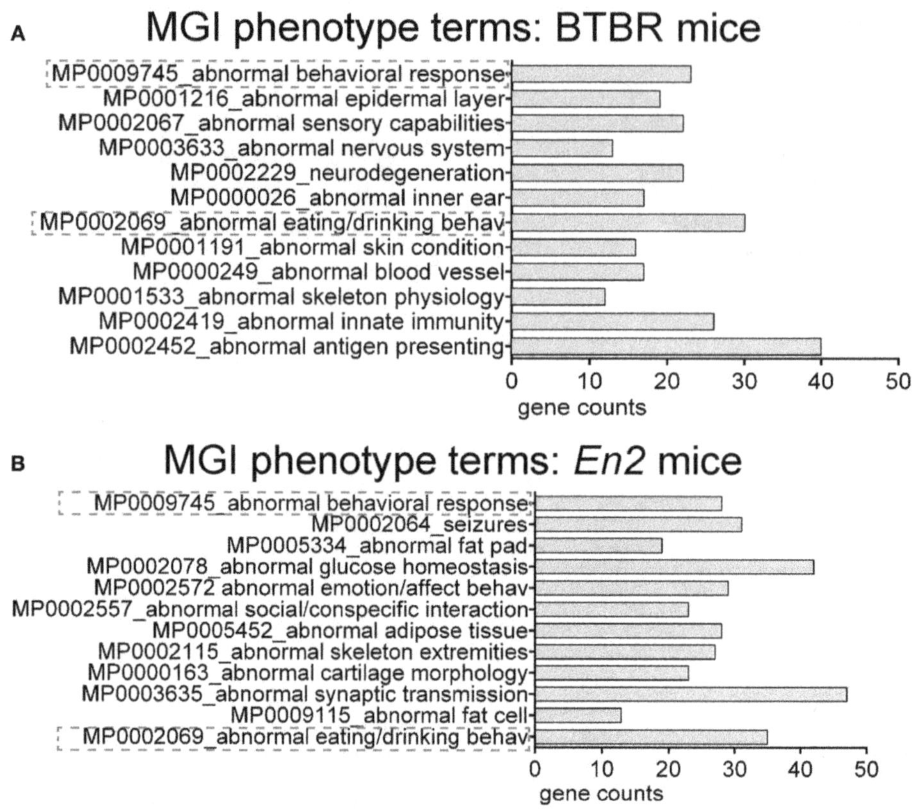

FIGURE 3 | Overrepresented mouse phenotype categories for differentially expressed genes in BTBR and *En2*$^{-/-}$ hippocampi. BTBR and *En2*$^{-/-}$ hippocampal DEGs were analyzed for enrichment in phenotype ontology categories using Enrichr, with an adjusted $p < 0.05$. For each category, the number of genes is indicated by the length of the horizontal bars (gene counts). Dashed red lines highlight phenotype categories common to BTBR **(A)** and *En2*$^{-/-}$ **(B)** DEGs.

To further investigate the presence of common molecular networks deregulated across autistic mice as compared to their respective controls, we analyzed the entire gene expression dataset (BTBR+*En2*$^{-/-}$ vs. B6+*En2*$^{+/+}$) using WGCNA (Zhang and Horvath, 2005). This analysis allows to identify discrete gene modules based on co-expression profiles (Voineagu et al., 2011). WGCNA identified 18 main modules for groups of genes with high topological overlap, ranging between 28 and 653 probes in size (**Supplementary Table 3**). The modules were correlated to the disease trait using a linear mixed regression framework and then ranked based on their enrichment in term of genes present in the SFARI list (retrieved on 2015). Six out of the eighteen modules were significantly enriched in ASD-related genes (Blue, p = 9.072043e-09; Brown, p = 6.297529e-08; Black, p = 7.691951e-06; Pink, p = 0.00021; Greenyellow, p = value 0.00054; Red, p = 0.0044) (**Figure 6A**). We next tested the association of each of the six ASD-enriched modules for enrichment analysis. Except the Greenyellow module, all modules shared a significant enrichment for neuronal markers, as well as for genes associated to epilepsy and SCZ (**Figure 6A**). The Greenyellow module was enriched only for FMRP-interacting and glutamatergic synapse genes. Brown and Red modules were significantly enriched for oligodendrocyte markers and genes associated with M2-microglial cell states. For a better functional characterization of ASD-associated modules, we also used Enrichr to assess the GO biological process annotation of the six ASD gene-enriched modules. Blue, Black, Pink, and Red modules, which are enriched for neuronal markers (**Figure 6A**) also contain genes with the GO term "regulation of ion transmembrane transport" or "synaptic transmission" (**Figure 6B**). The Brown module, one of most enriched for categories (neuronal markers, type 2 microglial markers, oligodendrocyte markers, postsynaptic density, FMRP interacting genes, GABAergic/glutamatergic/dopaminergic synapse, epilepsy, schizophrenia; **Figure 6A**), showed an over-representation of genes involved in cognition, learning, and memory. Finally, the Greenyellow module did not show any significant over-representation of GO categories (**Figure 6B**).

DISCUSSION

Brief Summary of Results

In this study, we compared the hippocampal transcriptome of BTBR and *En2*$^{-/-}$ adult mice, two robust animal models of ASD. We identified both common and distinct gene pathways represented in the BTBR and *En2*$^{-/-}$ transcriptome. Common pathways included chemokine and MAP kinase signaling, whereas genes involved in immune dysfunction and abnormal synaptic transmission were specifically represented among BTBR

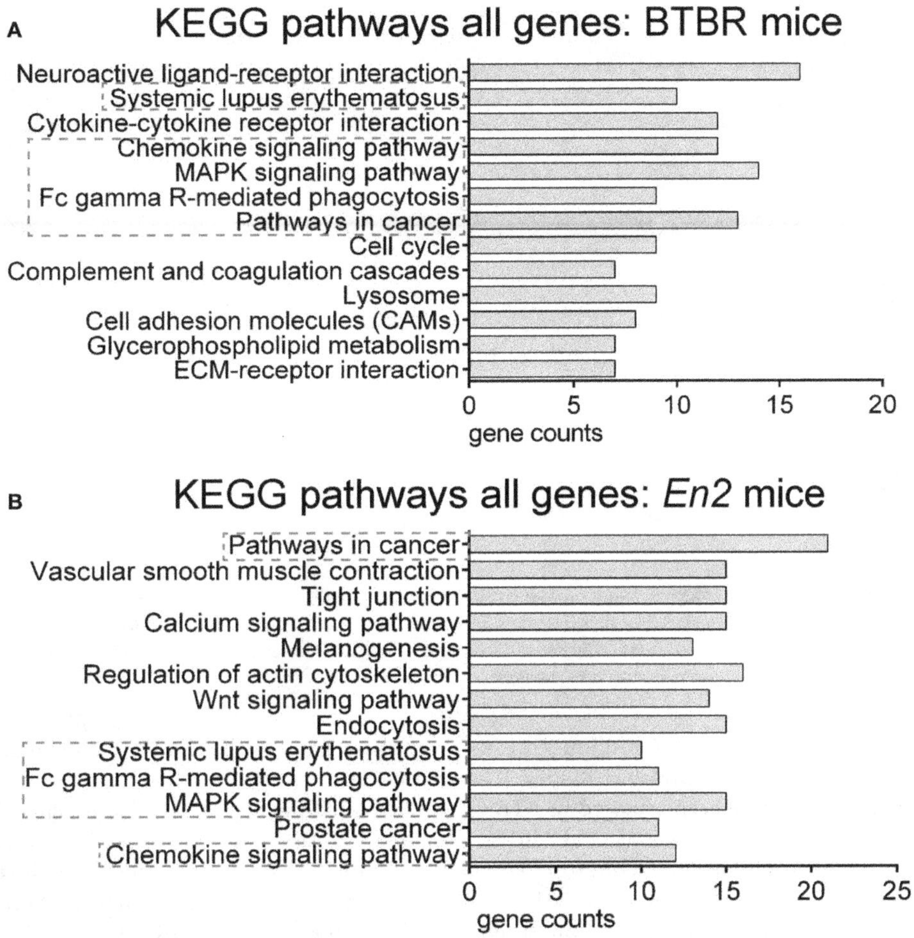

FIGURE 4 | Overrepresented pathways categories for differentially expressed genes in BTBR and *En2*$^{-/-}$ hippocampi. BTBR and *En2*$^{-/-}$ hippocampal DEGs were analyzed for enrichment in KEGG pathways categories using DAVID, with an adjusted $p < 0.05$. For each category, the number of genes is indicated by the length of horizontal bars (gene counts). Dashed red lines highlight pathways common to BTBR **(A)** and *En2*$^{-/-}$ **(B)** DEGs.

and *En2*$^{-/-}$ DEGs, respectively. Both BTBR and *En2*$^{-/-}$ hippocampal DEGs showed a significant enrichment of ASD and SCZ-associated genes, with specific gene sets enriched in the two models (glial genes in BTBR; GABAergic, glutamatergic FMRP-related and epilepsy-related genes in *En2*$^{-/-}$). Finally, network analysis (WGCNA) performed on BTBR and *En2*$^{-/-}$ hippocampal DEGs together identified six modules significantly enriched in ASD-associated genes, with specific enrichment profile in neuronal, glial, epilepsy-related, and SCZ-associated genes.

Common Pathways Deregulated in the BTBR and *En2*$^{-/-}$ Hippocampus

Our comparative microarray analysis revealed that 155 genes (out of a total of 44,000) are differentially expressed in both BTBR and *En2*$^{-/-}$ hippocampus (**Figure 1**), indicating that a very low of number of genes (0.35%) are commonly deregulated among these two ASD mouse models. Nevertheless, ontology analyses for phenotypes and cellular pathways revealed that some common gene categories are significantly over-represented among the genes differentially expressed in the BTBR and *En2*$^{-/-}$ hippocampus, as compared to their respective controls (B6, *En2*$^{+/+}$ mice). Mammalian Phenotype ontology revealed that genes involved in abnormal behavioral responses are significantly deregulated in both mouse models (**Figure 2**). Most importantly, KEGG pathways analysis showed that genes related to immune response and inflammation are significantly deregulated in both BTBR and *En2*$^{-/-}$ hippocampus (KEGG pathways: chemokine signaling, MAPK signaling, systemic lupus erythematosus, Fc gamma receptor mediated phagocytosis; **Figure 3**). This is in line with our current knowledge about the role of the immune system in ASD pathogenesis. Genetic studies indicate that several genes encoding components of the immune system are associated to ASD. In addition, data from both ASD individuals and animal models indicate a significant dysregulation of immune processes in ASD, such as up-regulation of pro-inflammatory cytokines/chemokines, increased expression of major histocompatibility complex, and activation

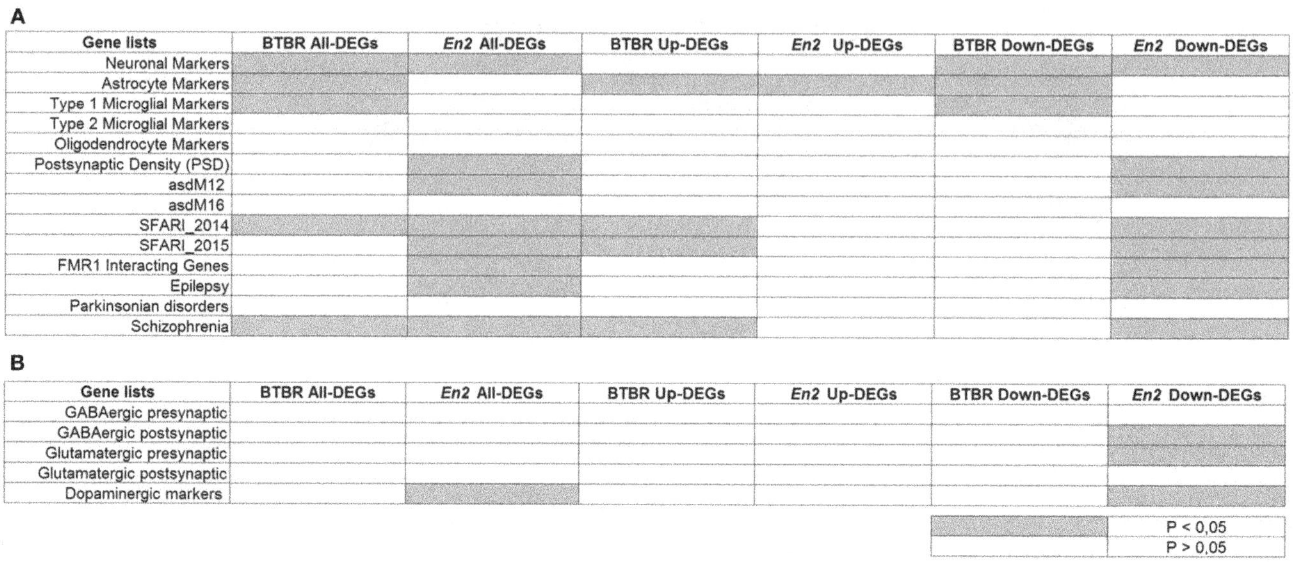

FIGURE 5 | Enrichment analysis on BTBR and *En2*$^{-/-}$ hippocampal DEGs. Lists of BTBR and *En2*$^{-/-}$ hippocampal DEGs (all, up-regulated and down-regulated) were analyzed for enrichment in genes belonging to specific categories relevant to the autistic phenotype **(A)** and neuronal subtypes **(B)**. Gene lists were compiled from the literature (see Materials and Methods and references therein). Significance of enrichment is indicated (white, $p > 0.05$; gray, $p < 0.05$).

of microglia in the brain (reviewed in Estes and McAllister, 2015). Significantly increased levels of pro-inflammatory cytokines (IL-1β, IL-6) and microglia activation have been reported in BTBR brains (Heo et al., 2011; Onore et al., 2013; Zhang et al., 2013), similarly to what observed in post-mortem brain tissue from ASD patients (Vargas et al., 2005; Li et al., 2009; Suzuki et al., 2013).

It is important to point out that, although the B6 strain is commonly used to compare with BTBR in molecular and behavioral studies (reviewed in Silverman et al., 2010), it exists the possibility that it is not an ideal or sufficient control for BTBR in gene expression studies. Indeed, linkage disequilibrium studies showed that B6 and BTBR mice are on different branches of the mouse genetic tree (Petkov et al., 2005). Thus, further genetic characterization is needed to identify the ideal control strain for inbred BTBR mice. In the absence of such a control, we conformed to previous studies using B6 as a control for BTBR in transcriptional profiling analyses (Daimon et al., 2015).

Differently from what reported in this study, our previous transcriptome profiling revealed a significant deregulation of immune- and inflammation-related genes in the cerebellum but not hippocampus of *En2*$^{-/-}$ adult mice (Sgadò et al., 2013b). One possible explanation is that our previous gene ontology analysis of the *En2*$^{-/-}$ hippocampal transcriptome was performed using different databases than those used for the present study. Preliminary unpublished data from our laboratory however indicate that the expression of several immune mediators (IL-1β, TNF-α, toll-like receptor 2, CCL2, CCL5) is significantly deregulated in the hippocampus (as well as neocortex and cerebellum) of *En2*$^{-/-}$ adult mice.

Our enrichment analyses revealed that both sets of BTBR and *En2*$^{-/-}$ hippocampal DEGs are enriched in ASD-related genes according to the SFARI 2014 dataset. *En2*$^{-/-}$ hippocampal DEGs also showed a significant enrichment in genes contained in two additional datasets of autism-related genes (asdM12 and SFARI15). This confirms that both BTBR and *En2*$^{-/-}$ mice are valuable mouse models to investigate ASD-relevant gene signatures. Most importantly, these enrichment analyses showed that both BTBR and *En2*$^{-/-}$ DEGs dataset are significantly enriched in SCZ-associated genes (**Figure 5**). This is in agreement with recent results from large-scale genomic studies showing that ASD and SCZ are neurodevelopmental disorders characterized by overlapping genetics and phenotypes (Murdoch and State, 2013). Genetic lesions at the origin of these disorders are thought to affect brain circuit formation and synaptic function during embryonic and/or postnatal development, ultimately leading to a varying range of (partially overlapping) pathological behaviors in ASD and SCZ. Recent genomic studies show that control subjects carrying copy-number variants (CNVs) conferring risk of ASD or SCZ poorly perform in cognitive tests (Stefansson et al., 2014), suggesting that conserved genetic mechanisms might underlie shared co-morbidities in these two neurodevelopmental disorders.

Enrichment analyses also showed that both sets of BTBR and *En2*$^{-/-}$ hippocampal DEGs are enriched in neuronal and astrocyte markers. The importance of glial cells in ASD pathophysiology was initially suggested by RNA sequencing studies showing a significant enrichment of glial genes belonging to immune/inflammatory categories in ASD brain tissues (Voineagu et al., 2011). These gene expression results are supported by neuroanatomical data showing glial cell activation in ASD postmortem brains (reviewed in Petrelli et al., 2016).

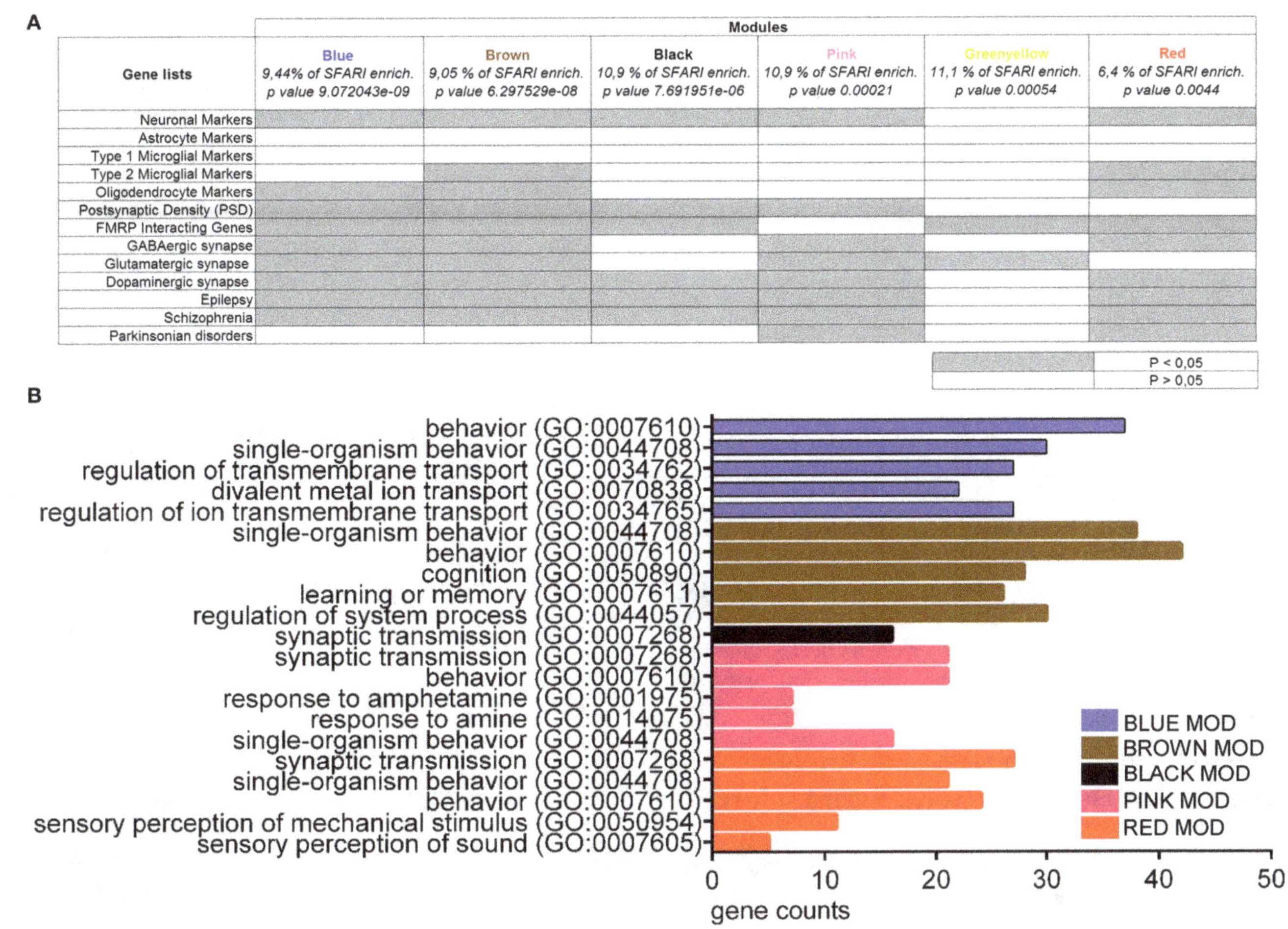

FIGURE 6 | Enrichment and gene ontology analyses on co-expression modules resulting from WGCNA on BTBR and *En2*$^{-/-}$ hippocampal DEGs. (A) Co-expression modules enriched in SFARI genes were analyzed for enrichment in genes belonging to specific categories relevant to the autistic phenotype, as indicated. Gene lists were as in **Figure 5**. Significance of enrichment is indicated (white, $p > 0.05$; gray, $p < 0.05$). **(B)** Co-expression modules were analyzed for enrichment in GO categories using Enrichr, with an adjusted $p < 0.05$. For each category, the number of genes is indicated by the length of horizontal bars (gene counts). Modules are indicated in their respective colors. The Greenyellow module is not indicated in the graph since it did not show any significant over-representation of GO terms.

Distinct Pathways Deregulated in the BTBR and *En2*$^{-/-}$ Hippocampus

Phenotype and gene ontology analyses, along with enrichment analyses, also confirmed that marked differences are present between the hippocampal gene expression profiles of BTBR and *En2*$^{-/-}$ adult mice. Mammalian Phenotype ontology analysis showed that the "abnormal innate immunity" and "seizure/abnormal synaptic transmission" pathways are significantly over-represented among hippocampal DEGs in BTBR and *En2*$^{-/-}$ adult mice, respectively (**Figure 2**). Abnormal immune response has been clearly demonstrated in BTBR mice (see Careaga et al., 2015, and references above). As an example, when pregnant dams of BTBR and C57BL/6J inbred strains were exposed to the viral mimic polyinosinic-polycytidylic acid (polyI:C), severe ASD-like behaviors and persistent dysregulation of adaptive immune system function were only observed in BTBR offspring (Schwartzer et al., 2013).

The gene expression signature of the BTBR hippocampus resulting from the present study is markedly different from that previously published by other authors. We detected a total of 1016 BTBR DEGs, whereas the number of BTBR DEGs detected by Daimon et al. (2015) was significantly lower (301). Only 69 BTBR DEGs were common to the two datasets. In both studies, the hippocampal BTBR transcriptome was compared to that of C57BL/6J inbred mice, and adult mice of comparable age were used (5 months in our study, 4 months in Daimon et al., 2015). However, Daimon et al. (2015) used a different microarray platform (Illumina), microarray analysis software (DIANE 6.0) and pathways analysis software (WebGestalt, http://bioinfo.vanderbilt.edu/), which can justify the difference in the obtained results.

As for the specific gene expression signature of the *En2*$^{-/-}$ hippocampus, KEGG pathway analysis performed in the present study confirmed our previous analysis (Sgadò et al., 2013b). Indeed, a marked excitation/inhibition unbalance is present in the *En2*$^{-/-}$ hippocampus and neocortex, as suggested by the increased seizure susceptibility (Tripathi et al., 2009) and loss of GABAergic interneurons (Sgadò et al., 2013a; Allegra et al., 2014; Provenzano et al., 2014) observed in *En2*$^{-/-}$ mice. These data are also supported by this study (**Figure 5**), which reveals a significant enrichment of GABAergic/glutamatergic postsynaptic markers among the genes down-regulated in the *En2*$^{-/-}$ hippocampus; genes interacting with fragile X mental retardation protein (FMRP) are also enriched, in keeping with the marked down-regulation of the FMRP pathway detected in the *En2*$^{-/-}$ hippocampus (Provenzano et al., 2015). Finally, dopaminergic markers are also enriched among the genes down-regulated in the *En2*$^{-/-}$ hippocampus, in keeping with the established role of Engrailed proteins in regulating the development and function of dopaminergic neurons (Gherbassi and Simon, 2006). Conversely, microglia markers are significantly enriched among genes down-regulated in the BTBR hippocampus, thus confirming the marked dysregulation of glial cell function in this ASD model. Accordingly, histopathological studies revealed glial cells but not GABAergic neurons alterations in the hippocampus of BTBR mice (Stephenson et al., 2011).

Weighted Correlation Network Analysis Reveals ASD-Relevant Gene Expression Modules

Based on the significant similarities detected between the BTBR and *En2*$^{-/-}$ hippocampal DEGs (**Figures 2, 3**), we considered the gene expression signature of these two ASD mouse models together, and compared it to that of their respective control strains (C57Bl/6J and *En2*$^{+/+}$). We then performed weighted gene co-expression network analysis (WGCNA; Langfelder and Horvath, 2008) to identify correlation patterns among genes across the ASD models vs. control microarray samples, and find gene clusters (modules) whose expression is highly correlated. Genes differentially expressed in ASD mouse models were clustered in 18 modules, and our WGCNA showed that 6 out of these 18 modules were significantly enriched in ASD-related genes. Each of these 6 ASD genes-enriched modules showed a specific enrichment profile in neuronal and glial genes, as well as in genes associated to epilepsy and SCZ. This is in line with WGCNA performed on gene signatures from ASD post-mortem cortical brain tissue, which showed a significant deregulation of glial and neuronal activity-dependent genes in autism (Gupta et al., 2014). It is also important to note that ASD and epilepsy show a high degree of comorbidity (Buckley and Holmes, 2016), and conserved genetic mechanisms have been proposed to underlie ASD and SCZ (see above in this discussion; Stefansson et al., 2014). Thus, WGCNA performed on microarray samples from autistic vs. control mouse strains is able to identify conserved gene expression signatures across different ASD mouse models.

CONCLUSIONS

The present study reveals significant transcriptional similarities and differences between the BTBR and *En2*$^{-/-}$ hippocampus, confirming the idea that transcriptome profiling of specific brain areas from ASD mouse models may contribute to identify novel molecular targets for pharmacological studies.

AUTHOR CONTRIBUTIONS

GP designed and performed experiments, analyzed data and wrote the paper. ZC and LR performed experiments. KM and TF analyzed data. MS conceived the study and provided funding. YB conceived the study, analyzed data, provided funding, and wrote the paper. ZC and KM equally contributed to this study.

ACKNOWLEDGMENTS

We thank Erik Dassi (CIBIO, University of Trento) for help with bioinformatic analyses, and Michael Pancher and Valentina Adami (High-Throughput Facility, CIBIO, University of Trento) for assistance with microarray experiments. We are grateful to the technical/administrative staff of CIBIO (University of Trento) and CNR Institute of Neuroscience (Pisa, Italy) for assistance. This work was funded by grants from the Italian Ministry of University and Research (PRIN 2010-11 grant 2010N8PBAA_002 to YB), University of Trento (CIBIO start-up to YB) and Italian Ministry of Health Grant (GR-2010-2315883 to MS). GP is supported by a grant fellowship from the Fondazione Umberto Veronesi (Milan, Italy).

REFERENCES

Alexander, A. L., Lee, J. E., Lazar, M., Boudos, R., DuBray, M. B., Oakes, T. R., et al. (2007). Diffusion tensor imaging of the corpus callosum in Autism. *Neuroimage* 34, 61–73. doi: 10.1016/j.neuroimage.2006.08.032

Allegra, M., Genovesi, S., Maggia, M., Cenni, M. C., Zunino, G., Sgadò, P., et al. (2014). Altered GABAergic markers, increased binocularity and reduced plasticity in the visual cortex of Engrailed-2 knockout mice. *Front. Cell. Neurosci.* 8:163. doi: 10.3389/fncel.2014.00163

Benayed, R., Choi, J., Matteson, P. G., Gharani, N., Kamdar, S., Brzustowicz, L. M., et al. (2009). Autism-associated haplotype affects the regulation of the homeobox gene, ENGRAILED 2. *Biol. Psychiatry* 66, 911–917. doi: 10.1016/j.biopsych.2009.05.027

Blake, J. A., Bult, C. J., Eppig, J. T., Kadin, J. A., and Richardson, J. E. (2009). The mouse genome database genotypes: phenotypes. *Nucleic Acids Res.* 37, D712–D719. doi: 10.1093/nar/gkn886

Brielmaier, J., Matteson, P. G., Silvermanm, J. L., Senerth, J. M., Kelly, S., Genestine, M., et al. (2012). Autism-relevant social abnormalities and cognitive deficits in engrailed-2 knockout mice. *PLoS ONE* 7:e40914. doi: 10.1371/journal.pone.0040914

Brielmaier, J., Senerth, J. M., Silverman, J. L., Matteson, P. G., Millonig, J. H., DiCicco-Bloom, E., et al. (2014). Chronic desipramine treatment rescues depression-related, social and cognitive deficits in Engrailed-2 knockout mice. *Genes Brain Behav.* 13, 286–298. doi: 10.1111/gbb.12115

Buckley, A. W., and Holmes, G. L. (2016). Epilepsy and autism. *Cold Spring Harb. Perspect Med.* 6:a022749. doi: 10.1101/cshperspect.a022749

Careaga, M., Schwartzer, J., and Ashwood, P. (2015). Inflammatory profiles in the BTBR mouse: how relevant are they to autism spectrum disorders? *Brain Behav. Immun.* 43, 11–16. doi: 10.1016/j.bbi.2014.06.006

Cheh, M. A., Millonig, J. H., Roselli, L. M., Ming, X., Jacobsen, E., Kamdar, S., et al. (2006). En2 knockout mice display neurobehavioral and neurochemical alterations relevant to autism spectrum disorder. *Brain Res.* 1116, 166–176. doi: 10.1016/j.brainres.2006.07.086

Choi, J., Ababon, M. R., Soliman, M., Lin, Y., Brzustowicz, L. M., Matteson, P. G., et al. (2014). Autism associated gene, engrailed2, and flanking gene levels are altered in post-mortem cerebellum. *PLoS ONE* 9:e87208. doi: 10.1371/journal.pone.0087208

Crespi, B., Stead, P., and ans Elliot, M. (2010). Evolution in health and medicine Sackler colloquium: Comparative genomics of autism and schizophrenia. *Proc. Natl. Acad. Sci. U.S.A.* 107, 1736–1741. doi: 10.1073/pnas.0906080106

Daimon, C. M., Jasien, J. M., Wood, W. H. III, Zhang, Y., Becker, K. G., Silverman, J. L., et al. (2015). Hippocampal transcriptomic and proteomic alterations in the BTBR mouse model of autism spectrum disorder. *Front. Physiol.* 6:324. doi: 10.3389/fphys.2015.00324

Darnell, J. C., Van Driesche, S. J., Zhang, C., Hung, K. Y., Mele, A., Fraser, C. E., et al. (2011). FMRP stalls ribosomal translocation on mRNAs linked to synaptic function and autism. *Cell* 146, 247–261. doi: 10.1016/j.cell.2011.06.013

de la Torre-Ubieta, L., Won, H., Stein, J. L., and Geschwind, D. H. (2016). Advancing the understanding of autism disease mechanisms through genetics. *Nat. Med.* 22, 345–361. doi: 10.1038/nm.4071

Egaas, B., Courchesne, E., and Saitoh, O. (1995). Reduced size of corpus callosum in autism. *Arch. Neurol.* 52, 794–801. doi: 10.1001/archneur.1995.00540320070014

Ellegood, J., Anagnostou, E., Babineau, B. A., Crawley, J. N., Lin, L., Genestine, M., et al. (2015). Clustering autism: using neuroanatomical differences in 26 mouse models to gain insight into the heterogeneity. *Mol. Psychiatry* 20, 118–125. doi: 10.1038/mp.2014.98

Ellegood, J., and Crawley, J. N. (2015). Behavioral and neuroanatomical phenotypes in mouse models of autism. *Neurotherapeutics* 12, 521–533. doi: 10.1007/s13311-015-0360-z

Estes, M. L., and McAllister, A. K. (2015). Immune mediators in the brain and peripheral tissues in autism spectrum disorder. *Nat. Rev. Neurosci.* 16, 469–486. doi: 10.1038/nrn3978

Fatemi, S. H., Reutiman, T. J., Folsom, T. D., Rooney, R. J., Patel, D. H., and Thuras, P. D. (2010). mRNA and protein levels for GABAAalpha4, alpha5, beta1 and GABABR1 receptors are altered in brains from subjects with autism. *J. Autism Dev. Disord.* 40, 743–750. doi: 10.1007/s10803-009-0924-z

Genestine, M., Lin, L., Durens, M., Yan, Y., Jiang, Y., Prem, S., et al. (2015). Engrailed-2 (En2) deletion produces multiple neurodevelopmental defects in monoamine systems, forebrain structures and neurogenesis and behavior. *Hum. Mol. Genet.* 24, 5805–5827. doi: 10.1093/hmg/ddv301

Gherbassi, D., and Simon, H. H. (2006). The engrailed transcription factors and the mesencephalic dopaminergic neurons. *J. Neural Transm. Suppl.* 70, 47–55. doi: 10.1007/978-3-211-45295-0_9

Gupta, S., Ellis, S. E., Ashar, F. N., Moes, A., Bader, J. S., Zhan, J., et al. (2014). Transcriptome analysis reveals dysregulation of innate immune response genes and neuronal activity-dependent genes in autism. *Nat. Commun.* 5:5748. doi: 10.1038/ncomms6748

Heo, Y., Zhang, Y., Gao, D., Miller, V. M., and Lawrence, D. A. (2011). Aberrant immune responses in a mouse with behavioral disorders. *PLoS ONE* 6:e20912. doi: 10.1371/journal.pone.0020912

James, S. J., Shpyleva, S., Melnyk, S., Pavliv, O., and Pogribny, I. P. (2013). Complex epigenetic regulation of Engrailed-2 (EN-2) homeobox gene in the autism cerebellum. *Transl. Psychiatry* 3:e232. doi: 10.1038/tp.2013.8

James, S. J., Shpyleva, S., Melnyk, S., Pavliv, O., and Pogribny, I. P. (2014). Elevated 5-hydroxymethylcytosine in the Engrailed-2 (EN-2) promoter is associated with increased gene expression and decreased MeCP2 binding in autism cerebellum. *Transl. Psychiatry* 4:e460. doi: 10.1038/tp.2014.87

Johnson, W. E., Li, C., and Rabinovic, A. (2007). Adjusting batch effects in microarray expression data using empirical Bayes methods. *Biostatistics* 8, 118–127. doi: 10.1093/biostatistics/kxj037

Jones-Davis, D. M., Yang, M., Rider, E., Osbun, N. C., da Gente, G. J., Li, J., et al. (2013). Quantitative trait loci for interhemispheric commissure development and social behaviors in the BTBR T+ tf/J mouse model of autism. *PLoS ONE* 8:e61829. doi: 10.1371/journal.pone.0061829

Joyner, A. L., Herrup, K., Auerbach, B. A., Davis, C. A., and Rossant, J. (1991). Subtle cerebellar phenotype in mice homozygous for a targeted deletion of the En-2 homeobox. *Science* 251, 1239–1243. doi: 10.1126/science.1672471

Kadanga, A. K., Leroux, C., Bonnet, M., Chauvet, S., Meunier, B., Cassar-Malek, I., et al. (2008). Image analysis and data normalization procedures are crucial for microarray analyses. *Gene Regul. Syst. Bio.* 2, 107–112.

Kratsman, N., Getselter, D., and Elliott, E. (2016). Sodium butyrate attenuates social behavior deficits and modifies the transcription of inhibitory/excitatory genes in the frontal cortex of an autism model. *Neuropharmacology* 102, 136–145. doi: 10.1016/j.neuropharm.2015.11.003

Kuemerle, B., Zanjani, H., Joyner, A., and Herrup, K. (1997). Pattern deformities and cell loss in Engrailed-2 mutant mice suggest two separate patterning events during cerebellar development. *J. Neurosci.* 17, 7881–7889.

Langfelder, P., and Horvath, S. (2008). WGCNA: an R package for weighted correlation network analysis. *BMC Bioinformatics* 9:559. doi: 10.1186/1471-2105-9-559

Leek, J., Johnson, W., Parker, H., Jaffe, A., and Storey, J. (2012). *SVA: Surrogate Variable Analysis. R package version* 3.2.1.

Li, X., Chauhan, A., Sheikh, A. M., Patil, S., Chauhan, V., Li, X. M., et al. (2009). Elevated immune response in the brain of autistic patients. *J. Neuroimmunol.* 207, 111–116. doi: 10.1016/j.jneuroim.2008.12.002

Murdoch, J. D., and State, M. W. (2013). Recent developments in the genetics of autism spectrum disorders. *Curr. Opin. Genet. Dev.* 23, 310–315. doi: 10.1016/j.gde.2013.02.003

Onore, C. E., Careaga, M., Babineau, B. A., Schwartzer, J. J., Berman, R. F., and Ashwood, P. (2013). Inflammatory macrophage phenotype in BTBR T+tf/J mice. *Front. Neurosci.* 7:158. doi: 10.3389/fnins.2013.00158

Petkov, P. M., Graber, J. H., Churchill, G. A., DiPetrillo, K., King, B. L., and Paigen, K. (2005). Evidence of a large-scale functional organization of mammalian chromosomes. *PLoS Genet.* 1:e33. doi: 10.1371/journal.pgen.0010033

Petrelli, F., Pucci, L., and Bezzi, P. (2016). Astrocytes and microglia and their potential link with autism spectrum disorders. *Front. Cell. Neurosci.* 10:21. doi: 10.3389/fncel.2016.00021

Prilutsky, D., Kho, A. T., Palmer, N. P., Bhakar, A. L., Smedemark-Margulies, N., Kong, S. W., et al. (2015). Gene expression analysis in Fmr1KO mice identifies an immunological signature in brain tissue and mGluR5-related signaling in primary neuronal cultures. *Mol. Autism* 6:66. doi: 10.1186/s13229-015-0061-9

Provenzano, G., Pangrazzi, L., Poli, A., Pernigo, M., Sgadò, P., Genovesi, S., et al. (2014). Hippocampal dysregulation of neurofibromin-dependent pathways is associated with impaired spatial learning in engrailed 2 knock-out mice. *J. Neurosci.* 34, 13281–13288. doi: 10.1523/JNEUROSCI.2894-13.2014

Provenzano, G., Sgadò, P., Genovesi, S., Zunino, G., Casarosa, S., and Bozzi, Y. (2015). Hippocampal dysregulation of FMRP/mGluR5 signaling in engrailed-2 knockout mice: a model of autism spectrum disorders. *Neuroreport* 26, 1101–1105. doi: 10.1097/WNR.0000000000000477

Scattoni, M. L., Gandhy, S. U., Ricceri, L., and Crawley, J. N. (2008). Unusual repertoire of vocalizations in the BTBR T+tf/J mouse model of autism. *PLoS ONE* 3:e3067. doi: 10.1371/journal.pone.0003067

Scattoni, M. L., Martire, A., Cartocci, G., Ferrante, A., and Ricceri, L. (2013). Reduced social interaction, behavioural flexibility and BDNF signalling in the BTBR T+ tf/J strain, a mouse model of autism. *Behav. Brain Res.* 251, 35–40. doi: 10.1016/j.bbr.2012.12.028

Schwartzer, J. J., Careaga, M., Onore, C. E., Rushakoff, J. A., Berman, R. F., and Ashwood, P. (2013). Maternal immune activation and strain specific interactions in the development of autism-like behaviors in mice. *Transl. Psychiatry* 3:e240. doi: 10.1038/tp.2013.16

Sgadò, P., Genovesi, S., Kalinovsky, A., Zunino, G., Macchi, F., Allegra, M., et al. (2013a). Loss of GABAergic neurons in the hippocampus and cerebral cortex of Engrailed-2 null mutant mice: implications for autism spectrum disorders. *Exp. Neurol.* 247, 496–505. doi: 10.1016/j.expneurol.2013.01.021

Sgadò, P., Provenzano, G., Dassi, E., Adami, V., Zunino, G., Genovesi, S., et al. (2013b). Transcriptome profiling in engrailed-2 mutant mice reveals common molecular pathways associated with autism spectrum disorders. *Mol. Autism* 4:51. doi: 10.1186/2040-2392-4-51

Silverman, J. L., Yang, M., Lord, C., and Crawley, J. N. (2010). Behavioural phenotyping assays for mouse models of autism. *Nat. Rev. Neurosci.* 11, 490–502. doi: 10.1038/nrn2851

Stefansson, H., Meyer-Lindenberg, A., Steinberg, S., Magnusdottir, B., Morgen, K., Arnarsdottir, S., et al. (2014). CNVs conferring risk of autism or schizophrenia affect cognition in controls. *Nature* 505, 361–366. doi: 10.1038/nature 12818

Stephenson, D. T., O'Neill, S. M., Narayan, S., Tiwari, A., Arnold, E., Samaroo, H. D., et al. (2011). Histopathologic characterization of the BTBR mouse model of autistic-like behavior reveals selective changes in neurodevelopmental proteins and adult hippocampal neurogenesis. *Mol. Autism* 2:7. doi: 10.1186/2040-23 92-2-7

Suzuki, K., Sugihara, G., Ouchi, Y., Nakamura, K., Futatsubashi, M., Takebayashi, K., et al. (2013). Microglial activation in young adults with autism spectrum disorder. *JAMA Psychiatry* 70, 49–58. doi: 10.1001/jamapsychiatry.20 13.272

Tilot, A. K., Bebek, G., Niazi, F., Altemus, J. B., Romigh, T., Frazier, T. W., et al. (2016). Neural transcriptome of constitutional Pten dysfunction in mice and its relevance to human idiopathic autism spectrum disorder. *Mol. Psychiatry* 21, 118–125. doi: 10.1038/mp.2015.17

Tripathi, P. P., Sgadò, P., Scali, M., Viaggi, C., Casarosa, S., Simon, H. H., et al. (2009). Increased susceptibility to kainic acid-induced seizures in Engrailed-2 knockout mice. *Neuroscience* 159, 842–849. doi: 10.1016/j.neuroscience.2009.01.007

Vargas, D. L., Nascimbene, C., Krishnan, C., Zimmerman, A. W., and Pardo, C. A. (2005). Neuroglial activation and neuroinflammation in the brain of patients with autism. *Ann. Neurol.* 57, 67–81. doi: 10.1002/ana.20315

Viaggi, C., Gerace, C., Pardini, C., Corsini, G. U., and Vaglini, F. (2015). Serotonin abnormalities in Engrailed-2 knockout mice: New insight relevant for a model of Autism Spectrum Disorder. *Neurochem. Int.* 87, 34–42. doi: 10.1016/j.neuint.2015.05.004

Voineagu, I., Wang, X., Johnston, P., Lowe, J. K., Tian, Y., Horvath, S., et al. (2011). Transcriptomic analysis of autistic brain reveals convergent molecular pathology. *Nature* 474, 380–384. doi: 10.1038/nature10110

Wahlsten, D., Metten, P., and Crabbe, J. C. (2003). Survey of 21 inbred mouse strains in two laboratories reveals that BTBR T/+ tf/tf has severely reduced hippocampal commissure and absent corpus callosum. *Brain Res.* 971, 47–54. doi: 10.1016/S0006-8993(03)02354-0

Zhang, B., and Horvath, S. (2005). A general framework for weighted gene co-expression network analysis. *Stat. Appl. Genet. Mol. Biol.* 4:17. doi: 10.2202/1544-6115.1128

Zhang, Y., Gao, D., Kluetzman, K., Mendoza, A., Bolivar, V. J., Reilly, A., et al. (2013). The maternal autoimmune environment affects the social behavior of offspring. *J. Neuroimmunol.* 258, 51–60. doi: 10.1016/j.jneuroim.2013.02.019

8

Defining Precision Medicine Approaches to Autism Spectrum Disorders: Concepts and Challenges

Eva Loth[1,2], Declan G. Murphy[1,2] and Will Spooren[3]*

[1] Department of Forensic and Neurodevelopmental Sciences, Institute of Psychiatry, Psychology and Neuroscience, King's College London, London, UK, [2] Sackler Institute for Translational Neurodevelopment, Institute of Psychiatry, Psychology and Neuroscience, King's College London, London, UK, [3] Roche Pharmaceutical Research and Early Development, NORD Discovery and Translational Area, Roche Innovation Center, Basel, Switzerland

Edited by:
Yuri Bozzi,
University of Trento, Italy

Reviewed by:
Stephanie Ameis,
Hospital for Sick Children, Canada
Enrico Domenici,
University of Trento, Italy

***Correspondence:**
Eva Loth
eva.loth@kcl.ac.uk

The tremendous clinical and etiological variability between individuals with autism spectrum disorder (ASD) has made precision medicine the most promising treatment approach. It aims to combine new pathophysiologically based treatments with objective tests (stratification biomarkers) to predict which treatment may be beneficial for a particular person. Here we discuss significant advances and current challenges for this approach: rare monogenic forms of ASD have provided a major breakthrough for the identification of treatment targets by providing a means to trace causal links from a gene to specific molecular alterations and biological pathways. To estimate whether treatment targets thus identified may be useful for larger patient groups we need a better understanding of whether different etiologies (i.e., genetic and environmental risk factors acting at different critical time points) lead to convergent or divergent molecular mechanisms, and how they map onto differences in circuit-level brain and cognitive development, and behavioral symptom profiles. Several recently failed clinical trials with syndromic forms of ASD provide valuable insights into conceptual and methodological issues linked to limitations in the translatability from animal models to humans, placebo effects, and a need for mechanistically plausible, objective outcome measures. To identify stratification biomarkers that enrich participant selection in clinical trials, large-scale multi-modal longitudinal observational studies are underway. Addressing these different factors in the next generation of research studies requires a translatable developmental perspective and multidisciplinary, collaborative efforts, with a commitment to sharing protocols and data, to increase transparency and reproducibility.

Keywords: autism spectrum disorder, biomarkers, precision medicine

INTRODUCTION

When parents first receive a diagnosis of autism spectrum disorder (ASD) of their child, some of their most pressing questions are: what is the prognosis of my child? What has caused his/her autism? And what are the treatment options?

Autism spectrum disorder is a clinically and etiologically heterogeneous condition, currently estimated to affect between 1 and 1.5% of children and adults worldwide (1, 2). Diagnostic ascertainment is based on the behavioral symptom profile alone; the co-occurrence of social-communicative deficits, repetitive and restricted behaviors and interests, and sensory processing anomalies [DSM-5 (3)]. In addition, up to 70% of individuals have one or more psychiatric and/or medical comorbidities, such as intellectual disability, ADHD, irritability, aggression, anxiety, depression, epilepsy, and sleep anomalies (4).

The prognosis is very variable. A recent large-scale longitudinal study showed distinct developmental trajectories in children between the ages of 2 and 14 years (5). Children whose symptoms were least severe at first diagnosis showed the most symptom improvement. However, a subgroup of around 10% of children who presented with the most severe social deficits at age 3 years made significant gains in their social trajectory across childhood. Nevertheless, for the majority of people with ASD, outcome in adulthood has been estimated to be "poor" (46%) or even "very poor" (12%) (6). IQ and language level are widely considered the best predictors of outcome. Beyond this, it is currently largely unknown whether different developmental trajectories may reflect different biological subgroups, and why some individuals develop comorbidities but others do not.

To date, no effective medical treatments are available that significantly improve the core symptoms of ASD. Only two medications (the second-generation antipsychotics risperidone and aripiprazole) have been approved in ASD by the US Food and Drugs Administration (FDA) and one (risperidone) by the European Medicines Agency (EMA). Both medications are not specific for ASD and target associated symptoms, such as aggression or irritability. Instead, the management of ASD relies heavily on behavioral and educational interventions (7). Although several of these programs report significant improvements, difficulties in generalizing skills to "real-world" settings, and access to these treatments and their expense, remain common limitations (8).

THE CALL FOR A PRECISION MEDICINE APPROACH

Recognition of the phenotypic and etiological variability between individuals on the autism spectrum and the lack of effective treatments has called for a precision medicine approach. This approach aims to identify targeted treatments based on the understanding of the underlying pathophysiology and to then combine the drug (or intervention) with a companion diagnostic (stratification biomarker) to select or exclude patients for a particular treatment. Below we review current progress and discuss some of the challenges and requirements that still lie ahead.

Perhaps the biggest breakthrough for drug discovery in ASD came from the identification of syndromic and monogenic forms of ASD (where the disorder is thought to be caused by a highly penetrant single gene). Hundreds of ASD risk genes have been identified (9, 10), and more are expected to be found over the next years through whole-genome sequencing and studies with larger sample sizes. The significance of these discoveries lies in their potential ability to identify a causal link from a gene to cellular and molecular mechanisms underlying ASD symptoms (11). Moreover, although each of these monogenic forms is rare (i.e., found in less than 1% of individuals with ASD) different genes have been shown to converge on affecting a much smaller number of common pathways (12). This finding is crucial as it means that a particular biological pathway could be a treatment target rather than individual gene products. Treatments thus identified may therefore, potentially, be applicable for broader patient groups. Many of these risk genes modulate pathways involved in synapse formation and function, as well as other cellular functions, such as chromatin remodeling and transcription, protein synthesis and degradation, and receptor signaling (10). Any of these mutations may therefore alter essential developmental processes *in utero* or shortly after birth (13). For example, abnormalities in synapse development, function, and plasticity may broadly impact the balance between excitation (mainly modulated by glutamate) and inhibition (mainly modulated by gamma-aminobutyric acid, GABA) In particular, it has been suggested that (some forms of) ASD may be linked to disproportionally high levels of excitation and cortical network function (14).

Animal models of syndromic and monogenic forms showed significant pre-clinical promise such that several molecular aberrations and behavioral phenotypes could be reversed through pharamacological treatment or genetic rescue – sometimes even in adulthood (15, 16). Subsequent Phase I clinical trials using mGluR antagonists, or a $GABA_B$ agonist, also reported promising results.

However, well-powered (Phase IIb or Phase III) double-blind placebo-controlled clinical trials with individuals with Fragile X syndrome so far produced disappointing results (17). For example, two clinical trials, led by Roche and Novartis, respectively, reported a lack of efficacy of their mGluR-inhibiting drugs (RG7090 and mavoglurant) in Fragile X syndrome. Similarly, a trial with arbaclofen, led by Seaside Therapeutics, failed to find significant improvements in individuals with Fragile X and idiopathic autism relative to placebo. This highlights several factors.

First, even monogenic or syndromic forms also involve considerably heterogeneous symptom expression. For example, although a SHANK3 haploinsufficiency (thought to cause Phelan McDermid Syndrome) is one of most penetrant genetic risk factors for ASD [approximately 70% (18)], it can also lead to ADHD, schizophrenia, or bipolar disorder in a smaller number of individuals (19). About 30% of people with Fragile X syndrome have ASD (20). Others present with ADHD, anxiety and avoidance behavior, mood instability, or aggressive behavior (21). This variable expressivity appears to be not solely explained by the size or location of the deletion alone. What are the factors that may influence shared vs. distinct developmental outcomes; and at what level(s) can divergence or variability be observed?

FACTORS THAT IMPACT DEVELOPMENTAL OUTCOME

Figure 1 outlines the interplay between four factors that may impact on developmental outcome.

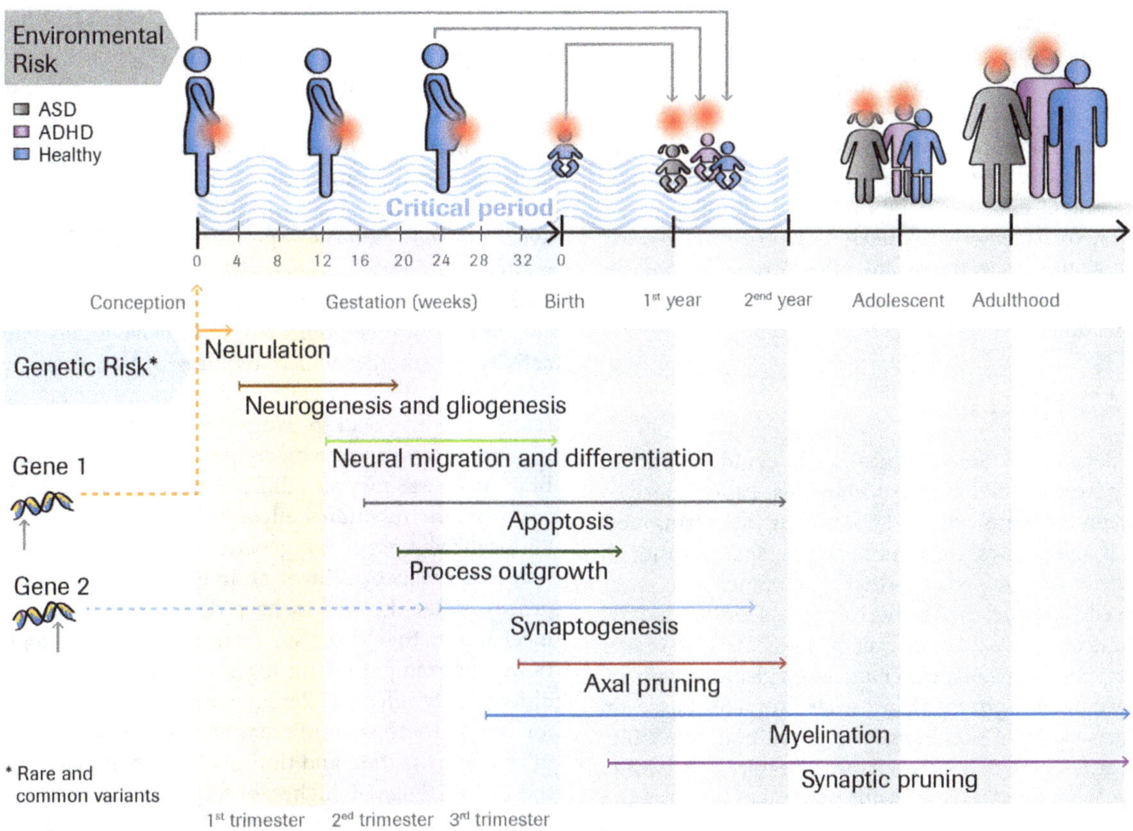

FIGURE 1 | Rare and common genetic variants, as well as environmental risk factors (e.g., toxins, maternal infection) acting at different time points impact on the developmental outcome. For example, the same rare genetic mutation can either lead to ASD, ASD + ADHD, or ADHD, depending on the person's genomic background (the sum of common variants). Or the effect of a genetic variant could be modulated by environmental insults that occur during the first, second or third trimester of the pregnancy. Many ASD risk genes are involved in essential developmental processes including proliferation, neuronal growth and differentiation, and synapse formation. These genes are expressed at different times in brain development.

Common Variants and Genomic Background

The impact of rare mutations on phenotypic outcome may depend on genomic background (the sum of common variants). It may act as a "buffer" that diminishes or increases the deleterious effect of rare variants (CNVs) – for example, by modulating synaptic homeostasis (10). For an individual with a genetic background that contains a high load of common ASD risk variants, a small burden of rare risk genes may suffice to cause ASD. By contrast, an individual whose genetic background only includes a small number of common risk variants may require a higher burden of deleterious mutations to cause ASD. The rare genetic mutation may still have some penetrance, but the effect may be "milder," including sub-threshold clinical symptoms (10).

Environmental Risk Factors

In addition to genetic factors, it is likely that environmental influences – notably those acting during the embryonic stage – modulate risk for ASD. This includes maternal infections and prenatal exposure to teratogenic agents such as valproate acid, exposure to toxins, and dysfunction of the immune system (22). For instance, human studies comparing monozygotic and dizygotic twins have consistently revealed significant environmental influences that account for approximately 5–6% (23) of the observed variance in ASD. Moreover, higher concordance rates of ASD and other neurodevelopmental disorders in dizygotic twins than (singleton) siblings suggest a specific role of the fetal environment because both the twins and singletons share 50% of their genes (24).

Critical Periods

The time when different factors impact on neuronal development likely plays a crucial factor in determining developmental outcome. Brain development is initially determined by distinct temporal and spatial stages of gene expression (25) and intrinsic neuronal activity (26) but then becomes actively refined by interactions with the environment. Timing could be influenced either by genetic factors as different genes are expressed at different times in brain development [e.g., in humans genes involved in cell proliferation are expressed earlier than those involved in synaptogenesis or myelination (25)] or the time when an environmental insult occurs.

By altering the developmental window during which genetic/environmental insults are applied, animal studies can trace these effects across cellular, molecular, brain systems, and behavioral levels. However, the vast majority of animal studies have only tested adult animals. Therefore, we only know the end state – and not how abnormalities developed or changed across development. To understand this is vital because it is possible that some treatment effects may be different in developing vs. adult brains. A treatment that is likely only effective in early development would raise important ethical implications for clinical trial designs that usually first test safety, efficacy and side-effects in adults.

TRANSLATABILITY

One potential factor in failed clinical trials could be limited translatability from animal models to humans. Patient-derived induced pluripotent stem cells (iPSCs) are an interesting new approach that overcomes inter-species differences, although the technology is still in need of further development. Recently, protocols have been developed to derive iPSCs from peripheral blood mononuclear cells (27) or hair roots (28). This makes sample collection significantly easier and more viable for vulnerable and larger patient groups than earlier protocols based on fibroplasts (derived from skin biopsies). In addition, the ability to freeze keratinocytes themselves now offers great flexibility in generating lines from patients with particular genetics and phenotypic characteristics. For example, by comparing lines from patients with a particular monogenic defect (e.g., with SHANK3), but different clinical symptoms we may be able to account for differences in genomic background (which is difficult in animal models) and identify which cellular alterations may be linked to the gene vs. particular phenotypic differences. Comparison of phenotypes between cells derived from patients with monogenic vs. "idiopathic" forms of ASD provides valuable information on how generalizable cellular or molecular alterations identified from specific genetic/environmental processes may be for wider patient groups. Currently, the iPSC methodology is very costly. However, by studying cell lines of patients that are also comprehensively characterized in terms of their systems level (MRI, EEG, and PET) and neurocognitive profile we will be able to advance our understanding of the relationship between cellular, morphological and molecular, and higher level phenotypes in the same person. New systems level features of brain anatomy, function, and connectivity are now developed that offer higher resolution and greater translatability to brain phenotypes studied in animal models (29).

WE NEED TO BRIDGE LEVELS OF ANALYSES – COGNITION AS A BLACK BOX

One of the current challenges for neurobiological hypotheses, such as the E/I imbalance hypothesis, lies in its broadness: both glutamate and GABA are ubiquitous in the brain. Is the E/I imbalance in ASD cell and/or circuit-specific? Or might phenotypic differences linked to E/I imbalances across disorders (e.g., ASD vs. schizophrenia, ID) depend on a critical period during which they occur? And how do E/I imbalances give rise to characteristic cognitive profiles of ASD that involves both weaknesses and strengths?

The immature brain undergoes progressive alterations in molecular composition and in synchronized currents that underpin the development of functional neuronal circuits. Synchronized patterns of neuronal activity engage many neurons of developing networks, possibly because of efficient feed-forward GABA-ergic inhibition. These immature signals stop at critical time points to enable behaviorally relevant brain activity to emerge, which requires sparse fired, time-locked oscillations. Whereas early perturbations during basic circuit refinement may lead to widespread abnormalities, later occurring ones may produce more specific and localized disruptions. Brain networks may also differ in their resilience to gene dosage such that the functional effects of abnormal gene dosage could be localized even if the genetic abnormalities are widespread (30). Brain networks involved in evolutionarily older biological processes are thought to have developed more compensatory mechanisms than those supporting more recent cognitive functions. For example, the timing of insults in synapse development differentially affects different cortical regions as the timeline for synaptogenesis is different across the cortex (31). Changes in synaptic function and timing might then particularly disrupt the connectivity of higher order association areas, including frontal–parietal, frontal–temporal, and frontal–striatal circuits (32). This coincides with brain systems supporting higher level social-cognitive function or language development, which spike in synaptogenesis and plasticity between 1 and 3 years of age (31); roughly the time when social and language-related symptoms often become first apparent in ASD. Transcriptomics studies of co-expression patterns showed enrichment of ASD genes in cortical projection neurons (33), including glutamatergic projection neurons in superficial cortical layers (34).

Recently, some efforts were also made in linking glutamate or GABA neurotransmission to sensory processing abnormalities. For example, deficits in binocular rivalry (35) as well as paradoxical motion perception (36) in ASD are taken as indirect proxies for reduced GABA-ergic signaling. However, this approach makes the strong assumption that anomalies in circuits underpinning sensory anomalies are "primary deficits" in autism (37, 38) with down-stream effects on networks supporting higher level (and later developing) cognitive and social-cognitive functions – a premise that remains to be further tested.

Finally, some brain circuits may be more affected than others because glutamate and GABA modulate and are modulated by other neurotransmitter systems in particular brain regions and that are crucial for cognitive functions. For example, at birth, GABA-ergic signaling shifts from excitation to inhibition due to a reduction in intracellular chloride concentration, which in turn is mediated by endogenous oxytocin release. This shift in GABA-ergic polarity is abolished in mouse models of fragile X syndrome and rodents treated with valproate *in utero*; and some evidence indicates that "immature" excitatory GABA-ergic activity may persist in people with ASD (39). This provides a potential link of GABA to a cascade effect of social-motivational abnormalities that are thought to be modulated by oxytocin.

Well-Validated Translated Cognitive Tests for Large-scale Investigations

Cognitive measures that map onto specific circuits are needed to bridge our understanding between systems level and behavioral anomalies. For many commonly used tests, psychometric properties (e.g., test–retest reliability), age norms, are not available. We need to invest in well-validated cognitive batteries that are equally suitable and meaningful for both children and adults, or for which different comparable versions exist. As most syndromic and monogenic forms of ASD involve varying degrees of intellectual disability, these tests should also be sensitive across the ability ranges, including profound intellectual disability levels to understand whether mechanisms are shared or different between these forms of ASD.

WHAT ARE MECHANISTICALLY PLAUSIBLE CLINICAL ENDPOINTS?

International regulators, such as the FDA, require clinical trials to select only one assessment as the primary endpoint against which the success of a study is measured. Currently, the lack of a truly mechanistic understanding of the link between molecular, neuroanatomical/functional, and cognitive processes impedes informed selection of "primary endpoints." For example, in a pilot trial of insulin-like growth factor-1 (IGF-1) in Phelan McDermid Syndrome the Aberrant Behavior Checklist (ABC) social withdrawal subscale was chosen as the primary outcome measure because it is well validated in ASD and ID and accepted within pediatric psychopharmacology research (40). In the STX209 arbaclofen trial with volunteers with "idiopathic" ASD, the ABC-irritability subscale was used as the primary outcome measure; again because the measure is known to be sensitive to change in pharmacologic trials. However, in both examples there was no mechanistic reason why the growth-stimulating hormone should primarily affect social symptoms or a specific $GABA_B$ receptor agonist should "specifically" affect irritability (rather than core social deficits of ASD). Also, in some instances, the clinical outcome measure (irritability) did not directly translate to the most consistent behavioral changes identified in the mouse model (learning) (17).

PLACEBO EFFECTS

Placebo effects are a major difficulty for testing treatment efficacy in double-blind randomized control trials, which result from participants' expectation that they are receiving a treatment and may lead to conscious or unconscious behavioral changes. Even the support, attention, and interest from the research team compared to the person or family's everyday experience may have a "therapeutic" effect. The effect size of the placebo response in medication trials for ASD is estimated to be "moderate" (41). Recently, trial designs have been proposed that aim to address the interaction between those behavioral changes and treatment (42). In addition, demonstration of target engagement using objective measures may be one way forward to evaluate the efficacy of the treatment in clinical trials, even when – by virtue of the placebo effects – changes in overall outcome may not be significantly different between the treatment and control groups.

STRATIFICATION BIOMARKERS

The next important step is to select particular patients groups for clinical trials that are more likely to respond to the treatment under consideration. Despite an explosion of biomarker research over the past years, we currently do not have a single validated or clinically useful biomarker for ASD. Biomarkers have been defined as "a characteristic that is objectively measured and evaluated as an indication of normal biological processes, pathogenic processes, or pharmacologic responses to a therapeutic intervention" (43). In the past, using case–control designs, the majority of research studies focused on the identification of *diagnostic biomarkers* to provide a discrete and objective indication of diagnostic status (i.e., whether or not someone has an ASD). Although many studies reported significant *mean group* differences in, for example, performances on a range of cognitive tests, or in brain structure, function, or connectivity (using MRI methods), inconsistencies in findings and failure to replicate are common problems. Moreover, it is important to note that a mean group difference alone (especially with moderate effect sizes) by no means indicates that that measure has diagnostic biomarker utility. This further requires an almost complete non-overlap of the distributions of individuals in the case and control groups (and, according to traditional categorical classifications, individuals with other neurodevelopmental or neuropsychiatric conditions).

Stratification biomarkers divide a group of patients into subgroups with shared biological characteristics. These subgroups may differ in terms of their clinical symptom profile and/or etiology. Stratification markers may be primarily clinically relevant if they have either *prognostic* value, i.e., they assess the (untreated) progression and outcome of the disorder, or *predictive* value, i.e., they estimate the probability of response to a given treatment. Stratification biomarker research in ASD is still in its infancy. Difficulties for stratification research have been primarily studies with small sample sizes, such that the majority of cognitive or neuroimaging studies include 15–30 participants per group – which are associated with limited power, especially if a group were divided into two or more subgroups.

Large-scale multi-center multidisciplinary observational studies, such as the EU-AIMS Longitudinal European Autism Project (LEAP) are currently underway that have sufficient power to identify stratification markers (44). Multi-modal assessments of each individual allow us to identify genetic, molecular, circuit-based, and behavioral markers.

One approach to stratification is to split the sample based on *a priori* participant criteria (e.g., sex, developmental level). For example, there is some evidence that females with ASD differ from males with ASD in terms of their cognitive profile, neuroanatomy, or function (45) and that females may require a higher burden of genetic risk factors to develop ASD [i.e., being more protected from developing ASD (46)]. There may also be differences between individuals with ASD with/without distinct co-occurring conditions, such as ADHD or anxiety. In addition, unsupervised, data-driven methods may be particularly useful to identify subtypes based on differences in, for example, brain anatomy, function, and/or cognitive profile. To do this, hierarchical clustering methods (47) or normative modeling approaches to neuroimaging data (48), have recently been used. Larger-scale neuroimaging studies of ASD [e.g., EU-AIMS LEAP (44); Province of Ontario Neurodevelopmental Disorders Network, POND (49)] or efforts to aggregate neuroimaging data from different laboratories [Autism Brain Image Data Exchange, ABIDE (50)] now begin to provide cohorts of sufficient sizes and to enable replication. In contrast to the relative high costs of MRI scans, electrophysiological methods are relatively less expensive, and easy to use in young children and even infants, and individuals with intellectual disabilities (51). Valid EEG stratification markers may therefore be in principle more feasible to implement in clinical practice. Many circuits underpinning fundamental bio-behavioral dimensions affected in ASD (e.g., social cognition, reward processing) cut across different neurodevelopmental and neuropsychiatric disorders. Therefore, a biomarker that estimates deficits in, for example, (neural activation underlying) emotional reactivity or reward sensitivity does not necessarily have to be specific to ASD but instead may predict dimensional symptom severity (52).

Multi-modal biomarkers (e.g., combining resting-state EEG and fMRI) likely have improved prognostic as well predictive value relative to markers based on one modality. For example, abnormalities in gamma band oscillations could indicate either increased excitatory (e.g., glutamatergic) or reduced inhibitory (e.g., GABA-ergic) signaling. Additional information on glutamate vs. GABA concentrations as derived from MRS or behavioral proxies of GABA signaling may help to interpret an individual's score on the EEG measure. For a stratification biomarker to be predictive of treatment response those differences are critical as it may indicate whether – broadly – a GABA agonist or glutamate (receptor) antagonist may be more likely to be effective for a particular individual. Also a fuller understanding of an individual's cognitive profile across domains, and the relationship between cognitive strengths and weaknesses is crucial, as individuals with ASD and their families may be more likely to accept future medical treatments if they could be reassured that those strengths, which form an important part of a person's identity, are not blunted by them.

Longitudinal designs with at least three time points are needed that concurrently track changes in the clinical, neurocognitive, functional, and anatomical trajectories to ascertain the prognostic value of stratification biomarkers. This way, we can begin to model whether a person whose social-communicative skills improve between, say childhood and adolescence has a different neurobiological profile to someone whose symptoms stay the same or worsen. Identification of convergent/divergent pathways into the disorder (risk biomarkers) would be particularly useful to estimate whether a child will develop an ASD before it is clinically manifest and to offer intervention or treatments during early development. Research on risk biomarkers typically employs the high-risk infant sibling design, which capitalizes on the finding that siblings of a child with ASD have a 20-fold increased risk to also developing ASD. So far, the majority of infant-at-risk studies have treated "high-risk" infants as a relatively homogeneous group and only typically stratified by whether or not they developed ASD at age 2–3 years. Identification of "prodromal" subgroups is difficult given that this design is so costly and the number of children who develop ASD in these cohorts is relatively small.

Validation of stratification biomarker requires determining their accuracy (i.e., sensitivity, specificity, positive and negative predictive values), plausibility (causal or mechanistically understandable), reliability in relating to a certain clinical endpoint, and reproducibility across clinically relevant settings (53). To increase reproducibility, large-scale consortium studies, such as the IMI-funded EU-AIMS (54) and the NIMH funded Autism Biomarker Consortium-Clinical Trials, are committed to sharing protocols and data.

CONCLUSION

The current assumption that ASD involves multiple etiologies and pathophysiological mechanisms makes precision medicine the most promising approach to effective treatments for individuals with the overall umbrella condition. Because in the majority of individuals with ASD (including most with IQ in the normal range) the etiology is currently not known, the approach hinges on a better understanding of whether cellular or molecular mechanisms are shared. The recently failed clinical trials with monogenic forms of ASD point to further obstacles: conceptual and methodological issues linked to translatability from animal models to humans, clinical trial design, placebo effects, and selection of mechanistically plausible, objective outcome measures. Addressing these different factors in the next generation of research studies requires a translatable developmental perspective and multidisciplinary, collaborative initiatives.

AUTHOR CONTRIBUTIONS

EL has produced the first and final draft of the paper. DM and WS have commented on and revised several versions of this manuscript.

FUNDING

This work was supported by EU-AIMS (European Autism Interventions), which receives support from the Innovative Medicines Initiative Joint Undertaking under grant agreement no. 115300, the resources of which are composed of financial contributions from the European Union's Seventh Framework Programme (grant FP7/2007-2013), from the European Federation of Pharmaceutical Industries and Associations companies' in-kind contributions, and from Autism Speaks.

REFERENCES

1. Baird G, Simonoff E, Pickles A, Chandler S, Loucas T, Meldrum D, et al. Prevalence of disorders of the autism spectrum in a population cohort of children in South Thames: the Special Needs and Autism Project (SNAP). *Lancet* (2006) 368(9531):210–5. doi:10.1016/S0140-6736(06)69041-7
2. Autism and Developmental Disabilities Monitoring Network Surveillance Year 2008 Principal Investigators, Centers for Disease Control and Prevention. Prevalence of autism spectrum disorders – Autism and Developmental Disabilities Monitoring Network, 14 sites, United States, 2008. *MMWR Surveill Summ* (2012) 61(3):1–19.
3. American Psychiatric Association. *Diagnostic and Statistical Manual of Mental Disorders*. 5th ed. Arlington, VA: American Psychiatric Publishing (2013).
4. Simonoff E, Pickles A, Charman T, Chandler S, Loucas T, Baird G. Psychiatric disorders in children with autism spectrum disorders: prevalence, comorbidity, and associated factors in a population-derived sample. *J Am Acad Child Adolesc Psychiatry* (2008) 47(8):921–9. doi:10.1097/CHI.0b013e318179964f
5. Fountain C, Winter AS, Bearman PS. Six developmental trajectories characterize children with autism. *Pediatrics* (2012) 129(5):e1112–20. doi:10.1542/peds.2011-1601
6. Howlin P. Outcome in high-functioning adults with autism with and without early language delays: implications for the differentiation between autism and Asperger syndrome. *J Autism Dev Disord* (2003) 33(1):3–13. doi:10.1023/A:1022270118899
7. Warren Z, McPheeters ML, Sathe N, Foss-Feig JH, Glasser A, Veenstra-Vanderweele J. A systematic review of early intensive intervention for autism spectrum disorders. *Pediatrics* (2011) 127:e1303–11. doi:10.1542/peds.2011-0426
8. Oono IP, Honey EJ, McConachie H. Parent-mediated early intervention for young children with autism spectrum disorders (ASD). *Cochrane Database Syst Rev* (2013) 4:CD009774. doi:10.1002/14651858.CD009774.pub2
9. Betancur C. Etiological heterogeneity in autism spectrum disorders: more than 100 genetic and genomic disorders and still counting. *Brain Res* (2011) 1380:42–77. doi:10.1016/j.brainres.2010.11.078
10. Bourgeron T. From the genetic architecture to synaptic plasticity in autism spectrum disorder. *Nat Rev Neurosci* (2015) 16(9):551–63. doi:10.1038/nrn3992
11. Spooren W, Lindemann L, Ghosh A, Santarelli L. Synapse dysfunction in autism: a molecular medicine approach to drug discovery in neurodevelopmental disorders. *Trends Pharmacol Sci* (2012) 33:669–84. doi:10.1016/j.tips.2012.09.004
12. Voineagu I, Wang X, Johnston P, Lowe JK, Tian Y, Horvath S, et al. Transcriptomic analysis of autistic brain reveals convergent molecular pathology. *Nature* (2011) 474:380–4. doi:10.1038/nature10110
13. Williams EL, Casanova MF. Above genetics: lessons from cerebral development in autism. *Transl Neurosci* (2011) 2(2):106–20. doi:10.2478/s13380-011-0016-3
14. Rubenstein JL, Merzenich MM. Model of autism: increased ratio of excitation/inhibition in key neural systems. *Genes Brain Behav* (2003) 2(5):255–67. doi:10.1034/j.1601-183X.2003.00037.x
15. Bear MF, Huber KM, Warren ST. The mGluR theory of fragile X mental retardation. *Trends Neurosci* (2004) 27(7):370–7. doi:10.1016/j.tins.2004.04.009
16. Baudouin SJ, Gaudias J, Gerharz S, Hatstatt L, Zhou K, Punnakkal P, et al. Shared synaptic pathophysiology in syndromic and nonsyndromic rodent models of autism. *Science* (2012) 338(6103):128–32. doi:10.1126/science.1224159
17. Berry-Kravis E, Des Portes V, Hagerman R, Jacquemont S, Charles P, Visootsak J, et al. Mavoglurant in fragile X syndrome: results of two randomized, double-blind, placebo-controlled trials. *Sci Transl Med* (2016) 8(321):321ra325. doi:10.1126/scitranslmed.aab4109
18. Soorya L, Kolevzon A, Zweifach J, Lim T, Dobry Y, Schwartz L, et al. Prospective investigation of autism and genotype-phenotype correlations in 22q13 deletion syndrome and SHANK3 deficiency. *Mol Autism* (2013) 4:18. doi:10.1186/2040-2392-4-18
19. Guilmatre A, Huguet G, Delorme R, Bourgeron T. The emerging role of SHANK genes in neuropsychiatric disorders. *Dev Neurobiol* (2014) 74(2):113–22. doi:10.1002/dneu.22128
20. Richards C, Jones C, Groves L, Moss J, Oliver C. Prevalence of autism spectrum disorder phenomenology in genetic disorders: a systematic review and meta-analysis. *Lancet Psychiatry* (2015) 2(10):909–16. doi:10.1016/S2215-0366(15)00376-4
21. Wadell PM, Hagerman RJ, Hessl DR. Fragile X syndrome: psychiatric manifestations, assessment and emerging therapies. *Curr Psychiatry Rev* (2013) 9(1):53–8. doi:10.2174/157340013805289644
22. Patterson PH. Maternal infection and immune involvement in autism. *Trends Mol Med* (2011) 17(7):389–94. doi:10.1016/j.molmed.2011.03.001
23. Hallmayer J, Cleveland S, Torres A, Phillips J, Cohen B, Torigoe T, et al. Genetic heritability and shared environmental factors among twin pairs with autism. *Arch Gen Psychiatry* (2011) 68(11):1095–102. doi:10.1001/archgenpsychiatry.2011.76
24. Szatmari P. Is autism, at least in part, a disorder of fetal programming? *Arch Gen Psychiatry* (2011) 68(11):1091–2. doi:10.1001/archgenpsychiatry.2011.99
25. Kang HJ, Kawasawa YI, Cheng F, Zhu Y, Xu X, Li M, et al. Spatio-temporal transcriptome of the human brain. *Nature* (2011) 478(7370):483–9. doi:10.1038/nature10523
26. Marin O, Valiente M, Ge X, Tsai LH. Guiding neuronal cell migrations. *Cold Spring Harb Perspect Biol* (2010) 2(2):a001834. doi:10.1101/cshperspect.a001834
27. DeRosa BA, Van Baaren JM, Dubey GK, Lee JM, Cuccaro ML, Vance JM, et al. Derivation of autism spectrum disorder-specific induced pluripotent stem cells from peripheral blood mononuclear cells. *Neurosci Lett* (2012) 516(1):9–14. doi:10.1016/j.neulet.2012.02.086
28. Cocks G, Curran S, Gami P, Uwanogho D, Jeffries AR, Kathuria A, et al. The utility of patient specific induced pluripotent stem cells for the modelling of autistic spectrum disorders. *Psychopharmacology (Berl)* (2014) 231(6):1079–88. doi:10.1007/s00213-013-3196-4
29. Ecker C, Bookheimer SY, Murphy DG. Neuroimaging in autism spectrum disorder: brain structure and function across the lifespan. *Lancet Neurol* (2015) 14(11):1121–34. doi:10.1016/S1474-4422(15)00050-2
30. Toro R, Konyukh M, Delorme R, Leblond C, Chaste P, Fauchereau F, et al. Key role for gene dosage and synaptic homeostasis in autism spectrum disorders. *Trends Genet* (2010) 26(8):363–72. doi:10.1016/j.tig.2010.05.007
31. Huttenlocher PR. *Neural Plasticity*. Cambridge: Harvard University Press (2002).
32. Abrahams BS, Geschwind DH. Connecting genes to brain in the autism spectrum disorders. *Arch Neurol* (2010) 67(4):395–9. doi:10.1001/archneurol.2010.47
33. Willsey AJ, Sanders SJ, Li M, Dong S, Tebbenkamp AT, Muhle RA, et al. Coexpression networks implicate human midfetal deep cortical projection neurons in the pathogenesis of autism. *Cell* (2013) 155(5):997–1007. doi:10.1016/j.cell.2013.10.020
34. Parikshak NN, Luo R, Zhang A, Won H, Lowe JK, Chandran V, et al. Integrative functional genomic analyses implicate specific molecular pathways and circuits in autism. *Cell* (2013) 155(5):1008–21. doi:10.1016/j.cell.2013.10.031
35. Robertson CE, Ratai EM, Kanwisher N. Reduced GABAergic action in the autistic brain. *Curr Biol* (2016) 26(1):80–5. doi:10.1016/j.cub.2015.11.019
36. Foss-Feig JH, Tadin D, Schauder KB, Cascio CJ. A substantial and unexpected enhancement of motion perception in autism. *J Neurosci* (2013) 33(19):8243–9. doi:10.1523/JNEUROSCI.1608-12.2013
37. Varcin KJ, Nelson CA III. A developmental neuroscience approach to the search for biomarkers in autism spectrum disorder. *Curr Opin Neurol* (2016) 29(2):123–9. doi:10.1097/WCO.0000000000000298
38. LeBlanc JJ, Fagiolini M. Autism: a "critical period" disorder? *Neural Plast* (2011) 2011:921680. doi:10.1155/2011/921680
39. Ben-Ari Y. Is birth a critical period in the pathogenesis of autism spectrum disorders? *Nat Rev Neurosci* (2015) 16(8):498–505. doi:10.1038/nrn3956
40. Kolevzon A, Bush L, Wang AT, Halpern D, Frank Y, Grodberg D, et al. A pilot controlled trial of insulin-like growth factor-1 in children with Phelan-McDermid syndrome. *Mol Autism* (2014) 5(1):54. doi:10.1186/2040-2392-5-54
41. Masi A, Lampit A, Glozier N, Hickie IB, Guastella AJ. Predictors of placebo response in pharmacological and dietary supplement treatment trials in pediatric autism spectrum disorder: a meta-analysis. *Transl Psychiatry* (2015) 5:e640. doi:10.1038/tp.2015.143

42. Chassang S, Snowberg E, Seymour B, Bowles C. Accounting for behavior in treatment effects: new applications for blind trials. *PLoS One* (2015) 10(6):e0127227. doi:10.1371/journal.pone.0127227
43. Biomarkers Definition Working Group. Biomarkers and surrogate end points: preferred definitions and conceptual framework. *Clin Pharmacol Ther* (2001) 69(3):89–95. doi:10.1067/mcp.2001.113989
44. Loth E, Spooren W, Ham LM, Isaac MB, Auriche-Benichou C, Banaschewski T, et al. Identification and validation of biomarkers for autism spectrum disorders. *Nat Rev Drug Discov* (2015) 15(1):70–3. doi:10.1038/nrd.2015.7
45. Lai MC, Lombardo MV, Auyeung B, Chakrabarti B, Baron-Cohen S. Sex/gender differences and autism: setting the scene for future research. *J Am Acad Child Adolesc Psychiatry* (2015) 54(1):11–24. doi:10.1016/j.jaac.2014.10.003
46. Jacquemont S, Coe BP, Hersch M, Duyzend MH, Krumm N, Bergmann S, et al. A higher mutational burden in females supports a "female protective model" in neurodevelopmental disorders. *Am J Hum Genet* (2014) 94(3):415–25. doi:10.1016/j.ajhg.2014.02.001
47. Lombardo MV, Lai M-C, Auyeung B, Holt RJ, Allison C, Smith P, et al. Unsupervised data-driven stratification of mentalizing heterogeneity in autism. (2016). Available from: http://biorxiv.org/content/early/2016/04/29/034454
48. Marquand AF, Rezek I, Buitelaar J, Beckmann CF. Understanding heterogeneity in clinical cohorts using normative models: beyond case-control studies. *Biol Psychiatry* (2016) 80(7):552–61. doi:10.1016/j.biopsych.2015.12.023
49. Sussman D, Leung RC, Vogan VM, Lee W, Trelle S, Lin S, et al. The autism puzzle: diffuse but not pervasive neuroanatomical abnormalities in children with ASD. *Neuroimage Clin* (2015) 8:170–9. doi:10.1016/j.nicl.2015.04.008
50. Di Martino A, Yan CG, Li Q, Denio E, Castellanos FX, Alaerts K, et al. The autism brain imaging data exchange: towards a large-scale evaluation of the intrinsic brain architecture in autism. *Mol Psychiatry* (2014) 19(6):659–67. doi:10.1038/mp.2013.78
51. McPartland JC. Considerations in biomarker development for neurodevelopmental disorders. *Curr Opin Neurol* (2016) 29(2):118–22. doi:10.1097/WCO.0000000000000300
52. Insel T, Cuthbert B, Garvey M, Heinssen R, Pine DS, Quinn K, et al. Research domain criteria (RDoC): toward a new classification framework for research on mental disorders. *Am J Psychiatry* (2010) 167(7):748–51. doi:10.1176/appi.ajp.2010.09091379
53. Prata D, Mechelli A, Kapur S. Clinically meaningful biomarkers for psychosis: a systematic and quantitative review. *Neurosci Biobehav Rev* (2014) 45:134–41. doi:10.1016/j.neubiorev.2014.05.010
54. Murphy D, Spooren W. EU-AIMS: a boost to autism research. *Nat Rev Drug Discov* (2012) 11(11):815–6. doi:10.1038/nrd3881

9

A Developmental and Sequenced One-to-One Educational Intervention for Autism Spectrum Disorder

Antoine Tanet[1,2,3], Annik Hubert-Barthelemy[3], Graciela C. Crespin[4], Nicolas Bodeau[2], David Cohen[1,2], Catherine Saint-Georges[1,2,5] and The GPIS Study Group[†]*

[1] Institut des Systèmes Intelligents et de Robotiques, Université Pierre et Marie Curie, Paris, France, [2] Departement de Psychiatrie de l'Enfant et de l'Adolescent, APHP, Groupe Hospitalier Pitié-Salpêtrière et Université Pierre et Marie Curie, Paris, France, [3] Croix Rouge Française, Paris, France, [4] Association Programme de Recherche et d'Etudes sur l'Autisme, Paris, France, [5] Hôpital de jour Centre André Boulloche, Paris, France

Edited by:
Yuri Bozzi,
University of Trento, Italy

Reviewed by:
Munis Dundar,
Erciyes University, Turkey
Umberto Balottin,
University of Pavia, Italy

***Correspondence:**
David Cohen
david.cohen@aphp.fr

[†]The members of the GPIS Study Group are listed at the end of the article.

Introduction: Individuals with autism spectrum disorder (ASD) who also exhibit severe-to-moderate ranges of intellectual disability (ID) still face many challenges (i.e., less evidence-based trials, less inclusion in school with peers).

Methods: We implemented a novel model called the "Developmental and Sequenced One-to-One Educational Intervention" (DS1-EI) in 5- to 9-year-old children with co-occurring ASD and ID. The treatment protocol was adapted for school implementation by designing it using an educational agenda. The intervention was based on intensity, regular assessments, updating objectives, encouraging spontaneous communication, promoting skills through play with peers, supporting positive behaviors, providing supervision, capitalizing on teachers' unique skills, and providing developmental and sequenced learning. Developmental learning implies that the focus of training is what is close to the developmental expectations given a child's development in a specific domain. Sequenced learning means that the teacher changes the learning activities every 10–15 min to maintain the child's attention in the context of an anticipated time agenda. We selected 11 French institutions in which we implemented the model in small classrooms. Each institution recruited participants per dyads matched by age, sex, and developmental quotient. Patients from each dyad were then randomized to a DS1-EI group or a Treatment as usual (TAU) group for 36 months. The primary variables – the Childhood Autism Rating scale (CARS) and the psychoeducational profile (PEP-3) – will be blindly assessed by independent raters at the 18-month and 36-month follow-up.

Discussion and baseline description: We enrolled 75 participants: 38 were randomized to the DS1-EI and 37 to the TAU groups. At enrollment, we found no significant differences in participants' characteristics between groups. As expected, exposure to school was the only significant difference [9.4 (±4.1) h/week in the DS1-EI group vs. 3.4 (±4.5) h/week in the TAU group, Student's *t*-test, $t = 5.83$, $p < 0.001$].

Ethics and dissemination: The protocol was authorized by the competent national regulatory authority (*Agence nationale de sécurité du médicament et des produits de santé*) and approved by the local Ethics Committee (*Comité de Protection des Personnes*) at the University Hospital Saint-Antoine (May 7, 2013). The findings will be disseminated through peer-reviewed journals and national and international conferences.

Keywords: autism, intellectual disability, randomized controlled trial

BACKGROUND

Autism spectrum disorder (ASD) is characterized by the presence of atypical social communicative interaction and behaviors. The role of some genetic factors in ASD is known. However, there is a growing body of neurobiological research that indicates the presence of complex gene–environment interactions. Despite these findings, there is no approved biological treatment for this disorder and the first-line treatments pertain to psychosocial domains (1). Typically, ASD is diagnosed by means of a behavioral analysis during the 3- to 5-year-old age range; once diagnosed, the treatment is primarily delivered through behavioral interventions following different models. In essence, these models try to promote cognitive, communication, and behavioral skills that are considered essential to improve social skills in the long run (2, 3).

Several global interventions for core deficits in ASD have been proposed and assessed within clinical trials. The Treatment and Education of Autistic and Communication Handicapped Children (TEACCH) program uses many technical interventions to meet the individual needs of people with autism. The work program is tailored to some seminal aspects of ASD. First, it is centered on the individual. Individual needs are assessed through a comprehensive assessment of several developmental dimensions while taking into account emerging capacities. Second, it requires an understanding of autism, the adoption of appropriate adaptations and a broadly based intervention strategy (e.g., structured teaching, visual understanding, object manipulation, social communication skills) that builds on existing skills and interests. Third, the environment is organized to help children and adults understand and remember what to do (e.g., visual agendas, making expectations clear, and explicit, visual materials, structured architecture). The focus is on positive strategies to support behavioral and teaching strategies (4, 5).

Applied Behavioral Analysis (ABA) is a one-to-one intensive method that uses reinforcement of adaptative and acquired skills (6). The first structured attempts by Lovaas (7) were criticized (difficulties in generalization of learned behaviors; mechanical responses; lack of spontaneity) despite their encouraging first results. These criticisms led to the development of Pivotal Response Training [PRT], a more naturalistic behavioral treatment that has good documented effectiveness (8). PRT is a home-based intervention that includes parents in the routines. The method is based on choosing "pivotal" skills as the target of the treatment; following the child's choice of activities and games; reinforcing not only the correct answer expected by the professional but also all (meaning complete or incomplete) forms of attempts to respond; alternating between acquisition and maintenance; and using intrinsic reinforcers.

The Early Start Denver Model (ESDM) is an early and intensive intervention approach for young children. The interventions are based on the following: (i) a curriculum that evaluates the child's development across different developmental domains; (ii) specific procedures for learning and incorporating ABA principles, such as PRT; (iii) sessions focusing on interactions with children, interpersonal exchanges, and shared commitment with materials and activities of daily living; (iv) a positive affect, adults being responsive and sensitive to child cues; (v) verbal and non-verbal communication cues; (vi) proximal developmental windows, meaning that the focus of training is what is close to the developmental expectations given a child's development in the according domain; and (vii) parents' involvement. This program is implemented in small groups or individually at a specialized center or at home (3, 9).

The Developmental, Individual Differences, and Relationship-based (DIR) method is built on three axes: (i) the level of functional and emotional development reached by the child; (ii) the individual differences in information processing and motor planning; and (iii) the types of interactions that the child establishes with his/her partners (10). Floor Time is the core of the DIR method. It consists of sequences of guided play (15–20 min) that are repeated several times by parents throughout the day and are supervised by an expert. The DIR principles that should always be respected are to follow the child's lead and support his/her initiative; to focus on joint attention; to close circles of communication; to create semi-structured problem solving; to contrast repetitiveness with playful obstruction; to support visual attention; and to work on imitation (10, 11).

In an attempt to capture the common components among these models and what could be learned from evidence-based studies, Narzisi and colleagues (12) delineated the following principles: the first group regards timing: (1) starting as early as possible; (2) minimizing the gap between diagnosis and treatment; (3) being intensive (not less than 3–4 h of treatment per day); the second group is based on viewing parents as partners and involving family; the third group gathers principles related to treatment program: (1) providing regular assessments, supervision and updating the goals of treatment; (2) encouraging spontaneous communication; (3) promoting skills through play with peers; (4) finalizing the acquisition of new skills and their generalization and maintenance in natural contexts; and (5) supporting positive behaviors rather than tackling challenging behaviors.

Why Should We Implement a School-Based Intervention?

Despite the encouraging results presented earlier, most of those programs (a notable exception being TEACCH) do not target school-aged children and are not proposed to occur in a school setting. This is unfortunate because schools are a favorable location for autism interventions (13). Additionally, many children with ASD do not receive a sufficient amount of treatment (14), even in countries with free access to health care (15). Because children with ASD benefit from being with other peers at school, the gap between education research and education practice (16) may be a missed opportunity to offer more support to these children. Additionally, larger doses of treatment could be offered in school contexts, especially when interventions are administered 1:1 (17). Several agencies have recommended conducting interventions in school-based settings (18, 19). Two objectives should be combined: school-based core deficit interventions and school-based social communication practice (20). There are already several studies that have shown that school-based interventions are able to reach larger numbers of children with ASD. This may improve challenges with generalization by using learned skills regarding communication in a natural environment, such as in the classroom (21, 22). Additionally, the preschool context seems to offer opportunities to develop communication skills (23, 24), and by offering opportunities to enter into play groups, teachers can supply reinforcements of the non-verbal ASD child requests (25).

However, there are very few school-based social communication interventions, and in many cases, teachers at school do their best without guided specific interventions for ASD children in the classroom. Consequently, there is a lack of response from teachers to the communicative acts produced by children with ASD (26). General educational teachers provide infrequent verbal prompting with ASD children (27), and they more frequently engage in functional play than symbolic play (28). They also lack supervision (20). Thus, there is a paradox between the need for appropriate intensive interventions for ASD and what is proposed in most school settings. For example, Mudford and colleagues (29) showed that the implementation of an evidence-based ABA program in preschoolers was not complete: 93% of the participants were not provided the dose of treatment (40 h/week). Additionally, from an efficiency perspective, although several programs support the concept of tailoring interventions to the child's needs and skills, to our knowledge, no one has questioned whether programs could be adapted according to teaching local skills.

Why Should We Study Children with ASD and Intellectual Disability?

As expressed in the dimensional approach of the new classifications in the DSM-5 (30), intellectual disability (ID) is a frequent challenge and comorbidity in ASD. According to studies, ID co-occurs in 50 to 75% of ASD cases (31). Risk factors of comorbid ID in ASD are gender (despite the high number of males with ASD, the male/female ratio decreases in ASD comorbid with ID) and the existence of seizures or of a neurodevelopmental or genetic syndrome (32, 33). The co-occurrence of ID also appears to be a prognostic factor for long-term outcomes of ASD (12, 34) and a risk factor of the incidence of challenging behaviors that provoke severe morbidity in some cases (35). To date, very few models have specifically addressed ASD comorbid with ID, in particular when ID is in the severe-to-moderate range. Therefore, the need to focus on this understudied population is warranted. Here, we wonder whether or not children with comorbid ASD and severe ID may be receptive to a pedagogical content? For such children over 5 years, could an adapted and one-to-one cognitive program in school be a road to improve non-verbal and verbal communication and to promote social skills?

METHODS/DESIGN

Objectives

In this paper, our aims are to describe a school-based intervention program (a developmental and sequenced one-to-one educational intervention, DS1-EI) that was adapted to the French health and education system; to justify the principles that were followed to implement the method and adapt it to a low-functioning population (i.e., ASD comorbid with ID); to describe the randomized controlled trial we began; and to present the sociodemographic and clinical characteristics of the participants at baseline.

Participants and Recruitment

All participants were recruited in outpatient French health care institutions that are specialized in treating children with autism and intellectual handicaps. At the request of the French national health regulatory authority [*Agence nationale de sécurité du médicament et des produits de santé* (ANSM)] and the main sponsor [*Caisse Nationale de Solidarité pour l'Autonomie* (CNSA)], we balanced day care hospitals and special education clinics to have a representative sample of French institutions. In each institution, we obtained a specific commitment to accept the implementation of a DS1-EI school-based program as described below and to recruit the same number of participants to be randomized into a DS1-EI exposed group (called the DS1-EI group) or a treatment as usual (TAU) group who would serve as controls. The commitment also entailed having the required resources from local school authorities to implement the DS1-EI and to have the leading teacher from the classroom be supervised. To avoid bias in the TAU group as a result of the diversity of institutions, we decided to randomize participants by site. **Figure 1** summarizes the list of institutions involved in the protocol and the number of patients by site. In total, we enrolled 75 participants.

Each parent provided informed written consent before inclusion. The inclusion criteria were a current diagnosis of ASD confirmed by a clinical assessment based on the International Classification of Diseases, 10th edition criteria and the Autism Diagnostic Interview-Revised (ADI-R) (36); an intellectual handicap with financial compensation from local agencies [*Maison Départementale du Handicap* (MDPH)]; being aged between 5 and 9 years; and having a communication developmental age of 24 months and under based on a Vineland assessment or a 3-year speech delay based on a Psycho-Educational Profile, third edition.

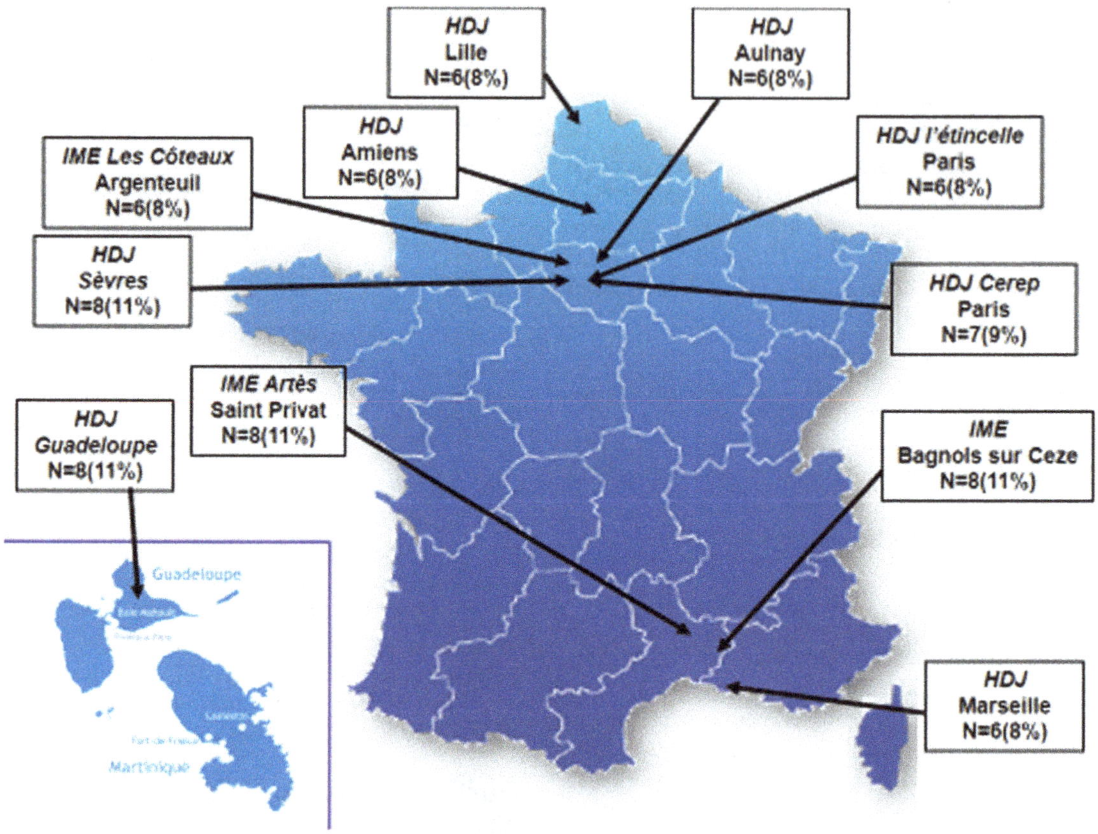

FIGURE 1 | Institutions and participants' enrollment in the DS1-EI trial by site. HDJ, *Hopital de Jour* (Day care medical center); IME, *Institut Medico-Educatif* (Special education center).

We did not exclude children with known organic syndromes and/or non-stabilized neuropaediatric (e.g., seizures) or medical (e.g., diabetes mellitus) comorbidities. However, during the medical assessment, we specifically listed comorbidities. The exclusion criteria were limited to parents' refusal to participate; family's plans to change institutions in the short term for any reason; and patient's severe behavioral impairments that would challenge treatment adherence. Of note, this last exclusion criterion was based on local institution staff decision. Before randomization, each site was requested to assess the IQ of the participants based on the Kaufman Assessment Battery for Children second edition (KABC-II) or, failing that, Vineland scores. Based on these results, dyads of participants matched for sex, age, and developmental quotient (DQ) were formed to limit the risk of bias between groups. Randomization before group allocation to TAU or DS1-EI group was performed by drawing lots in each dyad per site so that each site could have a TAU group and a DS1-EI group of three to four participants each. Randomization was performed by the methodological coordinating team at the Salpêtrière Hospital and was independent from local inclusion sites. TAU was defined as all therapeutic interventions given to a specific child. Given the study duration, we did not recommend not to change children's therapeutic protocol in the TAU group during the study period. The trial duration was defined as 36 months but included 12-, 18-, and 24-month intermediate assessments.

DS1-EI Treatment Principles

Participants randomized to the DS1-EI group received the specific experimental protocol four mornings per week (2 h 30 min); the rest of the week they continued to receive the usual protocol of each site. The treatment principles are summarized in **Table 1**. The setting was a small classroom with four pupils, but an adapted environment was proposed. Following the principles of TEACCH (5), each child was offered a desk, two chairs (one for the child, one for the adult working with the child), a screen where pictures of the child's schedule and activities were provided, and a locker with his or her picture. In contrast to TEACCH, the child sat with his back close to the wall where the screen was placed (see pictures in the supplementary material S1). The setting also included a large table for mid-session group collaboration and a place offering benches and carpets where group participants (both children and adults) met at the beginning and ending of a session. Although the program did not reach the 40 h per week recommended by some programs (37), it remained intensive, with 10 h of DS1-EI plus other therapeutic practices according to each institution (e.g., occupational therapy; speech therapy; social skill group activities). The program followed developmental rules, meaning the training was focused on the nearest expected activity/skill of a given child's development in a specific domain as recommended by the ESDM (9). In terms of timing, the program was sequenced in two ways. First, as in TEACCH,

TABLE 1 | A developmental and sequenced one-to-one educational intervention (DS1-EI) for autism spectrum disorder: main principles.

Characteristics	Brief definition	Justification
Setting	To be implemented in a small classroom with four pupils In an adapted environment	TEACCH, Barton et al. (13) TEACCH
Intensive	One-to-one support 10 h per week in addition to other treatment practices (e.g., occupational therapy, speech therapy, psychotherapy)	ABA, ESDM
Developmental	The focus of training is what is close to the developmental expectation given a child's development within a domain	ESDM
Sequenced	The 2 h 30 min sessions follow an anticipated and structured agenda Teachers change learning activities every 10–15 min to keep a child's attention	TEACCH Original
Curriculum based	A detailed assessment/curriculum is required to follow the developmental approach and to choose the appropriate cognitive/motor activity to be taught in each domain for preschoolers	ESDM, TEACCH
Educational objectives	Given the developmental quotient of the targeted children, the educational objectives are those of a second grade program for preschoolers (see **Table 2** below for details)	French Ministry for National Education
Reinforcers	Supporting positive behaviors rather than tackling challenging behaviors Using positive emotion engagement from teachers	ABA, ESDM ESDM
Group	Group activities are organized within the time schedule to encourage spontaneous communication and promote social skills through play with peers	Many programs
Supervision	Regular supervision of teachers with children's objectives being updated	ESDM, ABA, DIR
Exploiting teachers' unique skills	Implementation of the program will benefit from using teachers' individual skills, such as their knowledge of a specific method (e.g., the use of Picture Exchange Program) or of a particular child	COMVOOR

TEACCH, Treatment and Education of Autistic and Communication Handicapped Children; ABA, Applied Behavioral Analysis; ESDM, Early Start Denver Model; DIR, Developmental, Individual Differences and Relationship-based method; COMVOOR, Voorlopers in Communicatie.

the 2 h 30 min sessions followed an anticipated and structured agenda that was presented for each child on a screen. When a novel activity started, the corresponding pictogram was shown on the child's desk. Second, teachers were asked to change desk and activities every 10–15 min to maintain the child's attention and to help him improve by challenging patient's need of sameness. Thus, each 10–15 min, the child has a new activity and a new teacher. The program was also curriculum based and had specific educational objectives (see details below).

Academic Training

Because DS1-EI was a program implemented in classrooms, both the curriculum and the objectives followed academic recommendations from the French Ministry of National Education. The curriculum was adapted from the French program for nursery and primary schools and *handiscol* principles (http://eduscol.education.fr). This was decided based on the idea that these recommendations were part of a teacher's area of expertise and that it would promote participation in the program. Additionally, each classroom of N children was under the responsibility of one teacher helped by $(N - 1)$ assistants, according to the 1-to-1 design of the program. In the same vein, one of the principles of the program was capitalizing on teachers' individual skills. We believed that implementation of the program would benefit from using teachers' specific knowledge (e.g., the use of the Picture Exchange Program). A detailed assessment/curriculum was a prerequisite of each child's academic program because the DS1-EI was designed to follow a developmental approach, which required the selection of appropriate cognitive/motor activities for training within each domain. The curriculum is described in detail in the supplementary material S2. Regarding the academic/educational objectives, they were grouped into four domains: mathematics, language and communication, intermodality, and autonomy. **Table 2** provides some examples of the activities by domain and level of child's performance.

Teachers' Training and Supervision

Each teacher and each assistant were trained by Annik Hubert-Barthelemy during a 1-week session. They were provided with a method presentation and were trained to use positive affect, shared engagement, responsiveness, and sensitivity to child cues, to focus on both verbal and non-verbal communication, and to support positive behaviors rather than tackle challenging behaviors. The DS1-EI detailed assessment/curriculum was explained, including how to keep learning proposals close to a given child's developmental needs. The last 2 days of the training session was dedicated to define new objectives and adaptations. During the morning, the teacher with the help of his/her assistants had to fulfill children curriculums and to have related written observation. During the afternoon, curriculum was discussed and first learning activities for all domains were decided for each child.

Supervision was organized in three different steps: (i) daily sessions of verbal exchanges and written observations after the class about each child in each domain with all professionals (the teacher and the assistants); (ii) weekly supervisions by a psychologist; (iii) monthly supervisions by the main investigator to ensure the conformity of the program application and to help the teacher adapting the directives according to each child outcome.

Primary and Secondary Variables

Table 3 summarizes the variables that we planned to measure at enrollment and at several time points throughout the trial.

TABLE 2 | DS1-EI learning by domain and hierarchical proposals: examples of tasks.

	Level 1	Level 2
Domain 1: Mathematics		
Numeration	Nursery rhyme to 5	Nursery rhyme to 39
Problem solving	Organizing stickers	Constructing a logical paradigm
Domain 2: Language and communication		
Communication	Improving joint attention	Asking for help
Oral language	Naming five objects	Making sentences to express a wish
Written language	Knowing letters from own name	Knowing all letters of classroom names
Graphics	Using sticks	Copying words with a model
Domain 3: Intermodality		
Writing/drawing and listening	Using various tools (paint, pastels, markers…)	Using different techniques (cut, paste, stencils…)
Musical activities	Imitating a rhythm	Learning songs with body movements
Domain 4: Autonomy		
Motor activities	Walking/Running/Swimming	Walking on a beam
Drawing activities	Using felt	Cut/Paste
Discovering the world	Describing a tree	Drawing a tree
Social skills	Waiting one's turn	Improving autonomous work

TABLE 3 | DS1-EI study procedure and evaluation criteria.

	Selection	Inclusion	M12	M18	M24	M36
Inclusion criteria	X	–	–	–	–	–
Informed consent	X	–	–	–	–	–
CIM-10 diagnosis	–	X	–	X	–	X
Comorbidity	–	X	–	X	–	X
ADI-R	–	X	–	X	–	X
Vineland	–	X	X	X	X	X
CARS	–	X	–	X	–	X
CGAS	–	X	X	X	–	X
CGI	–	X	X	X	–	X
KABC	–	X	–	X	–	X
PEP-III	–	X	–	X	–	X
School assessment	–	X	X	X	X	X

ADI-R, Autism Diagnostic Interview-Revised; CARS, Childhood Autism Rating Scale; CGI, Clinical Global Impression; CGAS, Clinical Global Assessment Score; PEP-3, Psychoeducational Profile, 3rd Edition; DQ, developmental quotient; KABC, Kaufmann Assessment Battery for Children.

The primary outcome variables were (i) the Childhood Autism Rating scale (CARS), which measures autism severity (38); (ii) the psychoeducational profile, third edition (PEP-3), which measures the total DQ and 5-dimensional DQs related to cognition, receptive language, expressive language, fine motor skills, gross motor skills, and imitation, and (iii) the school's assessment (39). Secondary variables included the following measures: (i) the *Vineland Adaptive Behavior Scale II* (VABS-II) as a behavioral scale of independence; this scale is assessed through a parent/educator interview and is used to assess the ability of children to perform the daily activities required for personal and social sufficiency. The VABS-II examines four specific domains: Communication, Daily Living Skills, Socialization, and Motor Skills. The subscale scores are totaled to yield an Adaptive Behavior Composite score (40). (ii) The KABC-II standardized neuropsychological assessment to measure intelligence skills. This battery measures Verbal, Performance, Working Memory, Processing Speed and Total quotients (41). (iii) The *Clinical Global Impression* (CGI), which was used to assess global severity (42). (iv) Finally, the *Children Global Assessment Scale* (CGAS) (43). To assess clinical change during the 36-month study, we used a single-blind procedure (independent raters were blind to study group allocation) for all clinical assessments (PEP-3, KABC-II, CARS). Blind assessment was not possible for the measures that required 2-week observations of the participants (CGI, CGAS, school tests) or a parental interview (ADI-R, VABS-II).

Number of Participants

From previous studies that showed significant results in terms of efficacy it appears that the minimal number of patients in parallel design was 50 (2). This was the case for behavioral ABA approach [e.g., Ref. (6)] or for developmental ESDM approach [e.g., Ref. (3)]. The number of patients to enroll was based on the following theoretical statistics estimation: for a moderate effect size ($\alpha = 0.6$), a power fixed at 80%, and a level of significance for a p-value fixed at <0.05, 80 patients randomized into two groups are required for a student t-test. Given our choice to use linear mixed models (see below) to take into account participant's effect, we planned to recruit from 70 to 80 participants.

Statistical Analysis

Statistical analyses will be performed using R Software, Version 2.12.2. To assess whether improvement occurs in both primary and secondary variables, we will use linear mixed models with change in a given variable explained by group exposure (DS1-EI vs. TAU), time (baseline vs. 18 vs. 36 months) and their interaction (group exposure × time). We will also include a random effect and a site effect. This should account for individual heterogeneity, site heterogeneity, variable scores at inclusion, and change specific to DS1-EI within the same statistical regression. For missing data when available, we will use the last observation carried forward. In case of a non-Gaussian distribution, we will study the log transformation (or other transformation when appropriate) to achieve a normal distribution. Lost or drop-out patients will also be compared between groups using a separate non-parametric comparison.

TABLE 4 | Sociodemographic and clinical characteristics of the participants after group randomization.

	DS1-EI group (N = 38)	TAU group (N = 36)	Test, p
Sociodemographics			
Age, mean (± SD), year			
Male–Female	6.92 ± 1.57	7.34 ± 1.55	$t = -1.15$, $p = 0.254$
Socioeconomic status	32 (84%)/6 (16%)	30 (83%)/6 (17%)	Fisher, $p = 1$
Clinical characteristics			
ADI-R, current, mean (± SD)			
Social impairment score	21 ± 5.7	19.9 ± 5.8	$t = 0.81$, $p = 0.423$
Communication score	11.8 ± 4	10.9 ± 3.2	$t = 1.12$, $p = 0.266$
Repetitive interest score	6 ± 2.7	5.7 ± 3.1	$t = 0.44$, $p = 0.654$
Developmental score	4.2 ± 0.8	3.9 ± 1.1	$t = 1.29$, $p = 0.202$
CARS score	41.3 ± 7	40.2 ± 7.1	$t = 0.67$, $p = 0.504$
CGI score	5.8 ± 1	5.7 ± 0.9	$t = 0.44$, $p = 0.661$
CGAS score	27 ± 11.5	25.9 ± 11.1	$t = 0.38$, $p = 0.705$
PEP-3 (all scores in DQ): mean ± SD			
Cognition	22.3 ± 11.1	23.4 ± 11.1	$t = -0.44$, $p = 0.663$
Receptive language	14 ± 5.6	15.6 ± 8.6	$t = 0.85$, $p = 0.4$
Expressive language	16.2 ± 5.8	16.8 ± 6.6	$t = 0.4$, $p = 0.692$
Fine motor skills	26.6 ± 10.1	26.6 ± 9.7	$t = 0.0$, $p = 0.99$
Gross motor skills	23.7 ± 8	24.8 ± 6.2	$t = -0.62$, $p = 0.534$
Imitation	23.1 ± 7.8	25.8 ± 6.7	$t = -1.57$, $p = 0.12$
Vineland (all scores in DQ): mean ± SD			
Communication	13.3 ± 8.2	14.2 ± 7.6	$t = -0.49$, $p = 0.628$
Adaptation	26.5 ± 13.6	26.2 ± 12.5	$t = 0.07$, $p = 0.94$
Socialization	13.7 ± 9	13.3 ± 9.4	$t = 0.15$, $p = 0.88$
Daily living skills	30.9 ± 14.7	30 ± 12	$t = 0.26$, $p = 0.79$
Comorbidity			
Intellectual disability level (< or > 40 using KABC)	27 (90%)/3 (10%)	26 (90%)/3 (10%)	Fisher, $p = 1$
Known medical condition (no/yes)	34 (89%)/4 (11%)	27 (7589%)/9 (25%)	Fisher, $p = 0.183$

TAU, treatment as usual; ADI-R, Autism Diagnostic Interview-Revised; CARS, Childhood Autism Rating Scale; CGI, Clinical Global Impression; CGAS, Clinical Global Assessment Score; PEP-3, Psychoeducational Profile, 3rd Edition; DQ, developmental quotient; KABC, Kaufmann Assessment Battery for Children.

RESULTS

Participants at t0 after Randomization

Table 4 summarizes the participants' sociodemographic and clinical characteristics at enrollment. As expected, we found no significant differences at enrollment between the DS1-EI and TAU groups, indicating that the randomization by site did not introduce bias. As expected, exposure to school was the only significant difference found between the two groups: 9.4 (±4.1) hours per week in the DS1-EI group vs. 3.4 (±4.5) hours per week in the TAU group, Student's t-test, $t = 5.83$, $p < 0.001$.

DISCUSSION

We hope that the current trial will help demonstrate the feasibility of adapting and task-shifting a group of interventions used primarily as early interventions for autism to a school-based context and for use with older individuals with autism and intellectual disabilities. The school-based intervention program [the developmental and sequenced one-to-one educational intervention (DS1-EI)] was adapted from several methods including TEACCH (4, 5), ESDM (3), and ABA (6, 37). The key principles of the method are the intensity, the regular assessments and updating of objectives, the encouragement of spontaneous communication, promotion of skills through play with peers, support of positive behaviors instead of tackling challenging behaviors, regular team supervision, capitalization on teachers' unique skills, and developmental and sequenced learning (2). The use of sequenced learning (i.e., teacher and activity change every 10–15 min to keep the child's attention in the context of an anticipated time agenda) is likely the most original proposal. We are aware that treating children with autism and ID is very challenging. The effect sizes are typically small. To balance this risk of failure, we chose to have a rather long study duration with two single-blind assessments at 18 and 36 months. Given the number of sites, which may have introduced bias, we are satisfied that we did not find differences between the groups at baseline.

We are aware that there are several limitations to this trial. First, given the severity of the patients' conditions, the study duration and the nature of the intervention, only a single-blind for the primary variables was feasible. Second, the method used to randomize participants (to limit the bias of TAU) combined with the study duration and the supervision of local teams is likely to modify local staff practice and to lead to some DS1-EI principles being used in the TAU group as well. Third, because our public sponsors required us to balance hospital/academic/large city sites and non-hospital/remote rural area sites, we cannot assume that we will achieve a uniform level of adherence to the program from one site to another. Finally, given the study duration, we do not know whether we will retain a sufficient number of patients in the program to maintain the statistical power needed for per protocol analyses.

DECLARATIONS

Ethics Approval and Consent to Participate

The current trial protocol was authorized by the competent national health regulatory authority [*Agence nationale de sécurité du médicament et des produits de santé* (ANSM)]. The trial registration number (ANSM 130282B-31) was obtained on April 16, 2013. The protocol was approved by the local Ethics Committee (*Comité de Protection des Personnes*) of the University Hospital Saint-Antoine on May 7, 2013. Also, it was registered on the Australian New Zealand Clinical Trial Registry for public information availability (ACTRN12616000592448). Potential participants received oral and accessible information about the study given participants' cognitive profiles, and all parents/guardians were provided a written information leaflet about the trial. The information leaflet adhered to the current French guidelines for researchers on writing information sheets and consent forms. Only after written consent was obtained from the parents of potential participants did randomization occur.

Trial Committees

A pilot study committee has been formed and includes the principal investigator of the trial and all local investigators and study collaborators. They will meet three times a year. A scientific study committee has also been established and includes two administrative members of the promotor (*La Croix Rouge Française*), four members of the pilot study committee and four other independent members (two professionals, two family representatives). They will meet once a year.

AUTHOR NOTES

Antoine Tanet is neuropsychologist at the Child and Adolescent Psychiatry department of the Pitié-Salpêtrière Hospital and PhD Student at IMI2S group (Institut des Systèmes Intelligents et Robotiques, CNRS, UMR 7222, Pierre et Marie Curie University Paris 6). Annick Hubert-Barthélémy is clinical psychologist and supervisor of the DSI-E1 program at the Croix Rouge Française. Graciela Crespin in clinical psychologist and head of the Programme de Recherche et d'Etudes sur l'Autisme. Nicolas Bodeau is a statistician at the Child and Adolescent Psychiatry department of the Pitié-Salpêtrière Hospital. David Cohen is Professor and head of the Department of Child and Adolescent Psychiatry at Pitié-Salpêtrière Hospital, and senior member of IMI2S group (Institut des Systèmes Intelligents et Robotiques, CNRS, UMR 7222, Pierre et Marie Curie University Paris 6). Catherine Saint-George is a child psychiatrist, member of IMI2S group (Institut des Systèmes Intelligents et Robotiques, CNRS, UMR 7222, Pierre et Marie Curie University Paris 6).

AUTHOR CONTRIBUTIONS

DC, CS-G, and AH-B designed the study; AH-B and GC created the treatment program; AH-B and AT implemented the program in each study site; NB created the data base for implementation of the program; DC and NB performed the statistical analysis; AT, CS-G and DC did a first version of the manuscript; all authors critically revised the final version of the manuscript.

FUNDING

The study was funded by the *Caisse Nationale de Solidarité pour l'Autonomie* (CNSA), the *Croix Rouge Française*, the *Fondation Bettencourt-Schueller*, and the *Fondation EDF*.

MEMBERS OF THE GPIS (GROUPE DE PÉDAGOGIE INTENSIF ET SÉQUENTIEL) STUDY GROUP

Véronique Bur, Aude Brellier, Marie-Noëlle Clément, Christophe Chartier, Claire Ducateau, Jean-Louis Sarradet, Paris; Danièle Scellier, Hélène Petiton, Amiens; François Soumille, Marc Colombel, Marseille; Marc Bandelier, Louisa Garnil, Argenteuil; Emmanuel Damville, Isabelle Gylbert, Lille; Anne Juteau, Anne Vautrin, Aulnay-sous-Bois; Jean-François Havreng, Elisabeth Simonet, Sèvres; Georges Lançon, Yves Faure, Bagnols sur Cèze; Aurélie Broche, Myriam Garing, Saint Privat des Vieux; Carole Devaux, Sophie Michalak, Guadeloupe.

REFERENCES

1. Tordjman S, Somogyi E, Coulon N, Kermarrec S, Cohen D, Bronsard G, et al. Gene X environment interactions in autism spectrum disorders: role of epigenetic mechanisms. *Front Psychiatry* (2014) 5:e53,17. doi:10.3389/fpsyt.2014.00053
2. Ospina MB, Krebs Seida J, Clark B, Karkhaneh M, Hartling L, Tjosvold L, et al. Behavioural and developmental interventions for autism spectrum disorder: a clinical systematic review. *PLoS One* (2008) 3:e3755. doi:10.1371/journal.pone.0003755
3. Dawson G, Rogers S, Munson J, Smith M, Winter J, Greenson J, et al. Randomized, controlled trial of an intervention for toddlers with autism: the Early Start Denver Model. *Pediatrics* (2010) 125:e17–23. doi:10.1542/peds.2009-0958
4. Schopler E, Mesibov G, Baker A. Evaluation of treatment for autistic children and their parents. *J Am Acad Child Psychiatry* (1982) 21(3):262–7. doi:10.1016/S0002-7138(09)60881-5
5. Mesibov GB, Shea V. The TEACCH program in the era of evidence-based practice. *J Autism Dev Disord* (2010) 40(5):570–9. doi:10.1007/s10803-009-0901-6
6. Smith T, Groen AD, Wynn JW. Randomized trial of intensive early intervention for children with pervasive developmental disorder. *Am J Ment Retard* (2000) 105:269–85. doi:10.1352/0895-8017(2000)105<0269:RTOIEI>2.0.CO;2 (erratum appears in *Am J Ment Retard* 2000;105: 508).

7. Lovaas OI. Behavioral treatment and normal education and intellectual functioning in young autistic children. *J Consult Clin Psychol* (1987) 55:3–9. doi:10.1037/0022-006X.55.1.3
8. Koegel RL, Koegel LK, McNerney EK. Pivotal areas in intervention for autism. *J Clin Child Psychol* (2001) 30(1):19–32. doi:10.1207/S15374424JCCP3001_4
9. Rogers SJ, Hall T, Osaky D, Reaven J, Herbison J. The Denver model: a comprehensive, integrated educational approach to young children with autism and their families. 2nd ed. In: Handleman JS, Harris SL, editors. *Preschool Education Program for Children with Autism*. Austin, TX: Pro-Ed (2001). p. 95–134.
10. Mahoney G, Perales F. Relationship-focused early intervention with ASD children: a comparative study. *J Dev Behav Pediatrics* (2005) 26(2):77–85. doi:10.1097/00004703-200504000-00002
11. Greenspan SI, Wieder S. Can children with autism master the core deficits and become empathetic, creative and reflective? *J Dev Learn Disord* (2005) 9:39–61.
12. Narzisi A, Costanza C, Umberto B, Filippo M. Non-pharmacological treatments in autism spectrum disorders: an overview on early interventions for pre-schoolers. *Curr Clin Pharmacol* (2014) 9(1):17–26. doi:10.2174/1574884 7113086660071
13. Barton E, Lawrence K, Deurloo F. Individualizing interventions for young children with autism in preschool. *J Autism Dev Disord* (2012) 42:1205–17. doi:10.1007/s10803-011-1195-z
14. Bitterman A, Daley TC, Misra S, Carlson E, Markowitz J. A national sample of preschoolers with autism spectrum disorders: special education services and parent satisfaction. *J Autism Dev Disord* (2008) 38:1509–17. doi:10.1007/s10803-007-0531-9
15. Chamak B, Bonniau B, Oudaya L, Ehrenberg A. The autism diagnostic experiences of French parents. *Autism* (2011) 15:83–97. doi:10.1177/1362361309 354756
16. Dunst C, Trivette C. Using research evidence to inform and evaluate early childhood intervention practices. *Topics Early Child Spec Educ* (2009) 29:40–52. doi:10.1177/0271121408329227
17. Kohler FW, Strain PS, Hoyson M, Jamieson B. Merging naturalistic teaching and peer-based strategies to address the IEP objectives of preschoolers with autism: an examination of structural and child behavior outcomes. *Focus Autism Other Dev Disabl* (1997) 12:196–208. doi:10.1177/108835769701200402
18. ANESM, HAS. *Autisme et autres troubles envahissants du développement: interventions éducatives et thérapeutiques coordonnées chez l'enfant et l'adolescent*. Saint-Denis: ANESM (2012).
19. Interagency Autism Coordinating Committee. *Strategic Plan for Autism Spectrum Disorder Research*. (2012). Available from: https://iacc.hhs.gov/publications/strategic-plan/2012/strategic_plan_2012.pdf
20. Lawton K, Hannigan S, Ellawadi AB. Moving beyond the status quo: using evidence-based practice to improve autism core deficits in preschool classroom. *Int Rev Res Dev Disabil* (2014) 47:99–150. doi:10.1016/B978-0-12-800278-0.00004-X
21. Goldstein H. Communication intervention for children with autism: a review of treatment efficacy. *Autism Dev Disord* (2002) 32(5):373–96. doi:10.1023/A:1021215300163
22. Woods JJ, Wetherby AM. Early identification of and intervention for infants who are at risk for autism spectrum disorder. *Lang Speech Hear Serv Sch* (2003) 34:180–93. doi:10.1044/0161-1461(2003/015)
23. Reszka S, Odom S, Hume K. Ecological features of preschools and the social engagement of children with autism. *J Early Intervention* (2012) 34:40–56. doi:10.1177/1053815112452596
24. Schepis MM, Reid DH, Ownbey J, Parsons MB. Training support staff to embed teaching within natural routines of young children with disabilities in an inclusive preschool. *J Appl Behav Anal* (2001) 34:313–27. doi:10.1901/jaba.2001.34-313
25. Johnston S, Nelson C, Evans J, Palazolo K. The use of visual supports in teaching children with autism spectrum disorder to initiate interactions. *Augment Altern Commun* (2003) 19:86–103. doi:10.1080/0743461031000112016
26. Keen D, Sigafoos J, Woodyatt G. Teacher responses to the communicative attempts of children with autism. *J Dev Phys Disabil* (2005) 17:19–33. doi:10.1007/s10882-005-2198-5
27. Chiang H. Naturalistic observations of elicited expressive communication of children with autism: an analysis of teacher instructions. *Autism* (2009) 13:165–78. doi:10.1177/1362361308098513
28. Mudford OC, Martin NT, Eikeseth S, Bibby P. Parent-managed behavioral treatment for preschool children with autism: some characteristics of UK programs. *Res Dev Disabil* (2001) 22:173–82. doi:10.1016/S0891-4222(01)00066-X
29. Wong VC, Kwan QK. Randomized controlled trial for early intervention for autism: a pilot study of the Autism 1-2-3 project. *J Autism Dev Disord* (2010) 40(6):677–88. doi:10.1007/s10803-009-0916-z
30. Xavier J, Bursztejn C, Stiskin M, Canitanod R, Cohen D. Autism spectrum disorders: a historical synthesis and dimensional approach toward a tailored therapeutic program. *Res Autism Spectr Disord* (2015) 18:21–33. doi:10.1016/j.rasd.2015.06.011
31. Amiet C, Gourfinkel-An I, Bouzamondo A, Tordjman S, Baulac M, Lechat P, et al. Epilepsy in autism is associated with mental retardation and gender: evidence from a meta-analysis. *Biol Psychiatry* (2008) 64:577–82. doi:10.1016/j.biopsych.2008.04.030
32. Amiet C, Gourfinkel-An I, Laurent C, Bodeau N, Génin B, Leguern E, et al. Epilepsy in multiplex autism pedigrees is associated with intellectual disability and known genetic and non-genetic causes, but not with gender. *Mol Autism* (2013) 4:e47. doi:10.1186/2040-2392-4-47
33. Cohen D, Pichard N, Tordjman S, Baumann C, Burglen L, Excoffier E, et al. Specific genetic disorders and autism: clinical contribution towards identification. *J Autism Dev Disord* (2005) 35:103–16. doi:10.1007/s10803-004-1038-2
34. Baghdadli A, Assouline B, Sonié S, Pernon E, Darrou C, Michelon C, et al. Developmental trajectories of adaptive behaviors from early childhood to adolescence in a cohort of 152 children with autism spectrum disorders. *J Autism Dev Disord* (2012) 42:1314–25. doi:10.1007/s10803-011-1357-z
35. Guinchat V, Cravero C, Diaz L, Périsse D, Xavier J, Amiet C, et al. Acute behavioral crises in psychiatric inpatients with autism spectrum disorder (ASD): recognition of concomitant medical or non-ASD psychiatric conditions predicts enhanced improvement. *Res Dev Disabil* (2015) 38:242–55. doi:10.1016/j.ridd.2014.12.020
36. Lord C, Rutter M, Le Couteur A. Autism diagnostic interview-revised: a revised version of a diagnostic interview for caregivers of individuals with possible pervasive developmental disorders. *J Autism Dev Disord* (1994) 24(5):659–85. doi:10.1007/BF02172145
37. Reichow B, Wolery M. Comprehensive synthesis of early intensive behavioral interventions for young children with autism based on the UCLA young autism project model. *J Autism Dev Disord* (2009) 39:23–41. doi:10.1007/s10803-008-0596-0
38. Schopler E, Reichler RJ, DeVellis RF, Daly K. Toward objective classification of childhood autism: Childhood Autism Rating Scale (CARS). *J Autism Dev Disord* (1980) 10(1):91–103. doi:10.1007/BF02408436
39. Schopler E, Lansing MD, Reichler RJ, Marcus LM. *PEP-3 Psychoeducational Profile*. 3rd ed. Austin: Pro-Ed (2005).
40. Sparrow SS, Cicchetti DV, Balla DA. *Vineland Adaptive Behavior Scales*. 2nd ed. San Antonio, TX: Pearson (2005).
41. Kaufman AS, Kaufman NL. *Kaufman Assessment Battery for Children Second Edition*. Circle Pines, MN: American Guidance Service (2004).
42. Guy W. Clinical global impressions. Revised ed. In: Guy W, editor. *ECDEU Assessment Manual for Psychopharmacology*. Rockville, MD: National Institute of Mental Health (1976). p. 217–22.
43. Endicott J, Spitzer RL, Fleiss JL, Cohen J. The global assessment scale: a procedure for measuring overall severity of psychiatric disturbance. *Arch Gen Psychiatry* (1976) 33:766–71. doi:10.1001/archpsyc.1976.01770060 086012

10

Autism Spectrum Disorders and Schizophrenia Spectrum Disorders: Excitation/Inhibition Imbalance and Developmental Trajectories

Roberto Canitano[1] and Mauro Pallagrosi[2]*

[1] Division of Child Neuropsychiatry, University Hospital of Siena, Siena, Italy, [2]Department of Psychiatry, Sapienza University of Rome, Rome, Italy

Edited by:
Ashok Mysore,
St. John's Medical College Hospital, India

Reviewed by:
Joseph Gonzalez-Heydrich,
Harvard Medical School, USA
Bart P. F. Rutten,
Maastricht University, Netherlands

***Correspondence:**
Roberto Canitano
r.canitano@ao-siena.toscana.it,
canitano@unisi.it

Autism spectrum disorders (ASD) and schizophrenia spectrum disorders (SSD) share clinical and genetic components that have long been recognized. The two disorders co-occur more frequently than would be predicted by their respective prevalence, suggesting that a complex, multifactor association is involved. However, DSM-5 maintains the distinction between ASD, with core social and communication impairments, and SSD, including schizophrenia (SCZ), with hallucinations, delusions, and thought disorder as essential features. ASD and SSD have common biological underpinnings that may emerge early in development and unfold over time. One of the hypotheses supporting the similarities in the social and cognitive disturbances of ASD and SSD relates to abnormalities in the ratio of excitatory to inhibitory cortical activity (E/I imbalance). E/I imbalance in neurodevelopmental disorders could be the consequence of abnormalities in genes coding for glutamatergic and GABAergic receptors or synaptic proteins followed by system derangements. SSD and ASD have been characterized as polygenic disorders in which to the onset and progression of disease is triggered by interactions among multiple genes. Mammalian target of rapamycin signaling is under intense investigation as a convergent altered pathway in the two spectrum disorders. Current understanding of shared and divergent patterns between ASD and SSD from molecular to clinical aspects is still incomplete and may be implemented by the research domain criteria approach.

Keywords: autism spectrum disorders, schizophrenia spectrum disorders, psychosis, children and adolescents, excitation/inhibition imbalance

AUTISM SPECTRUM DISORDER (ASD) AND SCHIZOPHRENIA SPECTRUM DISORDER (SSD): CURRENT UNDERSTANDING

The clinical interplay and overlap between SSD and ASD have long been recognized as the two classes of disorder that share phenotypic and clinical features and a number of individuals diagnosed with ASD subsequently develop SSD symptoms (1). Currently, the relationship is further emphasized after controversies on the shared patterns and differences of the two disorders.

It has been demonstrated that the two types of disorder co-occur more frequently than would be that predicted by their respective prevalence. DSM-5 maintains a nosological distinction between ASD and schizophrenia (SCZ) in spite of overlapping in clinical characteristics. Examining the specific definition of core symptoms, there are two major criteria for ASD: "(1) persistent deficits in social communication, social interactions, social-emotional reciprocity and communicative behaviors and

(2) restricted, repetitive patterns of behavior, interests or activities, including stereotyped or repetitive movements, behavioral rigidity, odd or intense interests," and as an important additional criterion, abnormally high or low reactivity to sensory stimuli. On the other hand, the DSM-5 diagnostic criteria for SCZ specify that at least two of the following symptoms must be present: "hallucinations, delusions, disorganized speech, grossly disorganized or catatonic behavior and negative symptoms." Furthermore, in DSM-5, the criteria have been reorganized to emphasize the variability in the severity of the psychopathology and the severity dimensions have been updated (2).

Childhood-onset schizophrenia (COS) is a subtype of SCZ defined by onset of psychotic symptoms before 13 years and the absence of any other neuropsychiatric diagnosis. Re-examination of the overlap between COS and ASD has highlighted the clinical and genetic commonalities. Remarkably, in almost half the cases of COS identified in the largest longitudinal study to date, a pervasive developmental disorder was present before the onset of psychosis (3). In contrast, and somewhat unexpectedly, prospective longitudinal studies following children with ASD into young adulthood rarely report the appearance of psychotic symptoms. SSD includes SCZ, schizofreniform disorder, schizoaffective disorder, and schizotypal personality disorder. In ASD, it is not rare to detect unusual preoccupations, unusual perceptual experiences, odd thinking, and speech. Both the shared clinical features and frequent co-occurrence point to a close relationship between SSD and ASD. To further strength this relationship, it has been reported that about 30% of children and adolescents with COS had co-morbid ASD (4). In addition, the well-known difficulty to recognize social cues from the actions of others is tightly related to deficit in theory of mind that is a characteristic feature common to both SSD and ASD (5).

In this context, it is critically important to underscore that the negative symptoms of SSD are often more disabling and more resistant to treatment than the so-called positive ones, e.g., hallucinations and delusions (6). These negative symptoms include social avoidance and emotional flatness and might be regarded as closely linked to impairments in social communication and motivation. These so-called negative symptoms of SSD might be considered to fall within the same domain of social impairment as the social difficulties characteristic of ASD. Furthermore, the disorganized or abnormal behaviors characteristic of SSD include behaviors which would meet ASD Criterion B, e.g., repeated and stereotyped movements and verbal expressions, as to DSM-5. Other pathognomonic features common to both conditions include impairments in facial recognition and emotion processing (7, 8). Patients with both ASD and SSD have been shown to have significant difficulties in interpreting social cues associated with eye gaze and deficits on theory of mind tasks—one of the hallmarks of ASD.

Autism spectrum disorders and SSD share biological underpinnings that may emerge in early neural development and unfold during subsequent childhood development (9). Abnormal neural development has been ascertained in cortical projection neurons from different brain areas including prefrontal and somatosensory regions in ASD and dorsolateral/ventrolateral prefrontal regions in SSD. It has to be mentioned that neurodevelopmental disorders are associated with known genetic abnormalities both in ASD and SSD phenotypes, as detailed in **Table 1**. Furthermore, epigenetic effects and alterations in copy number variants (CNVs) have been reported to contribute to abnormalities of neural circuits associated with SSD and ASD (**Table 2**). The risk of both disorders is increased by advanced paternal age and maternal infection/immune activation during pregnancy (10, 11). These shared patterns suggest that the two spectra are likely to represent

TABLE 1 | Candidate genes validated in autism spectrum disorders (ASD) and schizophrenia spectrum disorders (SSD).

Gene	Function	Other phenotypes
RELN	Neuronal migration, polarization	Lissencephaly, Alzheimer's disease
DISC1	Neural development, synaptic plasticity, mammalian target of rapamycin (mTOR) regulation	Depression, bipolar disorder
FOXP2	Regulates DISC1, CTNAP2, language, and neural development	Developmental verbal dyspraxia
BDNF	Neurotrophic factor, regulates mTOR/AKT	Alzheimer's disease, Huntington disease
MECP2	Epigenetic regulator	Rett syndrome
UBE3A	Epigenetic regulator	Angelmann syndrome
NLGN3	Postsynaptic component coupled with NRXN	Undefined
NLG4	Postsynaptic component coupled with NXRN	ID
NRXN1	Presynaptic component coupled with NXRN	Pitt–Hopkins phenotype
SHANK3	Postsynaptic protein in glutamatergic neuron	Phelan–McDermid syndrome
CNTAP2 CNTAP4	Cell adhesion and differentiation	ID, epilepsy, language impairment
GRIN2B	NMDA receptor subunit	ID, epilepsy
NTGN1	Axon guidance	Bipolar disorder
GABRB3 GABRA5	GABA receptor subunits	Bipolar disorder
GAD	Conversion of glutamate to GABA	Epilepsy
CACNA1C	Voltage-dependent calcium channel subunit	Bipolar disorder, Brugada, and Timothy syndromes
SLC25A12	Mitochondrial membrane, solute channel protein	Mitochondrial disorders
OXTR/OXT	Oxytocin receptor/oxytocin gene	Undefined
ZNF804A	Transcription regulator of PRSS16, COMT	Bipolar disorders

Modified by de Lacy and King (9).
ID, intellectual disability.

TABLE 2 | Copy number variants (CNVs) implicated in ASD and SSD.

Region and type	Candidate genes	Phenotypes
1q21.1 Del	Unidentified	SCZ, ASD, ID, ADHD, deficit IGE
1q21.1 Dup	Unidentified	ASD, ID, ADHD
2p16.3 Del	NRXN1	SCZ, ASD, ID
3q29 Del	PAK2	ACZ, ID, ADHD
3q29 Dup	Unidentified	ID
15q11.2 Del	CYF1P1	ID, DD, SCZ, ASD, IGE, OCD, MDD
15q11-13 Dup	GABRA5, GABRB3, GABG3, and others	SCZ, ASD, ID, Ataxia
15q13.3 Del	CHRNA7	SCZ, ASD, ID
16p11.2 Del	DOC2A, ERK1	SCZ, ASD, ID, learning disorder
16p11.2 Dup	DOC2A, ERK1	SCZ, ASD, ID, DD
16p13.11 Del	NDE1	SCZ, ASD, ID
16p13.11 Dup	NDE1	SCZ, ASD, ID, ADHD, IGE
17q12	Undefined	SCZ, ASD, ID
22q11.2	PRODH, COMT, DGCR6, TRX1	SCZ, ASD, ID, epilepsy
22q11.21	PRODH, COMT, DGCR6, TRX1	ID, DD
22q13.3	SHANK3	ID, DD, ASD, SCZ

Modified by de Lacy and King (9).
ID, intellectual disability; ADHD, attention-deficit hyperactivity disorder, DD, developmental delay; OCD, obsessive–compulsive disorder; MMDD, major depressive disorder; IGE, immunoglobulin E deficit.

outcomes of common pathophysiological mechanisms. The next sections describe the E/I imbalance as a candidate mechanism possibly involved.

E/I IMBALANCE IN ASD AND SSD

An emerging hypothesis for the similarities in the social and cognitive disturbances associated with ASD and SSD is based on alterations in the ratio of excitatory to inhibitory cortical activity (E/I imbalance). Glutamate and GABA are, respectively, the two main neurotransmitters involved in excitatory and inhibitory signaling in the brain. Increased glutamatergic signaling alongside decreased GABAergic signaling would represent an E/I imbalance. Such imbalances may arise from disturbances in neural circuit formation or, abnormalities in the genes which code for proteins involved in these processes and linkage and association studies have been implicated in ASD and SSD (12). Postmortem studies have reported structural changes in both excitatory glutamatergic and inhibitory GABAergic circuits in individuals with ASD and SCZ (13–15).

In neurodevelopmental disorders, an E/I imbalance could arise directly through alterations in genes coding for glutamatergic receptors or synaptic proteins (16–18). The synapse organizers neurexins and their binding neuroligins are implicated in the formation and maintenance of excitatory and inhibitory synapses. Heterozygous deletions eliminating exons of the neurexin-1α gene in patients with ASD and SCZ have been detected and the functional significance of this recurrent deletion is still unclear. However, the availability of mice with deletion of the promoter and first exon of neurexin-1α provided evidence of the effects of neurexin-1α disruption on phenotypes relevant to ASD and SCZ and supported the role of neuroxins in neurodevelopmental disorders (19, 20).

In addition to the synaptic dysfunction, there is increasing evidence that E/I balance is also modulated by glial mechanisms that regulate glutamate activity (21, 22). Abnormalities in astrocyte gene expression in both ASD and SCZ have been detected (23), and reduced numbers of oligodendrocytes, impaired cell maturation, and altered gene expression of myelin/oligodendrocyte-related genes have been ascertained in SCZ (24). In turn, an increased number of activated microglia cells in adults with ASD have been found (25). As a result, glia deserves specific attention in the evaluation of E/I imbalance in these conditions.

ASD AND E/I IMBALANCE

The net effect of changes in glutamatergic and GABAergic systems in ASD may be an overall increase in the ratio of excitation to inhibition (E/I). Such an increase is likely to be implicated in seizures, macrocephaly, and core ASD symptoms (26). The E–I ratio in neocortical structures is determined by pyramidal glutamatergic neurons and inhibitory GABAergic parvalbumin (PV)-positive interneurons that are modulated and fine-tuned by minicolumns (groups of functionally autonomous neurons whose afferent and efferent connections influence the functioning of microcircuits) which have been found to be abnormal in ASD (27, 28). There are a number of candidate mechanisms for glutamatergic hyperactivity-driven hyperexcitability. Neuroligins (NL1–4) and neurexins (Nrxns 1–3) have been linked with ASD via point mutations and truncations, and chromosomal rearrangements have been identified in the region of interest (29–31). SHANK1, SHANK2, and SHANK3 are scaffolding proteins which influence the postsynaptic density of glutamatergic synapses and are of primary importance in ASD. SHANK3 is reported to be involved in Phelan–McDermid syndrome a form of ASD associated with moderate to severe intellectual disability (ID) and poor language skills (32). Regarding SHANK2 and SHANK1, they were found altered in ASD associated with mild ID as well as in high functioning individuals (33).

As to the mechanisms of GABAergic inhibitory dysfunction, the link with core ASD symptoms in humans is still under investigation. Deficit in binocular rivalry, a visual function that is thought to rely on the balance of excitation/inhibition in visual cortex has been observed in ASD individuals. The link between GABA and binocular rivalry dynamics was found specifically absent in ASD pointing to an insufficient GABA inhibitory function (34). Postmortem studies have provided evidence of alterations in GABAergic circuits in ASD individuals; there have been reports of significantly reduced GAD65/GAD67 levels in the parietal cortex and cerebellum (35).

Induced pluripotent stem cells (iPSCs) have been used to investigate putative abnormalities in neural substrate of individuals with ASD. Even if no known underlying genomic mutation could be identified in a new study herein presented, interestingly, transcriptome and gene network analyses revealed upregulation of genes involved in cell proliferation, neuronal differentiation, and synaptic formation. The main finding was that overexpression of the transcription factor FOXG1 was responsible for the overproduction of GABAergic neurons, shifting the E/I balance toward inhibition (36).

SSD AND E/I IMBALANCE

Several postmortem studies detected lower levels of PV mRNA and GAD67, the principal synthesizing enzyme for GABA, in dorso-lateral-prefrontal cortex (DLPFC) PV neurons of patients with SCZ. Markers of GABA neurotransmission between chandelier neurons and their synaptic targets are altered in the DLPFC of subjects with SCZ (37, 38).

NMDA receptors are ionotropic glutamate receptors involved in synaptic regulation of E/I balance and there are multiple subtypes of NMDA receptor with different functions and distributions (39). Dysfunction of NMDARs has been documented in SCZ both in experimental models and human studies. In the NMDA-hypofunction model of the disease, changes in E/I balance and the resulting changes in behaviors have been hypothesized (40). Disrupted NMDAR function is implicated in altered neurodevelopment and may play a role in the progression of symptoms for SCZ especially for cognitive deficits (41–43). NMDA receptor hypofunction has been proposed in ASD as well and the NR2A, NR2B, and NR2C genes abnormalities have been associated with ASD (44).

Remarkably, two *de novo* mutations in the *GRIN2A*-coded subunit of NMDA receptors have been detected in patients with SCZ and one *de novo* mutation in *GRIN2B*-coded subunit in a patient with ASD. Truncating mutations in *GRIN2C, GRIN3A,* and *GRIN3B* were identified in both patients and controls, but no truncating mutations were found in the *GRIN1, GRIN2A, GRIN2B,* and *GRIN2D* genes (45).

NRG1and ErbB4 genes deserve attention, are expressed at excitatory synapses, and regulate spine structure and function. ErbB4 deletion is associated with neurodevelopmental abnormalities that are consistent with SSD (46, 47). The disrupted in SCZ 1 gene (*DISC1*) is another important candidate gene implicated at different levels of neurodevelopment through a scaffolding protein and different mutations have been detected in SCZ emphasizing its role (48, 49).

E/I imbalance has been proposed as a mechanism for hallucinations, one of the main positive symptoms of SSD. Hallucinations have been linked to inhibitory deficits such as impaired GABA transmission unfolding in a series of abnormalities such as impaired NDMA receptor plasticity, reductions in gamma frequency oscillations, sensory cortical hyperactivity, and cognitive inhibition deficits. However, the mechanisms by which E/I dysfunctions at the cellular level might be linked to clinical symptoms and cognitive deficits remain unclear (50).

The 22q11 microdeletion syndrome is the most common CNV associated with SCZ as it is present in 1–2% of cases, further there is a very high association of the syndrome with SCZ, up to 30–40%. This elevated risk is not associated with any other neurogenetic syndrome. Social cognition is impaired in 22q11.2 deletion syndrome and remarkably this feature is correlated with psychotic symptoms. The role of this microdeletion as a potential contributor to E/I imbalance is undefined (51).

CONVERGENT PATHWAYS VS. DIVERGENT PHENOTYPE IN ASD AND SSD

Schizophrenia spectrum disorders and ASD have been described as polygenic disorders in which the onset and progression of disease are triggered by interactions among multiple susceptibility genes.

Overlaps of risk genes among ASD and SSD have been documented. Two lines of mutant mice with *Shank3* mutations linked to ASD and SSD have been documented with shared and distinct synaptic and behavioral phenotypes. Mice with the ASD-linked InsG3680 mutation manifest striatal synaptic transmission defects before weaning age and impaired juvenile social interaction, coinciding with the early onset of ASD symptoms. On the other hand, adult mice carrying the SCZ-linked R1117X mutation demonstrated synaptic defects in prefrontal cortex and social dominance behavior. This is a paradigmatic example of different alleles of the same gene that have distinct phenotypes at molecular, synaptic, and circuit levels which may inform exploration of these divergences in human patients (52).

MAMMALIAN TARGET OF RAPAMYCIN (mTOR) SIGNALING IN ASD AND SSD

The mTOR pathway is directly involved in the physiological maintenance of the synaptic E/I ratio and is implicated in ASD by virtue of its role in upstream signaling and downstream regulatory mechanisms (12). Dysregulation of mTOR increases excitability and decreases inhibition thus contributing to E/I imbalance. mTOR activation is found in tuberous sclerosis complex mutations (TSC1/TSC2) occurring in tuberous sclerosis, which is frequently associated with ASD. Dysregulation of the mTOR pathway in these conditions provides clues to the molecular pathophysiology of ASD as the synaptic and cellular alterations involved may converge to produce the core social impairment of these disorders (53). In addition, mTOR inhibitor compounds have the potential to reverse many of the behavioral and neurophysiological abnormalities associated with ASD (54).

Recent investigations have linked SSD to the mTOR signaling cascade (55). Dysfunction of diverse upstream activators and environmental stressors, that have been previously implicated in SCZ, can lead to either over-activation or inhibition of the signaling pathway. Alterations in GABA signaling may be involved in the dysfunction of inhibitory circuits in SSD through the DISC1–Akt–mTOR pathway. As well, a putative depression of mTOR signaling with possible variation between and within brain regions affecting neuronal functioning in variable fashion has been proposed. Consistently, a preponderant decrease in glutamatergic activity with respect to GABAergic activity has been reported (56). In this functional and still undefined background, abnormal synaptic function may be related to positive and negative symptoms of SSD (57). Lastly, mTOR signaling undergoes variations as neurodevelopment unfold and environment plays a significant role especially through early life experiences that needs to be thoroughly considered (58).

FINAL REMARKS AND FUTURE DIRECTIONS

There is epidemiological, clinical, neurobiological, and genetic evidence for a close relationship between ASD and SSD, and significant overlap in symptoms is frequently observed; however, there are also differences in clinical presentation, behavioral phenotype, and developmental trajectory.

The complex pathways that control E/I balance provide a framework for understanding how different genetic alterations implicated in these two distinct disorders can interact to disrupt excitatory and inhibitory neuronal function, neuronal circuit organization thus eventually influence complex social and cognitive behaviors. Nonetheless, it has to be clearly stated that current knowledge of the mechanistic relationships between E/I imbalance and the two spectrum disorders is still exploratory and need further evidence. The ways in which these shared mechanisms contribute to specific phenotypes such as ASD and SSD are still largely unknown. There are a number of open questions that need to be addressed such as whether there is a critical period for an E/I imbalance that mediates ASD- and SSD-associated behavior, or whether the E/I imbalance is circuit specific. Furthermore, an E/I imbalance may arise not only from synaptic dysfunction but also from altered cell fate that can lead to abnormal proportions of inhibitory and excitatory cells.

Shedding light on the shared functions of candidate genes for involvement in ASD and SSD is the key to translating genetic findings into descriptions of developmental and clinical subtypes. As to neuronal dysfunction hypothesized, abnormalities might be specific affecting only a subset of synapses in a selective group of neurons responsible of distinct symptoms but all that is still an hypothesis as evidence on the brain circuits potentially involved is lacking.

Research domain criteria (RDoC) project seems particularly indicated to this scope as it is directed to implement all the above level of understanding. One of the main purpose is to investigate mental illness through the dimensional approach to the fundamental components of behavior, through individual symptoms or symptom clusters, that cut across diagnoses, in this case specifically in ASD and SSD domains (59). Aim and legacy of RDoC novel approach is to build a research perspective that reflects advances in genetics, neuroscience, and behavioral science to provide a foundation for precision diagnosis and treatment of complex mental disorders such as those herein examined. The details obtained by the use of RDoC matrix likely will help to shed light on ASD and SSD relationships as well as on the longitudinal monitoring of emerging convergent and divergent symptoms of the two spectra (60).

It should also be noted that there is a subset of individuals with complex neurodevelopmental disorders whose symptoms span multiple functional domains including cognition and social communication. These individuals do not fit under any of the current diagnostic labels listed under ASD and SSD and further research through an RDoC approach holds promise to describe the specific biobehavioral profiles and thus eventually establish the diagnostic category in which they should be included. Consistent developmental designs are awaited to capture changes in the underlying neural circuitry, molecular pathways including E/I balance, and other biological components in ASD and SSD, relating them to changes in their corresponding cognitive and affective determinants as they emerge over time and alter behavior under the influencing role of environment.

AUTHOR CONTRIBUTIONS

RC and Mauro Pallagrosi equally participated in the substantial contribution to the conception or design of the work; drafted the work and revised it critically for important intellectual content; approved the final version to be published; and are accountable for all aspects of the work in ensuring that questions related to the accuracy or integrity of any part of the work are appropriately investigated and resolved.

REFERENCES

1. Hommer RE, Swedo SE. Schizophrenia and autism-related disorders. *Schizophr Bull* (2015) 41(2):313–4. doi:10.1093/schbul/sbu188
2. American Psychiatric Association. *Diagnostic and Statistical Manual of Mental Disorders*. 5th ed. Washington, DC: American Psychiatric Association (2013).
3. Rapoport J, Chavez A, Greenstein D, Addington A, Gogtay N. Autism spectrum disorders and childhood-onset schizophrenia: clinical and biological contributions to a relation revisited. *J Am Acad Child Adolesc Psychiatry* (2009) 48(1):10–8. doi:10.1097/CHI.0b013e31818b1c63
4. Driver DI, Gogtay N, Rapoport J. Childhood onset schizophrenia and early onset schizophrenia spectrum disorders. *Child Adolesc Psychiatr Clin N Am* (2013) 22(4):539–55. doi:10.1016/j.chc.2013.04.001

5. King BH, Lord C. Is schizophrenia on the autism spectrum? *Brain Res* (2011) 1380:34–41. doi:10.1016/j.brainres.2010.11.031
6. Cochran DM, Dvir Y, Frazier JA. 'Autism-plus' spectrum disorders: intersection with psychosis and the schizophrenia spectrum. *Child Adolesc Psychiatr Clin N Am* (2013) 22(4):609–27. doi:10.1016/j.chc.2013.04.005
7. Marwick K, Hall J. Social cognition in schizophrenia: a review of face processing. *Br Med Bull* (2008) 88(1):3–58. doi:10.1093/bmb/ldn035
8. Sasson NJ, Pinkham AE, Weittenhiller LP, Faso DJ, Simpson C. Context effects on facial affect recognition in schizophrenia and autism: behavioral and eye-tracking evidence. *Schizophr Bull* (2016) 42(3):675–8. doi:10.1093/schbul/sbv176.3
9. de Lacy N, King BH. Revisiting the relationship between autism and schizophrenia: toward an integrated neurobiology. *Annu Rev Clin Psychol* (2013) 9:555–87. doi:10.1146/annurev-clinpsy-050212-185627
10. McGrath JJ, Petersen L, Agerbo E, Mors O, Mortensen PB, Pedersen CB. A comprehensive assessment of parental age and psychiatric disorders. *JAMA Psychiatry* (2014) 71(3):301–9. doi:10.1001/jamapsychiatry.2013.4081
11. Knuesel I, Chicha L, Britschgi M, Schobel SA, Bodmer M, Hellings JA, et al. Maternal immune activation and abnormal brain development across CNS disorders. *Nat Rev Neurol* (2014) 10(11):643–60. doi:10.1038/nrneurol.2014.187
12. Gao R, Penzes P. Common mechanisms of excitatory and inhibitory imbalance in schizophrenia and autism spectrum disorders. *Curr Mol Med* (2015) 15(2):146–67. doi:10.2174/1566524015666150303003028
13. Chattopadhyaya B, Cristo GD. GABAergic circuit dysfunctions in neurodevelopmental disorders. *Front Psychiatry* (2012) 3:51. doi:10.3389/fpsyt.2012.00051
14. Glausier JR, Lewis DA. Dendritic spine pathology in schizophrenia. *Neuroscience* (2013) 251:90–107. doi:10.1016/j.neuroscience.2012.04.044
15. Hutsler JJ, Zhang C. Increased dendritic spine densities on cortical projection neurons in autism spectrum disorders. *Brain Res* (2010) 1309:83–94. doi:10.1016/j.brainres.2009.09.120
16. Silverman JL, Smith DG, Rizzo SJ, Karras MN, Turner SM, Tolu SS, et al. Negative allosteric modulation of the mGluR5 receptor reduces repetitive behaviors and rescues social deficits in mouse models of autism. *Sci Transl Med* (2012) 4(131):131–51. doi:10.1126/scitranslmed.3003501
17. Silverman JL, Pride MC, Hayes JE, Puhger KR, Butler-Struben HM, Baker S, et al. GABAB receptor agonist r-baclofen reverses social deficits and reduces repetitive behavior in two mouse models of autism. *Neuropsychopharmacology* (2015) 40(9):2228–39. doi:10.1038/npp.2015.66
18. Spooren W, Lindemann L, Ghosh A, Santarelli L. Synapse dysfunction in autism: a molecular medicine approach to drug discovery in neurodevelopmental disorders. *Trends Pharmacol Sci* (2012) 33(12):669–84. doi:10.1016/j.tips.2012.09.004
19. Reichelt AC, Rodgers RJ, Clapcote SJ. The role of neurexins in schizophrenia and autistic spectrum disorder. *Neuropharmacology* (2012) 62(3):1519–26. doi:10.1016/j.neuropharm.2011.01.024
20. Grayton HM, Missler M, Collier DA, Fernandes C. Altered social behaviours in neurexin 1alpha knockout mice resemble core symptoms in neurodevelopmental disorders. *PLoS One* (2013) 8:e67114. doi:10.1371/journal.pone.0067114
21. Di Benedetto B, Rupprecht R. Targeting glia cells: novel perspectives for the treatment of neuropsychiatric diseases. *Curr Neuropharmacol* (2013) 11:171–85. doi:10.2174/1570159X11311020004
22. Durieux AMS, Fernandes C, Murphy D, Labouesse MA, Giovanoli S, Meyer U, et al. Targeting glia with N-acetylcysteine modulates brain glutamate and behaviors relevant to neurodevelopmental disorders in C57BL/6J mice. *Front Behav Neurosci* (2015) 9:343. doi:10.3389/fnbeh.2015.00343
23. Fatemi SH, Reutiman TJ, Folsom TD, Thuras PD. GABA(A) receptor downregulation in brains of subjects with autism. *J Autism Dev Disord* (2009) 39(2):223–30. doi:10.1007/s10803-008-0646-7
24. Bernstein HG, Steiner J, Guest PC, Dobrowolny H, Bogerts B. Glial cells as key players in schizophrenia pathology: recent insights and concepts of therapy. *Schizophr Res* (2015) 161(1):4–18. doi:10.1016/j.schres.2014.03.035
25. Onore C, Careaga M, Ashwood P. The role of immune dysfunction in the pathophysiology of autism. *Brain Behav Immun* (2012) 26(3):383–92. doi:10.1016/j.bbi.2011.08.007
26. Uzunova G, Pallanti S, Hollander E. Excitatory/inhibitory imbalance in autism spectrum disorders: implications for interventions and therapeutics. *World J Biol Psychiatry* (2016) 17(3):174–86. doi:10.3109/15622975.2015.1085597
27. Hutsler JJ, Casanova M. Review: cortical construction in autism spectrum disorder: columns, connectivity and the subplate. *Neuropathol Appl Neurobiol* (2016) 42(2):115–34. doi:10.1111/nan.12227
28. Opris I, Casanova MF. Prefrontal cortical minicolumn: from executive control to disrupted cognitive processing. *Brain* (2014) 137(7):1863–75. doi:10.1093/brain/awt359
29. Etherton MR, Tabuchi K, Harma SM, Ko J, Sudhof TC. An autism-associated point mutation in the neuroligin cytoplasmic tail selectively impairs AMPA receptor-mediated synaptic transmission in hippocampus. *EMBO J* (2011) 30(14):2908–19. doi:10.1038/emboj.2011.182
30. Zhang C, Milunsky JM, Newton S, Ko J, Zhao G, Maher TA, et al. A neuroligin-4 missense mutation associated with autism impairs neuroligin-4 folding and endoplasmic reticulum export. *J Neurosci* (2009) 29(35):10843–54. doi:10.1523/JNEUROSCI.1248-09.2009
31. Gauthier J, Siddiqui TJ, Huashan P, Yokomaku D, Hamdan FF, Champagne N, et al. Truncating mutations in NRXN2 and NRXN1 in autism spectrum disorders and schizophrenia. *Hum Genet* (2011) 130(4):563–73. doi:10.1007/s00439-011-0975-z
32. Kolevzon A, Angarita B, Bush L, Wang AT, Frank Y, Yang A, et al. Phelan-McDermid syndrome: a review of the literature and practice parameters for medical assessment and monitoring. *J Neurodev Disord* (2014) 6:39. doi:10.1186/1866-1955-6-39
33. Leblond CS, Nava C, Polge A, Jauthier G, Huguet G, Lumbroso S, et al. Meta-analysis of SHANK mutations in autism spectrum disorders: a gradient of severity in cognitive impairments. *PLoS Genet* (2014) 10(9):e1004580. doi:10.1371/journal.pgen.1004580
34. Robertson CE, Ratai EM, Kanwisher N. Reduced GABAergic action in the autistic brain. *Curr Biol* (2016) 26(1):80–5. doi:10.1016/j.cub.2015.11.019
35. Oblak AL, Gibbs TT, Blatt GJ. Decreased GABA(B) receptors in the cingulate cortex and fusiform gyrus in autism. *J Neurochem* (2010) 114(5):1414–23. doi:10.1111/j.1471-4159.2010.06858.x
36. Mariani J, Coppola G, Zhang P, Abyzov A, Provini L, Tomasini L, et al. FOXG1-dependent dysregulation of GABA/glutamate neuron differentiation in autism spectrum disorders. *Cell* (2015) 16(162):375–90. doi:10.1016/j.cell.2015.06.034
37. Lewis DA. The chandelier neuron in schizophrenia. *Dev Neurobiol* (2011) 1(71):118–27. doi:10.1002/dneu.20825
38. Gonzalez-Burgos G, Lewis DA. GABA neurons and the mechanisms of network oscillations: implications for understanding cortical dysfunction in schizophrenia. *Schizophr Bull* (2008) 34(5):944–61. doi:10.1093/schbul/sbn070
39. Paoletti R, Bellone C, Zhou Q. NMDA receptor subunit diversity: impact on receptor properties, synaptic plasticity and disease. *Nat Rev Neurosci* (2013) 14(6):383–400. doi:10.1038/nrn3504
40. Kehrer C, Maziashvili N, Dugladze T, Gloveli T. Altered excitatory-inhibitory balance in the NMDA-hypofunction model of schizophrenia. *Front Mol Neurosci* (2008) 8(1):6. doi:10.3389/neuro.02.006.2008
41. Balu DT. The NMDA receptor and schizophrenia: from pathophysiology to treatment. *Adv Pharmacol* (2016) 76:351–82. doi:10.1016/bs.apha.2016.01.006
42. Fromer M, Pocklington AJ, Kavanagh DH, Williams HJ, Dwyer S, Gormley P, et al. De novo mutations in schizophrenia implicate synaptic networks. *Nature* (2014) 506(7487):179–84. doi:10.1038/nature12929
43. Snyder MA, Gao WJ. NMDA hypofunction as a convergence point for progression and symptoms of schizophrenia. *Front Cell Neurosci* (2013) 27(7):31. doi:10.3389/fncel.2013.00031
44. Voineagau I, Wang X, Johnston P, Tian Y, Horvath S, Mill J, et al. Transcriptomic analysis of autistic brain reveals convergent molecular pathology. *Nature* (2011) 474(7351):380–4. doi:10.1038/nature10110
45. Tarabeux J, Kebir O, Gauthier J, Hamdan FF, Xiong L, Piton A, et al. Rare mutations in N-methyl-D-aspartate glutamate receptors in autism spectrum disorders and schizophrenia. *Transl Psychiatry* (2011) 15(1):e55. doi:10.1038/tp.2011.52
46. Banerjee A, Macdonald ML, Borgmann-Winter KE, Hahn CG. Neuregulin 1-erbB4 pathway in schizophrenia: from genes to an interactome. *Brain Res Bull* (2010) 83(3–4):132–9. doi:10.1016/j.brainresbull.2010.04.011
47. Perez-Garcia CG. ErbB4 in laminated brain structures: a neurodevelopmental approach to schizophrenia. *Front Cell Neurosci* (2015) 18(9):472. doi:10.3389/fncel.2015.00472

48. Mackie S, Millar JK, Porteous DJ. Role of DISC1 in neural development and *schizophrenia. Curr Opin Neurobiol* (2007) 17(1):95–102. doi:10.1016/j.conb.2007.01.007
49. Bradshaw NJ, DJ Porteous DJ. DISC1-binding proteins in neural development, signalling and schizophrenia. *Neuropharmacology* (2012) 62(3):1230–41. doi:10.1016/j.neuropharm.2010.12.027
50. Jardri R, Hugdahl K, Hughes M, Brunelin J, Waters F, Alderson-Day B, et al. Are hallucinations due to an imbalance between excitatory and inhibitory influences on the brain? *Schizophr Bull* (2016) 42(5):1124–34. doi:10.1093/schbul/sbw075
51. Schneider M, Debbane M, Bassett AS, Chow EW, Fung WL, van den Bree M, et al. Psychiatric disorders from childhood to adulthood in 22q11.2 deletion syndrome: results from the International Consortium on Brain and Behavior in 22q11.2 Deletion Syndrome. *Am J Psychiatry* (2014) 171(6):627–39. doi:10.1176/appi.ajp.2013.13070864
52. Zhou Y, Kaiser T, Monteiro P, Zhang X, Van der Goes MS, Wang D, et al. Mice with Shank3 mutations associated with ASD and schizophrenia display both shared and distinct defects. *Neuron* (2016) 89(1):147–62. doi:10.1016/j.neuron.2015.11.023
53. Sato A. mTOR, a potential target to treat autism spectrum disorder. *CNS Neurol Disord Drug Targets* (2016) 15(5):533–43. doi:10.2174/1871527315666160413120638
54. Wang H, Doering LC. Reversing autism by targeting downstream mTOR signaling. *Front Cell Neurosci* (2013) 7:28. doi:10.3389/fncel.2013.00028
55. Gururajan A, van den Buuse M. Is the mTOR-signalling cascade disrupted in schizophrenia? *J Neurochem* (2014) 129(3):377–87. doi:10.1111/jnc.12622
56. Weston MC, Chen H, Swann JW. Multiple roles for mammalian target of rapamycin signaling in both glutamatergic and GABAergic synaptic transmission. *J Neurosci* (2012) 32(33):11441–52. doi:10.1523/JNEUROSCI.1283-12.2012
57. Fatemi SH, Folsom TD. The neurodevelopmental hypothesis of schizophrenia, revisited. *Schizophr Bull* (2009) 35(3):528–48. doi:10.1093/schbul/sbn187
58. Costa-Mattioli M, Monteggia LM. mTOR complexes in neurodevelopmental and neuropsychiatric disorders. *Nat Neurosci* (2013) 16(11):1537–43. doi:10.1038/nn.3546
59. Garvey M, Avenevoli S, Anderson K. The National Institute of Mental Health research domain criteria and clinical research in child and adolescent psychiatry. *J Am Acad Child Adolesc Psychiatry* (2016) 55(2):93–8. doi:10.1016/j.jaac.2015.11.002
60. Cuthbert BN. The RDoC framework: facilitating transition from ICD/DSM to dimensional approaches that integrate neuroscience and psychopathology. *World Psychiatry* (2014) 13(1):28–35. doi:10.1002/wps.20087

11

Genetic Syndromes, Maternal Diseases and Antenatal Factors Associated with Autism Spectrum Disorders (ASD)

Asher Ornoy [1]*, *Liza Weinstein-Fudim* [1] *and Zivanit Ergaz* [1,2]

[1] *Laboratory of Teratology, Department of Medical Neurobiology, Hadassah Medical School, Hebrew University, Jerusalem, Israel,* [2] *Department of Neonatology, Hadassah-Hebrew University Medical Center, Jerusalem, Israel*

Autism spectrum disorder (ASD) affecting about 1% of all children is associated, in addition to complex genetic factors, with a variety of prenatal, perinatal, and postnatal etiologies. In addition, ASD is often an important clinical presentation of some well-known genetic syndromes in human. We discuss these syndromes as well as the role of the more important prenatal factors affecting the fetus throughout pregnancy which may also be associated with ASD. Among the genetic disorders we find Fragile X, Rett syndrome, tuberous sclerosis, Timothy syndrome, Phelan–McDermid syndrome, Hamartoma tumor syndrome, Prader-Willi and Angelman syndromes, and a few others. Among the maternal diseases in pregnancy associated with ASD are diabetes mellitus (PGDM and/or GDM), some maternal autoimmune diseases like antiphospholipid syndrome (APLS) with anti-β2GP1 IgG antibodies and thyroid disease with anti-thyroid peroxidase (TPO) antibodies, preeclampsia and some other autoimmune diseases with IgG antibodies that might affect fetal brain development. Other related factors are maternal infections (rubella and CMV with fetal brain injuries, and possibly Influenza with fever), prolonged fever and maternal inflammation, especially with changes in a variety of inflammatory cytokines and antibodies that cross the placenta and affect the fetal brain. Among the drugs are valproic acid, thalidomide, misoprostol, and possibly SSRIs. β2-adrenergic receptor agonists and paracetamol have also lately been associated with increased rate of ASD but the data is too preliminary and inconclusive. Associations were also described with ethanol, cocaine, and possibly heavy metals, heavy smoking, and folic acid deficiency. Recent studies show that heavy exposure to pesticides and air pollution, especially particulate matter <2.5 and $10\,\mu m$ in diameter (PM2.5 and PM10) during pregnancy is also associated with ASD. Finally, we have to remember that many of the associations mentioned in this review are only partially proven, and not all are "clean" of different confounding factors. The associations described in this review emphasize again how little we know about the etiology and pathogenesis of ASD. It is obvious that we need more epidemiologic data to establish many of these associations, but if proven, they might be promising avenues for prevention.

Keywords: ASD, genetic syndromes, autoimmune diseases, prenatal factors, inflammation, drugs, chemicals, pollution

Edited by:
Benjamin Gesundheit, Cell El Ltd, Israel

Reviewed by:
Munis Dundar, Erciyes University, Turkey
Martine A. Jaworski, Carleton University, Canada

Correspondence:
Ornoy Asher
ornoy@cc.huji.ac.il

INTRODUCTION

ASD is defined by the DSM 5 as a neurobehavioral disorder manifested by persistent deficits in social and communication interaction, deficits in developing, understanding and maintaining relationships, as well as abnormal and fixed interests and repetitive behavior (Kogan et al., 2009; American Psychiatric Association, 2013). Symptoms must be present at early childhood and interfere with daily function. ASD is 4 times more prevalent in males than in females, but in experimental animal models where ASD is induced by neuro-teratogens, there are little gender differences. Mental impairment is common among children with ASD, and a variety of learning and behavioral changes are also prominent in autistic animals. The etiology is diverse, largely unknown, and seems to be the result of genetic and environmental interaction (Kogan et al., 2009; Tchaconas and Adesman, 2013).

Environmental exposures are increasingly being recognized as potential risk factors for ASD, and the possibility that the prenatal and perinatal environment affect fetal programming is an expanding direction for research. Prenatal environment include maternal use of medication, maternal infection and inflammations, and prenatal or perinatal exposure to various substances such as alcohol and heavy air pollution. Of special relevance are prematurity and maternal diabetes.

Epidemiology

The reported prevalence of autism has increased dramatically over time, from 4 to 5 cases per 10,000 in 1966 to ~1% today (Kogan et al., 2009; Tchaconas and Adesman, 2013). The increase is thought to result increased public awareness, changing diagnostic standards, earlier age of diagnosis, and development of treatment modes. It was also shown that many of the children and adults who were previously diagnosed as having mental retardation meet the DSM 4 and DSM 5 diagnostic criteria of ASD (Shattuck, 2006; Elsabbagh et al., 2012). Some increase, however, may result from "new" environmental causes such as pollution and changing life style.

In the US, for example, the autism and developmental disabilities monitoring network (ADDM network) found in children aged 8 years in 2008 an increase from 1/150 in year 2000 to 1/88 in 2008 and in the 2010 monitoring the rate increased to 1/68 children (Autism Developmental Disabilities Monitoring Network Surveillance Year Principal Centers for Disease Prevention, 2012).

In Israel, judging from the number of children who received childhood disability benefits by the Israeli Insurance Institute because of ASD, the cumulative incidence at 8 years of age at 2011 has increased 10-folds from 1991 and reached 0.49% with a ratio of males/females of about 5 (Raz et al., 2015b).

The more recent global prevalence of autism was estimated to be 0.62% (Autism Developmental Disabilities Monitoring Network Surveillance Year Principal Centers for Disease Prevention, 2012; Elsabbagh et al., 2012). In spite of a wide variation in prevalence between the studies, the authors conclude that there is no evidence of a significant impact of ethnic or socioeconomic factors on the rate of ASD.

It can be presumed that in developed countries the great progress in the diagnosis and treatment of ASD reached a relatively steady state at least in the last 10 years. However, both the incidence and prevalence of ASD continued to rise, implying that some of the increase results from a true increase in ASD rate. For example, in the UK in 1988–92 the incidence was 0.40/10,000 person years and it raised to 2.98/10,000 person years in 2000–2001 (Smeeth et al., 2004) and an in the US an increase was reported in the same states in the US between 2000 and 2008 and a further increase between 2008 and 2010 (Fombonne, 2009; Autism Developmental Disabilities Monitoring Network Surveillance Year Principal Centers for Disease Prevention, 2012). An increased incidence was also reported in Israel (Davidovitch et al., 2013). If this is correct, it may largely result from prenatal environmental causes because genetic, ethnic, socioeconomic, and geographic factors did not change significantly during that time. Recent meta-analysis of seven studies including 1,140,210 children evaluated the association between inter-pregnancy interval and increased risk of ASD, and found OR of 1.9 for interval <12 months and 1.37 interval >5 years. Proposed mechanisms included folate deficiency, maternal stress, and sustained post-partum inflammation from previous pregnancy for short interval and infertility, unintended pregnancy, and inflammation for long one (Conde-Agudelo et al., 2016). Genetic predisposition was offered by Darbro et al. who found decreased risk of cancer among ASD patients. Despite increased prevalence of rare coding single-nucleotide variations in oncogenes they tend to develop fewer neoplasms. They hypothesized that the protective effect may be due to defects in cellular proliferation and aging (Darbro et al., 2016).

The prenatal causes of ASD can be divided into environmental chemicals (i.e., drugs such as valproic acid, thalidomide, misoprostol; alcohol, cocaine, and toxic metals taken by the mother during pregnancy), exposure to particulate matter air pollution of up to 2.5 micron in diameter (PM2.5), maternal infections during pregnancy (i.e., rubella, CMV), maternal and fetal inflammation (Fox et al., 2012) and maternal diseases (i.e., diabetes mellitus), including autoimmune diseases (Brown et al., 2015) or allergic diseases such as asthma (Croen et al., 2005). In addition, perinatal factors such as perinatal asphyxia, IUGR, RDS, and others were also associated with an increase in the prevalence of ASD (Gardener et al., 2011).

Numerous mechanisms for ASD have been offered, based also on experimental animal models. In addition to complex genetic susceptibility, epigenetic changes have also been proposed (Kogan et al., 2009). Other mechanisms are: immune dysregulation that include abnormal levels of cytokines and growth factors and various fetal and maternal antibodies to brain tissue (Rossignol and Frye, 2012). Additional proposed mechanisms are increased oxidative stress, mitochondrial dysfunction, abnormalities in brain serotonin, abnormal white matter connectivity, decrease number of Purkinje cells in the cerebellum, and neuronal migration defects (Billeci et al., 2012; Grabrucker, 2012; Rossignol and Frye, 2012).

The purpose of the present review is to summarize the data describing genetic syndromes with ASD like behavior and the maternal diseases associated with increased prevalence of ASD.

In addition, we summarize the antenatal injurious factors that are known to be related to the etiology and pathogenesis of ASD.

GENETIC SYNDROMES ASSOCIATED WITH OR PREDISPOSING TO ASD

ASD phenomenology varies between syndromes, but in some it is more common than in the general population (Richards et al., 2015). Several human syndromes derived from a single gene mutation increase the risk for ASD. The more common aberrations are Fragile X syndrome, a mutation in FMR1 (Kaiser-McCaw et al., 1980), Rett syndrome, a mutation in MECP2 (Meloni et al., 2000), tuberous sclerosis, mutations in TSC1 or TSC2 (Green et al., 1994), Timothy syndrome, a mutation in CACNA1C (Gillis et al., 2012), and Hamartoma tumor syndrome, a mutation of the PTEN gene. Copy-number variants that lead to inherited maternal 15q11–13 duplication resulting in Prader-Willi and Angelman syndromes (Ogata et al., 2014) and other duplications like the NPHP1 gene (Yasuda et al., 2014) are also associated with autistic traits. Patients with other syndromes like 22q.11.2 deletion—DiGeorge syndrome (Swillen and McDonald-McGinn, 2015) and neurofibromatosis type 1 (Huijbregts et al., 2015) show behavioral changes that are also common among ASD patients. Multiple other syndromes were associated with ASD, however cases are sporadic (Moss and Howlin, 2009). The development in strategies for the identification of genetic variants led to the description of new syndromic forms of ASD and enabled the association between phenotype and genetic traits.

Fragile X (FMR1)

Children with Fragile X syndrome which is the most frequent inherited cause of mental retardation have increased rates of ASD. Current estimates suggest that ASD occurs in 21–50% of males with fragile X syndrome, with increased prevalence among individuals with a greater degree of intellectual disability (Moss and Howlin, 2009; Wadell et al., 2013). The Fragile Mental Retardation 1 locus (FMR1) resides in the X chromosome and expansion of triplet repeats in the untranslated region of the FMR1 gene prevents synthesis of the FMR1 gene product FMRP. FMRP is a RNA-binding protein that modulates mRNA trafficking, dendritic maturation and synaptic plasticity. FMRP deficiency leads to dysregulation of other pathways including metabotropic glutamate receptors (mGluR1 and 5), aminobutyric acid A and B pathways, phosphatidylinositol 3-kinase, and mammalian target of rapamycin pathways. FMRP regulates proteins known to be mutated in autism including neuroligins, neurorexins, SHANK, phosphatase, and tensin homolog (Darnell et al., 2011). Deficits in global network organization and decreased clustering with connectome that shift toward randomness were found by Bruno et al among fragile X patients by structural brain network topology evaluation with magnetic resonance imaging (MRI), a finding that was qualitatively similar to what has been described in ASD (Bruno et al., 2016). When 47 children and adolescents with fragile X were assessed for ASD symptoms, most were engaged in self injury behavior, aggression, and stereotypy (Newman et al., 2015). Compared to children with fragile X, those who also had ASD developed slower, had lower developmental level for age that improved over time and performed worse at language tasks (Ballantyne and Nunez, 2016). Boys with fragile X were found to have social smiling less impaired and complex mannerisms more impaired compared to boys with non-syndromic ASD (McDuffie et al., 2015). Besides behavioral Interventions that were proven beneficial, medical therapy based on the pathophysiology of fragile X is currently investigated (Newman et al., 2015). Waddell et al revised the medical treatment modalities based on the up-regulation of the metabotropic glutamate receptor 5 (mGluR5) pathway and down-regulation of the GABA A pathway. The mGluR5 antagonists evaluated in human studies, Fenobam and AFQ056, improved behavior. The GABA B agonist Arbaclofen which is the R-isomer of baclofen and a GABA B agonist that works at a presynaptic receptor improved social behavior of patients with fragile X and ASD. Minocycline, which lowers the levels of matrix metalloproteinase 9 (MMP9), one of a family of proteins important for synaptic plasticity, improved language and behavior among adolescents and young adults with fragile X, however minocycline may cause in young children graying of the permanent teeth when they emerge (Wadell et al., 2013). Human studies with antioxidants like melatonin (Karaaslan and Suzen, 2015; Kwon et al., 2015) and omega 3 fatty acid, vitamin C, vitamin E, and N acetyl cysteine have been tried in single cases. Acetylcarnitine (LAC) was proven beneficial among fragile x patients with ADHD (Wadell et al., 2013).

Rett Syndrome and MECP2 Mutations

Rett syndrome, an X linked disease that affects girls, is characterized by neurodevelopmental delay, ASD and seizures. Estimates of rates of ASD in Rett syndrome range from 25 to 40% and up to 97% in individuals with the preserved speech variant of Rett syndrome (Moss and Howlin, 2009). It is caused by mutations in the gene encoding for the methyl-CpG binding protein 2 (MeCP2) that binds to methylated-CpG dinucleotides and influences gene expression. MeCP2 is expressed widely, but is most abundant in neurons of the mature nervous system. MeCP2 duplication syndrome is characterized by autism, intellectual disability, motor dysfunction, anxiety, epilepsy, recurrent respiratory tract infections and early death. The MET receptor tyrosine kinase gene which is a part of the biological network that includes several ASD-associated transcriptional regulators, including FOXP2 and MeCP2 was found reduced in the temporal lobe of subjects with ASD. Regulation of MET transcription by MeCP2 was found *in vitro* in primary human neural progenitors from the olfactory epithelium. Analyses of postmortem temporal cortex samples from Rett syndrome and ASD cases demonstrated sex-based differences in reduced MET expression, with males' perturbation in ASD and females in Rett syndrome (Plummer et al., 2013). In a UK national sample of 91 women with Rett syndrome aged from 4 to 47 years behavioral disturbances included hand stereotypies (99%), low mood/changeable mood (77%), anxiety or inappropriate fear (73%), sleeping difficulties and night-time laughing (64%), teeth grinding (58%), and breath holding (63%) (Cianfaglione et al., 2015). Despite autistic traits Rett syndrome patients have some phenotypic features that differ from ASD patients like increased visual fixation at social stimuli (Schwartzman et al., 2015). Rett patients exhibited a decrease in visual evoked potential (VEP) amplitude that was most striking in the later stages of the disorder and a slower recovery from the peak of the VEP response that was impacted by MeCP2 mutation type (Leblanc et al., 2015). Based on animal studies in which IGF-1 and BDNF supplementation therapies improved neuronal developmental, synaptic maturation and plasticity exerted through the key cell-signaling pathways, PI3K/Akt and MAPK in MeCP2 mutant mice (Castro et al., 2013), a clinical trial in 10 Rett syndrome patients showed improvement in social and cognitive ability with recombinant human Insulin-Like Growth Factor 1 supplementation (Pini et al., 2016).

Tuberous Sclerosis TSC1 or TSC2

Tuberous sclerosis complex is an autosomal dominant disorder caused by mutations in either the TSC1 or TSC2 gene. The syndrome is associated with cerebral cortical tubers and may be complicated by astrocytomas. About 90% suffer from behavioral, intellectual, psychiatric and psychosocial difficulties and up to 60% have the diagnosis of ASD. There is disagreement regarding the association of ASD with the presence of temporal-lobe tubers (Moss and Howlin, 2009). The protein products of TSC1, hamartin and TSC2, tuberin, inhibit Ras homolog enriched in the brain (Rheb) that activates mammalian target of rapamycin (mTOR) complex 1 (mTORC1). Heterozygous defects in either TSC gene prevents the Rheb inhibition and allows for excessive mTOR activation, which induce cell growth and proliferation. Upregulation of the mTOR pathway leads to abnormal dendritic protein synthesis with reduced or dysmorphic dendritic spines and alterations in postsynaptic glutamate receptor-mediated long-term depression, similar to synaptic abnormalities described in ASD. Owing to the presence of cardiac rhabdomyomas being detected by pre/perinatal ultrasonography patients are diagnosed early, allowing prompt detection of ASD symptoms (Davis et al., 2015). In a recent study evaluating 42 patients aged 4–44 years that were diagnosed with Tuberous sclerosis 17 (40%) had ASD that worsened with intellectual disabilities. None of the patients with normal or borderline mental abilities had ASD. The Social Communication Questionnaire (SQL) score was positively associated with epilepsy, seizure onset before age 1 year, infantile spasms and mutations in TSC2, but not tubers localization and gender (Vignoli et al., 2015). The mTOR inhibitors used in treatment of TSC patients for various manifestations were also evaluated for ASD symptoms. Clinical trials with Rapamycin supplementation were inconclusive, some due to the severe intellectual deficits of the evaluated patients. TSC patients with infantile spasms had higher response rates compare to other patients when treated with Vigabatrin which increase GABA availability in the synaptic cleft. It is hypothesized that it may be associated with mTOR suppression found in a murine model (Davis et al., 2015)

Timothy Syndrome—CACNA1C Mutation

Timothy syndrome (TS) is a rare dysmorphic disease presenting with cardiac arrhythmias, syndactyly; immune deficiency, intermittent hypoglycemia and neurologic morbidities including seizures, mental retardation, and autism. It is a single nucleotide mutation in the gene encoding the pore-forming subunits of an L-type calcium channel (CaV1.2). The sporadic glycine-to-arginine mutation is located at position 406 in exon 8A (Splawski's terminology). Both variants of TS (the milder TS1 and the more severe TS2) arise from missense mutations in alternatively spliced exons that cause the same G406R replacement in the CaV1.2 L-type calcium channel. Association between non-syndromatic ASD and two SNPs in CACNA1C was found in families of Chinese Han ancestry (Li et al., 2015). Currently there is no specific treatment for ASD in patients with Timothy syndrome. Mexiletine, a voltage-gated sodium channel blocker improved cardiac symptoms in a 2 years old girl; however no data concerning her psychological situation is given (Gao et al., 2013).

Phelan–McDermid Syndrome—*SHANK3* Deletion

Deletion of the human *SHANK3* gene near the terminus of chromosome 22q13 is associated with Phelan–McDermid syndrome and autism. Clinical manifestations include dysmorphic face with wide nasal bridge, pointed chin, deep-set eyes, flat mid-face, large ears, long eyelashes, bulbous nose and high-arched palate, hypotonia, developmental delay, and delayed or absent speech. SHANK genes code for large synaptic scaffold proteins of the post-synaptic density. SHANK deletions or mutations were found in about 1% of cases of ASD. Among 760 ASD patients evaluated SHANK1 mutations were found in 0.04% and were present in males with normal IQ and autism, SHANK2 mutations were present in 0.17% of patients with ASD and mild intellectual disability and mutations in SHANK3 were present in 0.69% of the patients with ASD. Those with SHANK3 deletions presented manifestations of the Phelan–McDermid syndrome (Leblond et al., 2014). Using functional MRI to evaluate neural response to communicative vocal sounds, infants with Phelan–McDermid syndrome differed from infants with ASD by their better neural response to communicative vocal sounds in the right superior temporal gyrus (Wang et al., 2016). Children with Phelan–McDermid syndrome were found to have less sensory sensitivity as compared to children with ASD (Mieses et al., 2016).

Hamartoma Tumor Syndrome—PTEN Mutation

Phosphatase and tensin homolog on chromosome 10 (PTEN) is a tumor suppressor gene that has been reported in autistic individuals with macrocephaly, and also in some syndromes including the Hippocampus Cowdon, the Lhermitte-Duclos disease, and the Bannayan Riley Ruvalcaba Syndrome. More recently, the term PTEN Hamartoma Tumor Syndrome (PHTS) has been used to encompass the range of symptoms identified in PTEN mutation carriers (Leslie and Longy, 2016). McBride et al found in their ASD cohort that 7/99 (7.1%) of the ASD patients and 8/100 (8.0%) of those with mental retardation or developmental delay had PTEN mutations, all of them also had macrocephaly (McBride et al., 2010).

CNTNAP2 Mutations

The CNTNAP2 gene is located in chromosomal region 7q35. A recessive nonsense mutation in the contactin associated protein-like 2 (CNTNAP2) gene was shown to cause a syndromic form of ASD, cortical dysplasia and focal epilepsy syndrome (CDFE). This is a rare disorder resulting in epileptic seizures, language regression, intellectual disability, hyperactivity, and ASD. Neuronal migration defects were found in about half of the patients (Strauss et al., 2006). The CNTNAP2 variant that increases risk for the language impairments in autism was shown to lead to abnormal functional brain connectivity in human subjects (Scott-Van Zeeland et al., 2010). Besides ASD, mutations in the CNTNAP2 gene were also found among patients with Gilles de la Tourette syndrome, ADHD, language disturbances, epilepsy, and schizophrenia (Poot, 2015).

15q11-13 Deletion or Duplication Maternal/Paternal

Mutations in 15q11-13 are associated with either duplication or gene deletion. Prader-Willi syndrome results from the loss of imprinted genomic material within the paternal 15q11.2-13 locus and deletions, unbalanced translocations, or uniparental maternal disomy. The loss of maternal genomic material at the 15q11.2-13 locus results in Angelman syndrome since normally, only the maternal copy of the Ube3A gene is active in the brain (Lasalle et al., 2015). Region duplications are the most frequent genetic abnormality in autism and the penetrance rate in individuals with a maternally derived duplication is >85% (Cook and Scherer, 2008). Maternally inherited 15q11-13 duplications and triplications are among the most common genomic copy number variants identified in patients with autism. The dosage of an imprinted gene or genes within the duplicated region underlies the autism risk in these patients. E3 ubiquitin-protein ligase, Ube3a is the only gene within the 15q11-13 duplicated segment consistently expressed solely from the maternal allele in mature neurons, and inactivating mutations or deletions of Ube3a cause Angelman syndrome. Treatment attempts to hypermethylate the maternal locus by using pro-methylation oral supplements with folic acid and betaine (Peters et al., 2010) or L-5-methyltetrahydrofolate, vitamin B12, betaine, and creatine (Bird et al., 2011) failed to improve biochemical or behavioral parameters.

Oxytocin (OXT Gene)

Oxytocin is a hormone known for its role in childbirth and lactation. It is synthesized in neurons in the paraventricular and supraoptic nuclei of the hypothalamus and transported via axonal processing to the posterior pituitary, where it is stored in secretory vesicles for release into the portal vascular system to affect target organs, mainly the uterine and mammary glands. Additionally, oxytocin neurons directly project from the hypothalamus to the forebrain, the amygdala, the hippocampus, and the nucleus accumbens. Recent publications showed its role in interpersonal bonding behaviors and psychiatric disorders (Kirsch, 2015). The oxytocin receptor gene is a neuropeptide that contains many single-nucleotide polymorphisms (SNPs) with inconsistency in the effect of these variants on ASD. LoParo et al. revised data from eight studies evaluating 16 SNPs in oxytocin receptor using data from 3941 individuals with ASD from 11 independent samples and found significant associations between ASD and the SNPs rs7632287, rs237887, rs2268491, and rs2254298 (Loparo and Waldman, 2015). Another meta-analysis which also included data bases from Germany found an association with rs237889-A (Kranz et al., 2016). Studies on plasma oxytocin concentrations in children with ASD reported conflicting results, either lower levels (Modahl et al., 1998) or without significant difference to healthy controls (Taurines et al., 2014). Recently Francis et al showed association between OXT rs6084258 and ASD (Francis et al., 2016). Despite no difference between ASD children and controls, higher oxytocin blood levels were found in girls, and were associated with anxiety among the girls and less language impairment in the boys and girls of both groups (Miller et al., 2013). The validity of plasma oxytocin as a potential marker for brain levels was not evaluated among ASD patients, however, blood and CSF levels among non-psychiatric patients undergoing spinal anesthesia for minor procedures failed to show correlation between blood and CSF levels (Kagerbauer et al., 2013).

Oxytocin supplementation can be given either intravenously or intranasal with intranasal being superior due to its being well tolerated and easy to use. Reduction in repetitive behaviors (Hollander et al., 2003) and improved affective speech comprehension (Hollander et al., 2007) were found in ASD adults following oxytocin infusion. Studies evaluating ASD patients showed tasks improvement following a single dose (Aoki et al., 2015). However, some failed to show treatment effects (Althaus et al., 2015). Recent studies used continuous administration in order to evaluate treatment effects on daily life. Continuous intranasal administration over 6-weeks reduced autism core symptoms specific to social reciprocity among adults (Watanabe et al., 2015). Another study that failed to show improvement in social cognition and repetitive behaviors after 6 weeks of treatment found improvements in measures of social cognition and quality of life (Anagnostou et al., 2012). In a double-blind, randomized, placebo-controlled, crossover clinical trial, children with ASD at the age 3–8 years showed global improvement and significant improvement in caregiver-rated social responsiveness following a 5 week course of oxytocin (Yatawara et al., 2015).

The possible role of oxytocin in the etiology of ASD, and its potential use for the improvement of symptoms, is not yet understood and needs more studies.

MATERNAL DISEASES AND ASD IN THE OFFSPRING

Diabetes, several autoimmune diseases, infections and inflammatory diseases during pregnancy have been associated with an increased rate of ASD in the offspring. These diseases may apparently occur at any time during pregnancy.

ASD in Offspring of Diabetic Mothers

Diabetic pregnancies, both pregestational diabetes (PGD) and gestational diabetes (GD) are associated with a large number of pregnancy complications. While PGD may increase the rate of congenital anomalies in the offspring and affect fetal well-being and growth, GD is mainly associated with disturbed fetal growth and increased rate of a variety of pregnancy complications. Both PGD and GD are associated with slight disturbances in postnatal growth and development, also affecting fine and gross motor development and increasing the rate of learning difficulties and Attention Deficit Hyperactivity Disorder (Ornoy et al., 2001). Both also seem to be associated with a slight but significant increase in the rate of ASD in the offspring (Ornoy et al., 2015a).

Most, but not all studies on the possible association of maternal diabetes and ASD show an increased rate, and only recently is the type of diabetes in the mother (T1DM or T2DM or GDM) in relation to ASD in the offspring being considered. Lyall et al. (2012) assessed the possible association of maternal diabetes and ASD in 793 children with ASD from a cohort of 66,445 pregnancies. The highest association was found with maternal GD, as the OR of ASD among children born to mothers with GD was 1.76. This is in slight contrast to other studies which found that the risk for ASD is higher among offspring of mothers with PGD compared to mothers with GDM. Gardener et al. (2009) assessed the possible association of a variety of antenatal maternal factors with ASD in the offspring. Maternal diabetes was among the leading factors associated with ASD, with an odds ratio of 2.07 (95% CI 1.24–3.47). In a very recent study by Li et al. (2016) using the Boston Birth Cohort, both maternal diabetes and pregestational obesity were highly associated with ASD in the offspring. In mothers with PGD and obesity, the hazard ratio (HR) for ASD was 3.91 (95% CI 1.76–8.68) and in obesity and GD the HR was 3.04 (95% CI 1.21–7.63). As cohort and case-control studies are being published, there appears to be a more significant trend toward an association with ASD (Krakowiak et al., 2012). However, there are also studies that could not demonstrate such associations. For example, Hultman et al. (2002) in their case control study on 408 Swedish children with ASD compared to 2040 matched controls, found an association of ASD with a variety of pregnancy associated factors but not with maternal diabetes. Xiang et al. (2015) found in a recent study on pregnant women with preexisting type 2 diabetes. They found an adjusted odds ratio for ASD incidence in the offspring of only 1.21, that was insignificant, but in the offspring of women with GD diagnosed before the 26th week of pregnancy the HR was significant—1.42 (95% CI 1.15–1.74). Guinchat et al. (2012) in their review of 85 studies on the possible association between prenatal, perinatal and neonatal factors and ASD did not find a strong association of maternal diabetes and ASD. In contrast to this review, Xu et al. (2014) culled from 167 publications twelve; three cohort and nine case control studies. For the cohort studies, the pooled risk of maternal diabetes was 1.48 (1.25–1.75, $p < 0.001$), and for the case-control studies, the pooled odds ratio was 1.72 (1.24–2.41, $p = 0.001$). The OR for offspring of mothers with GD was generally lower than for that of mothers with PGD.

In a very recent study looking at the neuropsychiatric morbidity in offspring of 12,642 women with gestational diabetes compared to 218,629 non-diabetic women the investigators found an adjusted odds ratio of 4.4 (95% confidence interval: 1.55–12.69) for ASD. They examined children born during 1991–2014, and excluded prematurity, congenital anomalies, offspring of mothers with pregestational diabetes and other possible etiologic factors (Nahum Sacks et al., 2016).

The mechanism of the association between diabetes and ASD is largely unknown. We should remember that the increased risk found may be related to a variety of pregnancy complications that are common in diabetes, or to effects on fetal growth rather than to complications of hyperglycemia. Judging from the proposed mechanisms of the effects of maternal diabetes on the embryo and fetus, the increase in the rate of ASD in diabetic pregnancies may result from increased fetal oxidative stress, from epigenetic changes in the expression of several genes and it may also be related to the other neurodevelopmental changes induced by maternal diabetes (Ornoy et al., 2015b). It was shown repeatedly that good control of diabetes in pregnancy may reduce the different diabetic complications, but apparently will not completely prevent them. Hence, this is probably also the best way to reduce the diabetic—related ASD. There seem to be no studies relating the prevalence of ASD to the degree of diabetic control.

Maternal Autoimmune Diseases

In utero exposure to maternal antibodies and cytokines are known potential risk factors for ASD. Recent studies associated familial autoimmune diseases with the development of ASD. Most results come from cohort studies. However, due to the limited number of infants with ASD born to mothers with autoimmune diseases, many studies are small. Three Swedish registries including 1227 children with ASD [childhood autism, Asperger syndrome, or pervasive developmental disorder (PDD)] and 30,693 matched controls (25 controls for each case) evaluated linkage for 19 parental autoimmune disorders and found them weakly associated (maternal OR = 1.6, paternal OR = 1.4). A positive history of rheumatic fever was increased in both parents of ASD children, while type 1 diabetes, idiopathic thrombocytopenic purpura and myasthenia gravis were increased only among mothers (Keil et al., 2010). Out of 689,196 children born in Denmark from 1993 through 2004, a total of 3325 children were diagnosed with ASD. ASD diagnoses included infantile autism (1089 children), atypical autism, Asperger syndrome, and PDD. Children were evaluated for parental autoimmune diseases diagnosed before pregnancy. Increased ASD risk was found in offspring of families with type 1 diabetes, offspring of fathers with endocrine autoimmune diseases and mothers with rheumatoid arthritis and celiac disease. Thyrotoxicosis in the family and the mother, specifically, were related to lower risk of ASD (Atladottir et al., 2009).

Studies on the inter-relation of maternal autoimmune disorders with ASD also showed increased susceptibility to ASD among the offspring. A population-based cohort of 719 children born to 509 mothers with SLE, and a matched control group of 8493 children born to 5824 mothers without SLE found that children born to women with SLE had 1.4% recorded ASD diagnoses compared to 0.6% among the controls (OR 2.25). However, the numbers were small with 10 children of mothers with SLE and 53 children of controls. In addition to maternal SLE, other potential predictors of ASD in the adjusted multivariate analysis were gestational diabetes and male sex (Vinet et al., 2015). The association between maternal autoimmune thyroid disease and childhood autism was evaluated in 1.2 million singleton births with 1132 cases of childhood autism (not including Asperger disorder or PDD) in the Finnish cohort. The cases were matched 1:1 to comparison subjects drawn from the birth cohort who were without ASD. The odds of childhood autism were increased by nearly 80% among offspring of mothers who were positive for anti thyroperoxidase antibodies (TPO-Ab+) during pregnancy, compared to mothers negative for this autoantibody. The association was similar in males and females. There were no associations between maternal clinical or subclinical hypothyroidism or hyperthyroidism, maternal TSH or free T4 and autism (Brown et al., 2015). A follow-up study of 23 mothers with antiphospholipid syndrome (APLS) and their 36 children, and nine SLE mothers with 12 children revealed ASD in 3 children of the APLS mothers. Four children of the APLS mothers, of them the 3 ASD children had persistent anti-β2GP1 IgG antibodies. None of the offspring of the SLE mothers had either neurodevelopmental disorders or anti-β2GP1 IgG antibodies. The ASD cases born to mothers with APLS had normal birth weight, and normal genetic and metabolic work-up. Cerebral MRI performed at the ages of 2.5, 2.6, and 3.4 years were normal in two cases and revealed punctuate hyperintensities in the white matter of one case. None of the children had thrombosis or other antiphospholipid symptomatology (Abisror et al., 2013).

A prospective follow-up of a European multicenter cohort evaluated the long-term outcome and immunological status of children born to mothers with APLS at 3, 9, 24 months and 5 years. Of 134 children, four displayed behavioral abnormalities, which consisted with: autism (1), hyperactive behavior (1), feeding disorder with language delay (1), and axial hypotonicity with psychomotor delay (1). It is noteworthy that the mother of the ASD offspring also suffered from gestational diabetes (Mekinian et al., 2013).

Two large meta-analyses published lately found a significant increase in ASD prevalence among children born to parents with autoimmune diseases. Chen et al. evaluated nine case-control studies and one cohort study published from 1999 to 2015 and comprising of 9775 ASD cases born to mothers with autoimmune diseases and 952,211 controls. Of them, six studies reported a positive association while four did not reveal a substantially significant association. While evaluating the entire cohort they found that children of mothers with autoimmune diseases during pregnancy had a 30% greater risk of ASD. A positive association was identified between maternal autoimmune thyroid disease and ASD in the offspring. No significant difference was found for maternal SLE, inflammatory bowel disease, idiopathic thrombocytopenic purpura (ITP), psoriasis. and rheumatoid arthritis (Chen et al., 2016).

Wu et al evaluated the relationship between family history of autoimmune diseases and risk of ASD in children by a meta-analysis of 11 articles, including 3 cohort studies, 6 case-control studies. and 2 cross-sectional studies published up to Dec 2014. They found in the pooled analysis that family history of all autoimmune diseases combined was associated with a 28% higher risk of autism. Maternal autoimmune diseases were not associated with childhood autism and significant relative risks were only found in case-control studies. Type 1 diabetes in either of the parents, family history of rheumatoid arthritis, hypothyroidism, and psoriasis were significantly associated with higher risk of ASD in children (Wu et al., 2015).

In summary: there is insufficient data to associate maternal autoimmune diseases with increased rate of ASD. However, autoimmune diseases with specific IgG antibodies like TPO-Ab, or anti-β2GP1 that cross the placenta seem to increase significantly the rate of ASD in the offspring

Pre-Eclampsia

Preeclampsia may trigger aberrant neurodevelopment through placental, maternal, and fetal pathophysiologic mechanisms. Preeclampsia results from shallow placentation that may lead to fetal hypoperfusion. Association between pre-eclampsia and ASD was offered when brain MRI of 7–10 years old children (5 boys and 5 girls), offspring of pre-eclamptic pregnancies, revealed enlarged brain regional volumes in the cerebellum, temporal lobe, brain stem, and right and left amygdalae. These offspring also displayed reduced cerebral vessel radii in the occipital and parietal lobes. Enlarged left and right amygdalae were described in ASD and temporal lobe epilepsy (Ratsep et al., 2016).

Recent cohort studies suggested an association between pre-eclampsia and ASD. In the Swedish, population-based, case-control study that included 1216 subjects with autism who were born between 1987 and 2002 and 6080 controls, preeclampsia was associated with 50% increased risk of an autism spectrum disorder (Buchmayer et al., 2009). A recent study from the California Department of Developmental Services that compared 517 ASD cases to 350 controls found that pre-eclampsia complicated the pregnancy of children with ASD more than twice as often as those of controls and the association was more robust in those pregnancies complicated by severe disease (Walker et al., 2015). Two cohort data showed increased prevalence of ASD among pre-eclamptic pregnancies. Analysis of 87,677 births between 1996 and 2002, of the South Carolina Medicaid program, found greater odds of ASD with (OR = 1.69) or without (OR = 1.85) controlling for birth weight (Mann et al., 2010). Analysis of 218,890 singleton live births in Alberta, Canada, between 1998 and 2004 also found greater odds of ASD (OR = 1.49; Burstyn et al., 2010). Compared to these studies there was no association between pre-eclampsia and ASD among 28,967 children born between 1995 and 2008 in Aberdeen city and district (Love et al., 2012). A meta-analysis of 85 studies of pre-, peri,- and neonatal hazards related to PDD, including autism, concluded that there was not enough data in order to determine risk for PDD (Guinchat et al., 2012).

In conclusion: Preeclampsia seems to be an additional risk factor for ASD, but more studies are needed for the conclusive confirmation of such an association.

THE INFLAMMATORY AND INFECTIOUS ORIGIN OF ASD

Adverse intrauterine environment resulting from maternal bacterial and viral infections during pregnancy represent a significant risk factor for several neuropsychiatric disorders including ASD (Adams Waldorf and McAdams, 2013). The association between intrauterine inflammation, infection and ASD is based on both epidemiological studies and case reports.

Many studies associate maternal infection with ASD, and some studies even found that the season or month of birth was significantly related to the risk of ASD. For example, Gardener et al. (2011) found in a meta-analysis that March and August were both suggested as birth months associated with an elevated risk of ASD and hypothesized that a relationship may be caused by seasonal variation in viral or other infections.

Epidemiological Population Studies

An increased rate of ASD was found among children born to mothers that were hospitalized due to infection during pregnancy. Atladottir et al. (2010) matched the Danish Medical Birth Register of children born between 1980 and 2005, the Danish National Hospital Register and the cohort data in the Danish Psychiatric Central Register (1,612,342 children with 10,133 cases of ASD). They found that admission to hospital due to maternal viral infection in the first trimester of pregnancy increased the adjusted hazard ratio for ASD in the offspring by 2.98, and due to maternal bacterial infection in the second trimester by 1.42. No specific infectious category was associated with ASD in the offspring. Later, these authors (Atladottir et al., 2012) evaluated in the Danish cohort the association between self-reported maternal common infections and ASD among children born between years 1997–2003, and found that infection with influenza resulted in a hazard ratio of 2.3.

Lee et al. (2015) investigated the Swedish nationwide register-based birth cohort of children born in Sweden in 1984–2007 and followed until December 31, 2011. They found that 3.7% of ASD cases and 2.6% of non-ASD cases had mothers that were hospitalized with a diagnosis of infection during pregnancy. Maternal inpatient diagnosis of infection during pregnancy was associated with increased OR of ASD regardless of whether the infection was bacterial, viral, or other/unknown. The higher risk of ASD was observed during all trimesters: the 1st trimester (OR = 1.24), 2nd trimester (OR = 1.38), and 3rd trimester (OR = 1.36). In a subsample of the total Swedish population, the Stockholm Youth Cohort, the odds ratio for ASD with intellectual disability was 1.50, not related to the type of infection. Contradictory to these findings, Dodds et al. (2011) found that maternal infection during pregnancy did not increase the rate of ASD.

In a meta-analysis of 40 papers published until 2007 Gardener et al. (2009) evaluated the relationships between autism and pregnancy-related factors. Combined together there was no statistical increase in ASD except for maternal rubella with an OR of 1.66. However, when the analysis was limited to the four studies that controlled for multiple covariates or used sibling controls exposure to intra-uterine infections, a significant increase in risk for autism in OR was observed: 1.82 (1.01–3.30).

Case control studies comparing complications of pregnancy including maternal infection have also shown an association between viral maternal infections and ASD (Wilkerson et al., 2002). A similar association was found in women hospitalized during pregnancy due to bacterial infection (Zerbo et al., 2013). There were, however, case control studies that did not find any association of ASD with either maternal viral or bacterial infections (Langridge et al., 2013).

In summary: many but not all population or case control studies have shown a slight to moderate association of maternal infections with ASD. The controversy might be related to the fact that only several specific maternal infections (subgroups of women with infection during pregnancy) are associated with ASD. These are mainly Rubella, CMV and possibly influenza.

Congenital Rubella

The association between Rubella and ASD is based on few population studies and case reports. Berger et al. (2011) calculated that the rubella vaccination prevented an estimated number of congenital rubella cases that ranged from 8300 to 62,250 and that the corresponding ASD prevention estimates ranged from 614 to 4607 cases, depending on the infectious rate and prevalence of ASD among offspring of infected mothers. We should remember that at the time of the rubella epidemics, ASD definition was not the same as nowadays.

The largest study associating congenital rubella with ASD was reported in 1978 by Chess et al. (1978) who evaluated 243 children with congenital rubella, most of them followed until 9 years. Eighteen (7.4%) had autism compared to expected 0.07 (0.35/1000) in the general population at that time. All the children with autism also had other rubella associated anomalies including cardiac, neurologic, hearing and visual problems. Desmond et al. (1978) reported behavioral disturbances among 45% of *29* non-retarded children with congenital rubella at the age of 9–12 years. Carvill et al. (Carvill and Marston, 2002) described 12 young males with congenital Rubella who suffered from sensory imbalance and ASD. Associated morbidities included: visual and hearing impairment and seizures in three. Feldman et al. (1973) evaluated 12 children with autism or autistic traits and compared them with 25 children with a variety of psychiatric diagnoses, 21 children with language delay and 26 normal controls. None had a history of rubella. Sero-positivity for rubella was found to be significantly higher among the children with language delay, 8/21 and among children with autism, 3/12 compared to the other groups and the general population. All the mothers of the sero-positive children were sero-positive for rubella as well. Other reported cases of congenital rubella also described ASD children who suffered from hearing and visual impairment, iris hypoplasia, heart malformations, retinopathy, and seizures (Assumpcao and Kuczynski, 2002; Hwang and Chen, 2010).

CMV

The diagnosis of maternal CMV is based on medical history, serological studies for CMV or late diagnosis by preserved blood, mostly from Guthrie cards or dried umbilical cord. Koyano et al. (2004) and Sakamoto et al. (2015) used dried umbilical cords for retrospective diagnosis of congenital CMV infection in Japan where obstetric hospitals customarily provide dried umbilical cord to every parent as a symbol of the bond between mother and child.

Yamashita et al. studied seven children with congenital CMV, two of them had ASD. Neuroimaging studies did not vary between those who developed or did not develop autism when seven infants with congenital CMV were evaluated. Three had sub-ependymal cysts and two had calcifications. All had mental retardation (Yamashita et al., 2003).

When children with ASD were assessed, those seropositive for CMV tended to test worse in the major severity scales than the seronegative ones (Gentile et al., 2014). Additionally, Yamazaki et al. found that ASD cases with cochlear implants had lower language and social function than other children with corresponding developmental quotients (Yamazaki et al., 2012). Some studies showed that CMV DNA was detected among ASD cases in a higher prevalence than in the general population; however the numbers were small: 2/27 by Sakamoto et al. compared to incidence of ASD in Nagasaki which was 0.31%, $p = 0.004$ (Sakamoto et al., 2015); 3/76 by Stubbs et al. even though two had multifactorial prenatal causes for autism (Stubbs et al., 1984); 4/26 by Engman et al. with two of them also having cerebral cortical malformations (Engman et al., 2010). Townsend et al. (2013) evaluated 176 infants with congenital CMV born in Sweden and the United Kingdom between 1977 and 1986, and followed them until at least 5 years; none was diagnosed with ASD.

The role of individual placentas in the protection of the fetus against congenital CMV infection is exemplified by the different outcome in association with CMV stigmata, as described by Kitajima (Kitajima et al., 2012) in a triamniotic- trichorionic triplet born at 31 weeks after maternal febrile illness at 24 weeks. Two girls were asymptomatic; the third, a boy, had lower birth weight, increased IGM titer, thrombocytopenia, hepatosplenomegaly, retinitis, brain calcifications, and suffered from ASD. The triamniotic- trichorionic placentas had no fusion or structural abnormalities. Examination of the placenta of the third-born triplet showed that it was paler than the other two and had more severe villitis.

Other reported cases of ASD and congenital CMV also had associated anomalies including brain calcifications and chorioretinitis (Stubbs, 1978; Stubbs et al., 1984; Ivarsson et al., 1990; Sweeten et al., 2004; Lopez-Pison et al., 2005; Ikeda et al., 2006; Kawatani et al., 2010; Dogan et al., 2011).

In summary: There seem to be sufficient studies to associate maternal CMV infection in pregnancy to an increased rate of ASD in the offspring, especially in the children who suffer from other brain manifestations of congenital CMV.

Influenza

Studies associating maternal influenza and ASD are based on maternal reports. As stated above, Atladottir et al. (2012) found self-reported maternal infection with influenza to be associated with increased risk for infantile autism (adjusted HR: 2.3 [95% CI: 1.0–5.3]). The highest association was found with prolonged episodes of fever.

Zerbo et al. (2013) in a telephone interview, evaluated cases and controls in the Childhood Autism Risk from Genetics and Environment (CHARGE) Study. While comparing data from 538 children with ASD and 421 normal controls in association with maternal influenza during pregnancy, they found that the weighted odds ratio (wOR) between mothers of ASD children and those of children with normal development was 1.26. When they analyzed the association between fever and ASD, the odds ratio for mothers of children with ASD and fever during pregnancy doubled that of mothers of normal controls (wOR = 2.12). They also found that the wOR for ASD was 2.55, for children whose mothers reported fever but did not take anti-pyretic medication. For women who reported fever and took anti-pyretic medications, the wOR for ASD was only 1.30. Hence, if there is an association, it is weak, and apparently due to fever.

Inflammation

Maternal immune activation and cytokine dysregulation was also shown to be a mediator in the neuro-pathological behavior observed in autism. Maternal immune system and animal models were used to evaluate the role of cytokines in brain dysregulation together with *in-vitro* studies that evaluated the association between inflammatory mediators and neurological components.

Studies Evaluating Maternal Immune System

Increased levels of inflammatory mediators obtained from stored samples were found in large population studies. Abdallah et al. (2012, 2013) used a pool of samples from more than 100,000 pregnant women in Denmark and had their biologic samples stored from 1980 to 2004, and matched 421 singleton ASD cases born between 1982 and 2000 for gender and birth year with 820 controls. Levels of Monocyte Chemotactic Protein-1 (MCP-1) which play a role in the maturation of cerebellar Purkinje cells and may serve as a useful marker of abnormal neuronal development, were significantly elevated among ASD cases compared to controls. Using the same cohort amniotic fluid they found that samples from 331 ASD cases compared to 698 controls, had significantly elevated levels of IL-4, IL-10, TNF-α, and TNF- β. Goines et al. (2011) also found Increased levels of IL-4, IL-5, and IFN-gamma in banked serum collected from women at 15–19 weeks of gestation who gave birth to a child ultimately diagnosed with ASD ($n = 84$). Grether et al. (2010) found by examining screening filter paper blood specimens from the California Genetic Disease Screening Program of 213 ASD cases and 265 controls that children with ASD had lower total IgG and that the median value, for Herpes Simplex type 1 Virus IgG was significantly lower compared to controls.

Braunschweig et al. (2008) found reactivity to two protein bands against fetal brain at approximately 73kDa and 37kDa in plasma from 7 of 61 (11.5%) mothers of children with autism. These bands were not found in controls. These children also showed behavioral regression. It is assumed that the presence of specific anti-fetal brain antibodies in the circulation of mothers during pregnancy is a potential trigger to induce a downstream effect on neurodevelopment that may lead to autism. Mazina et al. (2015) investigated the gene-environment interaction by evaluating the interactive effects of maternal infection in pregnancy and the presence of copy number variants which are considered likely to play a contributing role in symptoms of ASD. Participants included 1971 children with ASD between the ages of 4 and 18 years with complete genetic, maternal pregnancy history, and phenotypic information. A statistically significant interactive effect of the presence of copy number variants and maternal infection on autistic symptomatology was observed.

C reactive protein (CRP) is an inflammatory marker that rises in response to infection or inflammation. Analysis of early gestational CRP levels in maternal sera and childhood autism in the Finish birth cohort (consisting of 1.2 million births from 1987-2007) revealed that increased maternal CRP levels were significantly associated with autism in the offspring (OR = 1.12). The increased risk was found in both sexes (Brown et al., 2014). Contradictory to these results, no association between maternal CRP blood levels during the first trimester of pregnancy and ASD in their offspring (children evaluated at 6 years) was found among 4165 pregnant women in Rotterdam that gave birth between 2002 and 2006 (Koks et al., 2016).

In Conclusion

In children affected by intrauterine infections with rubella or CMV, the association with ASD seems to result from the insult to the nervous system, as all also had other neurological problems as well as visual and hearing impairment, suggesting that ASD is secondary to the primary morbidity. Large population studies did not find a specific maternal infection to be associated with ASD, implying that the association between maternal infection during pregnancy and ASD is apparently related to maternal inflammatory process; hence, maternal immune activation may play a role in neuro-developmental perturbation.

EXPOSURE TO DRUGS AND CHEMICALS DURING PREGNANCY AND ASD IN THE OFFSPRING

Several drugs and chemicals have been associated with an increased rate of ASD following intrauterine exposure. However, the association was clearly demonstrated only in few drugs. In others, there are either few reports, or the existing literature is contradictory.

Exposure to SSRI's

Selective serotonin reuptake inhibitors (SSRIs) are among the most used drugs for the treatment of depression especially during pregnancy (Evans et al., 2001; Pereira et al., 2009). They increase extracellular serotonin and are recommended for first-line pharmacological management of depression because they are considered safer and better tolerated than other types of antidepressants. SSRIs and other antidepressant medications cross the placenta and are secreted in breast milk, thus raising concerns about possible adverse effects from fetal and infant exposure. Several studies show a possible association between SSRIs exposure during pregnancy and a higher risk of ASD in children (Croen et al., 2011b; Rai et al., 2013; Gidaya et al., 2014; Harrington et al., 2014). Three out of six recently published case-control studies reported a significantly positive association between SSRI exposure during pregnancy and ASD in children. Odds ratio in the different studies ranged from 2.2 (Croen et al., 2011b) with the strongest effect associated with treatment during the first trimester of pregnancy (OR, 3.8)—to 2.34 (Rai et al., 2013) and the highest was 2.91(Harrington et al., 2014). They found that the strongest association was following exposure in the first trimester of pregnancy. In addition, Gidaya et al. (2014) studied in Denmark a group of 5215 children diagnosed with ASD and 52,150 controls, all born between 1997 and 2006. The OR for ASD doubled among the children born to mothers who used SSRIs at any time during pregnancy.

Recently published large population based retrospective study by Boukhris et al. (2016) reported a significant association between maternal use of SSRI's during pregnancy and the risk of ASD in children. The study included 145,456 children born in Quebec, Canada from 1998 to 2009, of which1054 (0.72%) had at least one diagnosis of ASD. The authors reported that use of antidepressants during the second and/or third trimester was associated with the risk of ASD (31 exposed infants; adjusted hazard ratio, 1.87; 95% CI, 1.15–3.04). Stronger association was found if the mother used SSRI's antidepressants (22 exposed infants; adjusted hazard ratio, 2.17; 95% CI, 1.20–3.93) or used more than one class of antidepressants (5 exposed infants; adjusted HR, 4.39; 95% CI, 1.44–13.32). The risk was persistent even after taking into account maternal history of depression (29 exposed infants; adjusted hazard ratio, 1.75; 95% CI, 1.03–2.97). The use of other antidepressants during the first trimester or the year before pregnancy was not associated with the risk of ASD.

In contrast to these studies, Hviid et al. (2013) found no connection between the use of SSRIs during pregnancy and the increased risk for ASD (OR, 1.20; 95%CI, 0.90–1.61). Similarly, Sorensen et al. (2013) found that children who were exposed to SSRIs during pregnancy have indeed a 50% higher risk for ASD compared with unexposed children, but after controlling for important confounding factors such as maternal history of affective disorder and familial risk factors, they did not detect any significant association between maternal use of SSRI's during pregnancy and ASD in the offspring. Both researchers used data from the Danish civil registration system and Danish health registry systems about children who were born in Denmark between 1.1.96 and 31.12.2005 (Hviid) and until 31.12.2006 (Sorensen). The latest cohort study by Malm et al. from Finland (Malm et al., 2016) examined the rate of ASD among the offspring of 15,729 pregnant women exposed to SSRIs during pregnancy compared to 9651 women with psychiatric disease but no antidepressant treatment and 31,394 non-exposed women and without psychiatric disease. They did not find any increase in the rate of ASD among the SSRIs exposed children, as the rates of ASD were similar to the rate observed in the offspring of mothers with a psychiatric disorder but without treatment. The main finding in this study was an increase in the rate of depression in the SSRI exposed children at adolescence.

In summary: It is still unclear whether there is a direct association between the use of SSRIs during pregnancy and increased rate of ASD in the offspring. Alongside studies which show an association with ASD there are also negative studies. Of special importance is the recent negative study by Malm et al. (2016) as it examined the largest population of SSRI exposed children and adequately adjusted for confounders. It seems more reasonable that maternal depression itself, which is expressed by the use of antidepressants, or other causes, might be responsible for the association. Medical treatment during pregnancy of women with depression should apparently continue in spite of these, rather conflicting studies.

Exposure to Paracetamol

Several studies suggested a possible association between maternal use of paracetamol during pregnancy and a higher risk of ASD among the children. Bauer et al. (Bauer and Kriebel, 2013) examined the association between maternal paracetamol usage or early life paracetamol exposure in males and the prevalence of ASD. They reported positive correlations between ASD prevalence and indicators of both prenatal ($r = 0.80$) and very early life ($r = 0.98$) paracetamol exposures. Liew et al. (2015) followed 64,322 children and mothers enrolled in the Danish National Birth Cohort. They reported that maternal use of paracetamol in pregnancy was associated with ASD with hyperkinetic symptoms only (HR = 1.51 95% CI 1.19–1.92), but not with other types of ASD (HR = 1.06 95% CI 0.92–1.24). More than half of pregnant women in the USA and Europe report using paracetamol and it is the most common drug administered to children; as a result it is difficult to connect between these exposure and ASD). It is obvious that the data is insufficient to draw any conclusion from these studies.

Exposure to β2-Adrenergic Receptor Agonists

Connors et al. (2005) was the first to examine the effects of prenatal overstimulation of the beta2-adrenergic receptor (B2AR), in 37 dizygotic pair of ASD twins who were exposed to terbutaline, a B2AR agonists, commonly prescribed to treat asthma and other pulmonary disorders and to delay preterm labors. They found increased concordance for autism spectrum disorders in dizygotic twins (relative risk = 2.0), with a further increase in the risk for male twins with no other affected siblings (relative risk = 4.4) related to terbutaline exposure overall.

Croen et al. (2011a) examined maternal use of B2AR agonists during pregnancy among 291 children with and 284 without ASD. No evidence linking B2AR exposure during pregnancy with ASD risk was found. However, they reported that exposure to terbutaline only during the third trimester for more than 2 days may be associated with an increased risk of ASD.

A new case control study by Gidaya et al. (2016) investigated the associations between prenatal use of B2AR agonist drugs and the risk for ASD. They studied 5200 ASD diagnosed cases and 52,000 controls from the Denmark's health and population register. The frequency of B2AR agonist drug exposure in pregnancy was 3.7% (190) for cases and 2.9% (1489) in controls. B2AR agonist use during pregnancy was associated with increased risk of ASD, even after adjustment for maternal asthma and other covariates (OR: 1.3, 95% CI: 1.1–1.5). There was no difference regarding the trimesters of pregnancy during exposure.

Exposure to Valproic Acid

Antiepileptic drugs are among the most common teratogens prescribed to women of childbearing age, especially as some of them are also used for psychiatric indications and pain management. Prenatal exposure to antiepileptic drugs (AEDs) is associated with an increased risk of major congenital malformations and delayed cognitive development among the offspring, in a dose dependent manner (Meador et al., 2007; Tomson et al., 2011). Valporic acid (VPA), apparently the most teratogenic AED (Werler et al., 2011), was also found to be associated with impaired cognitive outcomes (Meador et al., 2009). Many reports demonstrate that prenatal exposure to VPA is also associated with a high risk for ASD in the prenatally exposed child in addition to other neurodevelopmental disorders, especially in language development (Moore et al., 2000; Williams et al., 2001; Rasalam et al., 2005; Bromley et al., 2008).

Christianson et al. (1994) were apparently the first to point to of a possible association between intrauterine exposure to VPA and ASD, as observed in four children exposed to VPA during pregnancy. All children had developmental delay and one of them had ASD.

Several years later, Williams et al. (2001) examined five children with ASD and found that VPA was used during pregnancy in all five, but in three in combination with another anticonvulsant. Moore et al. (2000) found among 57 children affected by antiepileptic drugs that four had autistic syndrome and two had Asperger syndrome. Five of them (10.8% of 46 exposed to VPA) were exposed to VPA alone or combined with another AED. Rasalam et al. (2005) evaluated the clinical features and frequency of autistic disorder or Asperger syndrome in 260 children exposed to anticonvulsant medication during pregnancy, by using the DSM IV criteria. They found that VPA was the drug most commonly associated with autistic disorder. The prevalence of ASD in children exposed to VPA alone was 8.9 and 11.7%, among children exposed to sodium valproate in combination with other AEDs. Bromley et al. (2008) examined 296 children of epileptic mothers and 336 children born to mothers without epilepsy. Out of the 632 children from both groups 10 have been diagnosed with ASD, 7 of them were exposed to AEDs. Of those seven children, four were exposed to VPA monotherapy (4/64 6.3%). In addition to these prospective studies, several large retrospective studies have also supported the findings that *in utero* VPA exposure may be linked to an increased risk of ASD (Ornoy, 2009).

Christensen et al. (2013) in a much larger Danish population-based study reviewed the National Population Register with prescription data, psychiatric register and birth records. Records were collated for 655,615 eligible children, with 508 exposed to VPA and 2136 to other anticonvulsants. An increased risk of ASD (Hazard Ratio-HR = 2.9, 95% CI, 1.7–4.9) was found in children exposed to VPA during pregnancy. The risk of ASD was elevated compared to non-exposure when VPA was taken in the first trimester of pregnancy or after the first trimester.

Animal models in rodents using different neurobehavioral measures fully support the human data. Exposure of mice and rats to VPA produced autism-like behaviors in the offspring (Schneider and Przewlocki, 2005; Wagner et al., 2006). Maternal exposure to VPA induced developmental delay, lifelong deficits in social behavior as well as motor deficits, anxiety-like behavior and alterations in postnatal growth and development in the offspring (Schneider and Przewlocki, 2005; Kolozsi et al., 2009; Bambini-Junior et al., 2011). As in humans, anatomical alterations such as reduced number of cerebellar Purkinje cells, damage to cranial nerve nuclei have been described (Rodier et al., 1997; Ingram et al., 2000) as well as enhanced synaptic plasticity of the prefrontal cortex (Sui and Chen, 2012).

In summary: VPA seems to be the drug with the highest association to ASD as proven in human and animal models and should therefore not be used as a first-line antiepileptic drug in pregnant women or in those who plan pregnancy. Similarly, it should not be used as a mood stabilizer for the treatment of psychiatric patients.

Exposure to Thalidomide

Thalidomide is a well-known human teratogen that caused multiple birth defects including limb reduction defects, ocular and cardiovascular anomalies. Thalidomide is still used in the treatment of leprosy and multiple myeloma (Ito et al., 2010). Stromland et al. (1994) have reported increased number of incidences of autism in children exposed prenatally to thalidomide. At least four of the 100 thalidomide embryopathy patients met full criteria for DSM III R autistic disorder- much higher prevalence then in the general population. The critical window of exposure to thalidomide was in the first trimester, mainly days 20–35 post fertilization. Because thalidomide is generally used in elder patients, no newer data was published regarding this possible effect, making it difficult to accept or deny this possible association, or to calculate the relative risk.

Exposure to Cocaine

Cocaine use during pregnancy has many deleterious effects on both the mother and the fetus, (Singer et al., 1993; Fox, 1994). Cocaine, which is used nowadays mainly as a recreational drug crosses the placenta and the fetal blood-brain barrier readily, and may affect the fetal central nervous system (Roe et al., 1990). Its use during pregnancy may have a variety of deleterious effects on the fetus including preterm delivery, intrauterine growth retardation, placental abruption, stillbirth, and neonatal death (Singer et al., 1993; Fox, 1994). Several studies reported a possible association between the use of cocaine during pregnancy and the development of ASD in the offspring.

Davis et al. (1992) examined 70 children with a history of prenatal cocaine exposure, in Harlem, New-York and found that nine of the children met the DMS III R criteria for autistic disorder—11.4%, much higher than the national average at that time. Harris et al. (1995) examined three, 25–36 month old children with prenatal exposure to cocaine, alcohol and other illicit drugs. They reported that all three children showed a notable pattern of autistic-like behaviors.

We could not find other studies associating prenatal cocaine exposure with ASD. Hence, judging from the paucity of studies, in spite of relatively high use, there seems to be insufficient data to support such association. Hence, the relative risk could not be calculated.

Exposure to Ethanol

Fetal alcohol syndrome (FAS) is a pattern of physical and neurodevelopmental abnormalities which develop in some of the children who were exposed to high levels of alcohol during pregnancy. It is characterized by prenatal and postnatal growth deficiency, CNS dysfunction including mental retardation and behavioral abnormalities, a distinctive pattern of facial features and major malformations of several organs. Some studies have shown a connection between FAS and an increased risk of ASD.

Nanson (1992) described six children aged 6–15 years, out of a data base of 326 FAS individuals who showed the physical phenotype of FAS and also presented a behavioral phenotype typical of autism spectrum disorder. The children also suffered from significant retardation of their cognitive and social skills. These data is representing an incidence of ASD in 1 of 54 cases of FAS.

Aronson et al. (1997) found that among 24 children born to mothers who used high doses of alcohol during pregnancy, two had Asperger syndrome and one had autistic-like behavior. There was a clear correlation between the occurrence and severity of ASD and the degree of alcohol exposure *in utero*. Landgren et al. (2010) assessed 71 children adopted from Eastern Europe between 4.8 and 10.5 years of age and found fetal alcohol syndrome in 37 of the children (52%) and autism in 6 of the children (9%), suggesting a positive association between prenatal alcohol consumption and ASD.

The association between maternal alcohol consumption in pregnancy and ASD does not seem to exist with low alcohol intake. In a large population-based cohort study Eliasen et al. (2010) evaluated a total of 80,522 mother-child pairs. Almost half of the women reported an average weekly intake of at least half a standard alcoholic drink (45%), and approximately one-quarter of the women reported at least one episode of binge drinking during pregnancy. They found no positive associations between ASD and average alcohol consumption or number of binge drinking episodes during pregnancy Adjusted hazard ratio for alcohol consumption of 0.5–1.5 glasses of wine per week (119 cases) = 0.84, 95% CI: 0.68–1.05; adjusted hazard ratio for single binge drinking episode (51 cases) = 0.72, 95% CI: 0.53–0.97.

In summary: Although the existing data of the association between high amounts of alcohol consumption in pregnancy and the risk for ASD in children (especially those with FAS) is well established, the relation to lower amounts ingested is not yet established.

Exposure to Misoprostol and Moebius Sequence

Misoprostol is a prostaglandin analog drug widely used to induce medical abortions (Gonzalez et al., 1998). It is also often prescribed for the prevention and treatment of gastric ulcers. Möbius sequence is a rare congenital disorder, characterized by uni-or bilateral eye-face palsy due to damage to cranial nerve nuclei, associated with muscle or skeletal malformations in the upper or lower limbs, with an estimated prevalence of 1:50,000 cases in the general population (Stromland et al., 2002; Verzijl et al., 2003). Among the etiological factors responsible for Möbius sequence, apart from genetic causes, is also intrauterine exposure to teratogens mainly misoprostol (Bandim et al., 2003; Vauzelle et al., 2013). Judging from the literature, it is expected that about 1% of children exposed *in utero* to misoprostol will have Möbius sequence (Gonzalez et al., 1993; Marques-Dias et al., 2003).

Johansson et al. (2001)analyzed 25 Swedish individuals with Möbius sequence. Six patients met all diagnostic DSM III R criteria for autism which is a much higher frequency than that of the general population. These findings suggest a strong association between Möbius sequence and ASD. All these patients also had mental retardation.

Bandim et al. (2003) examined 23 Brazilian patients with the age range of 1–11 years, which had been diagnosed as having Möbius sequence based on clinical findings. They identified seven children with ASD of whom four (57.1%) had a positive history of prenatal exposure to misoprostol during the first trimester of pregnancy. They concluded that the prevalence of ASD found in Möbius patients is around 26.1%, much higher than the general population, thus suggesting a strong association linking the two pathologies.

The correlation between misoprostol exposure during pregnancy and ASD is suggested on the basis of reports published in the literature. However, since most, if not all affected children also had Mobius syndrome, it is difficult to directly associate misoprostol exposure to ASD. We found no reports on an association of ASD to misoprostol exposure in exposed children that do not present the symptoms of Moebius syndrome. It should be remembered that the experimental models of VPA—induced ASD in rats and mice have also caused damage to the cranial nerve nuclei, similar to the damage observed in Mobius syndrome (Rodier et al., 1997; Ingram et al., 2000; Sui and Chen, 2012). Hence, it is possible that the relation of misoprostol—induced Mobius syndrome to ASD is not a result of the direct effects of misoprostol but rather from the damage to the cranial nerve nuclei.

Folic Acid Deficiency

Folic acid deficiency is associated with a variety of adverse outcomes in the offspring, especially Neural Tube Defects (NTD). Folic acid deficiency was therefore also proposed as a possible risk factor for ASD.

Schmidt et al. were the first to report that mothers of children with autism were less likely, than those of typically developing children, to report having taken prenatal vitamins, including folic acid, during the 3 months before pregnancy or the first month of pregnancy (OR, 0.62; 95% CI, 0.42–0.93). Later, Schmidt et al. (2012) examined the effect of maternal folic acid intake on the ASD risk in a group of 429 children with ASD and 278 normal children and found that mothers of normal children had a significantly greater mean folic acid intake during the first month of pregnancy compared to mothers of children with ASD. A mean daily folic acid intake of ≥600 μg during the first month of pregnancy was associated with reduced ASD risk (OR, 0.62), and risk estimates decreased with increased folic acid (P-trend = 0.001). The association between folic acid and reduced ASD risk was strongest for mothers and children with MTHFR 677 C > T variant genotypes.

In a prospective Norwegian cohort study, Surén et al. (2013) followed up 85,176 children of whom 270 had been diagnosed with ASD and found a significantly higher rate of Autism in children who were not exposed *in utero* to folic acid (0.21%) compared to children of mothers who took 400 μg or more folic acid (0.10%) during a month before and 2 month after the start of pregnancy (OR, 0.6).

Recently, DeVilbiss et al. (2015) summarized the existing literature regarding folic acid deficiency and ASD and discussed the limitations of the different studies. He concluded that the data associating Folate deficiency with a higher risk of autism is yet inconclusive. Hence, it is obvious that more studies are needed to elucidate the possible association of maternal folic acid deficiency with ASD.

EXPOSURE TO HIGH LEVELS OF ENVIRONMENTAL AGENTS

Exposure to Air Pollution

Increased air pollution is one of the more common signs of our modern life, and its possible effects on health are extensively investigated. In spite of great difficulties in measuring the extent of air pollution and the elucidation the large number of possible confounding factors, more and more studies are being published associating heavy air pollution to ASD.

The first study was apparently conducted in San Francisco Bay area in 2006 by Windham et al. (2006). They examined the effects of prenatal exposure to 19 hazardous air pollutants in 284 children with ASD compared to 657 controls. Elevated risk for ASD was found in adjusted analyses of the top quartile of exposure to chlorinated solvents and heavy metals [95% CI, 1.1–2.1]. In this study, however, the exposure was estimated 2 years after birth when ASD diagnosis was established. Hence the effects might be attributed to postnatal effects of these pollutants.

Kalkbrenner et al. (2010) examined prenatal exposure to 35 hazardous air pollutants in 383 children with ASD and 2829 control children with speech and language impairment. They found that prenatal exposure to hazardous air pollutants including methylene chloride (OR, 1.4; 95% CI, 0.7–2.5), quinoline (OR, 1.4; 95% CI, 1.0–2.2), and styrene (OR, 1.8; 95% CI, 1.0–3.1) were associated with a higher risk for ASD.

Volk et al. (2011) investigated the association between ASD and proximity of residence to freeways and major roadways during pregnancy and near the time of delivery, in a group of 304 children with ASD and 259 controls. They found that maternal residence during the third trimester (OR, 2.22; 95% CI, 1.16–4.42) and at the time of delivery (OR, 1.86; 95%CI, 1.04–3.45) were more likely to be near a freeway (≤309 m) for the ASD children than for the controls. They also found (Volk et al., 2013) in an additional study that, during gestation, children with

ASD were more likely to live at residencies that had the highest quartile of exposure to traffic-related air pollution (OR, 1.98; 95% CI, 1.20–3.31) compared with control children. Regional exposure during pregnancy with nitrogen dioxide and particulate matter <2.5 and 10 μm in diameter (PM2.5 and PM10) were also associated with autism.

Similarly, Becerra et al. (2013) studied the influence of exposures to traffic-related air pollution during pregnancy on the occurrence of ASD with controls matched by sex, birth year, and gestational age. They found a small but significant 12–15% relative increase, per interquartile range, in odds of autism for ozone (OR, 1.12, 95% CI: 1.06–1.19; per 11.54-ppb increase) and particulate matter ≤2.5 μm when mutually adjusting for both pollutants.

Roberts et al. (2013) estimated the association between levels of hazardous air pollutants at the time and place of birth and ASD in 325 children with ASD and 22,101 controls. Prenatal exposures to the highest quintile of air pollutants, such as diesel, lead, manganese, mercury, and methylene chloride, were significantly associated with ASD, with odds ratios ranging from 1.5 (for overall metals measure) to 2.0 (for diesel and mercury). For most pollutants, associations were stronger for boys (279 cases) than for girls (46 cases) suggesting a significant gender difference.

Raz et al. (2015a) examined the association between maternal exposure to particulate matter (PM) air pollution during pregnancy and the risk of ASD compared to controls. They found that PM2.5 exposure during pregnancy was associated with increased risk of ASD, with an adjusted odds ratio for ASD per interquartile range of 1.57 (95% CI: 1.22, 2.03). The association between ASD and PM2.5 was stronger for exposure during the third trimester (OR, 1.42 per inter-quartile range increase in PM2.5, 95% CI, 1.09–1.86).

In a recent, population based case–control study in Pennsylvania, Talbott et al. (2015) found that living in areas with higher ambient levels of styrene and chromium during pregnancy and the first and second years of life is associated with increased risk of ASD with borderline effects for polycyclic aromatic hydrocarbons (PAHs) and methylene chloride.

In contrast to these studies mostly carried out in the United States, showing a consistently positive association between exposure to several air pollutants during pregnancy and diagnosis of ASD, a much larger, recently published analysis of four European population-based cohorts appears to contradict those findings, reporting no associations between ASD and prenatal air pollution exposure (Guxens et al., 2016).

This research compared between nitrogen oxides and various sizes of particulate matter concentrations at the participants' birth home addresses during pregnancy and the presence of autistic traits, but not formal diagnoses of ASD, in more than 8000 children. No associations were found between the presence of autistic traits and prenatal exposure to any of the air pollutants (odds ratio = 0.94; 95% CI: 0.81, 1.10 per each 10-μg/m3 increase in NO2 pregnancy levels). The researchers explained the contradictory findings by the fact that previous case–control studies selected children with a diagnosis of ASD, whereas this study examined children with autistic traits from population-based birth/child cohorts. An alternative explanation could be the possible differences in air pollution levels and sources.

It can therefore be concluded that air pollution might be a contributing factor in the risk for ASD, but the data is as yet inconclusive.

In summary: these case control studies suggest that there is a positive association between maternal exposure to air pollution during pregnancy and ASD in children, especially following exposure in the third trimester. Although small PM may cross the placenta, there might also be other factors in the air pollutants that are associated and were not measured.

Exposure to Pesticides

Few studies have examined the effects of *in utero* exposure to pesticides such as organophosphates and carbamates on the neurobehavioral development and the risk of ASD in children. Each study reported an association with ASD.

Roberts et al. (2007) examined the association between maternal residence near agricultural pesticide applications during key periods of gestation and ASD in children. They reported that ASD risk was higher in children whose mothers lived near agricultural applications of organochlorines during the first trimester of pregnancy (OR 6.1) and decreased with increasing distance from such fields.

Shelton et al. (2014) evaluated whether residential proximity to agricultural areas and therefore increased exposures to pesticides during pregnancy is associated with ASD. They found that residence near organophosphates at some point during gestation was associated with a 60% increased risk for ASD, higher for third-trimester exposures (OR, 2.0), and second-trimester chlorpyrifos applications (OR, 3.3). Also, children of mothers residing near pyrethroid insecticide applications just before conception or during the third trimester were at greater risk for ASD with ORs ranging from 1.7 to 2.0. We can summarize that due to the paucity of studies in spite of extensive use, an association between ASD and pesticides is plausible, but it was not yet established.

Exposure to Heavy Metals

Maternal exposure to heavy metals, such as mercury, lead, and cadmium, has been suggested to be associated with neurodevelopmental disorders including mental retardation, inattention, learning difficulties, and possibly ASD (Mendola et al., 2002). Although there is more data on mercury, most available data suggests that maternal exposure to mercury does not play an important role in the development of ASD. Moreover, several of the studies were carried out on the affected children and not on their mothers, hence making the association with pregnancy an unproven possibility (Kern et al., 2007). In that respect we should add that Kern et al. (2007) found that sulfhydryl reactive metals: arsenic, cadmium, and lead were reduced in the hair of 45 children with ASD compared to controls. They suggested that the children with ASD have a problem in secreting these sulfhydryl reactive metals and their accumulation may contribute to the symptoms of ASD.

Geier et al. (2009) examined the association between maternal dental amalgams (containing 50% mercury) and the severity of ASD diagnosis in a group of 100 autistic children. They found that a rise in autism severity correlated with an elevation in the number of dental amalgams in the mother during pregnancy.

However, Yau et al. (2014) investigated the association between ASD and levels of total mercury measured in maternal serum from mid-pregnancy and infant blood shortly after birth in 84 children with ASD and 159 control children. They found no significant associations between ASD and mercury levels in maternal serum samples (OR, 0.96; 95% CI, 0.49–1.90) or in newborn blood samples (OR, 1.18; 95% CI, 0.71–1.95).

Van Wijngaarden et al. (2013) examined prenatal exposure to methyl mercury in 1784 children and young adults, by measuring maternal hair samples collected at or near the time of birth. They found no significant association between ASD and prenatal methyl mercury exposure.

It can therefore be concluded that there in insufficient data to associate prenatal exposure to heavy metals, especially mercury, to a higher occurrence of ASD in the offspring.

Exposure to Cigarette Smoking

Heavy maternal cigarette smoking during pregnancy is associated with an increased rate of spontaneous abortions, preterm delivery, reduced birth weight, immune system difficulties such as asthma and allergies and a relatively high rate of learning disabilities and attention deficit disorders later in life (Castles et al., 1999; Stene-Larsen et al., 2009; Kiechl-Kohlendorfer et al., 2010). Several studies have examined whether prenatal exposure to heavy tobacco smoke is also associated with ASD, and the findings are inconsistent. Hultman et al. (2002) and Larsson et al. (2009) found a mild association between smoking during pregnancy and the risk of childhood autism (OR, 1.4 and 2.09, respectively).

Kalkbrenner et al. (2012) assessed the association between maternal smoking during pregnancy and ASD among 3315 children with ASD and 630,674 control children at 8 years of age. A slightly positive association (OR 1.26) was found only for "ASD not otherwise specified" (ASD-NOS), which disappeared after correcting for possible confounding factors. Similarly Tran et al. (2013) examined 4019 ASD cases and 16, 123 controls, in a nested case-control study based on the Finnish Prenatal Study of Autism (FIPS-A) and found no connection between maternal smoking and childhood autism or Asperger syndrome, but found a slight association with PDD (OR, 1.2, 95% CI, 1.0- 1.5).

Other large studies also did not find any association between tobacco exposure and ASD. In a large registry based Swedish case-control study, that included 3958 ASD cases and 38,983 controls, Lee et al. (2012) found that maternal smoking during pregnancy is not associated with increased risk of ASD after adjustments for parental education, occupation, and income.

Several additional studies (Maimburg and Vaeth, 2006; Burstyn et al., 2010) and two recently published meta-analyses by Rosen et al. (2015) and Tang et al. (2015), also reported no significant association between maternal smoking during pregnancy and ASD.

It can be summarized maternal smoking does not increase the rate of ASD in the offspring.

CONCLUSIONS

The observed increase in the incidence of ASD in the last decades is considered to result directly from changes in definitions and better ascertainment. However, it is also possible that it reflects a real increase in the occurrence of ASD. In addition to well-defined genetic causes for ASD, examples of which we discussed in this review, the current search for prenatal environmental etiologic factors demonstrated real associations with a number of causes that may affect the developing fetal brain raising the vulnerability for ASD. Based on the findings reviewed here, we may conclude—with caution—that: (1) A possible association exists with maternal influenza in pregnancy, exposure to pesticides and insecticides, exposure to misoprostol, thalidomide, cocaine, SSRIs, or folic acid deficiency. (2) A probable association was found for maternal fever, autoimmune diseases, diabetes, preeclampsia, and exposure to heavy air pollution. (3) A definite association of ASD with maternal Rubella and CMV infections in pregnancy, maternal inflammation and immune activation, or exposure in pregnancy to VPA, and high levels of ethanol. (4) Although sometimes suggested, there seems to be sufficient evidence that there is no association with ASD for many maternal infections in pregnancy (i.e., herpes viruses, Epstein Barr virus, varicella—zoster virus, parvovirus), smoking, exposure to heavy metals or vitamin D deficiency.

Despite the increasing efforts in recent years, and support from animal studies, we still seem to be in a stage where the etiology of ASD is largely unknown and the associations described in the literature are, for many agents, inadequately proven. Hence, more research is needed to unravel environmental contribution to the genetic etiology of ASD. This type of research may ultimately lead to the establishment of possibilities for prevention.

AUTHOR CONTRIBUTIONS

Following the request by Dr. Joshua Rosenzweig and Dr. Benjamin Gesundheit, we attach our manuscript entitled Genetic syndromes, maternal diseases and antenatal factors associated with Autism Spectrum Disorders (ASD) by EZ, WL, and OA for consideration for publication in the special topic of the Journal-Autism Spectrum Disorders (ASD)—searching for the biological basis for behavioral symptoms and new therapeutic targets.

REFERENCES

Abdallah, M. W., Larsen, N., Grove, J., Norgaard-Pedersen, B., Thorsen, P., Mortensen, E. L., et al. (2012). Amniotic fluid chemokines and autism spectrum disorders: an exploratory study utilizing a Danish Historic Birth Cohort. *Brain Behav. Immun.* 26, 170–176. doi: 10.1016/j.bbi.2011.09.003

Abdallah, M. W., Larsen, N., Grove, J., Norgaard-Pedersen, B., Thorsen, P., Mortensen, E. L., et al. (2013). Amniotic fluid inflammatory cytokines: potential markers of immunologic dysfunction in autism spectrum disorders. *World J. Biol. Psychiatry* 14, 528–538. doi: 10.3109/15622975.2011.639803

Abisror, N., Mekinian, A., Lachassinne, E., Nicaise-Roland, P., De Pontual, L., Chollet-Martin, S., et al. (2013). Autism spectrum disorders in babies born to mothers with antiphospholipid syndrome. *Semin. Arthritis Rheum.* 43, 348–351. doi: 10.1016/j.semarthrit.2013.07.001

Adams Waldorf, K. M., and McAdams, R. M. (2013). Influence of infection during pregnancy on fetal development. *Reproduction* 146, R151–R162. doi: 10.1530/rep-13-0232

Althaus, M., Groen, Y., Wijers, A. A., Noltes, H., Tucha, O., and Hoekstra, P. J. (2015). Oxytocin enhances orienting to social information in a selective group of high-functioning male adults with autism spectrum disorder. *Neuropsychologia* 79, 53–69. doi: 10.1016/j.neuropsychologia.2015.10.025

Anagnostou, E., Soorya, L., Chaplin, W., Bartz, J., Halpern, D., Wasserman, S., et al. (2012). Intranasal oxytocin versus placebo in the treatment of adults with autism spectrum disorders: a randomized controlled trial. *Mol. Autism* 3:16. doi: 10.1186/2040-2392-3-16

Aoki, Y., Watanabe, T., Abe, O., Kuwabara, H., Yahata, N., Takano, Y., et al. (2015). Oxytocin's neurochemical effects in the medial prefrontal cortex underlie recovery of task-specific brain activity in autism: a randomized controlled trial. *Mol. Psychiatry* 20, 447–453. doi: 10.1038/mp.2014.74

Aronson, M., Hagberg, B., and Gillberg, C. (1997). Attention deficits and autistic spectrum problems in children exposed to alcohol during gestation: a follow-up study. *Dev. Med. Child Neurol.* 39, 583–587. doi: 10.1111/j.1469-8749.1997.tb07493.x

American Psychiatric Association (2013). *Diagnostic and Statistical Manual of Mental Disorders (DSM-5).* Washington, DC: American Psychiatric Association.

Assumpcao, F. B. Jr., and Kuczynski, E. (2002). [Autism, bipolar disorder and mental retardation in a male adolescent with congenital rubella: case report]. *Arq. Neuropsiquiatr.* 60, 324–327.

Atladottir, H. O., Henriksen, T. B., Schendel, D. E., and Parner, E. T. (2012). Autism after infection, febrile episodes, and antibiotic use during pregnancy: an exploratory study. *Pediatrics* 130, e1447–e1454. doi: 10.1542/peds.2012-1107

Atladottir, H. O., Pedersen, M. G., Thorsen, P., Mortensen, P. B., Deleuran, B., Eaton, W. W., et al. (2009). Association of family history of autoimmune diseases and autism spectrum disorders. *Pediatrics* 124, 687–694. doi: 10.1542/peds.2008-2445

Atladottir, H. O., Thorsen, P., Ostergaard, L., Schendel, D. E., Lemcke, S., Abdallah, M., et al. (2010). Maternal infection requiring hospitalization during pregnancy and autism spectrum disorders. *J. Autism Dev. Disord.* 40, 1423–1430. doi: 10.1007/s10803-010-1006-y

Autism Developmental Disabilities Monitoring Network Surveillance Year Principal and Centers for Disease and Prevention (2012). *Prevalence of Autism Spectrum Disorders–Autism and Developmental Disabilities Monitoring Network, 14 Sites, United States, 2008.* MMWR. Surveillance Summaries. 61, 1–19.

Ballantyne, C. J., and Nunez, M. (2016). Developmental trajectories of hierarchical visuo-spatial processing in fragile X syndrome and ASD: within- and cross-syndrome variability. *Res. Dev. Disabil.* 51–52, 103–115. doi: 10.1016/j.ridd.2015.12.016

Bambini-Junior, V., Rodrigues, L., Behr, G. A., Moreira, J. C., Riesgo, R., and Gottfried, C. (2011). Animal model of autism induced by prenatal exposure to valproate: behavioral changes and liver parameters. *Brain Res.* 1408, 8–16. doi: 10.1016/j.brainres.2011.06.015

Bandim, J. M., Ventura, L. O., Miller, M. T., Almeida, H. C., and Costa, A. E. (2003). Autism and Mobius sequence: an exploratory study of children in northeastern Brazil. *Arq. Neuropsiquiatr.* 61, 181–185. doi: 10.1590/S0004-282X2003000200004

Bauer, A. Z., and Kriebel, D. (2013). Prenatal and perinatal analgesic exposure and autism: an ecological link. *Environ. Health* 12:41. doi: 10.1186/1476-069X-12-41

Becerra, T. A., Wilhelm, M., Olsen, J., Cockburn, M., and Ritz, B. (2013). Ambient air pollution and autism in Los Angeles county, California. *Environ. Health Perspect.* 121, 380–386. doi: 10.1289/ehp.1205827

Berger, B. E., Navar-Boggan, A. M., and Omer, S. B. (2011). Congenital rubella syndrome and autism spectrum disorder prevented by rubella vaccination–United States, 2001-2010. *BMC Public Health* 11:340. doi: 10.1186/1471-2458-11-340

Billeci, L., Calderoni, S., Tosetti, M., Catani, M., and Muratori, F. (2012). White matter connectivity in children with autism spectrum disorders: a tract-based spatial statistics study. *BMC Neurol.* 12:148. doi: 10.1186/1471-2377-12-148

Bird, L. M., Tan, W. H., Bacino, C. A., Peters, S. U., Skinner, S. A., Anselm, I., et al. (2011). A therapeutic trial of pro-methylation dietary supplements in Angelman syndrome. *Am. J. Med. Genet. A* 155A, 2956–2963. doi: 10.1002/ajmg.a.34297

Boukhris, T., Sheehy, O., Mottron, L., and Berard, A. (2016). Antidepressant use during pregnancy and the risk of autism spectrum disorder in children. *JAMA Pediatr.* 170, 117–124. doi: 10.1001/jamapediatrics.2015.3356

Braunschweig, D., Ashwood, P., Krakowiak, P., Hertz-Picciotto, I., Hansen, R., Croen, L. A., et al. (2008). Autism: maternally derived antibodies specific for fetal brain proteins. *Neurotoxicology* 29, 226–231. doi: 10.1016/j.neuro.2007.10.010

Bromley, R. L., Mawer, G., Clayton-Smith, J., Baker, G. A., Liverpool and Manchester Neurodevelopment Group (2008). Autism spectrum disorders following *in utero* exposure to antiepileptic drugs. *Neurology* 71, 1923–1924. doi: 10.1212/01.wnl.0000339399.64213.1a

Brown, A. S., Sourander, A., Hinkka-Yli-Salomaki, S., McKeague, I. W., Sundvall, J., and Surcel, H. M. (2014). Elevated maternal C-reactive protein and autism in a national birth cohort. *Mol. Psychiatry* 19, 259–264. doi: 10.1038/mp.2012.197

Brown, A. S., Surcel, H. M., Hinkka-Yli-Salomaki, S., Cheslack-Postava, K., Bao, Y., and Sourander, A. (2015). Maternal thyroid autoantibody and elevated risk of autism in a national birth cohort. *Prog. Neuropsychopharmacol. Biol. Psychiatry* 57, 86–92. doi: 10.1016/j.pnpbp.2014.10.010

Bruno, J. L., Hosseini, S. M., Saggar, M., Quintin, E. M., Raman, M. M., and Reiss, A. L. (2016). Altered brain network segregation in fragile x syndrome revealed by structural connectomics. *Cereb. Cortex.* doi: 10.1093/cercor/bhw055. [Epub ahead of print].

Buchmayer, S., Johansson, S., Johansson, A., Hultman, C. M., Sparen, P., and Cnattingius, S. (2009). Can association between preterm birth and autism be explained by maternal or neonatal morbidity? *Pediatrics* 124, e817–e825. doi: 10.1542/peds.2008-3582

Burstyn, I., Sithole, F., and Zwaigenbaum, L. (2010). Autism spectrum disorders, maternal characteristics and obstetric complications among singletons born in Alberta, Canada. *Chronic Dis. Can.* 30, 125–134.

Carvill, S., and Marston, G. (2002). People with intellectual disability, sensory impairments and behaviour disorder: a case series. *J. Intellect. Disabil. Res.* 46, 264–272. doi: 10.1046/j.1365-2788.2002.00400.x

Castles, A., Adams, E. K., Melvin, C. L., Kelsch, C., and Boulton, M. L. (1999). Effects of smoking during pregnancy. Five meta-analyses. *Am. J. Prev. Med.* 16, 208–215. doi: 10.1016/S0749-3797(98)00089-0

Castro, J., Mellios, N., and Sur, M. (2013). Mechanisms and therapeutic challenges in autism spectrum disorders: insights from Rett syndrome. *Curr. Opin. Neurol.* 26, 154–159. doi: 10.1097/WCO.0b013e32835f19a7

Chen, S. W., Zhong, X. S., Jiang, L. N., Zheng, X. Y., Xiong, Y. Q., Ma, S. J., et al. (2016). Maternal autoimmune diseases and the risk of autism spectrum disorders in offspring: a systematic review and meta-analysis. *Behav. Brain Res.* 296, 61–69. doi: 10.1016/j.bbr.2015.08.035

Chess, S., Fernandez, P., and Korn, S. (1978). Behavioral consequences of congenital rubella. *J. Pediatr.* 93, 699–703. doi: 10.1016/S0022-3476(78)80921-4

Christensen, J., Gronborg, T. K., Sorensen, M. J., Schendel, D., Parner, E. T., Pedersen, L. H., et al. (2013). Prenatal valproate exposure and risk of autism spectrum disorders and childhood autism. *JAMA* 309, 1696–1703. doi: 10.1001/jama.2013.2270

Christianson, A. L., Chesler, N., and Kromberg, J. G. (1994). Fetal valproate syndrome: clinical and neuro-developmental features in two sibling pairs. *Dev. Med. Child Neurol.* 36, 361–369. doi: 10.1111/j.1469-8749.1994.tb11858.x

Cianfaglione, R., Clarke, A., Kerr, M., Hastings, R. P., Oliver, C., Moss, J., et al. (2015). A national survey of Rett syndrome: behavioural characteristics. *J. Neurodev. Disord.* 7, 11. doi: 10.1186/s11689-015-9104-y

Conde-Agudelo, A., Rosas-Bermudez, A., and Norton, M. H. (2016). Birth spacing and risk of autism and other neurodevelopmental disabilities: a systematic review. *Pediatrics.* doi: 10.1542/peds.2015-3482. [Epub ahead of print].

Connors, S. L., Crowell, D. E., Eberhart, C. G., Copeland, J., Newschaffer, C. J., Spence, S. J., et al. (2005). beta2-adrenergic receptor activation and genetic polymorphisms in autism: data from dizygotic twins. *J. Child Neurol.* 20, 876–884. doi: 10.1177/08830738050200110401

Cook, E. H. Jr., and Scherer, S. W. (2008). Copy-number variations associated with neuropsychiatric conditions. *Nature* 455, 919–923. doi: 10.1038/nature07458

Croen, L. A., Connors, S. L., Matevia, M., Qian, Y., Newschaffer, C., and Zimmerman, A. W. (2011a). Prenatal exposure to beta2-adrenergic receptor agonists and risk of autism spectrum disorders. *J. Neurodev. Disord.* 3, 307–315. doi: 10.1007/s11689-011-9093-4

Croen, L. A., Grether, J. K., Yoshida, C. K., Odouli, R., and Hendrick, V. (2011b). Antidepressant use during pregnancy and childhood autism spectrum disorders. *Arch. Gen. Psychiatry* 68, 1104–1112. doi: 10.1001/archgenpsychiatry.2011.73

Croen, L. A., Grether, J. K., Yoshida, C. K., Odouli, R., and Van de Water, J. (2005). Maternal autoimmune diseases, asthma and allergies, and childhood autism spectrum disorders: a case-control study. *Arch. Pediatr. Adolesc. Med.* 159, 151–157. doi: 10.1001/archpedi.159.2.151

Darbro, B. W., Singh, R., Zimmerman, M. B., Mahajan, V. B., and Bassuk, A. G. (2016). Autism linked to increased oncogene mutations but decreased cancer rate. *PLoS ONE* 11:e0149041. doi: 10.1371/journal.pone.0149041

Darnell, J. C., Van Driesche, S. J., Zhang, C., Hung, K. Y., Mele, A., Fraser, C. E., et al. (2011). FMRP stalls ribosomal translocation on mRNAs linked to synaptic function and autism. *Cell* 146, 247–261. doi: 10.1016/j.cell.2011.06.013

Davidovitch, M., Hemo, B., Manning-Courtney, P., and Fombonne, E. (2013). Prevalence and incidence of autism spectrum disorder in an Israeli population. *J. Autism Dev. Disord.* 43, 785–793. doi: 10.1007/s10803-012-1611-z

Davis, E., Fennoy, I., Laraque, D., Kanem, N., Brown, G., and Mitchell, J. (1992). Autism and developmental abnormalities in children with perinatal cocaine exposure. *J. Natl. Med. Assoc.* 84, 315–319.

Davis, P. E., Peters, J. M., Krueger, D. A., and Sahin, M. (2015). Tuberous Sclerosis: a new frontier in targeted treatment of autism. *Neurotherapeutics* 12, 572–583. doi: 10.1007/s13311-015-0359-5

Desmond, M. M., Fisher, E. S., Vorderman, A. L., Schaffer, H. G., Andrew, L. P., Zion, T. E., et al. (1978). The longitudinal course of congenital rubella encephalitis in nonretarded children. *J. Pediatr.* 93, 584–591. doi: 10.1016/S0022-3476(78)80892-0

DeVilbiss, E. A., Gardner, R. M., Newschaffer, C. J., and Lee, B. K. (2015). Maternal folate status as a risk factor for autism spectrum disorders: a review of existing evidence. *Br. J. Nutr.* 114, 663–672. doi: 10.1017/S0007114515002470

Dodds, L., Fell, D. B., Shea, S., Armson, B. A., Allen, A. C., and Bryson, S. (2011). The role of prenatal, obstetric and neonatal factors in the development of autism. *J. Autism Dev. Disord.* 41, 891–902. doi: 10.1007/s10803-010-1114-8

Dogan, Y., Yuksel, A., Kalelioglu, I. H., Has, R., Tatli, B., and Yildirim, A. (2011). Intracranial ultrasound abnormalities and fetal cytomegalovirus infection: report of 8 cases and review of the literature. *Fetal Diagn. Ther.* 30, 141–149. doi: 10.1159/000330636

Eliasen, M., Tolstrup, J. S., Nybo Andersen, A. M., Gronbaek, M., Olsen, J., and Strandberg-Larsen, K. (2010). Prenatal alcohol exposure and autistic spectrum disorders–a population-based prospective study of 80,552 children and their mothers. *Int. J. Epidemiol.* 39, 1074–1081. doi: 10.1093/ije/dyq056

Elsabbagh, M., Divan, G., Koh, Y. J., Kim, Y. S., Kauchali, S., Marcin, C., et al. (2012). Global prevalence of autism and other pervasive developmental disorders. *Autism Res.* 5, 160–179. doi: 10.1002/aur.239

Engman, M. L., Lewensohn-Fuchs, I., Mosskin, M., and Malm, G. (2010). Congenital cytomegalovirus infection: the impact of cerebral cortical malformations. *Acta Paediatr.* 99, 1344–1349. doi: 10.1111/j.1651-2227.2010.01852.x

Evans, J., Heron, J., Francomb, H., Oke, S., and Golding, J. (2001). Cohort study of depressed mood during pregnancy and after childbirth. *BMJ* 323, 257–260. doi: 10.1136/bmj.323.7307.257

Feldman, R. B., Pinsky, L., Mendelson, J., and Lajoie, R. (1973). Can language disorder not due to peripheral deafness be an isolated expression of prenatal rubella? *Pediatrics* 52, 296–299.

Fombonne, E. (2009). Epidemiology of pervasive developmental disorders. *Pediatr. Res.* 65, 591–598. doi: 10.1203/PDR.0b013e31819e7203

Fox, C. H. (1994). Cocaine use in pregnancy. *J. Am. Board Fam. Pract.* 7, 225–228.

Fox, E., Amaral, D., and Van de Water, J. (2012). Maternal and fetal antibrain antibodies in development and disease. *Dev. Neurobiol.* 72, 1327–1334. doi: 10.1002/dneu.22052

Francis, S. M., Kistner-Griffin, E., Yan, Z., Guter, S., Cook, E. H., and Jacob, S. (2016). Variants in adjacent oxytocin/vasopressin gene region and associations with ASD diagnosis and other autism related endophenotypes. *Front. Neurosci.* 10:195. doi: 10.3389/fnins.2016.00195

Gao, Y., Xue, X., Hu, D., Liu, W., Yuan, Y., Sun, H., et al. (2013). Inhibition of late sodium current by mexiletine: a novel pharmotherapeutical approach in timothy syndrome. *Circ. Arrhythm. Electrophysiol.* 6, 614–622. doi: 10.1161/CIRCEP.113.000092

Gardener, H., Spiegelman, D., and Buka, S. L. (2009). Prenatal risk factors for autism: comprehensive meta-analysis. *Br. J. Psychiatry* 195, 7–14. doi: 10.1192/bjp.bp.108.051672

Gardener, H., Spiegelman, D., and Buka, S. L. (2011). Perinatal and neonatal risk factors for autism: a comprehensive meta-analysis. *Pediatrics* 128, 344–355. doi: 10.1542/peds.2010-1036

Geier, D. A., Kern, J. K., and Geier, M. R. (2009). A prospective study of prenatal mercury exposure from maternal dental amalgams and autism severity. *Acta Neurobiol. Exp. (Wars).* 69, 189–197.

Gentile, I., Zappulo, E., Bonavolta, R., Maresca, R., Messana, T., Buonomo, A. R., et al. (2014). Prevalence and titre of antibodies to cytomegalovirus and epstein-barr virus in patients with autism spectrum disorder. *In Vivo* 28, 621–626.

Gidaya, N. B., Lee, B. K., Burstyn, I., Michael, Y., Newschaffer, C. J., and Mortensen, E. L. (2016). *In utero* exposure to beta-2-adrenergic receptor agonist drugs and risk for autism spectrum disorders. *Pediatrics* 137, 1–8. doi: 10.1542/peds.2015-1316

Gidaya, N. B., Lee, B. K., Burstyn, I., Yudell, M., Mortensen, E. L., and Newschaffer, C. J. (2014). *In utero* exposure to selective serotonin reuptake inhibitors and risk for autism spectrum disorder. *J. Autism Dev. Disord.* 44, 2558–2567. doi: 10.1007/s10803-014-2128-4

Gillis, J., Burashnikov, E., Antzelevitch, C., Blaser, S., Gross, G., Turner, L., et al. (2012). Long QT, syndactyly, joint contractures, stroke and novel CACNA1C mutation: expanding the spectrum of Timothy syndrome. *Am. J. Med. Genet. A* 158A, 182–187. doi: 10.1002/ajmg.a.34355

Goines, P. E., Croen, L. A., Braunschweig, D., Yoshida, C. K., Grether, J., Hansen, R., et al. (2011). Increased midgestational IFN-gamma, IL-4 and IL-5 in women bearing a child with autism: a case-control study. *Mol. Autism* 2:13. doi: 10.1186/2040-2392-2-13

Gonzalez, C. H., Marques-Dias, M. J., Kim, C. A., Sugayama, S. M., Da Paz, J. A., Huson, S. M., et al. (1998). Congenital abnormalities in Brazilian children associated with misoprostol misuse in first trimester of pregnancy. *Lancet* 351, 1624–1627. doi: 10.1016/S0140-6736(97)12363-7

Gonzalez, C. H., Vargas, F. R., Perez, A. B., Kim, C. A., Brunoni, D., Marques-Dias, M. J., et al. (1993). Limb deficiency with or without Mobius sequence in seven Brazilian children associated with misoprostol use in the first trimester of pregnancy. *Am. J. Med. Genet.* 47, 59–64. doi: 10.1002/ajmg.1320470113

Grabrucker, A. M. (2012). Environmental factors in autism. *Front. Psychiatry* 3:118. doi: 10.3389/fpsyt.2012.00118

Green, A. J., Johnson, P. H., and Yates, J. R. (1994). The tuberous sclerosis gene on chromosome 9q34 acts as a growth suppressor. *Hum. Mol. Genet.* 3, 1833–1834. doi: 10.1093/hmg/3.10.1833

Grether, J. K., Croen, L. A., Anderson, M. C., Nelson, K. B., and Yolken, R. H. (2010). Neonatally measured immunoglobulins and risk of autism. *Autism Res.* 3, 323–332. doi: 10.1002/aur.160

Guinchat, V., Thorsen, P., Laurent, C., Cans, C., Bodeau, N., and Cohen, D. (2012). Pre-, peri- and neonatal risk factors for autism. *Acta Obstet. Gynecol. Scand.* 91, 287–300. doi: 10.1111/j.1600-0412.2011.01325.x

Guxens, M., Ghassabian, A., Gong, T., Garcia-Esteban, R., Porta, D., Giorgis-Allemand, L., et al. (2016). Air pollution exposure during pregnancy and childhood autistic traits in four european population-based cohort studies: the ESCAPE project. *Environ. Health Perspect.* 124, 133–140. doi: 10.1289/ehp.1408483

Harrington, R. A., Lee, L. C., Crum, R. M., Zimmerman, A. W., and Hertz-Picciotto, I. (2014). Prenatal SSRI use and offspring with autism spectrum disorder or developmental delay. *Pediatrics* 133, e1241–e1248. doi: 10.1542/peds.2013-3406

Harris, S. R., MacKay, L. L., and Osborn, J. A. (1995). Autistic behaviors in offspring of mothers abusing alcohol and other drugs: a series of case reports. *Alcohol. Clin. Exp. Res.* 19, 660–665. doi: 10.1111/j.1530-0277.1995.tb01564.x

Hollander, E., Bartz, J., Chaplin, W., Phillips, A., Sumner, J., Soorya, L., et al. (2007). Oxytocin increases retention of social cognition in autism. *Biol. Psychiatry* 61, 498–503. doi: 10.1016/j.biopsych.2006.05.030

Hollander, E., Novotny, S., Hanratty, M., Yaffe, R., Decaria, C. M., Aronowitz, B. R., et al. (2003). Oxytocin infusion reduces repetitive behaviors in adults with autistic and Asperger's disorders. *Neuropsychopharmacology* 28, 193–198. doi: 10.1038/sj.npp.1300021

Huijbregts, S. C., Loitfelder, M., Rombouts, S. A., Swaab, H., Verbist, B. M., Arkink, E. B., et al. (2015). Cerebral volumetric abnormalities in Neurofibromatosis type 1: associations with parent ratings of social and attention problems, executive dysfunction, and autistic mannerisms. *J. Neurodev. Disord.* 7, 32. doi: 10.1186/s11689-015-9128-3

Hultman, C. M., Sparen, P., and Cnattingius, S. (2002). Perinatal risk factors for infantile autism. *Epidemiology* 13, 417–423. doi: 10.1097/00001648-200207000-00009

Hviid, A., Melbye, M., and Pasternak, B. (2013). Use of selective serotonin reuptake inhibitors during pregnancy and risk of autism. *N. Engl. J. Med.* 369, 2406–2415. doi: 10.1056/NEJMoa1301449

Hwang, S. J., and Chen, Y. S. (2010). Congenital rubella syndrome with autistic disorder. *J. Chin. Med. Assoc.* 73, 104–107. doi: 10.1016/S1726-4901(10)70011-3

Ikeda, S., Tsuru, A., Moriuchi, M., and Moriuchi, H. (2006). Retrospective diagnosis of congenital cytomegalovirus infection using umbilical cord. *Pediatr. Neurol.* 34, 415–416. doi: 10.1016/j.pediatrneurol.2005.10.006

Ingram, J. L., Peckham, S. M., Tisdale, B., and Rodier, P. M. (2000). Prenatal exposure of rats to valproic acid reproduces the cerebellar anomalies associated with autism. *Neurotoxicol. Teratol.* 22, 319–324. doi: 10.1016/S0892-0362(99)00083-5

Ito, T., Ando, H., Suzuki, T., Ogura, T., Hotta, K., Imamura, Y., et al. (2010). Identification of a primary target of thalidomide teratogenicity. *Science* 327, 1345–1350. doi: 10.1126/science.1177319

Ivarsson, S. A., Bjerre, I., Vegfors, P., and Ahlfors, K. (1990). Autism as one of several disabilities in two children with congenital cytomegalovirus infection. *Neuropediatrics* 21, 102–103. doi: 10.1055/s-2008-1071471

Johansson, M., Wentz, E., Fernell, E., Stromland, K., Miller, M. T., and Gillberg, C. (2001). Autistic spectrum disorders in Mobius sequence: a comprehensive study of 25 individuals. *Dev. Med. Child Neurol.* 43, 338–345. doi: 10.1017/S0012162201000627

Kagerbauer, S. M., Martin, J., Schuster, T., Blobner, M., Kochs, E. F., and Landgraf, R. (2013). Plasma oxytocin and vasopressin do not predict neuropeptide concentrations in human cerebrospinal fluid. *J. Neuroendocrinol.* 25, 668–673. doi: 10.1111/jne.12038

Kaiser-McCaw, B., Hecht, F., Cadien, J. D., and Moore, B. C. (1980). Fragile X-linked mental retardation. *Am. J. Med. Genet.* 7, 503–505. doi: 10.1002/ajmg.1320070411

Kalkbrenner, A. E., Braun, J. M., Durkin, M. S., Maenner, M. J., Cunniff, C., Lee, L. C., et al. (2012). Maternal smoking during pregnancy and the prevalence of autism spectrum disorders, using data from the autism and developmental disabilities monitoring network. *Environ. Health Perspect.* 120, 1042–1048. doi: 10.1289/ehp.1104556

Kalkbrenner, A. E., Daniels, J. L., Chen, J. C., Poole, C., Emch, M., and Morrissey, J. (2010). Perinatal exposure to hazardous air pollutants and autism spectrum disorders at age 8. *Epidemiology* 21, 631–641. doi: 10.1097/EDE.0b013e3181e65d76

Karaaslan, C., and Suzen, S. (2015). Antioxidant properties of melatonin and its potential action in diseases. *Curr. Top. Med. Chem.* 15, 894–903. doi: 10.2174/1568026615666150220120946

Kawatani, M., Nakai, A., Okuno, T., Kobata, R., Moriuchi, M., Moriuchi, H., et al. (2010). Detection of cytomegalovirus in preserved umbilical cord from a boy with autistic disorder. *Pediatr. Int.* 52, 304–307. doi: 10.1111/j.1442-200X.2010.03027.x

Keil, A., Daniels, J. L., Forssen, U., Hultman, C., Cnattingius, S., Soderberg, K. C., et al. (2010). Parental autoimmune diseases associated with autism spectrum disorders in offspring. *Epidemiology* 21, 805–808. doi: 10.1097/EDE.0b013e3181f26e3f

Kern, J. K., Grannemann, B. D., Trivedi, M. H., and Adams, J. B. (2007). Sulfhydryl-reactive metals in autism. *J. Toxicol. Environ. Health Part A* 70, 715–721. doi: 10.1080/15287390601188060

Kiechl-Kohlendorfer, U., Ralser, E., Pupp Peglow, U., Reiter, G., Griesmaier, E., and Trawoger, R. (2010). Smoking in pregnancy: a risk factor for adverse neurodevelopmental outcome in preterm infants? *Acta Paediatr.* 99, 1016–1019. doi: 10.1111/j.1651-2227.2010.01749.x

Kirsch, P. (2015). Oxytocin in the socioemotional brain: implications for psychiatric disorders. *Dialogues Clin. Neurosci.* 17, 463–476.

Kitajima, J., Inoue, H., Ohga, S., Kinjo, T., Ochiai, M., Yoshida, T., et al. (2012). Differential transmission and postnatal outcomes in triplets with intrauterine cytomegalovirus infection. *Pediatr. Dev. Pathol.* 15, 151–155. doi: 10.2350/11-05-1034-CR.1

Kogan, M. D., Blumberg, S. J., Schieve, L. A., Boyle, C. A., Perrin, J. M., Ghandour, R. M., et al. (2009). Prevalence of parent-reported diagnosis of autism spectrum disorder among children in the US, 2007. *Pediatrics* 124, 1395–1403. doi: 10.1542/peds.2009-1522

Koks, N., Ghassabian, A., Greaves-Lord, K., Hofman, A., Jaddoe, V. W., Verhulst, F. C., et al. (2016). Maternal C-reactive protein concentration in early pregnancy and child autistic traits in the general population. *Paediatr. Perinat. Epidemiol.* 30, 181–189. doi: 10.1111/ppe.12261

Kolozsi, E., MacKenzie, R. N., Roullet, F. I., Decatanzaro, D., and Foster, J. A. (2009). Prenatal exposure to valproic acid leads to reduced expression of synaptic adhesion molecule neuroligin 3 in mice. *Neuroscience* 163, 1201–1210. doi: 10.1016/j.neuroscience.2009.07.021

Koyano, S., Araki, A., Hirano, Y., Fujieda, K., Suzutani, T., Yagyu, K., et al. (2004). Retrospective diagnosis of congenital cytomegalovirus infection using dried umbilical cords. *Pediatr. Infect. Dis. J.* 23, 481–482. doi: 10.1097/00006454-200405000-00028

Krakowiak, P., Walker, C. K., Bremer, A. A., Baker, A. S., Ozonoff, S., Hansen, R. L., et al. (2012). Maternal metabolic conditions and risk for autism and other neurodevelopmental disorders. *Pediatrics* 129, e1121–e1128. doi: 10.1542/peds.2011-2583

Kranz, T. M., Kopp, M., Waltes, R., Sachse, M., Duketis, E., Jarczok, T. A., et al. (2016). Meta-analysis and association of two common polymorphisms of the human oxytocin receptor gene in autism spectrum disorder. *Autism Res.* doi: 10.1002/aur.1597. [Epub ahead of print].

Kwon, K. J., Lee, E. J., Kim, M. K., Jeon, S. J., Choi, Y. Y., Shin, C. Y., et al. (2015). The potential role of melatonin on sleep deprivation-induced cognitive impairments: implication of FMRP on cognitive function. *Neuroscience* 301, 403–414. doi: 10.1016/j.neuroscience.2015.05.079

Landgren, M., Svensson, L., Stromland, K., and Andersson Gronlund, M. (2010). Prenatal alcohol exposure and neurodevelopmental disorders in children adopted from eastern Europe. *Pediatrics* 125, e1178–e1185. doi: 10.1542/peds.2009-0712

Langridge, A. T., Glasson, E. J., Nassar, N., Jacoby, P., Pennell, C., Hagan, R., et al. (2013). Maternal conditions and perinatal characteristics associated with autism spectrum disorder and intellectual disability. *PLoS ONE* 8:e50963. doi: 10.1371/journal.pone.0050963

Larsson, M., Weiss, B., Janson, S., Sundell, J., and Bornehag, C. G. (2009). Associations between indoor environmental factors and parental-reported autistic spectrum disorders in children 6-8 years of age. *Neurotoxicology* 30, 822–831. doi: 10.1016/j.neuro.2009.01.011

Lasalle, J. M., Reiter, L. T., and Chamberlain, S. J. (2015). Epigenetic regulation of UBE3A and roles in human neurodevelopmental disorders. *Epigenomics* 7, 1213–1228. doi: 10.2217/epi.15.70

Leblanc, J. J., Degregorio, G., Centofante, E., Vogel-Farley, V. K., Barnes, K., Kaufmann, W. E., et al. (2015). Visual evoked potentials detect cortical processing deficits in Rett syndrome. *Ann. Neurol.* 78, 775–786. doi: 10.1002/ana.24513

Leblond, C. S., Nava, C., Polge, A., Gauthier, J., Huguet, G., Lumbroso, S., et al. (2014). Meta-analysis of SHANK Mutations in Autism Spectrum Disorders: a gradient of severity in cognitive impairments. *PLoS Genet.* 10:e1004580. doi: 10.1371/journal.pgen.1004580

Lee, B. K., Gardner, R. M., Dal, H., Svensson, A., Galanti, M. R., Rai, D., et al. (2012). Brief report: maternal smoking during pregnancy and autism spectrum disorders. *J. Autism Dev. Disord.* 42, 2000–2005. doi: 10.1007/s10803-01 1-1425-4

Lee, B. K., Magnusson, C., Gardner, R. M., Blomstrom, A., Newschaffer, C. J., Burstyn, I., et al. (2015). Maternal hospitalization with infection during pregnancy and risk of autism spectrum disorders. *Brain Behav. Immun.* 44, 100–105. doi: 10.1016/j.bbi.2014.09.001

Leslie, N. R., and Longy, M. (2016). Inherited PTEN mutations and the prediction of phenotype. *Semin. Cell Dev. Biol.* 52, 30–38. doi: 10.1016/j.semcdb.2016.01.030

Li, M., Fallin, M. D., Riley, A., Landa, R., Walker, S. O., Silverstein, M., et al. (2016). The association of maternal obesity and diabetes with autism and other developmental disabilities. *Pediatrics* 137:e20152206. doi: 10.1542/peds.2015-2206

Li, J., Zhao, L., You, Y., Lu, T., Jia, M., Yu, H., et al. (2015). Schizophrenia related variants in CACNA1C also confer risk of autism. *PLoS ONE* 10:e0133247. doi: 10.1371/journal.pone.0133247

Liew, Z., Ritz, B., Virk, J., and Olsen, J. (2015). Maternal use of acetaminophen during pregnancy and risk of autism spectrum disorders in childhood: a Danish national birth cohort study. *Autism Res.* doi: 10.1002/aur.1591. [Epub ahead of print].

Loparo, D., and Waldman, I. D. (2015). The oxytocin receptor gene (OXTR) is associated with autism spectrum disorder: a meta-analysis. *Mol. Psychiatry* 20, 640–646. doi: 10.1038/mp.2014.77

Lopez-Pison, J., Rubio-Rubio, R., Urena-Hornos, T., Omenaca-Teres, M., Sans, A., Cabrerizo de Diago, R., et al. (2005). [Retrospective diagnosis of congenital infection by cytomegalovirus in the case of one infant]. *Rev. Neurol.* 40, 733–736.

Love, E. R., Crum, J., and Bhattacharya, S. (2012). Independent effects of pregnancy induced hypertension on childhood development: a retrospective cohort study. *Eur. J. Obstet. Gynecol. Reprod. Biol.* 165, 219–224. doi: 10.1016/j.ejogrb.2012.08.015

Lyall, K., Pauls, D. L., Spiegelman, D., Ascherio, A., and Santangelo, S. L. (2012). Pregnancy complications and obstetric suboptimality in association with autism spectrum disorders in children of the Nurses' Health Study II. *Autism Res.* 5, 21–30. doi: 10.1002/aur.228

Maimburg, R. D., and Vaeth, M. (2006). Perinatal risk factors and infantile autism. *Acta Psychiatr. Scand.* 114, 257–264. doi: 10.1111/j.1600-0447.2006.00805.x

Malm, H., Brown, A. S., Gissler, M., Gyllenberg, D., Hinkka-Yli-Salomäki, S., et al. (2016). Gestational exposure to selective serotonin reuptake inhibitors and offspring psychiatric disorders: a national register-based study. *J. Am. Acad. Child Adolesc. Psychiatry.* 55, 359–366. doi: 10.1016/j.jaac.2016.02.013

Mann, J. R., McDermott, S., Bao, H., Hardin, J., and Gregg, A. (2010). Pre-eclampsia, birth weight, and autism spectrum disorders. *J. Autism Dev. Disord.* 40, 548–554. doi: 10.1007/s10803-009-0903-4

Marques-Dias, M. J., Gonzalez, C. H., and Rosemberg, S. (2003). Mobius sequence in children exposed *in utero* to misoprostol: neuropathological study of three cases. *Birth Defects Res. Part A Clin. Mol. Teratol.* 67, 1002–1007. doi: 10.1002/bdra.10144

Mazina, V., Gerdts, J., Trinh, S., Ankenman, K., Ward, T., Dennis, M. Y., et al. (2015). Epigenetics of autism-related impairment: copy number variation and maternal infection. *J. Dev. Behav. Pediatr.* 36, 61–67. doi: 10.1097/DBP.0000000000000126

McBride, K. L., Varga, E. A., Pastore, M. T., Prior, T. W., Manickam, K., Atkin, J. F., et al. (2010). Confirmation study of PTEN mutations among individuals with autism or developmental delays/mental retardation and macrocephaly. *Autism Res.* 3, 137–141. doi: 10.1002/aur.132

McDuffie, A., Thurman, A. J., Hagerman, R. J., and Abbeduto, L. (2015). Symptoms of autism in males with fragile X Syndrome: a comparison to nonsyndromic ASD using current ADI-R scores. *J. Autism Dev. Disord.* 45, 1925–1937. doi: 10.1007/s10803-013-2013-6

Meador, K. J., Baker, G., Cohen, M. J., Gaily, E., and Westerveld, M. (2007). Cognitive/behavioral teratogenetic effects of antiepileptic drugs. *Epilepsy Behav.* 11, 292–302. doi: 10.1016/j.yebeh.2007.08.009

Meador, K. J., Baker, G. A., Browning, N., Clayton-Smith, J., Combs-Cantrell, D. T., Cohen, M., et al. (2009). Cognitive function at 3 years of age after fetal exposure to antiepileptic drugs. *N. Engl. J. Med.* 360, 1597–1605. doi: 10.1056/NEJMoa0803531

Mekinian, A., Lachassinne, E., Nicaise-Roland, P., Carbillon, L., Motta, M., Vicaut, E., et al. (2013). European registry of babies born to mothers with antiphospholipid syndrome. *Ann. Rheum. Dis.* 72, 217–222. doi: 10.1136/annrheumdis-2011-201167

Meloni, I., Bruttini, M., Longo, I., Mari, F., Rizzolio, F., D'adamo, P., et al. (2000). A mutation in the rett syndrome gene, MECP2, causes X-linked mental retardation and progressive spasticity in males. *Am. J. Hum. Genet.* 67, 982–985. doi: 10.1086/303078

Mendola, P., Selevan, S. G., Gutter, S., and Rice, D. (2002). Environmental factors associated with a spectrum of neurodevelopmental deficits. *Ment. Retard. Dev. Disabil. Res. Rev.* 8, 188–197. doi: 10.1002/mrdd.10033

Mieses, A. M., Tavassoli, T., Li, E., Soorya, L., Lurie, S., Wang, A. T., et al. (2016). Brief report: sensory reactivity in children with Phelan-McDermid syndrome. *J. Autism Dev. Disord.* 46, 2508–2513. doi: 10.1007/s10803-016-2754-0

Miller, M., Bales, K. L., Taylor, S. L., Yoon, J., Hostetler, C. M., Carter, C. S., et al. (2013). Oxytocin and vasopressin in children and adolescents with autism spectrum disorders: sex differences and associations with symptoms. *Autism Res.* 6, 91–102. doi: 10.1002/aur.1270

Modahl, C., Green, L., Fein, D., Morris, M., Waterhouse, L., Feinstein, C., et al. (1998). Plasma oxytocin levels in autistic children. *Biol. Psychiatry* 43, 270–277. doi: 10.1016/S0006-3223(97)00439-3

Moore, S. J., Turnpenny, P., Quinn, A., Glover, S., Lloyd, D. J., Montgomery, T., et al. (2000). A clinical study of 57 children with fetal anticonvulsant syndromes. *J. Med. Genet.* 37, 489–497. doi: 10.1136/jmg.37.7.489

Moss, J., and Howlin, P. (2009). Autism spectrum disorders in genetic syndromes: implications for diagnosis, intervention and understanding the wider autism spectrum disorder population. *J. Intellect. Disabil. Res.* 53, 852–873. doi: 10.1111/j.1365-2788.2009.01197.x

Nahum Sacks, K., Friger, M., Shoham-Vardi, I., Abokaf, H., Speigel, E., Sergienko, R., et al. (2016). Prenatal exposure to gestational diabetes mellitus as an independent risk factor for long- term neuropsychiatric morbidity of the offspring. *Am. J. Obstet. Gynecol.* doi: 10.1016/j.ajog.2016.03.030. [Epub ahead of print].

Nanson, J. L. (1992). Autism in fetal alcohol syndrome: a report of six cases. *Alcohol. Clin. Exp. Res.* 16, 558–565. doi: 10.1111/j.1530-0277.1992.tb01417.x

Newman, I., Leader, G., Chen, J. L., and Mannion, A. (2015). An analysis of challenging behavior, comorbid psychopathology, and attention-deficit/hyperactivity disorder in fragile X syndrome. *Res. Dev. Disabil.* 38, 7–17. doi: 10.1016/j.ridd.2014.11.003

Ogata, H., Ihara, H., Murakami, N., Gito, M., Kido, Y., and Nagai, T. (2014). Autism spectrum disorders and hyperactive/impulsive behaviors in Japanese patients with Prader-Willi syndrome: a comparison between maternal uniparental disomy and deletion cases. *Am. J. Med. Genet. A* 164A, 2180–2186. doi: 10.1002/ajmg.a.36615

Ornoy, A. (2009). Valproic acid in pregnancy: how much are we endangering the embryo and fetus? *Reprod. Toxicol.* 28, 1–10. doi: 10.1016/j.reprotox.2009.02.014

Ornoy, A., Ratzon, N., Greenbaum, C., Wolf, A., and Dulitzky, M. (2001). School-age children born to diabetic mothers and to mothers with gestational diabetes exhibit a high rate of inattention and fine and gross motor impairment. *J. Pediatr. Endocrinol. Metab.* 14(Suppl. 1), 681–689. doi: 10.1515/jpem.2001.14.s1.681

Ornoy, A., Reece, E. A., Pavlinkova, G., Kappen, C., and Miller, R. K. (2015a). Effect of maternal diabetes on the embryo, fetus, and children: congenital anomalies, genetic and epigenetic changes and developmental outcomes. *Birth Defects Res. C Embryo Today* 105, 53–72. doi: 10.1002/bdrc.21090

Ornoy, A., Weinstein-Fudim, L., and Ergaz, Z. (2015b). Prenatal factors associated with autism spectrum disorder (ASD). *Reprod. Toxicol.* 56, 155–169. doi: 10.1016/j.reprotox.2015.05.007

Pereira, P. K., Lovisi, G. M., Pilowsky, D. L., Lima, L. A., and Legay, L. F. (2009). Depression during pregnancy: prevalence and risk factors among women attending a public health clinic in Rio de Janeiro, Brazil. *Cad. Saude Publica* 25, 2725–2736. doi: 10.1590/S0102-311X2009001200019

Peters, S. U., Bird, L. M., Kimonis, V., Glaze, D. G., Shinawi, L. M., Bichell, T. J., et al. (2010). Double-blind therapeutic trial in Angelman syndrome using betaine and folic acid. *Am. J. Med. Genet. A* 152A, 1994–2001. doi: 10.1002/ajmg.a.33509

Pini, G., Congiu, L., Benincasa, A., Dimarco, P., Bigoni, S., Dyer, A. H., et al. (2016). Illness severity, social and cognitive ability, and eeg analysis of ten patients with rett syndrome treated with mecasermin (recombinant human IGF-1). *Autism Res. Treat.* 2016:5073078. doi: 10.1155/2016/5073078

Plummer, J. T., Evgrafov, O. V., Bergman, M. Y., Friez, M., Haiman, C. A., Levitt, P., et al. (2013). Transcriptional regulation of the MET receptor tyrosine kinase gene by MeCP2 and sex-specific expression in autism and Rett syndrome. *Transl. Psychiatry* 3, e316. doi: 10.1038/tp.2013.91

Poot, M. (2015). Connecting the CNTNAP2 networks with neurodevelopmental disorders. *Mol. Syndromol.* 6, 7–22. doi: 10.1159/000371594

Rai, D., Lee, B. K., Dalman, C., Golding, J., Lewis, G., and Magnusson, C. (2013). Parental depression, maternal antidepressant use during pregnancy, and risk of autism spectrum disorders: population based case-control study. *BMJ* 346:f2059. doi: 10.1136/bmj.f2059

Rasalam, A. D., Hailey, H., Williams, J. H., Moore, S. J., Turnpenny, P. D., Lloyd, D. J., et al. (2005). Characteristics of fetal anticonvulsant syndrome associated autistic disorder. *Dev. Med. Child Neurol.* 47, 551–555. doi: 10.1017/S0012162205001076

Ratsep, M. T., Paolozza, A., Hickman, A. F., Maser, B., Kay, V. R., Mohammad, S., et al. (2016). Brain structural and vascular anatomy is altered in offspring of pre-eclamptic pregnancies: a pilot study. *AJNR Am. J. Neuroradiol.* 37, 939–945. doi: 10.3174/ajnr.A4640

Raz, R., Roberts, A. L., Lyall, K., Hart, J. E., Just, A. C., Laden, F., et al. (2015a). Autism spectrum disorder and particulate matter air pollution before, during, and after pregnancy: a nested case-control analysis within the nurses' health study ii cohort. *Environ. Health Perspect.* 123, 264–270. doi: 10.1289/ehp.1408133

Raz, R., Weisskopf, M. G., Davidovitch, M., Pinto, O., and Levine, H. (2015b). Differences in autism spectrum disorders incidence by sub-populations in israel 1992-2009: a total population study. *J. Autism Dev. Disord.* doi: 10.1007/s10803-014-2262-z

Richards, C., Jones, C., Groves, L., Moss, J., and Oliver, C. (2015). Prevalence of autism spectrum disorder phenomenology in genetic disorders: a systematic review and meta-analysis. *Lancet Psychiatry* 2, 909–916. doi: 10.1016/S2215-0366(15)00376-4

Roberts, A. L., Lyall, K., Hart, J. E., Laden, F., Just, A. C., Bobb, J. F., et al. (2013). Perinatal air pollutant exposures and autism spectrum disorder in the children of Nurses' Health Study II participants. *Environ. Health Perspect.* 121, 978–984. doi: 10.1289/ehp.1206187

Roberts, E. M., English, P. B., Grether, J. K., Windham, G. C., Somberg, L., and Wolff, C. (2007). Maternal residence near agricultural pesticide applications and autism spectrum disorders among children in the California Central Valley. *Environ. Health Perspect.* 115, 1482–1489. doi: 10.1289/ehp.10168

Rodier, P. M., Ingram, J. L., Tisdale, B., and Croog, V. J. (1997). Linking etiologies in humans and animal models: studies of autism. *Reprod. Toxicol.* 11, 417–422. doi: 10.1016/S0890-6238(97)80001-U

Roe, D. A., Little, B. B., Bawdon, R. E., and Gilstrap, L. C. III. (1990). Metabolism of cocaine by human placentas: implications for fetal exposure. *Am. J. Obstet. Gynecol.* 163, 715–718. doi: 10.1016/0002-9378(90)91054-G

Rosen, B. N., Lee, B. K., Lee, N. L., Yang, Y., and Burstyn, I. (2015). Maternal smoking and autism spectrum disorder: a meta-analysis. *J. Autism Dev. Disord.* 45, 1689–1698. doi: 10.1007/s10803-014-2327-z

Rossignol, D. A., and Frye, R. E. (2012). A review of research trends in physiological abnormalities in autism spectrum disorders: immune dysregulation, inflammation, oxidative stress, mitochondrial dysfunction and environmental toxicant exposures. *Mol. Psychiatry* 17, 389–401. doi: 10.1038/mp.2011.165

Sakamoto, A., Moriuchi, H., Matsuzaki, J., Motoyama, K., and Moriuchi, M. (2015). Retrospective diagnosis of congenital cytomegalovirus infection in children with autism spectrum disorder but no other major neurologic deficit. *Brain Dev.* 37, 200–205. doi: 10.1016/j.braindev.2014.03.016

Schmidt, R. J., Tancredi, D. J., Ozonoff, S., Hansen, R. L., Hartiala, J., Allayee, H., et al. (2012). Maternal periconceptional folic acid intake and risk of autism spectrum disorders and developmental delay in the CHARGE (CHildhood autism risks from genetics and environment) case-control study. *Am. J. Clin. Nutr.* 96, 80–89. doi: 10.3945/ajcn.110.004416

Schneider, T., and Przewlocki, R. (2005). Behavioral alterations in rats prenatally exposed to valproic acid: animal model of autism. *Neuropsychopharmacology* 30, 80–89. doi: 10.1038/sj.npp.1300518

Schwartzman, J. S., Velloso Rde, L., D'antino, M. E., and Santos, S. (2015). The eye-tracking of social stimuli in patients with Rett syndrome and autism spectrum disorders: a pilot study. *Arq. Neuropsiquiatr.* 73, 402–407. doi: 10.1590/0004-282X20150033

Scott-Van Zeeland, A. A., Abrahams, B. S., Alvarez-Retuerto, A. I., Sonnenblick, L. I., Rudie, J. D., Ghahremani, D., et al. (2010). Altered functional connectivity in frontal lobe circuits is associated with variation in the autism risk gene CNTNAP2. *Sci. Transl. Med.* 2, 56ra80. doi: 10.1126/scitranslmed.3001344

Shattuck, P. T. (2006). Diagnostic substitution and changing autism prevalence. *Pediatrics* 117, 1438–1439. doi: 10.1542/peds.2005-2911

Shelton, J. F., Geraghty, E. M., Tancredi, D. J., Delwiche, L. D., Schmidt, R. J., Ritz, B., et al. (2014). Neurodevelopmental disorders and prenatal residential proximity to agricultural pesticides: the CHARGE study. *Environ. Health Perspect.* 122, 1103–1109. doi: 10.1289/ehp.1307044

Singer, L., Arendt, R., and Minnes, S. (1993). Neurodevelopmental effects of cocaine. *Clin. Perinatol.* 20, 245–262.

Smeeth, L., Cook, C., Fombonne, P. E., Heavey, L., Rodrigues, L. C., Smith, P. G., et al. (2004). Rate of first recorded diagnosis of autism and other pervasive developmental disorders in United Kingdom general practice, 1988 to 2001. *BMC Med.* 2:39. doi: 10.1186/1741-7015-2-39

Sorensen, M. J., Gronborg, T. K., Christensen, J., Parner, E. T., Vestergaard, M., Schendel, D., et al. (2013). Antidepressant exposure in pregnancy and risk of autism spectrum disorders. *Clin. Epidemiol.* 5, 449–459. doi: 10.2147/CLEP.S53009

Stene-Larsen, K., Borge, A. I., and Vollrath, M. E. (2009). Maternal smoking in pregnancy and externalizing behavior in 18-month-old children: results from a population-based prospective study. *J. Am. Acad. Child Adolesc. Psychiatry* 48, 283–289. doi: 10.1097/CHI.0b013e318195bcfb

Strauss, K. A., Puffenberger, E. G., Huentelman, M. J., Gottlieb, S., Dobrin, S. E., Parod, J. M., et al. (2006). Recessive symptomatic focal epilepsy and mutant contactin-associated protein-like 2. *N. Engl. J. Med.* 354, 1370–1377. doi: 10.1056/NEJMoa052773

Stromland, K., Nordin, V., Miller, M., Akerstrom, B., and Gillberg, C. (1994). Autism in thalidomide embryopathy: a population study. *Dev. Med. Child Neurol.* 36, 351–356. doi: 10.1111/j.1469-8749.1994.tb11856.x

Stromland, K., Sjogreen, L., Miller, M., Gillberg, C., Wentz, E., Johansson, M., et al. (2002). Mobius sequence–a Swedish multidiscipline study. *Eur. J. Paediatr. Neurol.* 6, 35–45. doi: 10.1053/ejpn.2001.0540

Stubbs, E. G. (1978). Autistic symptoms in a child with congenital cytomegalovirus infection. *J. Autism Child. Schizophr.* 8, 37–43. doi: 10.1007/BF01550276

Stubbs, E. G., Ash, E., and Williams, C. P. (1984). Autism and congenital cytomegalovirus. *J. Autism Dev. Disord.* 14, 183–189. doi: 10.1007/BF02409660

Sui, L., and Chen, M. (2012). Prenatal exposure to valproic acid enhances synaptic plasticity in the medial prefrontal cortex and fear memories. *Brain Res. Bull.* 87, 556–563. doi: 10.1016/j.brainresbull.2012.01.011

Suren, P., Roth, C., Bresnahan, M., Haugen, M., Hornig, M., Hirtz, D., et al. (2013). Association between maternal use of folic acid supplements and risk of autism spectrum disorders in children. *JAMA* 309, 570–577. doi: 10.1001/jama.2012.155925

Sweeten, T. L., Posey, D. J., and McDougle, C. J. (2004). Brief report: autistic disorder in three children with cytomegalovirus infection. *J. Autism Dev. Disord.* 34, 583–586. doi: 10.1007/s10803-004-2552-y

Swillen, A., and McDonald-McGinn, D. (2015). Developmental trajectories in 22q11.2 deletion. *Am. J. Med. Genet. C Semin. Med. Genet.* 169, 172–181. doi: 10.1002/ajmg.c.31435

Talbott, E. O., Marshall, L. P., Rager, J. R., Arena, V. C., Sharma, R. K., and Stacy, S. L. (2015). Air toxics and the risk of autism spectrum disorder: the results of a population based case-control study in southwestern Pennsylvania. *Environ. Health* 14, 80. doi: 10.1186/s12940-015-0064-1

Tang, S., Wang, Y., Gong, X., and Wang, G. (2015). A meta-analysis of maternal smoking during pregnancy and autism spectrum disorder risk in offspring. *Int. J. Environ. Res. Public Health* 12, 10418–10431. doi: 10.3390/ijerph120910418

Taurines, R., Schwenck, C., Lyttwin, B., Schecklmann, M., Jans, T., Reefschlager, L., et al. (2014). Oxytocin plasma concentrations in children and adolescents with autism spectrum disorder: correlation with autistic symptomatology. *Atten. Defic. Hyperact. Disord.* 6, 231–239. doi: 10.1007/s12402-014-0145-y

Tchaconas, A., and Adesman, A. (2013). Autism spectrum disorders: a pediatric overview and update. *Curr. Opin. Pediatr.* 25, 130–144. doi: 10.1097/MOP.0b013e32835c2b70

Tomson, T., Battino, D., Bonizzoni, E., Craig, J., Lindhout, D., Sabers, A., et al. (2011). Dose-dependent risk of malformations with antiepileptic drugs: an analysis of data from the EURAP epilepsy and pregnancy registry. *Lancet Neurol.* 10, 609–617. doi: 10.1016/S1474-4422(11)70107-7

Townsend, C. L., Forsgren, M., Ahlfors, K., Ivarsson, S. A., Tookey, P. A., and Peckham, C. S. (2013). Long-term outcomes of congenital cytomegalovirus infection in Sweden and the United Kingdom. *Clin. Infect. Dis.* 56, 1232–1239. doi: 10.1093/cid/cit018

Tran, P. L., Lehti, V., Lampi, K. M., Helenius, H., Suominen, A., Gissler, M., et al. (2013). Smoking during pregnancy and risk of autism spectrum disorder in a Finnish National Birth Cohort. *Paediatr. Perinat. Epidemiol.* 27, 266–274. doi: 10.1111/ppe.12043

Van Wijngaarden, E., Davidson, P. W., Smith, T. H., Evans, K., Yost, K., Love, T., et al. (2013). Autism spectrum disorder phenotypes and prenatal exposure to methylmercury. *Epidemiology* 24, 651–659. doi: 10.1097/EDE.0b013e31829d2651

Vauzelle, C., Beghin, D., Cournot, M. P., and Elefant, E. (2013). Birth defects after exposure to misoprostol in the first trimester of pregnancy: prospective follow-up study. *Reprod. Toxicol.* 36, 98–103. doi: 10.1016/j.reprotox.2012.11.009

Verzijl, H. T., van der Zwaag, B., Cruysberg, J. R., and Padberg, G. W. (2003). Mobius syndrome redefined: a syndrome of rhombencephalic maldevelopment. *Neurology* 61, 327–333. doi: 10.1212/01.WNL.0000076484.91275.CD

Vignoli, A., La Briola, F., Peron, A., Turner, K., Vannicola, C., Saccani, M., et al. (2015). Autism spectrum disorder in tuberous sclerosis complex: searching for risk markers. *Orphanet J. Rare Dis.* 10, 154. doi: 10.1186/s13023-015-0371-1

Vinet, E., Pineau, C. A., Clarke, A. E., Scott, S., Fombonne, E., Joseph, L., et al. (2015). Increased risk of autism spectrum disorders in children born to women with systemic lupus erythematosus: results from a large population-based cohort. *Arthritis Rheumatol.* 67, 3201–3208. doi: 10.1002/art.39320

Volk, H. E., Hertz-Picciotto, I., Delwiche, L., Lurmann, F., and McConnell, R. (2011). Residential proximity to freeways and autism in the CHARGE study. *Environ. Health Perspect.* 119, 873–877. doi: 10.1289/ehp.1002835

Volk, H. E., Lurmann, F., Penfold, B., Hertz-Picciotto, I., and McConnell, R. (2013). Traffic-related air pollution, particulate matter, and autism. *JAMA Psychiatry* 70, 71–77. doi: 10.1001/jamapsychiatry.2013.266

Wadell, P. M., Hagerman, R. J., and Hessl, D. R. (2013). Fragile X syndrome: psychiatric manifestations, assessment and emerging therapies. *Curr. Psychiatry Rev.* 9, 53–58. doi: 10.2174/157340013805289644

Wagner, G. C., Reuhl, K. R., Cheh, M., McRae, P., and Halladay, A. K. (2006). A new neurobehavioral model of autism in mice: pre- and postnatal exposure to sodium valproate. *J. Autism Dev. Disord.* 36, 779–793. doi: 10.1007/s10803-006-0117-y

Walker, C. K., Krakowiak, P., Baker, A., Hansen, R. L., Ozonoff, S., and Hertz-Picciotto, I. (2015). Preeclampsia, placental insufficiency, and autism spectrum disorder or developmental delay. *JAMA Pediatr.* 169, 154–162. doi: 10.1001/jamapediatrics.2014.2645

Wang, A. T., Lim, T., Jamison, J., Bush, L., Soorya, L. V., Tavassoli, T., et al. (2016). Neural selectivity for communicative auditory signals in Phelan-McDermid syndrome. *J. Neurodev. Disord.* 8, 5. doi: 10.1186/s11689-016-9138-9

Watanabe, T., Kuroda, M., Kuwabara, H., Aoki, Y., Iwashiro, N., Tatsunobu, N., et al. (2015). Clinical and neural effects of six-week administration of oxytocin on core symptoms of autism. *Brain* 138, 3400–3412. doi: 10.1093/brain/awv249

Werler, M. M., Ahrens, K. A., Bosco, J. L., Mitchell, A. A., Anderka, M. T., Gilboa, S. M., et al. (2011). Use of antiepileptic medications in pregnancy in relation to risks of birth defects. *Ann. Epidemiol.* 21, 842–850. doi: 10.1016/j.annepidem.2011.08.002

Wilkerson, D. S., Volpe, A. G., Dean, R. S., and Titus, J. B. (2002). Perinatal complications as predictors of infantile autism. *Int. J. Neurosci.* 112, 1085–1098. doi: 10.1080/00207450290026076

Williams, G., King, J., Cunningham, M., Stephan, M., Kerr, B., and Hersh, J. H. (2001). Fetal valproate syndrome and autism: additional evidence of an association. *Dev. Med. Child Neurol.* 43, 202–206. doi: 10.1017/S001216220100038X

Windham, G. C., Zhang, L., Gunier, R., Croen, L. A., and Grether, J. K. (2006). Autism spectrum disorders in relation to distribution of hazardous air pollutants in the san francisco bay area. *Environ. Health Perspect.* 114, 1438–1444. doi: 10.1289/ehp.9120

Wu, S., Ding, Y., Wu, F., Li, R., Xie, G., Hou, J., et al. (2015). Family history of autoimmune diseases is associated with an increased risk of autism in children: a systematic review and meta-analysis. *Neurosci. Biobehav. Rev.* 55, 322–332. doi: 10.1016/j.neubiorev.2015.05.004

Xiang, A. H., Wang, X., Martinez, M. P., Walthall, J. C., Curry, E. S., Page, K., et al. (2015). Association of maternal diabetes with autism in offspring. *JAMA* 313, 1425–1434. doi: 10.1001/jama.2015.2707

Xu, G., Jing, J., Bowers, K., Liu, B., and Bao, W. (2014). Maternal diabetes and the risk of autism spectrum disorders in the offspring: a systematic review and meta-analysis. *J. Autism Dev. Disord.* 44, 766–775. doi: 10.1007/s10803-013-1928-2

Yamashita, Y., Fujimoto, C., Nakajima, E., Isagai, T., and Matsuishi, T. (2003). Possible association between congenital cytomegalovirus infection and autistic disorder. *J. Autism Dev. Disord.* 33, 455–459. doi: 10.1023/A:1025023131029

Yamazaki, H., Yamamoto, R., Moroto, S., Yamazaki, T., Fujiwara, K., Nakai, M., et al. (2012). Cochlear implantation in children with congenital cytomegalovirus infection accompanied by psycho-neurological disorders. *Acta Otolaryngol.* 132, 420–427. doi: 10.3109/00016489.2011.653442

Yasuda, Y., Hashimoto, R., Fukai, R., Okamoto, N., Hiraki, Y., Yamamori, H., et al. (2014). Duplication of the NPHP1 gene in patients with autism spectrum disorder and normal intellectual ability: a case series. *Ann. Gen. Psychiatry* 13, 22. doi: 10.1186/s12991-014-0022-2

Yatawara, C. J., Einfeld, S. L., Hickie, I. B., Davenport, T. A., and Guastella, A. J. (2015). The effect of oxytocin nasal spray on social interaction deficits observed in young children with autism: a randomized clinical crossover trial. *Mol. Psychiatry.* doi: 10.1038/mp.2015.162. [Epub ahead of print].

Yau, V. M., Green, P. G., Alaimo, C. P., Yoshida, C. K., Lutsky, M., Windham, G. C., et al. (2014). Prenatal and neonatal peripheral blood mercury levels and autism spectrum disorders. *Environ. Res.* 133, 294–303. doi: 10.1016/j.envres.2014.04.034

Zerbo, O., Iosif, A. M., Walker, C., Ozonoff, S., Hansen, R. L., and Hertz-Picciotto, I. (2013). Is maternal influenza or fever during pregnancy associated with autism or developmental delays? Results from the CHARGE (CHildhood Autism Risks from Genetics and Environment) study. *J. Autism Dev. Disord.* 43, 25–33. doi: 10.1007/s10803-012-1540-x

12

Can Mouse Imaging Studies Bring Order to Autism Connectivity Chaos?

Adam Liska[1,2] *and Alessandro Gozzi*[1*]

[1] *Functional Neuroimaging Laboratory, Center for Neuroscience and Cognitive Systems @ UniTn, Istituto Italiano di Tecnologia, Rovereto, Italy,* [2] *Center for Mind/Brain Sciences, University of Trento, Rovereto, Italy*

Edited by:
Roberto Canitano,
University Hospital of Siena, Italy

Reviewed by:
Jason Lerch,
The Hospital for Sick Children, Canada
Shruti Gopal,
University of Miami, USA

***Correspondence:**
Alessandro Gozzi
alessandro.gozzi@iit.it

Functional Magnetic Resonance Imaging (fMRI) has consistently highlighted impaired or aberrant functional connectivity across brain regions of autism spectrum disorder (ASD) patients. However, the manifestation and neural substrates of these alterations are highly heterogeneous and often conflicting. Moreover, their neurobiological underpinnings and etiopathological significance remain largely unknown. A deeper understanding of the complex pathophysiological cascade leading to aberrant connectivity in ASD can greatly benefit from the use of model organisms where individual pathophysiological or phenotypic components of ASD can be recreated and investigated via approaches that are either off limits or confounded by clinical heterogeneity. Despite some obvious limitations in reliably modeling the full phenotypic spectrum of a complex developmental disorder like ASD, mouse models have played a central role in advancing our basic mechanistic and molecular understanding of this syndrome. Recent progress in mouse brain connectivity mapping via resting-state fMRI (rsfMRI) offers the opportunity to generate and test mechanistic hypotheses about the elusive origin and significance of connectional aberrations observed in autism. Here we discuss recent progress toward this goal, and illustrate initial examples of how the approach can be employed to establish causal links between ASD-related mutations, developmental processes, and brain connectional architecture. As the spectrum of genetic and pathophysiological components of ASD modeled in the mouse is rapidly expanding, the use of rsfMRI can advance our mechanistic understanding of the origin and significance of the connectional alterations associated with autism, and their heterogeneous expression across patient cohorts.

Keywords: fMRI, functional connectivity, autism, mouse, resting-state, DMN, CNTNAP2, pathoconnectomics

THE CONNECTIVITY THEORY OF AUTISM: OPEN QUESTIONS AND CONTROVERSIES

Autism is a heterogeneous syndrome characterized by core behavioral features including deficits in social communication and interaction, as well as restricted, repetitive patterns of behavior, and interests (Association AP, 2013). Although a primary and unitary etiology for autism spectrum disorder (ASD) has not been identified, its high heritability has been consistently documented, revealing a contribution of complex and highly heterogeneous genetic mutations (Geschwind, 2009; Geschwind and State, 2015; Sanders et al., 2015). Remarkably, although previously identified mutations, genetic syndromes, and *de novo* copy number variations (CNVs) account for about 10–20% of ASD cases, none of these single known genetic causes accounts for more than

1–2% of cases (reviewed in Abrahams and Geschwind, 2008). The phenotypic expression (i.e., "penetrance") of these genetic components is also highly variable, ranging from fully penetrant point mutations to polygenic forms with multiple gene–gene and gene–environment interactions. Remarkable variability exists also in the extent of cognitive and behavioral abnormalities presented by affected individuals (Georgiades et al., 2013; Lai et al., 2014; Chang et al., 2015), making heterogeneity a dominant theme for this group of disorders.

The advent of non-invasive brain imaging raised hopes that such clinical heterogeneity could be narrowed down to a small number of identifiable "imaging endophenotypes" that could help ASD diagnosis, patient stratification, and possibly provide clues as to the elusive etiology of this group of disorders. Unfortunately, the results of imaging studies have proven overall as variable as the clinical manifestations of ASD (Stanfield et al., 2008; Ecker et al., 2015). A notable exception to this scenario was the initial observation of reduced connectivity between brain regions in ASD patients, a finding first reported by Horwitz et al. (1988) using PET, and later corroborated by task-based (Just et al., 2004) and resting-state fMRI (rsfMRI) studies (Cherkassky et al., 2006; Kennedy and Courchesne, 2008; Assaf et al., 2010), which revealed impaired long-range synchronization in spontaneous brain activity. Together with evidence of reduced white matter connectivity detected with MRI (reviewed in Anagnostou and Taylor, 2011), these observations form the basis of the so called "under-connectivity theory of autism" (Anagnostou and Taylor, 2011; Just et al., 2012), according to which deficient long-range communication between brain regions may underlie ASD symptoms and pathophysiology. However, recent imaging studies have strongly challenged this view, highlighting a much more heterogeneous picture (see Vasa et al., 2016 for a recent review). For example, rsfMRI mapping in a large cohort of patients has revealed the presence of concomitant hypo- and hyper-connectivity (Di Martino et al., 2014), although a clear prevalence of hypo-connected regions was apparent. Similarly, widespread hyper-connectivity during childhood has also been recently described (Keown et al., 2013; Supekar et al., 2013; Uddin et al., 2013a), suggesting a possible neurodevelopmental origin for these alterations. More recently, the hypothesis that such conflicting findings could reflect greater inter-subject variability in ASD patients than in neurotypical controls (i.e., idiosyncratic connectivity) has been proposed (Hahamy et al., 2015). A putative confounding contribution of ASD-related motion and its effect on functional connectivity readouts is also the subject of an open controversy in the imaging community (Deen and Pelphrey, 2012; Power et al., 2012, 2015; Pardoe et al., 2016).

Collectively, the extensive literature published to date points at the presence of major functional connectivity alterations in ASD populations, although the identified regional patterns vary considerably across studies and patient cohorts (Kana et al., 2011; Müller, 2014; Ecker and Murphy, 2014; Ameis and Catani, 2015; Ecker et al., 2015; Bernhardt et al., 2016; Vasa et al., 2016). Despite this rapidly accumulating evidence, many fundamental questions as to the origin and significance of connectional alterations in ASD remain unanswered. For one, the neurophysiological underpinnings of these connectional aberrancies are largely unknown, and a causal etiopathological contribution of specific genetic variants to impaired connectivity in ASD remains to be firmly established. More broadly, it is unclear whether these abnormalities are a causative or epiphenomenal consequence of the disease, and whether their heterogeneous expression reflects cohort effects, different genetic etiologies, or neurodevelopmental trajectories. The exact relationship between connectivity alterations and the severity of ASD manifestation remains also obscure, with the vast majority of the human neuroimaging literature being focused on high-functioning ASD cohorts (Vissers et al., 2012).

A deeper understanding of the origin and significance of these phenomena is greatly complicated by our very limited understanding of the neurobiological foundations of macro-scale neuroimaging readouts commonly employed in ASD research, such as white matter microstructural parameters (e.g., fractional anisotropy, Owen et al., 2014) or the elusive functional couplings underlying rsfMRI-based functional connectivity. This has left us with a major explanatory gap between mechanistic models of brain function at the cellular and microcircuit level, and the emergence of macroscale functional activity in health and pathological states such as those that are observed in autism. As a result, we are currently unable to properly interpret and back-translate clinical evidence of aberrant connectivity into interpretable neurophysiological events/models that can help understand, diagnose or treat these disorders. It is also becoming apparent that a full disambiguation of the multifactorial and complex determinants of aberrant functional connectivity in ASD can only be obtained through the combined use of refined clinical imaging methods and multimodal-multiscale investigational approaches that currently can only be applied in experimental animal models.

BRIDGING THE GAP: FUNCTIONAL CONNECTIVITY MAPPING IN MOUSE AUTISM MODELS

The identification of several high-confidence ASD-risk genes involved in syndromic forms of autism (Sanders et al., 2015) has been paralleled by the generation of mouse lines recapitulating human mutations. Despite predictable limitations in reliably modeling the full phenotypic spectrum of a complex (and possibly only human) developmental disorder like ASD, mouse models can be harnessed to understand how genetic alterations translate into relevant changes in cells and circuits, and ultimately to identify points of convergence for molecular pathways, cells, circuits, and systems that may result in a deeper understanding of the pathophysiology of ASD and related behavioral deficits (Arguello and Gogos, 2012; Nelson and Valakh, 2015; Vasa et al., 2016). For example, molecular investigations in ASD mouse models have been instrumental in the identification of a limited set of molecular pathways to which ASD-involved genes seem to converge, including, among others, synaptogenesis, synaptic function, and neuronal translational regulation (reviewed in de la Torre-Ubieta et al., 2016). This effort has been accompanied by the development of ASD-relevant behavioral phenotyping assays, primarily targeted at social, communication, and repetitive behaviors (Silverman et al., 2010a; Wöhr and Scattoni, 2013; Kas et al., 2014; Homberg et al., 2016). Interestingly, many—but not all—models showed autism-like traits, with manifestations ranging from repetitive behaviors to reduced social communication (ultrasonic vocalizations) and social interest (reviewed in Ellegood and Crawley, 2015). However, despite the widespread application and high face validity of ASD behavioral phenotyping, the significance and translational relevance of mouse behavioral alterations to human ASD remain debated (Wöhr and Scattoni, 2013) and should be extrapolated with caution.

Recent advances in mouse rsfMRI mapping (reviewed in Gozzi and Schwarz, 2016) offer the opportunity of extending mouse modeling of ASD to the investigation of the neurobiological underpinnings and etiopathological significance of ASD-related connectivity aberrations. Specifically, improvements in MRI imaging hardware, together with tighter control of physiological and motion artifacts (Weber et al., 2006; Ferrari et al., 2012) have led to robust and reproducible identification of homotopic rsfMRI networks covering known cortical and subcortical systems in the mouse by several research groups (Mechling et al., 2014; Nasrallah et al., 2014; Sforazzini et al., 2014; Zerbi et al., 2015; Shah et al., 2016). Interestingly, distributed networks encompassing heteromodal prefrontal and posterior cortical regions have also been identified (Sforazzini et al., 2014; Zerbi et al., 2015; Shah et al., 2016), leading to the suggestive hypothesis of the presence of evolutionary precursors of the human salience network and default mode network (DMN) in this species (reviewed in Gozzi and Schwarz, 2016). This notion is empirically corroborated by the recent observation that cytoarchitecturally homologous regions such as anterior cingulate and retrosplenial cortices (Vogt and Paxinos, 2014) similarly serve as connectivity hubs in humans and mice (Cole et al., 2010; Tomasi and Volkow, 2011; Liska et al., 2015). Moreover, the application of rsfMRI to the mouse brain comes with several important advantages, including the possibility to use quantitative imaging modalities for an objective endo-phenotypic characterization of ASD-related pathology complementary to behavioral assays, and to validate its readouts with invasive techniques that are off limits for human research, including local field potentials (LFPs) coherence mappings (Zhan et al., 2014), local injection of neuronal tracers (Sforazzini et al., 2016), as well as an ever-increasing array of histopathological, stereological, or immunohistochemical post-mortem analyses.

Collectively, these correspondences strongly support the use of rsfMRI as a means to bridge research of functional connectivity aberrancies in autism across species (human vs. mouse) and levels of inquiry (from cellular- and microscale to meso- and macroscale, **Figure 1**), along two main investigational routes. First, rsfMRI can be used to establish *causal* (rather than *associative*) etiopathological contributions between specific ASD-associated genetic variants and macroscale connectivity, thus complementing analogous clinical research efforts using imaging genetics (Scott-Van Zeeland et al., 2010; Rudie et al., 2012). One notable experimental advantage of mouse imaging with respect to current human imaging genetic approaches is the possibility of mapping and comparing the effect of multiple mutations (via the use of different autism mouse models) under rigorously controlled experimental conditions, thus reducing the confounding contribution of experimental variables that can be only minimally controlled in human research, such as genetic and environmental variability, age (Uddin et al., 2013b), ASD-related motion, and group differences in cognitive states (Vasa et al., 2016). The main goal of this line of investigation is to assess whether seemingly unrelated ASD-risk mutations do converge on a limited number of distinct functional connectivity endophenotypes. An elegant demonstration of this approach has been recently described using morpho-anatomical MRI. Brain-volumetric phenotypes of 26 ASD mouse models as defined by structural MRI methods exhibited clustering into three main groups, each with a distinct set of concomitant changes in size across different brain regions (Ellegood et al., 2015). Such reduction of morpho-anatomical heterogeneity is not surprising, given the wide (and sometimes opposing) stream of pathophysiological alterations observed in syndromic forms of autism, which range from basic molecular or synaptic mechanism such as protein synthesis (Geschwind and Levitt, 2007; Auerbach et al., 2011) up to homeostatic regulations of excitatory and inhibitory neurotransmission (Nelson and Valakh, 2015). Analogous analyses with regards to functional connectivity phenotypes should be possible in the future to associate basic pathophysiological traits with macroscale connectional aberrancies.

A second main line of investigation is the combined use of mouse rsfMRI and multiscale neurobiological techniques to obtain a mechanistic description of ASD-related phenotypes and pathophysiological pathways leading to aberrant functional connectivity. This research can include, but is not limited to, a deeper investigation of syndromic ASD mutations associated with specific pathological traits [e.g., Tuberous Sclerosis 2 as a key mediator of impaired autophagy and increased synaptic density (Tang et al., 2014)], and can possibly be extended to investigate risk factors that have been also more loosely implicated in autism. This research effort may generate crucial mechanistic information that can be used to back-translate clinical evidence of aberrant connectivity into interpretable neurophysiological events/models that can help understand, diagnose, or treat these disorders. A brief description of initial steps toward these two main goals is reported in the next two sections.

FUNCTIONAL CONNECTIVITY MAPPING IN GENETIC MODELS OF AUTISM

An outstanding question in ASD connectivity studies is whether genetic mutations associated with syndromic forms of autism are sufficient to produce aberrant macroscale functional connectivity. Initial mouse rsfMRI studies seem to corroborate this hypothesis. Specifically, Haberl and colleagues have recently investigated functional and structural connectivity in the

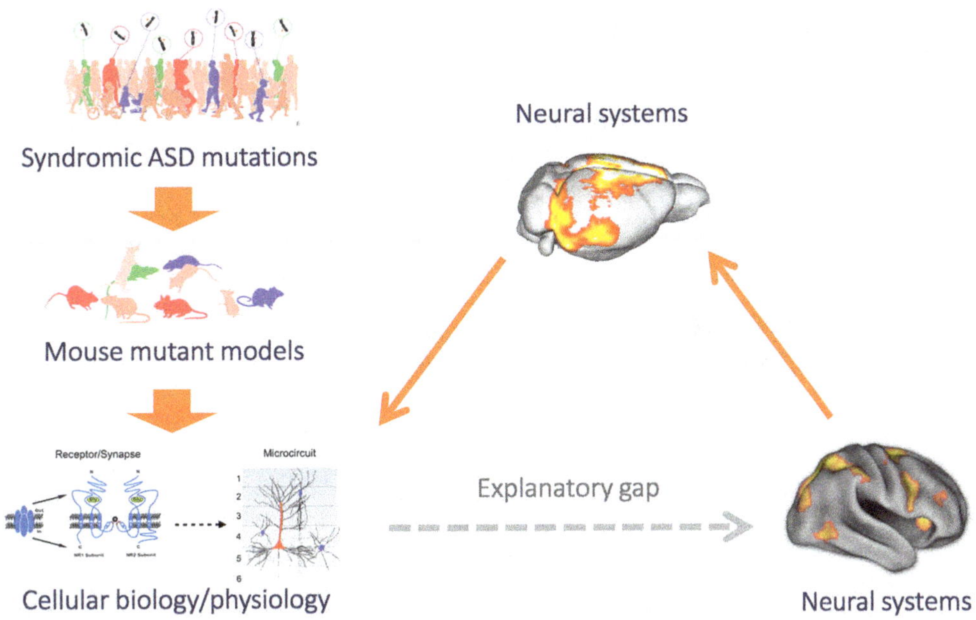

FIGURE 1 | Mouse imaging can bridge the gap between microscale models of brain function and clinical research of macroscale functional connectivity. Mouse models provide a powerful reductive platform that can be employed to link etiological determinants of ASD, such as syndromic mutation or neurodevelopmental traits, to basic molecular and cellular signatures of pathology (left, top to down). However, until recently we have been unable to use this approach to study the neurobiological underpinnings of macroscale functional connectivity, owing to difficulty in translating models of brain function across levels of inquiry. This results in a major explanatory gap between clinical research (heavily relying on macroscale neuroimaging measures of brain function, such as rsfMRI) and preclinical neurobiological investigation in rodent models (bottom, right). The implementation of functional connectivity mapping via rsfMRI in the mouse (right) can bridge this gap, by permitting to causally relate connectional changes with basic molecular or cellular processes, and by permitting a direct translation of these findings from and to humans owing to the shared biophysical principle underlying these measurements (figure adapted from Arguello and Gogos, 2012; Anticevic et al., 2013 with permission).

$Fmr1^{-/y}$ model of fragile X syndrome (FXS; Budimirovic and Kaufmann, 2011) and described connectional aberrations in sensory networks (Haberl et al., 2015). These included reduced structural integrity of the corpus callosum and an increase in local connectivity of the primary visual cortex, as probed by viral tracers, an effect accompanied by reduced rsfMRI coupling between visual and other neighboring sensory cortical regions. The authors suggested that the observed decoupling could explain sensory processing defects that are often observed in FXS patients (Boyd et al., 2010).

In another recent study, homozygous mice lacking the ASD-risk gene CNTNAP2 (Peñagarikano et al., 2011) exhibited reduced long-range and local functional connectivity in cingulate and prefrontal regions (Liska et al., 2016), two key heteromodal areas of the mouse brain previously characterized as functional connectivity hubs, owing to their rich connectivity with other brain areas (Liska et al., 2015). Interestingly, impaired antero-posterior prefrontal connectivity between components of the mouse DMN was associated with reduced social investigation, a behavioral measure regarded as a core "autism trait" in mice (Wöhr and Scattoni, 2013). This finding recapitulates analogous imaging results obtained in human carriers of CNTNAP2 gene polymorphisms (Scott-Van Zeeland et al., 2010), hence providing a first example of the translational value of this approach. This finding is consistent with the presence of impaired GABAergic neurotransmission in these animals (Peñagarikano et al., 2011), a trait that could result in aberrant oscillatory rhythms. It is interesting to note that analogous prefrontal hypo-connectivity has been observed using rsfMRI in BTBR mice, an idiopathic model of autism characterized by agenesis of the corpus callosum and by analogous excitatory/inhibitory imbalances (Sforazzini et al., 2016).

rsfMRI mapping has also been recently carried out in a mouse model of human 15q13.3 microdeletion, a CNV associated with schizophrenia, intellectual disability, and ASD (Shinawi et al., 2009). Compared to wild-type mice, 15q13.3 mice showed widespread patterns of hyper-connectivity along the hippocampal-prefrontal axis, a network commonly affected in schizophrenic patients (Gass et al., 2016). Notably, Gass and colleagues also showed that aberrant functional connectivity could be acutely rescued by pharmacological stimulation of nicotinic acetylcholine alpha 7 receptors, in keeping with a contribution of this mechanism to the development of schizophrenia-related phenotypes in these mice (Gass et al., 2016). Although the phenotypic traits of this mouse line appear to be more closely related to schizophrenia rather than to ASD (Fejgin et al., 2014), the results of this study are important as they show that CNVs and genetic alterations with partial penetrance to ASD could produce divergent connectional phenotypes (e.g., hyper- and hypo-connectivity), suggesting a plausible contribution of genetic heterogeneity to some of the discrepant imaging findings in humans. Importantly, these initial mouse studies argue against an artifactual (e.g., motion-driven) origin of connectivity aberrations reported in human ASD research, because the use of light sedation in mice along with artificial ventilation allows for the acquisition of virtually motion-free images.

NEUROBIOLOGICAL PATHWAYS LEADING TO ABERRANT FUNCTIONAL CONNECTIVITY

A few recent studies have provided important mechanistic investigations of ASD-relevant phenotypes associated with aberrant functional connectivity. In the first of such studies, Zhan et al. (2014) investigated whether deficits in synaptic pruning, a putative pathophysiological determinant of autism (Hutsler and Zhang, 2010), result in connectivity alterations. To probe this hypothesis, the authors measured rsfMRI connectivity in $Cx3cr1^{KO}$ mice, a mouse line characterized by microglia-dependent synaptic pruning deficits as a result of deficient neuronal-microglia signaling (Paolicelli et al., 2011). Synaptic pruning deficits in $Cx3cr1^{KO}$ were found to be associated with long-range functional connectivity impairments, a finding corroborated by LFPs coherence recordings in freely-behaving animals. Interestingly, the authors also showed that impaired pruning was associated with core mouse "autism traits," and that long-range fronto-hippocampal connectivity was a good predictor of social behavior. This study is of special importance, as it was the first to suggest a role for dysfunctional synaptic maturation in shaping long-range functional synchronization and to postulate a contribution of immune system mediators to this cascade. Empirical evidence in support of this hypothesis comes from another recent study (Kim et al., 2016), where analogous phenotypes where observed in mice characterized by defective autophagy in microglia, including increased synaptic density, impaired social activity, and a trend for impaired connectivity between posterior-sensory and prefrontal regions. Similarly, Filiano et al. (2016) recently showed that deficiency in interferon-γ, a key immune signaling protein, is associated with social deficits and frontal rsfMRI hyper-connectivity in SCID mice, thus corroborating a putative mechanistic link between immune dysfunction, impaired social behavior, and functional connectivity. Although promising and mechanistically relevant, these initial results should be extrapolated to autism research with great caution, as a pathophysiological contribution of immune and microglia deficits to ASD has yet to be unambiguously demonstrated (Estes and McAllister, 2015). They, however, powerfully illustrate how the combined use of rsfMRI, mouse genetics and state-of-the-art neuro-biological approaches can elucidate pathways leading to aberrant functional connectivity, an approach that can be extended to investigate the role of multiple ASD-relevant pathophysiological factors, including syndromic genetic mutations.

LIMITATIONS AND FUTURE PERSPECTIVES

Like any other experimental approach, mouse rsfMRI is accompanied by limitations that should be taken into account when the approach is used to investigate the basis of connectivity alterations in ASD. First and foremost, as mouse rsfMRI experiments normally employ sedation to minimize stress and motion of animals during scans, the contribution of possible genotype-dependent differences in sensitivity to anesthesia (Petrinovic et al., 2016) should be controlled. The fact that to date only a minority of studies (Zhan et al., 2014; Liska et al., 2016; Sforazzini et al., 2016) have reported genotype-dependent measures of anesthesia sensitivity is a factor for concern, as differences in anesthesia depth/sensitivity can affect connectivity strength and distribution of the imaged networks (Nasrallah et al., 2014). The impact of anesthesia *per-se* as a putative modifier of intrinsic connectional architecture appears to be less of an issue, as a large body of human and rodent research shows that, under light controlled sedation, the regional patterns of functional correlation seem to be largely preserved (reviewed in Gozzi and Schwarz, 2016). As pointed out in previous work, a rigorous control of motion and physiological state is also of paramount importance to obtain reliable network mapping (Jonckers et al., 2015; Gozzi and Schwarz, 2016). It should also be mentioned that, although the field is still lacking in standardized protocols and methods that would facilitate comparison of experimental results across studies and sites, this issue is receiving increased attention and collaborative efforts are underway to address it.

The initial studies described here represent only the first step toward a greater understanding of the origin and underpinnings of connectional alterations in ASD. Future investigations are required to describe commonalities and differences between brain functional networks in the mouse and human from multiple points of view, including topology (Sporns and Betzel, 2016; van den Heuvel et al., 2016a), biological underpinnings (Richiardi et al., 2015; Wang et al., 2015; van den Heuvel et al., 2016b), and functional equivalence (Li et al., 2015). Similarly, studies of additional genetic etiologies associated with ASDs, covering heterogeneous pathophysiological pathways, are crucial to achieve a deeper understanding of whether the connectional signatures are mutation specific or can be regarded as a generalizable phenomenon. When coupled to analogous clinical efforts aimed at identification of connectional aberrancies in genetically homogeneous populations [e.g., 16p11.2 deletion (Simons Vip Consortium, 2012; Owen et al., 2014)], the method can also be used to investigate the cellular and physiological basis of clinically relevant neuroimaging readouts and, via a comparison between human and mouse imaging findings, to obtain an assessment of the translational and construct validity of mouse models of ASD. The developmental trajectory of these alterations could in principle also be investigated in mouse models, although critical limitations in the accuracy of physiological control in young mice and pups exist.

Much of mouse ASD modeling has been so far primarily addressed at monogenic ASD syndromes, which represent ~10%

of ASDs (Silverman et al., 2010a; Nelson and Valakh, 2015). The recapitulation, in mice, of high-confidence genetic etiologies associated with ASD offers the opportunity to probe specific hypotheses about circuit dysfunction and ASD pathology that can be directly extrapolated to homologous clinical populations [e.g., 16p11.2 microdeletion (Simons Vip Consortium, 2012; Owen et al., 2014)]. An important limitation of current ASD translational research is its inability to reliably model "idiopathic" autism, which is the most frequent diagnostic label for ASD-related behavioral manifestations. Attempts to use forward genetic approaches in inbred mouse lines exhibiting ASD-like behaviors without a specific genetic determinant have been proposed, with the inbred BTBR mouse line probably being the most notable example in the field (Silverman et al., 2010b; Gogolla et al., 2014; Squillace et al., 2014). Translational relevance of neuro-behavioral findings obtained by comparing genetically homogeneous inbred lines like asocial BTBR and "normosocial" B6 mice is, however, debated (Dodero et al., 2013; Squillace et al., 2014). Nevertheless, novel neuromolecular approaches and the use of induced pluripotent stem cells (iPSCs) from patients have begun to reveal common downstream neurobiological pathways in idiopathic forms of autism characterized by shared neuroanatomical features [e.g., macrocephaly (Nicolini et al., 2015; Marchetto et al., 2016)]. Controlled manipulation of such signaling and molecular pathways in animal models is a foreseeable strategy that can be employed to expand our translational framework to the investigation of macroscale brain network aberrancies in idiopathic forms of ASD.

Finally, studies in which connectivity alterations are pharmacologically or genetically rescued may help clarify the relevance of functional connectional alterations to ASD pathology and its behavioral manifestations. Specifically, if connectivity alterations are an underlying cause of observed behavioral deficits, then behavioral phenotypic "rescue" should be accompanied by normalized patterns of brain functional connectivity. This research could indicate whether connectivity alterations are *necessary* for the expression of ASD-related behaviors in mice, or are instead an epiphenomenal manifestation of underlying pathophysiology, thus providing an empirical assessment of the pathophysiological relevance of connectivity aberrancies in ASD. "Rescue" studies may also help identify putative endo-phenotypes (complementary to behavior) that could serve as measurable readouts for early clinical translation and evaluation of novel ASD treatments in genetically defined autism syndromes (Smucny et al., 2014).

In conclusion, functional imaging of the mouse has now reached a turning point such that accurate modeling and investigation of ASD-connectivity aberrations is currently possible, via the use of readouts amenable to direct translation to human research (e.g., rsfMRI). Despite caveats, in the next few years the approach is poised to offer breakthroughs in our understanding of the pathogenesis of ASD-related connectivity aberrancies, possibly bringing some order to the intricate and often contradictory body of research detailing connectional alterations in patient populations.

AUTHOR CONTRIBUTIONS

AG conceived and wrote the manuscript with input from AL.

ACKNOWLEDGMENTS

AG has received funding by the Simons Foundation (SFARI 314688 and 400101).

REFERENCES

Abrahams, B. S., and Geschwind, D. H. (2008). Advances in autism genetics: on the threshold of a new neurobiology. *Nat. Rev. Genet.* 9, 341–355. doi: 10.1038/nrg2346

Ameis, S. H., and Catani, M. (2015). Altered white matter connectivity as a neural substrate for social impairment in Autism Spectrum Disorder. *Cortex* 62, 158–181. doi: 10.1016/j.cortex.2014.10.014

Anagnostou, E., and Taylor, M. J. (2011). Review of neuroimaging in autism spectrum disorders: what have we learned and where we go from here. *Mol. Autism* 2:4. doi: 10.1186/2040-2392-2-4

Anticevic, A., Cole, M. W., Repovs, G., Savic, A., Driesen, N. R., Yang, G., et al. (2013). Connectivity, pharmacology, and computation: toward a mechanistic understanding of neural system dysfunction in schizophrenia. *Schizophrenia* 4:169. doi: 10.3389/fpsyt.2013.00169

Arguello, P. A., and Gogos, J. A. (2012). Genetic and cognitive windows into circuit mechanisms of psychiatric disease. *Trends Neurosci.* 35, 3–13. doi: 10.1016/j.tins.2011.11.007

Assaf, M., Jagannathan, K., Calhoun, V. D., Miller, L., Stevens, M. C., Sahl, R., et al. (2010). Abnormal functional connectivity of default mode sub-networks in autism spectrum disorder patients. *Neuroimage* 53, 247–256. doi: 10.1016/j.neuroimage.2010.05.067

Association AP (2013). *Diagnostic and Statistical Manual of Mental Disorders, 5th Edn., DSM-5.* Washington, DC: American Psychiatric Publishing.

Auerbach, B. D., Osterweil, E. K., and Bear, M. F. (2011). Mutations causing syndromic autism define an axis of synaptic pathophysiology. *Nature* 480, 63–68. doi: 10.1038/nature10658

Bernhardt, B. C., Di Martino, A., Valk, S. L., and Wallace, G. L. (2016). "Neuroimaging-based phenotyping of the autism spectrum," in *Current Topics in Behavioral Neurosciences* (Berlin; Heidelberg: Springer), 1–15. Available online at: http://link.springer.com/chapter/10.1007/7854_2016_438 (Accessed July 10, 2016).

Boyd, B. A., Baranek, G. T., Sideris, J., Poe, M. D., Watson, L. R., Patten, E., et al. (2010). Sensory features and repetitive behaviors in children with autism and developmental delays. *Autism Res.* 3, 78–87. doi: 10.1002/aur.124

Budimirovic, D. B., and Kaufmann, W. E. (2011). What can we learn about autism from studying fragile X syndrome? *Dev. Neurosci.* 33, 379–394. doi: 10.1159/000330213

Chang, J., Gilman, S. R., Chiang, A. H., Sanders, S. J., and Vitkup, D. (2015). Genotype to phenotype relationships in autism spectrum disorders. *Nat. Neurosci.* 18, 191–198. doi: 10.1038/nn.3907

Cherkassky, V. L., Kana, R. K., Keller, T. A., and Just, M. A. (2006). Functional connectivity in a baseline resting-state network in autism. *Neuroreport* 17, 1687–1690. doi: 10.1097/01.wnr.0000239956.45448.4c

Cole, M. W., Pathak, S., and Schneider, W. (2010). Identifying the brain's most globally connected regions. *Neuroimage* 49, 3132–3148. doi: 10.1016/j.neuroimage.2009.11.001

Deen, B., and Pelphrey, K. (2012). Perspective: brain scans need a rethink. *Nature* 491, S20. doi: 10.1038/491S20a

de la Torre-Ubieta, L., Won, H., Stein, J. L., and Geschwind, D. H. (2016). Advancing the understanding of autism disease mechanisms through genetics. *Nat. Med.* 22, 345–361. doi: 10.1038/nm.4071

Di Martino, A., Yan, C.-G., Li, Q., Denio, E., Castellanos, F. X., Alaerts, K., et al. (2014). The autism brain imaging data exchange: towards a large-scale evaluation of the intrinsic brain architecture in autism. *Mol. Psychiatry* 19, 659–667. doi: 10.1038/mp.2013.78

Dodero, L., Damiano, M., Galbusera, A., Bifone, A., Tsaftsaris, S. A., Scattoni, M. L., et al. (2013). Neuroimaging evidence of major morpho-anatomical and functional abnormalities in the BTBR T+TF/J mouse model of autism. *PLoS ONE* 8:e76655. doi: 10.1371/journal.pone.0076655

Ecker, C., Bookheimer, S. Y., and Murphy, D. G. M. (2015). Neuroimaging in autism spectrum disorder: brain structure and function across the lifespan. *Lancet Neurol.* 14, 1121–1134. doi: 10.1016/S1474-4422(15)00050-2

Ecker, C., and Murphy, D. (2014). Neuroimaging in autism-from basic science to translational research. *Nat. Rev. Neurol.* 10, 82–91. doi: 10.1038/nrneurol.2013.276

Ellegood, J., Anagnostou, E., Babineau, B. A., Crawley, J. N., Lin, L., Genestine, M., et al. (2015). Clustering autism: using neuroanatomical differences in 26 mouse models to gain insight into the heterogeneity. *Mol. Psychiatry* 20, 118–125. doi: 10.1038/mp.2014.98

Ellegood, J., and Crawley, J. N. (2015). Behavioral and neuroanatomical phenotypes in mouse models of autism. *Neurotherapeutics* 12, 521–533. doi: 10.1007/s13311-015-0360-z

Estes, M. L., and McAllister, A. K. (2015). Immune mediators in the brain and peripheral tissues in autism spectrum disorder. *Nat. Rev. Neurosci.* 16, 469–486. doi: 10.1038/nrn3978

Fejgin, K., Nielsen, J., Birknow, M. R., Bastlund, J. F., Nielsen, V., Lauridsen, J. B., et al. (2014). A mouse model that recapitulates cardinal features of the 15q13.3 microdeletion syndrome including schizophrenia- and epilepsy-related alterations. *Biol. Psychiatry* 76, 128–137. doi: 10.1016/j.biopsych.2013.08.014

Ferrari, L., Turrini, G., Crestan, V., Bertani, S., Cristofori, P., Bifone, A., et al. (2012). A robust experimental protocol for pharmacological fMRI in rats and mice. *J. Neurosci. Methods* 204, 9–18. doi: 10.1016/j.jneumeth.2011.10.020

Filiano, A. J., Xu, Y., Tustison, N. J., Marsh, R. L., Baker, W., Smirnov, I., et al. (2016). Unexpected role of interferon-γ in regulating neuronal connectivity and social behaviour. *Nature* 535, 425–429. doi: 10.1038/nature18626

Gass, N., Weber-Fahr, W., Sartorius, A., Becker, R., Didriksen, M., Stensbøl, T. B., et al. (2016). An acetylcholine alpha7 positive allosteric modulator rescues a schizophrenia-associated brain endophenotype in the 15q13.3 microdeletion, encompassing CHRNA7. *Eur. Neuropsychopharmacol.* 26, 1150–1160. doi: 10.1016/j.euroneuro.2016.03.013

Georgiades, S., Szatmari, P., Boyle, M., Hanna, S., Duku, E., Zwaigenbaum, L., et al. (2013). Investigating phenotypic heterogeneity in children with autism spectrum disorder: a factor mixture modeling approach. *J. Child Psychol. Psychiatry* 54, 206–215. doi: 10.1111/j.1469-7610.2012.02588.x

Geschwind, D. H. (2009). Advances in autism. *Annu. Rev. Med.* 60, 367–380. doi: 10.1146/annurev.med.60.053107.121225

Geschwind, D. H., and Levitt, P. (2007). Autism spectrum disorders: developmental disconnection syndromes. *Curr. Opin. Neurobiol.* 17, 103–111. doi: 10.1016/j.conb.2007.01.009

Geschwind, D. H., and State, M. W. (2015). Gene hunting in autism spectrum disorder: on the path to precision medicine. *Lancet Neurol.* 14, 1109–1120. doi: 10.1016/S1474-4422(15)00044-7

Gogolla, N., Takesian, A. E., Feng, G., Fagiolini, M., and Hensch, T. K. (2014). Sensory integration in mouse insular cortex reflects GABA circuit maturation. *Neuron* 83, 894–905. doi: 10.1016/j.neuron.2014.06.033

Gozzi, A., and Schwarz, A. J. (2016). Large-scale functional connectivity networks in the rodent brain. *Neuroimage* 127, 496–509. doi: 10.1016/j.neuroimage.2015.12.017

Haberl, M. G., Zerbi, V., Veltien, A., Ginger, M., Heerschap, A., and Frick, A. (2015). Structural-functional connectivity deficits of neocortical circuits in the Fmr1(−/y) mouse model of autism. *Sci. Adv.* 1:e1500775. doi: 10.1126/sciadv.1500775

Hahamy, A., Behrmann, M., and Malach, R. (2015). The idiosyncratic brain: distortion of spontaneous connectivity patterns in autism spectrum disorder. *Nat. Neurosci.* 18, 302–309. doi: 10.1038/nn.3919

Homberg, J. R., Kyzar, E. J., Nguyen, M., Norton, W. H., Pittman, J., Poudel, M. K., et al. (2016). Understanding autism and other neurodevelopmental disorders through experimental translational neurobehavioral models. *Neurosci. Biobehav. Rev.* 65, 292–312. doi: 10.1016/j.neubiorev.2016.03.013

Horwitz, B., Rumsey, J. M., Grady, C. L., and Rapoport, S. I. (1988). The cerebral metabolic landscape in autism. Intercorrelations of regional glucose utilization. *Arch. Neurol.* 45, 749–755.

Hutsler, J. J., and Zhang, H. (2010). Increased dendritic spine densities on cortical projection neurons in autism spectrum disorders. *Brain Res.* 1309, 83–94. doi: 10.1016/j.brainres.2009.09.120

Jonckers, E., Shah, D., Hamaide, J., Verhoye, M., and Van der Linden, A. (2015). The power of using functional fMRI on small rodents to study brain pharmacology and disease. *Front. Pharmacol.* 6:231. doi: 10.3389/fphar.2015.00231

Just, M. A., Cherkassky, V. L., Keller, T. A., and Minshew, N. J. (2004). Cortical activation and synchronization during sentence comprehension in high-functioning autism: evidence of underconnectivity. *Brain J. Neurol.* 127, 1811–1821. doi: 10.1093/brain/awh199

Just, M. A., Keller, T. A., Malave, V. L., Kana, R. K., and Varma, S. (2012). Autism as a neural systems disorder: a theory of frontal-posterior underconnectivity. *Neurosci. Biobehav. Rev.* 36, 1292–1313. doi: 10.1016/j.neubiorev.2012.02.007

Kana, R. K., Libero, L. E., and Moore, M. S. (2011). Disrupted cortical connectivity theory as an explanatory model for autism spectrum disorders. *Phys. Life Rev.* 8, 410–437. doi: 10.1016/j.plrev.2011.10.001

Kas, M. J., Glennon, J. C., Buitelaar, J., Ey, E., Biemans, B., Crawley, J., et al. (2014). Assessing behavioural and cognitive domains of autism spectrum disorders in rodents: current status and future perspectives. *Psychopharmacology (Berl)* 231, 1125–1146. doi: 10.1007/s00213-013-3268-5

Kennedy, D. P., and Courchesne, E. (2008). The intrinsic functional organization of the brain is altered in autism. *Neuroimage* 39, 1877–1885. doi: 10.1016/j.neuroimage.2007.10.052

Keown, C. L., Shih, P., Nair, A., Peterson, N., Mulvey, M. E., and Müller, R.-A. (2013). Local functional overconnectivity in posterior brain regions is associated with symptom severity in autism spectrum disorders. *Cell Rep.* 5, 567–572. doi: 10.1016/j.celrep.2013.10.003

Kim, H.-J., Cho, M.-H., Shim, W. H., Kim, J. K., Jeon, E.-Y., Kim, D.-H., et al. (2016). Deficient autophagy in microglia impairs synaptic pruning and causes social behavioral defects. *Mol. Psychiatry* doi: 10.1038/mp.2016.103. [Epub ahead of print].

Lai, M.-C., Lombardo, M. V., and Baron-Cohen, S. (2014). Autism. *Lancet Lond. Engl.* 383, 896–910. doi: 10.1016/S0140-6736(13)61539-1

Li, J., Martin, S., Tricklebank, M. D., Schwarz, A. J., and Gilmour, G. (2015). Task-induced modulation of intrinsic functional connectivity networks in the behaving rat. *J. Neurosci.* 35, 658–665. doi: 10.1523/JNEUROSCI.3488-14.2015

Liska, A., Galbusera, A., Schwarz, A. J., and Gozzi, A. (2015). Functional connectivity hubs of the mouse brain. *Neuroimage* 115, 281–291. doi: 10.1016/j.neuroimage.2015.04.033

Liska, A., Gomolka, R., Sabbioni, M., Galbusera, A., Panzeri, S., Scattoni, M. L., et al. (2016). Homozygous loss of autism-risk gene CNTNAP2 results in reduced local and long-range prefrontal functional connectivity. *bioRxiv* 60335. doi: 10.1101/060335

Marchetto, M. C., Belinson, H., Tian, Y., Freitas, B. C., Fu, C., Vadodaria, K. C., et al. (2016). Altered proliferation and networks in neural cells derived from idiopathic autistic individuals. *Mol. Psychiatry.* doi: 10.1038/mp.2016.95. [Epub ahead of print].

Mechling, A. E., Hübner, N. S., Lee, H.-L., Hennig, J., von Elverfeldt, D., and Harsan, L.-A. (2014). Fine-grained mapping of mouse brain functional connectivity with resting-state fMRI. *Neuroimage* 96, 203–215. doi: 10.1016/j.neuroimage.2014.03.078

Müller, R.-A. (2014). "Anatomical and functional connectivity in autism spectrum disorders," in *Comprehensive Guide to Autism*, eds V. B. Patel, V. R. Preedy, and C. R. Martin (New York, NY: Springer), 49–75. Available online at: http://link.springer.com/referenceworkentry/10.1007/978-1-4614-4788-7_192 (Accessed July 10, 2016).

Nasrallah, F. A., Tay, H.-C., and Chuang, K.-H. (2014). Detection of functional connectivity in the resting mouse brain. *Neuroimage* 86, 417–424. doi: 10.1016/j.neuroimage.2013.10.025

Nelson, S. B., and Valakh, V. (2015). Excitatory/inhibitory balance and circuit homeostasis in autism spectrum disorders. *Neuron* 87, 684–698. doi: 10.1016/j.neuron.2015.07.033

Nicolini, C., Ahn, Y., Michalski, B., Rho, J. M., and Fahnestock, M. (2015). Decreased mTOR signaling pathway in human idiopathic autism and in rats exposed to valproic acid. *Acta Neuropathol. Commun.* 3:3. doi: 10.1186/s40478-015-0184-4

Owen, J. P., Chang, Y. S., Pojman, N. J., Bukshpun, P., Wakahiro, M. L. J., Marco, E. J., et al. (2014). Aberrant white matter microstructure in children with

16p11.2 deletions. *J. Neurosci.* 34, 6214–6223. doi: 10.1523/JNEUROSCI.4495-13.2014

Paolicelli, R. C., Bolasco, G., Pagani, F., Maggi, L., Scianni, M., Panzanelli, P., et al. (2011). Synaptic pruning by microglia is necessary for normal brain development. *Science* 333, 1456–1458. doi: 10.1126/science.1202529

Pardoe, H. R., Kucharsky Hiess, R., and Kuzniecky, R. (2016). Motion and morphometry in clinical and nonclinical populations. *Neuroimage* 135, 177–185. doi: 10.1016/j.neuroimage.2016.05.005

Peñagarikano, O., Abrahams, B. S., Herman, E. I., Winden, K. D., Gdalyahu, A., Dong, H., et al. (2011). Absence of CNTNAP2 leads to epilepsy, neuronal migration abnormalities, and core autism-related deficits. *Cell* 147, 235–246. doi: 10.1016/j.cell.2011.08.040

Petrinovic, M. M., Hankov, G., Schroeter, A., Bruns, A., Rudin, M., von Kienlin, M., et al. (2016). A novel anesthesia regime enables neurofunctional studies and imaging genetics across mouse strains. *Sci. Rep.* 6:24523. doi: 10.1038/srep24523

Power, J. D., Barnes, K. A., Snyder, A. Z., Schlaggar, B. L., and Petersen, S. E. (2012). Spurious but systematic correlations in functional connectivity MRI networks arise from subject motion. *Neuroimage* 59, 2142–2154. doi: 10.1016/j.neuroimage.2011.10.018

Power, J. D., Schlaggar, B. L., and Petersen, S. E. (2015). Recent progress and outstanding issues in motion correction in resting state fMRI. *Neuroimage* 105, 536–551. doi: 10.1016/j.neuroimage.2014.10.044

Richiardi, J., Altmann, A., Milazzo, A.-C., Chang, C., Chakravarty, M. M., Banaschewski, T., et al. (2015). BRAIN NETWORKS. Correlated gene expression supports synchronous activity in brain networks. *Science* 348, 1241–1244. doi: 10.1126/science.1255905

Rudie, J. D., Hernandez, L. M., Brown, J. A., Beck-Pancer, D., Colich, N. L., Gorrindo, P., et al. (2012). Autism-associated promoter variant in MET impacts functional and structural brain networks. *Neuron* 75, 904–915. doi: 10.1016/j.neuron.2012.07.010

Sanders, S. J., He, X., Willsey, A. J., Ercan-Sencicek, A. G., Samocha, K. E., Cicek, A. E., et al. (2015). Insights into autism spectrum disorder genomic architecture and biology from 71 risk loci. *Neuron* 87, 1215–1233. doi: 10.1016/j.neuron.2015.09.016

Scott-Van Zeeland, A. A., Abrahams, B. S., Alvarez-Retuerto, A. I., Sonnenblick, L. I., Rudie, J. D., Ghahremani, D., et al. (2010). Altered functional connectivity in frontal lobe circuits is associated with variation in the autism risk gene CNTNAP2. *Sci. Transl. Med.* 2:56ra80. doi: 10.1126/scitranslmed.3001344

Sforazzini, F., Bertero, A., Dodero, L., David, G., Galbusera, A., Scattoni, M. L., et al. (2016). Altered functional connectivity networks in acallosal and socially impaired BTBR mice. *Brain Struct. Funct.* 221, 941–954. doi: 10.1007/s00429-014-0948-9

Sforazzini, F., Schwarz, A. J., Galbusera, A., Bifone, A., and Gozzi, A. (2014). Distributed BOLD and CBV-weighted resting-state networks in the mouse brain. *Neuroimage* 87, 403–415. doi: 10.1016/j.neuroimage.2013.09.050

Shah, D., Blockx, I., Keliris, G. A., Kara, F., Jonckers, E., Verhoye, M., et al. (2016). Cholinergic and serotonergic modulations differentially affect large-scale functional networks in the mouse brain. *Brain Struct. Funct.* 221, 3067–3079. doi: 10.1007/s00429-015-1087-7

Shinawi, M., Schaaf, C. P., Bhatt, S. S., Xia, Z., Patel, A., Cheung, S. W., et al. (2009). A small recurrent deletion within 15q13.3 is associated with a range of neurodevelopmental phenotypes. *Nat. Genet.* 41, 1269–1271. doi: 10.1038/ng.481

Silverman, J. L., Tolu, S. S., Barkan, C. L., and Crawley, J. N. (2010b). Repetitive self-grooming behavior in the BTBR mouse model of autism is blocked by the mGluR5 antagonist MPEP. *Neuropsychopharmacology* 35, 976–989. doi: 10.1038/npp.2009.201

Silverman, J. L., Yang, M., Lord, C., and Crawley, J. N. (2010a). Behavioural phenotyping assays for mouse models of autism. *Nat. Rev. Neurosci.* 11, 490–502. doi: 10.1038/nrn2851

Smucny, J., Wylie, K. P., and Tregellas, J. R. (2014). Functional magnetic resonance imaging of intrinsic brain networks for translational drug discovery. *Trends Pharmacol. Sci.* 35, 397–403. doi: 10.1016/j.tips.2014.05.001

Sporns, O., and Betzel, R. F. (2016). Modular brain networks. *Annu. Rev. Psychol.* 67, 613–640. doi: 10.1146/annurev-psych-122414-033634

Squillace, M., Dodero, L., Federici, M., Migliarini, S., Errico, F., Napolitano, F., et al. (2014). Dysfunctional dopaminergic neurotransmission in asocial BTBR mice. *Transl. Psychiatry* 4:e427. doi: 10.1038/tp.2014.69

Stanfield, A. C., McIntosh, A. M., Spencer, M. D., Philip, R., Gaur, S., and Lawrie, S. M. (2008). Towards a neuroanatomy of autism: a systematic review and meta-analysis of structural magnetic resonance imaging studies. *Eur. Psychiatry* 23, 289–299. doi: 10.1016/j.eurpsy.2007.05.006

Supekar, K., Uddin, L. Q., Khouzam, A., Phillips, J., Gaillard, W. D., Kenworthy, L. E., et al. (2013). Brain hyperconnectivity in children with autism and its links to social deficits. *Cell Rep.* 5, 738–747. doi: 10.1016/j.celrep.2013.10.001

Tang, G., Gudsnuk, K., Kuo, S.-H., Cotrina, M. L., Rosoklija, G., Sosunov, A., et al. (2014). Loss of mTOR-dependent macroautophagy causes autistic-like synaptic pruning deficits. *Neuron* 83, 1131–1143. doi: 10.1016/j.neuron.2014.07.040

Tomasi, D., and Volkow, N. D. (2011). Functional connectivity hubs in the human brain. *Neuroimage* 57, 908–917. doi: 10.1016/j.neuroimage.2011.05.024

Uddin, L. Q., Supekar, K., Lynch, C. J., Khouzam, A., Phillips, J., Feinstein, C., et al. (2013a). Salience network-based classification and prediction of symptom severity in children with autism. *JAMA Psychiatry* 70, 869–879. doi: 10.1001/jamapsychiatry.2013.104

Uddin, L. Q., Supekar, K., and Menon, V. (2013b). Reconceptualizing functional brain connectivity in autism from a developmental perspective. *Front. Hum. Neurosci.* 7:458. doi: 10.3389/fnhum.2013.00458

van den Heuvel, M. P., Bullmore, E. T., and Sporns, O. (2016a). Comparative connectomics. *Trends Cogn. Sci.* 20, 345–361. doi: 10.1016/j.tics.2016.03.001

van den Heuvel, M. P., Scholtens, L. H., Turk, E., Mantini, D., Vanduffel, W., and Feldman Barrett, L. (2016b). Multimodal analysis of cortical chemoarchitecture and macroscale fMRI resting-state functional connectivity. *Hum. Brain Mapp.* 37, 3103–3113. doi: 10.1002/hbm.23229

Vasa, R. A., Mostofsky, S. H., and Ewen, J. B. (2016). The disrupted connectivity hypothesis of autism spectrum disorders: time for the next phase in research. *Biol. Psychiatry* 1, 245–252. doi: 10.1016/j.bpsc.2016.02.003

Simons Vip Consortium (2012). Simons Variation in Individuals Project (Simons VIP): a genetics-first approach to studying autism spectrum and related neurodevelopmental disorders. *Neuron* 73, 1063–1067. doi: 10.1016/j.neuron.2012.02.014

Vissers, M. E., Cohen, M. X., and Geurts, H. M. (2012). Brain connectivity and high functioning autism: a promising path of research that needs refined models, methodological convergence, and stronger behavioral links. *Neurosci. Biobehav. Rev.* 36, 604–625. doi: 10.1016/j.neubiorev.2011.09.003

Vogt, B. A., and Paxinos, G. (2014). Cytoarchitecture of mouse and rat cingulate cortex with human homologies. *Brain Struct. Funct.* 219, 185–192. doi: 10.1007/s00429-012-0493-3

Wang, G.-Z., Belgard, T. G., Mao, D., Chen, L., Berto, S., Preuss, T. M., et al. (2015). Correspondence between resting-state activity and brain gene expression. *Neuron* 88, 659–666. doi: 10.1016/j.neuron.2015.10.022

Weber, R., Ramos-Cabrer, P., Wiedermann, D., van Camp, N., and Hoehn, M. (2006). A fully noninvasive and robust experimental protocol for longitudinal fMRI studies in the rat. *Neuroimage* 29, 1303–1310. doi: 10.1016/j.neuroimage.2005.08.028

Wöhr, M., and Scattoni, M. L. (2013). Behavioural methods used in rodent models of autism spectrum disorders: current standards and new developments. *Behav. Brain Res.* 251, 5–17. doi: 10.1016/j.bbr.2013.05.047

Zerbi, V., Grandjean, J., Rudin, M., and Wenderoth, N. (2015). Mapping the mouse brain with rs-fMRI: an optimized pipeline for functional network identification. *Neuroimage* 123, 11–21. doi: 10.1016/j.neuroimage.2015.07.090

Zhan, Y., Paolicelli, R. C., Sforazzini, F., Weinhard, L., Bolasco, G., Pagani, F., et al. (2014). Deficient neuron-microglia signaling results in impaired functional brain connectivity and social behavior. *Nat. Neurosci.* 17, 400–406. doi: 10.1038/nn.3641

13

Developmental Profile and Diagnoses in Children Presenting with Motor Stereotypies

Francesco Cardona[1]*, Francesca Valente[1], Daniela Miraglia[1], Caterina D'Ardia[2], Valentina Baglioni[1] and Flavia Chiarotti[3]

[1] Dipartimento di Pediatria e Neuropsichiatria Infantile, Università degli Studi di Roma "La Sapienza", Rome, Italy, [2] Università degli Studi Niccolò Cusano, Rome, Italy, [3] Dipartimento di Biologia Cellulare e Neuroscienze, Istituto Superiore di Sanità, Rome, Italy

Edited by:
Roberto Canitano,
Azienda Ospedaliera Universitaria Senese, Italy

Reviewed by:
Roger Dante Freeman,
University of British Columbia, Canada
Vivek Agarwal,
King George's Medical University, India
Om Sai Ramesh Vallamkonda,
Lady Hardinge Medical College, India

****Correspondence:***
Francesco Cardona
francesco.cardona@uniroma1.it

Introduction: Motor stereotypies represent a typical example of the difficulty in distinguishing non-clinical behaviors (physiological and transient) from symptoms or among different disorders ["primary stereotypies," associated with autistic spectrum disorder (ASD), intellectual disabilities, genetic syndromes, and sensory impairment]. The aim of this study was to obtain an accurate assessment on the relationship between stereotypies and neurodevelopmental disorders.

Methods: We studied 23 children (3 girls), aged 36–95 months, who requested a consultation due to the persistence or increased severity of motor stereotypies. None of the patients had a previous diagnosis of ASD. The assessment included the Motor Severity Stereotypy Scale (MSSS), the Repetitive Behavior Scale-Revised (RBS-R), the Raven's Colored Progressive Matrices, the Child Behavior CheckList for ages 1½–5 or 4–18 (CBCL), the Social Responsiveness Scale (SRS), and the Autism Diagnostic Observation Schedule-second edition (ADOS 2).

Results: All patients were showing motor stereotypies for periods of time varying from 6 to 77 months. The MSSS showed that each child had a limited number of stereotypies; their frequency and intensity were mild. The interference of stereotypies was variable; the impairment in daily life was mild. The RBS-R scores were positive for the subscale of "stereotypic behaviors" in all children. Moreover, several children presented other repetitive behaviors, mainly "ritualistic behavior" and "sameness behavior." All patients showed a normal cognitive level. The CBCL evidenced behavioral problems in 22% of the children: internalizing problems, attention, and withdrawn were the main complaints. On the SRS, all but one of the tested patients obtained clinical scores in the clinical range for at least one area. On the ADOS 2, 4 patients obtained scores indicating a moderate level of ASD symptoms, 4 had a mild level, and 15 showed no or minimal signs of ASD.

Discussion: Motor stereotypies in children with normal cognitive level represent a challenging diagnostic issue for which a finely tailored assessment is mandatory in order to define a precise developmental profile. Thus, careful and cautious use of standardized tests is warranted to avoid misdiagnosis. Furthermore, it is hard to consider motor stereotypies, even the primary ones, exclusively as a movement disorder.

Keywords: stereotypies, autistic spectrum disorder, children, repetitive behaviors, neurodevelopmental disorders, complex motor stereotypies, DSM 5

INTRODUCTION

Stereotypies are a pattern of repetitive non-functional motor behavior that can interfere with the quality of social interactions, academic or other activities, or may result in injury (1, 2). Hand/arm flapping and waving, hand rotating, and finger wiggling are the stereotypies more frequently reported even if a wide range of other repetitive movements, sometimes accompanied by sounds or vocalizations, can be observed. Stereotypic movements generally last for seconds to minutes, tend to occur in clusters, and may appear many times throughout the day (3, 4). They are often triggered by periods of excitement, being engrossed in activities, stress, fatigue or boredom, and by daydreaming (5–7).

Stereotypies typically begin during the early developmental period, and they often represent a physiological and transient stage of development. Sixty percent of neurologically typical children show some stereotypic movements or behaviors between 2 and 5 years (8, 9). Besides the physiological ones, stereotypies are a main symptom of several developmental disorders, such as autistic spectrum disorder (ASD), intellectual disabilities (ID), genetic syndromes (Rett syndrome, Lesch–Nyhan syndrome, X-fragile syndrome, and others), and are also reported in sensory impaired individuals (10–12). In particular, stereotypies, together with other restricted, repetitive patterns of behavior, interest, or activities, represent a core symptom of ASD (13). Recent research suggests that restricted and repetitive behaviors can be subdivided into at least two subcategories, repetitive sensory motor and insistence on sameness behaviors, exhibiting different relationships with age and IQ (14). Moreover, stereotypic behaviors seem to be one of the four principal pathogenetic components in ASD, possibly differing in developmental trajectories and response to treatment (15).

If the above-mentioned conditions are ruled out, the stereotypies can be categorized as "primary" complex motor stereotypies (CMS) (16–18). Therefore, in the field of child neuropsychiatry, stereotypies represent a typical example of the difficulty in distinguishing non-clinical behaviors from symptoms or among different disorders.

In the DSM 5, the categorization into "primary" or "secondary" is not present: stereotypies are classified as stereotypic movement disorder (SMD) if they occur as a primary diagnosis or secondary to another disorder. It should be mentioned that the DSM 5 permits coding of SMD also in the presence of a neurodevelopmental disorder, adding the specifier of the associated condition (e.g., SMD associated with Lesch–Nyhan syndrome). On the other hand, when ASD is present, SMD is diagnosed only when there is self-injury or when the stereotypic behaviors are sufficiently severe to become a focus of treatment.

Some of the clinical conditions associated with stereotypies are relatively easy to diagnose. For instance, most genetic syndromes have evident phenotypic traits; moreover, in some of them, repetitive behaviors show specific profiles (19). In the same way, severe intellectual disability, sensory impairment, and low-functioning autism are conditions that can be ruled out without difficulty. On the other hand, major problems can be encountered in disentangling primary CMS from stereotypies occurring in high-functioning ASD. It should be mentioned that ASD was an exclusionary criterion in many studies on primary CMS: the children with a previous history of ASD diagnosis (based on a review of medical records) and those with overt risk of ASD (based on the Autism Spectrum Screening Questionnaire, carried out during a telephone screening) were excluded from the studies (20, 21).

From a differential diagnosis perspective, little help comes from previous studies aimed at comparing primary and secondary stereotypies. Previous studies have shown that individuals with autism had higher levels and intensity of stereotypy than individuals with mental retardation (22). These findings are consistent with other studies that have reported higher levels of stereotypy in individuals with disabilities than in age-matched individuals without disabilities (23). In a comparison study between typically developing children and patients with autism and PDD-NOS, the first ones showed constant and low levels of stereotypic behavior whereas levels increased with age in the children with autism and PDD-NOS (24). In a large cohort of 277 children, which included children with autism and non-autistic developmental disorders, Goldman and Greene (25) showed that the presence of stereotypies at preschool was more strongly linked with autism than with cognitive incompetence. Moreover, the number of stereotypies per child and the variety of stereotypies has been reported to be greater in low-functioning autism group, with head/trunk, hand/finger, and gait (e.g., spinning and pacing) stereotypies being the most frequent in this group (26). Finally, in a recent study comparing primary and secondary stereotypies, Ghosh et al. (27) found that the primary ones were simple, prevalently motor, of shorter duration, and of less frequency, whereas secondary had more vocalization, complexity, longer durations, and higher frequency; unexpectedly, worsening of stereotypies was noted in a higher percentage of the primary cases. Overall, these studies have limited usefulness when dealing with individual cases.

The aim of this study was to obtain an accurate analysis on the relationship between stereotypies and neurodevelopmental disorders. Therefore, we assessed a group of children requesting a consultation due to the presence, persistence, or increased severity of motor stereotypies.

MATERIALS AND METHODS

Participants

We studied 23 children, aged from 36 to 95 months, consecutively enrolled between September 2015 and June 2016 at the Outpatients Division of the Department of Pediatrics and Child Neuropsychiatry of "Sapienza" University of Rome. They were referred to our childhood movement disorder unit by their pediatrician. In all cases, the consultation was requested for the presence, persistence, or increased severity of motor stereotypies.

The only inclusion criterion was the presence of motor stereotypies, observed during the consultation, reported by parents or by home videos.

Exclusion criteria for the study were:

(1) known or suspected genetic syndromes;
(2) presence of other clinical neurological signs;
(3) presence of sensory impairment;
(4) previous diagnosis of ASD.

Procedures

After the first medical examination, eligible subjects were asked to participate in the study. Participants received a complete assessment with standardized tests, including an evaluation of cognitive profile [using Raven's Colored Progressive Matrices (CPM)]. Parents were asked to fill in questionnaires to check for other neuropsychiatric conditions: the Child Behavior CheckList for ages 1½–5 or 4–18 (CBCL), and the Social Responsiveness Scale (SRS) for children aged over 48 months. The Motor Severity Stereotypy Scale (MSSS) and the Repetitive Behavior Scale-Revised (RBS-R) were used to assess the stereotypies. The Autism Diagnostic Observation Schedule-Second edition (ADOS 2) was administered to the patients by fully qualified personnel, blinded to the clinical diagnosis. The study was approved by the "Sapienza - University of Rome" Ethics Committee (Ref. 3477). The parents gave their informed consent at the time of enrollment in the study.

Statistical Analysis

Quantitative data were summarized by means ± SD and categorical data by absolute and percent frequencies. Differences in total and subtotal scores of CBCL and SRS among groups based on the ADOS 2 calibrated severity score were assessed by the analysis of variance, followed by the Tukey test for multiple comparisons. The Pearson linear correlation coefficient r was computed to estimate the correlation between the CBCL pervasive developmental problem score and the ADOS 2 and SRS scores. To take into account possible violations of assumptions of parametric tests, non-parametric Kruskal–Wallis analysis of variance and Spearman's rank correlation coefficient were also applied. Since the results perfectly overlapped those of parametric analyses, only the latter are presented. Statistical analyses were performed by STATA Release 8.1.

RESULTS

The sample consisted of 23 children - 20 boys and 3 girls - aged between 36 and 95 months (mean = 53; SD = 15). The review of medical records showed that four patients had a history of motor delay (walking alone after 18 months of age), eight had motor coordination problems or immaturity in graphomotor skills, and seven had delay in expressive language. None of the children had a previous history of ASD diagnosis. At the time of consultation, all patients were showing motor stereotypies for periods of time varying from 6 to 77 months (mean = 33; SD = 16). The onset of stereotypies was reported between 4 and 51 months of age (mean = 19; SD = 14).

Their semiology had remained unchanged over time, mostly characterized by CMS: patients presented a single repetitive movement or complex sequences involving the entire body such as jumping, kicking, flapping hands, moving hands in front of the face or the eyes, or involving movements and "dystonic" postures of the trunk. Sounds or vocalizations accompanied the motor stereotypies in three patients. From the time of their onset, increasing frequency of stereotypies has been reported. Excitement or boredom was described as common triggers.

The MSSS showed that each child had a limited number of stereotypies, between 1 and 3 (mean = 1.6); their frequency and intensity were mild (range 1–4; mean = 2.8 for both). The interference of stereotypies was variable, from 0 to 4 (mean = 1.6). The mean MSSS final score was 21.1, suggestive of a mild impairment in daily life.

On the RBS-R, items in the subscale of "stereotypic behaviors" were scored by all children; moreover, the questionnaire revealed the presence of other repetitive behaviors in several children, mainly "ritualistic behavior" and "sameness behavior," even if at a lower degree (**Table 1**).

All patients showed a normal cognitive level: in particular, on the Raven's CPM, they obtained scores ranging between 32 and 95 percentiles (mean = 80, SD = 16), corresponding to IQ levels superior to 85.

The CBCL evidenced behavioral problems in 22% of the children (**Table 2**); internalizing problems, attention, and withdrawn were the main complaints reported by parents. Among the DSM-oriented scales, the pervasive developmental problems were the principal affected domain: indeed, three children obtained borderline and four clinical scores.

Symptoms of ASD were assessed by the SRS questionnaire (in the 15 children older than 48 months) and by the ADOS 2.

On the SRS, all but one of the 15 patients obtained clinical scores in the clinical range at least in one area (**Table 3**). Obviously, the more frequently affected domain was "restricted interests and repetitive behavior," which indicated the clinical range in 11 out of 15 children. Moreover, "social motivation" and "SRS total score" were affected in 56% of children.

For the ADOS 2, four patients obtained scores indicating a moderate level of ASD symptoms (calibrated severity score = 6–7), four had a mild level (calibrated severity score = 4–5), and 15 showed no or minimal signs of ASD (calibrated severity score = 0–3).

TABLE 1 | RBS-R: subscale scores and number endorsed.

	Subscale scores (mean ± SD)	Number endorsed[a] (mean ± SD)	Number of patients with number endorsed ≠ 0
I – stereotypic behavior	3.6 ± 2.3	2.0 ± 1.1	23
II – self-injurious behavior	0.4 ± 1.1	0.3 ± 0.6	4
III – compulsive behavior	1.1 ± 1.9	0.7 ± 1.2	9
IV – ritualistic behavior	1.4 ± 2	0.9 ± 1.1	12
V – sameness behavior	1.9 ± 2.5	1.6 ± 1.7	15
VI – restricted behavior	0.9 ± 1.5	0.5 ± 0.7	8

[a]*Number of items endorsed for each subscale (any rating other than 0).*

TABLE 2 | Number of patients obtaining borderline or clinical scores at the Child Behavior CheckList – ages 1½–5 or 4–18, according to chronological age.

	Borderline	Clinical
CBCL total	2	5
CBCL internalizing problems	3	5
CBCL externalizing problems	4	2
Symptoms scales		
Emotionally reactive	2	1
Anxious/depressed	0	1
Somatic complaints	0	2
Withdrawn	3	2
Sleep problems	0	2
Attention problems	3	3
Aggressive behavior	1	0
DSM-oriented scales		
Anxiety problems	1	0
Pervasive developmental problems	3	4
ADHD problems	2	1
Oppositional defiant problems	0	0

TABLE 3 | Number of patients obtaining clinical scores at the Social Responsiveness Scale (SRS).

	Mild range (*T* score: 60–65)	Moderate range (*T* score: 66–75)	Severe range (*T* score >76)
Total score	4	1	3
Social awareness	1	4	2
Social cognition	2	2	1
Social communication	3	2	1
Social motivation	5	3	1
Restricted interests and repetitive behavior	2	4	5

In the whole sample, no correlation was found between the ADOS 2 scores (calibrated severity score, total, and subtotal raw score) and the measures of stereotypic behavior (MSSS and RBS-R scores, subtotal, and total).

No statistical differences were found between subgroups of patients – divided on the basis of the ADOS 2 calibrated severity score – with regard to the total and subtotal scores of CBCL and SRS (**Table 4**). However, in the 15 patients aged above 48 months, a moderate correlation was found between the CBCL pervasive developmental problem scores and the following SRS scores: total ($r = 0.370$) and social communication ($r = 0.585$).

DISCUSSION

In this study, we focused on the assessment of a group of children seeking medical attention for the presence or the persistence of motor stereotypies. According to our data, the impairment due to the stereotypies was mild, without a clear interference in daily activities. The referral of children with mild stereotypies could be due to parents' concerns about a movement disorder that lasts over time and/or to an increased sensitivity to the ASD issue. Some of these children have a history of slight developmental delay in some areas (motor or language), but all had a normal cognitive level and no previous diagnosis of ASD.

Based on our assessment, most of them – 65% of the sample – can be easily diagnosed as having primary CMS. Namely, they showed a few stereotypies, with mild impairment; moreover, the ADOS 2 evidenced no or minimal risk of ASD. Notably, in many of these children, the RBS-R questionnaire disclosed the presence of other symptoms, mainly ritualistic behaviors, sameness, and restricted interests.

TABLE 4 | Comparison of CBCL and SRS *T* scores and number of patients with clinical scores in subgroups (following ADOS 2 score).

ADOS 2 – calibrated severity score	0–3	4–5	6–7
Number of patients	15	4	4
Mean age (range) (months)	57 (36–95)	37 (36–39)	57 (55–60)
CBCL			
Total score	Mean = 57 B = 1; C = 4	Mean = 53 B = 1; C = 0	Mean = 57 B = 0; C = 1
PDD subscale	Mean = 57 B = 0; C = 3	Mean = 60 B = 0; C = 1	Mean = 65 B = 3; C = 0
SRS			
Total score	Mean = 61 M = 3; Mo = 1; S = 2		Mean = 61 M = 1; Mo = 0; S = 1
Social awareness	Mean = 63 M = 1; Mo = 2; S = 2		Mean = 59 M = 0; Mo = 2; S = 0
Social cognition	Mean = 57 M = 1; Mo = 1; S = 1		Mean = 56 M = 1; Mo = 1; S = 0
Social communication	Mean = 59 M = 2; Mo = 1; S = 1		Mean = 54 M = 1; Mo = 1; S = 0
Social motivation	Mean = 58 M = 2; Mo = 2; S = 1		Mean = 65 M = 3; Mo = 1; S = 0
Restricted interests/repetitive behaviors	Mean = 71 M = 1; Mo = 3; S = 4		Mean = 70 M = 1; Mo = 1; S = 1

B, borderline; C, clinical; M, mild; Mo, moderate; S, severe.

These features constitute core symptoms of ASD and their presence, even if at a low level, in our "primary" patients, highlights the difficulty to define the boundaries between transient stereotypic movements in otherwise typically developing children, the primary motor stereotypies with or without comorbidity, and the stereotypic movements in the course of ASD.

Moreover, in some previous studies on children with primary CMS (4, 20), a series of comorbid conditions have already been reported; in particular, ADHD, tic disorders, developmental coordination disorder (DCD), and other neuropsychological problems were described in a significant percentage of cases. Thus, as the DSM 5 clearly states, the presence of stereotypic movements may indicate an undetected neurodevelopmental problem. Among these comorbidities, DCD seems to take on great interest, being present in school age (20) as well as preschool age patients (Baglioni et al., in preparation).

On the basis of all these observations, it is difficult to consider motor stereotypies, even the primary ones, exclusively as a movement disorder (28). A limited number of our patients showed behaviors compatible with a diagnosis of non-autistic ASD or autism, following the calibrated severity score of ADOS 2. This index is considered to be reliable and stable over time (29). These findings were unexpected mainly because, in the past, many of our patients underwent clinical consultations for developmental delay and the diagnosis of ASD was never suspected. A possible explanation for this could be that problems of communication or socialization were overlooked due to their normal cognitive level and/or that subsequent evaluations might be sensitive to developmental changes in social and communication goals that have to be progressively attained during development.

On the other hand, it should be noted that in the whole sample, important discrepancies between the results of different tests were disclosed. In particular, high rates of clinical scores on the SRS were also found in patients who showed no or minimal risk of ASD according to the ADOS 2.

The SRS is an instrument developed to measure social impairment, but many items also describe other core features of ASD, including communication deficits and repetitive behaviors (30), as well as symptoms not exclusively related to ASD diagnostic criteria (31). Moreover, when using the SRS as a quantitative phenotype measure, the effects of non-ASD-specific factors must be considered; if not, SRS scores are more appropriately interpreted as indicating general levels of impairment, rather than severity of ASD-specific symptoms or social impairment (32).

Our study has some limitations. First of all, a small number of children participated. Second, the wide age range of the subjects hampered gathering more homogeneous data (i.e., the SRS is validated from the age of 4 years, while the SRS-2, which can be administered from the age of 1.5 years, is not yet available in Italian). Third, we did not use the Autism Diagnostic Interview that, together with the ADOS 2 and the criteria of DSM 5, could have allowed us to gain more firm diagnostic conclusions within the study.

Nonetheless, our study highlights the challenge of establishing a categorical diagnosis in children with motor stereotypies. Obviously, beyond the classification, this issue is important in terms of treatment of stereotypies that is still a debated problem (33–36).

Waiting for the results of studies investigating the pathophysiological aspects of stereotypies in ASD subjects as in "primary" cases and possibly supporting current hypotheses (37–41), a dimensional approach to the diagnosis of stereotypic behaviors could be particularly suitable. In this perspective, the view of the DSM 5, that puts together the stereotypies (with the exceptions described above) and permits coding additional conditions, seems to be more useful than the rigid categorization of "primary" and "secondary."

In conclusion, complex stereotypies in children with normal cognitive level represent a challenging diagnostic issue for which a finely tailored assessment is mandatory in order to evaluate their peculiar developmental sentinel role. Notably, a careful and cautious use of standardized tests is warranted to avoid misdiagnosis.

AUTHOR CONTRIBUTIONS

FC made a substantial contribution to the conception of the work and in writing the paper; FV, DM, and VB contributed to the acquisition of data; CD contributed to the interpretation of data and literature analysis; FCh contributed to statistical analysis and critically reviewed the manuscript. All the authors read and approved the final version of the manuscript.

REFERENCES

1. American Psychiatric Association. *Diagnostic and Statistical Manual of Mental Disorders*. 5th ed. Arlington, VA: American Psychiatric Publishing (2013). 947 p.
2. Sanger TD, Chen D, Fehlings DL, Hallett M, Lang AE, Mink JW, et al. Definition and classification of hyperkinetic movements in childhood. *Mov Disord* (2010) 25:1538–49. doi:10.1002/mds.23088
3. Singer HS. Motor stereotypies. *Semin Pediatr Neurol* (2009) 16:77–81. doi:10.1016/j.spen.2009.03.008
4. Freeman RD, Soltanifar A, Baer S. Stereotypic movement disorder: easily missed. *Dev Med Child Neurol* (2010) 52:733–8. doi:10.1111/j.1469-8749.2010.03627.x
5. Barry S, Baird G, Lascelles K, Bunton P, Hedderly T. Neurodevelopmental movement disorders – an update on childhood motor stereotypies. *Dev Med Child Neurol* (2011) 53:979–85. doi:10.1111/j.1469-8749.2011.04058.x
6. Robinson S, Woods M, Cardona F, Baglioni V, Hedderly T. Intense imagery movements: a common and distinct paediatric subgroup of motor stereotypies. *Dev Med Child Neurol* (2014) 56:1212–8. doi:10.1111/dmcn.12518
7. Robinson S, Woods M, Cardona F, Hedderly T. Intense imagery movements (IIM): more to motor stereotypies than meets the eye. *Eur J Paediatr Neurol* (2016) 20:61–8. doi:10.1016/j.ejpn.2015.10.006
8. Evans DW, Leckman JF, Carter A, Reznick JS, Henshaw D, King RA, et al. Ritual, habit, and perfectionism: the prevalence and development of compulsive-like behavior in normal young children. *Child Dev* (1997) 68:58–68. doi:10.2307/1131925
9. Leekam S, Tandos J, McConachie H, Meins E, Parkinson K, Wright C, et al. Repetitive behaviours in typically developing 2-year-olds. *J Child Psychol Psychiatry* (2007) 48:1131–8. doi:10.1111/j.1469-7610.2007.01778.x
10. Tierney E, Nwokoro NA, Porter FD, Freund LS, Ghuman JK, Kelley RI. Behavior phenotype in the RSH/Smith-Lemli-Opitz syndrome. *Am*

J Med Genet (2001) 98:191–200. doi:10.1002/1096-8628(20010115) 98:2<191::AID-AJMG1030>3.0.CO;2-M
11. Temudo T, Ramos E, Dias K, Barbot C, Vieira JP, Moreira A, et al. Movement disorders in Rett syndrome: an analysis of 60 patients with detected MECP2 mutation and correlation with mutation type. *Mov Disord* (2008) 23:1384–90. doi:10.1002/mds.22115
12. Galéra C, Taupiac E, Fraisse S, Naudion S, Toussaint E, Rooryck-Thambo C, et al. Socio-behavioral characteristics of children with Rubinstein-Taybi syndrome. *J Autism Dev Disord* (2009) 39:1252–60. doi:10.1007/s10803-009-0733-4
13. Elison JT, Wolff JJ, Reznick JS, Botteron KN, Estes AM, Gu H, et al. Repetitive behavior in 12-month-olds later classified with autism spectrum disorder. *J Am Acad Child Adolesc Psychiatry* (2014) 53:1216–24. doi:10.1016/j.jaac.2014.08.004
14. Bishop SL, Hus V, Duncan A, Huerta M, Gotham K, Pickles A, et al. Subcategories of restricted and repetitive behaviors in children with autism spectrum disorders. *J Autism Dev Disord* (2013) 43:1287–97. doi:10.1007/s10803-012-1671-0
15. Sacco R, Curatolo P, Manzi B, Militerni R, Bravaccio C, Frolli A, et al. Principal pathogenetic components and biological endophenotypes in autism spectrum disorders. *Autism Res* (2010) 3:237–52. doi:10.1002/aur.151
16. Mahone EM, Bridges D, Prahme C, Singer HS. Repetitive arm and hand movements (complex motor stereotypies) in children. *J Pediatr* (2004) 145:391–5. doi:10.1016/j.jpeds.2004.06.014
17. Harris KM, Mahone EM, Singer HS. Nonautistic motor stereotypies: clinical features and longitudinal follow-up. *Pediatr Neurol* (2008) 38:267–72. doi:10.1016/j.pediatrneurol.2007.12.008
18. Muthugovindan D, Singer HS. Motor stereotypy disorders. *Curr Opin Neurol* (2009) 22:131–6. doi:10.1097/WCO.0b013e328326f6c8
19. Moss J, Oliver C, Arron K, Burbidge C, Berg K. The prevalence and phenomenology of repetitive behavior in genetic syndromes. *J Autism Dev Disord* (2009) 39:572–88. doi:10.1007/s10803-008-0655-6
20. Mahone EM, Ryan M, Ferenc L, Morris-Berry C, Singer HS. Neuropsychological function in children with primary complex motor stereotypies. *Dev Med Child Neurol* (2014) 56:1001–8. doi:10.1111/dmcn.12480
21. Oakley C, Mahone EM, Morris-Berry C, Kline T, Singer HS. Primary complex motor stereotypies in older children and adolescents: clinical features and longitudinal follow-up. *Pediatr Neurol* (2015) 52:398.e–403.e. doi:10.1016/j.pediatrneurol.2014.11.002
22. Bodfish JW, Symons FJ, Parker DE, Lewis MH. Varieties of repetitive behavior in autism: comparisons to mental retardation. *J Autism Dev Disord* (2000) 30:237–43. doi:10.1023/A:1005596502855
23. Smith EA, Van Houten R. A comparison of the characteristics of self-stimulatory behaviors in "normal" children and children with developmental delays. *Res Dev Disabil* (1996) 17:253–68. doi:10.1016/0891-4222(96)00007-8
24. MacDonald R, Green G, Mansfield R, Geckeler A, Gardenier N, Anderson J, et al. Stereotypy in young children with autism and typically developing children. *Res Dev Disabil* (2007) 28:266–77. doi:10.1016/j.ridd.2006.01.004
25. Goldman S, Greene PE. Stereotypies in autism: a video demonstration of their clinical variability. *Front Integr Neurosci* (2013) 6:121. doi:10.3389/fnint.2012.00121
26. Goldman S, Wang C, Salgado MW, Greene PE, Kim M, Rapin I. Motor stereotypies in children with autism and other developmental disorders. *Dev Med Child Neurol* (2009) 51:30–8. doi:10.1111/j.1469-8749.2008.03178.x
27. Ghosh D, Rajan PV, Erenberg G. A comparative study of primary and secondary stereotypies. *J Child Neurol* (2013) 28:1562–8. doi:10.1177/0883073812464271
28. Lemiere J. Do children with primary complex motor stereotypies only have movement problems? *Dev Med Child Neurol* (2014) 56:923–4. doi:10.1111/dmcn.12506
29. Shumway S, Farmer C, Thurm A, Joseph L, Black D, Golden C. The ADOS calibrated severity score: relationship to phenotypic variables and stability over time. *Autism Res* (2012) 5:267–76. doi:10.1002/aur.1238
30. Constantino JN, Przybeck T, Friesen D, Todd RD. Reciprocal social behavior in children with and without pervasive developmental disorders. *J Dev Behav Pediatr* (2000) 21:2–11. doi:10.1097/00004703-200002000-00002
31. Grzadzinski R, Di Martino A, Brady E, Mairena MA, O'Neale M, Petkova E, et al. Examining autistic traits in children with ADHD: does the autism spectrum extend to ADHD? *J Autism Dev Disord* (2011) 41:1178–91. doi:10.1007/s10803-010-1135-3
32. Hus V, Bishop S, Gotham K, Huerta M, Lord C. Factors influencing scores on the Social Responsiveness Scale. *J Child Psychol Psychiatry* (2013) 54:216–24. doi:10.1111/j.1469-7610.2012.02589.x
33. Rajapakse T, Pringsheim T. Pharmacotherapeutics of Tourette syndrome and stereotypies in autism. *Semin Pediatr Neurol* (2010) 17:254–60. doi:10.1016/j.spen.2010.10.008
34. Carrasco M, Volkmar FR, Bloch MH. Pharmacologic treatment of repetitive behaviors in autism spectrum disorders: evidence of publication bias. *Pediatrics* (2012) 129:e1301–10. doi:10.1542/peds.2011-3285
35. Specht MW, Mahone EM, Kline T, Waranch R, Brabson L, Thompson CB, et al. Efficacy of parent-delivered behavioral therapy for primary complex motor stereotypies. *Dev Med Child Neurol* (2016). doi:10.1111/dmcn.13164
36. Hedderly T. Childhood motor stereotypies: questions of definition and management. *Dev Med Child Neurol* (2016). doi:10.1111/dmcn.13181
37. Langen M, Durston S, Kas MJ, van Engeland H, Staal WG. The neurobiology of repetitive behavior:...and men. *Neurosci Biobehav Rev* (2011) 35:356–65. doi:10.1016/j.neubiorev.2010.02.005
38. Gao S, Singer HS. Complex motor stereotypies: an evolving neurobiological concept. *Future Neurol* (2013) 8:273–85. doi:10.2217/fnl.13.4
39. Houdayer E, Walthall J, Belluscio BA, Vorbach S, Singer HS, Hallett M. Absent movement-related cortical potentials in children with primary motor stereotypies. *Mov Disord* (2014) 29:1134–40. doi:10.1002/mds.25753
40. Harris AD, Singer HS, Horska A, Kline T, Ryan M, Edden RA, et al. GABA and glutamate in children with primary complex motor stereotypies: an 1H-MRS study at 7T. *AJNR Am J Neuroradiol* (2016) 37:552–7. doi:10.3174/ajnr.A4547
41. Mahone EM, Crocetti D, Tochen L, Kline T, Mostofsky SH, Singer HS. Anomalous putamen volume in children with complex motor stereotypies. *Pediatr Neurol* (2016) S887–8994. doi:10.1016/j.pediatrneurol.2016.08.023

14

Insulin-Like Growth Factor 1 and Related Compounds in the Treatment of Childhood-Onset Neurodevelopmental Disorders

*Cyrus Vahdatpour[1], Adam H. Dyer[1] and Daniela Tropea[2]**

[1] School of Medicine, Trinity College Dublin, Dublin, Ireland, [2] Department of Psychiatry, Trinity College Dublin, Dublin, Ireland

Edited by:
Roberto Canitano,
University Hospital of Siena, Italy

Reviewed by:
Enrico Tongiorgi,
University of Trieste, Italy
Hansen Wang,
University of Toronto, Canada
Om Sai Ramesh Vallamkonda,
Lady Hardinge Medical College, India

***Correspondence:**
Daniela Tropea
daniela.tropea@tcd.ie

Insulin-Like Growth Factor 1 (IGF-1) is a neurotrophic polypeptide with crucial roles to play in Central Nervous System (CNS) growth, development and maturation. Following interrogation of the neurobiology underlying several neurodevelopmental disorders and Autism Spectrum Disorders (ASD), both recombinant IGF-1 (mecasermin) and related derivatives, such as (1-3)IGF-1, have emerged as potential therapeutic approaches. Clinical pilot studies and early reports have supported the safety/preliminary efficacy of IGF-1 and related compounds in the treatment of Rett Syndrome, with evidence mounting for its use in Phelan McDermid Syndrome and Fragile X Syndrome. In ASD, clinical trials are ongoing. Here, we review the role of IGF-1 in the molecular etiologies of these conditions in addition to the accumulating evidence from early clinical studies highlighting the possibility of IGF-1 and related compounds as potential treatments for these childhood-onset neurodevelopmental disorders.

Keywords: IGF-1, autism spectrum disorders, Rett Syndrome, Fragile X Syndrome, Phelan-Mcdermid Syndrome

INTRODUCTION

Insulin-Like Growth Factor 1 (IGF1) is a polypeptide hormone and a member of a superfamily of related insulin like hormones termed Insulin Like Peptides (ILPs) (Fernandez and Torres-Alemán, 2012). IGF-1 is primarily released by hepatocytes in response to Growth Hormone, but is also produced in the Central Nervous System (CNS) where it has pleiotrophic effects on all major CNS cell types (Bach et al., 1991; O'Kusky and Ye, 2012). IGF-1 has crucial roles to play in the development, growth and maturation of the CNS and its synapses, roles which have been reviewed extensively elsewhere (Bach et al., 1991; Popken et al., 2004; Aberg et al., 2006; Llorens-Martín et al., 2009; Corvin et al., 2012; O'Kusky and Ye, 2012; Supeno et al., 2013; Huat et al., 2014; Dyer et al., 2016).

IGF-1 and IGF1 receptor (IGF1R) expression levels have a definite spatio-temporal patterns (Bach et al., 1991; Bartlett et al., 1992; Bondy and Lee, 1993; Zhang et al., 2007). Of note, the abundance of IGF-1R expression over IGF-1 hints at the importance of peripherally produced IGF-1 in mediating the effects of IGF-1 on the CNS (Fernandez and Torres-Alemán, 2012). IGF-1 acts on its glycoprotein receptor (IGF1R), a tyrosine kinase receptor, to activate canonical signaling pathways, including: (i) the PI3K (phosphatidylinositol-3 kinase)—AKT1 (serine-threonine-specific protein kinase)—FOXO (forkhead box protein O) and (ii) the RAS—MAPK (mitogen-activated protein kinases)—ERK (extracellular signal regulated kinases) pathway. Both of these pathways have important roles to play including cell cycle regulation, gene expression, protein synthesis, autophagy, apoptosis and remodeling of the cytoskeleton (Fernandez and Torres-Alemán, 2012; Costales and Kolevzon, 2015).

Once released in the serum, IGF-1 can be cleaved to yield an amino terminal glycine-proline-glutamate (GPE tripeptide) and a truncated IGF-1 form called des-N-(1-3)-IGF-1, lacking the N-terminal GPE tripeptide, which has greatly reduced affinity for IGFBPs and is therefore, is more potent than IGF-1. (1-3)IGF-1 is an active metabolite with neuroprotective effects as well as effects on excitatory synaptic markers such as synapsin 1 and post-synaptic density 95 (PSD-95), recapitulating many of the effects of IGF-1 on synaptic maturation and plasticity (Guan et al., 1999; Corvin et al., 2012). Of note, this effect of (1-3) IGF-1 may be different in neuronal and non-neuronal cell populations. In one report studying the effects of IGF-1 acting on its canonical pathways in neuronal and non-neuronal cells, IGF-1 was found to increase pAkt statining in neurons but not glial cells, whilst (1-3) IGF-1 increased staining in glial cells but not neurons (Corvin et al., 2012). Thus, signaling by IGF-1 and its active tripeptide may demonstrate different effects in different CNS cell populations, adding further to the biological complexity of IGF-1 signaling. One mechanism of action of (1-3)IGF-1 may be to indirectly activate the IGF-1R via an increase in endogenous IGF-1 release (Corvin et al., 2012). Another important aspect of IGF-1 physiology is its binding to IGF Binding Proteins (IGFBP), which regulate its bioavailability, localization and activity (Ocrant et al., 1990; Clemmons, 1998; Hwa et al., 1999; Firth and Baxter, 2002).

Disruption of IGF-1 function has profound phenotypic consequences both in murine models and in humans, underscoring the important role of IGF-1 in CNS development and maturation (Beck et al., 1995; Woods et al., 1996; Netchine et al., 2011). In the present Mini-Review, we address the role of perturbed IGF-1 signaling and the therapeutic potential of IGF-1 and (1-3)IGF-1 in neurodevelopmental disorders such as Rett Syndrome (RTT), Fragile X Syndrome (FXS), Phelan McDermid Syndrome (PMDS) as well as broader Autism Spectrum Disorder (ASD).

RETT SYNDROME

Rett Syndrome (RTT) is a pervasive X-Linked neurodevelopmental disorder affecting 1:10,000 female (Percy and Lane, 2004). RTT is characterized by an apparently normal development, followed by a subsequent regression in psychomotor, social and cognitive abilities, deficits in social interaction and a loss of acquired fine motor skills and purposive hand movements. In the CNS, RTT is characterized by microcephaly, neuronal atrophy and leads to cardiorespiratory problems (Julu et al., 2001; Hagberg, 2002). At present, the treatment of RTT represents an unmet therapeutic need.

More than 85% of RTT is caused by a mutation in methyl CpG-binding protein 2 (*MeCP2*), encoding the protein MECP2, which has roles both inside and outside the nucleus (Kaufmann et al., 2005; Chahrour et al., 2008). Atypical cases of RTT may also be caused, in less than 10% cases, by mutations in cyclin-dependent kinase-like 5 (CDK-L5) and in the Forkead Box G1 (FOXG1) in 1% cases (Cahrour and Zoghbi, 2007).

The deletion of the *MeCP2* gene in mouse models recapitulates many of the autonomic, motor and cognitive features of the human RTT phenotype (Banerjee et al., 2012; Castro et al., 2014; Katz et al., 2016), together with reduced connectivity (Armstrong, 2005; Chapleau et al., 2009) and defects in neurotransmitter and receptor expression. *MeCP2* loss in mice results in an alteration in excitatory-inhibitory balance with reduced excitation/increased inhibition in cortical samples/tissue (Dani et al., 2005; Durand et al., 2012).

MeCP2 deficient brains demonstrate large numbers of modest transcriptional changes, both positive and negative (Katz et al., 2016). One well characterized target of MECP2 function is Brain Derived Neurotrophic Factor (BDNF), an important modulator of CNS growth, which shows synergy with IGF1 in the CNS (Ding et al., 2006). BDNF is down-regulated in murine models of RTT as well as patients with RTT (Chang et al., 2006; Zhou et al., 2006). Although studies in rats have shown that there is clear exchange of BDNF between the brain and the periphery (Pan et al., 1998) and *viceversa* (Poduslo and Curran, 1996), other studies have failed to raise BDNF in the brain to therapeutic levels, suggesting crossing through the blood-brain barrier (BBB) of this neurotrophin to be insufficient for clinical purposes (Pardridge et al., 1994). IGF-1 is a potential alternative, which on crossing the BBB acts on the same pathways as BDNF (such as the PI3K-Akt and MAP-ERK pathways) and appears important for BNDF effects on activity dependent plasticity (Pardridge et al., 1994; Ding et al., 2006).

In *Mecp2* mutant mice, administration of both IGF-1 and (1-3)IGF-1 reverses many of the features of the RTT phenotype (Chen and Russo-Neustadt, 2007; Castro et al., 2014). Castro et al. (2014) demonstrated reduced IGF-1 levels in *MeCP2* mutant mice, with subsequent daily administration of IGF-1 resulting in an improved lifespan, weight and autonomic parameters in the knockout mice. IGF-1 significantly improved abnormalities in activity dependent plasticity in *MeCP2* mutant mice (using a monocular deprivation paradigm). Similar effects are observed with (1-3) IGF-1 administration (Tropea et al., 2009), together with improved spine density, synaptic amplitude and increased excitatory synaptic markers (Tropea et al., 2009). Furthermore, in a mouse model of atypical RTT with mutations in CDLK5, IGF-1 was demonstrated to rescue deficits in dendritic spine instability and expression of PSD-95 adding further support to IGF-1 as a potential treatment in RTT (Della Sala et al., 2016).

One mechanism by which IGF-1 exerts its effects in RTT may be by acting on its canonical signaling pathways (such as PI3K and MAPK pathways as above). Interestingly, a recent study demonstrates that IGF-1 application may actually increase nuclear *MeCP2* transcript and protein (Tropea et al., 2016). Activity dependent plasticity was also shown to modulate MeCP2 expression and this additionally demonstrates the profound effects of IGF-1 on cellular neuroplasticity in the CNS. Restoration of these abnormalities in activity-dependent plasticity may be one important way in which IGF-1 may exert its effects in RTT. Interestingly, MeCP2 may affect IGF-1 levels by regulation of IGFBPs which has been demonstrated for IGFBP3 in both murine models and humans (Itoh et al., 2007).

IGF-1 is already indicated in the pediatric population for severe growth failure and IGF-1 deficiency. In RTT patients, two early studies have been performed demonstrating the tolerability and safety of IGF-1 as a potential treatment (Pini et al., 2012; Khwaja et al., 2014). Khwaja et al. (2014) demonstrated the safety of IGF-1 in 12 patients with *MeCP2* mutations (9 with RTT) with a 4 week multiple ascending dose (40–120 ug/kg bd) followed by a 20 week open label extension, without any serious adverse events or hypoglycamia. A previous clinical study had demonstrated safety in 6 patients with RTT receiving twice daily injections of IGF-1 for a 6 month period (Pini et al., 2012). This was followed by a single case study of one of the patients reporting the safety of repeated treatment with IGF-1 for a second 6 month cycle (Pini et al., 2014).

Preliminary efficacy analysis by Khwaja et al. (2014) demonstrated an improvement in cardiorespiratory parameters, some neurobehavioral parameters and EEG measures of mood and anxiety (reversed frontal alpha band asymmetry). Pini et al. analyzed 10 patients whom had received IGF-1 treatment in a clinical study and compared various parameters to age and disease severity matched controls (Pini et al., 2016). They reported a significant improvement in disease severity as assessed by clinicians as well as two independent and blinded observers using a novel video based scoring system. Whilst this evidence is preliminary, this early data demonstrating efficacy of IGF-1 in RTT is encouraging. The results of ongoing Phase 2 clinical trials using IGF-1 in RTT are eagerly awaited (NCT01777542). Furthermore, an analog of (1-3)IGF-1, NNZ-2566 (administered orally) has demonstrated efficacy in both clinician and caregiver assessments in an industry-led Phase 2 trial on patients with RTT aged 15-45 (NCT01703533), with a Phase 2 trial on younger patients in progress (NCT02715115). Taken together, there is encouraging evidence for the use of IGF-1 and (1-3) IGF-1 in the treatment of RTT (see **Tables 1, 2**).

FRAGILE X SYNDROME

Fragile X Syndrome (FXS) results from a mutation in the *Fmr1* gene, encoding the protein Fragile X Mental Retardation Protein (FMRP1). The disorder is characterized by learning disability, social anxiety and attention deficit disorder, impaired social interactions and seizures as well as an abnormal physical phenotype with macro-orchidism and facial dysmorphism (Hagerman, 1997; Garber et al., 2008). The treatment of FXS represents a largely unmet clinical need.

FMRP, an mRNA binding protein, expressed in neuronal cell bodies and dendrites acts to regulate protein translation at the synapse, with important roles to play in activity-dependent plasticity (e.g., inhibition of translation triggered by mGluR1/5 in response to neuronal stimulation) (Bhakar et al., 2012). FMRP may also have important presynaptic effects on neuronal transmission, mediated via its effects on large conductance Ca^{2+} activated K^{+} channels (Deng et al., 2013).

Several studies have reported disruptions in MAPK/ERK signaling in FXS. Weng et al. (2008) have demonstrated delayed early-phase phosphorylation of ERK in mice deficient in FMRP whilst Curia et al. (2013) demonstrate a resistance to seizures with dephosphorylation of p-ERK in Fmr1 mice (Weng et al., 2008; Curia et al., 2013). In the PI3K pathway, the p110beta catalytic subunit can be regulated by FMRP, with p110beta and PI3K activity elevated in *Fmr1* knockout neurons. This suggests that dysregulation of PI3K signaling may be involved in the synaptic deficits seen in FXS. Indeed, inhibition of PI3K activity may correct dysregulated synaptic protein synthesis, AMPA internalization and spine density defects in knockout neurons (Gross et al., 2010). Thus, alterations in the same canonical pathways stimulated by IGF-1 and other neurotrophins may underlie a large part of the synaptic pathology seen in FXS.

Impressive preclinical evidence comes from a study by Deacon et al. (2015) using an analog of (1-3)IGF-1, NNZ-2566. In *Fmr1* knockout mice, NNZ-2566 demonstrated a significantly reduced brain phospho-ERK and phospho-Akt. Similarly, NNZ-2566 resulted in a significant reduction in spine numbers, which are increased in the *Fmr1* mice in comparison to controls. Improvement in hyperactivity and anxiety, learning and memory deficits was also observed (Deacon et al., 2015). In patients with FXS, a Phase 2 industry-led clinical trial has been completed using NNZ-2566, with clinical improvement in many of the core symptoms of FXS as disclosed by Neuren Pharmaceuticals (NCT01894958). The exact efficacy of IGF-1 related compounds such as NNZ-2566 awaits further clarification, but this early clinical evidence is encouraging.

PHELAN-MCDERMID SYNDROME

Phelan-McDermid Syndrome (PMDS) is another monogenic neurodevelopmental disorder and results from deletions in the SHANK3 gene on chromosome 22q13.3. Affected patients demonstrate global developmental delay, severe impairments in speech and intellectual disability (Phelan and McDermid, 2012). The protein product of SHANK3 is a key scaffolding protein present in the post-synaptic density of excitatory synapses, with key roles in activity-dependent plasticity and the functional maintenance of these synapses.

In 3-week old hippocampal neurons treated with siRNA to inhibit SHANK3 synthesis, there was a decreased number and an increased length of dendritic spines (Roussignol et al., 2005). Similarly, application of SHANK3 resulted in the formation of spine-like protrusions containing SHANK3 in aspiny neurons supporting the role of SHANK3 in spine formation and synaptic plasticity. Further, application of SHANK3 increased immunoreactivity for AMPAR subunits in cell body and dendritic spines (but not for GABA subunits), supporting its role in the function and maintenance of excitatory synapses (Roussignol et al., 2005). Using mice deficient in *Shank3*, Bozdagi et al. found reduced amplitude of miniature excitatory post-synaptic currents (mEPSCs) in the hippocampus and impaired Long Term Potentiation (LTP), with only transient spine expansion present (Bozdagi et al., 2010).

TABLE 1 | Previous studies and trials examining IGF-1 as a potential treatment in several childhood-onset neurodevelopmental disorders.

References	Disorder	Treatment	Dose	Sample SIze	Study type	Treatment duration	Findings	Conclusion	Company (if applicable)
Khwaja et al., 2014	RTT	rhIGF-1	40–120 ug/kg bd (MAD) followed by 12 weeks at max. dose	12	Clinical trial	6 months	Improvement in apnoea index neurobehavioural parameters, measures of mood and anxiety Reversal of alpha band desynchronization on EEG	Safety and preliminary efficacy supported	–
Pini et al., 2012	RTT	rhIGF-1	0.05 mg/kg bd first and last week; 0.1 mg/kg bd in between	6	Clinical study	6 months	No adverse events	Safety of IGF-1 supported	–
Pini et al., 2014	RTT	rhIGF-1	0.1 mg/kg bd	Single case study		6 months	No adverse events	Demonstrated safety of repeated doses in a single patient	–
Pini et al., 2016	RTT	rhIGF-1	0.05 mg/kg bd first and last week; 0.1 mg/kg bd in between	10 (incl. Pini et al., 2012)	Clinical study	6 months	Significant improvement in Rett Severity Score (RSS) and International Scoring System (RSS) Significant improvement in social/cognitive testing endurance	Prelimary efficacy of IGF-1 supported	–
NCT01703533	RTT	NNZ-2566	35 mg/kg or 70 mg/kg bd (note: oral administration)	56	Phase II Trial	28 days	No adverse events Significant improvement in Motor-Behavior Assessment Change Index, Clinical Global Impression of Improvement and Caregiver Top 3 Concerns	Safety and preliminary efficacy supported	Neuren Pharmaceuticals Ltd. see disclosure (Neuren Pharmaceuticals Ltd.)[a]
NCT01894958	FXS	NNZ-2566	35 mg/kg or 70 mg/kg bd (note: oral administration)	45	Phase II Trial	56 days	No serious adverse events Significant improvement in group and individual level analysis of specified core measures	Safety and preliminary efficacy supported	Neuren Pharmaceuticals Ltd.[b]
Kolevzon et al., 2014	PMDS	rhIGF-1	0.04 mg/kg bd to a maximum of 0.12 mg/kg bd	9	Phase II Trial	3 months	No serious adverse events Significant improvement on both the Aberrant Behavior Checklist and Repetitive Behavior Scale	Safety and preliminary efficacy supported	Neuren Pharmaceuticals Ltd.

RTT, Rett Syndrome; FXS, Fragile X Syndrome; PMDS, Phelan McDermid Syndrome, ASD, Autism Spectrum Disorder.

[a] *Neuren Pharmaceuticals Ltd. ASX Announcement 7th Dec 2015. Melbourne, Australia. Neuren's trofinetide successful in proof of concept Phase 2 clnical trial in Fragile X Syndrome. http://www.neurenpharma.com/IRM/PDF/1557/TrofinetidesuccessfulinPhase2trialinFragileX Last accessed 28th July 2016.*

[b] *Neuren Pharmaceuticals Ltd. Neuren (Neu) ASX Announcement 12th Nov 2014. Melbourne, Australia. Neuren's NZ-2566 successful in demonstrating clinical benefit in Rett syndrome Phase 2 trial. http://www.neurenpharma.com/IRM/PDF/1447/NeurensuccessfulinRettsyndromePhase2trial Last accessed 28th July 2016.*

TABLE 2 | Ongoing trials examining IGF-1 as a potential treatment in several childhood-onset neurodevelopmental disorders.

References	Disorder	Treatment	Dose	Sample size	Study type	Treatment duration	Findings	Company (if applicable)
NCT01777542	RTT	rhIGF-1	Unknown	In progress	Phase II Trial	10 months	In progress	–
NCT02715115	RTT	NNZ-2566	Various	In progress	Phase II Trial	11 weeks (avg.)	In progress	Neuren Pharmaceuticals Ltd.
NCT01970345	ASD	rhIGF-1	0.04 mg/kg bd to a maximum of 0.12 mg/kg bd	In progress	Phase II Trial	12 weeks	In progress	–

RTT, Rett Syndrome; FXS, Fragile X Syndrome; PMDS, Phelan McDermid Syndrome; ASD, Autism Spectrum Disorder.

In *Shank3* deficient mice, intraperitoneal injection of IGF-1, administered daily for a 2 week period reversed deficits in AMPAR receptors and LTP described above. Similar results were also seen for the active tripeptide (1-3) IGF-1 (Bozdagi et al., 2013). Recently, similar effects for IGF-1 on *Shank3* deficient human neurons has been demonstrated. By using induced pluripotent stem cells (iPSCs) from patients with PMDS and using them to produce functional neurons, Shcheglovitov et al. demonstrated that these neurons had a reduced expression of SHANK3 with accompanying defects in excitatory synaptic transmission as seen in the murine models above (Shcheglovitov et al., 2013). Treatment of the SHANK3 deficient neurons with IGF-1 increased the amplitude and frequency of EPSCs, restored the amplitude of evoked AMPA and NMDAR EPSCs and restored NMDA receptor currents on application of NMDA (Shcheglovitov et al., 2013). IGF-1 also caused a 340% increase in the fraction of puncta expressing PSD-95 in PMDS neurons (Shcheglovitov et al., 2013).

In a double blind, placebo controlled Phase 2 trial reported by Kolevzon et al., the safety and preliminary efficacy of IGF-1 treatment in PMDS were reported on 9 patients with PMDS aged 5–15 (Kolevzon et al., 2014). IGF-1 treatment was associated with significant improvements in social impairment and restrictive behaviors (Aberrant Behavior Checklist and Repetitive Behavior Scale). No serious adverse events occurred with the main side effects including sleep disturbance, hypoglycemia (<50 mg/dL), constipation, increased appetite and mood changes/irritability. This encouraging evidence awaits further confirmation and exploration in further clinical trials in the PMDS population.

AUTISM SPECTRUM DISORDER

Autism Spectrum Disorder is a heterogenous neurodevelopmental disorders characterized by deficits in social interaction and in speech and language with narrowed interests and repetitive behaviors (Wang and Doering, 2015). Autism affects about 3–6 per 1000 of the population, although recent estimates place its prevalence higher at 1 in 68 (CDC, 2012). The most substantial clue to ASD etiology is its substantial heritability (−90%) (Freitag, 2007). ASD demonstrates complex genetics, and whilst it is a genetically heterogenous disorder, evidence repeatedly implicates genes involved in synaptic development, function and activity-dependent plasticity by both common and rare variation (Wang et al., 2009; Hussman et al., 2011; De Rubeis et al., 2014). The potent effects of IGF-1 on synaptic function, maintenance and plasticity make it a potentially attractive target for the treatment of ASDs.

Vanhala et al. reported low levels of IGF-1 in children with autism, however sample sizes were small ($n = 11$) (Vanhala et al., 2006). In 25 young children with a diagnosis of autism, it was subsequently shown that IGF-1 levels were significantly reduced (Riikonen et al., 2001), and in those with a diagnosis of autism, Cerebrospinal Fluid (CSF) IGF-1 was correlated with head size (Mills et al., 2007). On measuring urinary IGF-1 excretion, Anlar et al. (2007) demonstrated that IGF-1 level was significantly lower in autistic children than in age matched controls. In contrast, a larger study has demonstrated significantly higher levels of IGF-1 in children with autism (Marchetto et al., 2016). The exact role of the IGF-1 axis in ASD awaits further clarification.

Interestingly, in a recent report using neurons derived from patients with ASD, Marchetto et al. found a partial rescue of deficits in neuronal networks (neuronal spike number and activity) on application of IGF-1 (Marchetto et al., 2016). At present, clinical trials of IGF-1 in Autism Spectrum Disorder are ongoing, with a phase 2 trial currently recruiting (NCT01970345). The trial aims to pilot the use of IGF-1 as a novel treatment for the core symptoms of ASD. The results of this trial are eagerly awaited. If successful, further trials will be needed in the ASD population to determine the exact efficacy of IGF-1 as a potential treatment, as well as studies to investigate the specific groups of patients with ASD which benefit the most from treatment with recombinant IGF-1.

POTENTIAL MOLECULAR MECHANISMS OF IGF1 AND DERIVATES IN DIFFERENT DISORDERS

There are three potential mechanisms by which IGF-1 may exert its effects in these neurodevelopmental disorders. The first is increased glutamatergic transmission, as seen in various preclinical studies (Tropea et al., 2009; Corvin et al., 2012; Castro et al., 2014; Marchetto et al., 2016). A potential consequence of this includes effects related to increased synaptic potentiation and plasticity (Bozdagi et al., 2013). A second potential action of IGF-1 in these neurodevelopmental disorders includes activation of molecular pathways involved in growth and connectivity (PI3K and MAPK). In RTT models, where these pathways are down-regulated, IGF1 induces an increase in the relative markers of neuronal function (Tropea et al., 2009; Castro et al., 2014), whilst in FXS models, where they are up-regulated, an (1-3)IGF1 analog induces a decrease in the cellular pathways (Deacon et al., 2015). This may be the result of a homeostatic action of IGF-1, in re-establishing basal levels of activity in these canonical signaling pathways. The third potential mechanism relates to effects on transcription. This has been demonstrated in recent studies of IGF-1 on mecp2 transcript (Tropea et al., 2016). More work is needed to clarify the direct and indirect effects of IGF1 and derivates, and their action in different cell types.

CONCLUSION

Preliminary evidence is beginning to emerge from well validated murine models and early clinical studies, that treatment with recombinant human IGF-1 (rhIGF-1/mecasermin) and derived compounds may be of benefit in several childhood onset neurodevelopmental disorders. Whilst the evidence base is preliminary, further clinical trials and studies are needed in order to quantify the effects of IGF-1 on patients with these disorders, as well as identifying particular patients which may derive maximum benefit from treatment with IGF-1 and related compounds. The results of ongoing clinical trials are eagerly awaited.

AUTHOR CONTRIBUTIONS

CV, AD, and DT had substantial roles in the drafting, writing and editing of the review and final manuscript.

REFERENCES

Aberg, N. D., Brywe, K. G., and Isgaard, J. (2006). Aspects of growth hormone and insulin-like growth factor-I related to neuroprotection, regeneration, and functional plasticity in the adult brain. *ScientificWorldJournal* 6, 53–80. doi: 10.1100/tsw.2006.22

Anlar, B., Oktem, F., Bakkaloglu, B., Haliloglu, M., Oguz, H., Unal, F., et al. (2007). Urinary epidermal and insulin-like growth factor excretion in autistic children. *Neuropediatrics* 38, 151–153. doi: 10.1055/s-2007-990282

Armstrong, D. D. (2005). Neuropathology of Rett syndrome. *J. Child Neurol.* 20, 747–753. doi: 10.1177/08830738050200082401

Bach, M. A., Shen-Orr, Z., Lowe, W. L. Jr., Roberts, C. T. Jr., and LeRoith, D. (1991). Insulin-like growth factor I mRNA levels are developmentally regulated in specific regions of the rat brain. *Brain Res. Mol. Brain Res.* 10, 43–48. doi: 10.1016/0169-328X(91)90054-2

Banerjee, A., Castro, J., and Sur, M. (2012). Rett syndrome: genes, synapses, circuits, and therapeutics. *Front. Psychiatry* 3:34. doi: 10.3389/fpsyt.2012.00034

Bartlett, W. P., Li, X. S., and Williams, M. (1992). Expression of IGF-1 mRNA in the murine subventricular zone during postnatal development. *Brain Res. Mol. Brain Res.* 12, 285–291. doi: 10.1016/0169-328X(92)90131-T

Beck, K. D., Powell-Braxton, L., Widmer, H. R., Valverde, J., and Hefti, F. (1995). Igf1 gene disruption results in reduced brain size, CNS hypomyelination, and loss of hippocampal granule and striatal parvalbumin-containing neurons. *Neuron* 14, 717–730. doi: 10.1016/0896-6273(95)90216-3

Bhakar, A. L., Dölen, G., and Bear, M. F. (2012). The pathophysiology of fragile X (and what it teaches us about synapses). *Annu. Rev. Neurosci.* 35, 417–443. doi: 10.1146/annurev-neuro-060909-153138

Bondy, C. A., and Lee, W. H. (1993). Patterns of insulin-like growth factor and IGF receptor gene expression in the brain. Functional implications. *Ann. N.Y. Acad. Sci.* 692, 33–43.

Bozdagi, O., Sakurai, T., Papapetrou, D., Wang, X., Dickstein, D. L., Takahashi, N., et al. (2010). Haploinsufficiency of the autism-associated Shank3 gene leads to deficits in synaptic function, social interaction, and social communication. *Mol. Autism* 1:15. doi: 10.1186/2040-2392-1-15

Bozdagi, O., Tavassoli, T., and Buxbaum, J. D. (2013). Insulin-like growth factor-1 rescues synaptic and motor deficits in a mouse model of autism and developmental delay. *Mol. Autism* 4:9. doi: 10.1186/2040-2392-4-9

Cahrour, M., and Zoghbi, H. Y. (2007). The story of Rett syndrome: from clinic to neurobiology. *Neuron* 56, 422–437. doi: 10.1016/j.neuron.2007.10.001

Castro, J., Garcia, R. I., Kwok, S., Banerjee, A., Petravicz, J., Woodson, J., et al. (2014). Functional recovery with recombinant human IGF1 treatment in a mouse model of Rett Syndrome. *Proc. Natl. Acad. Sci. U.S.A.* 111, 9941–9946. doi: 10.1073/pnas.1311685111

Centers for Disease Control and Prevention (2012). *Prevalence and Characteristics of Autism Spectrum Disorder Among Children Aged 8 Years—Autism and Developmental Disabilities Monitoring Network, 11 Sites, United States, 2012.* Available online at: http://www.cdc.gov/mmwr/volumes/65/ss/ss6503a1.htm (Accessed on: September 26, 2016).

Chahrour, M., Jung, S. Y., Shaw, C., Zhou, Z., Wong, S. T., Qin, J., et al. (2008). MeCP2, a key contributor to neurological disease, activates and represses transcription. *Science* 320, 1224–1229. doi: 10.1126/science.1153252

Chang, Q., Khare, G., Dani, V., Nelson, S., and Jaenisch, R. (2006). The disease progression of Mecp2 mutant mice is affected by the level of BDNF expression. *Neuron* 49, 341–348. doi: 10.1016/j.neuron.2005.12.027

Chapleau, C. A., Calfa, G. D., Lane, M. C., Albertson, A. J., Larimore, J. L., Kudo, S., et al. (2009). Dendritic spine pathologies in hippocampal pyramidal neurons from Rett syndrome brain and after expression of Rett-associated MECP2 mutations. *Neurobiol. Dis.* 35, 219–233. doi: 10.1016/j.nbd.2009.05.001

Chen, M. J., and Russo-Neustadt, A. A. (2007). Running exercise- and antidepressant-induced increases in growth and survival-associated signaling molecules are IGF-dependent. *Growth Factors* 25, 118–131. doi: 10.1080/08977190701602329

Clemmons, D. R. (1998). Role of insulin-like growth factor binding proteins in the control of IGF actions. *Mol. Cell. Endocrinol.* 140, 19–24.

Corvin, A. P., Molinos, I., Little, G., Donohoe, G., Gill, M., Morris, D. W., et al. (2012). Insulin-like growth factor 1 (IGF1) and its active peptide (1-3)IGF1 enhance the expression of synaptic markers in neuronal circuits through different cellular mechanisms. *Neurosci. Lett.* 520, 51–56. doi: 10.1016/j.neulet.2012.05.029

Costales, J. L., and Kolevzon, A. (2015). The therapeutic potential of insulin-like growth factor-1 in central nervous system disorders. *Neurotherapeutics* 12, 620–630. doi: 10.1007/s13311-015-0352-z

Curia, G., Gualtieri, F., Bartolomeo, R., Vezzalo, R., and Biagini, G. (2013). Resilience to audiogenic seizures is associated with p-ERK1/2 dephosphorylation in the subiculum of Fmr1 knockout mice. *Front. Cell. Neurosci.* 25:46. doi: 10.3389/fncel.2013.00046

Dani, V. S., Chang, Q., Maffei, A., Turrigiano, G. G., Jaenisch, R., Nelson, S. B., et al. (2005). Reduced cortical activity due to a shift in the balance between excitation and inhibition in a mouse model of Rett syndrome. *Proc. Natl. Acad. Sci. U.S.A.* 102, 12560–12565. doi: 10.1073/pnas.0506071102

Deacon, R. M., Glass, L., Snape, M., Hurley, M. J., Altimiras, F. J., Biekofsky, R. R., et al. (2015). NNZ-2566, a novel analog of (1-3) IGF-1, as a potential therapeutic agent for fragile X syndrome. *Neuromol. Med.* 17, 71–82. doi: 10.1007/s12017-015-8341-2

Della Sala, G., Putignano, E., Chelini, G., Melani, R., Calcagno, E., Michele Ratto, G., et al. (2016). Dendritic spine instability in a mouse model of CDKL5 disorder is rescued by insulin-like growth factor 1. Mol. *Psychiatry.* 80, 302–311. doi: 10.1016/j.biopsych.2015.08.028

Deng, P. Y., Rotman, Z., Blundon, J. A., Cho, Y., Cui, J., Cavalli, V., et al. (2013). FMRP regulates neurotransmitter release and synaptic information transmission by modulating action potential duration via BK channels. *Neuron* 77, 696–711. doi: 10.1016/j.neuron.2012.12.018

De Rubeis, S., He, X., Goldberg, A. P., Poultney, C. S., Samocha, K., Cicek, A. E., et al. (2014). Synaptic, transcriptional and chromatin genes disrupted in autism. *Nature* 515, 209–215. doi: 10.1038/nature13772

Ding, Q., Vaynman, S., Akhavan, M., Ying, Z., and Gomez-Pinilla, F. (2006). Insulin-like growth factor I interfaces with brain-derived neurotrophic factor-mediated synaptic plasticity to modulate aspects of exercise-induced cognitive function. *Neuroscience* 140, 823–833. doi: 10.1016/j.neuroscience.2006.02.084

Durand, S., Patrizi, A., Quast, K. B., Hachingian, L., Pavlyuk, R., and Saxena, A. (2012). NMDA receptor regulation prevents regression of visual cortical function in the absence of Mecp2. *Neuron* 76, 1078–10790. doi: 10.1016/j.neuron.2012.12.004

Dyer, A. H., Vahdatpour, C., Sanfeliu, A., and Tropea, D. (2016). The role of Insulin-Like Growth Factor 1 (IGF-1) in brain development, maturation and neuroplasticity. *Nueroscience* 325, 89–99. doi: 10.1016/j.neuroscience.2016.03.056

Fernandez, A. M., and Torres-Alemán, I. (2012). The many faces of insulin-like peptide signalling in the brain. *Nat. Rev. Neurosci.* 13, 225–239. doi: 10.1038/nrn3209

Firth, S. M., and Baxter, R. C. (2002). Cellular actions of the insulin-like growth factor binding proteins. *Endocr. Rev.* 23, 824–854. doi: 10.1210/er.2001-0033

Freitag, C. M. (2007). The genetics of autistic disorders and its clinical relevance: a review of the literature. *Mol. Psychiatry* 12, 2–22. doi: 10.1038/sj.mp.4001896

Garber, K. B., Visootsak, J., and Warren, S. T. (2008). Fragile X syndrome. *Eur. J. Hum. Genet.* 16, 666–6672. doi: 10.1038/ejhg.2008.61

Gross, C., Nakamoto, M., Yao, X., Chan, C. B., Yim, S. Y., Ye, K., et al. (2010). Excess phosphoinositide 3-kinase subunit synthesis and activity as a novel therapeutic target in fragile X syndrome. *J. Neurosci.* 30, 10624–10638. doi: 10.1523/jneurosci.0402-10.2010

Guan, J., Waldvogel, H. J., Faull, R. L., Gluckman, P. D., and Williams, C. E. (1999). The effects of the N-terminal tripeptide of insulin-like growth factor-1, glycine-proline-glutamate in different regions following hypoxic-ischemic brain injury in adult rats. *Neuroscience* 89, 649–659. doi: 10.1016/S0306-4522(98)00338-8

Hagberg, B. (2002). Clinical manifestations and stages of Rett syndrome. *Ment. Retard. Disabil. Res. Rev.* 8, 61–65. doi: 10.1002/mrdd.10020

Hagerman, R. J. (1997). Fragile X syndrome. molecular and clinical insights and treatment issues. *West J. Med.* 166, 129–137.

Huat, T. J., Khan, A. A., Pati, S., Mustafa, Z., Abdullah, J. M., and Jaafar, H. (2014). IGF-1 enhances cell proliferation and survival during early differentiation of mesenchymal stem cells to neural progenitor-like cells. *BMC Neurosci.* 15:91. doi: 10.1186/1471-2202-15-91

Hussman, J. P., Chung, R. H., Griswold, A. J., Jaworski, J. M., Salyakina, D., Ma, D., et al. (2011). A noise-reduction GWAS analysis implicates altered regulation of neurite outgrowth and guidance in autism. *Mol. Autism* 2:1. doi: 10.1186/2040-2392-2-1

Hwa, V., Oh, Y., and Rosenfeld, R. G. (1999). The insulin-like growth factor-binding protein (IGFBP) superfamily. *Endocr. Rev.* 20, 761–787. doi: 10.1210/er.20.6.761

Itoh, M., Ide, S., Takashima, S., Kudo, S., Nomura, Y., Segawa, M., et al. (2007). Methyl CpG-binding protein 2 (a mutation of which causes Rett syndrome) directly regulates insulin-like growth factor binding protein 3 in mouse and human brains. *Neuropathol. Exp. Neurol.* 66, 117–123. doi: 10.1097/nen.0b013e3180302078

Julu, P. O., Kerr, A. M., Apartopoulos, F., Al-Rawas, S., Engerstrom, I. W., Engerström, L., et al. (2001). Characterisation of breathing and associated central autonomic dysfunction in the Rett disorder. *Arch. Dis. Child.* 85, 29–37. doi: 10.1136/adc.85.1.29

Katz, D. M., Bird, A., Coenraads, M., Gray, S. J., Menon, D. U., Philpot, B. D., et al. (2016). Rett syndrome: crossing the threshold to clinical translation. *Trends Neurosci.* 39, 100–113. doi: 10.1016/j.tins.2015.12.008

Kaufmann, W. E., Johnston, M. V., and Blue, M. E. (2005). MeCP2 expression and function during brain development: implications for Rett syndrome's pathogenesis and clinical evolution. *Brain Dev.* 27(Suppl. 1), S77–S87. doi: 10.1016/j.braindev.2004.10.008

Khwaja, O. S., Ho, E., Barnes, K. V., O'Leary, H. M., Pereira, L. M., and Finkelstein, Y. (2014). Safety, pharmacokinetics, and preliminary assessment of efficacy of mecasermin (recombinant human IGF-1) for the treatment of Rett syndrome. *Proc. Natl. Acad. Sci. U.S.A.* 111, 4596–4601. doi: 10.1073/pnas.1311141111

Kolevzon, A., Bush, L., Wang, A. T., Halpern, D., Frank, Y., Grodberg, D., et al. (2014). A pilot controlled trial of insulin-like growth factor-1 in children with Phelan-McDermid syndrome. *Mol. Autism* 5:54. doi: 10.1186/2040-2392-5-54

Llorens-Martín, M., Torres-Alemán, I., and Trejo, J. L. (2009). Mechanisms mediating brain plasticity: IGF1 and adult hippocampal neurogenesis. *Neuroscientist* 15, 134–148. doi: 10.1177/1073858408331371

Marchetto, M. C., Belinson, H., Tian, Y., Freitas, B. C., Fu, C., Vadodaria, K. C., et al. (2016). Altered proliferation and networks in neural cells derived from idiopathic autistic individuals. *Mol. Psychiatry*. doi: 10.1038/mp.2016.95. [Epub ahead of print].

Mills, J. L., Hediger, M. L., Molloy, C. A., Chrousos, G. P., Manning-Courtney, P., Yu, K. F., et al. (2007). Elevated levels of growth-related hormones in autism and autism spectrum disorder. *Clin. Endocrinol.* 67, 230–237. doi: 10.1111/j.1365-2265.2007.02868.x

Netchine, I., Azzi, S., Le Bouc, Y., and Savage, M. O. (2011). IGF1 molecular anomalies demonstrate its critical role in fetal, postnatal growth and brain development. *Best Pract. Res. Clin. Endocrinol. Metab.* 25, 181–190. doi: 10.1016/j.beem.2010.08.005

Ocrant, I., Fay, C. T., and Parmelee, J. T. (1990). Characterization of insulin-like growth factor binding proteins produced in the rat central nervous system. *Endocrinology* 127, 1260–1267. doi: 10.1210/endo-127-3-1260

O'Kusky, J., and Ye, P. (2012). Neurodevelopmental effects of insulin-like growth factor signaling. *Front. Neuroendocrinol.* 33, 230–251. doi: 10.1016/j.yfrne.2012.06.002

Pan, W., Banks, W. A., Fasold, M. B., Bluth, J., and Kastin, A. J. (1998). Transport of brain-derived neurotrhophic factor across the blood brain barrier. *Nueropharmacology* 37, 1553–1561. doi: 10.1016/S0028-3908(98)00141-5

Pardridge, W. M., Kang, Y. S., and Buckiak, J. L. (1994). Transport of human recombinant brain-derived neurotrophic factor (BDNF) through the rat blood-brain barrier *in vivo* using vector-mediated peptide drug delivery. *Pharm. Res.* 11, 738–746. doi: 10.1023/A:1018940732550

Percy, A. K., and Lane, J. B. (2004). Rett syndrome: clinical and molecular update. *Curr. Opin. Paediatr.* 16, 670–677. doi: 10.1097/01.mop.0000143693.59408.ce

Phelan, K., and McDermid, H. E. (2012). The 22q13.3 deletion syndrome (Phelan-McDermid syndrome). *Mol. Syndromol.* 2, 186–201. doi: 10.1159/000334260

Pini, G., Congiu, L., Benicasa, A., DiMarco, P., Bigoni, S., Dyer, A. H., et al. (2016). Illness severity, social and cognitive ability, and EEG analysis of ten patients with rett syndrome treated with mecasermin (recombinant human IGF-1). *Autism Res. Treat.* 2016:5073078. doi: 10.1155/2016/5073078

Pini, G., Scusa, M. F., Benincasa, A., Bottliglioni, I., Congiu, L., Vahdatpour, C., et al. (2014). Repeated insulin-like growth factor 1 treatment in a patient with rett syndrome: a single case study. *Front. Paediatry* 2:52. doi: 10.3389/fped.2014.00052

Pini, G., Scusa, M. F., Congiu, L., Benincasa, A., Morescalchi, P., Bottliglioni, I., et al. (2012). IGF1 as a potential treatment for rett syndrome: safety assessment in six rett patients. *Autism Res. Treat.* 2012:679801. doi: 10.1155/2012/679801

Poduslo, J. F., and Curran, G. L. (1996). Permeability at the blood-brain and blood-nerve barriers of the neurotrophic factors: NGF, CNTF, NT-3, BDNF. *Brain Res. Mol. Brain Res.* 36, 280–286. doi: 10.1016/0169-328X(95)00250-V

Popken, G. J., Hodge, R. F., Ye, P., Zhang, J., Ng, W., O'Kusky, J. R., et al. (2004). *In vivo* effects of insulin-like growth factor-I (IGF-I) on prenatal and early postnatal development of the central nervous system. *Eur. J. Neurosci.* 19, 2056–2068. doi: 10.1111/j.0953-816X.2004.03320.x

Riikonen, R., Turpeinen, U., and Riikonen, R. (2001). Cerebrospinal fluid insulin-like growth factors IGF-1 and IGF-2 in infantile autism. *Dev. Med. Chlild Neurol.* 43, 614–616. doi: 10.1017/S0012162201001116

Roussignol, G., Ango, F., Romorini, S., Tu, J. C., Sala, C., Worley, P. F., et al. (2005). Shank expression is sufficient to induce functional dendritic spine synapses in aspiny neurons. *J. Neurosci.* 25, 3560–3570. doi: 10.1523/jneurosci.4354-04.2005

Shcheglovitov, A., Shcheglovitova, O., Yazawa, M., Portmann, T., Shu, R., Sebastino, V., et al. (2013). SHANK3 and IGF1 restore synaptic deficits in neurons from 22q13 deletion syndrome patients. *Nature* 503, 267–271. doi: 10.1038/nature12618

Supeno, N. E., Pati, S., Hadi, R. A., Ghani, A. R., Mustafa, Z., Abdullah, J. M., et al. (2013). IGF-1 acts as controlling switch for long-term proliferation and maintenance of EGF/FGF-responsive striatal neural stem cells. *Int. J. Med. Sci.* 10, 522–531. doi: 10.7150/ijms.5325

Tropea, D., Diacometti, E., Wilson, N. R., Beard, C., McCurry, C., Fu, D. D., et al. (2009). Partial reversal of Rett Syndrome-like symptoms in MeCP2 mutant mice. *Proc. Natl. Acad. Sci. U.S.A.* 106, 2029–2034. doi: 10.1073/pnas.0812394106

Tropea, D., Mortimer, N., Bellini, S., Molinos, I., Sanfeliu, A., Shovlin, S., et al. (2016). Expression of nuclear Methyl-CpG binding protein 2 (Mecp2) is dependent on neuronal stimulation and application of Insulin-like growth factor 1. *Neurosci. Lett.* 621, 111–116. doi: 10.1016/j.neulet.2016.04.024

Vanhala, R., Turpeinen, U., and Riikonen, R. (2006). Low levels of insulin-like growth factor-I in cerebrospinal fluid in children with autism. *Dev. Med. Child Neurol.* 48, 751–755. doi: 10.1017/S0012162206001605

Wang, H., and Doering, L. C. (2015). Autism spectrum disorders: emerging mechanisms and mechanism-based treatment. *Front. Cell Neursci.* 9:183. doi: 10.3389/fncel.2015.00183

Wang, K., Zhang, H., Ma, D., Bucan, M., Glessner, J. T., Abrahams, B. S., et al. (2009). Common genetic variants on 5p14.1 associate with autism spectrum disorders. *Nature* 459, 528–533. doi: 10.1038/nature07999

Weng, N., Weller, I. J., Sumis, A., Berry-Kravis, E., and Greenough, W. T. (2008). Early-phase ERK activation as a biomarker for metabolic status in fragile X syndrome. *Am. J. Med. Genet. B Neuropsychiatr. Genet.* 147B, 1253–1257. doi: 10.1002/ajmg.b.30765

Woods, K. A., Camacho-Hübner, C., Savage, M. O., and Clark, A. J. (1996). Intrauterine growth retardation and postnatal growth failure associated with deletion of the insulin-like growth factor I gene. *N. Engl. J. Med.* 335, 1363–1367. doi: 10.1056/NEJM199610313351805

Zhang, J., Moats-Staats, B. M., Ye, P., and D'Ercole, A. J. (2007). Expression of insulin-like growth factor system genes during the early postnatal neurogenesis in the mouse hippocampus. *J. Neurosci. Res.* 85, 1618–1627. doi: 10.1002/jnr.21289

Zhou, Z., Hong, E. J., Cohen, S., Zhao, W. N., Ho, H. Y., and Schmidt, L. (2006). Brain-specific phosphorylation of MeCP2 regulates activity-dependent Bdnf transcription, dendritic growth, and spine maturation. *Neuron* 52, 255–269. doi: 10.1016/j.neuron.2006.09.037

15

Language Impairments in ASD Resulting from a Failed Domestication of the Human Brain

Antonio Benítez-Burraco[1], *Wanda Lattanzi*[2†] *and Elliot Murphy*[3*†]

[1] Department of Philology, University of Huelva, Huelva, Spain, [2] Institute of Anatomy and Cell Biology, Università Cattolica del Sacro Cuore, Rome, Italy, [3] Division of Psychology and Language Sciences, University College London, London, UK

Edited by:
Yuri Bozzi,
University of Trento, Italy

Reviewed by:
Suhash Chakraborty,
Hindustan Aeronautics Limited Hospital, India
Roberto Canitano,
University Hospital of Siena, Italy

***Correspondence:**
Elliot Murphy
elliotmurphy91@gmail.com

† These authors have contributed equally to this work.

Autism spectrum disorders (ASD) are pervasive neurodevelopmental disorders entailing social and cognitive deficits, including marked problems with language. Numerous genes have been associated with ASD, but it is unclear how language deficits arise from gene mutation or dysregulation. It is also unclear why ASD shows such high prevalence within human populations. Interestingly, the emergence of a modern faculty of language has been hypothesized to be linked to changes in the human brain/skull, but also to the process of self-domestication of the human species. It is our intention to show that people with ASD exhibit less marked domesticated traits at the morphological, physiological, and behavioral levels. We also discuss many ASD candidates represented among the genes known to be involved in the "domestication syndrome" (the constellation of traits exhibited by domesticated mammals, which seemingly results from the hypofunction of the neural crest) and among the set of genes involved in language function closely connected to them. Moreover, many of these genes show altered expression profiles in the brain of autists. In addition, some candidates for domestication and language-readiness show the same expression profile in people with ASD and chimps in different brain areas involved in language processing. Similarities regarding the brain oscillatory behavior of these areas can be expected too. We conclude that ASD may represent an abnormal ontogenetic itinerary for the human faculty of language resulting in part from changes in genes important for the "domestication syndrome" and, ultimately, from the normal functioning of the neural crest.

Keywords: autism, domestication, language evolution, neural oscillations, language deficits

INTRODUCTION

Autism spectrum disorders (ASD) are pervasive neurodevelopmental conditions characterized by several and severe cognitive and social deficits, including language and communication problems, repetitive and stereotypical behavior, and problems with social interaction (Bailey et al., 1996). In DSM-V, language deficits are no longer explicitly postulated as a central feature of ASD because they are subsumed in its distinctive communication problems. Nevertheless, it is clear that ASD entails a typical language profile and language developmental path (reviewed in Benítez-Burraco and Murphy, 2016; see also Tager-Flusberg et al., 2005; Tager-Flusberg, 2006; Eigsti et al., 2007; Bourguignon et al., 2012). Because of the masking effect of a variable IQ, and the variable degree of functionality exhibited by ASD patients, it is difficult to hypothesize a core language deficit in this condition. The impairment of the oromotor function has been claimed to account for expressive language problems in some autistic subjects (Belmonte et al., 2013). Comprehension problems seemingly result from other underlying deficit(s), including a reduced effect of semantic priming (Preissler, 2008), problems with phonological processing (Lindgren et al., 2009), or impairment of procedural memory (Walenski et al., 2006).

At the neural level, ASD entails atypical development, wiring and interconnection of areas involved in language processing (Stefanatos and Baron, 2011; Bourguignon et al., 2012). Not surprisingly, functional differences in language processing tasks of ASD compared with unaffected subjects have been attested as well (Courchesne and Pierce, 2005; Scott-Van Zeeland et al., 2010a,b). For instance, microstructural anomalies and reduced lateralization patterns have been observed in the arcuate fasciculus of ASD patients (Fletcher et al., 2010), suggesting that a constraint on the integrative processes during development may contribute to language impairment in this condition (Schipul et al., 2011). We also wish to highlight both increased and decreased intra- and inter-hemispheric connectivity (Hahamy et al., 2015), and abnormal responses to linguistic stimuli (reviewed in Stefanatos and Baron, 2011, pp 259–262). Intriguingly, the ASD phenotype is characterized by increased intrinsic functional connectivity during the first years of life (the time window where language is acquired) and reduced connectivity in adolescent and adult states (Uddin et al., 2013).

In spite of this growing body of neurobiological data, a comprehensive view of language processing in the ASD brain is still lacking. Specifically, ASD studies need to move beyond simplistic models of language processing and focus instead on how collections of brain areas jointly engaged in specific, impaired cognitive operations (see Fedorenko and Thompson-Schill, 2014, for a general discussion). This is a real challenge, provided that abnormal brain profiles are not expected to easily map on to anomalous categories or computations of linguistic theories (see Poeppel, 2012; Murphy, 2016a, for discussion). We have recently proposed a translational theory of language deficits in ASD as amounting to abnormal patterns of brain rhythms (Benítez-Burraco and Murphy, 2016); although a clarification and empirical validation of this hypothesis is still pending.

Finally, we wish to emphasize that ASD has been associated with sequence variants, copy number variation (CNVs), and/or changes in the expression patterns of an extensive number of genes (Geschwind and State, 2015). Despite the remarkable genetic heterogeneity, it is noteworthy that all these genes tend to converge on specific pathways and neural mechanisms, functionally relevant in this condition and expected to account for its associated deficits (Willsey and State, 2015). Specifically, several candidates for language impairment in ASD have been proposed, including *MET*, *CTTNBP2*, *EN2*, *NBEA*, *HRAS*, and *PTEN* (Comings et al., 1996; Naqvi et al., 2000; Cheung et al., 2001; Castermans et al., 2003; Benayed et al., 2005; Campbell et al., 2006). Nonetheless, the gap between genes and language deficits in ASD still remains open (see Jeste and Geschwind, 2014, for a general discussion, and Benítez-Burraco and Murphy, 2016, for a specific discussion on candidates for language dysfunction in ASD).

The aim of this paper is to contribute to the bridging of the gap between the genetic backdrop and language deficits observed in ASD. To this end, we will primarily focus on language evolution. There exists a strong, deep link between evolution and (abnormal) development. Recently-evolved neural networks seem to be more sensitive to damage because of their lower levels of resilience (Toro et al., 2010). As a consequence, aspects of brain development and function that are preferably impaired in modern populations are expected to be involved in recently evolved, human-specific cognitive abilities. Some comprehensive accounts of the human condition set against the cognitive profiles of other primates have been recently put forth (Seed and Tomasello, 2010; Platt et al., 2016). Comparative genomics also provides valuable information about the sources of the observed differences and similarities in the human genome (Rogers and Gibbs, 2014; Franchini and Pollard, 2015). Likewise, we are beginning to achieve an advanced understanding of the genetic changes that occurred after our split from extinct hominins (Pääbo, 2014; Zhou et al., 2015). We expect that the same factors that prompted the transition from an ape-like cognition to our specific mode of cognition are involved in the etiology of cognitive disorders involving language deficits and, particularly, of ASD (see Benítez-Burraco, 2016a, for a general discussion).

In what follows, the focus is placed on one aspect of this evolutionary process: the self-domestication of the human species. At present, we have a decent understanding of how our language-readiness (that is, our species-specific ability to learn and use language) may have evolved. Accordingly, among the changes brought about by human evolution, one very relevant aspect is the ability to transcend (better than other species) the signature limits of core knowledge systems and thus go beyond modular boundaries (Mithen, 1996; Spelke, 2003; Carruthers, 2006; Hauser, 2009; Boeckx, 2011; Wynn and Coolidge, 2011). As hypothesized in Boeckx and Benítez-Burraco (2014a), our language-readiness boils down to this enhanced cognitive ability, but also to its embedding inside cognitive systems responsible for interpretation (*thought*) and externalization (*speech*). This language-readiness was seemingly brought about by specific changes in the skull/brain developmental path (resulting in a more globular brain), which entailed new patterns of long-distance connections among distributed neurons and, ultimately, new patterns of brain rhythmicity, including an adequate degree and pattern of cortical inhibition. Interestingly, brain rhythms are heritable components of brain function (Linkenkaer-Hansen et al., 2007; Hall et al., 2011) and have been linked to computational primitives of language (Murphy, 2015a,b, 2016a), allowing for a good explanation (and not just a description) of linguistic computation (and of language deficits) at the brain level, and specifically, for a satisfactory mapping of language deficits to neural dysfunction and its genetic basis in ASD (Benítez-Burraco and Murphy, 2016). We have found many candidates for ASD among the genes known to be involved in the emergence of language-readiness (Benítez-Burraco and Boeckx, 2015).

At the same time, the emergence of modern-like languages (and perhaps of core aspects of language too) was seemingly favored by changes in the cultural niche of our ancestors. The archeological record shows that cognitive modernity (encompassing language-readiness) did not automatically entail behavioral modernity (seemingly resulting from using fully-fledged languages), which only appeared long after the emergence of anatomically-modern humans (AMHs) together with changes in human cultural dynamics. Current linguistic research has shown that aspects of linguistic complexity (including core aspects of grammatical knowledge) correlate with aspects of social complexity (Wray and Grace, 2007; Lupyan and Dale, 2010). Moreover, core properties of human languages (like duality of patterning) can develop in response to environmental pressure, as research into emergent sign languages has nicely illustrated, implying that they cannot be regarded as part of the biological endowment (see Benítez-Burraco, 2016b, for discussion). Importantly, language acquisition by the child demands a prolonged socialization window that enables her to receive the proper amount of triggering stimuli and to interact with other conspecifics. All this means that the intrinsic cognitive machinery may be not enough for granting the acquisition of a successful tool for linguistic cognition and that the environment has to be of the right kind too (see Sterelny, 2011 on behavioral modernity set against cognitive modernity).

It has been hypothesized that the social conditions (or the *cultural niche*) that facilitated the enhancement of linguistic structure through a cultural mechanism were brought about by a process of human self-domestication (see Thomas, 2014, for details, and Hare and Tomasello, 2005; Deacon, 2009, on relaxed selective pressures resulting from self-domestication as explanations of the emergence of key aspects of behavioral modernity). Different factors may have contributed to human self-domestication, from adaptation to the human-made environment to selection against aggression to sexual selection. We have hypothesized (Benítez-Burraco et al., in press) that the very changes that brought about our globular skull/brain and our language-readiness may have also fuelled the emergence of a (self-domesticated) phenotype in the human species. Accordingly, we have found numerous links between the candidates for globularization and language-readiness, and genes important for the development and function of neural crest cells (NCC). Indeed, the hypofunction of the neural crest (NC) has been claimed to account for the constellation of distinctive traits observed in domestic mammals (the "domestication syndrome") (Wilkins et al., 2014).

Because of the deep link between evolution and development, we expect that examining the signatures of the domesticated phenotype in people with ASD contributes to a better understanding of etiology of ASD, and specifically, of language deficits in this condition. In a recent paper Reser (2014) found similarities between autism and species of solitary mammals. Although the focus was put on behavior, the author suggests that future research will benefit from investigating the neurobiological, genetic and epigenetic causes of these similarities. Here we try to push research in this direction. The paper is structured as follows. First, we provide a general account of the domesticated traits that are absent or attenuated in ASD. Then we move to the genes and focus on candidates for ASD that are found among the set of genes involved in the domestication syndrome and the evolution of language-readiness, as characterized in Benítez-Burraco et al. (in press), showing that they exhibit a distinctive expression profile in the brain of autists. Finally, we compare the ASD phenotype with wild primates, focusing on the expression profile of these genes, but also on oscillatory signatures of areas important for language processing, considering that language impairment in ASD can be interpreted as an "oscillopathic" condition (see Benítez-Burraco and Murphy, 2016). We will conclude that ASD (and language deficits in ASD) can be viewed as an abnormal ontogenetic itinerary for the human faculty of language, resulting in part from changes in genes important for the domestication syndrome and seemingly from changes in the normal functioning of the NC.

DOMESTIC TRAITS IN THE ASD PHENOTYPE

Wilkins et al. (2014) provide a comprehensive summary of traits known to be modified in domesticated mammals, many of them concerning the cranial region. These include changes in ear size and shape, changes in the orofacial area (including shorter snouts and smaller jaws), changes in dentition (particularly, smaller teeth), and a reduced brain capacity (specifically, of components of the forebrain such as the amygdala or parts of the limbic system). Other distinctive traits commonly found in domesticated strains are depigmentation, neoteny, shorter reproductive cycles, and increased docility, which is thought to result from adrenal size reduction and adrenal hypofunction as well as from reduced levels of stress hormones (including adrenocorticoids, adrenocorticotropic hormone, cortisol, and corticosterone). This delayed adrenal maturation also involves a hypofunction of the sympathetic nervous system and an increase of the duration of the immaturity of the hypothalamic-pituitary-adrenal system (the HPA axis), which provides the animal with a longer socialization window. According to Wilkins et al. (2014), the multiple phenotypic traits that characterize the domestication syndrome emerge as unselected by-products from a developmental reduction in NCC inputs, resulting from selection for tameness. Interestingly, compared to extinct hominins, AMHs exhibit a number of domesticated traits, including reduced brains (at least during the last 50,000 years), changes in dentition, reduction of aggressiveness, and retention of juvenile characteristics (see Thomas, 2014, for details). Intriguingly, most of these features are generally attenuated in ASD (**Figure 1**).

To begin with, ASD subjects show significant differences with healthy controls regarding minor physical anomalies, particularly in the craniofacial region (assumed to result from deviations during fetal development and suggested to constitute external markers of atypical brain growth) (Tripi et al., 2008; Manouilenko et al., 2014). Specifically, in adults the abnormal shape of the ears is robustly associated with autistic traits, with

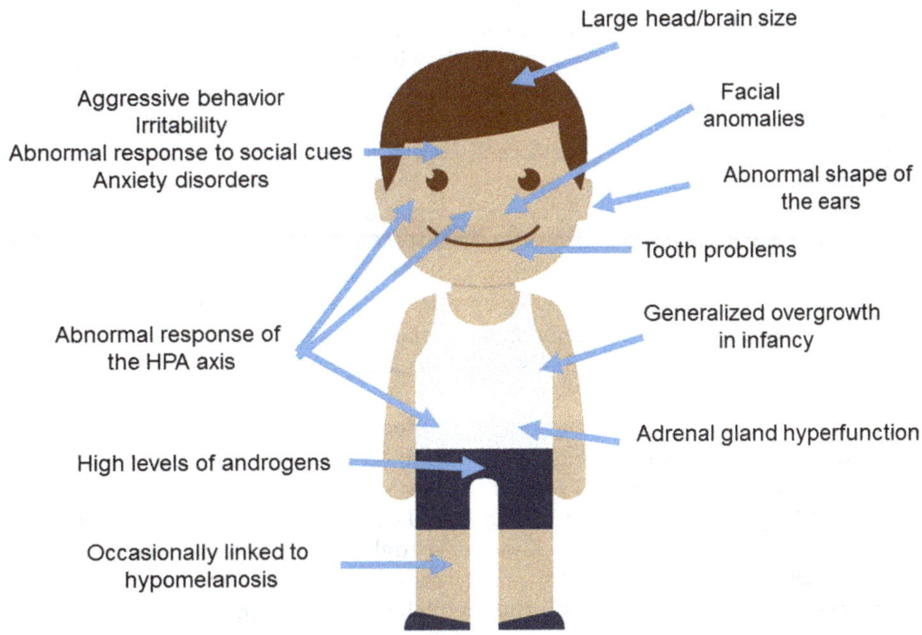

FIGURE 1 | Anomalous presentation of domesticated traits in people with ASD. Main clinical features observed in ASD patients and concerning the domestication syndrome are shown. The child diagram was gathered from Iconfinder output (available at http://www.iconfinder.com/icons/525448/boy_child_kid_male_man_person_white_icon).

higher scores correlating with poorer functioning (Manouilenko et al., 2014). Regarding the changes in the orofacial region, prepubertal boys with ASD show significant differences in facial morphology compared to typically developing (TD) boys (Aldridge et al., 2011). This distinctive facial phenotype is more pronounced in subjects with severe symptoms, significant cognitive impairment, and language regression (Obafemi-Ajayi et al., 2015). Concerning tooth peculiarities, children with ASD show greater abnormalities in dentition, including missing teeth, diastemas, or reverse overjets (Luppanapornlarp et al., 2010). With respect to brain size, head circumference is significantly larger in people with ASD, with nearly 15% suffering from macrocephaly. Higher brain volumes correlate with lower functioning abilities; indeed nearly 9% ASD individuals exhibit brain overgrowth (Sacco et al., 2015). It is worth noticing that higher head circumference and brain size values are observed only during early childhood (Fukumoto et al., 2008; Courchesne et al., 2011, although see Raznahan et al., 2013), particularly when ASD is presented with regression (Nordahl et al., 2011). Typically, early brain overgrowth is followed by a decrease in structural volumes (Courchesne et al., 2011). Although brain overgrowth may result from a dysregulation of the overall systemic growth (see below), it is thought to impact on cognition. This is believed to occur as a result of the reduced networking efficiency among widespread regions of the cortex, due to the increased long-distance connections (Lewis et al., 2013). Specifically, people with ASD show increased volumes of the amygdala (Mosconi et al., 2009; Murphy et al., 2012), which correlate with the severity of their social and communication impairments (Schumann et al., 2009). In the TD population, higher amygdala volumes are associated with poorer language abilities in infancy (Ortiz-Mantilla et al., 2010).

Regarding the behavioral traits associated with the domestication syndrome, we wish to highlight that aggressive behaviors are frequent in children with ASD (with about 25% of them having scores in the clinical range), and correlate with lower cognitive outcomes (Hill et al., 2014). Children with ASD display more reactive than proactive aggression attitudes (Farmer et al., 2015). Likewise, irritability is also commonly observed in affected individuals (Mikita et al., 2015). Additionally, ASD is commonly found to be comorbid with generalized anxiety disorder (Hollocks et al., 2014; Bitsika et al., 2015). Several studies have been carried out to learn more about the physiological basis of this anomalous response to the social environment. Interestingly, higher serum cortisol responses are usually found in children with ASD, particularly after stressor stimulation, when prolonged duration and recovery of cortisol elevation is also observed (Spratt et al., 2012). Moreover, children with ASD show a distinctive diurnal rhythm of cortisol compared to their TD peers; this involves elevated cortisol levels at the end of the day and dampened linear decline across the day in some children (Tomarken et al., 2015). Dysregulation of the diurnal rhythm as a whole has been found in low functioning ASD (Taylor and Corbett, 2014). Also, anxiety symptoms correlate with high cortisol levels in ASD pediatric patients (Bitsika et al., 2015). Plasma levels of adrenocorticotropic hormone are also significantly higher in children with ASD, and correlate positively with the severity of the symptoms (Hamza et al., 2010). The HPA axis in ASD responds in a more sluggish way to physiological or physical manipulation. Accordingly, Taylor and Corbett (2014) found hyper-responsiveness of the HPA axis when unpleasant stimuli or relatively benign social situations are involved, whereas they observed hypo-responsiveness in conditions involving social evaluative threat. On the whole, the HPA axis may be more reactive to stress in social anxiety disorder and ASD (Spratt et al., 2012; Jacobson, 2014). Because children with autism and anxiety disorders show a blunted cortisol response to psychosocial stress, and given that reduced cortisol responsiveness is significantly related to increased anxiety symptoms, Hollocks et al. (2014) suggested that a non-adaptive physiological response to psychosocial stress may exist in ASD.

Finally, it is worth considering some other traits commonly observed in domesticated mammals: neoteny, alterations of reproductive cycles, and pigmentation changes. Regarding neotenic features, it is noteworthy that children with ASD exhibit an early generalized overgrowth (van Daalen et al., 2007; Fukumoto et al., 2008; Chawarska et al., 2011). Typically, boys with ASD show increased body size at birth and during infancy, with postnatal overgrowth correlating with lower adaptive functioning, greater severity of social deficits, and poorer verbal skills (Chawarska et al., 2011; Campbell et al., 2014). Interestingly, higher levels of androgens are found in children and adolescents with ASD. This correlates with the severity of autistic traits and might account for the precocious puberty also reported in this condition (El-Baz et al., 2014). These findings emphasize the role of elevated pre- and postnatal testosterone levels in the liability for ASD (see Hauth et al., 2014). Testosterone significantly affects brain development, particularly targeting the hypothalamus, the amygdala and the hippocampus, impacting on aspects of memory consolidation (Filová et al., 2013). High perinatal testosterone concentration negatively correlates with early vocabulary development in TD boys (Hollier et al., 2013). Interestingly, children with elevated androgen levels due to congenital adrenal hyperplasia show atypical patterns of brain asymmetry in the perisylvian areas, and language/learning disabilities (Plante et al., 1996). Less data on reproductive functions in females is available, due to the lower prevalence of ASD among women. Nevertheless, women with ASD reported significantly more irregular menstrual cycles and dysmenorrhea (Ingudomnukul et al., 2007; Hamilton et al., 2011). Likewise, an increase in premenstrual syndrome has been observed in women with ASD (Obaydi and Puri, 2008; Hamilton et al., 2011), who are more likely to exhibit behavioral issues related to the onset of periods (Burke et al., 2009). In addition, delayed age of menarche seems to correlate with the severity of autistic traits (Hergüner and Hergüner, 2016). These findings lend support to the androgen theory of ASD, according to which elevated levels of testosterone during fetal development may contribute to the development of ASD. Finally, concerning changes in pigmentation, it is of interest that hypomelanotic diseases usually entail autistic symptoms, as is commonly observed in hypomelanosis of Ito (OMIM#300337; Akefeldt and Gillberg, 1991; von Aster et al., 1997; Gómez-Lado et al., 2004). It has been hypothesized that the comorbidity between hypomelanosis and ASD may result from a deficiency in vitamin D (Eyles, 2010; Bakare et al., 2011). In fact, core symptoms of ASD improve after vitamin D supplementation (Jia et al., 2015). Interestingly, core candidates for the globularization of the AMH skull/brain and the evolution of language-readiness are involved in vitamin D homeostasis and function (see Benítez-Burraco and Boeckx, 2015, for details).

As noted above, regardless of the different selectionist scenarios that may account for the traits commonly found in domesticated mammals, a role for NC hypofunction during embryonic development has been proposed (see Wilkins et al., 2014, for details). No comprehensive view of the role (if any) of the NC in the aetiopathogenesis of ASD has been provided to date. Still, it is important to note that neurocristopathies (that is, conditions resulting from NC defects) commonly involve autistic features. For instance, in CHARGE syndrome (OMIM#214800) autistic traits coexist with developmental abnormalities affecting endocrine, reproductive, urinary and digestive systems, along with skeletal and craniofacial features (Fernell et al., 1999). Given this background, we will now examine whether candidates for ASD are overrepresented among the genes believed to play a central role in NC development and function, with a special emphasis on those that interact with genes important for the globularization of the AMH skull/brain.

ASD AND THE GENETICS OF THE DOMESTICATION SYNDROME

In order to improve our characterization of the domesticated traits in ASD, it is of interest to assess whether candidate genes for this condition (with a particular emphasis on language disabilities) are overrepresented among, or are functionally related to, candidates for domestication. We have relied on an extended list of candidates, which includes the core set of genes proposed by Wilkins et al. (2014), plus a subset of the genes involved in the globularization of the AMH skull/brain and the emergence of language-readiness that are functionally related to them, through direct interaction, and/or that play a role in the development and function of the NC (see Benítez-Burraco et al., in press, for details). Our list also comprises NC-related genes known to play a key role in craniofacial development and/or disorders. As noted above, most of the domesticated traits result from the modification of the cranial region and many of the ASD distinctive features concern the skull, face and brain. Moreover, as reasoned in Boeckx and Benítez-Burraco (2014a,b), we expect that our language-readiness resulted from changes in the development of the skull/brain, but also from the refinement of the externalization devices, specifically, the orofacial region: As also noted above, the impairment of oromotor function has been hypothesized to account for some language deficits in ASD. **Table 1** provides a full list and a schematic characterization of these genes.

When we tried to identify ASD-candidates among this extended list of genes via PubMed (http://www.ncbi.nlm.nih.gov/pubmed), we found out that nearly 25% of them have been suggested to play a role in the aetiopathogenesis of ASD. If we also consider genes that we found differentially expressed in postmortem brain tissues isolated from patients (as discussed

TABLE 1 | List of putative candidate genes for domestication and ASD.

Gene symbol	Gene name	Domestication[a]	Language-readiness[b]	NCC[c]	Craniofacial[d]	Brain rhythmicity[e]	ASD	
							Candidate[f]	Differentially expressed[g]
ALX1	Aristaless-like homeobox protein 1			+	+			
ALX3	Aristaless-like homeobox protein 3			+	+			
ALX4	Aristaless-like homeobox protein 4			+	+			
AXIN2	Axin 2			+	+			+
BAZ1B	Bromodomain adjacent to zinc finger domain 1B	+		+				
BMP2	Bone morphogenetic protein 2	+	+	+	+			
BMP7	Bone morphogenetic protein 7	+	+	+				+
CDC42	Cell division cycle 42		+	+				+
CHD7	Chromodomain helicase DNA binding protein 7	+		+			+	+
CITED2	Cbp/p300 interacting transactivator with Glu/Asp rich carboxy-terminal domain 2		+	+				+
CTNNB1	Catenin Beta 1		+	+			+	+
DLX1	Distal-less homeobox 1		+	+				+
DLX2	Distal-less homeobox 2	+	+	+				
DLX5	Distal-less homeobox 5	+	+	+	+	+	+	
DLX6	Distal-less homeobox 6		+	+	+	+	+	
EDN1	Endothelin 1			+	+			+
EDN3	Endothelin 3	+		+				+
EDNRA	Endothelin receptor type A			+	+			+
EDNRB	Endothelin receptor type B	+		+				+
ERF	ETS2 repressor factor			+	+			+
FGF7	Fibroblast growth factor 7		+	+				
FGF8	Fibroblast growth factor 8	+	+	+				+
FGFR1	Fibroblast growth factor receptor 1	+	+	+	+			
FGFR2	Fibroblast growth factor receptor 2			+	+		+	
FOXD3	Forkhead box D3	+		+			+	
FOXP2	Forkhead box P2	+	+					
FREM1	FRAS1 related extracellular matrix 1			+	+			
GDNF	Glial-derived neurotrophic factor	+		+				
GLI3	GLI family zinc finger 3	+	+	+	+			
GRHL3	Grainyhead like transcription factor 3			+	+			
GSC	Goosecoid homeobox			+	+			
HES1	Hes family bHLH transcription factor 1	+	+	+				+
HOXA2	Homeobox A2			+	+	+		
HSH2D	Hematopoietic SH2 domain containing			+	+			
KIT	KIT proto-oncogene receptor tyrosine kinase	+		+			+	+
MAGOH	Mago homolog, exon junction complex core component	+		+				+
MITF	Microphthalmia-associated transcription factor	+		+				+
MSX1	Msh homeobox 1			+	+		+	+
MSX2	Msh homeobox 2			+	+			+
NCAM1	Neural cell adhesion molecule 1	+	+				+	+
NODAL	Nodal growth differentiation factor	+	+					+
NOG	Noggin			+	+			
NTN1	Netrin 1			+	+			+

(Continued)

TABLE 1 | Continued

Gene symbol	Gene name	Domestication[a]	Language-readiness[b]	NCC[c]	Craniofacial[d]	Brain rhythmicity[e]	ASD	
							Candidate[f]	Differentially expressed[g]
PAX3	Paired box 3	**+**	+	+				
PAX6	Paired box 6		+	+		+	+	+
PAX7	Paired box 7				+			+
POLR1A	Polymerase (RNA) I subunit A				+		+	
POU3F2	POU class 3 homeobox 2	+	+				+	+
PQBP1	Polyglutamine binding protein 1	+	+					+
PTCH1	Patched 1			+	+		+	+
RET	Ret proto-oncogene	**+**		+				+
ROBO1	Roundabout guidance receptor 1		+	+				+
ROBO2	Roundabout guidance receptor 2		+	+			+	
RUNX2	Runt related transcription factor 2	+	+	+	+			
SATB2	Special AT-rich sequence binding-homeobox 2		+	+				+
SHH	Sonic hedgehog	+	+	+	+			
SIX2	Sine oculis-related homeobox 2			+	+			
SLIT1	Slit guidance ligand 1		+	+				
SLIT2	Slit guidance ligand 2		+	+				+
SOX2	Sex determining region Y-box 2	**+**	+	+				+
SOX9	Sex determining region Y-box 9	**+**	+	+	+		+	+
SOX10	Sex determining region Y-box 10	**+**	+	+			+	
SPECC1L	Sperm antigen with calponin homology and coiled-coil domains 1-like			+	+			+
TCF12	Trascription factor 12			+	+			+
TCOF1	Treacle ribosome biogenesis factor 1	**+**		+				
VCAN	Versican		+	+				+
ZIC1	Zinc finger protein family member 1			+	+			+

[a]*Core candidates for the "domestication syndrome" according to Wilkins et al. (2014) (bold italicized tags) plus language-readiness genes functionally interacting with them according to Benítez-Burraco et al. (in press) (regular tags).*
[b]*Genes highlighted as candidates for globularization of the AMH skull/brain and the emergence of language-readiness according to Boeckx and Benítez-Burraco (2014a,b) and Benítez-Burraco and Boeckx (2015).*
[c]*Involved in neural crest (NC) development and function.*
[d]*Involved in craniofacial development and/or found mutated in craniofacial syndromes.*
[e]*Involved in brain oscillation and rhythmicity.*
[f]*Candidate for ASD as resulting from genomic studies (pathogenic SNPs, association studies, CNVs, functional studies, etc.).*
[g]*Differentially expressed in postmortem brain tissues of ASD-vs.-control individuals (see text for details).*

in the subsequent section), the percentage rises above 50%. Interestingly, some of these genes are thought to be involved in brain rhythmicity (see **Table 1**), plausibly contributing to the oscillopathic signature of the ASD brain during language processing.

We expect that the genes we highlight here are functionally interconnected and map on to specific pathways, signaling cascades, or aspects of brain development and function, of interest for language processing and the aetiopathology of ASD. *In silico* analyses offer promising insights. Accordingly, String 10 (http://www.string-db.org) predicts quite robust links between most of these genes (**Figure 2**). Likewise, ontology analyses by Panther (http://www.pantherdb.org) suggest that they might play biological functions important for ASD and be part of signaling pathways known to be impaired in this condition (**Table 2**).

Candidate Genes: A Functional Characterization

Some of Wilkins et al.'s (2014) original candidates for the domestication syndrome are candidates for ASD. *KIT* mutations have been found in patients featuring ASD symptoms (Kilsby et al., 2013). KIT is a tyrosine kinase receptor (Kasamatsu et al., 2008), which acts as a key developmental regulator in the NC-derived processes of hematopoiesis, melanogenesis, and gametogenesis (Rothschild et al., 2003). In rats mutations of *Kit* impair hippocampal synaptic potentiation and spatial learning and memory (Katafuchi et al., 2000). Likewise, whole-genome sequencing analyses have identified deleterious variants of *CHD7* in ASD probands (Jiang et al., 2013). *CHD7* is known to be the main candidate for CHARGE syndrome (Vissers et al., 2004; Lalani et al., 2006), mentioned above. Interestingly, CHARGE

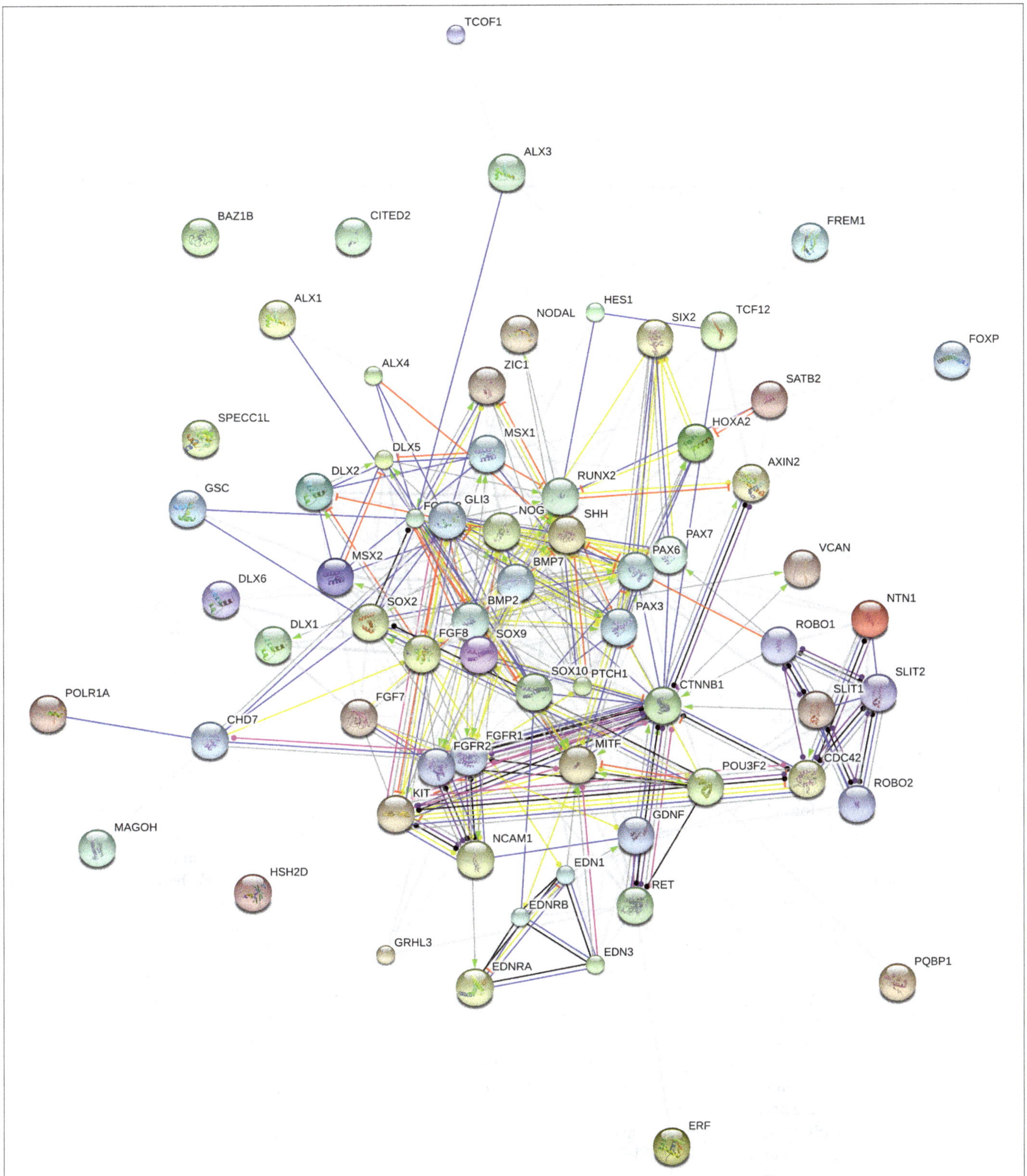

FIGURE 2 | Functional links among candidates for domestication and ASD. The chart shows the network of known and predicted interactions among all genes listed in **Table 1**. The colored nodes symbolize proteins: small nodes are proteins with unknown 3D structure, while large nodes are those with known 3D structures. The color of the edges represent different kind of known protein-protein associations. Green: activation, red: inhibition, dark blue: binding, light blue: phenotype, dark purple: catalysis, light purple: posttranslational modification, black: reaction, yellow:

(Continued)

FIGURE 2 | Continued
transcriptional regulation. Edges ending in an arrow symbolize positive effects, edges ending in a bar symbolize negative effects, whereas edges ending in a circle symbolize unspecified effects. Gray edges symbolize predicted links based on literature search ((co-mention in PubMed abstracts). Stronger associations between proteins are represented by thicker lines. The medium confidence value was 0.0400 (a 40% probability that a predicted link exists between two enzymes in the same metabolic map in the KEGG database: http://www.genome.jp/kegg/pathway.html). String 10 predicts associations between proteins that derive from a limited set of databases: genomic context, high-throughput experiments, conserved coexpression, and the knowledge previously gained from text mining (Szklarczyk et al., 2015). This is why the figure does not represent a fully connected graph (evidence for additional links are provided in the main text). Importantly, the diagram only represents the potential connectivity between the involved proteins, which has to be mapped onto particular biochemical networks, signaling pathways, cellular properties, aspects of neuronal function, or cell-types of interest that can be confidently related to aspects of language development and function.

TABLE 2 | GO classifications of candidates for domestication and ASD.

Biological process	%[a]	Pathway	
Metabolic process (GO:0008152)	21.60%	Axon guidance mediated by Slit/Robo (P00008)	12.20%
Biological regulation (GO:0065007)	18.80%	TGF-beta signaling pathway (P00052)	10.20%
Developmental process (GO:0032502)	17.00%	Endothelin signaling pathway (P00019)	8.20%
Cellular process (GO:0009987)	13.80%	Gonadotropin releasing hormone receptor pathway (P06664)	8.20%
Multicellular organismal process (GO:0032501)	11.50%	Wnt signaling pathway (P00057)	8.20%
Immune system process (GO:0002376)	4.10%	FGF signaling pathway (P00021)	8.20%
Apoptotic process (GO:0006915)	3.20%	Angiogenesis (P00005)	6.10%
Response to stimulus (GO:0050896)	3.20%	Hedgehog signaling pathway (P00025)	6.10%
Biological adhesion (GO:0022610)	3.20%	Axon guidance mediated by netrin (P00009)	4.10%
Localization (GO:0051179)	1.80%	CCKR signaling map (P06959)	4.10%

[a]*Numbers refer to percent of gene hit against total of process or pathway hits. Only the top 10 functions, filted after Bonferroni post-hoc correction, have been included.*

syndrome also involves microcephaly, face asymmetry, cleft lip/palate, along with variable degrees of intellectual disability (Pisano et al., 2014; Hale et al., 2016, for review). Changes in the expression pattern of *CDH7* can also result in behavioral anomalies resembling the autistic phenotype. Accordingly, *in utero* exposure to heavy metals in mice increases autism-like behavioral phenotypes in adult animals through inducing the hypomethylation of *Chd7* (Hill et al., 2015). *FOXD3*, encoding a transcription factor, is downregulated by DISC1 (Drerup et al., 2009), a robust candidate for schizophrenia that has been also associated to ASD (Williams et al., 2009; Zheng et al., 2011; Kanduri et al., 2016). *FOXD3* maps within one of the present-day human-specific differentially-methylated genomic regions (DMRs) (Gokhman et al., 2014). Interestingly, loss of *Disc1* results in abnormal NCC migration and differentiation (Drerup et al., 2009). Also, DISC1 downregulates *SOX10*, another NC gene, involved in the maintenance of precursor NCC pools, in the timing of NCC migration onset, and in the induction of their differentiation; it is also implicated in oligodendrocyte differentiation (Hattori et al., 2014). In turn, SOX10 interacts with PAX3, another core candidate proposed by Wilkins et al. (2014), and with POU3F2 (Smit et al., 2000). Sequence and CNVs affecting *POU3F2* have been found in subjects with ASD, and in individuals with different developmental and language delays (Huang et al., 2005; Lin et al., 2011). POU3F2 is a known interactor of *FOXP2*, the renowned "language gene" (Maricic et al., 2013). AMHs bear a derived allele of the binding site which is less efficient in activating transcription than the Neanderthal/Denisovan counterpart (Maricic et al., 2013). Likewise, *POU3F2* has been associated with human accelerated conserved non-coding sequences (haCNSs) (Miller et al., 2014). Also, it interacts with PQBP1, which has been linked to intellectual disability (Wang et al., 2013) and developmental delay and microcephaly (Li et al., 2013). Also *SOX9*, considered a master regulator of craniofacial development and related to several congenital skeletal malformations (Mansour et al., 2002; Gordon et al., 2009; Lee and Saint-Jeannet, 2011), is found among the candidates for ASD.

Accordingly, gene and miRNA expression profiling using cell-line derived total RNA has revealed *SOX9* as one of the genes dysregulated in ASD (Ghahramani Seno et al., 2011). As discussed in detail by Benítez-Burraco et al. (in press) *SOX9* interacts with *BMP2*, *BMP7*, *DLX2*, and *HES1*. All of them are core components of the network believed important for globularization and language-readiness (reviewed in Boeckx and Benítez-Burraco, 2014a). In addition, all of them are involved in NCC development and migration, and in the patterning of NC-derived tissues (Mallo, 2001; Gajavelli et al., 2004; Correia et al., 2007; Glejzer et al., 2011; Ishii et al., 2012). *BMP2* is a key osteogenic regulator, which has been associated to craniosynostosis (Justice et al., 2012; Lattanzi et al., 2013). *BMP2*, *BMP7*, and *DLX2* act upstream *SOX9* (Sperber et al., 2008; Li et al., 2013). In turn, *SOX9* mediates the retinoic acid-induced expression of *HES1*, known also to be involved in language function, craniofacial development, and neuron growth and interconnection (reviewed in Boeckx and Benítez-Burraco, 2014b). Importantly, retinoic acid also regulates the expression of other genes that are relevant for language, like *FOXP2* (Devanna et al., 2014), or for globularization, like *ASCL1* (see Benítez-Burraco and Boeckx, 2015, for details). Retinoic acid has proven to be important for brain plasticity (Luo et al., 2009), and memory and learning processes (Etchamendy et al., 2003; Jiang et al.,

2012). Recent whole-exome sequencing analyses have linked retinoic acid regulation pathways to ASD (Moreno-Ramos et al., 2015). In neuronal cells reduced levels of RORA downregulate multiple transcriptional targets that are significantly enriched in biological functions negatively impacted in ASD and which include known ASD-associated genes, like *A2BP1*, *CYP19A1*, *ITPR1*, *NLGN1*, and *NTRK2* (Sarachana and Hu, 2013a). *RORA* itself is downregulated in postmortem prefrontal cortex and cerebellum of subjects with ASD (Nguyen et al., 2010). *RORA* is differentially regulated in them by masculine and feminine hormones: Whereas it is under negative feedback regulation by androgens, it is under positive regulation by estrogens (Sarachana et al., 2011; Sarachana and Hu, 2013b). In certain regions of the brain this sexually dimorphic expression is also found in several of RORA's targets and this correlation is much higher in the cortex of males (Hu et al., 2015). Perhaps not surprisingly, synthetic RORα/γ agonist improve autistic symptoms in animal models of the disease, particularly, repetitive behavior (Wang et al., 2016).

We wish to highlight two other genes thought to be involved in the changes that brought about modern language that are also candidates for ASD and interact with core candidates for the domestication syndrome as posited by Wilkins et al. The first one is *DLX5*, involved in crucial aspects of NC development (McLarren et al., 2003; Ruest et al., 2003), but also of skull and brain development (Kraus and Lufkin, 2006; Wang et al., 2010). Accordingly, it plays a role in thalamic development (Jones and Rubenstein, 2004) and contributes to regulate the migration and differentiation of precursors of GABA-expressing neurons in the forebrain (Cobos et al., 2006). *DLX5* is a candidate for ASD (Nakashima et al., 2010), due to an ultraconserved cis-regulatory element (Poitras et al., 2010), which is bound by GTF2I, encoded by one of the genes commonly deleted in Williams-Beuren syndrome (OMIM#194050) and a candidate for ASD too (Malenfant et al., 2012). Additionally, *DLX5* is regulated by MECP2 (Miyano et al., 2008), encoded by the main candidate for Rett syndrome (OMIM#312750), a condition entailing problems for motor coordination, autistic behavior, and language regression (Uchino et al., 2001; Veenstra-VanderWeele and Cook, 2004). Interestingly, Dlx5/6(±) mice exhibit abnormal pattern of γ rhythms resulting from alterations in GABAergic interneurons, particularly in fast-spiking interneurons (Cho et al., 2015). In addition, DLX5 interacts with key candidates for language evolution, in particular, with *RUNX2* and *FOXP2* (see Boeckx and Benítez-Burraco, 2014a, for details). The second one is *NCAM1*, which is also a target of both RUNX2 (Kuhlwilm et al., 2013) and FOXP2 (Konopka et al., 2009). In mice mutations in the gene affect working/episodic-like memory (Bisaz et al., 2013), whereas overexpression of the Ncaml extracellular proteolytic cleavage fragment impacts on GABAergic innervation, affecting long- and short-term potentiation in the prefrontal cortex (Brennaman et al., 2011). *NCAM1* encodes a cell adhesion protein involved in axonal and dendritic growth and synaptic plasticity (Rønn et al., 2000; Hansen et al., 2008). It interacts with VCAM1 which is involved in cell adhesion and the control of neurogenesis (Kokovay et al., 2012), and which bears a fixed (D414G) change in AMHs compared to Neanderthals/Denisovans (Pääbo, 2014). *VCAM1* is upregulated by CLOCK, which plays a key role in the modulation of circadian rhythm (Gao et al., 2014). Together with other circadian-relevant genes *CLOCK* seems to be involved in the psychopathology of ASD cases entailing sleep disturbances (Yang et al., 2016). The circadian modulation of synaptic function has been hypothesized to contribute decisively to ASD (Bourgeron, 2007). In turn, *CLOCK* interacts with *RUNX2* and with several other candidates for language-readiness, like *DUSP1*, involved in vocal learning (Doi et al., 2007), and *USF1*, which regulates synaptic plasticity, neuronal survival and differentiation (Tabuchi et al., 2002; Steiger et al., 2004). USF1 binds the promoter of *FMR1* (Kumari and Usdin, 2001), a strong candidate for Fragile-X syndrome (OMIM#300624), which presents with language problems and ASD features (Kaufmann et al., 2004; Smith et al., 2012). The regulatory region of *USF1* shows many fixed or high frequency changes compared to Denisovans (Meyer et al., 2012).

As shown in **Table 1**, several of the genes important for globularization and language-readiness are involved in NC development and function and some of them are also candidates for ASD. Accordingly, we expect them to contribute to the abnormal domesticated features observed in patients with ASD, and also to their distinctive language profile. Among them we wish mention *CTNNB1*, *DLX1*, *DLX6*, *PAX6*, and *ROBO2*. CTNNB1 is a component of the Wnt/β-catenin signaling pathway, known to be impaired in ASD (Cao et al., 2012; Zhang et al., 2012; Martin et al., 2013). CTNNB1 controls aspects of NC development, from NC induction, lineage decisions, to differentiation (Hari et al., 2012). As noted in Boeckx and Benítez-Burraco (2014b), CTNNB1 is expected to interact with many of the genes highlighted as important for the evolution of language-readiness, specifically with RUNX2 and SLIT2/ROBO1 signals. Regarding DLX1, it is a robust NC marker (Ishii et al., 2012), involved in patterning and morphogenetic processes in NC-derived tissues (Mallo, 2001). It also regulates the development of the skull and the brain (Andrews et al., 2003; Jones and Rubenstein, 2004). In mice *Dlx1* downregulation results in reduced glutamatergic input to the hippocampus (Jones et al., 2011), as well as in changes in interneuron subtypes and migration patterns in the cortex (Ghanem et al., 2008). *DLX1* is found to be downregulated in ASD (Voineagu et al., 2011; McKinsey et al., 2013). ROBO2 is one of the DLX1 interactors. Slit/Robo signaling regulates early NCC migration (Jia et al., 2005) *ROBO2* is also involved in thalamocortical axons (TCA) development, known to be important for the modulation of cognitive functions (López-Bendito et al., 2007; Marcos-Mondéjar et al., 2012). *ROBO2* is a candidate for ASD (Suda et al., 2011), but also for different types of language disorders, like dyslexia (Fisher et al., 2002) and speech-sound disorder and reading (Stein et al., 2004). It has been related as well to expressive vocabulary growth in the normal population (St Pourcain et al., 2014). Finally, *PAX6* controls the migration of NCCs from the anterior midbrain (Matsuo et al., 1993). *PAX6* is involved as well in the development of the brain (Valverde et al., 2000; Tyas et al., 2003; Caballero et al., 2014). Mutations on *PAX6* have been reported in some forms of ASD (Maekawa et al., 2009), although they also impact in working memory (Bamiou et al., 2007). Alterations of *PAX6* expression in the brain of people with ASD may account for the observed imbalance in excitatory/inhibitory neuronal activity (Kim et al., 2014). And like many of the genes reviewed above, *PAX6* is functionally related to both *FOXP2* and *RUNX2*, and it also targets *POU3F2* (see Benítez-Burraco and Boeckx, 2015, for details).

Most of the NCC-genes mentioned here are known to play a key role in the development and patterning of the craniofacial complex, and to be associated to congenital craniofacial defects (**Table 1**) (see Twigg and Wilkie, 2015 for review). Many of these genes are known candidates for ASD, including *DLX5* and *DLX6* (reviewed above), *FGFR2*, *MSX1*, *POLR1A*, and *PTCH1*. Both *DLX5* and *DLX6* are indeed required for NC-derived facial morphogenesis (Gitton et al., 2011) FGFRs are among the main craniosynostosis-associated genes. In particular, gain-of-function mutations in *FGFR2* are typically associated to Apert (OMIM#101200) and Crouzon (OMIM#123500) syndromes, while both *FGFR1* and *FGFR2* are found mutated in Pfeiffer syndrome (OMIM#101600) (Lattanzi et al., 2012). All these syndromic craniosynostoses occasionally present with variable degree of ASD-like mental retardation (Morey-Canellas et al., 2003). *MSX1* encodes a transcriptional repressor involved in craniofacial development and shaping (particularly in odontogenesis) (Alappat et al., 2003; Lattanzi, forthcoming). It is expressed in the NC (Khadka et al., 2006), where it acts as a master regulator of gene expression (Attanasio et al., 2013). Although it has not been associated to ASD, *MSX1* is a direct downstream target of DLX5 during early inner ear formation (Sajan et al., 2011). The gene is also a critical intrinsic dopaminergic neuron determinant (Andersson et al., 2006) and is found mutated in some patients with Wolf-Hirschhorn syndrome (OMIM#194190), a clinical condition entailing profound mental retardation and craniofacial dysmorphism (Campbell et al., 1989). *POLR1A*, found mutated in acrofacial dysostosis (Cincinnati type, OMIM#616462) involving microcephaly, plays a role in the regulation of NC-derived skeletal precursor cells (Weaver et al., 2015). In some ASD subjects CNVs result in fusion transcripts involving *POLR1A*, although no fusion transcripts have been detected to date (Holt et al., 2012).

Finally, it is worth mentioning that genes encoding primary cilium signaling molecules, such as *SHH*, *GLI3*, and *PTCH1*, are all primarily involved in congenital malformations affecting the midline craniofacial compartment (Brugmann et al., 2010; Rice et al., 2010). Specifically, *PTCH1* is required in the NC-dependent orofacial development and gives rise to orofacial clefting, when mutated (Metzis et al., 2013). Heterozygous mutations of either *SHH* or *PTCH1* are typically found in holoprosencephaly (OMIM#610828, and #236100), a genetically heterogeneous, highly prevalent congenital forebrain anomaly in humans, associated with mental retardation and craniofacial malformations (Ming et al., 2002; Mercier et al., 2011). In addition, a 22-bp deletion in this gene has been found in a girl with ASD and Gorlin syndrome, a complex condition involving macrocrania and hypertelorism (Delbroek et al., 2011).

Candidate Genes: Expression Profiles in the ASD Brain

If our hypothesis is on the right track, we expect that the genes we highlight here are dysregulated in the brain of people with ASD, particularly in areas important for language processing. Accordingly, we surveyed the Gene Expression Omnibus (GEO) repository (https://www.ncbi.nlm.nih.gov/gds) searching for their expression profiles in the cerebellum and the temporal cortex (but also in the frontal and occipital cortices) in patients with ASD. This should help identify new candidates for ASD in the context of domestication and language-readiness (**Table 1**). Overall, we could find significant expression values for some of our candidates and learnt that they are up- or downregulated in the brain of autists (**Figure 3**).

Among the genes that are significantly downregulated in the cerebellum we found *AXIN2*, *EDNRB*, *SOX2*, *SPECC1L*, *TCF12*, and *VCAN*, whereas *CDC42*, and *PQBP1* are found upregulated in this region (**Figure 3**). Although none of them has been associated to ASD, they stroke us as promising candidates for the atypical presentation of the domestication syndrome in ASD. *AXIN2* is expressed in the cranial NC and is needed for NC-derived frontal bone osteogenesis (Yu et al., 2005; Li et al., 2015a). This gene is also expressed as a specific marker for suture stem cells (Maruyama et al., 2016), but also acts as a negative regulator of canonical Wnt pathway, contributing to the stability of CTNNB1 (Li et al., 2015a). Speech alterations are also observed in people with *AXIN2* mutations causing non-syndromic oligodontia (Liu et al., 2015). *EDNRB* encodes a receptor for endothelins, known to be potent vasoactive peptides. Mutations in this gene are associated to increased susceptibility to Hirschsprung disease (OMIM#600155), a neurocristopathy characterized by congenital absence of intrinsic ganglion cells in the enteric nervous plexa (Amiel et al., 2008). Waardenburg syndrome (OMIM#277580), a genetically heterogeneous condition which may involve developmental delay subsidiary to sensorineural hearing loss, has also been associated with mutations in *EDNRB* (Read and Newton, 1997). *SOX2*, one of core candidates for domestication (Wilkins et al., 2014), encodes an interactors of the GLI factors as part of the SHH-GLI signaling pathway involved in NCC fate (Oosterveen et al., 2012, 2013; Peterson et al., 2012), but also in the globularization of the AMH skull/brain (see Boeckx et al., submitted for details). SOX2 interacts as well with the BMP signaling (Li et al., 2015b). Interestingly, SOX2 regulates *PQBP1*, highlighted above as one of POU3F2 interactors. *SPECC1L* is found mutated in Opitz G/BBB syndrome (OMIM# #145410) and in facial clefting (Kruszka et al., 2015). This gene functions in NC development (Wilson et al., 2016) and is specifically involved in facial morphogenesis (Saadi et al., 2011). *TCF12* is highly expressed in embryonic precursors of skull/brain structures, including NC-derived head mesenchyme (Uittenbogaard and Chiaramello, 2002). *TCF12* directly interacts with *TWIST1*, mutated in Saethre-Chotzen syndrome (OMIM#601622), which features complex craniosynostosys with variable degrees of intellectual disability, including ASD traits (Maliepaard et al., 2014). Indeed, loss-of-function mutations of *TCF12* have been identified in patients with coronal synostosis, which sometimes involves intellectual disability (Sharma et al., 2013; di Rocco et al., 2014; Paumard-Hernández et al., 2015; Piard et al., 2015). *VCAN* encodes versican-1, a protein that guides migratory NCCs (Dutt et al., 2006) and which shows a fixed N3042D change in AMHs (Pääbo, 2014). Finally, *CDC42* controls NC stem

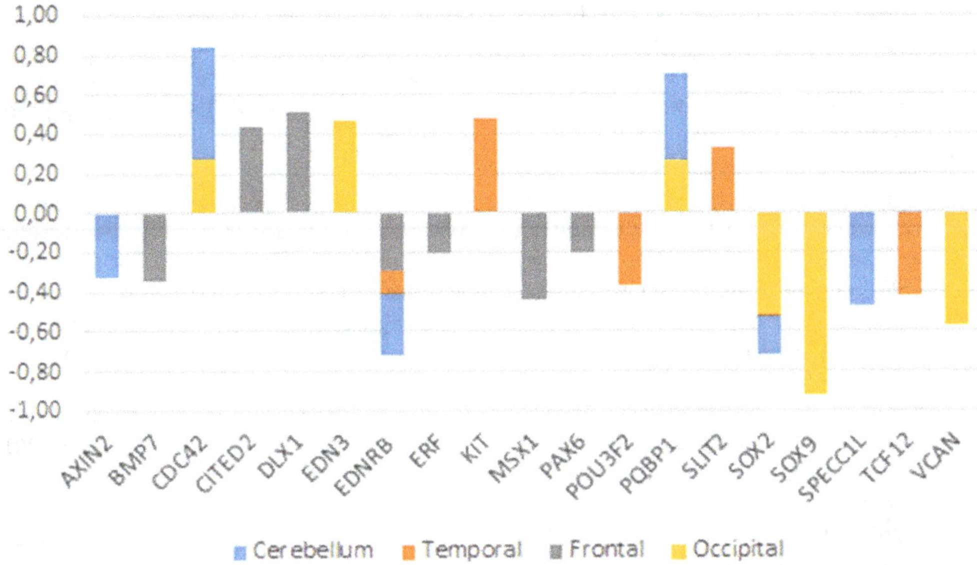

FIGURE 3 | Expression profiles of candidate genes in the ASD brain. Data were gathered from the following microarray expression datasets available on the Gene Expression Omnibus database (GEO datasets, http://www.ncbi.nlm.nih.gov/gds): GSE28521 (Voineagu et al., 2011) for the temporal and frontal cortices, GSE38322 (Ginsberg et al., 2012) for the cerebellum and the occipital cortex. Data are shown as log transformation of fold changes (logFC) between patients and corresponding controls. Only genes showing statistically significant ($p < 0.05$) differential expression were considered. Additional details may be found in the Supplemental information file.

cell proliferation (Fuchs et al., 2009). Inactivation of Cdc42 in NCCs causes craniofacial and cardiovascular morphogenesis defects (Liu et al., 2013). As discussed in detail in Boeckx and Benítez-Burraco (2014b) *CDC42* is an important gene regarding language evolution, because of its functional connections with core candidates for globularization and the externalization of language (including *FOXP2*, *RUNX2*, *SLIT2*, and *ROBO1*), with genes related to language disorders (like *CMIP*), and with genes known to have changed after our split from Neanderthals and Denisovans (like *ITGB4*, *ARHGAP32*, *ANAPC10*, and *CDC42EP4*).

With regards to the temporal cortex, we found that *EDNRB*, *POU3F2*, *SOX2*, *VCAN*, and *TCF12* are downregulated in subjects with ASD, whereas *KIT*, *PQBP1*, and *SLIT2* are upregulated in them (**Figure 3**). As noted above, *POU3F2*, *SOX2*, *KIT* are known candidates for ASD. We have already reviewed all these genes. Concerning the frontal cortex we found that *BMP7*, *EDNRB*, *PAX6*, *ERF*, and *MSX1* are significantly downregulated, whereas *CITED2* and *DLX1* are significantly upregulated (**Figure 3**). As noted in **Table 1**, *DLX1*, *PAX6*, and *MSX1* have been previously associated to ASD. Most of these genes have been already reviewed. *BMP7* is a NCC gene involved in regulation of osteogenesis (Cheng et al., 2003; Anderson et al., 2006) and in skull and brain development (Yuge et al., 2011; Segklia et al., 2012). *BMP7* is also closely related to some of the core candidates for globularization and language- readiness, like *BMP2*, *DLX1*, *DLX2*, and *RUNX2*. BMP7 is predicted (according to String 10) to interact with SOX2 via NOG, involved in dopamine neuron production and an inhibitor of BMP signaling (Chiba et al., 2008). Developmental delay and learning disabilities are commonly observed in people with mutations in *BMP7* (Wyatt et al., 2010). *ERF* encodes a member of the ETS family of transcription factors, expressed in migratory cells, including NCCs (Paratore et al., 2002). *ERF* haploinsufficiency gives rise to either coronal or multisuture synostosis, midface hypoplasia, often associated with behavioral and learning difficulties (Twigg et al., 2013). Concerning *CITED2*, this is a functional partner of both FOXP2 and RUNX2 (Luo et al., 2005; Vernes et al., 2011; Nelson et al., 2013), two important genes for the emergence of modern language. *CITED2* is also involved in craniofacial development (Bhattacherjee et al., 2009) and in the establishment of left-right axis through interactions with the BMP signaling and Nodal (Preis et al., 2006; Lopes Floro et al., 2011). Interestingly, 99% of AMHs bear a highly disruptive intergenic change near *CITED2* compared to Altai Neanderthals and Denisovans (Prüfer et al., 2014).

Finally, regarding the occipital cortex, we found that *EDN3*, *CDC42*, and *PQBP1* are significantly upregulated in ASD, whereas *SOX2*, *SOX9*, and *VCAN* are downregulated. We have already considered all these genes, with the exception of *EDN3*. This gene encodes an endothelium-derived vasoactive peptide which binds the product of *EDNRB*, playing a key role in the development of neural crest-derived cell lineages, such as melanocytes and enteric neurons. Although *EDN3* is a candidate for Waardenburg syndrome and Hirschsprung disease, the gene has been found significantly dysregulated in children with ASD (Glatt et al., 2011).

As shown in **Figure 3**, genes that exhibit significant changes in their expression levels in the ASD brain are consistently down- or upregulated across all the regions under analysis. Considering their functions and the phenotypes resulting from their mutation, the most promising of these genes are *CDC42* and *PQBP1* (which are upregulated) and *EDNRB* and *SOX2* (which are found downregulated). As noted above, to date none of them have been associated to ASD, but they emerge as reasonably involved in the pathogenesis of this condition.

Noteworthy age-related differences in the intrinsic functional connectivity of the brain are observed in ASD: adult patients show reduced connectivity while children tend to exhibit an increased connectivity (Uddin et al., 2013). Therefore, we have further analyzed ASD brain expression data in an age-matched fashion. Due to the available sample characteristics, only expression data obtained from the cerebellum could be analyzed (see Supplemental file for further details). The reduction of the age-related bias in the patients-vs.-controls comparison, enabled finding a higher number of statistically significant dysregulated genes in the ASD brain. Accordingly, we found that in the cerebellum of ASD children (below 11 years old), *CDC42, MSX1, MSX2, NODAL, PQBP1,* and *SLIT2* were downregulated, whereas, *AXIN2, CHD7, CITED2, EDNRB, FGF8, NCAM1, PAX7, PTCH1, RET, ROBO1, SOX2, SPECC1L, TCF12, VCAN,* and *ZIC1* were upregulated. In turn, in the cerebellum of adult patients (aged 22–60 years) we found that *CDC42, CTNNB1, DLX1, EDNRA, EDNRB, HES1, KIT, MAGOH, MITF, NCAM1, NTN1, POU3F2, PQBP1, PTCH1, RET, ROBO1, SATB2, SOX2, SPECC1L, TCF12, VCAN,* and *ZIC1* are downregulated, whereas only *AXIN2, CTNNB1, DLX1, EDN1,* and *MSX1* are upregulated. Overall, we concluded that nearly one third of the candidates for domestication are dysregulated in the cerebellum of people with ASD, and that more than a half are specifically dysregulated in the cerebellum of either children and/or adults with this condition. Genes that are dysregulated in both children and adults with ASD can be regarded as significant contributors to the atypical presentation of the domestication syndrome in this condition. This list encompasses 14 genes: *AXIN2, CDC42, EDNRB, MSX1, NCAM1, PQBP1, PTCH1, RET, ROBO1, SOX2, SPECC1L, TCF12, VCAN,* and *ZIC1*. Interestingly, they exhibit opposite expression profiles in children and adults with ASD (**Figure 4**). Most of these genes have been already discussed here. In addition, *RET,* encoding a cadherin that plays a crucial role in NC development, is a candidate for Hirschsprung disease (OMIM# 142623; Edery et al., 1994) and is found to be differentially expressed after RUNX2 transfection in neuroblastoma cells (Kuhlwilm et al., 2013). *RET* is downstream *ASCL1* (another candidate for Hirschsprung disease) in noradrenergic brain stem neurons important for respiratory rhythm modulation (Dauger et al., 2001). Likewise, *ZIC1* is needed for NC development (along with *PAX3*) and plays a key role in craniofacial development (Milet et al., 2013; Plouhinec et al., 2014). Mutations in *ZIC1* result in severe coronal synostosis associated with learning difficulties (Twigg et al., 2015).

In the last section of the paper we attempt refining our characterization of ASD as an atypically-domesticated phenotype. In doing so, we will focus on brain function, with a special emphasis on brain oscillations. Accordingly, we will compare the oscillopathic profile of people with ASD during language processing with the oscillatory signature of the TD population and that of non-domesticated primates. Additionally, we will examine the expression profile in the primate brain of the candidate genes we highlight here.

ASD AND WILD PRIMATES: FROM BRAIN OSCILLATION TO GENE EXPRESSION PATTERNS

ASD and Primate Oscillomes

As we have discussed in detail in Benítez-Burraco and Murphy (2016) language impairment in ASD (as ASD itself) can be satisfactorily characterized as an oscillopathic condition. With cognitive disorders exhibiting disorder-specific abnormal oscillatory profiles, it is also noteworthy that species-specific oscillatory patterns seemingly emerge as slight variations within the network constellation that constitutes a universal brain syntax (Buzsáki and Watson, 2012; Buzsáki et al., 2013).

The differences in brain capacity between domesticated and non-domesticated animals (Wilkins et al., 2014) would be predicted to give rise to a corresponding alteration in oscillatory properties (i.e., features of neural oscillations which form part of an individual's "oscillome," as it is termed in Murphy and Benítez-Burraco, in press; Murphy, 2016a,b). Although we feel that current knowledge is too scarce to permit any reasonable linking hypotheses between the primate and ASD oscillomes, we would like to briefly sketch out a possible route to increasing our understanding of the neural signature of domestication (and failed domestication itineraries).

Call vocalizations have been found not to be impaired when the homolog of Broca's region in the monkey brain is lesioned, which suggests that other area (like the limbic system and brainstem) are involved (Sage et al., 2006). However, macaques appear to share similar call comprehension substrates with human language comprehension in the left posterior temporal gyrus (Heffner and Heffner, 1986). It would be of interest, for instance, to compare the rhythmic properties of this region of the TD brain with those of the primate brain to see if any particular activity (e.g., coupling and synchronization) is marked in humans. This would also yield insights into how the primate call comprehension system "interfaces" with other cognitive systems (given the appropriate experimental environment), and would also permit the exploration of similar interface properties of human language comprehension, which requires the transfer of information to two interfaces (**Figure 5**).

Discounting work on evoked potentials (which is itself fairly modest), there are currently only a handful of empirical studies of the monkey oscillome. Brincat and Miller (2015), for instance, discovered functional differences and frequency-specific interactions between the Rhesus hippocampus (HPC) and prefrontal cortex (PFC) during object pair association learning. θ synchrony was found to be greater after errors and decreased after learning; correct associations increased β-α synchrony, which was also greater in the HPC-PFC direction. Esghaei et al. (2015) also suggested that the macaque visual cortex employs phase-amplitude coupling to regulate inter-neuronal correlations, and so the potential for generic oscillomic processes to yield insights into cognitive (dys)function seems apparent. During the internally monitored continuation phase of a synchronization-continuation task, β also appears to increase in

FIGURE 4 | Expression profiles of candidates genes in the cerebellum of children and adults with ASD. Expression data were obtained from the microarray expression dataset GSE38322 (Ginsberg et al., 2012) available on the Gene Expression Omnibus database (GEO datasets, http://www.ncbi.nlm.nih.gov/gds). Data are shown as log transformation of fold changes (logFC) between patients and corresponding controls. Only genes showing statistically significant ($p < 0.05$) differential expression were considered. Additional details may be found in the Supplemental information file.

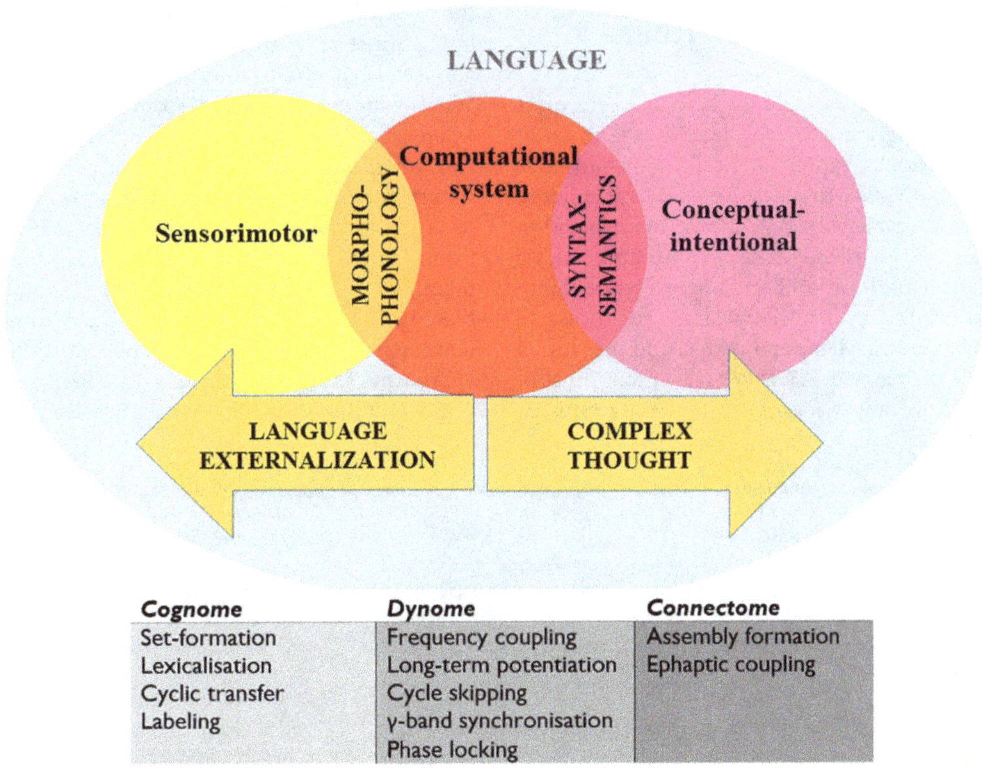

FIGURE 5 | A schematic view of language representing the systems and interfaces of interest and the levels of analysis. "Cognome" refers to the operations available to the human nervous system (Poeppel, 2012) and "dynome" refers to brain dynamics (Kopell et al., 2014; Murphy and Benítez-Burraco, in press). See text for details.

Rhesus monkeys (Bartolo and Merchant, 2015), suggesting that—as in humans (Murphy, 2015a)—β is responsible for maintaining the existing cognitive set in memory. β is also involved in "the attentive state and external cues as opposed to detailed muscle activities" in Japanese monkeys (*Macaca fuscata*) (Watanabe et al., 2015). Finally, pulvinar γ is involved in feedforward processing for snake images, and also in cortico-pulvinar-cortical integration for face images (Le et al., 2016), while Ramirez-Villegas et al.'s (2015) study of the macaque hippocampal CA3-CA1 network pointed to the role of γ in memory reactivation, transfer and consolidation.

Currently, there are no studies comparing the oscillome of domesticated and non-domesticated primates, but our prediction would be that non-domesticated primates display a degree of oscillomic difference with domesticated primates comparable to the difference between TD individuals and people with ASD. **Table 3** summarizes existing knowledge of the ASD and primate oscillome during a range of cognitive tasks, and it is hard to find any correlations or connections between the two. However, we feel that comparatively exploring these oscillomes will permit a greater understanding of the atavistic neural oscillations of the non-domesticated human and primate brains. Future research should also seek to compare the oscillomes of domesticated and non-domesticated primates in an effort to investigate neural signatures of domestication.

Candidate Genes: Expression Profiles in the Primate Brain

If our hypothesis turns to be on the right track, we further expect that the genes that we have found dysregulated in the brain of people with ASD show similar expression profiles in conditions where normal socialization failed to occur. Because feral children are scarce and not easily available we examined the expression profiles of these genes in wild primates (chimps). In particular, we selected available gene expression profiles obtained from chimp brain areas that are known to be involved in language processing in humans (the cerebellum, the temporal cortex, and the frontal cortex), as we did for people with ASD. We learnt that most of the genes that we had previously found differentially expressed in the ASD brain data exhibit the same expression pattern in the chimp brain, including *EDNRB* (in the cerebellum), *BMP7*, *DLX1*, *EDNRB*, *MSX1*, and *PAX6* (in the frontal cortex), and *VCAN* (in the temporal cortex) (**Figure 6**).

CONCLUSIONS

Socialization is a crucial step needed for the achievement of many cognitive abilities that are a signature of the human condition. Language is one of the most prominent of such abilities. Several high prevalent pathological conditions impact on human-specific cognitive abilities, including schizophrenia and ASD. In ASD, social abilities are seriously compromised, but other core cognitive skills, including language, also exhibit differences with the non-affected population. ASD is a multifactorial condition, with wide clinical and genetic heterogeneity. It is still not clear how ASD features emerge from genomic and/or environmental cues during development. In this paper we have focused on language deficits in ASD, although we expect that the lessons we draw here contribute to shedding light on the whole profile of this cognitive condition. In doing so we have adopted and evolutionary perspective, because of the robust link that exists between (abnormal) development and evolution. As we have shown, domesticated traits are absent or are attenuated in people with ASD, and genes that we believe important for the (self)domestication of our species and the evolution of our distinctive cognitive abilities (including language) show abnormal expression patterns in the brains of people with autism. What is more: abnormalities can be traced to the time window when crucial brain rewiring occurs during language acquisition and when changes in the normal configuration of the brain occurs in children with ASD. Additionally, some features of the ASD phenotype can be found (or expected to be found) in wild primates. On the whole, we think that our approach can help illuminate the etiology of ASD primarily because provides robust links between the genome and the environment, and between development and evolution, in line with the current evo-devo approaches to cognitive diseases (see Benítez-Burraco, 2016a, for review). In this sense, the putative involvement of the neural crest

TABLE 3 | Summary of the patterns of rhythmicity observed in wild primates and the observed oscillomic differences in ASD compared to TD subjects.

Frequency band	Oscillomic monkey profile	Oscillopathic profile of autism spectrum disorder
Delta (~0.5–4 Hz)	Decreased phase-amplitude coupling with γ yields increased visual attention, suggesting that cross-frequency coupling suppression modulates attention.	Increased in eyes-closed resting state exam; predicted to be disrupted in processing phrases involving raising and passives.
Theta (~4–10 Hz)	Decreased phase-amplitude coupling with γ yields increased visual attention; greater HPC-PFC synchrony after object pair association errors.	Reduced cross-frequency coupling with γ; does not synergistically engage with γ during speech; predicted to be disrupted in certain memory retrieval processes.
Alpha (~8–12 Hz)	Increased synchrony with β during correct object pair associations.	Reduced cross-cortically; reduced resting-state α-γ phase amplitude coupling; increased in resting state; predicted to be disrupted during certain lexicalizations.
Beta (~10–30 Hz)	Increased synchrony with α during object pair associations; increases during continuation phase of a synchronization-continuation task.	Reduced in picture-naming tasks; predicted to be disrupted in the maintenance of syntactic objects in raising, passives and *wh*-questions.
Gamma (~30–100 Hz)	Involved in processing snake and face images increases during action sequence updating and memory consolidation, reactivation, and transfer.	Over-connectivity gives rise to increased γ; reduced in rSTG and lIFG during picture naming; predicted to be disrupted quite generally in linguistic cognition.

FIGURE 6 | Comparative expression profiles in chimpanzees and subjects with ASD of candidate genes. Data were obtained from microarray expression datasets available on the Gene Expression Omnibus database (GEO datasets, http://www.ncbi.nlm.nih.gov/gds): GSE28521 (Voineagu et al., 2011) for the temporal and frontal cortices, and GSE38322 (Ginsberg et al., 2012) for the cerebellum of subjects with ASD; GSE22569 (Somel et al., 2011; Liu et al., 2012) for the cerebellum, GSE18142 (Konopka et al., 2009) for the frontal cortex, and GSE7540 (Cáceres et al., 2003) for the temporal cortex of chimps. Data are shown as log transformation of fold changes (logFC) between patients and corresponding controls. Only genes showing statistically significant ($p < 0.05$) differential expression were considered. Additional details may be found in the Supplemental information file. Note that the plot is intended to display the overall trend of gene expression, given that the relative expression values (i.e., logFC) were obtained from comparative analyses performed on different datasets (based on different designs, samples, and batches).

in the aetiopathogenesis of ASD emerges as a promising avenue for future research. At the same time, we expect that our approach with help illuminate the evolutionary history of our language-readiness: Our results support the view that language evolution benefitted from a favorable social context that may have resulted from our (self)-domestication.

AUTHOR CONTRIBUTIONS

AB contributed to all Sections and drafted the manuscript, WL contributed to Sections "Domestic Traits in the ASD Phenotype" and "ASD and the Genetics of the Domestication Syndrome" and revised the manuscript, EM contributed to Sections "Introduction" and "ASD and Wild Primates: from Brain Oscillation to Gene Expression Patterns" and revised the manuscript.

ACKNOWLEDGMENTS

Preparation of this work was supported in part by funds from the Spanish Ministry of Economy and Competitiveness (grant numbers FFI2014-61888-EXP and FFI-2013-43823-P to ABB), in part by "Linea D1- 2015" intramural funds from Università Cattolica S. Cuore (to WL), and in part by an Economic and Social Research Council scholarship (1474910) (to EM).

REFERENCES

Akefeldt, A., and Gillberg, C. (1991). Hypomelanosis of Ito in three cases with autism and autistic-like conditions. *Dev. Med. Child Neurol.* 33, 737–743. doi: 10.1111/j.1469-8749.1991.tb14953.x

Alappat, S., Zhang, Z. Y., and Chen, Y. P. (2003). Msx homeobox gene family and craniofacial development. *Cell Res.* 13, 429–442. doi: 10.1038/sj.cr.7290185

Aldridge, K., George, I. D., Cole, K. K., Austin, J. R., Takahashi, T. N., Duan, Y., et al. (2011). Facial phenotypes in subgroups of prepubertal boys with autism spectrum disorders are correlated with clinical phenotypes. *Mol. Autism.* 2:15. doi: 10.1186/2040-2392-2-15

Amiel, J., Sproat-Emison, E., Garcia-Barceo, M., Lantieri, F., Burzynski, G., Borrego, S., et al. (2008). Hirschsprung disease: associated syndromes and genetics: a review. *J. Med. Genet.* 45, 1–14. doi: 10.1136/jmg.2007.053959

Anderson, R. M., Stottmann, R. W., Choi, M., and Klingensmith, J. (2006). Endogenous bone morphogenetic protein antagonists regulate mammalian neural crest generation and survival. *Dev. Dyn.* 235, 2507–2520. doi: 10.1002/dvdy.20891

Andersson, E., Tryggvason, U., Deng, Q., Friling, S., Alekseenko, Z., Robert, B., et al. (2006). Identification of intrinsic determinants of midbrain dopamine neurons. *Cell* 124, 393–405. doi: 10.1016/j.cell.2005.10.037

Andrews, G. L., Yun, K., Rubenstein, J. L., and Mastick, G. S. (2003). Dlx transcription factors regulate differentiation of dopaminergic neurons of the ventral thalamus. *Mol. Cell Neurosci.* 23, 107–120. doi: 10.1016/S1044-7431(03)00016-2

Attanasio, C., Nord, A. S., Zhu, Y., Blow, M. J., Li, Z., Liberton, D. K., et al. (2013). Fine tuning of craniofacial morphology by distant-acting enhancers. *Science* 342:1241006. doi: 10.1126/science.1241006

Bailey, A., Phillips, W., and Rutter, M. (1996). Autism: towards an integration of clinical, genetic, neuropsychological, and neurobiological perspectives. *J. Child Psychol. Psychiatry* 37, 89–126. doi: 10.1111/j.1469-7610.1996.tb01381.x

Bakare, M. O., Munir, K. M., and Kinney, D. K. (2011). Association of hypomelanotic skin disorders with autism: links to possible etiologic role of vitamin-D levels in autism? *Hypothesis* 9:e2. doi: 10.5779/hypothesis.v9i1.200

Bamiou, D. E., Campbell, N. G., Musiek, F. E., Taylor, R., Chong, W. K., Moore, A., et al. (2007). Auditory and verbal working memory deficits in a child with congenital aniridia due to a PAX6 mutation. *Int. J. Audiol.* 46, 196–202. doi: 10.1080/14992020601175952

Bartolo, R., and Merchant, H. (2015). β oscillations are linked to the initiation of sensory-cued movement sequences and the internal guidance of regular tapping in the monkey. *J. Neurosci.* 35, 4635–4640. doi: 10.1523/JNEUROSCI.4570-14.2015

Belmonte, M. K., Saxena-Chandhok, T., Cherian, R., Muneer, R., George, L., and Karanth, P. (2013). Oral motor deficits in speech-impaired children with autism. *Front. Integr. Neurosci.* 7:47. doi: 10.3389/fnint.2013.00047

Benayed, R., Gharani, N., Rossman, I., Mancuso, V., Lazar, G., Kamdar, S., et al. (2005). Support for the homeobox transcription factor gene ENGRAILED 2 as an autism spectrum disorder susceptibility locus. *Am. J. Hum. Genet.* 77, 851–868. doi: 10.1086/497705

Benítez-Burraco, A. (2016a). "A biolinguistic approach to language disorders: towards a paradigm shift in clinical linguistics," in *Advances in Biolinguistics: The Human Language Faculty and Its Biological Basis*, eds C. A. Boeckx and K. Fujita (London: Routledge), 256–272.

Benítez-Burraco, A. (2016b). "A biolinguistic approach to sign languages," *in The Oxford Handbook of Deaf Studies: Language and Language Development*, eds M. Marschark and P. E. Spencer (Oxford: Oxford University Press), 247–263.

Benítez-Burraco, A., and Boeckx, C. (2015). Possible functional links among brain- and skull-related genes selected in modern humans. *Front. Psychol.* 6:794. doi: 10.3389/fpsyg.2015.00794

Benítez-Burraco, A., and Murphy, E. (2016). The oscillopathic nature of language deficits in autism: from genes to language evolution. *Front. Hum. Neurosci.* 10:120. doi: 10.3389/fnhum.2016.00120

Benítez-Burraco, A., Theofanopoulou, C., and Boeckx, C. (in press). Globularization and domestication. *Topoi.* doi: 10.1007/s11245-016-9399-7. Available online at: http://link.springer.com/article/10.1007/s11245-016-9399-7

Bhattacherjee, V., Horn, K. H., Singh, S., Webb, C. L., Pisano, M. M., and Greene, R. M. (2009). CBP/p300 and associated transcriptional co-activators exhibit distinct expression patterns during murine craniofacial and neural tube development. *Int. J. Dev. Biol.* 53, 1097–1104. doi: 10.1387/ijdb.072489vb

Bisaz, R., Boadas-Vaello, P., Genoux, D., and Sandi, C. (2013). Age-related cognitive impairments in mice with a conditional ablation of the neural cell adhesion molecule. *Learn. Mem.* 20, 183–193. doi: 10.1101/lm.030064.112

Bitsika, V., Sharpley, C. F., Andronicos, N. M., and Agnew, L. L. (2015). Hypothalamus-pituitary-adrenal axis daily fluctuation, anxiety and age interact to predict cortisol concentrations in boys with an autism spectrum disorder. *Physiol. Behav.* 138, 200–207. doi: 10.1016/j.physbeh.2014.11.010

Boeckx, C. (2011). "The emergence of the language faculty, from a biolinguistic point of view," in *Oxford Handbook of Language Evolution*, eds M. Tallerman and K. Gibson (Oxford: Oxford University Press), 492–501.

Boeckx, C., and Benítez-Burraco, A. (2014a). The shape of the human language-ready brain. *Front. Psychol.* 5:282. doi: 10.3389/fpsyg.2014.00282

Boeckx, C., and Benítez-Burraco, A. (2014b). Globularity and language-readiness: generating new predictions by expanding the set of genes of interest. *Front. Psychol.* 5:1324. doi: 10.3389/fpsyg.2014.01324

Bourgeron, T. (2007). The possible interplay of synaptic and clock genes in autism spectrum disorders. *Cold Spring Harb. Symp. Quant. Biol.* 72, 645–654. doi: 10.1101/sqb.2007.72.020

Bourguignon, N., Nadig, A., and Valois, D. (2012). The biolinguistics of autism: emergent perspectives. *Biolinguistics* 6, 124–165.

Brennaman, L. H., Kochlamazashvili, G., Stoenica, L., Nonneman, R. J., Moy, S. S., Schachner, M., et al. (2011). Transgenic mice overexpressing the extracellular domain of NCAM are impaired in working memory and cortical plasticity. *Neurobiol. Dis.* 43, 372–378. doi: 10.1016/j.nbd.2011.04.008

Brincat, S. L., and Miller, E. K. (2015). Frequency-specific hippocampal-prefrontal interactions during associative learning. *Nat. Neurosci.* 18, 576–581. doi: 10.1038/nn.3954

Brugmann, S. A., Allen, N. C., James, A. W., Mekonnen, Z., Madan, E., and Helms, J. A. (2010). A primary cilia-dependent etiology for midline facial disorders. *Hum. Mol. Genet.* 19, 1577–1592. doi: 10.1093/hmg/ddq030

Burke, L. M., Kalpakjian, C. Z., Smith, Y. R., and Quint, E. H. (2009). Gynecologic issues of adolescents with Down syndrome, autism, and cerebral palsy. *J. Pediatr. Adolesc. Gynecol.* 23, 11–15. doi: 10.1016/j.jpag.2009.04.005

Buzsáki, G., Logothetis, N., and Singer, W. (2013). Scaling brain size, keeping timing: evolutionary preservation of brain rhythms. *Neuron* 80, 751–764. doi: 10.1016/j.neuron.2013.10.002

Buzsáki, G., and Watson, B. O. (2012). Brain rhythms and neural syntax: implications for efficient coding of cognitive content and neuropsychiatric disease. *Dialogues Clin. Neurosci.* 14, 345–367.

Caballero, I. M., Manuel, M. N., Molinek, M., Quintana-Urzainqui, I., Mi, D., Shimogori, T., et al. (2014). Cell-autonomous repression of Shh by transcription factor Pax6 regulates diencephalic patterning by controlling the central diencephalic organizer. *Cell Rep.* 8, 1405–1418. doi: 10.1016/j.celrep.2014.07.051

Cáceres, M., Lachuer, J., Zapala, M. A., Redmond, J. C., Kudo, L., Geschwind, D. H., et al. (2003). Elevated gene expression levels distinguish human from non-human primate brains. *Proc. Natl. Acad. Sci. U.S.A.* 100, 13030–13035. doi: 10.1073/pnas.2135499100

Campbell, D. B., Sutcliffe, J. S., Ebert, P. J., Militerni, R., Bravaccio, C., Trillo, S., et al. (2006). A genetic variant that disrupts MET transcription is associated with autism. *Proc. Natl. Acad. Sci. U.S.A.* 103, 16834–16839. doi: 10.1073/pnas.0605296103

Campbell, D. J., Chang, J., and Chawarska, K. (2014). Early generalized overgrowth in autism spectrum disorder: prevalence rates, gender effects, and clinical outcomes. *J. Am. Acad. Child Adolesc. Psychiatry* 53, 1063–1073. doi: 10.1016/j.jaac.2014.07.008

Campbell, K., Flavin, N., Ivens, A., Robert, B., Buckingham, M., and Williamson, R. (1989). The human homeobox gene HOX7 maps to 4p16.1 and is deleted in Wolf-Hirschhorn syndrome patients. *Am. J. Hum. Genet.* 45, A179.

Cao, F., Yin, A., Wen, G., Sheikh, A. M., Tauqeer, Z., Malik, M., et al. (2012). Alteration of astrocytes and Wnt/β-catenin signaling in the frontal cortex of autistic subjects. *J. Neuroinflammation* 9:223. doi: 10.1186/1742-2094-9-223

Carruthers, P. (2006). *The Architecture of Mind.* Oxford: Oxford University Press.

Castermans, D., Wilquet, V., Parthoens, E., Huysmans, C., Steyaert, J., Swinnen, L., et al. (2003). The neurobeachin gene is disrupted by a translocation in a patient with idiopathic autism. *J. Med. Genet.* 40, 352–356. doi: 10.1136/jmg.40.5.352

Chawarska, K., Campbell, D., Chen, L., Shic, F., Klin, A., and Chang, J. (2011). Early generalized overgrowth in boys with autism. *Arch. Gen. Psychiatry* 68, 1021–1031. doi: 10.1001/archgenpsychiatry.2011.106

Cheng, H., Jiang, W., Phillips, F. M., Haydon, R. C., Peng, Y., Zhou, L., et al. (2003). Osteogenic activity of the fourteen types of human bone morphogenetic proteins (BMPs). *J. Bone Joint Surg. Am.* 85A, 1544–1552.

Cheung, J., Petek, E., Nakabayashi, K., Tsui, L. C., Vincent, J. B., and Scherer, S. W. (2001). Identification of the human cortactin-binding protein-2 gene from the autism candidate region at 7q31. *Genomics* 78, 7–11. doi: 10.1006/geno.2001.6651

Chiba, S., Lee, Y. M., Zhou, W., and Freed, C. R. (2008). Noggin enhances dopamine neuron production from human embryonic stem cells and improves behavioral outcome after transplantation into Parkinsonian rats. *Stem Cells* 26, 2810–2820. doi: 10.1634/stemcells.2008-0085

Cho, K. K., Hoch, R., Lee, A. T., Patel, T., Rubenstein, J. L., and Sohal, V. S. (2015). Gamma rhythms link prefrontal interneuron dysfunction with cognitive inflexibility in Dlx5/6(+/−) mice. *Neuron* 85, 1332–1343. doi: 10.1016/j.neuron.2015.02.019

Cobos, I., Long, J. E., Thwin, M. T., and Rubenstein, J. L. (2006). Cellular patterns of transcription factor expression in developing cortical interneurons. *Cereb. Cortex* 16, i82–i88. doi: 10.1093/cercor/bhk003

Comings, D. E., Wu, S., Chiu, C., Muhleman, D., and Sverd, J. (1996). Studies of the c-Harvey-Ras gene in psychiatric disorders. *Psychiatry Res.* 63, 25–32. doi: 10.1016/0165-1781(96)02829-6

Correia, A. C., Costa, M., Moraes, F., Bom, J., Nóvoa, A., and Mallo, M. (2007). Bmp2 is required for migration but not for induction of neural crest cells in the mouse. *Dev. Dyn.* 236, 2493–2501. doi: 10.1002/dvdy.21256

Courchesne, E., Campbell, K., and Solso, S. (2011). Brain growth across the life span in autism: age-specific changes in anatomical pathology. *Brain Res.* 1380, 138–145. doi: 10.1016/j.brainres.2010.09.101

Courchesne, E., and Pierce, K. (2005). Why the frontal cortex in autism might be talking only to itself: local over-connectivity but long-distance disconnection. *Curr. Opin. Neurobiol.* 15, 225–230. doi: 10.1016/j.conb.2005.03.001

Dauger, S., Guimiot, F., Renolleau, S., Levacher, B., Boda, B., Mas, C., et al. (2001). MASH-1/RET pathway involvement in development of brain stem control of respiratory frequency in newborn mice. *Physiol. Genomics* 7, 149–157. doi: 10.1152/physiolgenomics.00056.2001

Deacon, T. W. (2009). "Relaxed selection and the role of epigenesis in the evolution of language," in *Oxford Handbook of Developmental Behavioral Neuroscience*, eds M. Blumberg, J. Freeman, and J. Robinson (New York, NY: Oxford University Press), 730–752.

Delbroek, H., Steyaert, J., and Legius, E. (2011). An 8.9 year old girl with autism and Gorlin syndrome. *Eur J. Paediatr. Neurol.* 15, 268–270. doi: 10.1016/j.ejpn.2010.12.001

Devanna, P., Middelbeek, J., and Vernes, S. C. (2014). FOXP2 drives neuronal differentiation by interacting with retinoic acid signaling pathways. *Front. Cell. Neurosci.* 8:305. doi: 10.3389/fncel.2014.00305

di Rocco, F., Baujat, G., Arnaud, E., Rénier, D., Laplanche, J. L., Daire, V. C., et al. (2014). Clinical spectrum and outcomes in families with coronal synostosis and TCF12 mutations. *Eur. J. Hum. Genet.* 22, 1413–1416. doi: 10.1038/ejhg.2014.57

Doi, M., Cho, S., Yujnovsky, I., Hirayama, J., Cermakian, N., Cato, A. C., et al. (2007). Light-inducible and clock-controlled expression of MAP kinase phosphatase 1 in mouse central pacemaker neurons. *J. Biol. Rhythms* 22, 127–139. doi: 10.1177/0748730406298332

Drerup, C. M., Wiora, H. M., Topczewski, J., and Morris, J. A. (2009). Disc1 regulates foxd3 and sox10 expression, affecting neural crest migration and differentiation. *Development* 136, 2623–2632. doi: 10.1242/dev.030577

Dutt, S., Kléber, M., Matasci, M., Sommer, L., and Zimmermann, D. R. (2006). Versican V0 and V1 guide migratory neural crest cells. *J. Biol. Chem.* 17, 12123–12131. doi: 10.1074/jbc.M510834200

Edery, P., Lyonnet, S., Mulligan, L. M., Pelet, A., Dow, E., Abel, L., et al. (1994). Mutations of the RET proto-oncogene in Hirschsprung's disease. *Nature* 367, 378–380. doi: 10.1038/367378a0

Eigsti, I. M., Bennetto, L., and Dadlani, M. (2007). Beyond pragmatics: morphosyntactic development in autism. *J. Autism Dev. Disord.* 37, 1007–1023. doi: 10.1007/s10803-006-0239-2

El-Baz, F., Hamza, R. T., Ayad, M. S., and Mahmoud, N. H. (2014). Hyperandrogenemia in male autistic children and adolescents: relation to disease severity. *Int. J. Adolesc. Med. Health* 26, 79–84. doi: 10.1515/ijamh-2012-0116

Esghaei, M., Daliri, M. R., and Treue, S. (2015). Attention decreases phase-amplitude coupling, enhancing stimulus discriminability in cortical area MT. *Front. Neural Circuits* 9:82. doi: 10.3389/fncir.2015.00082

Etchamendy, N., Enderlin, V., Marighetto, A., Pallet, V., Higueret, P., and Jaffard, R. (2003). Vitamin A deficiency and relational memory deficit in adult mice: relationships with changes in brain retinoid signalling. *Behav. Brain Res.* 145, 37–49. doi: 10.1016/S0166-4328(03)00099-8

Eyles, D. W. (2010). Vitamin D and autism: does skin colour modify risk? *Acta Paediatr.* 99, 645–647. doi: 10.1111/j.1651-2227.2010.01797.x

Farmer, C., Butter, E., Mazurek, M. O., Cowan, C., Lainhart, J., Cook, E. H., et al. (2015). Aggression in children with autism spectrum disorders and a clinic-referred comparison group. *Autism* 19, 281–291. doi: 10.1177/1362361313518995

Fedorenko, E., and Thompson-Schill, S. L. (2014). Re-working the language network. *Trends Cogn. Sci.* 18, 120–126. doi: 10.1016/j.tics.2013.12.006

Fernell, E., Olsson, V. A., Karlgren-Leitner, C., Norlin, B., Hagberg, B., and Gillberg, C. (1999). Autistic disorders in children with CHARGE association. *Dev. Med. Child Neurol.* 41, 270–272. doi: 10.1017/S0012162299000572

Filová, B., Ostatníková, D., Celec, P., and Hodosy, J. (2013). The effect of testosterone on the formation of brain structures. *Cells Tissues Organs* 197, 169–177. doi: 10.1159/000345567

Fisher, S. E., Francks, C., Marlow, A. J., MacPhie, I. L., Newbury, D. F., Cardon, L. R., et al. (2002). Independent genome-wide scans identify a chromosome 18 quantitative-trait locus influencing dyslexia. *Nat. Genet.* 30, 86–91. doi: 10.1038/ng792

Fletcher, P. T., Whitaker, R. T., Tao, R., DuBray, M. B., Froehlich, A., Ravichandran, C., et al. (2010). Microstructural connectivity of the arcuate fasciculus in adolescents with high-functioning autism. *Neuroimage* 51, 1117–1125. doi: 10.1016/j.neuroimage.2010.01.083

Franchini, L. F., and Pollard, K. S. (2015). Genomic approaches to studying human-specific developmental traits. *Development* 142, 3100–3112. doi: 10.1242/dev.120048

Fuchs, S., Herzog, D., Sumara, G., Büchmann-Møller, S., Civenni, G., Wu, X., et al. (2009). Stage-specific control of neural crest stem cell proliferation by the small rho GTPases Cdc42 and Rac1. *Cell Stem Cell* 4, 236–247. doi: 10.1016/j.stem.2009.01.017

Fukumoto, A., Hashimoto, T., Ito, H., Nishimura, M., Tsuda, Y., Miyazaki, M., et al. (2008). Growth of head circumference in autistic infants during the first year of life. *J. Autism Dev. Disord.* 38, 411–418. doi: 10.1007/s10803-007-0405-1

Gajavelli, S., Wood, P. M., Pennica, D., Whittemore, S. R., and Tsoulfas, P. (2004). BMP signaling initiates a neural crest differentiation program in embryonic rat CNS stem cells. *Exp. Neurol.* 188, 205–223. doi: 10.1016/j.expneurol.2004.03.026

Gao, Y., Meng, D., Sun, N., Zhu, Z., Zhao, R., Lu, C., et al. (2014). Clock upregulates intercellular adhesion molecule-1 expression and promotes mononuclear cells adhesion to endothelial cells. *Biochem. Biophys. Res. Commun.* 443, 586–591. doi: 10.1016/j.bbrc.2013.12.022

Geschwind, G. H., and State, M. W. (2015). Gene hunting in autism spectrum disorder: on the path to precision medicine. *Lancet Neurol.* 14, 1109–1120. doi: 10.1016/S1474-4422(15)00044-7

Ghahramani Seno, M. M., Hu, P., Gwadry, F. G., Pinto, D., Marshall, C. R., Casallo, G., et al. (2011). Gene and miRNA expression profiles in autism spectrum disorders. *Brain Res.* 1380, 85–97. doi: 10.1016/j.brainres.2010.09.046

Ghanem, N., Yu, M., Poitras, L., Rubenstein, J. L., and Ekker, M. (2008). Characterization of a distinct subpopulation of striatal projection neurons expressing the Dlx genes in the basal ganglia through the activity of the I56ii enhancer. *Dev. Biol.* 322, 415–424. doi: 10.1016/j.ydbio.2008.07.029

Ginsberg, M. R., Rubin, R. A., Falcone, T., Ting, A. H., and Natowicz, M. R. (2012). Brain transcriptional and epigenetic associations with autism. *PLoS ONE* 7:e44736. doi: 10.1371/journal.pone.0044736

Gitton, Y., Benouaiche, L., Vincent, C., Heude, E., Soulika, M., Bouhali, K., et al. (2011). Dlx5 and Dlx6 expression in the anterior neural fold is essential for patterning the dorsal nasal capsule. *Development* 138, 897–903. doi: 10.1242/dev.057505

Glatt, S. J., Cohen, O. S., Faraone, S. V., and Tsuang, M. T. (2011). Dysfunctional gene splicing as a potential contributor to neuropsychiatric disorders. *Am. J. Med. Genet. B Neuropsychiatr. Genet.* 156, 382–392. doi: 10.1002/ajmg.b.31181

Glejzer, A., Laudet, E., Leprince, P., Hennuy, B., Poulet, C., Shakhova, O., et al. (2011). Wnt1 and BMP2: two factors recruiting multipotent neural crest progenitors isolated from adult bone marrow. *Cell. Mol. Life Sci.* 68, 2101–2114. doi: 10.1007/s00018-010-0558-5

Gokhman, D., Lavi, E., Prüfer, K., Fraga, M. F., Riancho, J. A., Kelso, J., et al. (2014). Reconstructing the DNA methylation maps of the Neandertal and the Denisovan. *Science* 344, 523–527. doi: 10.1126/science.1250368

Gómez-Lado, C., Eirís-Puñal, J., Blanco-Barca, O., del Río-Latorre, E., Fernández-Redondo, V., and Castro-Gago, M. (2004). Hypomelanosis of Ito. a possibly under-diagnosed heterogeneous neurocutaneous syndrome. *Rev. Neurol.* 38, 223–228.

Gordon, C. T., Tan, T. Y., Benko, S., Fitzpatrick, D., Lyonnet, S., and Farlie, P. G. (2009). Long-range regulation at the SOX9 locus in development and disease. *J. Med. Genet.* 46, 649–656. doi: 10.1136/jmg.2009.068361

Hahamy, A., Behrmann, M., and Malach, R. (2015). The idiosyncratic brain: distortion of spontaneous connectivity patterns in autism spectrum disorder. *Nat. Rev. Neurosci.* 18, 302–309. doi: 10.1038/nn.3919

Hale, C. L., Niederriter, A. N., Green, G. E., and Martin, D. M. (2016). Atypical phenotypes associated with pathogenic CHD7 variants and a proposal for broadening CHARGE syndrome clinical diagnostic criteria. *Am. J. Med. Genet. A.* 170, 344–354. doi: 10.1002/ajmg.a.37435

Hall, M. H., Taylor, G., Sham, P., Schulze, K., Rijsdijk, F., Picchioni, M., et al. (2011). The early auditory gamma-band response is heritable and a putative endophenotype of schizophrenia. *Schizophr. Bull.* 37, 778–787. doi: 10.1093/schbul/sbp134

Hamilton, A., Marshal, M. P., and Murray, P. J. (2011). Autism spectrum disorders and menstruation. *J. Adolesc. Health* 49, 443–445. doi: 10.1016/j.jadohealth.2011.01.015

Hamza, R. T., Hewedi, D. H., and Ismail, M. A. (2010). Basal and adrenocorticotropic hormone stimulated plasma cortisol levels among Egyptian autistic children: relation to disease severity. *Ital. J. Pediatr.* 36, 71. doi: 10.1186/1824-7288-36-71

Hansen, S. M., Berezin, V., and Bock, E. (2008). Signaling mechanisms of neurite outgrowth induced by the cell adhesion molecules NCAM and N-cadherin. *Cell Mol. Life Sci.* 65, 3809–3821. doi: 10.1007/s00018-008-8290-0

Hare, B., and Tomasello, M. (2005). Human-like social skills in dogs? *Trends Cogn. Sci.* 9, 439–444. doi: 10.1016/j.tics.2005.07.003

Hari, L., Miescher, I., Shakhova, O., Suter, U., Chin, L., Taketo, M., et al. (2012). Temporal control of neural crest lineage generation by Wnt/β-catenin signaling. *Development* 139, 2107–2117. doi: 10.1242/dev.073064

Hattori, T., Shimizu, S., Koyama, Y., Emoto, H., Matsumoto, Y., Kumamoto, N., et al. (2014). DISC1 (disrupted-in-schizophrenia-1) regulates differentiation of oligodendrocytes. *PLoS ONE* 9:e88506. doi: 10.1371/journal.pone.0088506

Hauser, M. (2009). The possibility of impossible cultures. *Nature* 460, 190–196. doi: 10.1038/460190a

Hauth, I., de Bruijn, Y. G., Staal, W., Buitelaar, J. K., and Rommelse, N. N. (2014). Testing the extreme male brain theory of autism spectrum disorder in a familial design. *Autism Res.* 7, 491–500. doi: 10.1002/aur.1384

Heffner, H. E., and Heffner, R. S. (1986). Effect of unilateral and bilateral auditory cortex lesions on the discrimination of vocalizations by Japanese macaques. *J. Neurophysiol.* 56, 683–701.

Hergüner, A., and Hergüner, S. (2016). Association between age at menarche and autistic traits in Turkish university students. *Am. J. Hum. Biol.* 28, 44–47. doi: 10.1002/ajhb.22739

Hill, A. P., Zuckerman, K. E., Hagen, A. D., Kriz, D. J., Duvall, S. W., van Santen, J., et al. (2014). Aggressive behavior problems in children with autism spectrum disorders: prevalence and correlates in a large clinical sample. *Res. Autism Spectr. Disord.* 8, 1121–1133. doi: 10.1016/j.rasd.2014.05.006

Hill, D. S., Cabrera, R., Wallis Schultz, D., Zhu, H., Lu, W., Finnell, R. H., et al. (2015). Autism-like behavior and epigenetic changes associated with autism as consequences of *in utero* exposure to environmental pollutants in a mouse model. *Behav. Neurol.* 2015:426263. doi: 10.1155/2015/426263

Hollier, L. P., Mattes, E., Maybery, M. T., Keelan, J. A., Hickey, M., and Whitehouse, A. J. (2013). The association between perinatal testosterone concentration and early vocabulary development: a prospective cohort study. *Biol. Psychol.* 92, 212–215. doi: 10.1016/j.biopsycho.2012.10.016

Hollocks, M. J., Howlin, P., Papadopoulos, A. S., Khondoker, M., and Simonoff, E. (2014). Differences in HPA-axis and heart rate responsiveness to psychosocial stress in children with autism spectrum disorders with and without co-morbid anxiety. *Psychoneuroendocrinology* 46, 32–45. doi: 10.1016/j.psyneuen.2014.04.004

Holt, R., Sykes, N. H., Conceição, I. C., Cazier, J. B., Anney, R. J., Oliveira, G., et al. (2012). CNVs leading to fusion transcripts in individuals with autism spectrum disorder. *Eur. J. Hum. Genet.* 20, 1141–1147. doi: 10.1038/ejhg.2012.73

Hu, V. W., Sarachana, T., Sherrard, R. M., and Kocher, K. M. (2015). Investigation of sex differences in the expression of RORA and its transcriptional targets in the brain as a potential contributor to the sex bias in autism. *Mol. Autism* 6:7. doi: 10.1186/2040-2392-6-7

Huang, Y. T., Iwamoto, K., Kurosaki, T., Nasu, M., and Ueda, S. (2005). The neuronal POU transcription factor Brn-2 interacts with Jab1, a gene involved in the onset of neurodegenerative diseases. *Neurosci. Lett.* 382, 175–178. doi: 10.1016/j.neulet.2005.03.008

Ingudomnukul, E., Baron-Cohen, S., Wheelwright, S., and Knickmeyer, R. (2007). Elevated rates of testosterone-related disorders in women with autism spectrum conditions. *Horm. Behav.* 51, 597–604. doi: 10.1016/j.yhbeh.2007.02.001

Ishii, M., Arias, A. C., Liu, L., Chen, Y. B., Bronner, M. E., and Maxson, R. E. (2012). A stable cranial neural crest cell line from mouse. *Stem Cells Dev.* 21, 3069–3080. doi: 10.1089/scd.2012.0155

Jacobson, L. (2014). Hypothalamic-pituitary-adrenocortical axis: neuropsychiatric aspects. *Compr. Physiol.* 4, 715–738. doi: 10.1002/cphy.c130036

Jeste, S. S., and Geschwind, D. H. (2014). Disentangling the heterogeneity of autism spectrum disorder through genetic findings. *Nat. Rev. Neurol.* 10, 74–81. doi: 10.1038/nrneurol.2013.278

Jia, F., Wang, B., Shan, L., Xu, Z., Staal, W. G., and Du, L. (2015). Core symptoms of autism improved after vitamin D supplementation. *Pediatrics* 135, e196–e198. doi: 10.1542/peds.2014-2121

Jia, L., Cheng, L., and Raper, J. (2005). Slit/Robo signaling is necessary to confine early neural crest cells to the ventral migratory pathway in the trunk. *Dev. Biol.* 282, 411–421. doi: 10.1016/j.ydbio.2005.03.021

Jiang, W., Yu, Q., Gong, M., Chen, L., Wen, E. Y., Bi, Y., et al. (2012). Vitamin A deficiency impairs postnatal cognitive function via inhibition of neuronal calcium excitability in hippocampus. *J. Neurochem.* 121, 932–943. doi: 10.1111/j.1471-4159.2012.07697.x

Jiang, Y. H., Yuen, R. K., Jin, X., Wang, M., Chen, N., Wu, X., et al. (2013). Detection of clinically relevant genetic variants in autism spectrum disorder by whole-genome sequencing. *Am. J. Hum. Genet.* 93, 249–263. doi: 10.1016/j.ajhg.2013.06.012

Jones, D. L., Howard, M. A., Stanco, A., Rubenstein, J. L., and Baraban, S. C. (2011). Deletion of Dlx1 results in reduced glutamatergic input to hippocampal interneurons. *J. Neurophysiol.* 105, 1984–1991. doi: 10.1152/jn.00056.2011

Jones, E. G., and Rubenstein, J. L. R. (2004). Expression of regulatory genes during differentiation of thalamic nuclei in mouse and monkey. *J. Comp. Neurol.* 477, 55–80. doi: 10.1002/cne.20234

Justice, C. M., Yagnik, G., Kim, Y., Peter, I., Jabs, E. W., Erazo, M., et al. (2012). A genome-wide association study identifies susceptibility loci for nonsyndromic sagittal craniosynostosis near BMP2 and within BBS9. *Nat. Genet.* 44, 1360–1364. doi: 10.1038/ng.2463

Kanduri, C., Kantojärvi, K., Salo, P. M., Vanhala, R., Buck, G., Blancher, C., et al. (2016). The landscape of copy number variations in Finnish families with autism spectrum disorders. *Autism Res.* 9, 9–16. doi: 10.1002/aur.1502

Kasamatsu, S., Hachiya, A., Higuchi, K., Ohuchi, A., Kitahara, T., and Boissy, R. E. (2008). Production of the soluble form of KIT, s-KIT, abolishes stem cell factor-induced melanogenesis in human melanocytes. *J. Invest. Dermatol.* 128, 1763–1772. doi: 10.1038/jid.2008.9

Katafuchi, T., Li, A. J., Hirota, S., Kitamura, Y., and Hori, T. (2000). Impairment of spatial learning and hippocampal synaptic potentiation in c-kit mutant rats. *Learn. Mem.* 7, 383–392. doi: 10.1101/lm.33900

Kaufmann, W. E., Cortell, R., Kau, A. S., Bukelis, I., Tierney, E., Gray, R. M., et al. (2004). Autism spectrum disorder in fragile X syndrome: communication, social interaction, and specific behaviors. *Am. J. Med. Genet. A.* 129, 225–234. doi: 10.1002/ajmg.a.30229

Khadka, D., Luo, T., and Sargent, T. D. (2006). Msx1 and Msx2 have shared essential functions in neural crest but may be dispensable in epidermis and axis formation in Xenopus. *Int. J. Dev. Biol.* 50, 499–502. doi: 10.1387/ijdb.052115dk

Kilsby, A. J., Cruwys, M., Kukendrajah, C., Russell-Eggitt, I., Raglan, E., Rajput, K., et al. (2013). Homozygosity for piebaldism with a proven KIT mutation resulting in depigmentation of the skin and hair, deafness, developmental delay and autism spectrum disorder. *Clin. Dysmorphol.* 22, 64–67. doi: 10.1097/MCD.0b013e32835e8ce5

Kim, K. C., Lee, D. K., Go, H. S., Kim, P., Choi, C. S., Kim, J. W., et al. (2014). Pax6-dependent cortical glutamatergic neuronal differentiation regulates autism-like behavior in prenatally valproic acid-exposed rat offspring. *Mol. Neurobiol.* 49, 512–528. doi: 10.1007/s12035-013-8535-2

Kokovay, E., Wang, Y., Kusek, G., Wurster, R., Lederman, P., Lowry, N., et al. (2012). VCAM1 is essential to maintain the structure of the SVZ niche and acts as an environmental sensor to regulate SVZ lineage progression. *Cell Stem Cell.* 11, 220–230. doi: 10.1016/j.stem.2012.06.016

Konopka, G., Bomar, J. M., Winden, K., Coppola, G., Jonsson, Z. O., Gao, F., et al. (2009). Human-specific transcriptional regulation of CNS development genes by FOXP2. *Nature* 462, 213–217. doi: 10.1038/nature08549

Kopell, N. J., Gritton, H. J., Whittington, M. A., and Kramer, M. A. (2014). Beyond the connectome: the dynome. *Neuron* 83, 1319–1328. doi: 10.1016/j.neuron.2014.08.016

Kraus, P., and Lufkin, T. (2006). Dlx homeobox gene control of mammalian limb and craniofacial development. *Am. J. Med. Genet. A.* 140, 1366–1374. doi: 10.1002/ajmg.a.31252

Kruszka, P., Li, D., Harr, M. H., Wilson, N. R., Swarr, D., McCormick, E. M., et al. (2015). Mutations in SPECC1L, encoding sperm antigen with calponin homology and coiled-coil domains 1-like, are found in some cases of autosomal dominant Opitz G/BBB syndrome. *J. Med. Genet.* 52, 104–110. doi: 10.1136/jmedgenet-2014-102677

Kuhlwilm, M., Davierwala, A., and Pääbo, S. (2013). Identification of putative target genes of the transcription factor RUNX2. *PLoS ONE* 8:e83218. doi: 10.1371/journal.pone.0083218

Kumari, D., and Usdin, K. (2001). Interaction of the transcription factors USF1, USF2, and alpha -Pal/Nrf-1 with the FMR1 promoter. Implications for Fragile X mental retardation syndrome. *J. Biol. Chem.* 276, 4357–4364.

Lalani, S. R., Safiullah, A. M., Fernbach, S. D., Harutyunyan, K. G., Thaller, C., Peterson, L., et al. (2006). Spectrum of CHD7 mutations in 110 individuals with CHARGE syndrome and genotype-phenotype correlation. *Am. J. Hum. Genet.* 78, 303–314. doi: 10.1086/500273

Lattanzi, W. (forthcoming). "Molecular genetics of craniosynostosis," in *eLS* (Chichester: John Wiley & Sons Ltd.). Available online at: http://www.els.net

Lattanzi, W., Barba, M., Novegno, F., Massimi, L., Tesori, V., Tamburrini, G., et al (2013). Lim mineralization protein is involved in the premature calvarial ossification in sporadic craniosynostoses. *Bone* 52, 474–484. doi: 10.1016/j.bone.2012.09.004

Lattanzi, W., Bukvic, N., Barba, M., Tamburrini, G., Bernardini, C., Michetti, F., et al. (2012). Genetic basis of single-suture synostoses: genes, chromosomes and clinical implications. *Childs Nerv. Syst.* 28, 1301–1310. doi: 10.1007/s00381-012-1781-1

Le, Q. V., Isbell, L. A., Matsumoto, J., Le, V. A., Nishimaru, H., Hori, E., et al (2016). Snakes elicit earlier, and monkey faces, later, gamma oscillations in macaque pulvinar neurons. *Sci. Rep.* 6:20595. doi: 10.1038/srep20595

Lee, Y. H., and Saint-Jeannet, J. P. (2011). Sox9 function in craniofacial development and disease. *Genesis* 49, 200–208. doi: 10.1002/dvg.20717

Lewis, J. D., Theilmann, R. J., Fonov, V., Bellec, P., Lincoln, A., Evans, A. C., et al. (2013). Callosal fiber length and interhemispheric connectivity in adults with autism: brain overgrowth and underconnectivity. *Hum. Brain Mapp.* 34, 1685–1695. doi: 10.1002/hbm.22018

Li, C., Ito, H., Fujita, K., Shiwaku, H., Qi, Y., Tagawa, K., et al. (2013). Sox2 transcriptionally regulates PQBP1, an intellectual disability-microcephaly causative gene, in neural stem progenitor cells. *PLoS ONE* 8:e68627. doi: 10.1371/journal.pone.0068627

Li, J., Feng, J., Liu, Y., Ho, T. V., Grimes, W., Ho, H. A., et al. (2015b). BMP-SHH signaling network controls epithelial stem cell fate via regulation of its niche in the developing tooth. *Dev. Cell.* 33, 125–135. doi: 10.1016/j.devcel.2015.02.021

Li, S., Quarto, N., Senarath-Yapa, K., Grey, N., Bai, X., and Longaker, M. T. (2015a). Enhanced activation of canonical Wnt signaling confers mesoderm-derived parietal bone with similar osteogenic and skeletal healing capacity to neural crest-derived frontal bone. *PLoS ONE* 10:e0138059. doi: 10.1371/journal.pone.0138059

Lin, M., Pedrosa, E., Shah, A., Hrabovsky, A., Maqbool, S., Zheng, D., et al. (2011). RNA-Seq of human neurons derived from iPS cells reveals candidate long non-coding RNAs involved in neurogenesis and neuropsychiatric disorders. *PLoS ONE* 6:e23356. doi: 10.1371/journal.pone.0023356

Lindgren, K., Folstein, S., Tomblin, J. B., and Tager-Flusberg, H. (2009). Language and reading abilities of children with autism spectrum disorders and specific language impairment and their first-degree relatives. *Autism Res.* 2, 22–38. doi: 10.1002/aur.63

Linkenkaer-Hansen, K., Smit, D. J., Barkil, A., van Beijsterveldt, T. E., Brussaard, A. B., Boomsma, D. I., et al. (2007). Genetic contributions to long-range temporal correlations in ongoing oscillations. *J. Neurosci.* 27, 13882–13889. doi: 10.1523/JNEUROSCI.3083-07.2007

Liu, H., Ding, T., Zhan, Y., and Feng, H. (2015). A novel AXIN2 missense mutation is associated with non-syndromic oligodontia. *PLoS ONE* 10:e0138221. doi: 10.1371/journal.pone.0138221

Liu, X., Somel, M., Tang, L., Yan, Z., Jiang, X., Guo, S., et al. (2012). Extension of cortical synaptic development distinguishes humans from chimpanzees and macaques. *Genome Res.* 22, 611–622. doi: 10.1101/gr.127324.111

Liu, Y., Jin, Y., Li, J., Seto, E., Kuo, E., Yu, W., et al. (2013). Inactivation of Cdc42 in neural crest cells causes craniofacial and cardiovascular morphogenesis defects. *Dev. Biol.* 383, 239–252. doi: 10.1016/j.ydbio.2013.09.013

Lopes Floro, K., Artap, S. T., Preis, J. I., Fatkin, D., Chapman, G., et al. (2011). Loss of Cited2 causes congenital heart disease by perturbing left-right patterning of the body axis. *Hum. Mol. Genet.* 20, 1097–1110. doi: 10.1093/hmg/ddq554

López-Bendito, G., Flames, N., Ma, L., Fouquet, C., Di Meglio, T., Chedotal, A., et al. (2007). Robo1 and Robo2 cooperate to control the guidance of major axonal tracts in the mammalian forebrain. *J. Neurosci.* 27, 3395–3407. doi: 10.1523/JNEUROSCI.4605-06.2007

Luo, T., Wagner, E., and Dräger, U. C. (2009). Integrating retinoic acid signaling with brain function. *Dev. Psychol.* 45, 139–150. doi: 10.1037/0012-1649.45.1.139

Luo, X., Ding, L., Xu, J., and Chegini, N. (2005). Gene expression profiling of leiomyoma and myometrial smooth muscle cells in response to transforming growth factor-beta. *Endocrinology* 146, 1097–1118. doi: 10.1210/en.2004-1377

Luppanapornlarp, S., Leelataweewud, P., Putongkam, P., and Ketanont, S. (2010). Periodontal status and orthodontic treatment need of autistic children. *World J. Orthod.* 11, 256–261.

Lupyan, G., and Dale, R. (2010). Language structure is partly determined by social structure. *PLoS ONE* 5:e8559. doi: 10.1371/journal.pone.0008559

Maekawa, M., Iwayama, Y., Nakamura, K., Sato, M., Toyota, T., Ohnishi, T., et al. (2009). A novel missense mutation (Leu46Val) of PAX6 found in an autistic patient. *Neurosci. Lett.* 462, 267–271. doi: 10.1016/j.neulet.2009.07.021

Malenfant, P., Liu, X., Hudson, M. L., Qiao, Y., Hrynchak, M., Riendeau, N., et al. (2012). Association of GTF2i in the Williams-Beuren syndrome critical region with autism spectrum disorders. *J. Autism Dev. Disord.* 42, 1459–1469. doi: 10.1007/s10803-011-1389-4

Maliepaard, M., Mathijssen, I. M., Oosterlaan, J., and Okkerse, J. M. (2014). Intellectual, behavioral, and emotional functioning in children with syndromic craniosynostosis. *Pediatrics* 133, e1608–e1615. doi: 10.1542/peds.2013-3077

Mallo, M. (2001). Formation of the middle ear: recent progress on the developmental and molecular mechanisms. *Dev. Biol.* 231, 410–419. doi: 10.1006/dbio.2001.0154

Manouilenko, I., Eriksson, J. M., Humble, M. B., and Bejerot, S. (2014). Minor physical anomalies in adults with autism spectrum disorder and healthy controls. *Autism Res. Treat.* 2014:743482. doi: 10.1155/2014/743482

Mansour, S., Offiah, A. C., McDowall, S., Sim, P., Tolmie, J., and Hall, C. (2002). The phenotype of survivors of campomelic dysplasia. *J. Med. Genet.* 39, 597–602. doi: 10.1136/jmg.39.8.597

Marcos-Mondéjar, P., Peregrín, S., Li, J. Y., Carlsson, L., Tole, S., and López-Bendito, G. (2012). The lhx2 transcription factor controls thalamocortical axonal guidance by specific regulation of robo1 and robo2 receptors. *J. Neurosci.* 32, 4372–4385. doi: 10.1523/JNEUROSCI.5851-11.2012

Maricic, T., Günther, V., Georgiev, O., Gehre, S., Curlin, M., Schreiweis, C., et al. (2013). A recent evolutionary change affects a regulatory element in the human FOXP2 gene. *Mol. Biol. Evol.* 30, 844–852. doi: 10.1093/molbev/mss271

Martin, P. M., Yang, X., Robin, N., Lam, E., Rabinowitz, J. S., Erdman, C. A., et al (2013). A rare WNT1 missense variant overrepresented in ASD leads to increased Wnt signal pathway activation. *Transl. Psychiatry* 3:e301. doi: 10.1038/tp.2013.75

Maruyama, T., Jeong, J., Sheu, T. J., and Hsu, W. (2016). Stem cells of the suture mesenchyme in craniofacial bone development, repair and regeneration. *Nat. Commun.* 7:10526. doi: 10.1038/ncomms10526

Matsuo, T., Osumi-Yamashita, N., Noji, S., Ohuchi, H., Koyama, E., Myokai, F., et al. (1993). A mutation in the Pax-6 gene in rat small eye is associated with impaired migration of midbrain. *Nat. Genet.* 3, 299–304. doi: 10.1038/ng0493-299

McKinsey, G., Lindtner, S., Trzcinski, B., Visel, A., Pennacchio, L. A., Huylebroeck, D., et al. (2013). Dlx1and2-dependent expression of Zfhx1b (Sip1, Zeb2) regulates the fate switch between cortical and striatal interneurons. *Neuron* 77, 83–98. doi: 10.1016/j.neuron.2012.11.035

McLarren, K. W., Litsiou, A., and Streit, A. (2003). DLX5 positions the neural crest and preplacode region at the border of the neural plate. *Dev. Biol.* 259, 34–47. doi: 10.1016/S0012-1606(03)00177-5

Mercier, S., Dubourg, C., Garcelon, N., Campillo-Gimenez, B., Gicquel, I., Belleguic, M., et al. (2011). New findings for phenotype-genotype correlations in a large European series of holoprosencephaly cases. *J. Med. Genet.* 48, 752–760. doi: 10.1136/jmedgenet-2011-100339

Metzis, V., Courtney, A. D., Kerr, M. C., Ferguson, C., Rondón Galeano, M. C., Parton, R. G., et al. (2013). Patched1 is required in neural crest cells for the prevention of orofacial clefts. *Hum. Mol. Genet.* 22, 5026–5035. doi: 10.1093/hmg/ddt353

Meyer, M., Kircher, M., Gansauge, M. T., Li, H., Racimo, F., Mallick, S., et al. (2012). A high-coverage genome sequence from an archaic Denisovan individual. *Science* 338, 222–226. doi: 10.1126/science.1224344

Mikita, N., Hollocks, M. J., Papadopoulos, A. S., Aslani, A., Harrison, S., Leibenluft, E., et al. (2015). Irritability in boys with autism spectrum disorders: an investigation of physiological reactivity. *J. Child Psychol. Psychiatry* 56, 1118–1126. doi: 10.1111/jcpp.12382

Milet, C., Maczkowiak, F., Roche, D. D., and Monsoro-Burq, A. H. (2013). Pax3 and Zic1 drive induction and differentiation of multipotent, migratory, and functional neural crest in Xenopus embryos. *Proc. Natl. Acad. U.S.A.* 110, 5528–5533. doi: 10.1073/pnas.1219124110

Miller, J. A., Ding, S. L., Sunkin, S. M., Smith, K. A., Ng, L., Szafer, A., et al. (2014). Transcriptional landscape of the prenatal human brain. *Nature* 508, 199–206. doi: 10.1038/nature13185

Ming, J. E., Kaupas, M. E., Roessler, E., Brunner, H. G., Golabi, M., Tekin, M., et al. (2002). Mutations in PATCHED-1, the receptor for SONIC HEDGEHOG, are associated with holoprosencephaly. *Hum. Genet.* 110, 297–301. doi: 10.1007/s00439-002-0695-5

Mithen, S. (1996). *The Prehistory of the Mind.* London: Thames and Hudson.

Miyano, M., Horike, S., Cai, S., Oshimura, M., and Kohwi-Shigematsu, T. (2008). DLX5 expression is monoallelic and Dlx5 is up-regulated in the Mecp2-null frontal cortex. *J. Cell Mol. Med.* 12, 1188–1191. doi: 10.1111/j.1582-4934.2008.00377.x

Moreno-Ramos, O. A., Olivares, A. M., Haider, N. B., de Autismo, L. C., and Lattig, M. C. (2015). Whole-exome sequencing in a South American cohort links ALDH1A3, FOXN1 and retinoic acid regulation pathways to autism spectrum disorders. *PLoS ONE* 10:e0135927. doi: 10.1371/journal.pone.0135927

Morey-Canellas, J., Sivagamasundari, U., and Barton, H. (2003). A case of autism in a child with Apert's syndrome. *Eur. Child Adolesc. Psychiatry* 12, 100–102. doi: 10.1007/s00787-003-0289-3

Mosconi, M. W., Cody-Hazlett, H., Poe, M. D., Gerig, G., Gimpel-Smith, R., and Piven, J. (2009). Longitudinal study of amygdala volume and joint attention in 2- to 4-year-old children with autism. *Arch. Gen. Psychiatry* 66, 509–516. doi: 10.1001/archgenpsychiatry.2009.19

Murphy, C. M., Deeley, Q., Daly, E. M., Ecker, C., O'Brien, F. M., Hallahan, B., et al. (2012). Anatomy and aging of the amygdala and hippocampus in autism spectrum disorder: an *in vivo* magnetic resonance imaging study of Asperger syndrome. *Autism Res.* 5, 3–12. doi: 10.1002/aur.227

Murphy, E. (2015a). The brain dynamics of linguistic computation. *Front. Psychol.* 6:1515. doi: 10.3389/fpsyg.2015.01515

Murphy, E. (2015b). Labels, cognomes and cyclic computation: an ethological perspective. *Front. Psychol.* 6:715. doi: 10.3389/fpsyg.2015.00715

Murphy, E. (2016a). The human oscillome and its explanatory potential. *Biolinguistics* 10, 6–20.

Murphy, E. (2016b). Evolutionary monkey oscillomics: generating linking hypotheses from preserved brain rhythms. *Theor. Linguist.* 42, 117–137. doi: 10.1515/tl-2016-0005

Murphy, E., and Benítez-Burraco, A. (in press). Language deficits in schizophrenia and autism as related oscillatory connectomopathies: an evolutionary account. *Neurosci. Biobehav. Rev.* doi: 10.1101/044198

Nakashima, N., Yamagata, T., Mori, M., Kuwajima, M., Suwa, K., and Momoi, M. Y. (2010). Expression analysis and mutation detection of DLX5 and DLX6 in autism. *Brain Dev.* 32, 98–104. doi: 10.1016/j.braindev.2008.12.021

Naqvi, S., Cole, T., and Graham, J. M. Jr. (2000). Cole-Hughes macrocephaly syndrome and associated autistic manifestations. *Am. J. Med. Genet.* 94, 149–152.

Nelson, C. S., Fuller, C. K., Fordyce, P. M., Greninger, A. L., Li, H., and DeRisi, J. L. (2013). Microfluidic affinity and ChIP-seq analyses converge on a conserved FOXP2-binding motif in chimp and human, which enables the detection of evolutionarily novel targets. *Nucleic Acids Res.* 41, 5991–6004. doi: 10.1093/nar/gkt259

Nguyen, A., Rauch, T. A., Pfeifer, G. P., and Hu, V. W. (2010). Global methylation profiling of lymphoblastoid cell lines reveals epigenetic contributions to autism spectrum disorders and a novel autism candidate gene, *RORA*, whose protein product is reduced in autistic brain. *FASEB. J.* 24, 3036–3051. doi: 10.1096/fj.10-154484

Nordahl, C. W., Lange, N., Li, D. D., Barnett, L. A., Lee, A., Buonocore, M. H., et al. (2011). Brain enlargement is associated with regression in preschool-age boys with autism spectrum disorders. *Proc. Natl. Acad. Sci. U.S.A.* 108, 20195–20200. doi: 10.1073/pnas.1107560108

Obafemi-Ajayi, T., Miles, J. H., Takahashi, T. N., Qi, W., Aldridge, K., Zhang, M., et al. (2015). Facial structure analysis separates autism spectrum disorder into meaningful clinical subgroups. *J. Autism Dev. Disord.* 45, 1302–1317. do 10.1007/s10803-014-2290-8

Obaydi, H., and Puri, B. K. (2008). Prevalence of premenstrual syndrome in autism: a prospective observer-rated study. *J. Int. Med. Res.* 36, 268–272. doi: 10.1177/147323000803600208

Oosterveen, T., Kurdija, S., Alekseenko, Z., Uhde, C. W., Bergsland, M., Sandberg, M., et al. (2012). Mechanistic differences in the transcriptional interpretation of local and long-range Shh morphogen signaling. *Dev. Cell* 23, 1006–1019. doi: 10.1016/j.devcel.2012.09.015

Oosterveen, T., Kurdija, S., Ensterö, M., Uhde, C. W., Bergsland, M., Sandberg, M., et al. (2013). SoxB1-driven transcriptional network underlies neural-specific interpretation of morphogen signals. *Proc. Natl. Acad. Sci. U.S.A.* 110, 7330–7335. doi: 10.1073/pnas.1220010110

Ortiz-Mantilla, S., Choe, M. S., Flax, J., Grant, P. E., and Benasich, A. A. (2010). Associations between the size of the amygdala in infancy and language abilities during the preschool years in normally developing children. *Neuroimage* 49, 2791–2799. doi: 10.1016/j.neuroimage.2009.10.029

Pääbo, S. (2014). The human condition-a molecular approach. *Cell* 157, 216–226. doi: 10.1016/j.cell.2013.12.036

Paratore, C., Brugnoli, G., Lee, H. Y., Suter, U., and Sommer, L. (2002). The role of the Ets domain transcription factor Erm in modulating differentiation of neural crest stem cells. *Dev. Biol.* 250, 168–180. doi: 10.1006/dbio.2002.0795

Paumard-Hernández, B., Berges-Soria, J., Barroso, E., Rivera-Pedroza, C. I., Pérez-Carrizosa, V., Benito-Sanz, S., et al. (2015). Expanding the mutation spectrum in 182 Spanish probands with craniosynostosis: identification and characterization of novel TCF12 variants. *Eur. J. Hum. Genet.* 23, 907–914. doi: 10.1038/ejhg.2014.205

Peterson, K. A., Nishi, Y., Ma, W., Vedenko, A., Shokri, L., Zhang, X., et al. (2012). Neural-specific Sox2 input and differential Gli-binding affinity provide context and positional information in Shh-directed neural patterning. *Genes Dev.* 26, 2802–2816. doi: 10.1101/gad.207142.112

Piard, J., Rozé, V., Czorny, A., Lenoir, M., Valduga, M., Fenwick, A. L., et al. (2015). TCF12 microdeletion in a 72-year-old woman with intellectual disability. *Am. J. Med. Genet. A.* 167A, 1897–1901. doi: 10.1002/ajmg.a.37083

Pisano, S., Milone, A., Gemo, I., and Masi, G. (2014). High-functioning autism spectrum disorder associated with CHARGE syndrome: a case report. *Clin. Dysmorphol.* 23, 35–37. doi: 10.1097/MCD.0000000000000014

Plante, E., Boliek, C., Binkiewicz, A., and Erly, W. K. (1996). Elevated androgen, brain development and language/learning disabilities in children with congenital adrenal hyperplasia. *Dev. Med. Child Neurol.* 38, 423–437. doi: 10.1111/j.1469-8749.1996.tb15100.x

Platt, M. L., Seyfarth, R. M., and Cheney, D. L. (2016). Adaptations for social cognition in the primate brain. *Philos. Trans. R. Soc. Lond. B Biol. Sci.* 371:20150096. doi: 10.1098/rstb.2015.0096

Plouhinec, J. L., Roche, D. D., Pegoraro, C., Figueiredo, A. L., Maczkowiak, F., Brunet, L. J., et al. (2014). Pax3 and Zic1 trigger the early neural crest gene regulatory network by the direct activation of multiple key neural crest specifiers. *Dev. Biol.* 386, 461–472. doi: 10.1016/j.ydbio.2013.12.010

Poeppel, D. (2012). The maps problem and the mapping problem: two challenges for a cognitive neuroscience of speech and language. *Cogn. Neuropsychol.* 29, 34–55. doi: 10.1080/02643294.2012.710600

Poitras, L., Yu, M., Lesage-Pelletier, C., Macdonald, R. B., Gagné, J. P., Hatch, G., et al. (2010). An SNP in an ultraconserved regulatory element affects Dlx5/Dlx6 regulation in the forebrain. *Development* 137, 3089–3097. doi: 10.1242/dev.051052

Preis, J. I., Wise, N., Solloway, M. J., Harvey, R. P., Sparrow, D. B., and Dunwoodie, S. L. (2006). Generation of conditional Cited2 null alleles. *Genesis* 44, 579–583. doi: 10.1002/dvg.20251

Preissler, M. A. (2008). Associative learning of pictures and words by low-functioning children with autism. *Autism* 12, 231–248. doi: 10.1177/1362361307088753

Prüfer, K., Racimo, F., Patterson, N., Jay, F., Sankararaman, S., Sawyer, S., et al. (2014). The complete genome sequence of a Neanderthal from the Altai Mountains. *Nature* 505, 43–49. doi: 10.1038/nature12886

Ramirez-Villegas, J. F., Logothetis, N. K., and Besserve, M. (2015). Sharp wave-ripple complexes in a reduced model of the hippocampal CA3-CA1 network of the macaque monkey. *BMC Neurosci.* 16(Suppl. 1):P15. doi: 10.1186/1471-2202-16-S1-P15

Raznahan, A., Wallace, G. L., Antezana, L., Greenstein, D., Lenroot, R., Thurm, A., et al. (2013). Compared to what? Early brain overgrowth in autism and the perils of population norms. *Biol. Psychiatry* 74, 563–575. doi: 10.1016/j.biopsych.2013.03.022

Read, A. P., and Newton, V. E. (1997). Waardenburg syndrome. *J. Med. Genet.* 34, 656–665. doi: 10.1136/jmg.34.8.656

Reser, J. E. (2014). Solitary mammals provide an animal model for autism spectrum disorders. *J. Comp. Psychol.* 128, 99–113. doi: 10.1037/a0034519

Rice, D. P., Connor, E. C., Veltmaat, J. M., Lana-Elola, E., Veistinen, L., Tanimoto, Y., et al. (2010). Gli3Xt-J/Xt-J mice exhibit lambdoid suture craniosynostosis which results from altered osteoprogenitor proliferation and differentiation. *Hum. Mol. Genet.* 19, 3457–3467. doi: 10.1093/hmg/ddq258

Rogers, J., and Gibbs, R. A. (2014). Comparative primate genomics: emerging patterns of genome content and dynamics. *Nat. Rev. Genet.* 15, 347–359. doi: 10.1038/nrg3707

Rønn, L. C., Berezin, V., and Bock, E. (2000). The neural cell adhesion molecule in synaptic plasticity and ageing. *Int. J. Dev. Neurosci.* 18, 193–199. doi: 10.1016/S0736-5748(99)00088-X

Rothschild, G., Sottas, C. M., Kissel, H., Agosti, V., Manova, K., Hardy, M. P., et al. (2003). A role for Kit receptor signaling in Leydig cell steroidogenesis. *Biol. Reprod.* 69, 925–932. doi: 10.1095/biolreprod.102.014548

Ruest, L. B., Hammer, R. E., Yanagisawa, M., and Clouthier, D. E. (2003). Dlx5/6-enhancer directed expression of Cre recombinase in the pharyngeal arches and brain. *Genesis* 37, 188–194. doi: 10.1002/gene.10247

Saadi, I., Alkuraya, F. S., Gisselbrecht, S. S., Goessling, W., Cavallesco, R., Turbe-Doan, A., et al. (2011). Deficiency of the cytoskeletal protein SPECC1L leads to oblique facial clefting. *Am. J. Hum. Genet.* 89, 44–55. doi: 10.1016/j.ajhg.2011.05.023

Sacco, R., Gabriele, S., and Persico, A. M. (2015). Head circumference and brain size in autism spectrum disorder: a systematic review and meta-analysis. *Psychiatry Res.* 234, 239–251. doi: 10.1016/j.pscychresns.2015.08.016

Sage, S. R., Jürgens, U., and Ehret, G. (2006). Audio-vocal interaction in the pontine brainstem during self-initiated vocalization in the squirrel monkey. *Eur. J. Neurosci.* 23, 3297–3308. doi: 10.1111/j.1460-9568.2006.04835.x

Sajan, S. A., Rubenstein, J. L., Warchol, M. E., and Lovett, M. (2011). Identification of direct downstream targets of Dlx5 during early inner ear development. *Hum. Mol. Genet.* 20, 1262–1273. doi: 10.1093/hmg/ddq567

Sarachana, T., and Hu, V. W. (2013a). Genome-wide identification of transcriptional targets of RORA reveals direct regulation of multiple genes associated with autism spectrum disorder. *Mol. Autism.* 4:14. doi: 10.1186/2040-2392-4-14

Sarachana, T., and Hu, V. W. (2013b). Differential recruitment of coregulators to the RORA promoter adds another layer of complexity to gene (dys) regulation by sex hormones in autism. *Mol. Autism* 4:39. doi: 10.1186/2040-2392-4-39

Sarachana, T., Xu, M., Wu, R. C., and Hu, V. W. (2011). Sex hormones in autism: androgens and estrogens differentially and reciprocally regulate RORA, a novel candidate gene for autism. *PLoS ONE* 6:e17116. doi: 10.1371/journal.pone.0017116

Schipul, S. E., Keller, T. A., and Just, M. A. (2011). Inter-regional brain communication and its disturbance in autism. *Front. Syst. Neurosci.* 5:10. doi: 10.3389/fnsys.2011.00010

Schumann, C. M., Barnes, C. C., Lord, C., and Courchesne, E. (2009). Amygdala enlargement in toddlers with autism related to severity of social and communication impairments. *Biol. Psychiatry* 66, 942–949. doi: 10.1016/j.biopsych.2009.07.007

Scott-Van Zeeland, A. A., Abrahams, B. S., Alvarez-Retuerto, A. I., Sonnenblick, L. I., Rudie, J. D., Ghahremani, D., et al. (2010b). Altered functional connectivity in frontal lobe circuits is associated with variation in the autism risk gene CNTNAP2. *Sci. Transl. Med.* 2:56ra80. doi: 10.1126/scitranslmed.3001344

Scott-Van Zeeland, A. A., McNealy, K., Wang, A. T., Sigman, M., Bookheimer, S. Y., and Dapretto, M. (2010a). No neural evidence of statistical learning during exposure to artificial languages in children with autism spectrum disorders. *Biol. Psychiatry* 68, 345–351. doi: 10.1016/j.biopsych.2010.01.011

Seed, A., and Tomasello, M. (2010). Primate cognition. *Top Cogn. Sci.* 2, 407–419. doi: 10.1111/j.1756-8765.2010.01099.x

Segklia, A., Seuntjens, E., Elkouris, M., Tsalavos, S., Stappers, E., Mitsiadis, T. A., et al. (2012). Bmp7 regulates the survival, proliferation, and neurogenic properties of neural progenitor cells during corticogenesis in the mouse. *PLoS ONE* 7:e34088. doi: 10.1371/journal.pone.0034088

Sharma, V. P., Fenwick, A. L., Brockop, M. S., McGowan, S. J., Goos, J. A., Hoogeboom, A. J., et al. (2013). Mutations in TCF12, encoding a basic helix-loop-helix partner of TWIST1, are a frequent cause of coronal craniosynostosis. *Nat. Genet.* 45, 304–307. doi: 10.1038/ng.2531

Smit, D. J., Smith, A. G., Parsons, P. G., Muscat, G. E., and Sturm, R. A. (2000). Domains of Brn2 that mediate homodimerization and interaction with general and melanocytic transcription factors. *Eur. J. Biochem.* 267, 6413–6422. doi: 10.1046/j.1432-1327.2000.01737.x

Smith, L. E., Barker, E. T., Seltzer, M. M., Abbeduto, L., and Greenberg, J. S. (2012). Behavioral phenotype of fragile X syndrome in adolescence and adulthood. *Am. J. Intellect. Dev. Disabil.* 117, 1–17. doi: 10.1352/1944-7558-117.1.1

Somel, M., Liu, X., Tang, L., Yan, Z., Hu, H., Guo, S., et al. (2011). MicroRNA-driven developmental remodeling in the brain distinguishes humans from other primates. *PLoS Biol.* 9:e1001214. doi: 10.1371/journal.pbio.1001214

Spelke, E. (2003). "What makes us smart?" in *Language in Mind*, eds D. Gentner and S. Goldin-Meadow (Cambridge, MA: MIT Press), 277–311.

Sperber, S. M., Saxena, V., Hatch, G., and Ekker, M. (2008). Zebrafish dlx2a contributes to hindbrain neural crest survival, is necessary for differentiation of sensory ganglia and functions with dlx1a in maturation of the arch cartilage elements. *Dev. Biol.* 314, 59–70. doi: 10.1016/j.ydbio.2007.11.005

Spratt, E. G., Nicholas, J. S., Brady, K. T., Carpenter, L. A., Hatcher, C. R., Meekins, K. A., et al. (2012). Enhanced cortisol response to stress in children in autism. *J. Autism Dev. Disord.* 42, 75–81. doi: 10.1007/s10803-011-1214-0

Stefanatos, G. A., and Baron, I. S. (2011). The ontogenesis of language impairment in autism: a neuropsychological perspective. *Neuropsychol. Rev.* 21, 252–270. doi: 10.1007/s11065-011-9178-6

Steiger, J. L., Bandyopadhyay, S., Farb, D. H., and Russek, S. J. (2004). cAMP response element-binding protein, activating transcription factor-4, and upstream stimulatory factor differentially control hippocampal GABABR1a and GABABR1b subunit gene expression through alternative promoters. *J. Neurosci.* 24, 6115–6126. doi: 10.1523/JNEUROSCI.1200-04.2004

Stein, C. M., Schick, J. H., Gerry Taylor, H., Shriberg, L. D., Millard, C., Kundtz-Kluge, A., et al. (2004). Pleiotropic effects of a chromosome 3 locus on speech-sound disorder and reading. *Am. J. Hum. Genet.* 74, 283–297. doi: 10.1086/381562

Sterelny, K. (2011). From hominins to humans: how sapiens became behaviourally modern. *Philos. Trans. R. Soc. Lond. B Biol. Sci.* 366, 809–822. doi: 10.1098/rstb.2010.0301

St Pourcain, B., Cents, R. A., Whitehouse, A. J., Haworth, C. M., Davis, O. S., O'Reilly, P. F., et al. (2014). Common variation near ROBO2 is associated with expressive vocabulary in infancy. *Nat. Commun.* 5, 4831. doi: 10.1038/ncomms5831

Suda, S., Iwata, K., Shimmura, C., Kameno, Y., Anitha, A., Thanseem, I., et al. (2011). Decreased expression of axon-guidance receptors in the anterior cingulate cortex in autism. *Mol. Autism.* 2:14. doi: 10.1186/2040-2392-2-14

Szklarczyk, D., Franceschini, A., Wyder, S., Forslund, K., Heller, D., Huerta-Cepas, J., et al. (2015). STRING v10: protein-protein interaction networks, integrated over the tree of life. *Nucleic Acids Res.* 43, D447–D452. doi: 10.1093/nar/gku1003

Tabuchi, A., Sakaya, H., Kisukeda, T., Fushiki, H., and Tsuda, M. (2002). Involvement of an upstream stimulatory factor as well as cAMP-responsive element-binding protein in the activation of brain-derived neurotrophic factor gene promoter I. *J. Biol. Chem.* 277, 35920–35931. doi: 10.1074/jbc.M204784200

Tager-Flusberg, H. (2006). Defining language phenotypes in autism. *Clin. Neurosci. Res.* 6, 219–224. doi: 10.1016/j.cnr.2006.06.007

Tager-Flusberg, H., Paul, R., and Lord, C. (2005). "Language and communication in autism," in *Handbook of Autism and Pervasive Developmental Disorders*, eds F. R. Volkmar, R. Paul, A. Klin, and D. Cohen (New York, NY: Wiley), 335–364.

Taylor, J. L., and Corbett, B. A. (2014). A review of rhythm and responsiveness of cortisol in individuals with autism spectrum disorders. *Psychoneuroendocrinology* 49, 207–228. doi: 10.1016/j.psyneuen.2014.07.015

Thomas, J. (2014). *Self-Domestication and Language Evolution.* Ph.D. thesis. University of Edinburgh, Edinburgh.

Tomarken, A. J., Han, G. T., and Corbett, B. A. (2015). Temporal patterns, heterogeneity, and stability of diurnal cortisol rhythms in children with autism spectrum disorder. *Psychoneuroendocrinology* 62, 217–226. doi: 10.1016/j.psyneuen.2015.08.016

Toro, R., Konyukh, M., Delorme, R., Leblond, C., Chaste, P., Fauchereau, F., et al. (2010). Key role for gene dosage and synaptic homeostasis in autism spectrum disorders. *Trends Genet.* 26, 363–372. doi: 10.1016/j.tig.2010.05.007

Tripi, G., Roux, S., Canziani, T., Bonnet Brilhault, F., Barthélémy, C., and Canziani, F. (2008). Minor physical anomalies in children with autism spectrum disorder. *Early Hum. Dev.* 84, 217–223. doi: 10.1016/j.earlhumdev.2007.04.005

Twigg, S. R., Forecki, J., Goos, J. A., Richardson, I. C., Hoogeboom, A. J., van den Ouweland, A. M., et al. (2015). Gain-of-function mutations in ZIC1 are associated with coronal craniosynostosis and learning disability. *Am. J. Hum. Genet.* 97, 378–388. doi: 10.1016/j.ajhg.2015.07.007

Twigg, S. R., Vorgia, E., McGowan, S. J., Peraki, I., Fenwick, A. L., Sharma, V. P., et al. (2013). Reduced dosage of ERF causes complex craniosynostosis in humans and mice and links ERK1/2 signaling to regulation of osteogenesis. *Nat. Genet.* 45, 308–313. doi: 10.1038/ng.2539

Twigg, S. R., and Wilkie, A. O. (2015). New insights into craniofacial malformations. *Hum. Mol. Genet.* 24, R50–R59. doi: 10.1093/hmg/ddv228

Tyas, D. A., Pearson, H., Rashbass, P., and Price, D. J. (2003). Pax6 regulates cell adhesion during cortical development. *Cereb. Cortex* 13, 612–619. doi: 10.1093/cercor/13.6.612

Uchino, J., Suzuki, M., Hoshino, K., Nomura, Y., and Segawa, M. (2001). Development of language in Rett syndrome. *Brain Dev.* 23, S233–S235. doi: 10.1016/S0387-7604(01)00367-9

Uddin, L. Q., Supekar, K., and Menon, V. (2013). Reconceptualizing functional brain connectivity in autism from a developmental perspective. *Front. Hum. Neurosci.* 7:458. doi: 10.3389/fnhum.2013.00458

Uittenbogaard, M., and Chiaramello, A. (2002). Expression of the bHLH transcription factor Tcf12 (ME1) gene is linked to the expansion of precursor cell populations during neurogenesis. *Brain Res. Gene Expr. Patterns* 1, 115–121. doi: 10.1016/S1567-133X(01)00022-9

Valverde, F., García, C., López-Mascaraque, L., and De Carlos, J. A. (2000). Development of the mammillothalamic tract in normal and Pax-6 mutant mice. *J. Comp. Neurol.* 419, 485–504. doi: 10.1002/(SICI)1096-9861(20000417)419:4<485::AID-CNE6>3.0.CO;2-1

van Daalen, E., Swinkels, S. H., Dietz, C., van Engeland, H., and Buitelaar, J. K. (2007). Body length and head growth in the first year of life in autism. *Pediatr. Neurol.* 37, 324–330. doi: 10.1016/j.pediatrneurol.2007.06.006

Veenstra-VanderWeele, J., and Cook, E. H. (2004). Molecular genetics of autism spectrum disorder. *Mol. Psychiatry* 9, 819–832. doi: 10.1038/sj.mp.4001505

Vernes, S. C., Oliver, P. L., Spiteri, E., Lockstone, H. E., Puliyadi, R., Taylor, J. M., et al. (2011). Foxp2 regulates gene networks implicated in neurite outgrowth in the developing brain. *PLoS Genet.* 7:e1002145. doi: 10.1371/journal.pgen.1002145

Vissers, L. E. L. M., van Ravenswaaij, C. M. A., Admiraal, R., Hurst, J. A., de Vries, B. B. A., Janssen, I. M., et al. (2004). Mutations in a new member of the chromodomain gene family cause CHARGE syndrome. *Nat. Genet.* 36, 955–957. doi: 10.1038/ng1407

Voineagu, I., Wang, X., Johnston, P., Lowe, J. K., Tian, Y., Horvath, S., et al. (2011). Transcriptomic analysis of autistic brain reveals convergent molecular pathology. *Nature* 474, 380–384. doi: 10.1038/nature10110

von Aster, M., Zachmann, M., Brandeis, D., Wohlrab, G., Richner, M., and Steinhausen, H. C. (1997). Psychiatric, neuropediatric, and neuropsychological symptoms in a case of hypomelanosis of Ito. *Eur. Child Adolesc. Psychiatry* 6, 227–233. doi: 10.1007/s007870050034

Walenski, M., Tager-Flusberg, H., and Ullman, M. (2006). "Language in autism," in *Understanding Autism: From Basic Neuroscience to Treatment*, eds S. O. Moldin and J. L. R. Rubenstein (Boca Raton, FL: Taylor and Francis Books), 175–203.

Wang, Q., Moore, M. J., Adelmant, G., Marto, J. A., and Silver, P. A. (2013). PQBP1, a factor linked to intellectual disability, affects alternative splicing associated with neurite outgrowth. *Genes. Dev.* 27, 615–626. doi: 10.1101/gad.212308.112

Wang, Y., Billon, C., Walker, J. K., and Burris, T. P. (2016). Therapeutic effect of a synthetic RORα/γ agonist in an animal model of autism. *ACS Chem. Neurosci.* 7, 143–148. doi: 10.1021/acschemneuro.5b00159

Wang, Y., Dye, C. A., Sohal, V., Long, J. E., Estrada, R. C., Roztocil, T., et al. (2010). Dlx5 and Dlx6 regulate the development of parvalbumin-expressing cortical interneurons. *J. Neurosci.* 30, 5334–5345. doi: 10.1523/JNEUROSCI.5963-09.2010

Wray, A., and Grace, G. W. (2007). The consequences of talking to strangers: evolutionary corollaries of socio-cultural influences on linguistic form. *Lingua* 117, 543–578. doi: 10.1523/JNEUROSCI.5963-09.2010

Watanabe, H., Takahashi, K., and Isa, T. (2015). "Phase locking of β oscillation in electrocorticography (ECoG) in the monkey motor cortex at the onset of EMGs and 3D reaching movements," in *Engineering in Medicine and Biology Society (EMBC), 37th Annual International Conference of the IEEE* (Milan), 55–58.

Weaver, K. N., Watt, K. E., Hufnagel, R. B., Navajas Acedo, J., Linscott, L. L., Sund, K. L., et al. (2015). Acrofacial dysostosis, Cincinnati type, a mandibulofacial dysostosis syndrome with limb anomalies, is caused by POLR1A dysfunction. *Am. J. Hum. Genet.* 96, 765–774. doi: 10.1016/j.ajhg.2015.03.011

Wilkins, A. S., Wrangham, R. W., and Fitch, W. T. (2014). The "domestication syndrome" in mammals: a unified explanation based on neural crest cell behavior and genetics. *Genetics* 197, 795–808. doi: 10.1534/genetics.114.165423

Williams, J. M., Beck, T. F., Pearson, D. M., Proud, M. B., Cheung, S. W., and Scott, D. A. (2009). A 1q42 deletion involving DISC1, DISC2, and TSNAX in an autism spectrum disorder. *Am. J. Med. Genet. A.* 149A, 1758–1762. doi: 10.1002/ajmg.a.32941

Willsey, A. J., and State, M. W. (2015). Autism spectrum disorders: from genes to neurobiology. *Curr. Opin. Neurobiol.* 30, 92–99. doi: 10.1016/j.conb.2014.10.015

Wilson, N. R., Olm-Shipman, A. J., Acevedo, D. S., Palaniyandi, K., Hall, E. G., Kosa, E., et al. (2016). SPECC1L deficiency results in increased adherens junction stability and reduced cranial neural crest cell delamination. *Sci. Rep.* 6:17735. doi: 10.1038/srep17735

Wyatt, A. W., Osborne, R. J., Stewart, H., and Ragge, N. K. (2010). Bone morphogenetic protein 7 (BMP7) mutations are associated with variable ocular, brain, ear, palate, and skeletal anomalies. *Hum. Mutat.* 31, 781–787. doi: 10.1002/humu.21280

Wynn, T., and Coolidge, F. (2011). *How to Think Like a Neanderthal.* Oxford: Oxford University Press.

Yang, Z., Matsumoto, A., Nakayama, K., Jimbo, E. F., Kojima, K., Nagata, K., et al. (2016). Circadian-relevant genes are highly polymorphic in autism spectrum disorder patients. *Brain Dev.* 38, 91–99. doi: 10.1016/j.braindev.2015.04.006

Yu, H. M., Jerchow, B., Sheu, T. J., Liu, B., Costantini, F., Puzas, J. E., et al. (2005). The role of Axin2 in calvarial morphogenesis and craniosynostosis. *Development* 132, 1995–2005. doi: 10.1242/dev.01786

Yuge, K., Kataoka, A., Yoshida, A. C., Itoh, D., Aggarwal, M., Mori, S., et al. (2011). Region-specific gene expression in early postnatal mouse thalamus. *J. Comp. Neurol.* 519, 544–561. doi: 10.1002/cne.22532

Zhang, Y., Sun, Y., Wang, F., Wang, Z., Peng, Y., and Li, R. (2012). Downregulating the canonical Wnt/β-catenin signaling pathway attenuates the susceptibility to autism-like phenotypes by decreasing oxidative stress. *Neurochem. Res.* 37, 1409–1419. doi: 10.1007/s11064-012-0724-2

Zheng, F., Wang, L., Jia, M., Yue, W., Ruan, Y., Lu, T., et al. (2011). Evidence for association between Disrupted-in-Schizophrenia 1 (DISC1) gene polymorphisms and autism in Chinese Han population: a family-based association study. *Behav. Brain Funct.* 7:14. doi: 10.1186/1744-9081-7-14

Zhou, H., Hu, S., Matveev, R., Yu, Q., Li, J., Khaitovich, P., et al. (2015). A chronological atlas of natural selection in the human genome during the past half-million years. *BioRxiv.* doi: 10.1101/018929. [Epub ahead of print].

16

GOLIAH: A Gaming Platform for Home-Based Intervention in Autism – Principles and Design

Valentina Bono[1], Antonio Narzisi[2], Anne-Lise Jouen[3], Elodie Tilmont[3,4], Stephane Hommel[1], Wasifa Jamal[1], Jean Xavier[4], Lucia Billeci[2], Koushik Maharatna[1], Mike Wald[1], Mohamed Chetouani[3], David Cohen[3,4], Filippo Muratori[2] and MICHELANGELO Study Group†*

[1] Electronics and Computer Science, University of Southampton, Southampton, UK, [2] Department of Developmental Neuroscience, IRCCS Stella Maris Foundation, Pisa, Italy, [3] Institute of Intelligent Systems and Robotics, University Pierre and Marie Curie, Paris, France, [4] Department of Child and Adolescent Psychiatry, APHP, Groupe Hospitalier Pitié-Salpêtrière et University Pierre and Marie Curie, Paris, France

Edited by:
Yuri Bozzi,
University of Trento, Italy

Reviewed by:
Munis Dundar,
Erciyes University, Turkey
Vijaya Raman,
St. John's Medical College Hospital, India

***Correspondence:**
Valentina Bono
vb2a12@ecs.soton.ac.uk

†The members of the MICHELANGELO Study Group are listed in Appendix A.

Children with Autism need intensive intervention and this is challenging in terms of manpower, costs, and time. Advances in Information Communication Technology and computer gaming may help in this respect by creating a nomadically deployable closed-loop intervention system involving the child and active participation of parents and therapists. An automated serious gaming platform enabling intensive intervention in nomadic settings has been developed by mapping two pivotal skills in autism spectrum disorder: Imitation and Joint Attention (JA). Eleven games – seven Imitations and four JA – were derived from the Early Start Denver Model. The games involved application of visual and audio stimuli with multiple difficulty levels and a wide variety of tasks and actions pertaining to the Imitation and JA. The platform runs on mobile devices and allows the therapist to (1) characterize the child's initial difficulties/strengths, ensuring tailored and adapted intervention by choosing appropriate games and (2) investigate and track the temporal evolution of the child's progress through a set of automatically extracted quantitative performance metrics. The platform allows the therapist to change the game or its difficulty levels during the intervention depending on the child's progress. Performance of the platform was assessed in a 3-month open trial with 10 children with autism (Trial ID: NCT02560415, Clinicaltrials.gov). The children and the parents participated in 80% of the sessions both at home (77.5%) and at the hospital (90%). All children went through all the games but, given the diversity of the games and the heterogeneity of children profiles and abilities, for a given game the number of sessions dedicated to the game varied and could be tailored through automatic scoring. Parents (N = 10) highlighted enhancement in the child's concentration, flexibility, and self-esteem in 78, 89, and 44% of the cases, respectively, and 56% observed an enhanced parents–child relationship. This pilot study shows the feasibility of using the developed gaming platform for home-based intensive intervention. However, the overall capability of the platform in delivering intervention needs to be assessed in a bigger open trial.

Keywords: autism spectrum disorder, Early Start Denver Model, serious game, intensive intervention, Imitation, Joint Attention, nomadic settings

INTRODUCTION

Autism spectrum disorder (ASD) is a spectrum of neurodevelopmental disorders characterized by the presence of atypical social communicative interaction and behaviors (1). Typically, ASD is diagnosed through behavioral analysis in the 3–5 years age range and, once diagnosed, its treatment is mainly delivered through behavioral intervention following different intervention models. In essence, these models try to teach a child cognitive, social, and behavioral skills that are considered essential for independent living in the long run and various techniques have been developed over the years (2–7). However, two major problems associated with such interventions are as follows: (1) a person's specific development intervention protocol, accounting for the actual difficulties and strengths of a child, needs to be designed to achieve maximal effects - ASD is a broad spectrum with significant inter-child variability, and it has already been established that tailor-made personalized intervention may be more effective compared to any generic type of intervention (8) and (2) at least 20 h/week are supposed to be needed for an intensive intervention (9, 10).

Characterization of a child is typically done through behavioral assessment by a trained therapist in clinical settings but such an approach is often prone to have subjective biases. To avoid such biases, one needs to employ a set of stimuli multiple times ensuring their repeatability and then extracting a set of objective measures for characterizing the outcomes. Repeatability is an essential criterion in this case so that an average performance measure in a stimulus-specific way could be obtained reflecting the child's actual ability for responding to the stimuli in question. Such repeatability and the 20 h/week intensive intervention are difficult to achieve (10). In fact, its implementation needs a trained therapist and, given the prevalence of ASD, the workload of a therapist could make the effective implementation of this strategy impractical. Moreover, the involvement of trained parents/caregivers to be part of intervention also in home setting seems to be an effective strategy in order to increase the learning opportunity for children with ASD (11, 12). This requires parent training and regular monitoring to check whether the parents are implementing and properly adhering to the intervention protocol outlined by the therapist. However, the economic implication of such process is quite substantial.

In recent years, computer-based approaches have been shown to be effective in improving the learning cognitive and social skills of children with various learning disability conditions (13–15). In these methods, the target intervention is mapped into a set of computer games and is thereby training the children since children enjoy playing games rather than going through the conventional learning process (16–18). Most of these computer applications designed for people with autism focus on the relationship between one user and one computer and aim to help with specific behavioral problems associated with autism. Computers are motivating for children with autism due to their predictability and consistency, compared with the unpredictable nature of human responses. In regard to social interaction, the computer does not send confusing social messages. Research on the use of computers (19) for students with autism revealed increase in (1) focused attention, (2) overall attention span, (3) sitting behavior, (4) fine motor skills, (5) generalization skills (from computer to related non-computer activities); and decrease in (6) agitation, (7) self-stimulatory behaviors, and (8) perseverative responses. The importance of assistive technology for children with autism has been established by the fact that this technology can be used in rehabilitation for daily activities.

Motivated by these facts, we conceived a closed-loop system with computer gaming at its center that allows the interaction between subjects with autism and a partner. This approach may help in mitigating the effect of isolation that could affect the traditional computer applications mentioned above. The solution we developed is innovative because it seeks to go over the actual lacuna in various computer games for children with ASD. In fact, in most computer games for ASD, the children are engaged only with a computer screen. In our protocol children are engaged with another person (therapist/caregiver) who has a computer and share the activity with the child.

The intensity of intervention for ASD plays a crucial role in terms of clinical outcome. However, the hours of intervention assigned to children with ASD are usually less than the real need of the children. To mitigate this problem, the gaming platform is an interesting solution to increase (1) the hours of treatment for children with ASD and (2) involve caregivers in the intervention. The intensity of the treatment and the involvement of caregivers are two important requirements of the intervention in ASD. In this sense, the gaming platform is in line with the recent recommendation about the intervention proposed by Ref. (11, 12).

The conceptual view of a closed-loop system that may enable effective intervention integrating both the home and clinical settings is shown in **Figure 1**.

At the heart of the system is a computerized gaming library [Gaming Open Library Intervention for Autism at Home (GOLIAH)] that consists of a set of computer games created by mapping the desired intervention stimuli, Imitation, and Joint Attention (JA) in this case, into the games. In theory, the library could be divided into two parts - assessment games and intervention games - although they could be used interchangeably without loss of any generality. At the beginning, the child would be asked to play a set of games carefully selected from the library by the therapist for characterizing the child's difficulties/strengths. Since a particular type of stimulus could be mapped in different ways in multiple games, this will allow using different games for ascertaining the child's difficulties/strengths pertaining to a type of stimulus in a repeatable way without inflicting boredom on the child and thereby obtaining a much more precise average assessment of the child. Once characterized, the therapist could choose appropriate games (designated as the intervention games for convenience) from the gaming library that the child needs to play at his/her home setting on a regular basis adhering to a protocol outlined by the therapist. The aim here is to enhance the cognitive performance of the child through playing these games at home so that the effective intervention hours could be increased. The games could be made flexible enough so that the child may play the games with his/her parents (actively involving the parents without requiring an extensive training process) on a regular basis and with the therapist remotely connected through the internet at pre-scheduled times. The gaming system could

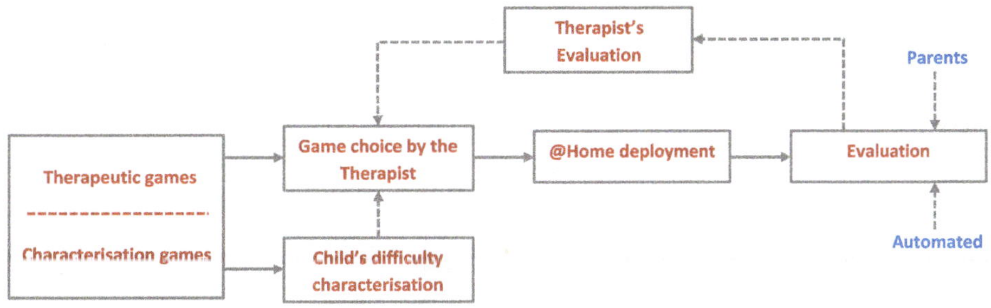

FIGURE 1 | The conceptual closed-loop intervention system. The games contained in the platform are used for assessing the child, first, and for intervention purposes later. The first aim is to characterize the starting cognitive skills of a child by playing games at different levels of difficulty. After identifying the current level of ability of the child, a series of games and difficulties will be planned by the therapist and employed at home. According to the evaluation, both automated and manual, a new set of games will be planned by the therapist.

have an automated evaluation process embedded in it that would extract a set of quantitative evaluation metrics, characterizing the child's performance with each game and thereby providing the temporal evolution characteristics of the child's performance. On the other hand, the parents could also assign a score manually according to a scoring criterion suggested by the therapist to signify how the child's performance has evolved against each stimulus according to their own perception. All the automated and manually evaluated scores could be transmitted to the therapist who may compare them to check, on the one hand, how the child is improving and, on the other hand, whether the parents are adhering to the prescribed protocol truthfully. This could act as the basis of the evaluation by the therapist when he/she plays the game remotely with the child at a pre-scheduled time. Depending on this final evaluation, the therapist may choose a set of different intervention games from the gaming library once the child achieves the target set by the therapist and the whole process may continue. This closed-loop approach may help in alleviating several problems currently encountered by the autism therapists and have many advantages as described below in **Table 1**.

TABLE 1 | Advantages of the closed-loop GOLIAH approach.

Tailoring intervention through careful assessment of the child

- Being computer based, the stimuli for assessment can be programed in an exact reproducible way
- The same type of stimulus could be mapped into different games giving the child the feeling that he/she plays different games. This is particularly important for assessing the child's difficulties since repetition of the same game may force them not to respond to his/her capability level out of boredom. This fact is also true during the intervention stage
- Different difficulty levels could be incorporated within the games to ascertain the child's performance even for a specific type of stimulus
- The whole process could be run automatically without incurring extra load on the therapist at the assessment phase
- A set of quantitative measures could be extracted in an automated way assessing the child objectively

Nomadic intervention

- The process could be deployed in nomadic environments where the child may play the game either with his/her parents or remotely with the therapist through internet connections
- Parents will need minimal training
- Automated measurements could give an objective idea about how the child's performance changes over time in stimulus-specific way
- The therapist can adjust the intervention remotely and dynamically by adding/removing games from the pre-stored library
- It also opens up the possibility of a batch-mode intervention where the therapist may deliver intervention to multiple children located at various locations in one session

Improving social interaction skills of children with autism is a difficult task for their families as well as for well-trained therapists (20, 21). Although ASD remains a devastating disorder with a poor outcome in adult life (22, 23), there have been important improvements in the condition with the development of various therapeutic approaches. The literature on interventions in ASD has become quite extensive, with increasing convergence between behavioral and developmental methods (24, 25). The focus of many interventions is directed toward the development of skills that are considered to be "pivotal," such as Imitation and JA (26–28).

Imitation plays a critical role in the development of every child. Among the several definitions of imitation, no definition is universally agreed upon: (1) Thorndike (26) offered a definition based on visual aspects: "learning to do an action by watching someone doing it." However, a full definition of imitation must consider multi-sensory aspects. (2) Wallon (28) defined imitation as a learning technique without reward (or reinforcement). (3) Whiten and Ham (29) defined imitation as the process by which the imitator learns some behavioral characteristics of the model. Imitation fulfils two essential functions for adaptation: it is used for learning and it serves to communicate without words (30). Two children involved in imitation are temporally synchronized; they respond to the perception of movements or actions to produce a similar behavior. Compared to imitation, JA introduces a third partner during interaction. Emery defined JA as a triadic interaction that showed that both agents focus on a single object (31). Some authors (32) have argued that JA implies viewing the behavior of other agents as intentionally driven. In that sense, JA is much more than gaze following or simultaneous looking (33).

Lack of Imitation and JA are the main problems when interacting with children with ASD. While playing a game or conducting other activities with a social partner, these children tend to not concentrate on what others are actually doing, switching to repetitive and stereotypical behaviors that are of interest for the child but that usually have no or few relations with the actual social context. Imitation is possible but the communicative value of early imitation seems poorly understood (30). Also, children with ASD can display concerted attention to toys or objects that they like, but they have difficulties in sharing attention or interests with others (34). For example, maintaining eye contact with the caregiver is especially complicated (35, 36) and the lack of JA is the consequence (37, 38).

Owing to the importance of Imitation and JA as core difficulties in ASD, we mapped a subset of related stimuli from the Early Start Denver Model (ESDM) protocol into the gaming platform containing a set of games with varying levels of difficulties that could be dynamically adjusted by the therapists. This program aims to meet the socio-emotional needs of children and their families, to identify and use validated and effective intervention techniques that are based on developmental needs (39). The ESDM recently received strong evidence of its efficacy at the level of clinical outcome (40) and brain plasticity (2).

Motivated by these facts, the purpose of the work is to design a novel computerized gaming platform that would allow: (1) delivering intensive intervention in nomadic environments for Imitation and JA tasks in children with autism, (2) tailoring and adapting intervention through child-specific assessment of difficulties, (3) enhancing effective intervention hours, and (4) without increasing the cost of delivery. The major point to note here is that GOLIAH is not intended to replace one of the state-of-the-art interventions for ASD but to supplement and expand it for achieving its maximal benefit.

METHODS

Participants

We tested the software in a 3-month open trial with 10 children with ASD (all boys, aged 5–9 years) to assess the performance of the software itself. All children were recruited in the Department of Child and Adolescent Psychiatry, Hôpital Pitié-Salpêtrière, Paris and in the Department of Child Neuropsychiatry, IRCCS Stella Maris Foundation, Calambrone, Pisa. The study was approved by the local ethics committees of each institution (*Comité de Protection des Personnes* Ile De France VI under agreement number CCP 21-14, and Comitato Etico of the Stella Maris under agreement number 05/2011) and was in accordance with the declaration of Helsinki. Each parent gave informed written consent before inclusion for participation and for publication of the individual clinical data. Clinical characteristics of the children are given in **Table 2**.

TABLE 2 | Socio-demographic and clinical characteristics of the participants.

	ASD (N = 10)
Age, mean (±SD)	6.8 (±1.4)
Male – female	10 – 0
ADI-R, current, mean (±SD)	
Social impairment score	14.14 (±4.58)
Communication score	10 (±5.82)
Repetitive interest score	4 (±2.91)
Cognitive Level (WISC3/WPPSI)	
VIQ	103.1 (±14)
PIQ	96.1 (±24.8)
Vineland: mean (±SD)	
Communication score	88.2 (±16.7)
Daily living score	84.3 (±13.4)
Socialization	79.5 (±10.3)

ASD: Autistic Spectrum Disorder; ADI-R: Autism Diagnostic Interview-Revised; WISC 3: Wechsler Intelligence Scale for Children 3; WPPSI: Wechsler Preschool and Primary Scale of Intelligence; VIQ: Verbal Intelligent Quotient; PIQ: Performance Intelligent Quotient.

Procedures

The intervention protocol used with children included six sessions per week (from Monday to Friday) of training with GOLIAH; five sessions per week were at home with the parents (mother or father) playing with their children in the afternoon; and one session per week was planned at the hospital. The duration of each session, both at home and at hospital, was equal to 20 min. The sessions at home and at hospital were the same in terms of tasks. The only differences were the different setting (i.e., home or hospital) and the partner (therapist or parent). Each child's plan was tailored on the basis of functional profile and adapted during the 3-months protocol according to children progress in playing the games. This open-trial aimed at assessing (1) the usefulness of the gaming platform with children–therapist interactions as well as with children–parents, (2) whether tailored intervention was useful when used at home and with non-professional therapist/parents, and (3) whether children performed as expected when using the different Imitation and JA games. To do so, we used both objective data computed from the platform and clinical annotations produced by therapists during weekly sessions at hospital. (4) Finally, subjective views from users were also explored through a questionnaire.

At the beginning of the study, a 3-month open trial was planned with 60 sessions (four sessions at home per week + one session at the hospital per week = five sessions per week × 12 weeks = 60 sessions). To assess in detail the usability of the gaming platform, we planned a systematic recording of the number of times each game was played in each session by each of the 10 children included in the 3-month study period. Details are shown individually in **Table 3**.

Instruments

Software Design

The game software has been developed in Microsoft Visual Studio 10 Platform in C# language. The platform has as many classes as the number of included mini-games; thus, creation of new games will not alter the existing ones. Real-time communication between two devices is performed through a multi-threading process that includes: (1) game flow thread in which all the game tasks are performed (including sending objects to the other user) and (2) receiving thread in which the objects sent by the other user are received and fire the semaphore in the game flow thread. The two players are connected to a server, developed in C#, which acts as a bridge between them. In fact, the objects exchange occurs through a Socket connection based on a TCP/IP protocol that ensures that the information exchange will not be lost during the transmission.

Choice of Stimuli

The ESDM is a comprehensive behavioral early intervention protocol for children with autism. It uses a combination of developmental and behavioral techniques in both therapist and parent-implemented early intervention models (41, 42). It is an intervention for infants with ASD aged 12–48 months that combines applied behavior analysis (ABA) with developmental

TABLE 3 | Number of sessions per game and per child during the 3-month study period.

Child	1	2	3	4	5	6	7	8	9	10	N of sessions per game for all children: mean (range)
Imitation games											
Imitate free drawing	11	4	4	6	3	19	16	19	15	16	11 (3–19)
Imitate step by step draw	17	13	24	10	5	20	11	18	13	9	14 (5–24)
Imitate speech	17	13	15	9	11	15	11	19	12	6	13 (6–19)
Imitate sounds	2	19	10	13	11	10	17	9	11	8	11 (2–19)
Imitate actions	15	23	7	6	10	14	11	14	4	16	12 (4–23)
Imitate actions and build	12	11	19	13	12	12	14	11	12	13	13 (11–19)
Guess the instrument	4	3	11	10	9	2	1	7	6	5	6 (1–11)
Joint attention games											
Follow the therapist's pointing	15	19	20	17	12	14	13	16	21	12	16 (12–21)
Cooperative drawing	2	19	15	11	13	9	11	11	18	18	13 (2–19)
Bake a cake	11	14	16	15	12	18	9	12	19	7	13 (7–19)
Receptive communication	21	25	31	20	17	16	15	25	9	12	19 (9–31)
No. of sessions per child for all games: mean (range)	12 (2–21)	15 (3–25)	16 (4–31)	12 (6–20)	10 (3–17)	14 (2–20)	12 (1–17)	15 (7–25)	13 (4–21)	11 (5–18)	

and relationship-based approaches. The intervention is provided by trained therapists (Antonio Narzisi is a certified therapist from MIND Institute, University of California Davis, Davis, CA, USA) and parents.

Each child's treatment program includes models based on development, functional profile, relational patterns, and modification of behaviors. The curriculum includes, among others, systematic activities on receptive and expressive communication, as well as social, play, cognitive, self-care, and fine and gross motor skills. Particular attention is devoted to specific tasks regarding Imitation and JA. ESDM considers JA as an activity in which two subjects are engaged with each other in the same cooperative activity, attending to the same objects, or playing or working together on a common activity. A JA routine is made up of several phases: (1) the opening or set-up phase that involves the acts that precede the establishment of the first shared play activity based on the theme of the play. (2) The child and adult are engaged in a definable play activity, either object centered, such as building blocks, pouring water, marking with crayons, or involving a social game, such as singing a song, dancing to music, or playing hide and seek. (3) The elaboration phase involves variation on the theme to keep it interesting or to highlight different aspects of the activity. This preserves the play from becoming repetitious and allows more skill areas to be addressed. (4) The closing is the fourth and final phase when attention is waning or the teaching value of the activity is all used up. It is a time to put materials away and to transit to something else. Closing allows nice transitions in changing activity, location, and time.

Regarding imitation, in the ESDM different tasks may be proposed to the children: (a) imitation of actions on objects, (b) imitation of gestures, and (c) vocal imitation of sounds and words. During intervention sessions, children are asked to imitate conventional or unconventional actions with and/or without objects using or not the vocalizations.

Mapping ESDM Stimuli for Imitation and JA into a Computerized Gaming Platform

The Imitation and JA stimuli are mapped into 11 games: seven Imitation and four JA games. Although currently the proposed platform consists of 11 games, it is flexible enough for developing/adding new games according to the need. A list of the games and the ESDM stimuli they address is depicted in **Table 4**. In developing the games, special attention has been devoted to their realistic resemblance to the real-life scenario, more importantly emulating human–human interactions during the game playing phase. Each of the games incorporates different levels of difficulty ranging from the application of one stimulus (e.g., the sound of a train), to a combination of different stimuli (e.g., the sound and the image of a train).

The seven Imitation-based games comprise of tasks involving the imitation of drawing, speech, sounds, and building actions. For instance, the one related to the sound imitation (Imitation game 4) requires the child to repeat the sound played on the device, either a tablet or a computer. Whereas in the building action game (Imitation game 6), the child would build an object, starting from simple cubes, in a similar way to a normal session with Lego toys. The other four games are based on JA stimuli, including the identification of objects (such as fruits, home furniture, and vehicles), described or pointed to by the therapist/parent.

The Gaming Platform

The multi-player gaming platform developed here requires two computers or tablets with an active internet connection. One computer/tablet is operated by the therapist or parent (depending upon the application scenario) acting as the *therapist/parent* and the other by the child designated as the *player*. Currently, the platform is available in three different languages (Italian, English, and French) for providing instructions to the child and the therapist/parent.

The choice of the language, the game to play as well as the goal setting is made by the therapist/parent. As instance, when playing the musical instrument game, the *therapist/parent* can select between two different goal settings: listen and recognize a sequence of (a) three or (b) six musical instruments. The role of the player is to achieve the goal set by the therapist/parent at the end of the game. In the game described above, the child will listen to a sequence of instruments and, depending on the goal selected, he will listen and recognize the sequence of three or six instruments.

TABLE 4 | Mapping of ESDM stimuli for JA and imitation into the games.

Game type	Description	ESDM stimuli
Imitation game 1: imitate free drawing	Imitation of the drawing done by the online therapist/parent	(lev.4) FM 4
Imitation game 2: imitate step by step drawing	Imitation of a drawing created step by step from the online therapist/parent (three difficulties)	(lev.4) FM 4
Imitation game 3: imitate speech	Imitation of words or phrases from the library (three difficulties)	(lev.2) IM 3, 9
Imitation game 4: imitate sounds	Imitation of sounds chosen from the library (four difficulties and two categories of stimuli)	(lev.2) IM 2
Imitation game 5: imitate actions	Imitation of the actions with balls made by the online therapist/parent (three difficulties and two types of task)	(lev.2) IM 6
Imitation game 6: imitate actions and build	Imitation of the actions with cubes made by the online therapist/parent (three difficulties and two types of task)	(lev.3) FM 3
Imitation game 7: guess the instrument	Identification of the musical instruments played and chosen by the therapist/parent from the library (two difficulties)	(lev. 1, 2) IM
Joint attention game 1: follow the therapist's pointing (both audio and visual)	Identification of the object indicated (verbally, visually or pointed) by the therapist on the video and chosen from the library (six difficulties and eight categories of stimuli)	(lev.1) RC 1, 4 (lev.2) JA 2, 4, 6
Joint attention game 2: cooperative drawing – connect dots	The therapist and the child cooperate to complete a figure shown on the right, by clicking on the corners of the figure itself (two difficulties and four categories of stimuli)	JA
Joint attention game 3: bake a cake	The child cooks a recipe by clicking and dragging into a bowl the ingredients chosen by the therapist/parent from the library of recipes (11 categories of stimuli)	JA
Joint attention game 4: receptive communication	The child identifies the objects described by the therapist/parent and chosen from the library (three difficulties and five categories of stimuli)	(lev.2) RC 5, (lev.1) RC 6, (lev.1) RC 4

FM, fine motor subset; IM, imitation subset; RC, receptive communication subset; JA, Joint Attention subset.

The games can also be categorized in (a) stand-alone operation game and (b) game requiring active co-operation between the therapist and the child. (a) The stand-alone operation games contain pre-developed libraries containing the stimuli and the instruction to achieve the goal. The imitation game 4 – Imitate Sound is an example of stand-alone game; the therapist/parent selects a list of animal's sounds to imitate: the player will listen to each sound and imitate it. (b) In the second category of games, the therapist/parent has an active role: he/she needs to cooperate with the child to achieve the goal of the game and can also create new stimuli. An example of this category is the JA game 2 – Cooperative drawing-connect dots: both therapist/parent and the child have to cooperate to connect the dots and create the final figure. Details and figures of these games can be found in the supplementary material.

All the games have different levels of difficulty allowing the therapist/parent to adjust the initial level of difficulty according to the cognitive skills identified by the therapist at the beginning of the treatment process or dynamically adjusting it as the player's performance progresses with time.

The performance of the player could be assessed mainly in two different ways: through an (a) automated evaluation based on a predefined scoring convention and through a (b) manual evaluation by the therapist/parent. (a) The automated evaluation does not require any action to the therapist/parent: the game will automatically assign a score to the performance of the child. For example, the game will assign a positive score if the child has selected the right musical instruments. (b) The manual evaluation requires to the therapist/parent to select among three different buttons: score 0 if the player did not achieve the goal, 1 for partial achievement, and 2 for successfully satisfying the goal. As instance, at the end of the imitation game 4 – Imitate Sound, the therapist/parent has to click among three buttons indicating score 0, 1, or 2. Without loss of generality, a more complicated scoring system could be programed easily according to the need of granularity to assess the achievement of the player.

Apart from the simple scores describing whether the player has achieved the goal, a set of objective metrics and an array of possible events are also extracted by the platform in an automated way. A list of such objective measurements is given in **Table 5** along with their definitions.

This set of objective metrics allows the therapist to analyze quantitatively the performance of the player in a stimulus-specific way not only at a particular time point but also the progression of the child's performance over a time window (hours, days, months, etc.) giving a holistic picture of the child's development. For example, the therapist might want to analyze if the child recognize a particular musical instruments and if this recognition becomes quicker throughout the sessions. In addition, the objective metrics allow the therapist to ascertain the appropriateness of scoring and adherence to the prescribed protocol by the parents. Such analysis could be done both online and offline by the therapist as the metrics are stored each time the player plays the game. For example, in the imitation game 1 – Free drawing, both the therapist/parent and the player's drawing are saved as well as the scores given by the parent. The therapist could then check if the parent's scores adhere to the scoring guidelines suggested by the therapist.

The gaming platform provides a flexible means for giving a reward to the player on successful completion of the goal capturing the essence of reward-based intervention. In the current version, a smiley face is shown at the end of each game in the player's device, regardless of the score obtained as a positive reinforcement that also gives an impression of feedback to the player. Such feedback is once again programmable and an appropriate reward could be set by the therapist depending on the player's motivation factors (such as playing music that the child likes, etc.).

Descriptions of the Games

At the start of the game, the main window, shown in **Figure 2** will appear on the therapist/parent's device. He/she will first

TABLE 5 | The objective metrics extracted by the gaming platform.

Measurement type	Measured metrics	Description
Automated	Name of stimulus	Type of the stimulus embedded within the game and the name of the object the player has to click or drag or draw
	Time of the stimulus	Defined by the difference $\Delta T_s = T_{ss} - T_{es}$ between a start time T_{ss} variable (the time instant the stimulus starts to be shown or played on the child's device) and an end time T_{es} variable (the time instant the stimulus is finished)
	Time of response	Defined by the difference $\Delta T_r = T_{sr} - T_{er}$ between a start time T_{sr} variable (the time instant the child starts to respond) and an end time T_{er} variable (the time instant the child complete his/her response)
	Type of response	Defined by the correctness of the child's response depending on whether the child performs action as intended by the therapist/parent (only Correct or Incorrect)
	Score of response	Assigned score to the response of the child, either 1 or 0 signifying whether the intended response has been achieved or not respectively – a more complicated scoring system could be programed
	Image of the stimulus and the response	A screenshot of the child's device obtained during imitation drawing and the action games – assisting the therapist to analyze the response further offline to ascertain the quality of response.
	Sound recording	The audio response of the player recorded during the sound and speech imitation games – allowing the therapist to check the quality of response
Manual	Therapist/parent evaluation	Defined as Complete/Partially complete/Incomplete response of the child according to the therapist/parent judgment
	Manual score	Assigned to 0/1/2 corresponding to the therapist/parent evaluation of the child's action – a more complicated scoring system could be programed

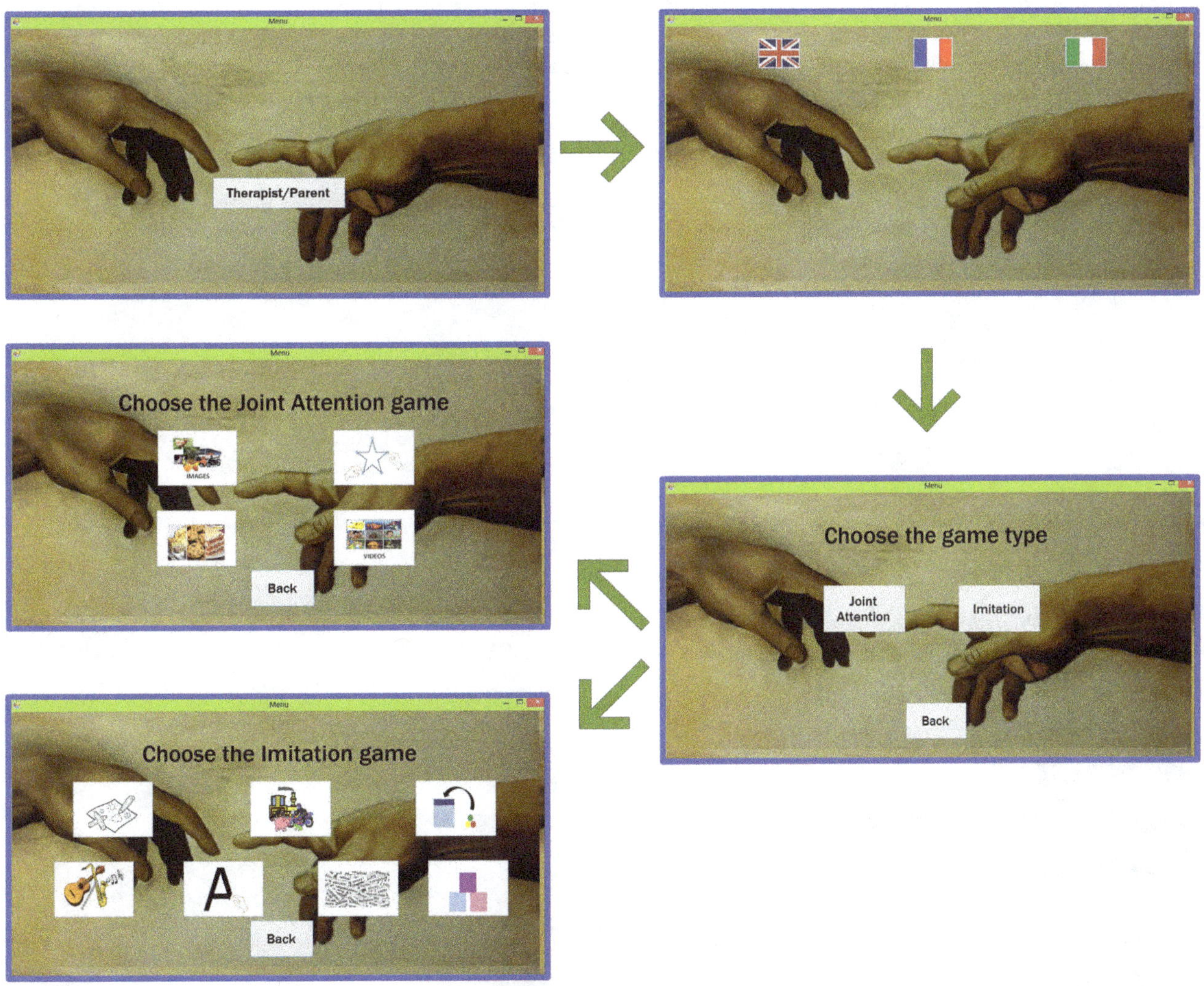

FIGURE 2 | Main windows of the therapist/parent during the beginning of the game. The therapist/parent (blue windows) will select the language, the category of the game (whether Joint Attention or Imitation), and the game, according to the category chosen.

choose the language in which the stimuli and instructions will be played. Thereafter, the therapist/parent selects the desired game that will automatically be launched on both devices.

Here, we report only the description of two games (Free drawing and Bake a recipe) and we use it to illustrate the children's performances through sessions of both Imitation and JA (a detailed description of all other games is reported on Supplementary Materials GamesDescription.doc).

Joint Attention Game 3 – Bake a Recipe

This game is targeted to cook a recipe by mixing six ingredients in a bowl, as shown in **Figure 3**. The therapist/parent selects the recipe to cook among 11 dishes from a standardized library, which includes pizza, tiramisu', lasagne, omelet, roasted chicken, pasta, etc. For each of the six ingredients, as soon as the therapist/parent clicks on it, an arrow connecting this ingredient to the bowl appears on the player's device, as shown in **Figure 3**. The player needs to drag the ingredients into the bowl. When all the ingredients have been dragged into the bowl, the player has to click on the Mix button and, finally, he/she has to choose the recipe they cooked among seven dishes.

As before, an event with positive or negative score is generated each time the player clicks on an ingredient and drags it into the bowl, as well as when the correct recipe is recognized.

Imitation Game 1 – Free Drawing

This imitation game is intended for examining the player's ability to imitate several objects drawn by the therapist/parent, starting from very basic drawings, such as scribbles and dots, to very complicated, such as letters and numbers. The whole process of this game is shown in **Figure 4**, where the blue window indicates the therapist/parent's window and the red window indicates the player's window. Once launched, a window will appear on both therapist/parent and player's device with clearly marked separate drawing panels. The therapist/parent can draw any object of any shape in the panel dedicated to him/her (on the right). Once completed, the therapist/parent's drawing appears on the player's device and the player needs to imitate that drawing in his/her dedicated panel (on the left). The live outline of the player's drawing will appear on the therapist/parent's device. Depending on whether the drawing is correct or not, the therapist/parent can decide to finish the game (by clicking on the tick button) or encourage the player to have another try (by clicking on the cross button). The quality of the imitation will be evaluated by the therapist/parent among three possibilities: correct, incorrect, or partially correct. To avoid discrepancies and to create normalization, the therapists involved in this study have reached an agreement, according to the ESDM, on how to evaluate the drawings and sounds imitation and train the parents to adhere to it.

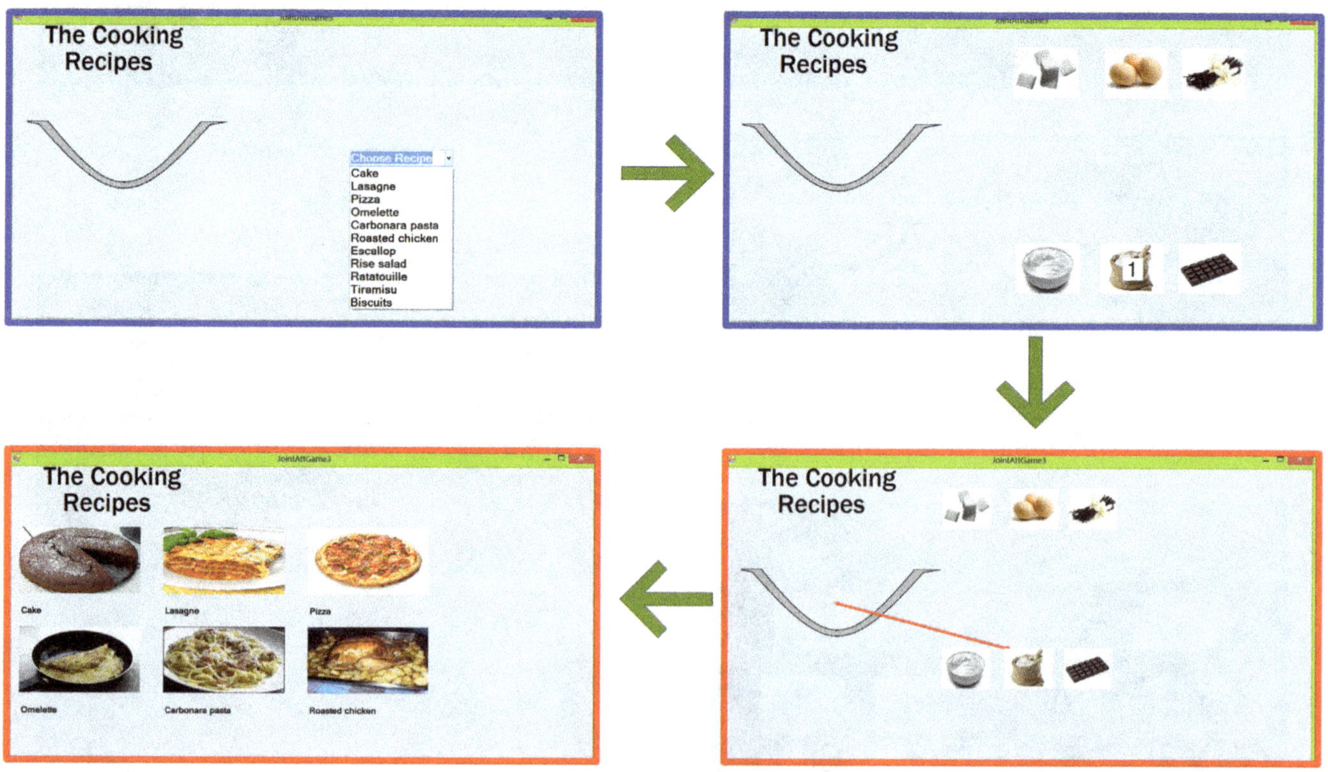

FIGURE 3 | Flow of the Joint Attention game 3 – Bake a recipe. The therapist/parent (blue windows), after selecting the recipe, will select each ingredient to be dragged into the bowl. The red arrow on the player's device (red window) will indicate the ingredient selected by the therapist/parent. After dragging all the ingredients, the player's will click on the recipe cooked.

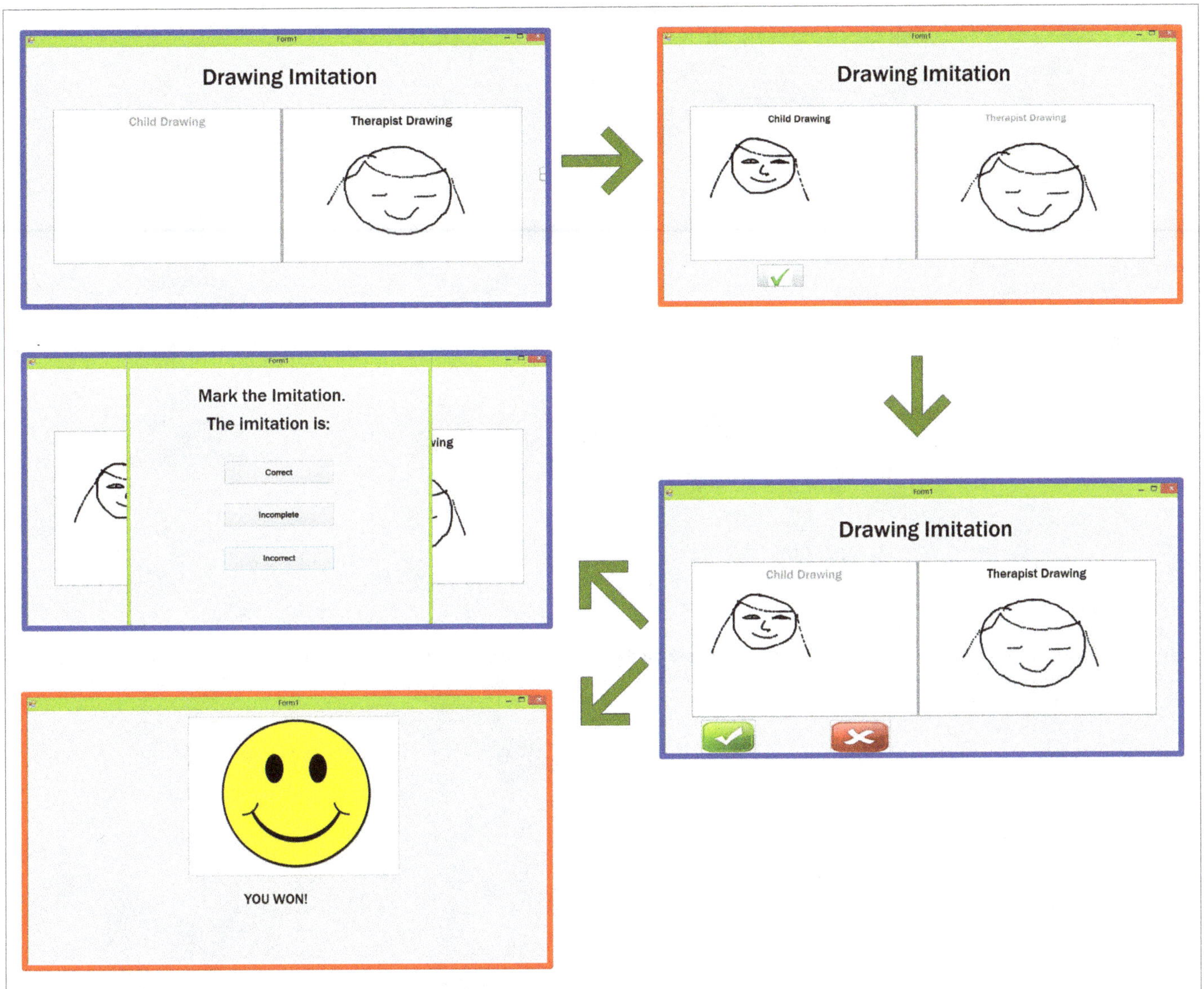

FIGURE 4 | Flow of the Imitation game 1 – Free drawing. The therapist/parent's drawing (blue window) appears on the player's window (red window) who will then imitate the drawing and send it to the therapist/parent. After the therapist/parent's feedback, the smiley will appear on the player's device, while the therapist/parent will evaluate the imitation as Correct/Incomplete/Incorrect.

RESULTS AND DISCUSSION

Validation by Testing with Children

Overall, during the study period, the children and the parents participated in 77.5% of the planned sessions at home and in 90% of the hospital sessions. All children went through all games (seven Imitation games and four JA games). Given the diversity of the games and the heterogeneity of children profile and abilities, for a given game the number of sessions dedicated to the game varied. Also given the levels of difficulty within a game, all the conditions of the games have not been exploited by the children at the end of the 3 months. All games were well tolerated and followed both by children and parents showing the robustness of the gaming platform and the feasibility of the course of the games. One family initially had troubles in using the two tablets system related to Wi-Fi connecting problems that could be easily corrected. Tailoring treatment during the hospital session and data transfer from home was easily achieved.

Children's Performance through Sessions and Games

We selected two games to illustrate the children's performances through sessions of both Imitation and JA by using either quantitative or qualitative scoring. Our goal here was to verify how meaningful the extracted scores were from each game session to follow the child's progress or difficulties.

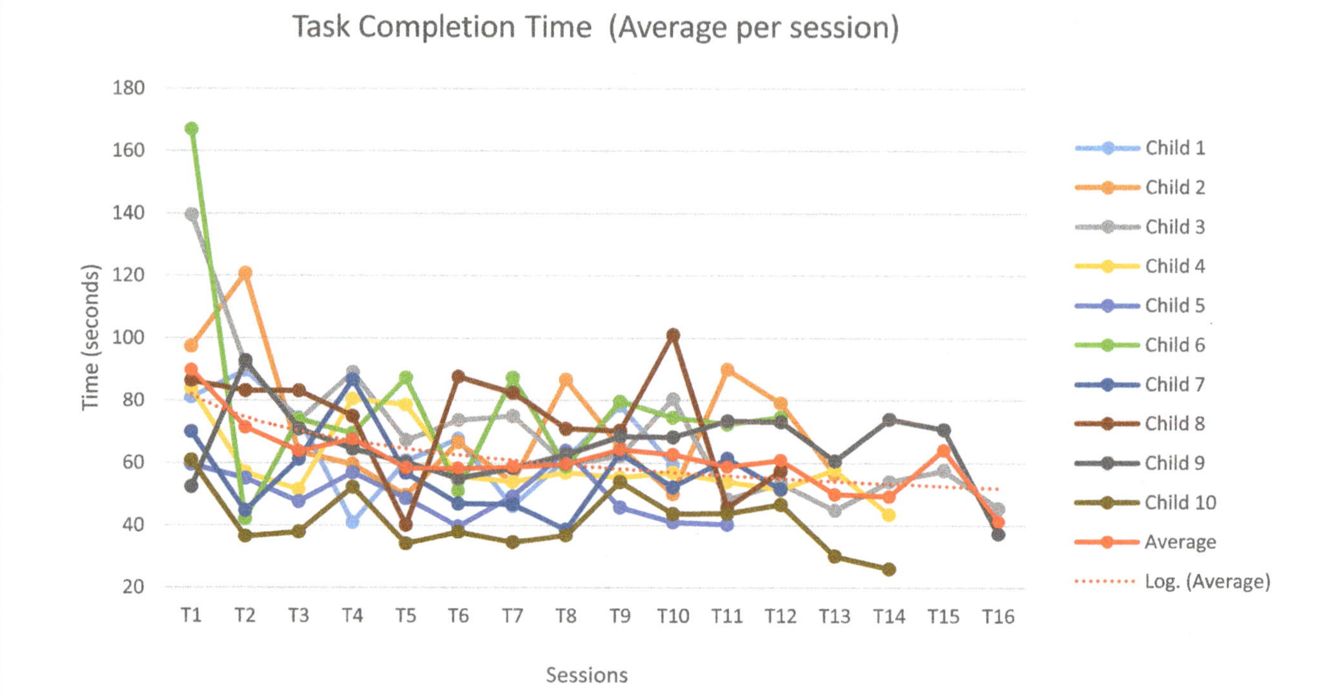

FIGURE 5 | Evolution of the time (in seconds) to complete the task for the Joint Attention game 3 – Bake a recipe. Evolution of the time occurred to complete the Joint Attention game 3 for each child (each color represents a child) across different sessions. The average across children, in dotted red, shows a decreasing trend across sessions.

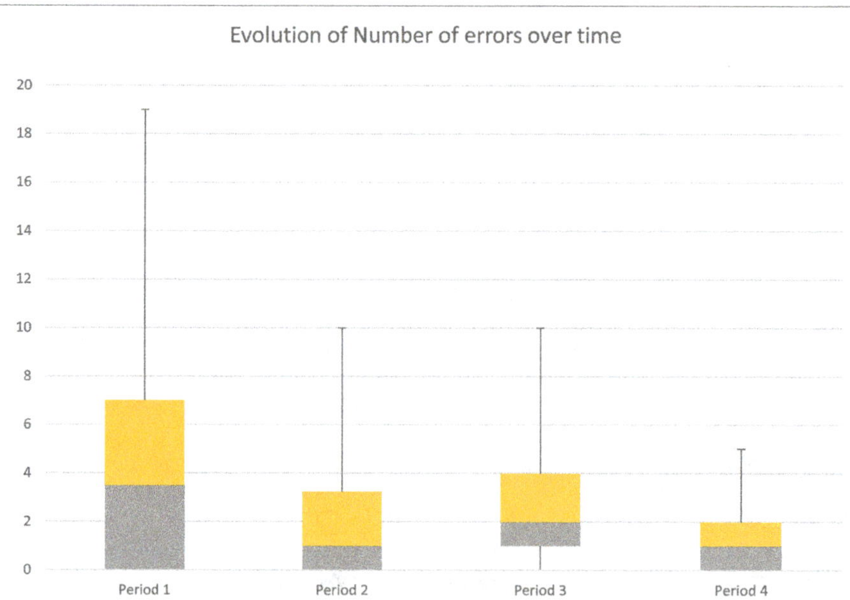

FIGURE 6 | Number of errors performed to complete the task for the Joint Attention game 3 during different periods. The figure contains the number of mistakes committed by the 10 children during the Joint Attention game 3. The total number of errors decreases across the different periods, as shown by the variability (from 19 to 5).

Bake a Recipe (Joint Attention Game 3 – Quantitative Scoring)

Figures 5 and **6** show children's performances for the JA game 3 – Bake a recipe. **Figure 5** represents the evolution of the time (in seconds) to complete the task for the JA game 3. For one session (T_i, T_{i+1} ...), completion time is averaged, as the children practice the game several times during one session. As sessions progressed over time, children become faster to achieve the task. Each line corresponds to the evolution of the task completion time across different sessions for a given child.

The red dot curve represents the evolution of task completion time averaged for all children ($N = 10$): a common overall decrease was observed in all subjects. To assess whether the task completion time significantly decreased over the sessions, we used a linear mixed model with the Log (time to complete the task) to be explained by the number of sessions as a continuous variable. The Log function was required to have a normal distribution. We found that the time to complete the task significantly decreased along sessions ($\beta = -0.021$, t-value $= -5.53$, $p < 0.001$).

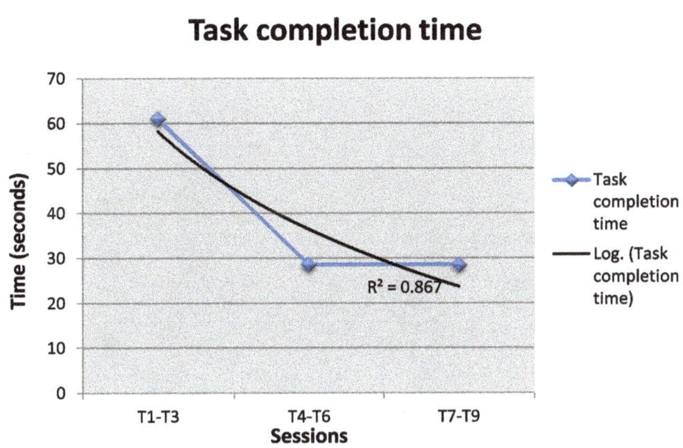

FIGURE 7 | Evolution of the time (in seconds) to complete the drawing in Imitation game 1. Evolution of the time occurred to complete the Imitation game 1 for one child across different sessions. Figure shows that the child becomes faster at reproducing the drawing model.

In parallel, the number of errors decreased also over time (**Figure 6**). For this game, the mistakes that have been taken into account are as follows: wrong and fake answers during the first "mixing ingredients" phase of the game (when the child selects the wrong ingredient or when he presses one or several wrong ingredients after selecting the correct one) and wrong answers during the "choose recipe" phase of the game (when he/she has to guess the cooked recipe). For reasons of readability of the boxplot type graph (**Figure 6**), the sessions have been grouped into four periods (period 1 = T_1, T_2, T_3, T_4; period 2 = T_5, T_6, T_7, T_8; period 3 = T_9, T_{10}, T_{11}, T_{12}; and period 4 = T_{13}, T_{14}, T_{15}, T_{16}).

According to our data, the children who had already good performances at the beginning (Period 1), kept their performances constant all along. But there is an important decrease of the number of errors per child across the four periods, particularly for the children who committed several mistakes initially. At the end (Period 4), the number of mistakes is very low for all children. To assess whether the number of errors significantly decreased over the number of sessions, we used a linear mixed model with a binomial variable (the probability of correct answers) to be explained by the number of sessions as a continuous variable. We found that the probability of correct answers significantly increased with the number of sessions ($\beta = 0.039$, z-value $= 2.78$, $p = 0.005$). In sum, for this game, the results after 3-month training are promising.

Free Drawing (Imitation Game 1 – Qualitative Scoring)

For the second game (Imitation game 1 – Free drawing), the evolution of performances is illustrated from the results of one

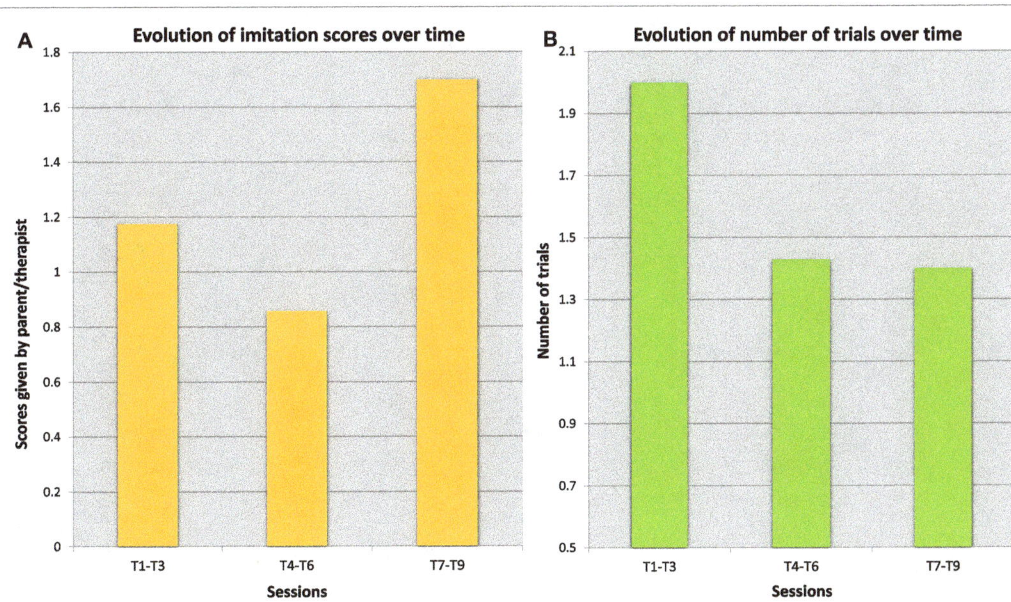

FIGURE 8 | Evolution of the performances of one child during the Imitation game 1. The error bars **(A)** describes the variations of the scores given by the therapist at hospital for different sessions. The quality of imitation improved throughout the sessions: the average score (av = 1.7) during the third period (T7–T9) is closer to the maximum score (score 2) and higher than the initial scores for the periods T1–T3 (av = 1.2), and T4–T6 (av = 0.9). The average number of trials required to complete the imitation, shown on the right **(B)**, has decreased as well across different sessions from the first period (T1–T3 with av = 2) to the next periods (T4–T6 and T7-T9 with av = 1.4).

FIGURE 9 | Evolution of the imitation skills of a child across three periods. Example of the evolution of the imitation skill for one of the children across different periods.

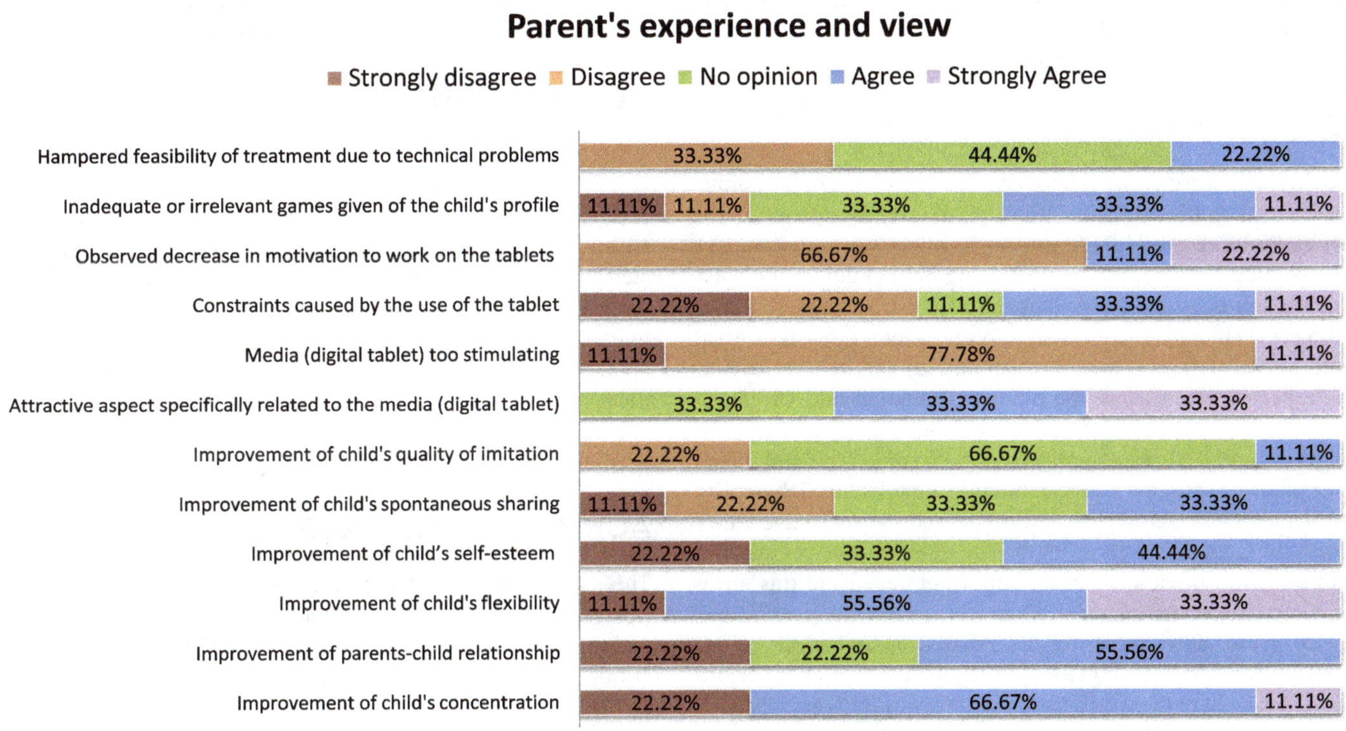

FIGURE 10 | Results related to the questionnaire proposed to the parents. Answers given by the parents of the children recruited for the study to the questionnaire containing the questions related to the use of the GOLIAH platform.

child, since the results are mainly qualitative and it is difficult to compare the drawing performances of one child with another (complexity of pictures, differences in drawing time, differences in fine motor skills, etc.).

Figure 7 shows that the child becomes faster at reproducing the drawing model ($R^2 = 0.867$). In addition, the quality of imitation improved throughout the sessions as shown by the evolution of the imitation scores (given by the therapist/parent) in **Figure 8**. The quality of the imitation is evaluated by the therapist/parent among three possibilities: correct (score 2), partially correct (score 1), and incorrect (score 0). **Figure 8A** shows that the average score (av = 1.7) during the third period (T_7–T_9) is closer to the maximum score (score 2) and different from the initial scores for the periods T_1–T_3 (av = 1.2) and T_4–T_6 (av = 0.9). Furthermore, as shown in **Figure 8B**, the child needed fewer trials to reproduce the therapist/parent's drawing. As an illustration, **Figure 9** represents the evolution of child's imitation skills in drawing across the three periods.

Parents Experience and View

At the end of the 3-month open trial, a web questionnaire was sent to the parents of children who participated in the open-trial (10 parents). The questionnaire contained 12 questions with a positive or negative orientation toward the serious game (see details at https://goo.gl/foMpPI). The questions asked about the use of the game (ease of use for parents, chosen media, technical problems, etc.) and the improvement in the child's skills (concentration, attention, imitation, self-esteem, etc.). The parents had to answer through a Likert scale from 1 to 5 (1 = strongly disagree, 2 = disagree, 3 = no opinion, 4 = agree, 5 = strongly agree). Results are summarized in **Figure 10** and show that parents have positively assessed the use of the serious game as a treatment. Sixty-seven percent of interrogated families did not observe a decrease in the child's motivation to work on tablets; 44% of them were not particularly disturbed by the constraints on daily activities caused by the use of the serious game on tablets, and 33% judged that the feasibility of treatment was not seriously hampered due to technical problems. The media (digital tablet) was not considered as too stimulating by 89% of the families and more than 67% of them thought that there was a specifically attractive aspect related to the media itself. Only one negative point was noted: 44% of the parents found that the games were inadequate given their children's profile. At the beginning of our pilot study, we were aware of this possible limitation. However, since our focus was to assess the feasibility and usability of the game, older participants were preferred because they could be more willing to collaborate and test the game.

Concerning progress on the children's skills, it seems that there is not so much progress on Imitation since the majority of the parents (67%) had no specific opinion on this topic. On the contrary, JA (spontaneous sharing) seemed to be slightly ameliorated (33% agreement). Interestingly, some skills that were not directly trained by the games strongly evolved during the course of the 3-month open trial according to parents: child's self-esteem, child's concentration, and child's flexibility. Moreover, the quality of parents–child relationship was qualified as enhanced for 56% of the parents. We could hypothesize that the interactive nature of GOLIAH and its pleasantness for the child had the effect of improving parent–child interaction also in other contexts, which is a generalization effect that often is lacking in treatments for autism.

CONCLUSION

In the current paper, we described a gaming platform for home-based intervention in ASD. Within the context of a pilot open trial, we showed the feasibility of the intervention. We found that (1) the gaming platform was useful during both children–therapist interaction at hospital as well as children–parents interaction at home, (2) tailored intervention was compatible with at home use and non-professional therapist/parents, (3) children performed as expected when using the different Imitation and JA games and no game appeared inaccurate, (4) data computed from the platform and clinical annotations produced by parents and therapists allowed session-to-session monitoring and helped therapists to dynamically reconfigure treatment, and (5) subjective views from users (mainly parents here) were overall positive. From the clinical point of view, the most important benefits of this novel method of intervention for children with autism are: (a) the rapid performance amelioration on tasks based on Imitation and JA that are considered pivotal for children with autism; (b) to create a scenario where the spontaneous, and usually lone, activity with video games is easily pushed to become a shared activity; (c) a general amelioration of attention and availability to discuss the results of a performance. Nevertheless, some limitations must be considered. First, the lack of more precise and external evaluation of improvements in Imitation and JA with specific methodology; second, a deeper analysis of the minority of parents who have signaled difficulties in applying GOLIAH is needed to individuate for which child and for which family it could be more indicated; third, in a future study, it will be important to study the gender differences than the current GOLIAH tasks and to evaluate the appropriateness of the GOLIAH tasks also with girls with ASD. Given the promising preliminary results, we are moving now within the context of FP7 MICHELANGELO project to further ascertain the efficacy of the gaming platform in the context of a bigger (N = 30) and longer (6 months) clinical trial, including a control group. Besides Imitation and JA, two cognitive skills directly targeted within the gaming platform, we plan to use external primary variables (i.e., Vineland scores and Social Communication Questionnaire) to assess generalization.

AUTHOR CONTRIBUTIONS

VB created the entire gaming platform with help from WJ and SH. KM and MW first conceptualized the gaming platform and KM coordinated the work. AN made critical evaluations of the stimuli to be selected from ESDM protocol, recruited and evaluated the children in Pisa, and ran the open trial; A-LJ adapted ESDM stimuli in serious game stimuli; JX recruited the children in Paris; ET recruited and evaluated children in Paris and ran the open trial; MC, DC, and FM provided supervision and reviewed the paper. The MICHELANGELO study group contributed to the overall project and study design, help in managing computational data and engineering issues.

ACKNOWLEDGMENTS

This work was supported by the European Commission (FP7: MICHELANGELO under grant agreement no. 288241) and the endowment fund "Entreprendre pour aider" and the Foundation "Initiative Autisme." Authors thank Nicolas Bodeau for statistical advice.

REFERENCES

1. American Psychiatric Association. *Diagnostic and Statistical Manual of Mental Disorders (4th ed., Text Revision).* Washington, DC: American Psychiatric Association (2000).
2. Dawson G, Rogers S, Munson J, Smith M, Winter J, Greenson J, et al. Randomized, controlled trial of an intervention for toddlers with autism: the Early Start Denver Model. *Pediatrics* (2010) **125**:e17. doi:10.1542/peds.2009-0958
3. Landa RJ. Diagnosis of autism spectrum disorders in the first 3 years of life. *Nat Clin Pract Neurol* (2008) **4**:138. doi:10.1038/ncpneuro0731
4. W. D. National Academy of Sciences-National Research Council. *Educating Children with Autism.* ERIC Clearinghouse. Washington, DC: National Academy Press (2001).
5. Reichow B, Wolery M. Comprehensive synthesis of early intensive behavioral interventions for young children with autism based on the UCLA young autism project model. *J Autism Dev Disord* (2009) **39**:23. doi:10.1007/s10803-008-0596-0
6. Stone WL, Yoder PJ. Predicting spoken language level in children with autism spectrum disorders. *Autism* (2001) **5**:341. doi:10.1177/1362361301005004002
7. Szatmari P, Bryson S, Boyle M, Streiner D, Duku E. Predictors of outcome among high functioning children with autism and Asperger syndrome. *J Child Psychol Psychiatry* (2003) **44**:520. doi:10.1111/1469-7610.00141
8. Picard R, Goodwin M. Developing innovative technology for future personalized autism research and treatment. *Autism Advocate* (2008) **50**:32.
9. Remington B, Hastings RP, Kovshoff H, degli Espinosa F, Jahr E, Brown T, et al. Early intensive behavioral intervention: outcomes for children with autism and their parents after two years. *Am J Ment Retard* (2007) **112**:418. doi:10.1352/0895-8017(2007)112[418:EIBIOF]2.0.CO;2
10. Johnson CP, Myers SM, American Academy of Pediatrics Council on Children With Disabilities. Identification and evaluation of children with autism spectrum disorders. *Pediatrics* (2007) **120**:1183. doi:10.1542/peds.2007-2361

11. Zwaigenbaum L, Bauman ML, Choueiri R, Fein D, Kasari C, Pierce K, et al. Early identification and interventions for autism spectrum disorder: executive summary. *Pediatrics* (2015) **136**:S1. doi:10.1542/peds.2014-3667B
12. Zwaigenbaum L, Bauman ML, Choueiri R, Kasari C, Carter A, Granpeesheh D, et al. Early intervention for children with autism spectrum disorder under 3 years of age: recommendations for practice and research. *Pediatrics* (2015) **136**:S60. doi:10.1542/peds.2014-3667E
13. Battocchi A, Pianesi F, Tomasini D, Zancanaro M, Esposito G, Venuti P, et al. *Collaborative Puzzle Game: A Tabletop Interactive Game for Fostering Collaboration in Children with Autism Spectrum Disorders (ASD)*. New York: ACM (2009). p. 197–204.
14. Cheng L, Kimberly G, Orlich F. *KidTalk: Online Therapy for Asperger's Syndrome (Technical Report No. MSR-TR-2002-08)*. Redmond, WA: Microsoft Research (2003).
15. Piper AM, O'Brien E, Morris MR, Winograd T. SIDES: a cooperative tabletop computer game for social skills development. *Proceedings of CSCW*. (2006). p. 1–10.
16. Mevarech ZR, Silber O, Fine D. Learning with computers in small groups: cognitive and affective outcomes. *J Educ Comput Res* (1991) **7**:233. doi:10.2190/BRCJ-P9K5-9E1D-2ALC
17. Moore M, Calvert S. Brief report: vocabulary acquisition for children with autism: teacher or computer instruction. *J Autism Dev Disord* (2000) **30**:359. doi:10.1023/A:1005535602064
18. Pascualvaca DM, Fantie BD, Papageorgiou M, Mirsky AF. Attentional capacities in children with autism: is there a general deficit in shifting focus? *J Autism Dev Disord* (1998) **28**:467. doi:10.1023/A:1026091809650
19. Boucenna S, Narzisi A, Tilmont E, Muratori F, Pioggia G, Cohen D, et al. Interactive technologies for autistic children: a review. *Cognit Comput* (2014) **6**:722. doi:10.1007/s12559-014-9276-x
20. Cohen D, Cassel RS, Saint-Georges C, Mahdhaoui A, Laznik M-C, Apicella F, et al. Do parentese prosody and fathers' involvement in interacting facilitate social interaction in infants who later develop autism? *PLoS One* (2013) **8**:e61402. doi:10.1371/journal.pone.0061402
21. Saint-Georges C, Mahdhaoui A, Chetouani M, Cassel RS, Laznik M-C, Apicella F, et al. Do parents recognize autistic deviant behavior long before diagnosis? Taking into account interaction using computational methods. *PLoS One* (2011) **6**:e22393. doi:10.1371/journal.pone.0022393
22. Howlin P, Moss P, Savage S, Rutter M. Social outcomes in mid-to later adulthood among individuals diagnosed with autism and average nonverbal IQ as children. *J Am Acad Child Adolesc Psychiatry* (2013) **52**:572. doi:10.1016/j.jaac.2013.02.017
23. Roux AM, Shattuck PT, Cooper BP, Anderson KA, Wagner M, Narendorf SC. Postsecondary employment experiences among young adults with an autism spectrum disorder. *J Am Acad Child Adolesc Psychiatry* (2013) **52**:931. doi:10.1016/j.jaac.2013.05.019
24. Narzisi A, Muratori F, Calderoni S, Fabbro F, Urgesi C. Neuropsychological profile in high functioning autism spectrum disorders. *J Autism Dev Disord* (2013) **43**:1895. doi:10.1007/s10803-012-1736-0
25. Ospina MB, Seida JK, Clark B, Karkhaneh M, Hartling L, Tjosvold L, et al. Behavioural and developmental interventions for autism spectrum disorder: a clinical systematic review. *PLoS One* (2008) **3**:e3755. doi:10.1371/journal.pone.0003755
26. Thorndike EL. Animal intelligence: an experimental study of the associative processes in animals. *Psychol Monogr* (1898) **2**(4):1–109. doi:10.1037/h0092987
27. Toth K, Munson J, Meltzoff AN, Dawson G. Early predictors of communication development in young children with autism spectrum disorder: joint attention, imitation, and toy play. *J Autism Dev Disord* (2006) **36**:993. doi:10.1007/s10803-006-0137-7
28. Wallon H. *De l'acte à la pensée*. Paris: Flammarion (1942).
29. Whiten A, Ham R. On the nature and evolution of imitation in the animal kingdom: reappraisal of a century of research. *Adv Study Behav* (1992) **21**:239. doi:10.1016/S0065-3454(08)60146-1
30. Nadel J. Does imitation matter to children with autism? In: Rogers SJ, Williams JHG, editors. *Imitation and the Social Mind*. New York: Guilford Press (2006). p. 118–37.
31. Emery N. The eyes have it: the neuroethology, function and evolution of social gaze. *Neurosci Biobehav Rev* (2000) **24**:581. doi:10.1016/S0149-7634(00)00025-7
32. Tomasello M. Joint attention as social cognition. In: Moore C, Dunham PJ, editors. *Joint Attention: Its Origins and Role in Development*. Hillsdale, NJ: Lawrence Erlbaum Associates (1995). p. 103–30.
33. Carpenter M, Nagell K, Tomasello M. Social cognition, joint attention, and communicative competence from 9 to 15 months of age. *Monogr Soc Res Child Dev* (1998) **63**:1–143. doi:10.2307/1166214
34. Rogers SJ, Dawson G. *Early Start Denver Model Curriculum Checklist for Young Children with Autism*. New York: Guilford Press (2009).
35. Maestro S, Muratori F, Cavallaro MC, Pecini C, Cesari A, Paziente A, et al. How young children treat objects and people: an empirical study of the first year of life in autism. *Child Psychiatry Hum Dev* (2005) **35**:383. doi:10.1007/s10578-005-2695-x
36. Saint-Georges C, Cassel RS, Cohen D, Chetouani M, Laznik M-C, Maestro S, et al. What studies of family home movies can teach us about autistic infants: a literature review. *Res Autism Spectr Disord* (2010) **4**:355. doi:10.1016/j.rasd.2009.10.017
37. Dominey PF, Dodane C. Indeterminacy in language acquisition: the role of child directed speech and joint attention. *J Neurolinguistics* (2004) **17**:121. doi:10.1016/S0911-6044(03)00056-3
38. Premack D, Woodruff G. Does the chimpanzee have a theory of mind? *Behav Brain Sci* (1978) **1**:515. doi:10.1017/S0140525X00076512
39. Smith M, Rogers S, Dawson G. The Early Start Denver Model: a comprehensive early intervention approach for toddlers with autism. In: Handelman S, Harris SL, editors. *Preschool Education Programs for Children with Autism*. (3rd ed). Austin, TX: Pro-Ed Corporation, Inc. (2008). p. 65–101.
40. Dawson G, Jones EJ, Merkle K, Venema K, Lowy R, Faja S, et al. Early behavioral intervention is associated with normalized brain activity in young children with autism. *J Am Acad Child Adolesc Psychiatry* (2012) **51**:1150. doi:10.1016/j.jaac.2012.08.018
41. Rogers SJ, Dawson G. *Early Start Denver Model for Young Children with Autism: Promoting Language, Learning, and Engagement*. New York: Guilford Press (2010).
42. Rogers S, Dawson G, Vismara L. *An Early Start for Your Child with Autism*. New York: Guilford Press (2012).

17

Paternal HLA-C and Maternal Killer-cell Immunoglobulin-Like Receptor Genotypes in the Development of Autism

*Moriya Gamliel[1], Karen L. Anderson[2], Richard P. Ebstein[3], Nurit Yirmiya[4] and David Mankuta[2]**

[1] *Department of Immunology and Cancer Research, Hadassah-Hebrew University Medical Center, Jerusalem, Israel,* [2] *Department of Obstetrics and Gynecology, Hadassah-Hebrew University Medical Center, Jerusalem, Israel,* [3] *Department of Psychology, National University of Singapore, Singapore,* [4] *Department of Psychology, The Hebrew University of Jerusalem, Jerusalem, Israel*

Edited by:
Benjamin Gesundheit, Cell El Ltd., Israel

Reviewed by:
Munis Dundar, Erciyes University, Turkey
Ganesan Venkatasubramanian, National Institute of Mental Health and Neurosciences, India

Correspondence:
David Mankuta
mankutad@gmail.com

Killer-cell immunoglobulin-like receptors (KIRs) are a family of cell surface proteins found on natural killer cells, which are components of the innate immune system. KIRs recognize MHC class I proteins, mainly HLA-C and are further divided into two groups: short-tailed 2/3DS activating receptors and long-tailed 2/3DL inhibitory receptors. Based on the Barker Hypothesis, the origins of illness can be traced back to embryonic development in the uterus, and since KIR:HLA interaction figures prominently in the maternal–fetal interface, we investigated whether specific KIR:HLA combinations may be found in autism spectrum disorders (ASD) children compared with their healthy parents. This study enrolled 49 ASD children from different Israeli families, and their healthy parents. Among the parents, a higher frequency of HLA-C2 allotypes was found in the fathers, while its corresponding ligand 2DS1 was found in higher percentage in the maternal group. However, such skewing in KIR:HLA frequencies did not appear in the ASD children. Additionally, analysis of "overall activation" indicated higher activation in maternal than in paternal cohorts.

Keywords: autism, pregnancy, natural killer, KIR, HLA

INTRODUCTION

Autism spectrum disorders (ASD) encompass a range of neurodevelopmental syndromes defined by difficulties in social communication and stereotyped behaviors (1). Recent data indicate a prevalence of up to 1 in 66 children (2). Although studies in families and twins (3) point toward a significant genetic component with a high sibling recurrence risk (4), in only a few cases can a clear genetic component be identified. Various factors – hormonal, immunological, and biochemical – have been implicated in autism's etiology, but their roles in the symptomology of the disease remain undefined (5). Immune system dysregulation reported in ASD patients includes differential cell fractions and reactivity, autoimmune phenomena, altered cytokine and antibody profiles, and genetic correlations (6). These findings partially corroborate the theory that chronic neurological inflammation in fetal or newborn brain underlies the development of ASD. Subsequent dysregulation of the immune system may contribute to ASD development in genetically susceptible children.

Abbreviations: ASD, autism spectrum disorders; HLA, histocompatibility leukocyte antigens; KIR, killer-cell immunoglobulin-like receptor; NK, natural killer.

Altered natural killer (NK) cell activity has been reported in the periphery of ASD patients (7). However, these innate immune cells' function in the pathogenesis of autism is yet unclear. NK cells act specifically against infected or transformed cells, with their actions governed by a balance between activating and inhibitory receptors, each recognizing specific molecules on a given target (8). Killer-cell immunoglobulin-like receptors (KIRs) are a group of cell surface molecules involved in regulating activity of NK (and some T) cells. KIRs are classified as either inhibitory or activating. Their nomenclature is based on the number of extracellular Ig-like domains, and whether the cytoplasmic domain is *long* (L) or *short* (S). The KIR gene family is clustered within the LRC leukocyte receptor complex on chromosome 19q13.4, encoding a total of 14 genes and 2 pseudo genes. KIR genes exhibit allelic and haplotypic variability, while each mature NK cell expresses a specific set of KIRs.

Killer-cell immunoglobulin-like receptor counterparts, the HLA class I ligands, are also extremely polymorphic. This generates an additional level of functional diversity. Both KIRs and their HLA ligands are encoded on different chromosomes (19 and 6, respectively), and therefore segregate independently of each other. This expands the repertoire of possible profiles within any given population (9). Specific KIR–HLA combinations have been suggested as underlying susceptibility as well as resistance to various diseases and conditions (10); the functional implications are less clear. Genetic associations have been reported in infectious diseases (11), autoimmunity (12), inflammatory conditions, reproductive failure, and cancer. Biological models in such studies need to incorporate these receptor:ligand interactions, beyond mere consideration of KIR–HLA genotyping. Indeed, several methods have been proposed to analyze the overall genotyping detected in a specific subject or whole population (13, 14).

The KIR family predominantly recognizes HLA class I molecules. Specifically, HLA-C is recognized by both inhibitory receptors (KIRs 2DL1, 2DL2, and 2DL3) and activating receptors (KIRs 2DS1, 2DS2, and 2DS4) (**Figure 1**). HLA-C group 1 (C1) allotypes have an asparagine residue at position 80 (C1:N[80]), and serve as ligands for KIRs 2DL2, 2DL3, and 2DS2. HLA-C group 2 (C2) allotypes function as ligands for KIRs 2DL1 and 2DS1; C2 allotypes have a lysine at position 80 (C2:K[80]). The interactional affinities of these groups may differ. KIR 2DS4 can bind to both HLA-C C1 and C2 allotypes, and certain HLA-A alleles. KIRs 3DL1 and (putatively) 3DS1 interact with HLA-A BW4:I80 as well as HLA-B allotypes [with either isoleucine (BW4:I80) or threonine (BW4:T80) at position 80].

The aim of our research was to genotype the KIR receptors known to interact with HLA ligands in autistic children and their non-autistic parents (mothers and fathers, separately), and to compare KIR receptor: HLA ligand frequencies between these groups. Our hypothesis was that a non-random distribution of these genes profiles should be found if interactions between these two classes of molecules are relevant to autism.

According to the Barker Hypothesis (15), the source of pathologies – including mental disorders such as ASD – can be traced back to embryonic existence in the intrauterine environment (16, 17). KIRs are expressed by maternal NK cells (decidua, uterine lining), which are in close contact with HLA-expressing fetal tissues (placenta). Such prenatal interaction between maternal KIR and the fetal HLA in the uterus may lead to either enhanced NK activation or NK inhibition, which in turn may exert influence upon the placenta and/or developing fetus (18–20). Resulting immune activation and effects upon the central nervous system may lead to neurological and psychiatric disorders in predisposed patients. A mouse model for intrauterine maternal immune activation has already been demonstrated as a possible mechanism for autism- and schizophrenia-related behaviors in offspring (21).

MATERIALS AND METHODS

Participants

This study comprised of 49 ASD-diagnosed children (38 males, 11 females, a male:female ratio of 3.4:1) from Jewish Israeli families, and their parents. Another six sets of parents of ASD-diagnosed children were enrolled, though no DNA samples were available from their children. DNA samples were collected in Israeli special education schools and treatment centers, by the Israeli Society for Autistic Children (ALUT).[1]

Many of the probands had already been diagnosed with ASD by independent clinicians; two trained clinicians confirmed the

[1] http://www.autismaroundtheglobe.org/countries/Israel.asp

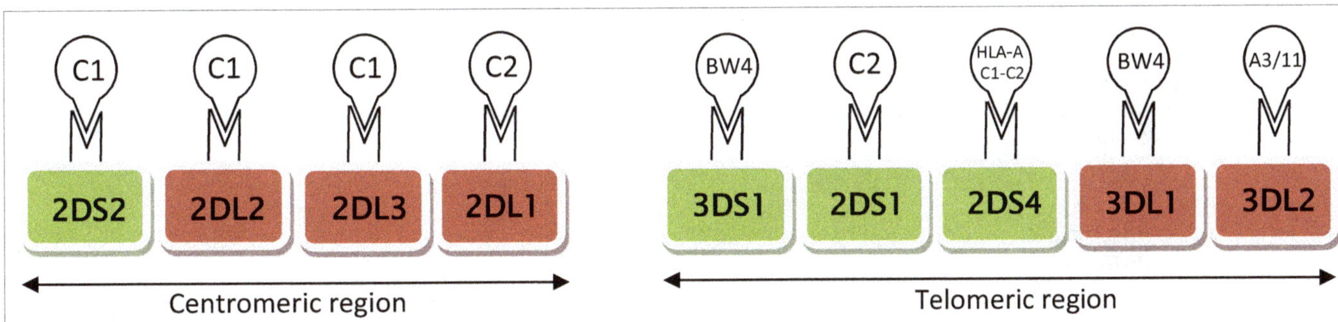

FIGURE 1 | Schematic diagram of activating (green) and inhibitory (red) receptors on natural killer cells, arranged according to centromic/telomeric location. These receptors are known to interact specifically with HLA ligands (HLA Cl or C2, HLA A and B BW4). HLA-C group 1 (Cl) allotypes serve as ligands for KIRs 2DS2, 2DL2, and 2DL3; HLA-C group 2 (C2) functions as ligands for KIRs 2DL1 and 2DS1.

diagnosis for autism or Pervasive Developmental Disorder-Not Otherwise Specified (PDD-NOS). All probands were diagnosed using the Autism Diagnostic Observation Scale-Generic (ADOS-G) and the Autism Diagnostic Interview-Revised (ADI-R). In addition, parents were interviewed using the Vineland Adaptive Behavior Scales-second edition (Vineland™-II) survey interview edition (VABS).

Probands ranged in age between 25 months to 33 years and 8 months. None of the subjects were known, according to parental reports, to have known genetic factors such as chromosomal aberrations, tuberous sclerosis, or other medical complications that could be related to autism. Parents were screened for psychiatric illness (including ASD); all results were found to be negative.

The Ethics Committee of the Israeli Health Ministry approved this study. All participants signed informed consent forms in advance.

Genotyping

DNA was extracted from either peripheral blood or buccal cells using a commercial DNA purification kit (Epicentre's Master Pure™, Madison, WI, USA).

The presence or absence of nine KIR genes known to interact with specific HLA ligands was determined by SSP-PCR (sequence-specific primer polymerase chain reaction), as previously described (22, 23), using nine pairs of primers specific for these KIR genes. This mapping enables verification of presence or absence of a KIR, without discriminating specific heterozygous or homozygote status. A 440/750-bp fragment of the CRP/CAMP, respectively, was included in each PCR as an internal control. The following KIR genes were amplified under identical conditions: 2DL2, 2DL1, 3DL1, 2DS2, 2DS4, and 3DS1. Their PCR thermo-profile comprised 2 min at 92°C; then 25 s at 91°C, 45 s at 65°C, and 45 s at 72°C for 4 cycles; 25 s at 91°C, 45 s at 60°C, and 45 s at 72°C for 26 cycles; 25 s at 91°C, 60 s at 55°C, and 45 s at 72°C for 5 cycles, and 10 min at 72°C (an extension step, in the case of 3DL1 and 3DS1 was set to 2 min). Other KIR amplifications (for 2DL3, 3DL2, and 2DS1) were initiated with denaturation for 2 min at 92°C; then 25 s at 91°C, 45 s at 57°C, and 45 s at 72°C for 4 cycles; 25 s at 91°C, 45 s at 54°C, and 45 s at 72°C for 26 cycles; 25 s at 91°C, 60 s at 50°C, and 45 s at 72°C for 5 cycles, and 10 min at 72°C. All primer sequences, expected PCR products and allelic recoveries are listed in **Table 1**.

The distinction of HLA-C KIR ligand groups C1 (N^{80}) and C2 (K^{80}) was also performed by SSP-PCR. The common HLA-C forward primer was either paired with the C1 (N^{80}) or C2 (K^{80}) reverse primers, leading to an amplification product of 139 bp (**Table 2**). This mapping enables discrimination between heterozygous/homozygous status, i.e., C1–C1, C1–C2, or C2–C2. In each HLA PCR reaction, a 440-bp fragment of the CRP gene was included as an internal PCR control. The thermo-profile comprised an initial denaturation of 3 min at 95°C; then 10 s at 95°C, 30 s at 65°C, and 45 s at 72°C for 10 cycles; 10 s at 95°C, 30 s at 58°C, 45 s at 72°C for 22 cycles, and 10 min at 72°C.

For HLA-C protocol validation, selected samples (n = 30; 10 homozygous C1/C1, 10 homozygous C2/C2 and 10 heterozygous C1/C2) that had previously been typed for HLA-C at high resolution by LIFECODES® HLA SSO Typing Kit (Gen-Probe, Inc.) (Later sequenced by Allele SEQR® HLA PCR/Sequencing Kit, Abbott Molecular) were analyzed by our SSP-PCR.

HLA-A BW4 and HLA-B BW4-I^{80}/T^{80} were identified under the same conditions as HLA-C. Validation for HLA-A and B was also performed by selected samples previously genotyped by high

TABLE 1 | KIR genotyping primers.

KIR	Forward primers (5′–3′) / Reverse primers (5′–3′)	Amplicon (bp)	Annealing temp (°C)	Control gene	Alleles not detected
2DS2	CGGGCCCCACGGTTT GGTCACTCGAGTTTGACCACTCA	240	60	CRP	
2DS4	TAGGCTCCCTGCAGTGCG GAGTTTGACCACTCGTAGGGAGC	129	63	CAMP	2DS4*003 2DS4*004 2DS4*006 2DS4*007 2DS4*009
2DS1	CTTCTCCATCAGTCGCAT AGGGTCACTGGGAGCTGACAA	102	53	CAMP	
3DS1	GCCCAGCGCTGTGGTGCCTCGC CTGCAAGGGCACGCATCATGGA	1958	71	CAMP	3DS1*047
2DL2	CTGGCCCACCCAGGTCG GGACCGATGGAGAAGTTGGCT	173	60	CRP	2DL2*004
2DL1	AACTTCTCCATCAGTCGCATGAC GGTCACTGGGAGCTGACAC	100	60	CRP	
2DL3	CTTCATCGCTGGTGCTG AGGCTCTTGGTCCATTACAA	516	54	CAMP	2DL3*007
3DL1	CTCCATCGGTCCCATGATGCT CGCTCTCTCCTGCCTGAACCT	1725	65	CAMP	
3DL2	CCCATGAACGTAGGCTCCG CACACGCAGGGCAGGG	130	54	CRP	

Expected PCR products, annealing temperature (°C), and allelic specificity are given per pair of primers. Primer reference is (22) for all KIRs except 2DS1, for which the primer reference is (23).

resolution methods. All primer sequences [based on Hong et al. (23)] and expected PCR products for HLA-A, -B, and -C genotyping are listed in **Table 2**.

All amplified SSP-PCR products were visualized by agarose gel electrophoresis using a non-mutagenic fluorescent reagent ("Novel Juice"; GeneDireX, Las Vegas City, NV, USA). Selected sample from each amplified band was sent for sequencing.

Statistical Analysis

The Wilcoxon Signed-Ranks test ($p < 0.05$) was determined using SPSS software. When combination of more than one factor to specific receptor was detected, some different aspects were detected. The first refers to all ligands equally, and compares the sum of all ligands (relevant to specific receptor) found in each person to determine the mean value. This is defined as "Ligand Composite" (**Table 7**). Secondly, an alternative designation of "Ligand One+" compares existence of at least one ligand to this specific receptor. This was the case in C1 + 2DL2/2DL3/2DS2, C2 + 2DL1/2DS1 (**Table 8**). In contrast, for overall signaling (**Table 9**) and in the case of A_BW4 + 3DL1/3DS1 and B_BW4 + 3DL1/3DS1 (**Table 7**) only the first option is shown. All HLAB genotyping analysis is described as "total," meaning having I^{80}/T^{80}.

RESULTS

HLA and KIRs Frequency Comparison

Comparison of the nine different KIR genes and HLA frequencies revealed several main differences between parents of autistic children (**Tables 3–5**).

The most surprising finding is higher frequency of HLA-C2 allotypes in fathers of ASD children (mean 0.73 vs. 0.52, $p = 0.038$), in contrast to C1 frequencies, which were the same in both mothers and fathers (0.88 vs. 0.91) (**Table 5**). On the other hand, 2DS1, which is known to interact specifically with HLA-C2, was found in higher percentage (0.55 vs. 0.34, $p = 0.022$) in the maternal group (**Table 4**). Additionally 3DS1, with its specificity against BW4 allotypes, was found to be higher in mothers than in their ASD children (0.51 vs. 0.36, $p = 0.044$) (**Table 4**). Other KIR frequencies (2DL2, 2DL1, 2DL3, 3DL1, 3DL2, 2DS2, and 2DS4) were similar in both mothers and fathers, and corresponded with values expected in Asian populations.[2] Most KIR and HLA frequencies in ASD children were similar to those detected in parents.

Positive correlation between parent (mother or father) and child, reflecting the likelihood of transferring the gene (**Tables 3–5**) were found relative to most of genes, which may reflect a high probability of homozygous genotyping for these genes.

KIR Signaling Through HLA Molecules

Relevant combinations between KIR receptors and their specific HLA ligands were detected (**Table 6**). ASD children did not exhibit

[2] http://www.allelefrequencies.net/kir6008a.asp

TABLE 2 | PCR primers for human leukocyte antigen (HLA) amplification.

HLA allotype	Direction	Forward primers (5′–3′) / Reverse primers (5′–3′)	Amplicon (bp)
HLA-C	Forward	CGCCGCGAGTCCGAGAGG	139
	Reverse (C1: N^{80})	GTTGTAGTAGCCGCGCAGG	
	Reverse (C2: K^{80})	GTTGTAGTAGCCGCGCAGT	
HLA-A	Forward	CCATTGGGTGTCGGGTTTC	569
BW4:I^{80}	Reverse	CTCTGGTTGTAGTAGCGGAGCGCG	
HLA-B	Forward	ACCCGGACTCAGAATCTCC	366
BW4:I^{80}	Reverse	CTCTGGTTGTAGTAGCGGAGCGCG	
HLA-B	Forward	ACCCGGACTCAGAATCTCC	369
BW4:T^{80}	Reverse	CTCTGGTTGTAGTAGCGGAGCAGG	

Expected PCR product sizes are given. In the case of HLA-C, forward primer was either paired with the C1 (N^{80}) or C2 (K^{80}) reverse primers, leading to an amplification product of 139 bp.
F, forward; R, reverse.

TABLE 3 | Inhibitory KIR frequencies in Israeli families with at least 1 ASD-diagnosed child.

Inhibitory KIR		Child^{ASD}	Father	Child^{ASD}	Mother	Father	Mother
2DL2	Mean	0.59	0.63	0.58	0.66	0.64	0.68
	Z	−0.577		−0.894		−0.408	
	Pearson's *r*	0.487*		0.204		NR	
2DL1	Mean	0.96	0.98	0.96	0.96	0.98	0.95
	Z	−1		0		−1	
	Pearson's *r*	0.7*		−0.039		NR	
2DL3	Mean	0.86	0.84	0.87	0.89	0.84	0.88
	Z	−0.302		−0.333		−0.535	
	Pearson's *r*	0.135		0.212		NR	
3DL1	Mean	0.94	0.94	0.94	0.89	0.93	0.89
	Z	0		−1.342		−0.707	
	Pearson's *r*	0.645*		0.428*		NR	
3DL2	Mean	1	1	1	1	1	1
	Z	0		0		0	
	Pearson's *r*	NR		NR		NR	

Z = Wilcoxon Signed-Ranks Test value.
NR = not relevant.
$^{*}p \leq 0.01$.

TABLE 4 | Activating KIR frequencies in Israeli families with at least 1 ASD-diagnosed child.

Activating KIR		Child^{ASD}	Father	Child^{ASD}	Mother	Father	Mother
2DS2	Mean	0.61	0.63	0.6	0.62	0.64	0.66
	Z	−0.302		−0.209		−0.209	
	Pearson's *r*	0.523**		0.086		NR	
2DS4	Mean	0.96	0.96	0.94	0.89	0.94	0.91
	Z	0		−1.342		−0.707	
	Pearson's *r*	0.478**		0.428**		NR	
2DS1	Mean	0.51	0.37	0.49	0.57	0.34	0.55
	Z	−1.528		−1.069		−2.268*	
	Pearson's *r*	0.154		0.478**		NR	
3DS1	Mean	0.37	0.39	0.36	0.51	0.39	0.5
	Z	−0.728		−2*		−1.279	
	Pearson's *r*	0.281*		0.419**		NR	

Z = Wilcoxon Signed-Ranks Test value.
NR = not relevant.
$^{*}p \leq 0.05$.
$^{**}p \leq 0.01$.

TABLE 5 | HLA ligand frequencies in Israeli families with at least 1 ASD-diagnosed child.

HLA Ligand		Child^{ASD}		Father	Child^{ASD}		Mother	Father		Mother
HLAC1	Mean	0.86		0.9	0.83		0.85	0.88		0.91
	Z		−0.707			−0.333			−0.577	
	Pearson's *r*		0.248			0.371**			NR	
HLAC2	Mean	0.65		0.72	0.68		0.57	0.73		0.52
	Z		−0.535			−1.342			−2.058*	
	Pearson's *r*		0.353**			0.214			NR	
HLA-A-BW4	Mean	0.33		0.37	0.3		0.28	0.36		0.3
	Z		−0.577			−0.229			−0.557	
	Pearson's *r*		0.462**			0.134			NR	
HLA-B-BW4	Mean	0.88		0.86	0.88		0.81	0.87		0.8
	Z		0.33			1.272			1	
	Pearson's *r*		0.203			0.248*			NR	

Z = Wilcoxon Signed-Ranks Test value.
NR = not relevant.
$^{*}p \leq 0.05$.
$^{**}p \leq 0.01$.

TABLE 6 | Frequency of each KIR detected and its corresponding ligand in Israeli ASD families, consisting of both parents and an ASD-diagnosed child.

KIR		Child^{ASD} – Father	Child^{ASD} – Mother	Father – Mother
2DL2 + C1	*Z*	−0.832	−1.342	−1.177
	Pearson's *r*	0.474**	0.259	NR
2DL1 + C2	*Z*	−0.535	−1.091	−1.859
	Pearson's *r*	0.372**	0.176	NR
2DL3 + C1	*Z*	0	0	−0.426
	Pearson's *r*	0.227	0.321*	NR
3DL1 + A_BW4	*Z*	−0.227	−0.243	−0.392
	Pearson's *r*	0.148	0.156	NR
3DL1 + B_BW4	*Z*	−0.302	−1.941*	−1.225
	Pearson's *r*	0.283*	0.359**	NR
2DS2 + C1	*Z*	−0.577	−0.853	−1
	Pearson's *r*	0.511**	0.174	NR
2DS4 + A_BW4	*Z*	−0.577	−0.243	−0.6
	Pearson's *r*	0.393**	0.156	NR
2DS4 + B_BW4	*Z*	−0.302	−1.941*	−1.279
	Pearson's *r*	0.211	0.359**	NR
2DS1 + C2	*Z*	−0.243	−0.775	−0.784
	Pearson's *r*	0.132	0.345**	NR
3DS1 + A_BW4	*Z*	0	−0.577	−0.535
	Pearson's *r*	0.456**	0.12	NR
3DS1 + B_BW4	*Z*	−0.728	−1.414	−0.853
	Pearson's *r*	0.25	0.295*	NR

Z = Wilcoxon Signed-Ranks Test value.
NR, not relevant.
$^{*}p \leq 0.05$.
$^{**}p \leq 0.01$.

high frequency of the combination HLA-C2 + KIR2DS1, despite elevated paternal HLA-C2 and maternal 2DS1 frequencies.

Correlational analysis between parent (mother or father) and child reflected the likelihood of transferring a gene with its corresponding ligand. Significant values were reported in most cases (**Table 6**). It is important to mention, these gene families are located on different autosomal chromosomes, supporting homozygous status for most of the genes.

The next evaluation involves the examination of particular HLA ligands with presence/absence of all relevant activating/inhibitory KIR genes (**Table 7**). "Ligand Composite" analysis (see Materials and Methods) was compared between ASD children and their parents, as well as "Ligand One+" values (**Table 8**). Significant differences were found between parental groups in the case of C2 + 2DL1/2DS1 "Ligand One+" ($p = 0.040$).

Overall Balance of Activation and Inhibition

Final analysis (**Table 9**) presents a full view of the genotyping. It may allow insight to the overall expected interaction of KIR/HLA in Israeli autistic individuals and their non-autistic parents,

TABLE 7 | Comparison of particular HLA ligands with presence/absence of all relevant activating/inhibitory KIR genes in Israeli ASD families.

Ligand composite		Child^{ASD} Father	Child^{ASD} Mother	Father Mother
C1 + 2DL2/2DL3/2DS2	*Z*	−0.363	−0.779	−1.178
C2 + 2DL1/2DS1	*Z*	−0.213	−0.288	−0.704
A_BW4 + 3DL1/3DS1	*Z*	−0.216	−0.378	−0.429
B_BW4 + 3DL1/3DS1	*Z*	−0.382	−0.177	−0.28

Z = Wilcoxon Signed-Ranks Test value.

TABLE 8 | Interactions of KIR and HLA in autistic Israeli patients and their parents, based on overall genotype mapping.

Ligand one+		Child^{ASD} Father	Child^{ASD} Mother	Father Mother
C1 + 2DL2/2DL3/2DS2	*Z*	−0.707	−0.333	−0.577
C2 + 2DL1/2DS1	*Z*	−0.535	−1.342	−2.058*

Z = Wilcoxon Signed-Ranks Test value.
**$p \leq 0.05$.*

TABLE 9 | Overall ligand and interaction summaries.

		Child^{ASD}		Father	Child^{ASD}		Mother	Father		Mother
KIRs: activating	Mean	2.4043		2.3191	2.3962		2.5849	2.2593		2.6667
	Pearson's *r*		0.331*			0.274*			0.104	
	t-Test		0.443			−1.121			−2.015*	
KIRs: inhibitory	Mean	4.3469		4.3878	4.3585		4.3962	4.4		4.3818
	Pearson's *r*		0.229			−0.023			0.153	
	t-Test		−0.362			−0.286			0.155	
Interactions: activating	Mean	1.9149		1.9787	1.9245		2.0377	1.9259		2.1111
	Pearson's *r*		0.216			0.142			−0.119	
	t-Test		−0.308			−0.636			−0.778	
Interactions: inhibitory	Mean	2.6939		2.7959	2.6981		2.6038	2.8214		2.6607
	Pearson's *r*		0.272			0.114			−0.099	
	t-Test		−0.647			0.582			0.903	

**$p \leq 0.05$.*
***$p \leq 0.01$.*

based on all genotype mapping. Mothers have significantly higher levels of activating signals than their male counterparts ($p = 0.049$).

DISCUSSION

Despite the increased attention garnered by autism research in recent years, the condition is currently diagnosed only after the infant reaches 2 or 3 years of age. Findings in autistic patients indicate multifactorial inheritance, while definitive genetic factors can be diagnosed in only a small percentage of cases. Immunological studies revealed a unique and distinguishing profile in ASD patients compared to controls. In the context of NK cells, altered gene expression, absolute number and function have been reported (7, 24, 25). Reports of modified NK function led us to investigate the highly polymorphic cell surface proteins on NK cells, called KIRs, to search for genetic background underlying the immune abnormalities. By interacting with MHC class I proteins expressed on all cell types, KIRs regulate the killing function of NK.

The most significant finding in this study is the unequal distribution of HLA-C2 (higher in fathers of ASD children) known to interact with KIR 2DS1 (higher in mothers of ASD children) to activate NK function. Analysis of "overall activation" (**Table 9**) signaling pointed to higher activation in maternal than paternal cohorts. Most HLA and KIR frequencies in ASD children ranged between those of their parents, indicating regular independent genetic inheritance from parents to children. This reinforced the importance of the specific HLA–KIR combinations between parents, though the mechanisms involved are still unclear. Our limitation in interpreting these findings lies in the absence of unusual prevalence of these genes or their combination in the ASD children, in comparison to their healthy parents.

Some reports correlated these initial interactions between parental cells as a possible mechanism for subsequent disease development or other complications. Hiby et al. (26) reported an increased HLA-C2 frequency in different cohorts of affected pregnancies: (a) recurrent miscarriage (RM) couples and their conception products, (b) fetal growth restriction (FGR), and (c) preeclampsia. Conversely, lack of activating KIR (in women affected by RM) or increased inhibitory KIR (in women with preeclampsia) (26, 27) has already been reported. Specifically, KIR 2DS1 seemed to be protective because of its significant lack in RM women. We find this plausible, since activating KIR 2DS1 compete with inhibitory KIR 2DL1 in interaction with HLA-C2, such that a predominance of KIR 2DS1 can overcome the strong inhibitory effect mediated by KIR 2DL1. All these findings support the importance of the innate immune system (mediated by maternal uterine NK and fetal trophoblast cells), modulated by KIR–HLA interaction to play a beneficial role in reproductive success.

Some papers have already pointed out differential segregation of KIR–HLA genes in autistic patients. Our study expands upon this by focusing within ASD families. Torres et al. (28) examined a large autistic cohort, revealing a highly significant increase in the activating KIR gene 2DS1 and its cognate HLA-C2 ligand. This increase in activating KIR may explain, at least partially, the high frequency of autoimmune diseases in autism patients. Guerini et al. (29) compared ASD children to their non-ASD mothers and showed both that activating KIR/HLA combinations were increased and inhibitory KIR/HLA were reduced in ASD children. This difference was proposed as having resulted from the genetic influence of the mothers, as these molecules' expression and interaction are relevant in the surrounding uterus.

Ethnic populations are known to differ in KIR genotype frequencies and genotype content (30). To the best of our knowledge, this is the first study to research KIR and HLA combinations in the Israeli Jewish population. As shown in the Allele Frequency Net Database,[3] our geographical location has higher frequency of HLA-C2 (around 0.4–0.7 in Africa and the Middle East). However, we showed here a significant skewing between maternal and paternal C2 frequencies. It raises an interesting question, since HLA clusters map in autosomal chromosomes, leading to independent segregation without respect to gender.

Genotype mapping of this system has certain limitations. While theoretically all gene segments identified by our SSP-PCR system may be expressed on the cell surface (meaning the functional KIR repertoire may depend on the KIR genotype), the transcription and translation processes may lead to different phenotype profiles. Another limitation of the SSP-PCR method in this context is the inability to determine the heterozygous/homozygous status of each of these KIRs. Our future plans are to determine not only genotype, but also RNA and protein levels. Another point to take into account is that NK cell function is a very complicated process determined upon the balance of an array of receptors, of which KIR is only one family. Moreover, the affinity of these interactions may differ (e.g., KIR 2DL3:HLA-C1 interaction is thought to be weak, compared to KIR 2DL2:HLA-C1 or KIR 2DL1:HLA-C2), such that one interaction may wield greater influence than another. It is also becoming increasingly clear that genetic factors, such as promoters and epigenetic mechanisms, are important in controlling NK cell receptor expression and function.

This study comprised a relatively small cohort of ASD-affected families – though statistically verified based on the minor allele frequency (MAF) of C2 (39.5%). In the absence of a control group, our findings were compared with the general population data of our geographical area. Additionally, the clinical patient data have not been thoroughly listed here, places limitations upon the reader in drawing parallels to other patient cohorts. The trends revealed in this preliminary investigation need to be further corroborated in ongoing and expanded research efforts.

Finally, we would like to emphasis another interesting aspect. On the one hand, different pregnancy complications (FGR, spontaneous abortion, placental abruption) are known to stem (at least to some degree) from immunological factors. On the other hand, perinatal factors unrelated to the immunological milieu may also be important in the pathogenesis of ASD. Certain complications during gestation were found to occur with increased frequency in mothers of ASD patients; an immunological basis has been suggested as underlying a portion of these. In some cases, intermediate factors may play a partial role in the association (e.g., reduced birth weight).

CONCLUSION

The aim of our research was to genotype the KIR receptors and their relevant HLA ligands in autistic children and their non-autistic parents, in order to screen for possible unique combinations. The most interesting finding in this study is higher frequency of HLA-C2 allotypes in the paternal group besides higher percentage of KIR 2DS1 in the maternal group. Such interaction may lead to NK activation. An absence of unusual prevalence of these genes or their combination in the ASD children, limited our ability to interpret these findings. Moreover, analysis of "overall activation" signaling pointed to higher activation in maternal than paternal cohorts.

AUTHOR CONTRIBUTIONS

Mrs. MG is a Ph.D. student. She is the major contributor to this manuscript doing the thinking, bench work, and manuscript writing. Mrs. KA contributed to the bench work as well as writing the manuscript. Prof. NY is an initiator of the original study and has performed the clinical diagnosis of all the participants of the study. Prof. RE is the initiator of original study recruited the families and the original head of the lab. Dr. DM is the head of the lab the study was conducted in, supported the study, and contributed to the manuscript writing and editing.

ACKNOWLEDGMENTS

This work was supported by a research grant (#232-12-13B) from the National Institute for Psychobiology in Israel, founded by the Charles E. Smith Family, and the Harris Foundation. The authors wish to thank Mrs. Shoshana Israel, Ph.D., and Mrs. Amal Halabi, M.Sc., for their help with validating HLA primers, and Dr. Lubov Nemanov for her assistance in processing patient samples. MG was supported by the Hoffman Leadership and Responsibility Fund, at the Hebrew University.

[3]http://www.allelefrequencies.net/

REFERENCES

1. Caronna EB, Milunsky JM, Tager-Flusberg H. Autism spectrum disorders: clinical and research frontiers. *Arch Dis Child* (2008) 93:518–23. doi:10.1136/adc.2006.115337
2. Blumberg SJ, Bramlett MD, Kogan MD, Schieve LA, Jones JR, Lu MC. Changes in prevalence of parent-reported autism spectrum disorder in school-aged U.S. children: 2007 to 2011-2012. *Natl Health Stat Report* (2013) 1-11:1following11.
3. Persico AM, Napolioni V. Autism genetics. *Behav Brain Res* (2013) 251:95–112. doi:10.1016/j.bbr.2013.06.012
4. Geschwind DH. Genetics of autism spectrum disorders. *Trends Cogn Sci* (2011) 15:409–16. doi:10.1016/j.tics.2011.07.003
5. Hu VW. From genes to environment: using integrative genomics to build a "systems-level" understanding of autism spectrum disorders. *Child Dev* (2013) 84:89–103. doi:10.1111/j.1467-8624.2012.01759.x
6. Noriega DB, Savelkoul HF. Immune dysregulation in autism spectrum disorder. *Eur J Pediatr* (2014) 173:33–43. doi:10.1007/s00431-013-2183-4
7. Enstrom AM, Lit L, Onore CE, Gregg JP, Hansen RL, Pessah IN, et al. Altered gene expression and function of peripheral blood natural killer cells in children with autism. *Brain Behav Immun* (2009) 23:124–33. doi:10.1016/j.bbi.2008.08.001
8. Biassoni R. Natural killer cell receptors. *Adv Exp Med Biol* (2008) 640:35–52. doi:10.1007/978-0-387-09789-3_4
9. Rajalingam R, Ashouri E. Gene-specific PCR typing of killer cell immunoglobulin-like receptors. *Methods Mol Biol* (2013) 1034:239–55. doi:10.1007/978-1-62703-493-7_12
10. Jamil KM, Khakoo SI. KIR/HLA interactions and pathogen immunity. *J Biomed Biotechnol* (2011) 2011:298348. doi:10.1155/2011/209348
11. De Re V, Caggiari L, De Zorzi M, Toffoli G. KIR molecules: recent patents of interest for the diagnosis and treatment of several autoimmune diseases, chronic inflammation, and B-cell malignancies. *Recent Pat DNA Gene Seq* (2011) 5:169–74. doi:10.2174/187221511797636266
12. Kulkarni S, Martin MP, Carrington M. The Yin and Yang of HLA and KIR in human disease. *Semin Immunol* (2008) 20:343–52. doi:10.1016/j.smim.2008.06.003
13. Holm SJ, Sakuraba K, Mallbris L, Wolk K, Stahle M, Sanchez FO. Distinct HLA-C/KIR genotype profile associates with guttate psoriasis. *J Invest Dermatol* (2005) 125:721–30. doi:10.1111/j.0022-202X.2005.23879.x
14. Zhi D, Sun C, Sedimbi SK, Luo F, Shen S, Sanjeevi CB. Killer cell immunoglobulin-like receptor along with HLA-C ligand genes are associated with type 1 diabetes in Chinese Han population. *Diabetes Metab Res Rev* (2011) 27:872–7. doi:10.1002/dmrr.1264
15. Barker DJ, Osmond C, Golding J, Kuh D, Wadsworth ME. Growth in utero, blood pressure in childhood and adult life, and mortality from cardiovascular disease. *BMJ* (1989) 298:564–7. doi:10.1136/bmj.298.6673.564
16. Gamliel M, Ebstein R, Yirmiya N, Mankuta D. Minor fetal sonographic findings in autism spectrum disorder. *Obstet Gynecol Surv* (2012) 67:176–86. doi:10.1097/OGX.0b013e31824bb5d6
17. Hagberg H, Gressens P, Mallard C. Inflammation during fetal and neonatal life: implications for neurologic and neuropsychiatric disease in children and adults. *Ann Neurol* (2012) 71:444–57. doi:10.1002/ana.22620
18. Bashirova AA, Martin MP, McVicar DW, Carrington M. The killer immunoglobulin-like receptor gene cluster: tuning the genome for defense. *Annu Rev Genomics Hum Genet* (2006) 7:277–300. doi:10.1146/annurev.genom.7.080505.115726
19. Chazara O, Xiong S, Moffett A. Maternal KIR and fetal HLA-C: a fine balance. *J Leukoc Biol* (2011) 90:703–16. doi:10.1189/jlb.0511227
20. Xiong S, Sharkey AM, Kennedy PR, Gardner L, Farrell LE, Chazara O, et al. Maternal uterine NK cell-activating receptor KIR2DS1 enhances placentation. *J Clin Invest* (2013) 123:4264–72. doi:10.1172/JCI68991
21. Patterson PH. Immune involvement in schizophrenia and autism: etiology, pathology and animal models. *Behav Brain Res* (2009) 204:313–21. doi:10.1016/j.bbr.2008.12.016
22. Chainonthee W, Bottcher G, Gagne K, Fussel M, Bignon JD, Wassmuth R. Improved KIR gene and HLA-C KIR ligand sequence-specific primer polymerase chain reaction genotyping using whole genome amplification. *Tissue Antigens* (2010) 76:135–43. doi:10.1111/j.1399-0039.2010.01479.x
23. Hong HA, Loubser AS, de Assis Rosa D, Naranbhai V, Carr W, Paximadis M, et al. Killer-cell immunoglobulin-like receptor genotyping and HLA killer-cell immunoglobulin-like receptor-ligand identification by real-time polymerase chain reaction. *Tissue Antigens* (2011) 78:185–94. doi:10.1111/j.1399-0039.2011.01749.x
24. Ashwood P, Corbett BA, Kantor A, Schulman H, Van de Water J, Amaral DG. In search of cellular immunophenotypes in the blood of children with autism. *PLoS One* (2011) 6:e19299. doi:10.1371/journal.pone.0019299
25. Vojdani A, Mumper E, Granpeesheh D, Mielke L, Traver D, Bock K, et al. Low natural killer cell cytotoxic activity in autism: the role of glutathione, IL-2 and IL-15. *J Neuroimmunol* (2008) 205:148–54. doi:10.1016/j.jneuroim.2008.09.005
26. Hiby SE, Walker JJ, O'Shaughnessy KM, Redman CW, Carrington M, Trowsdale J, et al. Combinations of maternal KIR and fetal HLA-C genes influence the risk of preeclampsia and reproductive success. *J Exp Med* (2004) 200:957–65. doi:10.1084/jem.20041214
27. Flores AC, Marcos CY, Paladino N, Arruvito L, Williams F, Middleton D, et al. KIR receptors and HLA-C in the maintenance of pregnancy. *Tissue Antigens* (2007) 69(Suppl 1):112–3. doi:10.1111/j.1399-0039.2006.762_8.x
28. Torres AR, Westover JB, Givvons C, Johnson RC, Ward DC. Activating killer-cell immunoglobulin-like receptors (KIR) and their cognate HLA ligands are significantly increased in autism. *Brain Behav Immun* (2012) 26:1122–7. doi:10.1016/j.bbi.2012.07.014
29. Guerini FR, Bolognesi E, Chiappedi M, Manca S, Ghezzo A, Agliardi C, et al Activating KIR molecules and their cognate ligands prevail in children with a diagnosis of ASD and in their mothers. *Brain Behav Immun* (2014) 36:54–60. doi:10.1016/j.bbi.2013.10.006
30. Takeshita LY, Gonzalez-Galarza FF, dos Santos EJ, Maia MH, Rahman MM, Zain SM, et al. A database for curating the associations between killer cell immunoglobulin-like receptors and diseases in worldwide populations. *Database (Oxford)* (2013) 2013:bat021. doi:10.1093/database/bat021

18

Dynamic Akt/mTOR Signaling in Children with Autism Spectrum Disorder

*Charity Onore[1,2], Houa Yang[1,2], Judy Van de Water[1,3] and Paul Ashwood[1,2]**

[1] The M.I.N.D. Institute, University of California Davis, Davis, CA, USA, [2] Department of Medical Microbiology and Immunology, University of California Davis, Davis, CA, USA, [3] Division of Rheumatology, Allergy and Clinical Immunology, University of California Davis, Davis, CA, USA

Autism spectrum disorder (ASD) is a behaviorally defined disorder affecting 1 in 68 children. Currently, there is no known cause for the majority of ASD cases nor are there physiological diagnostic tools or biomarkers to aid behavioral diagnosis. Whole-genome linkage studies, genome-wide association studies, copy number variation screening, and SNP analyses have identified several ASD candidate genes, but which vary greatly among individuals and family clusters, suggesting that a variety of genetic mutations may result in a common pathology or alter a common mechanistic pathway. The Akt/mammalian target of rapamycin (mTOR) pathway is involved in many cellular processes including synaptic plasticity and immune function that can alter neurodevelopment. In this study, we examined the activity of the Akt/mTOR pathway in cells isolated from children with ASD and typically developing controls. We observed higher activity of mTOR, extracellular receptor kinase, and p70S6 kinase and lower activity of glycogen synthase kinase 3 (GSK3)α and tuberin (TSC2) in cells from children with ASD. These data suggest a phosphorylation pattern indicative of higher activity in the Akt/mTOR pathway in children with general/idiopathic ASD and may suggest a common pathological pathway of interest for ASD.

Keywords: autism, signaling, phosphorylation, T cells, mTOR

Edited by:
Roberto Canitano,
University Hospital of Siena, Italy

Reviewed by:
Richard Eugene Frye,
Arkansas Children's Hospital Research Institute, USA
Laura Hewitson,
The Johnson Center for Child Health and Development, USA
Stefano Nardone,
Bar-Ilan University, Israel

Correspondence:
Paul Ashwood
pashwood@ucdavis.edu

INTRODUCTION

Autism spectrum disorder (ASD) is characterized by severe and pervasive impairment in reciprocal social interaction skills, communication skills, or the presence of stereotyped behavior, interests, and activities (1). According to the most recent studies by the US Centers for Disease Control and Prevention, ASD is estimated to affect 1 in 68 children younger than 8 years (2). ASD remains a behaviorally defined disorder with no current physiological diagnostic tools or biological signatures. The cause(s) for the majority of cases of ASD remain unknown. In genetically identical monozygotic twins, there is a concordance rate of 44–91%; in dizygotic twins, the concordance rate for ASD is 0–37%; and in non-twin siblings, the rate is 0–24%; data that suggest a strong heritable component for this disorder (3-9). Although there is evidence to suggest that the disorder is highly heritable, no single genetic cause for all ASD has been identified. Heritability of ASD may suggest a genetic component in the disorder's etiology; however, the genes involved vary greatly among individuals and family clusters and therefore suggest a more likely model that a variety of genetic mutations and/or environmental contributors may result in a common pathology or disruption of a common pathway.

Whole-genome linkage studies, genome-wide association studies, copy number variation screening, and SNP analyses have identified several ASD candidate genes (10). Associations between candidate genetic mechanisms and ASD have implicated a diverse range of functions including metabolism, immune function, neuronal migration, synapse formation, neuronal growth, and neurotransmission. Among some of the notable associations are mutations in *RELN* (11), *SHANK3* (12), *NLGN3*, *NLGN4X* (13), *MET* (14), *GABRB3* (15), *OXTR* (16), and *SLC6A4* (16). Furthermore, several single-gene mutation syndromic disorders incur increased risk of developing ASD including Rett syndrome (*MeCP2*), Fragile X (*FMR1*), Tuberous sclerosis (either *TSC1* or *TSC2*), Cowden syndrome (*PTEN*), Timothy syndrome (*CACNA1C*), and Angelman syndrome (*UBE3A*) (17–19). Even with the recent advancements in identifying candidate genes involved in ASD, all identified genetic risk factors combined account for only 10–20% of the total ASD population (10). The genetic mechanisms or mutations are clearly diverse and heterogeneous and may be influenced by environmental factors.

Among the potential candidate genes identified in ASD to date, those involved in Akt/mammalian target of rapamycin (mTOR) signaling and the downstream effects of this pathway are highly represented including *FMR1*, *PTEN*, *TSC1*, and *TSC2* (20). In addition, microarray analysis of peripheral blood suggests that there is abnormal activity in this pathway (21). The Akt/mTOR pathway is involved in many cellular processes that may impact neurodevelopment and have relevance to ASD symptoms. For example, in neurons, this pathway is believed to be important in the process of learning and memory formation by augmenting long-term potentiation (LTP) of synapses (22). The process of LTP involves the strengthening of synapses as a result of sustained signaling in the Akt/mTOR pathway (23).

The Akt/mTOR pathway is complex, and a defect in any of the proteins involved can lead to aberrant signaling. Increased Akt/mTOR activity is consistent with deficiencies of FMR1, TSC1/2, or PTEN found in Fragile X, TSC, and Cowden syndrome and suggests that increased Akt/mTOR activity may have a role in the pathophysiology of the general ASD population and not limited to single ASD genetic mutations. We hypothesized that there are a diverse collection of physiological abnormalities including genetic mutation or environment factors that converge to dysregulate the Akt/mTOR pathway in individuals with ASD.

To probe directly for dysregulation in the Akt/mTOR pathway, we examined the phosphorylation activity of several proteins in the Akt/mTOR pathway in children with ASD and typically developing (TD) controls. Protein phosphorylation was examined in freshly isolated T cells (24) and following stimulation from both ASD and TD control children of the same age. Phosphorylation levels of insulin receptor substrate-1 (IRS1), phosphatase and tensin homolog (PTEN), tuberin (*TSC2*), Akt, glycogen synthase kinase 3 (GSK3)α, GSK3β, mTOR, p70S6 kinase (p70S6K), ribosomal protein S6 (RPS6), and extracellular receptor kinase (ERK) were measured in T cells collected from peripheral blood of all subjects to cast a wide net over the entirety of the Akt/mTOR pathway. In this study, we describe a dysregulation of Akt/mTOR signaling in T cells isolated from children with ASD compared with TD control children, data that might help point to possible etiological mechanisms in ASD.

MATERIALS AND METHODS

Subjects and Behavioral Assessments

Study participants were recruited as part of the Autism Phenome Project (25, 26). The study protocol was approved and carried out in accordance with the recommendations of the Institutional Review Board for the UC Davis School of Medicine, and parents of each subject provided written informed consent for their child to participate in accordance with the Declaration of Helsinki. Participants consisted of 41 children with ASD [mean age (SD) = 6.13 (1.23) years, 32 males] and 31 TD controls [mean age (SD) = 5.95 (1.27) years, 22 males] (**Table 1**). Age and male:female ratios were not statistically different. Diagnostic instruments for ASD included the Autism Diagnostic Observation Schedule-Generic (ADOS-G) (27) and the Autism Diagnostic Interview—Revised (28). ADOS scores [mean (SD)] were 12.6 (3.8) for social affect, 4.6 (1.7) for restricted/repetitive behaviors, and 7.4 (1.9) for severity. All diagnostic assessments were conducted or directly observed by trained, licensed clinical psychologists who specialize in autism and had been trained according to research standards for these tools. Inclusion criteria for ASD were taken from the diagnostic definition of ASD in young children formulated and agreed upon by the Collaborative Programs of Excellence in Autism. Inclusion criteria for TD controls included developmental scores within two SDs of the mean on all subscales of the Mullen's scale of early learning.

TABLE 1 | Study population demographics.

Group	Autism spectrum disorder (ASD) (*N* = 41)	Controls (*N* = 32)
Age (years), median (range)	5.7 (4.6–9.3)	5.5 (4.5–9.9)
Gender		
Male	32 (72%)	22 (55%)
Female	9 (28%)	10 (45%)
Race/ethnicity		
Caucasian, non-Hispanic	26 (64%)	24 (75%)
African American, non-Hispanic	1 (2%)	–
Hispanic	8 (20%)	5 (16%)
Asian, non-hispanic	1 (2%)	–
Other, non-hispanic	5 (12%)	3 (9%)
Mullen, median [interquartile range (IQR)]		
Differential quotient (DQ)	56.1 (35.4–77.1)	105.8 (98.6–114.4)
Verbal differential quotient (VDQ)	69.1 (60.1–83.6)	105.8 (98.3–116)
Non-verbal differential quotient (NVDQ)	66.2 (48.4–78.9)	105.5 (99.2–112.1)
Autism Diagnostic Observation Schedule (ADOS), median (IQR)		
Social affect	12 (9–16)	N/A
Restricted and repetitive behavior	5 (3–6)	N/A
Severity	7 (6–9)	N/A

Controls with a sibling or first-degree relative with ASD were excluded from the study. Behavioral data include Mullen's Scales of Early Learning (DQ, VDQ, NVDQ) scores with median and interquartile range and ADOS (social affect, restricted and repetitive behavior, severity) scores with median and interquartile range.

For ASD differential quotient (DQ) [mean (SD)] = 59.8 (27.5), verbal differential quotient (VDQ) = 72.3 (18.5), and non-verbal differential quotient (NVDQ) = 66.2 (21.7); for TD, DQ = 105.8 (11.4), VDQ = 105.8 (12.7), and NVDQ = 105.5 (10.1). Exclusion criteria for TD controls included any known developmental, neurological, or behavioral problems; a diagnosis of mental retardation, pervasive developmental disorder, or specific language impairment. TD children were screened and excluded for autism with the Social Communication Questionnaire (29) (scores > 11) (SCQ—Lifetime Edition). All participants were native English speakers, were ambulatory, and had no suspected vision or hearing problems. The exclusion criteria for all subjects consisted of the presence of Fragile X or other serious neurological (e.g., seizures), psychiatric (e.g., bipolar disorder), the presence of any known genetic polymorphism that causes ASD, or known medical conditions including autoimmune disease and inflammatory bowel diseases/celiac disease. All subjects were screened *via* parental interview for current and past physical illness. Children with known endocrine, cardiovascular, pulmonary, liver, or kidney disease were excluded from enrollment in the study. No participant presented with a cold, fever, or other common illness, if such a condition occurred, the blood draw were delayed until the child's health status was stable for 48 h.

Peripheral Blood Mononuclear Cell (PBMC) Collection

Peripheral blood was collected in acid-citrate-dextrose Vacutainers (BD Biosciences, San Jose, CA, USA) following behavioral assessments. Whole blood was centrifuged at 960 *g* for 10 min to separate cell fractions from plasma. The cell fraction was diluted in 25 ml of Hank's Balanced Salt Solution (HBSS) (Mediatech, Manassas, VA, USA) and layered at room temperature over lymphocyte separation medium (LSM) (Mediatech) and centrifuged at 300 *g* for 30 min to isolate PBMCs. PBMCs were harvested at the interface between LSM and HBSS fractions and washed twice with 50 ml HBSS. The number of viable PBMC was determined by 1:1 dilution of Trypan Blue (Mediatech) exclusion counting on a Hausser phase contrast hemacytometer. Cells were then diluted in a chilled (4°C) magnetic separation buffer (MACS buffer) (Miltenyi Biotec, Auburn, CA, USA) to a concentration of 2.5×10^8/ml.

T Cell Isolation

T cells were isolated with a Pan T cell isolation kit according to the protocol provided by the manufacturer (Miltenyi Biotec). Briefly, a biotinylated antibody cocktail containing antibodies reactive to CD14, CD15, CD16, CD19, CD34, CD36, CD56, CD123, and CD235a (glycophorin A) was added at a concentration of 10 μl of antibody cocktail/10^7 cells and incubated for 10 min at 4°C. Following incubation, an additional 30 μl of MACS buffer per 10^7 cells was added followed by 10 μl of magnetic beads conjugated to antibiotin antibodies at a concentration of 20 μl/10^7 cells and incubated at 4°C for an additional 15 min. Cells were then washed in 20-fold incubation volume of MACS buffer and centrifuged at 300 *g* for 10 min. Supernatants were aspirated and discarded, and PBMC were resuspended in 500 μl. This suspension was transferred to a MACS LS column on a MACS magnetic platform. The column was washed with a total of 9 ml MACS buffer, and eluent was again collected. All of the T cell-enriched eluent that passed through the LS column from the column was collected and centrifuged at 300 *g* for 10 min. The T cell-enriched pellet was washed and centrifuged twice in 10 ml of Roswell Park Memorial Institute (RPMI) media (Life technologies) containing 10% low endotoxin, heat-inactivated fetal bovine serum (Life technologies, Carlsbad, CA, USA), 100 IU/ml penicillin, and 100 IU/ml streptomycin (Sigma, St. Louis, MO, USA) (complete RPMI). The T cells were then resuspended in 1×10^6 cell/ml and plated 1 ml/well in a 12-well sterile tissue culture plate (Greiner Bio-One, Monroe, NC, USA). T cells were allowed to rest in complete RPMI at 37°C for 16 h prior to stimulation and lysis.

T Cell Stimulation, Lysis, and Protein Quantification

T cells were either left unstimulated or stimulated with 10 nM phorbol myristate acetate (PMA) for 15 or 45 min in complete RPMI at 37°C. Following stimulation, T cells were quickly washed in 10 ml of ice-cold PBS and centrifuged for 10 min at 500 *g* at 4°C. Supernatants were aspirated, and cell pellet was resuspended in ice-cold lysis buffer (Cell Signaling Technology, Danvers, MA, USA) containing 20 mM Tris-HCl (pH 7.5), 150 mM NaCl, 1 mM Na_2EDTA, 1 mM EGTA, 1% Triton X, 2.5 mM sodium pyrophosphate, 1 mM beta-glycerophosphate, 1 mM Na_3VO_4, and 1 μg/ml leupeptin supplemented with freshly added 1% AEBSF. Cells were mixed in lysis buffer with vigorous pipetting and sonicated for 30 s. Cells were then incubated in lysis buffer on ice for 10 min. Following incubation, cell suspensions were centrifuged at 18,000 *g* for 10 min. Supernatants were collected, and aliquots were stored at −80°C until date of protein quantification or phosphorylation analysis. Protein levels were quantified using Bradford assay. In brief, diluted lysate and BSA standards were combined 1:1 with room temperature Bradford reagent (Bio-Rad, Hercules, CA, USA) and incubated for 10 min. Following incubation, optical density was measured with a 595 λ filter on a Bio-Rad spectrophotometer. Protein levels of T cell lysate samples were derived from a linear seven-point BSA standard curve (Bio-Rad).

Phosphorylation Assay

Relative levels of phosphorylated and total IRS1, PTEN, ERK1/2, Akt, GSK3α, GSK3β, TSC2, mTOR, p70S6K, and RPS6 were measured with Milliplex™ multiplexing bead immunoassays (Millipore, Billerica, MA, USA). This assay contains antibodies that have been standardized and optimized for sensitivity and specificity to detect the phosphorylation and total protein levels of the molecules tested. Assay detection of the total and phosphorylated proteins detected was confirmed using Western blot analysis of individual phosphorylated or total proteins prior to testing, as well as the manufacturer's own internal research quality controls. A subset of samples was also put through a second assay provided by Bio-Rad that contains many of standardized antibodies used in Western blot analyses, with strong correlation between assays (data not shown). Luminex technology provides a unique platform for analysis of limited sample volume, as is the case in this study, where precious blood samples from pediatric patients are used. GAPDH was used as an internal control for both phoshporylated and total protein assays, which were measured separately. The multiplex assay was performed according to the manufacturer's instructions. Briefly, lysates were incubated with antibody-conjugated beads at a total protein concentration of 500 μg/ml. After protein capture, beads were washed twice followed by incubation with biotinylated detection antibody. Beads were then incubated with streptavidin-conjugated phycoerythrin (PE), followed by several washes. Finally, the bead sets were analyzed using a flow-based Luminex™ 100 suspension array system to determine bead identity and corresponding PE mean fluorescent intensity (MFI) (Bio-Plex 200; Bio-Rad Laboratories). Relative levels of phosphorylated and total proteins were determined by dividing MFI signal of each protein by GAPDH signal for each sample. Relative phosphorylation was determined by further dividing the GAPDH relative levels of phosphorylated proteins to their respective GAPDH relative total protein levels. All phosphorylation values are expressed as ratios.

Statistical Analysis

The data were non-parametrically distributed, p values were determined with Mann–Whitney U-test. All analyses were two tailed, and values of $p < 0.05$ were considered statistically significant. For these novel and previously untested experiments, unadjusted p values are presented (30). All analyses were conducted using GraphPad Prism statistical software (GraphPad Software Inc., San Diego, CA, USA). Associations between Akt/mTOR/pathway measures and behaviors assessed by ADOS were calculated using a two-tailed, non-parametric Spearman's correlation test with 95% confidence intervals.

RESULTS

Given that Akt/mTOR genetic mutations are potentially associated with increased ASD risk, we hypothesized that aberrations in many parts of the Akt/mTOR pathway will contribute to an overall pattern of increased Akt/mTOR pathway activity. To test this theory, we examined several proteins in the Akt/mTOR pathway. We observed increased IRS1 and RSP6 total protein in children with ASD compared with TD controls under unstimulated conditions ($p < 0.03$; **Table 2**). Similarly, total IRS1 and RSP6 were increased, in T cells following 15 or 45 min of stimulation, in the ASD group compared to TD controls ($p < 0.04$). No other total protein levels were different between groups (**Table 2**). For phosphorylated proteins, in unstimulated T cells, GSK3α, GSK3β, PTEN, TSC2, and mTOR were increased in children with ASD compared to TD controls ($p < 0.006$; **Table 3**). After 15 min of stimulation, T cells from children with ASD had higher phosphorylation of proteins, p7056K, IRS1, GSK3α, GSK3β, AKT, PTEN, TSC2, mTOR, and ERK ($p < 0.04$; **Table 3**). After 45 min of T cell stimulation, levels of phosphorylated protein were still increased in children with ASD for p7056K, IRS1, GSK3α, GSK3β, AKT, PTEN, TSC2, mTOR, and ERK, as well as RPS6 ($p < 0.02$; **Table 3**).

By calculating the ratio of phosphorylated to total protein levels, we observed higher ratios for mTOR and GSK3β ($p < 0.02$) in unstimulated ASD T cells when compared to unstimulated TD control T cells (**Table 4**; and Figures S1 and S2 in Supplementary Material). Given the effects of phosphorylation on these proteins (**Table 5**), it would indicate increased activity of mTOR and decreased activity of GSK3β in ASD T cells. This may suggest

TABLE 2 | Akt/mTOR pathway total protein in T cells.

Protein	ASD		Control		p Value
	Median	Interquartile range (IQR)	Median	IQR	
Activating					
Unstimulated					
Akt	0.175	0.132	0.169	0.088	0.708
Mammalian target of rapamycin (mTOR)	0.016	0.012	0.015	0.005	0.741
p70S6 kinase (p70S6K)	0.250	0.092	0.221	0.094	0.406
Ribosomal protein S6 (RPS6)	0.005	0.002	0.004	0.001	**0.017**
Extracellular receptor kinase (ERK)	0.655	0.149	0.646	0.076	0.551
Stimulated (15 min)					
Akt	0.173	0.124	0.171	0.085	0.792
mTOR	0.014	0.008	0.016	0.007	0.377
p70S6K	0.263	0.110	0.265	0.109	0.474
RPS6	0.006	0.004	0.005	0.002	**0.001**
ERK	0.604	0.196	0.605	0.155	0.669
Stimulated (45 min)					
Akt	0.168	0.107	0.169	0.090	0.853
mTOR	0.018	0.008	0.016	0.009	0.071
p70S6K	0.270	0.089	0.273	0.141	0.966
RPS6	0.014	0.016	0.009	0.008	**0.003**
ERK	0.607	0.115	0.617	0.118	0.664
Inactivating					
Unstimulated					
Insulin receptor substrate-1 (IRS1)	0.027	0.026	0.018	0.022	**0.030**
PTEN	0.289	0.156	0.255	0.079	0.129
Glycogen synthase kinase 3 (GSK) 3α	0.282	0.275	0.254	0.203	0.729
GSK3β	0.269	0.238	0.260	0.130	0.544
TSC2	0.040	0.049	0.039	0.056	0.590
Stimulated (15 min)					
IRS1	0.030	0.023	0.021	0.020	**0.041**
PTEN	0.307	0.146	0.266	0.075	0.067
GSK3α	0.209	0.245	0.280	0.214	0.053
GSK3β	0.153	0.169	0.168	0.143	0.378
TSC2	0.043	0.050	0.036	0.056	0.538
Stimulated (45 min)					
IRS1	0.040	0.028	0.024	0.031	**0.004**
PTEN	0.284	0.114	0.245	0.074	0.078
GSK3α	0.210	0.186	0.276	0.131	0.065
GSK3β	0.115	0.109	0.159	0.128	0.147
TSC2	0.040	0.049	0.035	0.056	0.866

All p values were calculated with two-tailed Mann–Whitney U-tests.
Values in bold and gray shades signifies a p < 0.05.

TABLE 3 | Akt/mTOR pathway phosphorylated protein in T cells.

Protein	ASD		Control		*p* Value
	Median	Interquartile range (IQR)	Median	IQR	
Activating					
Unstimulated					
Akt	0.006	0.004	0.005	0.003	0.110
Mammalian target of rapamycin (mTOR)	0.024	0.017	0.015	0.012	**0.006**
p70S6 kinase (p70S6K)	0.011	0.007	0.008	0.004	0.064
Ribosomal protein S6 (RPS6)	0.009	0.006	0.009	0.005	0.473
Extracellular receptor kinase (ERK)	0.006	0.004	0.006	0.002	0.211
Stimulated (15 min)					
Akt	0.008	0.005	0.005	0.006	**0.013**
mTOR	0.099	0.088	0.057	0.088	**0.011**
p70S6K	0.093	0.142	0.027	0.125	**0.018**
RPS6	0.060	0.071	0.013	0.070	0.085
ERK	0.153	0.150	0.080	0.195	**0.029**
Stimulated (45 min)					
Akt	0.008	0.005	0.005	0.005	**0.006**
mTOR	0.127	0.094	0.071	0.107	**0.002**
p70S6K	0.142	0.140	0.069	0.145	**0.003**
RPS6	0.137	0.221	0.035	0.200	**0.023**
ERK	0.104	0.094	0.043	0.103	**0.005**
Inactivating					
Unstimulated					
Insulin receptor substrate-1 (IRS1)	0.005	0.004	0.004	0.003	0.064
PTEN	0.219	0.097	0.170	0.074	**0.000**
Glycogen synthase kinase 3 (GSK3)α	0.015	0.012	0.011	0.005	**0.002**
GSK3β	0.023	0.021	0.012	0.014	**0.000**
TSC2	0.016	0.012	0.013	0.006	**0.001**
Stimulated (15 min)					
IRS1	0.009	0.007	0.004	0.008	**0.009**
PTEN	0.208	0.119	0.175	0.111	**0.045**
GSK3α	0.317	0.326	0.161	0.361	**0.009**
GSK3β	0.116	0.099	0.064	0.118	**0.023**
TSC2	0.052	0.039	0.034	0.054	**0.027**
Stimulated (45 min)					
IRS1	0.010	0.016	0.005	0.006	**0.003**
PTEN	0.233	0.176	0.164	0.050	**0.001**
GSK3α	0.307	0.303	0.107	0.263	**0.001**
GSK3β	0.113	0.077	0.067	0.089	**0.002**
TSC2	0.054	0.046	0.028	0.039	**0.000**

Median and IQR of phosphorylated Akt/mTOR pathway proteins. All p values were calculated with two-tailed Mann-Whitney U-tests.
Values in bold and gray shades signifies a $p < 0.05$.

TABLE 4 | Akt/mTOR pathway phosphorylated/total protein ratios in T cells.

Protein	ASD		Control		*p* Value
	Median	Interquartile range (IQR)	Median	IQR	
Activating					
Unstimulated					
Akt	0.039	0.050	0.028	0.021	0.544
Mammalian target of rapamycin (mTOR)	1.262	1.529	0.941	0.866	**0.024**
p70S6 kinase (p70S6K)	0.041	0.038	0.035	0.019	0.254
Ribosomal protein S6 (RPS6)	1.685	1.532	1.995	1.395	0.590
Extracellular receptor kinase (ERK)	0.009	0.009	0.009	0.004	0.597
Stimulated (15 min)					
Akt	0.053	0.046	0.039	0.038	0.129
mTOR	5.954	6.491	2.770	5.730	**0.016**
p70S6K	0.342	0.653	0.104	0.357	**0.002**
RPS6	5.787	7.306	3.298	10.334	0.274
ERK	0.227	0.288	0.127	0.367	**0.027**
Stimulated (45 min)					
Akt	0.062	0.058	0.036	0.042	0.078
mTOR	6.769	6.872	3.929	5.815	**0.008**
p70S6K	0.503	0.588	0.225	0.417	**0.004**
RPS6	9.008	8.853	4.325	17.095	0.087
ERK	0.178	0.168	0.078	0.186	**0.050**
Inactivating					
Unstimulated					
Insulin receptor substrate-1 (IRS1)	0.235	0.294	0.250	0.224	0.346
PTEN	0.681	0.461	0.647	0.278	0.115
Glycogen synthase kinase 3 (GSK3)α	0.072	0.283	0.043	0.090	0.057
GSK3β	0.073	0.111	0.050	0.042	**0.010**
TSC2	0.428	2.717	0.360	1.653	0.153
Stimulated (15 min)					
IRS1	0.305	0.695	0.275	0.347	0.834
PTEN	0.680	0.452	0.673	0.276	0.636
GSK3α	1.409	6.295	0.505	1.964	**0.004**
GSK3β	0.808	0.921	0.484	0.969	0.055
TSC2	1.797	7.840	0.867	2.747	**0.039**
Stimulated (45 min)					
IRS1	0.232	0.374	0.254	0.352	0.874
PTEN	0.860	0.445	0.663	0.207	**0.025**
GSK3α	1.199	4.969	0.364	1.290	**0.004**
GSK3β	0.977	0.783	0.523	0.899	**0.017**
TSC2	1.548	5.008	0.786	1.909	**0.029**

Median and IQR of phosphorylated/total Akt/mTOR pathway proteins. All p values were calculated with two-tailed Mann–Whitney U-tests.
Values in bold and gray shades signifies a $p < 0.05$.

higher activity of Akt/mTOR signaling in ASD T cells (**Figure 1**). ASD T cells also trended toward increased phosphorylation of GSK3α under unstimulated conditions (**Table 5**), which would indicate lower activity of GSK3α consistent with higher Akt/mTOR pathway activity (**Table 1**). Together these data indicate Akt/mTOR signaling is higher in resting T cells of children with ASD when compared with T cells from TD controls.

After stimulation with PMA for 15 min, T cells from children with ASD exhibited higher phosphorylation of ERK, mTOR,

TABLE 5 | Effect of phosphorylation on target sites of Akt/mTOR pathway proteins.

Activating		Inactivating	
Akt	Ser473	IRS1	Ser312
mTOR	Ser2448	PTEN	Ser380
p70S6K	Thr412	GSK3α	Ser21
RPS6	Ser235/Ser236	GSK3β	Ser9
ERK	Thr185/Tyr187	TSC2	Ser939

Proteins are organized according to whether the effect of phosphorylation on a specific phosphorylation site is activating or inactivating. The sites listed in the table are those measured in this article.

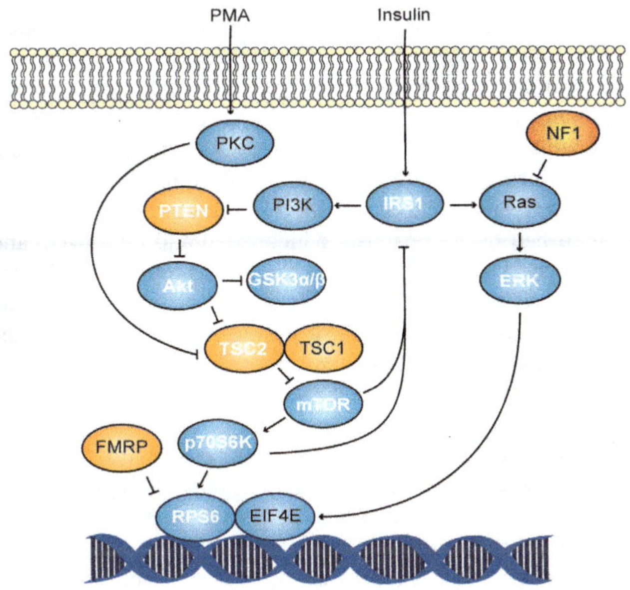

FIGURE 1 | Akt/mTOR signaling schematic. The PI3K pathway in response to stimulation with phorbol myristate acetate (PMA). Autism spectrum disorder-associated mutations are shown in orange, while all others are shown in blue. Molecules measured in this study are shown with white lettering.

p70S6K, GSK3α, and TSC2 compared with T cells from children with TD ($p < 0.04$; **Table 4**), indicating increased activity of ERK, mTOR, and p70S6K but a decreased activity of inhibitory signals by TSC2 and GSK3α, suggesting that Akt/mTOR pathway activity may be increased in stimulated ASD T cells (**Table 1**). ASD T cells also trended toward increased phosphorylation of GSK3β ($p < 0.054$), which would indicate lower activity of inhibitory GSK3β consistent with higher Akt/mTOR pathway activity. After 45 min of PMA stimulation, increased phosphorylation of ERK, mTOR, p70S6K, GSK3α, GSK3β, PTEN, and TSC2 were detected in ASD T cells (**Table 4**). There was also a trend for increased AKT but which did not quite reach statistical significance ($p = 0.077$). Together these data suggest overall increased AKT/mTOR pathway activity in ASD T cells following stimulation.

Associations were observed for total p7056k and autism severity at 15 min poststimulation ($r = 0.327$, $p = 0.04$). Restrictive and repetitive behaviors were associated with the PTEN ratio after 15 min stimulation also ($r = -0.3316$, $p = 0.03$). For social affect, several measures were associated including total p7056k and the IRIS ratio in unstimulated and 45 min after stimulation ($p < 0.05$).

DISCUSSION

In this study, we report differential activity of several Akt/mTOR signaling molecules in young children with ASD. To observe dynamic phosphorylation activity, freshly isolated T lymphocyte cells were chosen as a cellular representative that could be acquired efficiently, safely, and easily from relatively non-invasive blood samples. From our experiments, we determined that ASD T cells generally exhibit phosphorylation to total protein ratios that would indicate higher activity of mTOR, ERK, and p70S6K as well as lower activity of GSK3α, GSK3β, TSC2, and PTEN than TD control T cells. This indicates a shift toward higher Akt/mTOR pathway activity in the ASD group (**Table 5**; **Figure 1**). An increased Akt/mTOR activity is consistent with deficiencies of FMR1, TSC1/2, or PTEN found in Fragile X, TSC, and Cowden syndrome, respectively (31–33). Moreover, suppression of this increased Akt/mTOR activity has been demonstrated to improve ASD-associated symptoms in mice deficient for PTEN and TSC1 (34, 35). Together these data suggest that increased Akt/mTOR activity may have a role in the pathophysiology of the general ASD population and not limited to known ASD-associated Akt/mTOR genetic mutations.

The Akt/mTOR pathway is involved in a large number of physiological functions, in both the central nervous and immune systems (36–39). Atypical Akt/mTOR signaling may be related to many previous observations of abnormal T cell function (40–44) in children with ASD. The aberrancies in Akt/mTOR signaling observed in this study are likely not limited to T cells but will have relevance to signaling also in other immune cells and as such these data have relevance to other immune abnormalities previously observed in ASD involving multiple leukocyte subsets (25, 45–50). Aberrant Akt/mTOR signaling has the potential to impact cellular growth, proliferation, and cytokine production in the immune system (38), which can in turn affect behavior (26).

Our data show that immune dysfunction of children with ASD previously demonstrated may stem from aberrant T cells signaling *via* the Akt/mTOR pathway. To probe directly for dysregulation in the Akt/mTOR pathway, we sought to examine the phosphorylation activity of several proteins in the Akt/mTOR pathway in children with ASD and TD controls. As ASD manifests in early childhood, it is difficult to find suitable research tools and accessible tissues for experimentation. For example, postmortem human tissue can never provide the substrate for dynamic functional studies, and finding suitable control material is problematic. Immune cells, in contrast, provide a readily accessible model system that has many advantages including easy acquisition, high availability, and fine matching with controls. The advantages of using lymphocytes as an easily accessible "neural probe" in the investigation of psychiatric disorders in living subjects has been previously reviewed (24). We therefore utilized T lymphocytes as a neuronal surrogate in our experiments to examine dynamic signaling activity. T lymphocyte cells were chosen as a cellular model in which to test Akt/mTOR pathway activity for several characteristics including their long life span and high numbers within the blood. Moreover, the Luminex technology was chosen as it provides a platform for analyses of a number of analytes simultaneously from small volumes of tissue. As this study utilized pediatric blood samples, T cell numbers were limited, and thus, performing Western blot analyses on all phosphorylated or total proteins would be prohibitive. Importantly, the antibodies used had been previously standardized and optimized, and we also checked for detection of the same proteins in Western blot analysis and intracellular flow cytometry techniques, using Jurkat cells and primary T cells from adults, prior to running the Luminex assays. In addition, on a subset of samples, a number of phosphorylated or total proteins were compared between two Luminex assays from different manufacturer's, with similar results. Our results suggest that the Luminex platform provides a quick and efficient means of identifying possible changes in the Akt/mTOR pathway, in pediatric samples that are limited in volume. Although our data showed increased Akt/mTOR signaling in ASD, whether this reflects what happens *in vivo* or within other tissues such as the gastrointestinal tract or brain is not known and would need further investigation.

Further work needs to be performed to determine context-dependent effects on Akt/mTOR pathway in T cells and how they relate to the brain; however, many gene expression studies have taken the approach to look at primary or immortalized blood cells as a surrogate for inaccessible tissue such as the brain. The advantages of using lymphocytes as neural surrogates for *in vitro* examination has been previously established, but there is also evidence that the increased Akt/mTOR activity observed in Fragile X central nervous system (CNS) tissue is mirrored in lymphocytes (51), suggesting that Akt/mTOR signaling in T cells is applicable to cells of the CNS, including neurons and glial cells. In neurons, the Akt/mTOR pathway is essential in the regulation of dendritic arborization and spine formation (52), which are important features of synapse formation. Increased activity of this pathway in neuronal knockouts of *TSC1* or *PTEN* results in lower sociability and seizures in mouse models (53–55), suggesting that both sociability and seizures are Akt/mTOR pathway activity dependent. Increased activity of this pathway in glial cells can also have negative effects on neurobiology, such as aberrant neuronal organization and seizures in astrocyte-specific *TSC1* conditional knockout mice (56). Lack of social interactions is a central symptom of ASD (1), and seizures are a common comorbidity in the disorder (57). Together these data suggest that these ASD symptoms could be potentially related to the high Akt/mTOR signaling as described in this study in ASD cells (53, 56, 58).

Akt activation leads to a number of effects, some of which are mTOR independent. These include regulating cell survival and growth, such as phosphorylation of Forkhead box O family of transcription factors and of GSK3α and GSK3β (59–61). GSK3 exists in two genetically distinct isoforms but with near identical function. GSK3α and GSK3β share 85% amino acid identity and 98% amino acid sequence homology within their kinase domains (62). The GSK3 proteins are involved in regulating metabolic function and are phosphorylated and inhibited by Akt among other kinases such as p70S6K. Once phosphorylated, the kinase activity of GSK3 is inhibited, and their substrates such as glycogen synthase, Ap-1, β-catenin, c-myc, and p53, thereby initiating signaling mechanisms promoting cell survival and growth. GSK3s are expressed in virtually all cell types, but their expression is highly enriched in the CNS (63) and appears to be involved in regulating synaptic plasticity (64). These proteins have recently gained attention in the area of Alzheimer's disease (AD) research, and there have been several observations that both the activity and total levels of GSK3 is upregulated in AD patients (65). Interestingly, we observed lower GSK3 activity in children with ASD compared with TD controls. Current evidence suggests that low GSK3 activity impairs LTD (66), which could affect synaptic plasticity and in children with ASD.

Collectively, these data described in this study suggest a general dysregulation of the Akt/mTOR pathway in an idiopathic ASD population. This may suggest a convergent pathology in ASD that would affect multiple physiological symptoms. It is unclear whether Akt/mTOR aberrancies described in the study are due to as yet unknown genetic mutations, epigenetic changes, or environmental factors, and it is possible that it may be due to a combination of genetic and environmental influences. In fact, growth factors that imbue effects by signaling through the Akt/mTOR pathway such as HGF and MIF have also been reported as dysregulated in ASD (67, 68), suggesting that circulatory homeostatic factors can be an additional source of Akt/mTOR pathway activity. Similarly, a mutation in cMET, the receptor for HGF, has also been reported in ASD (69), suggesting that Akt/mTOR-associated receptors may also be a source for aberrant signaling activity. Together, these data present a novel finding Akt/mTOR pathway dysregulation in young children with ASD that could provide a focus for targeted therapeutics for at least a subset of individuals with ASD.

AUTHOR CONTRIBUTIONS

All authors designed the experiments, helped with data analysis and interpretation, and played a major role in writing the manuscript.

ACKNOWLEDGMENTS

This study was funded by the NIH grants R21HD065269, R01MH089626-01, P01 ES011269-11, U54HD079125, Autism Speaks Foundation (#7567), the Jane Botsford Johnson Foundation, National Alliance for Research on Schizophrenia and Depression, and the Peter Emch Foundation. We would like to thank the dedicated staff of both the UC Davis M.I.N.D. Institute and the APP study for their technical support. We also thank Milo Careaga and Tamanna Noyon for their technical support. The commitment of the families who took part in these studies, at both the M.I.N.D. Institute and as part of the APP study, is also gratefully acknowledged.

SUPPLEMENTARY MATERIAL

FIGURE S1 | Akt/mammalian target of rapamycin (mTOR) pathway activating phosphorylated/total protein ratios in T cells. Box and whisker plots show activating AKT/mTOR pathway (phosphorylated/total) protein levels after 0, 15, and 45 min of stimulation between autism spectrum disorder (ASD) (black bars) and controls (gray bars). Data are depicted as box showing the lower (25%) and upper (75%) quartiles and the middle line representing the median, whiskers showing the minimum and maximum. *p Value less than 0.05, calculated with two-tailed Mann–Whitney U-tests.

FIGURE S2 | Akt/mammalian target of rapamycin (mTOR) pathway inactivating phosphorylated/total protein ratios in T cells. Box and whisker plots show inactivating AKT/mTOR pathway (phosphorylated/total) protein levels after 0, 15, and 45 min of stimulation between autism spectrum disorder (ASD) (black bars) and controls (gray bars). Data are depicted as box showing the lower (25%) and upper (75%) quartiles and the middle line representing the median, whiskers showing the minimum and maximum. *p Value less than 0.05, calculated with two-tailed Mann–Whitney U-tests.

REFERENCES

1. American Psychiatric Association. *Diagnostic and Statistical Manual of Mental Disorders*. Arlington, VA: American Psychiatric Publishing, Inc. (2000).
2. Wingate M, Mulvihill B, Kirby RS, Pettygrove S, Cunniff C, Meaney F, et al. Prevalence of autism spectrum disorders – autism and developmental disabilities monitoring network, 14 sites, United States, 2008. *MMWR Surveill Summ* (2012) 61(3):1–19.
3. Constantino JN, Todd RD. Genetic structure of reciprocal social behavior. *Am J Psychiatry* (2000) 157(12):2043–5. doi:10.1176/appi.ajp.157.12.2043
4. Bailey A, Le Couteur A, Gottesman I, Bolton P, Simonoff E, Yuzda E, et al. Autism as a strongly genetic disorder: evidence from a British twin study. *Psychol Med* (1995) 25(1):63–77. doi:10.1017/S0033291700028099
5. Steffenburg S, Gillberg C, Hellgren L, Andersson L, Gillberg IC, Jakobsson G, et al. A twin study of autism in Denmark, Finland, Iceland, Norway and Sweden. *J Child Psychol Psychiatry* (1989) 30(3):405–16. doi:10.1111/j.1469-7610.1989.tb00254.x
6. Kates WR, Burnette CP, Eliez S, Strunge LA, Kaplan D, Landa R, et al. Neuroanatomic variation in monozygotic twin pairs discordant for the narrow phenotype for autism. *Am J Psychiatry* (2004) 161(3):539–46. doi:10.1176/appi.ajp.161.3.539
7. Lauritsen MB, Pedersen CB, Mortensen PB. Effects of familial risk factors and place of birth on the risk of autism: a nationwide register-based study. *J Child Psychol Psychiatry* (2005) 46(9):963–71. doi:10.1111/j.1469-7610.2004.00391.x
8. Jorde LB, Hasstedt SJ, Ritvo ER, Mason-Brothers A, Freeman BJ, Pingree C, et al. Complex segregation analysis of autism. *Am J Hum Genet* (1991) 49(5):932–8.
9. Bolton P, Macdonald H, Pickles A, Rios P, Goode S, Crowson M, et al. A case-control family history study of autism. *J Child Psychol Psychiatry* (1994) 35(5):877–900. doi:10.1111/j.1469-7610.1994.tb02300.x
10. Abrahams BS, Geschwind DH. Advances in autism genetics: on the threshold of a new neurobiology. *Nat Rev Genet* (2008) 9(5):341–55. doi:10.1038/nrg2346
11. Skaar DA, Shao Y, Haines JL, Stenger JE, Jaworski J, Martin ER, et al. Analysis of the RELN gene as a genetic risk factor for autism. *Mol Psychiatry* (2005) 10(6):563–71. doi:10.1038/sj.mp.4001614
12. Moessner R, Marshall CR, Sutcliffe JS, Skaug J, Pinto D, Vincent J, et al. Contribution of SHANK3 mutations to autism spectrum disorder. *Am J Hum Genet* (2007) 81(6):1289–97. doi:10.1086/522590
13. Jamain S, Quach H, Betancur C, Råstam M, Colineaux C, Gillberg IC, et al. Mutations of the X-linked genes encoding neuroligins NLGN3 and NLGN4 are associated with autism. *Nat Genet* (2003) 34(1):27–9. doi:10.1038/ng1136
14. Campbell DB, Sutcliffe JS, Ebert PJ, Militerni R, Bravaccio C, Trillo S, et al. A genetic variant that disrupts MET transcription is associated with autism. *Proc Natl Acad Sci U S A* (2006) 103(45):16834–9. doi:10.1073/pnas.0605296103
15. Buxbaum JD, Silverman JM, Smith CJ, Greenberg DA, Kilifarski M, Reichert J, et al. Association between a GABRB3 polymorphism and autism. *Mol Psychiatry* (2002) 7(3):311–6. doi:10.1038/sj.mp.4001011
16. Wu S, Jia M, Ruan Y, Liu J, Guo Y, Shuang M, et al. Positive association of the oxytocin receptor gene (OXTR) with autism in the Chinese Han population. *Biol Psychiatry* (2005) 58(1):74–7. doi:10.1016/j.biopsych.2005.03.013
17. Nagarajan RP, Patzel KA, Martin M, Yasui DH, Swanberg SE, Hertz-Picciotto I, et al. MECP2 promoter methylation and X chromosome inactivation in autism. *Autism Res* (2008) 1(3):169–78. doi:10.1002/aur.24
18. Belmonte MK, Bourgeron T. Fragile X syndrome and autism at the intersection of genetic and neural networks. *Nat Neurosci* (2006) 9(10):1221–5. doi:10.1038/nn1765
19. Wiznitzer M. Autism and tuberous sclerosis. *J Child Neurol* (2004) 19(9):675–9. doi:10.1177/08830738040190090701
20. Kelleher RJ III, Bear MF. The autistic neuron: troubled translation? *Cell* (2008) 135(3):401–6. doi:10.1016/j.cell.2008.10.017
21. Cuscó I, Medrano A, Gener B, Vilardell M, Gallastegui F, Villa O, et al. Autism-specific copy number variants further implicate the phosphatidylinositol signaling pathway and the glutamatergic synapse in the etiology of the disorder. *Hum Mol Genet* (2009) 18(10):1795–804. doi:10.1093/hmg/ddp092
22. Opazo P, Watabe AM, Grant SG, O'Dell TJ. Phosphatidylinositol 3-kinase regulates the induction of long-term potentiation through extracellular signal-related kinase-independent mechanisms. *J Neurosci* (2003) 23(9):3679–88.
23. Sanna PP, Cammalleri M, Berton F, Simpson C, Lutjens R, Bloom FE, et al. Phosphatidylinositol 3-kinase is required for the expression but not for the induction or the maintenance of long-term potentiation in the hippocampal CA1 region. *J Neurosci* (2002) 22(9):3359–65.
24. Gladkevich A, Kauffman HF, Korf J. Lymphocytes as a neural probe: potential for studying psychiatric disorders. *Prog Neuropsychopharmacol Biol Psychiatry* (2004) 28(3):559–76. doi:10.1016/j.pnpbp.2004.01.009
25. Breece E, Paciotti B, Nordahl CW, Ozonoff S, Van de Water JA, Rogers SJ, et al. Myeloid dendritic cells frequencies are increased in children with autism spectrum disorder and associated with amygdala volume and repetitive behaviors. *Brain Behav Immun* (2012) 31:69–75. doi:10.1016/j.bbi.2012.10.006
26. Onore C, Careaga M, Ashwood P. The role of immune dysfunction in the pathophysiology of autism. *Brain Behav Immun* (2011) 26(3):383–92. doi:10.1016/j.bbi.2011.08.007
27. Lord C, Risi S, Lambrecht L, Cook EH Jr, Leventhal BL, DiLavore PC, et al. The autism diagnostic observation schedule-generic: a standard measure of social and communication deficits associated with the spectrum of autism. *J Autism Dev Disord* (2000) 30(3):205–23. doi:10.1023/A:1005591205002
28. Lord C, Rutter M, Le Couteur A. Autism diagnostic interview-revised: a revised version of a diagnostic interview for caregivers of individuals with possible pervasive developmental disorders. *J Autism Dev Disord* (1994) 24(5):659–85. doi:10.1007/BF02172145
29. Berument SK, Rutter M, Lord C, Pickles A, Bailey A. Autism screening questionnaire: diagnostic validity. *Br J Psychiatry* (1999) 175:444–51. doi:10.1192/bjp.175.5.444
30. Rothman KJ. No adjustments are needed for multiple comparisons. *Epidemiology* (1990) 1(1):43–6. doi:10.1097/00001648-199001000-00010
31. Tavazoie SF, Alvarez VA, Ridenour DA, Kwiatkowski DJ, Sabatini BL. Regulation of neuronal morphology and function by the tumor suppressors Tsc1 and Tsc2. *Nat Neurosci* (2005) 8(12):1727–34. doi:10.1038/nn1566
32. Kwon CH, Luikart BW, Powell CM, Zhou J, Matheny SA, Zhang W, et al. Pten regulates neuronal arborization and social interaction in mice. *Neuron* (2006) 50(3):377–88. doi:10.1016/j.neuron.2006.03.023
33. Sharma A, Hoeffer CA, Takayasu Y, Miyawaki T, McBride SM, Klann E, et al. Dysregulation of mTOR signaling in fragile X syndrome. *J Neurosci* (2010) 30(2):694–702. doi:10.1523/JNEUROSCI.3696-09.2010
34. Zhou J, Blundell J, Ogawa S, Kwon CH, Zhang W, Sinton C, et al. Pharmacological inhibition of mTORC1 suppresses anatomical, cellular, and behavioral abnormalities in neural-specific Pten knock-out mice. *J Neurosci* (2009) 29(6):1773–83. doi:10.1523/JNEUROSCI.5685-08.2009
35. Ehninger D, Silva AJ. Rapamycin for treating tuberous sclerosis and autism spectrum disorders. *Trends Mol Med* (2011) 17(2):78–87. doi:10.1016/j.molmed.2010.10.002
36. Fukao T, Koyasu S. PI3K and negative regulation of TLR signaling. *Trends Immunol* (2003) 24(7):358–63. doi:10.1016/S1471-4906(03)00139-X

37. Waite K, Eickholt BJ. The neurodevelopmental implications of PI3K signaling. *Curr Top Microbiol Immunol* (2010) 346:245–65. doi:10.1007/82_2010_82
38. Koyasu S. The role of PI3K in immune cells. *Nat Immunol* (2003) 4(4):313–9. doi:10.1038/ni0403-313
39. Fruman DA, Bismuth G. Fine tuning the immune response with PI3K. *Immunol Rev* (2009) 228(1):253–72. doi:10.1111/j.1600-065X.2008.00750.x
40. Ashwood P, Krakowiak P, Hertz-Picciotto I, Hansen R, Pessah IN, Van de Water J. Altered T cell responses in children with autism. *Brain Behav Immun* (2010) 25(5):840–9. doi:10.1016/j.bbi.2010.09.002
41. Yonk LJ, Warren RP, Burger RA, Cole P, Odell JD, Warren WL, et al. CD4+ helper T cell depression in autism. *Immunol Lett* (1990) 25(4):341–5. doi:10.1016/0165-2478(90)90205-5
42. Ashwood P, Anthony A, Pellicer AA, Torrente F, Walker-Smith JA, Wakefield AJ. Intestinal lymphocyte populations in children with regressive autism: evidence for extensive mucosal immunopathology. *J Clin Immunol* (2003) 23(6):504–17. doi:10.1023/B:JOCI.0000010427.05143.bb
43. Ashwood P, Enstrom A, Krakowiak P, Hertz-Picciotto I, Hansen RL, Croen LA, et al. Decreased transforming growth factor beta1 in autism: a potential link between immune dysregulation and impairment in clinical behavioral outcomes. *J Neuroimmunol* (2008) 204(1–2):149–53. doi:10.1016/j.jneuroim.2008.07.006
44. Gupta S, Aggarwal S, Rashanravan B, Lee T. Th1- and Th2-like cytokines in CD4+ and CD8+ T cells in autism. *J Neuroimmunol* (1998) 85(1):106–9. doi:10.1016/S0165-5728(98)00021-6
45. Enstrom AM, Lit L, Onore CE, Gregg JP, Hansen RL, Pessah IN, et al. Altered gene expression and function of peripheral blood natural killer cells in children with autism. *Brain Behav Immun* (2009) 23(1):124–33. doi:10.1016/j.bbi.2008.08.001
46. Enstrom AM, Onore CE, Van de Water JA, Ashwood P. Differential monocyte responses to TLR ligands in children with autism spectrum disorders. *Brain Behav Immun* (2010) 24(1):64–71. doi:10.1016/j.bbi.2009.08.001
47. Sweeten TL, Posey DJ, McDougle CJ. High blood monocyte counts and neopterin levels in children with autistic disorder. *Am J Psychiatry* (2003) 160(9):1691–3. doi:10.1176/appi.ajp.160.9.1691
48. Jyonouchi H, Geng L, Cushing-Ruby A, Quraishi H. Impact of innate immunity in a subset of children with autism spectrum disorders: a case control study. *J Neuroinflammation* (2008) 5:52. doi:10.1186/1742-2094-5-52
49. Vojdani A, Mumper E, Granpeesheh D, Mielke L, Traver D, Bock K, et al. Low natural killer cell cytotoxic activity in autism: the role of glutathione, IL-2 and IL-15. *J Neuroimmunol* (2008) 205(1–2):148–54. doi:10.1016/j.jneuroim.2008.09.005
50. Warren RP, Foster A, Margaretten NC. Reduced natural killer cell activity in autism. *J Am Acad Child Adolesc Psychiatry* (1987) 26(3):333–5. doi:10.1097/00004583-198705000-00008
51. Hoeffer CA, Sanchez E, Hagerman RJ, Mu Y, Nguyen DV, Wong H, et al. Altered mTOR signaling and enhanced CYFIP2 expression levels in subjects with fragile X syndrome. *Genes Brain Behav* (2012) 11(3):332–41. doi:10.1111/j.1601-183X.2012.00768.x
52. Kumar V, Zhang MX, Swank MW, Kunz J, Wu GY. Regulation of dendritic morphogenesis by Ras-PI3K-Akt-mTOR and Ras-MAPK signaling pathways. *J Neurosci* (2005) 25(49):11288–99. doi:10.1523/JNEUROSCI.2284-05.2005
53. Meikle L, Talos DM, Onda H, Pollizzi K, Rotenberg A, Sahin M, et al. A mouse model of tuberous sclerosis: neuronal loss of Tsc1 causes dysplastic and ectopic neurons, reduced myelination, seizure activity, and limited survival. *J Neurosci* (2007) 27(21):5546–58. doi:10.1523/JNEUROSCI.5540-06.2007
54. Ogawa S, Kwon CH, Zhou J, Koovakkattu D, Parada LF, Sinton CM. A seizure-prone phenotype is associated with altered free-running rhythm in Pten mutant mice. *Brain Res* (2007) 1168:112–23. doi:10.1016/j.brainres.2007.06.074
55. Tsai PT, Hull C, Chu Y, Greene-Colozzi E, Sadowski AR, Leech JM, et al. Autistic-like behaviour and cerebellar dysfunction in Purkinje cell Tsc1 mutant mice. *Nature* (2012) 488(7413):647–51. doi:10.1038/nature11310
56. Uhlmann EJ, Wong M, Baldwin RL, Bajenaru ML, Onda H, Kwiatkowski DJ, et al. Astrocyte-specific TSC1 conditional knockout mice exhibit abnormal neuronal organization and seizures. *Ann Neurol* (2002) 52(3):285–96. doi:10.1002/ana.10283
57. Deykin EY, MacMahon B. The incidence of seizures among children with autistic symptoms. *Am J Psychiatry* (1979) 136(10):1310–2. doi:10.1176/ajp.136.10.1310
58. Flores AI, Narayanan SP, Morse EN, Shick HE, Yin X, Kidd G, et al. Constitutively active Akt induces enhanced myelination in the CNS. *J Neurosci* (2008) 28(28):7174–83. doi:10.1523/JNEUROSCI.0150-08.2008
59. Brunet A, Bonni A, Zigmond MJ, Lin MZ, Juo P, Hu LS, et al. Akt promotes cell survival by phosphorylating and inhibiting a Forkhead transcription factor. *Cell* (1999) 96(6):857–68. doi:10.1016/S0092-8674(00)80595-4
60. Fingar DC, Salama S, Tsou C, Harlow E, Blenis J. Mammalian cell size is controlled by mTOR and its downstream targets S6K1 and 4EBP1/eIF4E. *Genes Dev* (2002) 16(12):1472–87. doi:10.1101/gad.995802
61. Cross DA, Alessi DR, Cohen P, Andjelkovich M, Hemmings BA. Inhibition of glycogen synthase kinase-3 by insulin mediated by protein kinase B. *Nature* (1995) 378(6559):785–9. doi:10.1038/378785a0
62. Woodgett JR. Molecular cloning and expression of glycogen synthase kinase-3/factor A. *EMBO J* (1990) 9(8):2431–8.
63. Salcedo-Tello P, Ortiz-Matamoros A, Arias C. GSK3 function in the brain during development, neuronal plasticity, and neurodegeneration. *Int J Alzheimers Dis* (2011) 2011:189728. doi:10.4061/2011/189728
64. Bradley CA, Peineau S, Taghibiglou C, Nicolas CS, Whitcomb DJ, Bortolotto ZA, et al. A pivotal role of GSK-3 in synaptic plasticity. *Front Mol Neurosci* (2012) 5:13. doi:10.3389/fnmol.2012.00013
65. Hooper C, Killick R, Lovestone S. The GSK3 hypothesis of Alzheimer's disease. *J Neurochem* (2008) 104(6):1433–9. doi:10.1111/j.1471-4159.2007.05194.x
66. Peineau S, Taghibiglou C, Bradley C, Wong TP, Liu L, Lu J, et al. LTP inhibits LTD in the hippocampus via regulation of GSK3beta. *Neuron* (2007) 53(5):703–17. doi:10.1016/j.neuron.2007.01.029
67. Grigorenko EL, Han SS, Yrigollen CM, Leng L, Mizue Y, Anderson GM, et al. Macrophage migration inhibitory factor and autism spectrum disorders. *Pediatrics* (2008) 122(2):e438–45. doi:10.1542/peds.2007-3604
68. Sugihara G, Hashimoto K, Iwata Y, Nakamura K, Tsujii M, Tsuchiya KJ, et al. Decreased serum levels of hepatocyte growth factor in male adults with high-functioning autism. *Prog Neuropsychopharmacol Biol Psychiatry* (2007) 31(2):412–5. doi:10.1016/j.pnpbp.2006.10.010
69. Campbell DB, D'Oronzio R, Garbett K, Ebert PJ, Mirnics K, Levitt P, et al. Disruption of cerebral cortex MET signaling in autism spectrum disorder. *Ann Neurol* (2007) 62(3):243–50. doi:10.1002/ana.21180

Blocking and Binding Folate Receptor Alpha Autoantibodies Identify Novel Autism Spectrum Disorder Subgroups

Richard E. Frye [1], Leanna Delhey [1], John Slattery [1], Marie Tippett [1], Rebecca Wynne [1], Shannon Rose [1], Stephen G. Kahler [1], Sirish C. Bennuri [1], Stepan Melnyk [1], Jeffrey M. Sequeira [2] and Edward Quadros [2]*

[1] *Department of Pediatrics, Arkansas Children's Hospital Research Institute, University of Arkansas for Medical Sciences, Little Rock, AR, USA,* [2] *Department of Medicine, State University of New York–Downstate Medical Center, Brooklyn, NY, USA*

Edited by:
Roberto Canitano,
University Hospital of Siena, Italy

Reviewed by:
Munis Dundar,
Erciyes University, Turkey
Alka Anand Subramanyam,
Topiwala National Medical College & BYL Nair Charitable Hospital, India

****Correspondence:***
Richard E. Frye
refrye@uams.edu

Folate receptor α (FRα) autoantibodies (FRAAs) are prevalent in autism spectrum disorder (ASD). They disrupt the transportation of folate across the blood-brain barrier by binding to the FRα. Children with ASD and FRAAs have been reported to respond well to treatment with a form of folate known as folinic acid, suggesting that they may be an important ASD subgroup to identify and treat. There has been no investigation of whether they manifest unique behavioral and physiological characteristics. Thus, in this study we measured both blocking and binding FRAAs, physiological measurements including indices of redox and methylation metabolism and inflammation as well as serum folate and B12 concentrations and measurements of development and behavior in 94 children with ASD. Children positive for the binding FRAA were found to have higher serum B12 levels as compared to those negative for binding FRAAs while children positive for the blocking FRAA were found to have relatively better redox metabolism and inflammation markers as compared to those negative for blocking FRAAs. In addition, ASD children positive for the blocking FRAA demonstrated better communication on the Vineland Adaptive Behavior Scale, stereotyped behavior on the Aberrant Behavioral Checklist and mannerisms on the Social Responsiveness Scale. This study suggests that FRAAs are associated with specific physiological and behavioral characteristics in children with ASD and provides support for the notion that these biomarkers may be useful for subgrouping children with ASD, especially with respect to targeted treatments.

Keywords: folate receptor autoantibody, autism spectrum disorders, folinic acid, redox metabolism, glutathione

INTRODUCTION

Autism spectrum disorder (ASD) is a devastating neurodevelopmental disorder with life-long consequences that affects young children during critical times in their development. The Center for Disease Control estimates that 1 in 68 individuals in the United States (~1–2%) are affected by an ASD (Developmental Disabilities Monitoring Network Surveillance Year 2010 Principal Investigators; Centers for Disease Control and Prevention (CDC), 2014). Despite this alarming prevalence, the etiology of ASD is still poorly understood with several studies suggesting that both environmental and genetic components may contribute equally to the etiology of ASD (Hallmayer et al., 2011; Sandin et al., 2014).

Recent research has suggested that several physiological abnormalities such as dysfunctional mitochondrial and redox metabolism and immune abnormalities, alone, or in combination, are related to the underlying aberrant biological processes that results in ASD (Rossignol and Frye, 2012b). Folate is related to many of the physiological systems found to be abnormal in ASD (Frye and James, 2014) and has been shown to be protective against the development of ASD when supplemented in adequate amounts during or before pregnancy (Schmidt et al., 2012; Suren et al., 2013). Folate is a water-soluble B vitamin that is essential for numerous metabolic reactions and normal neurodevelopment (Greenblatt et al., 1994; Black, 2008).

In some individuals with ASD, the primary mechanism that transports folate across the blood-brain barrier may be compromised. The folate receptor alpha (FRα) along with the energy dependent endocytosis transports folate, attached to the FRα, from the apical to the basolateral side of the choroid plexus endothelium against a concentration gradient. Active transport of folate is necessary because the folate concentration in the central nervous system is several times higher than the folate concentration in the blood (Frye et al., 2013b).

A new neurometabolic disorder called cerebral folate deficiency (CFD) was described about a decade ago. CFD is characterized by abnormally low folate concentrations in the cerebrospinal fluid despite normal folate concentration in the serum (Ramaekers et al., 2002). CFD is associated with autoantibodies to the FRα which impair its function (Ramaekers et al., 2005). Serum titers of FRα autoantibodies (FRAAs) have been correlated with cerebrospinal fluid (CSF) folate concentrations in independent studies (Ramaekers et al., 2005; Frye et al., 2013b). Mitochondrial disorders can cause CFD because of the lack of energy for the active transportation of folate across the blood-brain barrier (Ramaekers et al., 2007b; Garcia-Cazorla et al., 2008; Frye and Naviaux, 2011). Early case-series of children with CFD described many with ASD features (Ramaekers and Blau, 2004; Ramaekers et al., 2005).

Recently, Frye et al. (2013b) measured blocking and binding FRAAs in 93 children with ASD using the assay developed by Dr Quadros (Ramaekers et al., 2005; Molloy et al., 2009). Overall, 60 and 44% were positive for the blocking and binding FRAAs, respectively. The high prevalence of FRAAs in ASD children was verified in a study from Belgium which demonstrated that 47% of children with ASD were positive for the blocking FRAA as compared to 3.3% of developmentally delayed non-ASD controls (Ramaekers et al., 2013b). These prevalence rates for blocking FRAAs are clearly higher than prevalence rates in healthy populations which vary from 10 to 15% (Frye et al., 2013b).

The importance of the FRα is related to the targeted treatment which can bypass the FRα when it is blocked and/or dysfunctional. Folinic acid can cross the blood-brain barrier using the reduced folate carrier (RFC) when the FRα is blocked by FRAAs or non-functional due to mitochondrial dysfunction and/or genetic mutations. The RFC has a lower affinity for folate than the FRα, so a high-dose of folinic acid is required for treatment. Case-reports (Moretti et al., 2005) and series (Ramaekers et al., 2005, 2007a) have described neurological, behavioral and cognitive improvements in children with CFD and ASD with high-dose folinic acid (0.5–2 mg/kg/day), including complete recovery of ASD symptom in some and substantial improvements in communication in many (Ramaekers et al., 2005, 2007a).

Frye et al. (2013b) treated 44 children positive for at least one FRAA with high-dose folinic acid in an open-label fashion. After 4 months of treatment, significant improvements in verbal communication, receptive and expressive language and stereotypical behavior were noted in the treated children as compared to a wait list control group who were also FRAA positive. About two-thirds (66%) of treated children showed some improvement in language, verbal communication and stereotyped behavior, with one-third (~33%) demonstrating moderate or much improvement in these areas.

Although, this promising evidence suggests that FRAAs are biomarkers that can identify an important subset of children with ASD who may respond to a specific treatment, an investigation into whether the subgroup of ASD children with FRAA have particular characteristics that can distinguish them from others with ASD, has not been conducted. Thus, in this study we examine a sample of children with ASD to determine the correspondence between FRAA status and behavior and developmental characteristics. Since the folate pathway is closely connected with methylation and redox regulation pathways (Frye and James, 2014), markers of glutathione and methylation metabolism are also examined. Since antibody production can be associated with immune activation and increases in inflammation can be associated with redox and methylation abnormalities (Rose et al., 2012; Rossignol and Frye, 2014), a marker of inflammation is also examined.

Since there are two different FRAAs, blocking and blinding, our analysis determines whether the characteristics investigated are an effect of blocking or binding FRAAs independently of one another. Since some individuals will have both blocking and binding FRAAs, a general linear model is used to investigate these independent effects. This will be the first time a difference between these two FRAAs has been investigated. Such information can not only help better identify children with ASD who are positive for FRAAs but can help us understand the consequence and significance of each FRAA in ASD.

MATERIALS AND METHODS

The data from the 94 children with ASD were obtained from two research protocols approved by the Institutional Review Board at the University of Arkansas for Medical Science (Little Rock, AR). Written informed consent was obtained from parents of participants and assent was waived.

A diagnosis of ASD, required for study entry, was defined by one of the following: (i) a gold-standard diagnostic instrument such as the Autism Diagnostic Observation Schedule and/or Autism Diagnostic Interview-Revised (ADI-R); (ii) the state of Arkansas diagnostic standard, defined as agreement of a physician, psychologist and speech therapist; and/or (iii) Diagnostic and Statistical Manual for Mental Disorders diagnosis by a physician along with standardized validated questionnaires and diagnosis confirmation by the Principal Investigator (REF). Reconfirmation of the diagnosis using the ADI-R by an independent research reliable rater was requested for a portion of participants to confirm that the criteria used for including the participants was equivalent to other high-quality studies. Excluded from the study were children on antipsychotic medications as well as children with well-defined genetic syndromes.

Folate Autoantibody Assay

About 1 ml of serum was analyzed at the State University of New York, Downstate (Brooklyn, NY) for blocking and binding FRAAs using the assay previously described (Ramaekers et al., 2005; Molloy et al., 2009). Blocking FRAAs are expressed as pmoles of folic acid blocked from binding to FRα per ml of serum, and binding FRAAs are expressed as pmoles of IgG antibody per ml of serum.

Redox, Methylation, Immune and Vitamin Biomarkers

Redox and methylation potential was measured by the total and free reduced-to-oxidized glutathione redox ratio (tGSH/GSSG and fGSH/GSSG) and the S-adenosylmethionine to S-adenosylhomocysteine ratio (SAM/SAH), respectively. 3-Chlorotyrosine (CT), a measure of myeloperoxidase activity, was used as a marker of immune system activation. Fasting blood (4 ml) was collected into an EDTA-Vacutainer tube, chilled on ice and centrifuged at 1500 × g for 15 min at 4°C. Plasma was stored at −80°C and analyzed by HPLC with electrochemical detection as previously described (Melnyk et al., 1999) within 2 weeks of collection. Total plasma folate and vitamin B12 were measured using MP Diagnostics SimulTRAC-SNB Radioassay Kit (Cat# 06B264806).

Cognitive and Behavioral Assessments

The Preschool Language Scale-4 (PLS) and two versions of the Clinical Evaluations of Language Fundamentals (CELF) were used to assess language ability. The CELF is one of the only standardized, well-validated language assessment instruments that spans the age range of most participants (using both CELF-preschool-2 and CELF-4; Semel et al., 2003; Wiig et al., 2004). It assesses a wide range of language skills that are only partially measured by other language tests, including high-level language skills that are abnormal in individuals with ASD, such as language pragmatics (Condouris et al., 2003) and has been used in several studies focusing on core language deficits in ASD (Verly et al., 2014; Edgar et al., 2015). The PLS is also a standardized, well-validated language assessment instrument that can measure subtle changes in language in children with poor language abilities (Zimmerman et al., 2002; Volden et al., 2011). Both instruments provide a standardized core language score which was used as the index of language ability. For each participant the most ability appropriate instrument was used in order to prevent floor and ceiling effects.

Adaptive behavior was assessed using the Vineland Adaptive Behavior Scales, 2nd Edition, Interview Edition, Survey Form (VABS), an instrument that has demonstrated good reliability and validity (Sparrow et al., 2005). Standardized scores for summary scales were examined: communication, daily living skills, social skills, motor skills and adaptive behavior composite.

The Aberrant Behavior Checklist (ABC) was designed to measure disruptive behaviors in individuals with developmental disabilities (Aman et al., 1985). The ABC has been shown to have convergent and divergent validity in ASD (Kaat et al., 2014) and has been used in multiple autism clinical trials (Frye et al., 2015).

The Social Responsiveness Scale (SRS) measures the severity of social skill deficits (Constantino, 2002). It has been validated and shown to be reliable and to have good correspondence to the gold-standard ADI-R, while being more time efficient and cost effective (Murray et al., 2011).

Statistical Analysis

The "glm" procedure of SAS 9.1 (SAS Institute Inc., Cary, NC) was used with a two-tailed alpha of 0.05. FRAA status was dichotomized into positive or negative for both blocking and/or binding FRAAs. These variables were entered into a general linear model to determine if differences in the dependent variable were related to blocking and/or binding FRAA status. In this sense, the analysis examined the independent effects of blocking and bindings FRAAs on the dependent variable while controlling for the effect of each FRAA. Because of the limited sample size, the interaction of the two FRAAs was not examined. Planned orthogonal contrasts were used to determine whether the blocking and binding FRAAs demonstrated significant differences in the dependent variable. Since ASD symptoms are often associated with developmental level, the VABS Adaptive Behavior Composite was used as a covariate in the analysis that examined behavior and developmental indices.

RESULTS

Participants

Basic participant characteristics are outlined in **Table 1** stratified across FRAA status. The average age and gender did not differ across the FRAA groups. Race and ethnicity was not different across FRAA groups. Overall, 84% were Caucasian, 7% African American, 5% Asian and 3% mixed race and 95% were non-Hispanic.

Participants were recruited from our research registry (35%), autism clinic (27%), word-of-mouth (15%), physician referrals (13%), and community advertisement and social media (11%). All participants evaluated by an independent research reliable rater exceeded the threshold for the autism diagnosis.

Overall, immune and neurological abnormalities did not differ across FRAA status. Of the children with immune disorders, 79% had recurrent infections, 35% were diagnosed with immune disorder not otherwise specified, 32% had eczema, 21% had Pediatric Acute-onset Neuropsychiatric Syndrome, 11% had hypogammaglobulinemia and 5% had complement deficiency. Of the children with neurological abnormalities, 42% had epilepsy, 27% had migraines, 23% had abnormal electroencephalograms without seizures, 20% had visual problems, 15% had macrocephaly, 8% had Chiari malformation,

TABLE 1 | Demographic and clinical characteristics by folate receptor alpha autoantibody groups.

Variable	FRAA Negative (n = 40)	FRAA Blocking Positive (n = 16)	FRAA Binding Positive (n = 48)
Age, years months	7 years 0 months (3 years 4 months)	6 years 5 months (3 years 0 months)	7 years 4 months (3 years 2 months)
Males, N (%)	34 (85%)	15 (94%)	39 (81%)
Vineland adaptive behavior composite,	64.9 (11.7)	66.7 (10.8)	63.2 (10.4)
Only blocking autoantibody positive, N (%)		6 (38%)	
Only binding autoantibody positive, N (%)			38 (79%)
Both folate autoantibodies positive, N (%)		10 (63%)	10 (21%)
Blocking titer (pmol/ml),		0.52 (0.36)	0.54 (0.44)
Binding titer (pmol/ml),		1.03 (0.81)	0.85 (0.66)
Glutathione redox ratio, total	30.72 (1.09)	29.67 (1.07)	34.92 (2.06)
Glutathione redox ratio, free	9.06 (1.83)	9.82 (1.82)	8.75 (1.62)
Methylation SAM/SAH Ratio	2.65 (0.48)	2.67 (0.42)	2.60 (0.46)
3-Chlorotyrosine	37.7 (7.6)	33.4 (6.6)	37.1 (7.7)
Folate (ng/ml) [Normal 5-21],	17.7 (4.3)	18.9 (5.3)	18.0 (4.1)
B12 (pg/ml) [Normal 200-900],	828.3 (451.3)	1426.0 (1589.8)	1383.0 (1495.4)
LANGUAGE TESTING, N (%)			
Preschool language scales	12 (30%)	4 (25%)	17 (35%)
Clinical evaluation of language fundamentals 2	14 (35%)	6 (38%)	10 (21%)
Clinical evaluation of language fundamentals 4	13 (33%)	6 (38%)	21 (44%)
DIAGNOSTIC DOCUMENTATION, N(%)			
Autism diagnostic observation schedule	20 (50%)	8 (50%)	22 (46%)
3 Practitioner agreement	30 (75%)	10 (63%)	31 (65%)
Single practitioner with standardized questionnaires	5 (13%)	5 (31%)	12 (25%)
AUTISM DIAGNOSTIC INTERVIEW-REVISED			
Participated in confirmation testing, N(%)	27 (68%)	11 (69%)	37 (77%)
Social interaction score,	21.41 (5.44)	22.18 (4.40)	22.76 (4.96)
Communication score: verbal,	16.64 (4.40)	18.88 (1.46)	19.43 (3.89)
Communication score: non-verbal,	12.69 (2.36)	12.33 (2.08)	13.07 (1.59)
Restricted and repetitive play score,	5.85 (1.83)	5.82 (2.71)	5.84 (2.39)
Summary score,	4.41 (0.93)	4.64 (0.50)	4.41 (0.93)
MEDICATIONS (CONCURRENT TREATMENTS), N (%)			
Melatonin	17 (43%)	1 (6%)	10 (21%)
Allergy/Asthma medications	13 (33%)	4 (25%)	10 (21%)
Gastrointestinal medications	15 (38%)	2 (13%)	9 (19%)
Alpha-adrenergic agonists	7 (18%)	1 (6%)	10 (21%)
Stimulant	6 (15%)	0 (0%)	8 (17%)
Antiepileptic medication	4 (10%)	0 (0%)	6 (13%)
Antimicrobial medications	5 (13%)	1 (6%)	4 (8%)
Selective serotonin reuptake inhibitors	0 (0%)	1 (6%)	6 (13%)
Other psychotropic medications	4 (10%)	0 (0%)	2 (4%)
Immunomodulatory medications	2 (5%)	1 (6%)	2 (4%)
Antipsychotic	2 (5%)	0 (0%)	0 (0%)
Beta blocker	1 (3%)	0 (0%)	0 (0%)
SUPPLEMENTS (CONCURRENT TREATMENTS), N (%)			
Multivitamin	13 (33%)	6 (38%)	12 (25%)
Minerals	8 (20%)	3 (19%)	11 (23%)
Fatty acids	7 (18%)	4 (25%)	10 (21%)
Folate	8 (20%)	0 (0%)	7 (15%)
Vitamin B-12	2 (5%)	2 (13%)	12 (25%)
Carnitine	6 (15%)	3 (19%)	7 (15%)
Other antioxidants	4 (10%)	1 (6%)	8 (17%)
Other vitamins	7 (18%)	1 (6%)	5 (10%)

(Continued)

TABLE 1 | Continued

Variable	FRAA Negative (n = 40)	FRAA Blocking Positive (n = 16)	FRAA Binding Positive (n = 48)
Other B vitamins	3 (8%)	3 (19%)	8 (17%)
CoEnzyme Q10	4 (10%)	1 (6%)	5 (10%)
Other supplements	1 (3%)	0 (0%)	3 (6%)
Amino acids	1 (3%)	1 (6%)	2 (4%)
Thyroid supplements	1 (3%)	0 (0%)	1 (2%)
COMORBID MEDICAL CONDITIONS, N (%)			
Allergic disorders	18 (45%)	6 (38%)	19 (40%)
Gastrointestinal disorders	18 (45%)	6 (38%)	17 (35%)
Neurological disorders	9 (23%)	5 (31%)	15 (31%)
Copy number variants	7 (18%)	4 (25%)	14 (29%)
Psychiatric disorders	5 (13%)	3 (19%)	14 (29%)
Immune abnormality	8 (20%)	1 (6%)	10 (21%)

Mean values with standard deviation in parenthesis.

8% had non-specific magnetic resonance imaging abnormalities of the brain, and 4% had microcephaly.

Folate Receptor Alpha Autoantibodies

Fifty seven percent of the participants were positive for either the blocking or binding FRAAs, with 17% positive for blocking FRAA and 51% positive for the binding FRAA; 11% were positive for both FRAAs. There was no significant difference in age across participants who were FRAA blocking positive vs. negative or FRAA binding positive vs. negative.

Folate and B12

B_{12} [$F_{(1, 92)} = 4.35, p = 0.03$], but not folate, was significantly higher in the binding FRAA positive participants as compared to binding FRAA negative participants (See **Figure 1**). Participants positive for the blocking FRAA were not, as a group, significantly different than those negative for the blocking FRAA with respect to B_{12} or folate. Neither, B_{12} nor folate was significantly different in those positive for blocking FRAAs vs. those positive for the binding FRAAs.

Redox, Methylation and Inflammation Biomarkers

As depicted in **Figure 2**, total and free GSH/GSSG was significantly higher in participants positive for the blocking FRAA as compared to those participants negative for the blocking FRAA [$F_{(1, 92)} = 9.52, p = 0.003$ and $F_{(1, 92)} = 5.35, p = 0.02$, respectively]. Total and free GSH/GSSG were significantly higher in participants positive for blocking FRAAs as compared to those positive for binding FRAAs [$F_{(1, 92)} = 9.06, p = 0.003$ and $F_{(1, 92)} = 6.76, p = 0.01$, respectively].

CT was significantly lower in participants positive for the blocking FRAA as compared to those negative for the blocking FRAA [$F_{(1, 92)} = 4.83, p = 0.03$] but CT was not significantly different between those positive for blocking FRAA vs those positive for binding FRAAs.

Since supplemental B_{12} can improve the GSH/GSSG ratio in clinical studies, we reanalyzed the difference in GSH/GSSG ratio across groups with B_{12} as a covariate but the results did not changed, indicating that the difference in GSH/GSSG ratio across groups was not due to differences in serum B_{12} concentrations.

The SAM/SAH methylation ratio was not significantly different between blocking FRAA positive and negative groups. Additionally, participants positive for the binding FRAA were not, as a group, significantly different than those negative for the binding FRAA with respect to GSH/GSSG or SAH/SAH ratio or CT.

Behavior and Cognition

The VABS Adaptive Behavior Composite was not significantly different in those positive for the blocking FRAA vs. those negative for the blocking FRAA or those positive for the binding FRAA vs. those negative for the binding FRAA, suggesting that any behavioral differences found across FRAA status were not due to developmental level.

As depicted in **Figure 3**, VABS Communication [$F_{(1, 86)} = 5.95, p = 0.02$], ABC Stereotyped Behavior [$F_{(1, 84)} = 5.30, p = 0.02$] and SRS Mannerisms [$F_{(1, 82)} = 5.19, p = 0.03$] were significantly better in participants positive for blocking FRAA as compared to those negative for blocking FRAA. Total SRS Score was significantly better in those positive for the blocking FRAA as compared to those positive for the binding FRAA [$F_{(1, 82)} = 4.04, p = 0.05$]. None of the behavioral or developmental measures were different across those positive vs. negative for the binding FRAA.

DISCUSSION

FRAAs (both blocking and binding) are believed to have pathologic consequences in ASD because of their role in blocking the transport of folate into the brain by interfering with FRα function and reducing folate availability in the brain (Frye et al., 2013b). Several studies have documented that individuals with FRAAs, including those with CFD, have ASD characteristics (Ramaekers and Blau, 2004; Ramaekers et al., 2005) and the prevalence of FRAAs appears to be high in individuals with ASD (Frye et al., 2013b; Ramaekers et al., 2013b). However, until

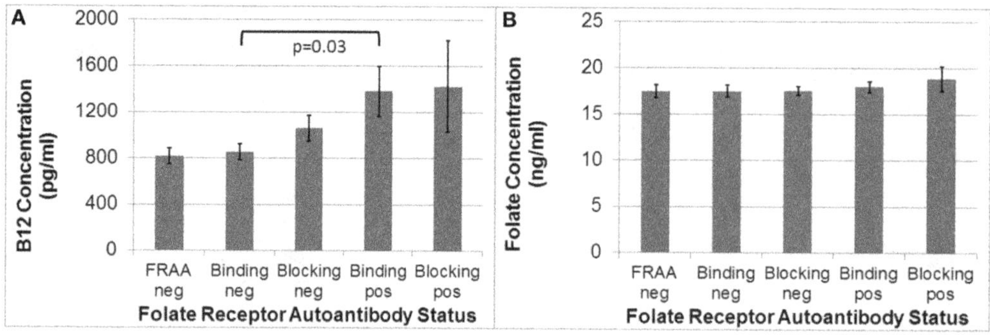

FIGURE 1 | (A) Children with Autism Spectrum Disorder who are positive for the binding Folate Receptor Alpha Autoantibody have higher serum B12 concentrations than children negative for the binding Folate Receptor Alpha Autoantibody; **(B)** Serum Folate concentration does not differ across Folate Receptor Alpha Autoantibody status in children with Autism Spectrum Disorder.

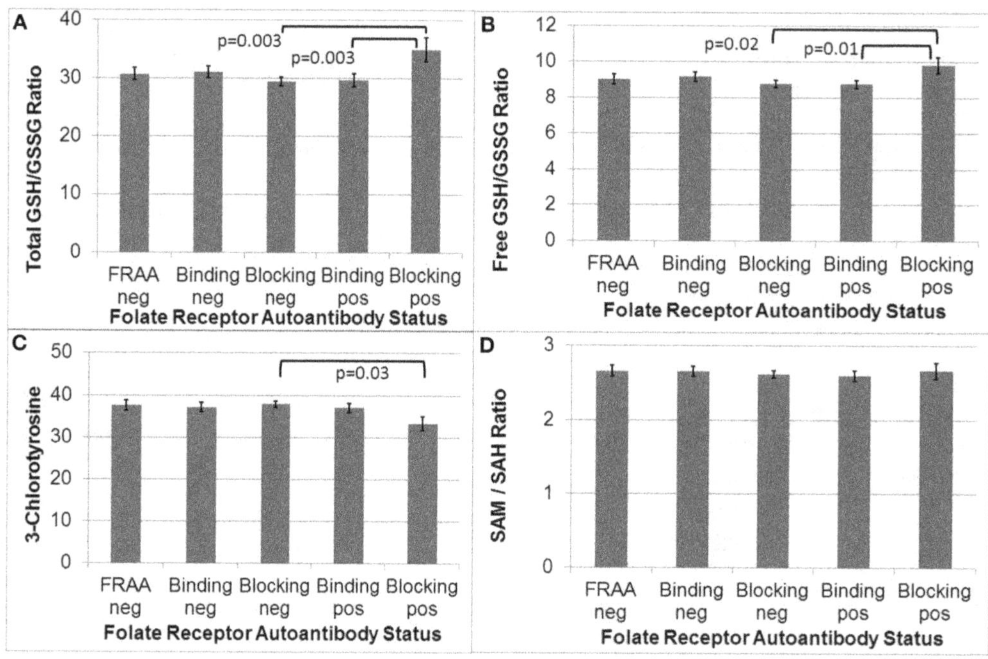

FIGURE 2 | Children with Autism Spectrum Disorder who are positive for the blocking Folate Receptor Alpha Autoantibody have more favorable total and free glutathione redox ratios (A,B) and marker of inflammation (C) as compared to those negative for the blocking FRAA. (D) Methylation metabolism was not different across Folate Receptor Alpha Autoantibody status.

this study no one has examined whether individuals with ASD who are FRAA positive have behavioral, developmental and/or physiological characteristics that are distinct from individuals with ASD who are negative for FRAAs.

In this study we found that individuals with ASD who were positive for the blocking FRAA demonstrated behavioral and physiological differences as compared to those negative for the blocking FRAA and as compared to those positive for the binding FRAA. Interestingly this subset of children appears to have better physiological and behavioral profiles, although their behavioral scores are well within the range for children with ASD. There is evidence that children positive for the FRAAs respond to folinic acid therapy, suggesting that these children are a subset of children with ASD that may be particularly responsive to therapy that addresses physiological abnormalities. The fact that children with FRAAs, at least blocking FRAAs, may have less severe ASD symptoms, suggests that these children may be a group to target early as they may be very likely to substantially improve their ASD symptoms and attain optimal outcomes with treatment. This may explain several reports of children with CFD recovering from ASD symptoms with high-dose folinic acid therapy—since they may have started out with milder ASD symptoms it may have been easier for them to recover.

Interestingly, ASD children with the blocking FRAA appear to have a more favorable redox and inflammation profile with relatively better glutathione and CT indices than FRAA blocking

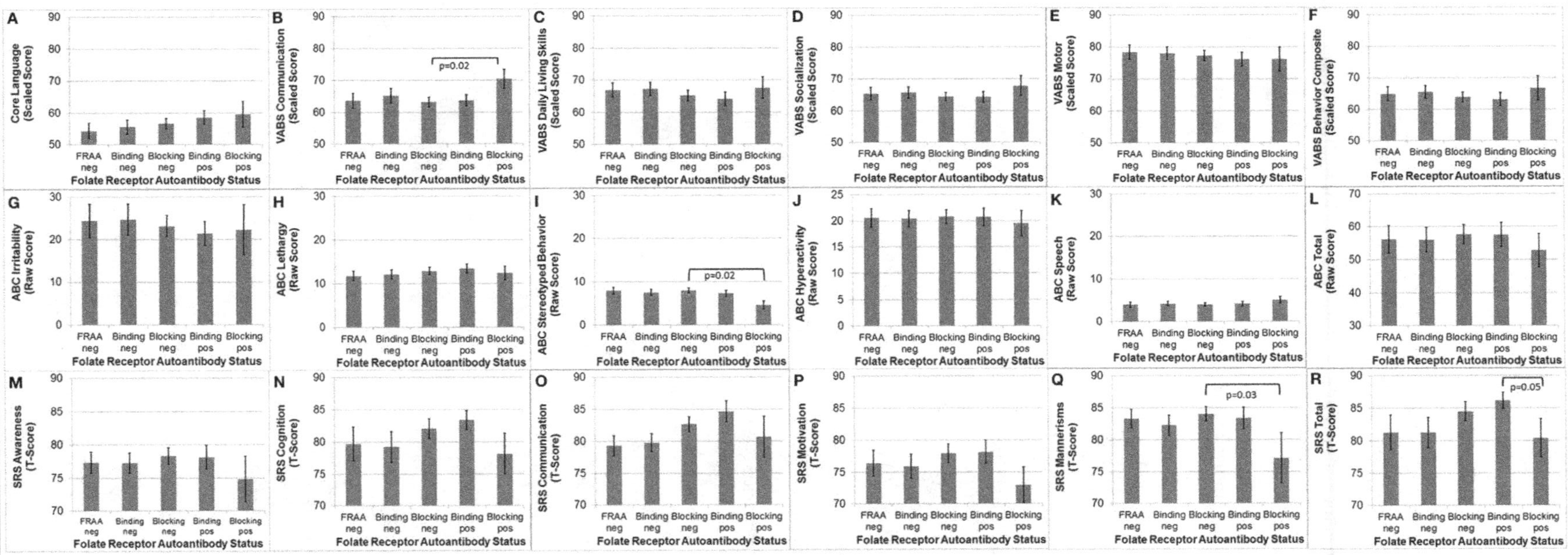

FIGURE 3 | Children with Autism Spectrum Disorder who are positive for the blocking Folate Receptor Alpha Autoantibody have more favorable (B) communication on the Vineland Adaptive Behavior Scale, (I) Stereotyped behavior on the Aberrant Behavior Checklist (ABC) and (Q) Mannerisms on the Social Responsiveness Scale (SRS) as compared to children negative for the blocking Folate Receptor Alpha Autoantibody. (R) In addition, children positive for the blocking FRAA have better total Social Responsiveness Scale score than those positive for the binding Folate Receptor Alpha Autoantibody. This figure depicts behavioral and Cognitive differences across Folate Receptor Alpha Autoantibody (FRAA) groups including difference in **(A)** Language, **(B–F)** Vineland Adaptive Behavioral Scale, **(G–L)** ABC, and **(M–R)** SRS.

negative children. A group of children with ASD and relatively unfavorable redox profiles have been described as having a distinct metabolic endophenotype in previous studies (James et al., 2006). It would appear that the group of ASD children with blocking FRAAs may be a complimentary metabolic endophenotype to the group with unfavorable redox metabolism that may have abnormalities specific to folate metabolism rather than redox metabolism. Importantly, this study demonstrates how multiple biomarkers can be used to differentiate subgroups of children with ASD who could potentially respond to different and/or synergistic treatments.

Children with ASD who are positive for the binding FRAA did not appear to have significant differences in behavioral, developmental or physiological measures when compared to children with ASD who were negative for the binding FRAA but the group did demonstrate significantly higher serum B12 concentrations. This may suggest that the binding FRAAs may interfere with cellular B12 uptake, resulting in a higher concentration of B12 in the blood. Indeed, polymorphisms in the B12 binding protein have been linked to an increased risk of ASD (James et al., 2006). Thus, the binding FRAAs may yet be another mechanism for interfering with B12 metabolism, resulting in methylation and glutathione abnormalities. Abnormalities in B12 metabolism, especially interference with B12 uptake into the cell, could result in the glutathione abnormalities seen in participants with the binding FRAAs. As B12 supplementation can correct glutathione metabolism abnormalities ASD (James et al., 2009) and improve adaptive behavior (Frye et al., 2013a) in children with ASD, it is very possible that a deficit in the cellular uptake of B12, either through a polymorphism in the B12 binding protein or binding FRAA interfering with B12 transport, could result in abnormal glutathione metabolism. Although, we used B12 as a covariate in the analysis of glutathione differences across groups, the covariate would only have been significant if it represented higher levels of intracellular B12. If indeed the higher B12 levels represent a failure of B12 entering the cell, then the covariate would have no relation to glutathione levels (or may have had the opposite predicted relationship). Thus, this is another indication that the elevated B12 levels associated with the binding FRAA do not represent intracellular levels and may be a reflection of a lack of cellular B12 uptake. If this is the case, the binding FRAA may interfere with both folate and B12 transportation, resulting in a more severe phenotype. Indeed, individuals positive for the binding FRAA appear to have worse social skills (as measured by the SRS) than children positive for the blocking FRAA.

Because of the limited sample size we might not have been able to detect small differences in physiology and behavior between the groups. Larger sample sizes could be helpful in detecting more subtle physiological and behavioral differences between groups. Perhaps an interesting study would be to measure the variation in FRAA titers within individuals. Titers tend to vary over short intervals of time (Ramaekers et al., 2013a), but this study only characterized the participants as FRAA positive or negative. It may be very useful to monitor changes in both FRAA titers and behavior within an individual over time as a more sensitive measure of the relationship between FRAAs titers and behavior, as examining intra-subject variation can control for the variation in physiology between individuals. Indeed, one study has demonstrated that the close relationship between aggression and blocking FRAA titers over a 6 week period in a 8 year old girl with ASD (Ramaekers et al., 2007a). Although, this study did not find any relationship between aggressive behavior and FRAA status, this may have been due to the large number of factors that can result in aggressive behavior within an individual with ASD (Matson and Jang, 2014). Thus, intra-subject studies may be most sensitive, especially if considering correlating FRAA titers.

It is important to appreciate that FRAAs could also work in concert with the defects in folate metabolism that have been associated with ASD, including polymorphisms in dihydrofolate reductase (Adams et al., 2007), the reduced folate carrier (James et al., 2006) and methylenetetrahydrofolate reductase (Frustaci et al., 2012), and mitochondrial dysfunction which appears to be rather common in children with ASD (Frye and Rossignol, 2011; Rossignol and Frye, 2012a). In addition, emerging evidence suggests that the enteric microbiome also has an important role for regulating the bioavailability of vitamins such as folate and B12 (Frye et al., 2015). Thus, a study which comprehensively assesses multiple folate pathway abnormalities in relationship to ASD behavior could be very insightful.

This study has helped define the importance of FRAAs in ASD and the effect of the FRAAs on physiology and behavior. It appears that blocking and binding FRAAs are associated with slightly different physiological and behavioral effects in children with ASD. Further, research will help better define their physiological roles and significance. Studying clinical subgroups in other disorders associated with FRAAs such as schizophrenia (Ramaekers et al., 2014) and subfertility (Berrocal-Zaragoza et al., 2009) may also yield important information. Ultimately, this information may be important to determining optimal treatments for certain children with ASD.

AUTHOR CONTRIBUTIONS

RF designed the study, analyzed the data and wrote the manuscript; LD collected and analyzed the data and edited the manuscript; JS collected and analyzed the data and designed the study and edited the manuscript; MT collected the data and edited the manuscript; RW collected and analyzed the data; SR collected and analyzed the data and edited the manuscript; SK edited the manuscript; SB analyzed the data; SM collected and analyzed the data and designed the study and edited the manuscript; JS collected and analyzed the data; EQ designed the study and wrote the manuscript.

ACKNOWLEDGMENTS

This study was supported, in part, by funding from the Arkansas Biosciences Institute, Autism Research Institute, the Jane Botsford Johnson Foundation and Autism Speaks grant #8202.

REFERENCES

Adams, M., Lucock, M., Stuart, J., Fardell, S., Baker, K., and Ng, X. (2007). Preliminary evidence for involvement of the folate gene polymorphism 19bp deletion-DHFR in occurrence of autism. *Neurosci. Lett.* 422, 24–29. doi: 10.1016/j.neulet.2007.05.025

Aman, M. G., Singh, N. N., Stewart, A. W., and Field, C. J. (1985). The aberrant behavior checklist: a behavior rating scale for the assessment of treatment effects. *Am. J. Ment. Defic.* 89, 485–491.

Berrocal-Zaragoza, M. I., Fernandez-Ballart, J. D., Murphy, M. M., Cavalle-Busquets, P., Sequeira, J. M., and Quadros, E. V. (2009). Association between blocking folate receptor autoantibodies and subfertility. *Fertil. Steril.* 91, 1518–1521. doi: 10.1016/j.fertnstert.2008.08.104

Black, M. M. (2008). Effects of vitamin B12 and folate deficiency on brain development in children. *Food Nutr. Bull.* 29, S126–S131. doi: 10.1177/15648265080292S117

Condouris, K., Meyer, E., and Tager-Flusberg, H. (2003). The relationship between standardized measures of language and measures of spontaneous speech in children with autism. *Am. J. Speech Lang. Pathol.* 12, 349–358. doi: 10.1044/1058-0360(2003/080)

Constantino, J. N. (2002). *The Social Responsiveness Scale.* Los Angeles, CA: Western Psychological Services.

Developmental Disabilities Monitoring Network Surveillance Year 2010 Principal Investigators; Centers for Disease Control and Prevention (CDC) (2014). Prevalence of autism spectrum disorder among children aged 8 years - autism and developmental disabilities monitoring network, 11 sites, United States, 2010. *MMWR. Surveill. Summ.* 63, 1–21.

Edgar, J. C., Khan, S. Y., Blaskey, L., Chow, V. Y., Rey, M., Gaetz, W., et al. (2015). Neuromagnetic oscillations predict evoked-response latency delays and core language deficits in autism spectrum disorders. *J. Autism Dev. Disord.* 45, 395–405. doi: 10.1007/s10803-013-1904-x

Frustaci, A., Neri, M., Cesario, A., Adams, J. B., Domenici, E., Dalla Bernardina, B., et al. (2012). Oxidative stress-related biomarkers in autism: systematic review and meta-analyses. *Free Radic. Biol. Med.* 52, 2128–2141. doi: 10.1016/j.freeradbiomed.2012.03.011

Frye, R. E., and James, S. J. (2014). Metabolic pathology of autism in relation to redox metabolism. *Biomark. Med.* 8, 321–330. doi: 10.2217/bmm.13.158

Frye, R. E., Melnyk, S., Fuchs, G., Reid, T., Jernigan, S., Pavliv, O., et al. (2013a). Effectiveness of methylcobalamin and folinic Acid treatment on adaptive behavior in children with autistic disorder is related to glutathione redox status. *Autism Res. Treat.* 2013:609705. doi: 10.1155/2013/609705

Frye, R. E., and Naviaux, R. K. (2011). Autistic disorder with complex IV overactivity: a new mitochondrial syndrome. *J. Pediatr. Neurol.* 9, 427–434. doi: 10.3233/JPN-2011-0507

Frye, R. E., and Rossignol, D. A. (2011). Mitochondrial dysfunction can connect the diverse medical symptoms associated with autism spectrum disorders. *Pediatr. Res.* 69, 41R–47R. doi: 10.1203/PDR.0b013e318212f16b

Frye, R. E., Sequeira, J. M., Quadros, E. V., James, S. J., and Rossignol, D. A. (2013b). Cerebral folate receptor autoantibodies in autism spectrum disorder. *Mol. Psychiatry* 18, 369–381. doi: 10.1038/mp.2011.175

Frye, R. E., Slattery, J., Macfabe, D. F., Allen-Vercoe, E., Parker, W., Rodakis, J., et al. (2015). Approaches to studying and manipulating the enteric microbiome to improve autism symptoms. *Microb. Ecol. Health Dis.* 26:26878. doi: 10.3402/mehd.v26.26878

Garcia-Cazorla, A., Quadros, E. V., Nascimento, A., Garcia-Silva, M. T., Briones, P., Montoya, J., et al. (2008). Mitochondrial diseases associated with cerebral folate deficiency. *Neurology* 70, 1360–1362. doi: 10.1212/01.wnl.0000309223.98616.e4

Greenblatt, J. M., Huffman, L. C., and Reiss, A. L. (1994). Folic acid in neurodevelopment and child psychiatry. *Prog. Neuropsychopharmacol. Biol. Psychiatry* 18, 647–660. doi: 10.1016/0278-5846(94)90074-4

Hallmayer, J., Cleveland, S., Torres, A., Phillips, J., Cohen, B., Torigoe, T., et al. (2011). Genetic heritability and shared environmental factors among twin pairs with autism. *Arch. Gen. Psychiatry* 68, 1095–1102. doi: 10.1001/archgenpsychiatry.2011.76

James, S. J., Melnyk, S., Fuchs, G., Reid, T., Jernigan, S., Pavliv, O., et al. (2009). Efficacy of methylcobalamin and folinic acid treatment on glutathione redox status in children with autism. *Am. J. Clin. Nutr.* 89, 425–430. doi: 10.3945/ajcn.2008.26615

James, S. J., Melnyk, S., Jernigan, S., Cleves, M. A., Halsted, C. H., Wong, D. H., et al. (2006). Metabolic endophenotype and related genotypes are associated with oxidative stress in children with autism. *Am. J. Med. Genet. B Neuropsychiatr. Genet.* 141B, 947–956. doi: 10.1002/ajmg.b.30366

Kaat, A. J., Lecavalier, L., and Aman, M. G. (2014). Validity of the aberrant behavior checklist in children with autism spectrum disorder. *J. Autism Dev. Disord.* 44, 1103–1116. doi: 10.1007/s10803-013-1970-0

Matson, J. L., and Jang, J. (2014). Treating aggression in persons with autism spectrum disorders: a review. *Res. Dev. Disabil.* 35, 3386–3391. doi: 10.1016/j.ridd.2014.08.025

Melnyk, S., Pogribna, M., Pogribny, I., Hine, R. J., and James, S. J. (1999). A new HPLC method for the simultaneous determination of oxidized and reduced plasma aminothiols using coulometric electrochemical detection. *J. Nutr. Biochem.* 10, 490–497. doi: 10.1016/S0955-2863(99)00033-9

Molloy, A. M., Quadros, E. V., Sequeira, J. M., Troendle, J. F., Scott, J. M., Kirke, P. N., et al. (2009). Lack of association between folate-receptor autoantibodies and neural-tube defects. *N. Engl. J. Med.* 361, 152–160. doi: 10.1056/NEJMoa0803783

Moretti, P., Sahoo, T., Hyland, K., Bottiglieri, T., Peters, S., Del Gaudio, D., et al. (2005). Cerebral folate deficiency with developmental delay, autism, and response to folinic acid. *Neurology* 64, 1088–1090. doi: 10.1212/01.WNL.0000154641.08211.B7

Murray, M. J., Mayes, S. D., and Smith, L. A. (2011). Brief report: excellent agreement between two brief autism scales (Checklist for Autism Spectrum Disorder and Social Responsiveness Scale) completed independently by parents and the Autism Diagnostic Interview-Revised. *J. Autism Dev. Disord.* 41, 1586–1590. doi: 10.1007/s10803-011-1178-0

Ramaekers, V., Sequeira, J. M., and Quadros, E. V. (2013a). Clinical recognition and aspects of the cerebral folate deficiency syndromes. *Clin. Chem. Lab. Med.* 51, 497–511. doi: 10.1515/cclm-2012-0543

Ramaekers, V. T., and Blau, N. (2004). Cerebral folate deficiency. *Dev. Med. Child Neurol.* 46, 843–851. doi: 10.1111/j.1469-8749.2004.tb00451.x

Ramaekers, V. T., Blau, N., Sequeira, J. M., Nassogne, M. C., and Quadros, E. V. (2007a). Folate receptor autoimmunity and cerebral folate deficiency in low-functioning autism with neurological deficits. *Neuropediatrics* 38, 276–281. doi: 10.1055/s-2008-1065354

Ramaekers, V. T., Hausler, M., Opladen, T., Heimann, G., and Blau, N. (2002). Psychomotor retardation, spastic paraplegia, cerebellar ataxia and dyskinesia associated with low 5-methyltetrahydrofolate in cerebrospinal fluid: a novel neurometabolic condition responding to folinic acid substitution. *Neuropediatrics* 33, 301–308. doi: 10.1055/s-2002-37082

Ramaekers, V. T., Quadros, E. V., and Sequeira, J. M. (2013b). Role of folate receptor autoantibodies in infantile autism. *Mol. Psychiatry* 18, 270–271. doi: 10.1038/mp.2012.22

Ramaekers, V. T., Rothenberg, S. P., Sequeira, J. M., Opladen, T., Blau, N., Quadros, E. V., et al. (2005). Autoantibodies to folate receptors in the cerebral folate deficiency syndrome. *N. Engl. J. Med.* 352, 1985–1991. doi: 10.1056/NEJMoa043160

Ramaekers, V. T., Thony, B., Sequeira, J. M., Ansseau, M., Philippe, P., Boemer, F., et al. (2014). Folinic acid treatment for schizophrenia associated with folate receptor autoantibodies. *Mol. Genet. Metab.* 113, 307–314. doi: 10.1016/j.ymgme.2014.10.002

Ramaekers, V. T., Weis, J., Sequeira, J. M., Quadros, E. V., and Blau, N. (2007b). Mitochondrial complex I encephalomyopathy and cerebral 5-methyltetrahydrofolate deficiency. *Neuropediatrics* 38, 184–187. doi: 10.1055/s-2007-991150

Rose, S., Melnyk, S., Pavliv, O., Bai, S., Nick, T. G., Frye, R. E., et al. (2012). Evidence of oxidative damage and inflammation associated with low glutathione redox status in the autism brain. *Transl. Psychiatry* 2, e134. doi: 10.1038/tp.2012.61

Rossignol, D. A., and Frye, R. E. (2012a). Mitochondrial dysfunction in autism spectrum disorders: a systematic review and meta-analysis. *Mol. Psychiatry* 17, 290–314. doi: 10.1038/mp.2010.136

Rossignol, D. A., and Frye, R. E. (2012b). A review of research trends in physiological abnormalities in autism spectrum disorders: immune dysregulation, inflammation, oxidative stress, mitochondrial dysfunction and environmental toxicant exposures. *Mol. Psychiatry* 17, 389–401. doi: 10.1038/mp.2011.165

Rossignol, D. A., and Frye, R. E. (2014). Evidence linking oxidative stress, mitochondrial dysfunction, and inflammation in the brain of individuals with autism. *Front. Physiol.* 5:150. doi: 10.3389/fphys.2014.00150

Sandin, S., Lichtenstein, P., Kuja-Halkola, R., Larsson, H., Hultman, C. M., and Reichenberg, A. (2014). The familial risk of autism. *JAMA* 311, 1770–1777. doi: 10.1001/jama.2014.4144

Schmidt, R. J., Tancredi, D. J., Ozonoff, S., Hansen, R. L., Hartiala, J., Allayee, H., et al. (2012). Maternal periconceptional folic acid intake and risk of autism spectrum disorders and developmental delay in the CHARGE (CHildhood Autism Risks from Genetics and Environment) case-control study. *Am. J. Clin. Nutr.* 96, 80–89. doi: 10.3945/ajcn.110.004416

Semel, E., Wiig, E. H., and Secord, W. A. (2003). *Clinical Evaluation of Language Fundamentals, 4th Edn, (CELF-4).* Toronto, ON: The Psychological Corporation/A Harcourt Assessment Company.

Sparrow, S., Cicchetti, D., and Balla, D. (2005). *Vineland Adaptive Behavior Scales, 2nd Edn.* Minneapolis, MN: Pearson Assessment.

Suren, P., Roth, C., Bresnahan, M., Haugen, M., Hornig, M., Hirtz, D., et al. (2013). Association between maternal use of folic acid supplements and risk of autism spectrum disorders in children. *JAMA* 309, 570–577. doi: 10.1001/jama.2012.155925

Verly, M., Verhoeven, J., Zink, I., Mantini, D., Van Oudenhove, L., Lagae, L., et al. (2014). Structural and functional underconnectivity as a negative predictor for language in autism. *Hum. Brain Mapp.* 35, 3602–3615. doi: 10.1002/hbm.22424

Volden, J., Smith, I. M., Szatmari, P., Bryson, S., Fombonne, E., Mirenda, P., et al. (2011). Using the preschool language scale, fourth edition to characterize language in preschoolers with autism spectrum disorders. *Am. J. Speech Lang. Pathol.* 20, 200–208. doi: 10.1044/1058-0360(2011/10-0035)

Wiig, E. H., Secord, W. A., and Semel, E. (2004). *Clinical Evaluation of Language Fundamentals—Preschool, 2nd Edn. (CELF Preschool-2).* Toronto, ON: The Psychological Corporation/A Harcourt Assessment Company.

Zimmerman, I. L., Steiner, V. G., and E., P. R. (2002). *Preschool Language Scale, 4th Edn.* San Antonio, TX: The Psychological Corporation.

Permissions

All chapters in this book were first published in ASDDTNBTU, by Frontiers; hereby published with permission under the Creative Commons Attribution License or equivalent. Every chapter published in this book has been scrutinized by our experts. Their significance has been extensively debated. The topics covered herein carry significant findings which will fuel the growth of the discipline. They may even be implemented as practical applications or may be referred to as a beginning point for another development.

The contributors of this book come from diverse backgrounds, making this book a truly international effort. This book will bring forth new frontiers with its revolutionizing research information and detailed analysis of the nascent developments around the world.

We would like to thank all the contributing authors for lending their expertise to make the book truly unique. They have played a crucial role in the development of this book. Without their invaluable contributions this book wouldn't have been possible. They have made vital efforts to compile up to date information on the varied aspects of this subject to make this book a valuable addition to the collection of many professionals and students.

This book was conceptualized with the vision of imparting up-to-date information and advanced data in this field. To ensure the same, a matchless editorial board was set up. Every individual on the board went through rigorous rounds of assessment to prove their worth. After which they invested a large part of their time researching and compiling the most relevant data for our readers.

The editorial board has been involved in producing this book since its inception. They have spent rigorous hours researching and exploring the diverse topics which have resulted in the successful publishing of this book. They have passed on their knowledge of decades through this book. To expedite this challenging task, the publisher supported the team at every step. A small team of assistant editors was also appointed to further simplify the editing procedure and attain best results for the readers.

Apart from the editorial board, the designing team has also invested a significant amount of their time in understanding the subject and creating the most relevant covers. They scrutinized every image to scout for the most suitable representation of the subject and create an appropriate cover for the book.

The publishing team has been an ardent support to the editorial, designing and production team. Their endless efforts to recruit the best for this project, has resulted in the accomplishment of this book. They are a veteran in the field of academics and their pool of knowledge is as vast as their experience in printing. Their expertise and guidance has proved useful at every step. Their uncompromising quality standards have made this book an exceptional effort. Their encouragement from time to time has been an inspiration for everyone.

The publisher and the editorial board hope that this book will prove to be a valuable piece of knowledge for researchers, students, practitioners and scholars across the globe.

List of Contributors

Blythe A. Corbett
Department of Psychiatry and Behavioral Sciences, Vanderbilt University, Nashville, TN, USA
Vanderbilt Brain Institute, Neuroscience Graduate Program, Vanderbilt University, Nashville, TN, USA

Rachael A. Muscatello
Vanderbilt Brain Institute, Neuroscience Graduate Program, Vanderbilt University, Nashville, TN, USA

Scott D. Blain
Department of Psychology and Human Development, Vanderbilt University, Nashville, TN, USA

Martina Franchini
Office Médico-Pédagogique, University of Geneva, Geneva, Switzerland
Psychology and Educational Sciences, University of Geneva, Geneva, Switzerland

Hilary Wood de Wilde and Bronwyn Glaser
Office Médico-Pédagogique, University of Geneva, Geneva, Switzerland

Edouard Gentaz
Psychology and Educational Sciences, University of Geneva, Geneva, Switzerland

Stephan Eliez
Department of Medical Genetics, Geneva University Medical School, Geneva, Switzerland
Office Médico-Pédagogique, University of Geneva, Geneva, Switzerland

Marie Schaer
Office Médico-Pédagogique, University of Geneva, Geneva, Switzerland,
Stanford Cognitive & Systems Neuroscience Laboratory, Stanford University, Palo Alto, CA, USA

Eleonora Napoli, Catherine Ross-Inta, Gyu Song and Sarah Wong
Department of Molecular Biosciences, School of Veterinary Medicine, Davis, CA, USA

Randi Hagerman
Medical Investigations of Neurodevelopmental Disorders Institute, University of California, Davis, Davis, CA, USA
Department of Pediatrics, University of California Davis Medical Center, Sacramento, CA, USA

Louise W. Gane
Medical Investigations of Neurodevelopmental Disorders Institute, University of California, Davis, Davis, CA, USA

Jennifer T. Smilowitz
Department of Food Science and Technology and Foods for Health Institute, University of California, Davis, Davis, CA, USA

Flora Tassone
Medical Investigations of Neurodevelopmental Disorders Institute, University of California, Davis, Davis, CA, USA
Department of Biochemistry and Molecular Medicine, School of Medicine, University of California, Davis, Davis, CA, USA

Cecilia Giulivi
Department of Molecular Biosciences, School of Veterinary Medicine, Davis, CA, USA
Medical Investigations of Neurodevelopmental Disorders Institute, University of California, Davis, Davis, CA, USA

Richard E. Frye and John C. Slattery
Autism Research Program, Arkansas Children's Research Institute, Little Rock, AR, USA
Department of Pediatrics, University of Arkansas for Medical Sciences, Little Rock, AR, USA

Manuel F. Casanova
Department of Biomedical Sciences, University of South Carolina School of Medicine Greenville, Greenville, SC, USA

S. Hossein Fatemi, Timothy D. Folsom, and Teri J. Reutiman
Department of Psychiatry, University of Minnesota Medical School, Minneapolis, MN, USA

Gregory L. Brown
Serenity Health Care Center, Waukesha, WI, USA

Stephen M. Edelson
Autism Research Institute, San Diego,CA, USA

James B. Adams
School for Engineering of Matter, Transport, and Energy, Arizona State University, Tempe, AZ, USA

Lucia Billeci, Camilla Gesi, Claudia Carmassi and Liliana Dell'Osso
Department of Clinical and Experimental Medicine, University of Pisa, Pisa, Italy

Sara Calderoni
IRCCS Stella Maris Foundation, Pisa, Italy

Eugenia Conti
Department of Clinical and Experimental Medicine, University of Pisa, Pisa, Italy
Department of Sciences for Health Promotion and Mother and Child Care G. D'Alessandro, University of Palermo, Palermo, Italy

Giovanni Cioni, Filippo Muratori and Andrea Guzzetta
Department of Clinical and Experimental Medicine, University of Pisa, Pisa, Italy
IRCCS Stella Maris Foundation, Pisa, Italy

Bernard J. Crespi
Department of Biological Sciences and Human Evolutionary Studies Program, Simon Fraser University, Burnaby, BC, Canada

Giovanni Provenzano, Zelia Corradi and Katia Monsorno
Laboratory of Molecular Neuropathology, Centre for Integrative Biology, University of Trento, Trento, Italy

Tarcisio Fedrizzi
Bioinformatics Core Facility, Centre for Integrative Biology, University of Trento, Trento, Italy

Laura Ricceri and Maria L. Scattoni
Neurotoxicology and Neuroendocrinology Section, Department of Cell Biology and Neuroscience, Istituto Superiore di Sanità, Rome, Italy,

Yuri Bozzi
Laboratory of Molecular Neuropathology, Centre for Integrative Biology, University of Trento, Trento, Italy
National Research Council Neuroscience Institute,Pisa, Italy

Eva Loth and Declan G. Murphy
Department of Forensic and Neurodevelopmental Sciences, Institute of Psychiatry, Psychology and Neuroscience, King'sCollege London, London, UK
Sackler Institute for Translational Neurodevelopment, Institute of Psychiatry, Psychology and Neuroscience, King's College London, London, UK

Will Spooren
Roche Pharmaceutical Research and Early Development, NORD Discovery and Translational Area, Roche Innovation Center, Basel, Switzerland

Antoine Tanet
Institut des Systèmes Intelligents et de Robotiques, Université Pierre et Marie Curie, Paris, France
Departement de Psychiatrie de l'Enfant et de l'Adolescent, APHP, Groupe Hospitalier Pitié-Salpêtrière et Université Pierre et Marie Curie, Paris, France
Croix Rouge Française, Paris, France

Annik Hubert-Barthelemy
Croix Rouge Française, Paris, France

Graciela C. Crespin
Association Programme de Recherche et d'Etudes sur l'Autisme, Paris, France

Nicolas Bodeau
Departement de Psychiatrie de l'Enfant et de l'Adolescent, APHP, Groupe Hospitalier Pitié-Salpêtrière et Université Pierre et Marie Curie, Paris, France

David Cohen
Institut des Systèmes Intelligents et de Robotiques, Université Pierre et Marie Curie, Paris, France
Departement de Psychiatrie de l'Enfant et de l'Adolescent, APHP, Groupe Hospitalier Pitié-Salpêtrière et Université Pierre et Marie Curie, Paris, France

Catherine Saint-Georges
Institut des Systèmes Intelligents et de Robotiques, Université Pierre et Marie Curie, Paris, France
Departement de Psychiatrie de l'Enfant et de l'Adolescent, APHP, Groupe Hospitalier Pitié-Salpêtrière et Université Pierre et Marie Curie, Paris, France
Hôpital de jour Centre André Boulloche, Paris, France

Roberto Canitano
Division of Child Neuropsychiatry, University Hospital of Siena, Siena, Italy

Mauro Pallagrosi
Department of Psychiatry, Sapienza University of Rome, Rome, Italy

Asher Ornoy and Liza Weinstein- Fudim
Laboratory of Teratology, Department of Medical Neurobiology, Hadassah Medical School, Hebrew University, Jerusalem,Israel

Zivanit Ergaz
Laboratory of Teratology, Department of Medical Neurobiology, Hadassah Medical School, Hebrew University, Jerusalem,Israel
Department of Neonatology, Hadassah-Hebrew University Medical Center, Jerusalem

Alessandro Gozzi
Functional Neuroimaging Laboratory, Center for Neuroscience and Cognitive Systems @ UniTn, Istituto Italiano di Tecnologia, Rovereto, Italy

Adam Liska
Functional Neuroimaging Laboratory, Center for Neuroscience and Cognitive Systems @ UniTn, Istituto Italiano di Tecnologia, Rovereto, Italy
Center for Mind/Brain Sciences, University of Trento, Rovereto, Italy

Francesco Cardona, Francesca Valente, Daniela Miraglia and Valentina Baglioni
Dipartimento di Pediatria e Neuropsichiatria Infantile, Università degli Studi di Roma "La Sapienza", Rome, Italy

Caterina D'Ardia
Università degli Studi Niccolò Cusano, Rome, Italy

Flavia Chiarotti
Dipartimento di Biologia Cellulare e Neuroscienze, Istituto Superiore di Sanità, Rome, Italy

H. Dyer
School of Medicine, Trinity College Dublin, Dublin, Ireland

Daniela Tropea
Department of Psychiatry, Trinity College Dublin, Dublin, Ireland

Antonio Benítez-Burraco
Department of Philology, University of Huelva, Huelva, Spain

Wanda Lattanzi
Institute of Anatomy and Cell Biology, Università Cattolica delSacro Cuore, Rome, Italy

Elliot Murphy
Division of Psychology and Language Sciences, University College London, London, UK

Valentina Bono, Koushik Maharatna, Mike Wald, Stephane Hommel and Wasifa Jamal
Electronics and Computer Science, University of Southampton, Southampton, UK

Antonio Narzisi, Lucia Billeci and Filippo Muratori
Department of Developmental Neuroscience, IRCCS Stella Maris Foundation, Pisa, Italy

Anne-Lise Jouen and Mohamed Chetouani
Institute of Intelligent Systems and Robotics, University Pierre and Marie Curie, Paris, France

Elodie Tilmont and David Cohen
Institute of Intelligent Systems and Robotics, University Pierre and Marie Curie, Paris, France
Department of Child and Adolescent Psychiatry, APHP, Groupe Hospitalier Pitié-Salpêtrière et University Pierre and Marie Curie, Paris, France

Jean Xavier
Department of Child and Adolescent Psychiatry, APHP, Groupe Hospitalier Pitié-Salpêtrière et University Pierre and Marie Curie, Paris, France

Moriya Gamliel
Department of Immunology and Cancer Research, Hadassah-Hebrew University Medical Center, Jerusalem, Israel

Karen L. Anderson and David Mankuta
Department of Obstetrics and Gynecology, Hadassah-Hebrew University Medical Center, Jerusalem, Israel

Richard P. Ebstein
Department of Psychology, National University of Singapore, Singapore

Nurit Yirmiya
Department of Psychology, The Hebrew University of Jerusalem, Jerusalem, Israel

Charity Onore, Houa Yang and Paul Ashwood
The M.I.N.D. Institute, University of California Davis, Davis, CA, USA
Department of Medical Microbiology and Immunology, University of California Davis, Davis, CA, USA

Judy Van de Water
The M.I.N.D. Institute, University of California Davis, Davis, CA, USA
Division of Rheumatology, Allergy and Clinical Immunology, University of California Davis, Davis, CA, USA

Frye, Leanna Delhey, John Slattery, Marie Tippett, Rebecca Wynne, Shannon Rose, Stephen G. Kahler, Sirish C. Bennuri and Stepan Melnyk
Department of Pediatrics, Arkansas Children's Hospital Research Institute, University of Arkansas for Medical Sciences, Little Rock, AR, USA

Jeffrey M. Sequeira and Edward Quadros
Department of Medicine, State University of New York–Downstate Medical Center, Brooklyn, NY, USA

Index

CPSIA information can be obtained
at www.ICGtesting.com
Printed in the USA
LVHW061513020922
727480LV00006B/667

9 781639 890644